India Studies in Business and Economics

The Indian economy is considered to be one of the fastest growing economies of the world with India amongst the most important G-20 economies. Ever since the Indian economy made its presence felt on the global platform, the research community is now even more interested in studying and analyzing what India has to offer. This series aims to bring forth the latest studies and research about India from the areas of economics, business, and management science. The titles featured in this series will present rigorous empirical research, often accompanied by policy recommendations, evoke and evaluate various aspects of the economy and the business and management landscape in India, with a special focus on India's relationship with the world in terms of business and trade.

More information about this series at http://www.springer.com/series/11234

Rajendra P. Mamgain
Editor

Growth, Disparities and Inclusive Development in India

Perspectives from the Indian State of Uttar Pradesh

Editor
Rajendra P. Mamgain
Development Studies
Giri Institute of Development Studies
Lucknow, India

ISSN 2198-0012 ISSN 2198-0020 (electronic)
India Studies in Business and Economics
ISBN 978-981-13-6442-6 ISBN 978-981-13-6443-3 (eBook)
https://doi.org/10.1007/978-981-13-6443-3

Library of Congress Control Number: 2019930578

© Springer Nature Singapore Pte Ltd. 2019
This work is subject to copyright. All rights are reserved by the Publisher, whether the whole or part of the material is concerned, specifically the rights of translation, reprinting, reuse of illustrations, recitation, broadcasting, reproduction on microfilms or in any other physical way, and transmission or information storage and retrieval, electronic adaptation, computer software, or by similar or dissimilar methodology now known or hereafter developed.
The use of general descriptive names, registered names, trademarks, service marks, etc. in this publication does not imply, even in the absence of a specific statement, that such names are exempt from the relevant protective laws and regulations and therefore free for general use.
The publisher, the authors and the editors are safe to assume that the advice and information in this book are believed to be true and accurate at the date of publication. Neither the publisher nor the authors or the editors give a warranty, express or implied, with respect to the material contained herein or for any errors or omissions that may have been made. The publisher remains neutral with regard to jurisdictional claims in published maps and institutional affiliations.

This Springer imprint is published by the registered company Springer Nature Singapore Pte Ltd.
The registered company address is: 152 Beach Road, #21-01/04 Gateway East, Singapore 189721, Singapore

Foreword

India's high economic growth trajectory along with a substantial reduction in poverty over the last two and half decades is also marked by rising regional inequalities largely due to unequal access to opportunities. Alongside interstate regional disparities, there exist significant gaps in different indicators of development across various social/religious groups, gender and regions within states like Uttar Pradesh. Being the most populous state in India, Uttar Pradesh has been the bedrock of the country's economic, social and political development for long. It has made significant achievements in the spheres of economic, social and cultural well-being. However, the per capita income in Uttar Pradesh still remains less than half of the Indian average. Uttar Pradesh faces the challenge of its low human development levels including educational and health development.

The book, *Growth, Disparities and Inclusive Development in India: Perspectives from the Indian State of Uttar Pradesh*, provides a holistic assessment of the economic and social development achieved by Uttar Pradesh so far and suggests strategies for faster and inclusive development of the state. The strategies suggested focus on (i) promoting high and sustained economic growth; (ii) broadening social inclusiveness through greater access to economic and social opportunities at a faster pace; (iii) strengthening social protection through social safety nets to protect the chronically poor; and (iv) mitigating the risks and vulnerabilities of people, supported by good governance and institutions.

The Chief Minister of Uttar Pradesh, Yogi Adityanath, is working with great clarity of purpose. Some of the strategies that come out from this book could be incorporated into the new template of governance in Uttar Pradesh.

I congratulate Prof. Rajendra P. Mamgain of the Giri Institute of Development Studies, Lucknow, for his efforts to edit the volume and putting issues, concerns and prospects pertaining to inclusive development in Uttar Pradesh. I hope the rich analyses and findings in the book are very useful to policy-makers, researchers, students, entrepreneurs and donor agencies interested in the issues of inclusive development.

New Delhi, India
September 2018

Dr. Rajiv Kumar
Vice Chairman
National Institution for Transforming India
NITI Aayog, Government of India

Preface

The high growth trajectory of India over the last two and half decades is also marked by rising inequalities largely due to unequal access to opportunities. Due to weak convergence in economic growth across various regions in India, achieving 'inclusive growth' remains a formidable development challenge for government as well as policy-makers. The slow pace of structural transformation in employment and deficit of opportunities for stable employment with reasonably remunerative income and social security continue to be major constraining blocks in the path of inclusive growth. Though there has been a marked improvement in several social indicators of development, the major challenges remain in poorer states like Uttar Pradesh, which remains at the bottom among Indian states, just above Bihar in various indicators of development. Alongside interstate disparities, there are striking inter-regional differences in various indicators of development for population belonging to different genders and socio-religious groups in states like Uttar Pradesh, which are yet to disappear. The per person income in Uttar Pradesh is less than half of the national average. The per capita income in the eastern region of the state is almost half of its western region. The incidence of poverty in Bundelkhand region is almost double than that of western region of the state. Uttar Pradesh suffers from a huge deficit of remunerative employment opportunities and also faces the challenge of its lower human development levels including educational and health development. Such lower outcomes in human development act as 'cause and effect' of lower income levels in the state. The rise in distress-induced migration is another major concern largely due to the lack of adequate employment opportunities in the state.

In brief, the pace of catching-up process in the state has been less than desired. It has enormous potential to shift to a development path characterised by remunerative jobs for its increasing labour force, access to quality education, health and other basic amenities, which also form the important pillars of achieving sustainable development goals in the state. For this, Uttar Pradesh needs substantial investment supported by active public policy support particularly progressing towards improved access to quality infrastructure, credit, technology, skill training and market.

A modest attempt is made in this book to fill this gap by providing a holistic assessment of economic and social development achieved by the state in specific areas, viz. employment, agriculture, industry, education, health and related reduction in poverty and inequalities, within the overarching framework of inclusive growth. These issues assume critical importance as the nature and pace of development of Uttar Pradesh would significantly shape the overall development of the country. This book suggests a road map for facilitating fuller utilisation of the state's potential in the coming years by promoting high and sustained economic growth, broadening social inclusiveness through greater access to economic and social opportunities at a faster pace, strengthening social protection through social safety nets for the chronically poor and mitigating their risks and vulnerabilities by good governance and effective institutions. While the Constitution of India is quite clear on the whole issue of promoting inclusiveness, the challenge is how to realise the dreams of its makers for inclusive development. Towards this end, the sustainable development goal (SDG) framework can become a basis to initiate and monitor the progress of inclusive development in the state. Some of the strategies that emerge out of this book could be incorporated into the new template of SDGs in Uttar Pradesh.

The selected, freshly written and thoroughly revised articles in the book have been contributed by senior researchers, which were earlier presented in an international seminar on 'Growth, Disparities and Inclusive Development in Uttar Pradesh: Experiences, Challenges and Policy Options' during 23–25 September 2016. The seminar was organised by the Giri Institute of Development Studies (GIDS), Lucknow, with the valuable financial support from the Indian Council of Social Science Research (ICSSR), New Delhi; Department of Planning, Government of Uttar Pradesh; and the International Labour Organisation (ILO). The seminar was a huge success as it was attended by about 80 academicians, policy-makers and social activists, who clearly identified the challenges and made suggestions to accelerate the process of faster yet inclusive growth in the state.

I owe a debt of gratitude to a number of institutions and individuals who have helped me in several ways in publishing this book. Special thanks are due to ICSSR; Department of Planning, Government of Uttar Pradesh; and ILO for their valuable financial support for the seminar. My sincere thanks are due to Prof. Sukhadeo Thorat, the then Chairman of ICSSR, and Dr. Sher Verick, Deputy Director of ILO for their valuable support and academic insights. I am grateful to Dr. Rajiv Kumar, Vice-Chairman, NITI Aayog, for writing the foreword of this book despite his busy schedule. I express my thanks to the director, faculty colleagues, and support staff of GIDS, for extending their full cooperation and support towards making the seminar successful. I am indebted to Prof. S. R. Hashim, the then Chairman of the GIDS; Mr. N. C. Bajpei, the then Vice-Chairman of State Planning Commission; Professor Ravi Srivastava, Jawaharlal Nehru University; and Mr. Alok Ranjan, the then Chief Adviser to the Chief Minister of Uttar Pradesh, for their valuable guidance and support. I am sincerely grateful to the paper contributors for their patience and support while complying with my frequent requests to send their revised papers on time. I also thank all the seminar participants including the chairpersons and discussants of various sessions of the seminar for their valuable contributions. I also take this opportunity to thank Ms. Sudha Passi for her careful copyediting work and Ms. Nupoor Singh and her entire team at Springer Nature publication for efficient handling of the manuscript and its speedy publication.

Last but not least, I dedicate this volume to my parents who tirelessly supported me towards my career development despite their vulnerable economic conditions.

Lucknow, India

Rajendra P. Mamgain
Professor of Economics
Giri Institute of Development Studies

Contents

Growth, Disparities and Inclusive Development: An Introduction and Overview 1
Rajendra P. Mamgain

Part I   Growth, Employment and Inequality

Deciphering Growth and Development: Past and Present 23
Ravi Srivastava and Rahul Ranjan

Employment, Its Quality and Inequality 49
Rajendra P. Mamgain

Labour Market Outcomes and Inclusive Development: Experiences of South Asian Countries 75
Rizwanul Islam

Regional Disparities in Economic and Social Development 103
Nomita P. Kumar

Part II   Poverty, Vulnerability and Inclusion

Poverty and Inequality: A Disaggregated Analysis................ 133
Amaresh Dubey and Shivakar Tiwari

Inclusion and Marginalization: Economic and Food Security Dimensions.. 155
M. H. Suryanarayana

Migration, Remittances and Poverty Reduction 177
Imtiyaz Ali, Abdul C. P. Jaleel and R. B. Bhagat

Violation of Civil Rights, Atrocities and Deprivation 191
G. C. Pal

Part III Agriculture Development: Challenges and Opportunities

Agricultural Growth: Performance, Constraints and Strategy for Future Development 215
Ajit Kumar Singh

Public and Private Capital Formation in Agriculture and Contribution of Institutional Credit to Private Investment 243
Seema Bathla and Shiv Jee

Access to Credit and Indebtedness Among Rural Households in Uttar Pradesh: Implications for Farm Income and Poverty 261
Anjani Kumar and Sunil Saroj

Part IV Industrial Development and Informality

Regional Pattern of Industrialisation and Urbanisation 289
S. P. Singh and Divyanshu Kumar Dixit

Employment and Livelihood Potential of Rural Non-farm Informal Enterprises 313
Nripendra Kishore Mishra

Part V Human Development Concerns

Trends in Private and Public Schooling 343
Geeta Gandhi Kingdon

Health Status: Progress and Challenges 371
Mohammad Zahid Siddiqui, Srinivas Goli, Md Juel Rana and Swastika Chakravorty

Burden of Private Healthcare Expenditure: A Study of Three Districts 393
C. S. Verma and Shivani Singh

Editor and Contributors

About the Editor

Rajendra P. Mamgain is a Development Economist from India. With more than three decades of research experience, he is currently a Professor at Giri Institute of Development Studies, Lucknow, India. He is also an Adjunct Professor in Doon University, and a Visiting Professor and former Director of Indian Institute of Dalit Studies (IIDS), New Delhi. In addition he was a Senior Academic Consultant at the Indian Council of Social Science Research from 2012–13, a Senior Fellow at the Institute for Human Development, New Delhi, and a member of the faculty at the Institute of Applied Manpower Research (now National Institute of Labour Economics Research and Development or NILERD), New Delhi. He obtained PhD in Economics from the Jawaharlal Nehru University, New Delhi, and specialises in the areas of labour, employment, migration, skill development, human poverty, inclusive development, and impact evaluation of government programmes. He has considerable expertise in large field-based research and has authored/co-authored nine books and more than 65 research papers in reputed national and international journals. He serves on the editorial boards of numerous journals and has been the Managing Editor of the *Indian Journal of Labour Economics* (published by Springer since 2015) for more than twenty five years. He has been a consultant to various national and international organizations. Dr. Mamgain has been a member of many policy advisory bodies of leading institutions in India and abroad.

Contributors

Imtiyaz Ali International Institute for Population Sciences, Mumbai, India

Seema Bathla Centre for the Study of Regional Development, Jawaharlal Nehru University, New Delhi, India

R. B. Bhagat Department of Migration and Urban Studies, International Institute for Population Sciences, Mumbai, India

Swastika Chakravorty Centre for the Study of Regional Development, Jawaharlal Nehru University, New Delhi, India

Divyanshu Kumar Dixit Department of Humanities and Social Sciences, IIT Roorkee, Roorkee, India

Amaresh Dubey Centre for the Study of Regional Development, Jawaharlal Nehru University, New Delhi, India

Srinivas Goli Centre for the Study of Regional Development, Jawaharlal Nehru University, New Delhi, India

Rizwanul Islam Formerly of the Employment Sector, International Labour Office, Geneva, Switzerland

Abdul C. P. Jaleel International Institute for Population Sciences, Mumbai, India

Shiv Jee Centre for the Study of Regional Development, Jawaharlal Nehru University, New Delhi, India

Geeta Gandhi Kingdon UCL Institute of Education, University College London, London, UK

Anjani Kumar International Food Policy Research Institute, New Delhi, India

Nomita P. Kumar Giri Institute of Development Studies, Lucknow, India

Rajendra P. Mamgain Giri Institute of Development Studies, Lucknow, Uttar Pradesh, India

Nripendra Kishore Mishra Department of Economics, Banaras Hindu University, Varanasi, India

G. C. Pal Indian Institute of Dalit Studies, New Delhi, India

Md. Juel Rana Centre for the Study of Regional Development, Jawaharlal Nehru University, New Delhi, India

Rahul Ranjan Centre for the Study of Regional Development, Jawaharlal Nehru University, New Delhi, India

Sunil Saroj International Food Policy Research Institute, New Delhi, India

Mohammad Zahid Siddiqui Centre for the Study of Regional Development, Jawaharlal Nehru University, New Delhi, India

Ajit Kumar Singh Formerly of Giri Institute of Development Studies, Lucknow, India

S. P. Singh Department of Humanities and Social Sciences, IIT Roorkee, Roorkee, India

Shivani Singh Giri Institute of Development Studies, Lucknow, India

Ravi Srivastava Centre for the Study of Regional Development, Jawaharlal Nehru University, New Delhi, India

M. H. Suryanarayana Indira Gandhi Institute of Development Research, Mumbai, India

Shivakar Tiwari Giri Institute of Development Studies, Lucknow, India

C. S. Verma Giri Institute of Development Studies, Lucknow, India

List of Figures

Deciphering Growth and Development: Past and Present

Fig. 1	UP per capita income as percentage of India.	25
Fig. 2	Percentage growth in income: UP and India	26

Employment, Its Quality and Inequality

Fig. 1	Trends in income inequality in Uttar Pradesh (Share of workers by MPCE Quintiles). 1993–94, 2004–05 and 2011–12	62
Fig. 2	Income inequality across types of employment in Uttar Pradesh (share of workers by MPCE quintiles). 2011–12.	62
Fig. 3	Region-wise income inequality in Uttar Pradesh, 2011–12	63
Fig. 4	Major or severe difficulties in operating business enterprises in UP, 2015.	66

Labour Market Outcomes and Inclusive Development: Experiences of South Asian Countries

Fig. 1	Social protection index and informal employment in select countries of South Asia.	92
Fig. 2	Social protection index and GDP per capita at current prices, 2009.	92
Fig. 3	Bangladesh—Increase (%) in nominal wages and consumer price index.	94

Regional Disparities in Economic and Social Development

Fig. 1	Impact of social infrastructure on economic development (income)	119
Fig. 2	Impact of economic infrastructure on income levels	119

Poverty and Inequality: A Disaggregated Analysis

Fig. 1	Average annual growth rate of GSDP; 2004–05 to 2011–12.....	136
Fig. 2	Change in structure of SDP in two decades..................	137
Fig. 3	Inter-regional variation in per capita income, 2011–12	137
Fig. 4	Inter-divisional variations in per capita income, 2011–12	138
Fig. 5	Urbanisation level in different divisions of Uttar Pradesh, 2011.....	139
Fig. 6	Trends in HCR in Uttar Pradesh in different NSS regions.......	141
Fig. 7	HCR in different districts of Uttar Pradesh, 1993–94	146
Fig. 8	HCR in different districts of Uttar Pradesh, 2004–05	146
Fig. 9	HCR in different districts of Uttar Pradesh, 2011–12	147
Fig. 10	Trend in consumption inequality (Gini)....................	147
Fig. 11	Change in income inequality; UP and all India...............	148

Inclusion and Marginalization: Economic and Food Security Dimensions

Fig. 1	Monthly per capita food of the poorest sample household: rural Uttar Pradesh (2011/12)	172
Fig. 2	Monthly per capita food of the poorest sample household: urban Uttar Pradesh (2011/12)...........................	173

Violation of Civil Rights, Atrocities and Deprivation

Fig. 1	Patterns and trends of the total crimes and PCR and PoA crimes together against SCs in India and U.P. during 2002–15. **a** India, **b** Uttar Pradesh	195
Fig. 2	Percentage share of PCR and PoA crimes together to the total crimes against SCs in India and U.P......................	196
Fig. 3	Annual percentage share of various registered crimes against SCs in U.P. to total crimes in India during 2002–15...........	198
Fig. 4	Disposal of crimes against SCs by the police and courts........	199

Agricultural Growth: Performance, Constraints and Strategy for Future Development

Fig. 1	Index of agricultural outputs and inputs	223
Fig. 2	Agricultural price parity index...........................	224
Fig. 3	Index of public investment in agriculture and irrigation and agricultural GSDP.................................	226

List of Figures

Regional Pattern of Industrialisation and Urbanisation

Fig. 1 Region-wise level of urbanisation in Uttar Pradesh (2011) 292
Fig. 2 Region-wise percentage distribution of registered working factories in Uttar Pradesh 297
Fig. 3 Region-wise per capita gross value of industrial production (GVI) in Uttar Pradesh 299

Employment and Livelihood Potential of Rural Non-farm Informal Enterprises

Fig. 1 CAGR of population and enterprises during 1999–2000 to 2010–11 318

Trends in Private and Public Schooling

Fig. 1 **Distribution of private-unaided schools' fee levels, age 6–14, India, 2014–15. a** Distribution of (annual) fee level without constraining the fee values. Notice that a very tiny number of students report paying fee from Rupees 50,000 to Rupees 200,000 per annum (above about Rs. 4000 pm). **b** Distribution of (annual) fee level after constraining the fee values to be below Rs. 30,000 pa (Rs. 2500 pm). Even here, it is visible that only a very small number of students pay fees above around Rs. 12,000 pa or Rs. 1000 pm. **c** This shows the distribution of **log of course fee**, rather than of the course fee. It is apparent that this is much more normally distributed (much closer to the bell-shaped 'Gaussian' distribution) than graphs 1a and 1b 354

Health Status: Progress and Challenges

Fig. 1 Life expectancy at birth (LEB) for all persons, males and females in the districts of Uttar Pradesh during 2001 and 2011 381
Fig. 2 Change in life expectancy at birth in all persons, male and females in the districts of Uttar Pradesh during 2001 and 2011 382
Fig. 3 Change in LEB during 1981–2011 for districts of Uttar Pradesh by LEB levels in the initial period, 2001, separately for males, females and all persons 384
Fig. 4 Non-parametric test of convergence in health across the districts of Uttar Pradesh, 2001–2011................................ 387

Burden of Private Healthcare Expenditure: A Study of Three Districts

Fig. 1 Impoverishment effect of cost of healthcare.................. 406

List of Tables

Deciphering Growth and Development: Past and Present

Table 1	Growth across different periods—Uttar Pradesh and India	26
Table 2	Region-wise share in net state domestic product	28
Table 3	Per capita net domestic product as percentage of western region	28
Table 4	Regions' MPCE as percentage of MPCE in western UP	28
Table 5	Quality of employment, UP and India (2011–12)	30
Table 6	Period-wise and region-wise growth rate of agricultural output value in UP	31
Table 7	Value of output per cropped hectare and per agricultural worker as per cent of western UP	32
Table 8	Annual average growth rate of manufacturing in UP in different sub-periods	36
Table 9	Percentage share of regions in total invested capital (TIC), net value added (NVA) and total persons engaged (TPE)	37

Employment, Its Quality and Inequality

Table 1	Workforce participation rates (15–59 years), 2011–12	52
Table 2	Workforce participation rates (15–59 years), 2011–12 by social groups	52
Table 3	Share of workers by employment status, (15–59 years) (%)	53
Table 4	Gender-wise trends in share of workers by employment status (15–59 years) (%)	54
Table 5	Region-wise trends in share of workers by employment status in Uttar Pradesh (15–59 years) (%)	55
Table 6	Quality of employment, 2010–11 (%)	56
Table 7	Growth rate (%) in employment in Uttar Pradesh and India	57
Table 8	Growth rate in employment in Uttar Pradesh and India by social group of workers	58

Table 9	Industrial structure of employment, 2011–12	59
Table 10	Industry-wise growth in employment (compound annual growth rates)	60
Table 11	Distribution of workers across MPCE quintiles	61
Table 12	Average annual growth of establishments and employment between the fifth (2005) and sixth (2013) Economic Census (%)	64
Table 13	Per worker market value of fixed capital (INR'000) during 2006–07	65
Table 14	Trends in workforce participation rates (15–59 years) in Uttar Pradesh	68
Table 15	Trends in workforce participation rates (15–59 years) in India	69
Table 16	Workforce participation rates (15–59 years) by social groups—Uttar Pradesh	69
Table 17	Workforce participation rates (15–59 years) by social groups—India	70
Table 18	Trends in nature of employment—Uttar Pradesh (%)	70
Table 19	Trends in nature of employment—India (%)	71

Labour Market Outcomes and Inclusive Development: Experiences of South Asian Countries

Table 1	Per capita (2014) income in South Asian Countries	78
Table 2	Growth of output in South Asian countries, 1990–2014 (% per annum)	79
Table 3	Structure of output of South Asian countries, 2000 and 2014 (in %)	80
Table 4	Elasticity of employment with respect to output, select South Asian countries	83
Table 5	Growth of labour productivity (% per annum)	84
Table 6	Change in the sector composition of GDP in select developing countries, 1960–2010	86
Table 7	Sector composition of employment in South Asia (% of total employment)	87
Table 8	Share (%) of informal employment in total non-agricultural employment	89
Table 9	Real wages of agricultural workers in countries of South Asia	95
Table 10	Gender difference in real wages in select countries of South Asia	97
Table 11	India: average daily wages of male and females, 1983 to 2011–12 (wages in Rs.)	97
Table 12	India: ratio of female wage to male wage	98

Regional Disparities in Economic and Social Development

Table 1	Inter-district disparities in the availability of social infrastructure.	106
Table 2	Weights of the economic infrastructure indicators in Uttar Pradesh	108
Table 3	Weights of the social infrastructure indicators in Uttar Pradesh	109
Table 4	Number of principal components with variance explained in each infrastructure sub-groups.	110
Table 5	Region-wise ranks of districts for economic and social infrastructure in Uttar Pradesh.	111
Table 6	Correlation matrix between the ranks in composite indices of economic and social infrastructure	116
Table 7	Region-wise Gini index and CV for per capita income.	118
Table 8	Stepwise regression estimates of determinants of per capita income in Uttar Pradesh—2011–12.	120
Table 9	Correlation matrix for indicators of economic infrastructure: 2011–12	124
Table 10	Correlation matrix for indicators of social infrastructure: 2011–12	126
Table 11	Factor scores for economic and social infrastructure.	127
Table 12	Inequality indices (Gini index) for infrastructure indices.	129
Table 13	Value of correlation coefficient between factor scores of economic and social infrastructure and per capita income.	129

Poverty and Inequality: A Disaggregated Analysis

Table 1	Gender-wise literacy rate in different divisions of Uttar Pradesh, 2011	140
Table 2	States with lowest and highest level of poverty	140
Table 3	Change in HCR (% per annum) in Uttar Pradesh; NSS region and sectors	142
Table 4	Poverty incidence across social groups	143
Table 5	Change in HCR (% per annum); region and social groups	144
Table 6	Level and trends of poverty incidence (HCR) in different divisions.	145
Table 7	Decomposition results of the per annum change in HCR (rural)	149
Table 8	Decomposition results of the per annum change in HCR (urban).	149
Table 9	Correlation matrix, 2011–12	150

Inclusion and Marginalization: Economic and Food Security Dimensions

Table 1	Estimates of median consumption per person and measures of inclusion/exclusion: all India	163
Table 2	Mainstreaming/marginalization: all India	164
Table 3	Estimates of median consumption per person and measures of inclusion/exclusion: Uttar Pradesh	164
Table 4	Mainstreaming/marginalization: Uttar Pradesh	165
Table 5	Estimates of median consumption per person and measures of inclusion/exclusion: all India and Uttar Pradesh (NSS region wise) 2011/12	166
Table 6	Mainstreaming/marginalization: all India and Uttar Pradesh (region-wise)	167
Table 7	Estimates of incidence of outlier food insecurity across NSS regions by sector: Uttar Pradesh (2011/12)	171
Table 8	Per capita food consumption of the poorest across social groups by NSS regions: Uttar Pradesh (2011/12) (kg/capita/month)	172

Migration, Remittances, and Poverty Reduction

Table 1	Out-migrants and remittances receiving households in Uttar Pradesh and Bihar, 2007–08	181
Table 2	Composition of households in Uttar Pradesh and Bihar by remittances and poverty status (in %)	182
Table 3	Determinants of remittances in Uttar Pradesh and Bihar, India, 2007–08	184
Table 4	Utilization of remittances by remittances receiving household in Uttar Pradesh and Bihar, 2007–08	185
Table 5	Determinants of utilization of remittances (as first priority) by remittance receiving households, 2007–08	186
Table 6	Description of propensity scores in Uttar Pradesh and Bihar	187
Table 7	Propensity score matching estimators in Uttar Pradesh and Bihar	187

Violation of Civil Rights, Atrocities and Deprivation

Table 1	Rate of registered crimes against Scheduled Castes in select states, 2012–15	197

Agricultural Growth: Performance, Constraints and Strategy for Future Development

Table 1	Region-wise productivity of major crops in U.P. (2014–15) (Quintl./Ha.)	216
Table 2	Compound growth rate of output, area and yield of major crops in U.P. (% per annum)	218
Table 3	Region-wise agricultural growth in U.P.: 2001–14	219
Table 4	District-wise growth rate of food grains output during 2000–01 to 2013–14 (% per annum)	220
Table 5	District-wise CAGR of NDDP (agriculture and animal husbandry) at 2004–05 prices during 2004–05 to 2013–14 (%)	222
Table 6	CAGR of agricultural inputs since 1980–81 by sub-periods (per cent per annum)	223
Table 7	CAGR of agricultural parity prices 1981–2015 in U.P. (% per annum)	224
Table 8	Indicators of private investment in agriculture in U.P. 1981–2015	225
Table 9	CAGR of public investment in agriculture and GSDPAG (per cent)	225
Table 10	Trends in distribution of land holdings by size in U.P.: 1971–2013	227

Public and Private Capital Formation in Agriculture and Contribution of Institutional Credit to Private Investment

Table 1	Public expenditure on agriculture-irrigation in UP and India; Rs. billion at 2004–05 prices	247
Table 2	Per ha public investment in agriculture–irrigation in UP and India (Rs. at 2004–05 prices)	248
Table 3	Private investment in agriculture and allied activities (FCE FB) at 2004–05 prices	250
Table 4	Per cent share of components of fixed capital expenditure in agriculture in rural households	251
Table 5	General characteristics of rural HHs as per institutional and non-institutional borrowings in Uttar Pradesh (nominal prices)	253
Table 6	FCE of rural HH as per land size in Uttar Pradesh during 2012–13 (nominal prices)	254
Table 7	FCE FB (agriculture) and extent of borrowing (Rs./hh)	254

Table 8	Share of borrowings and non-borrowings in private FCE FB (%)	255
Table 9	Impact of institutional credit on private investment in agriculture in UP	256

Access to Credit and Indebtedness Among Rural Households in Uttar Pradesh: Implications for Farm Income and Poverty

Table 1	Share of institutional borrowings in UP: 1991–92, 2002–03 and 2013–14 (per cent)	266
Table 2	Amount of institutional and non-institutional borrowings: 1991–92, 2002–03 and 2013–14 (Rs./ha at 1993–94 price)	267
Table 3	Distribution of loans by sources	268
Table 4	Farmers' access to credit from formal and informal sectors, 2012–13	268
Table 5	Distribution of borrower households by operational holding, 2012–13	269
Table 6	Socio-economic characteristics of institutional and non-institutional borrower	270
Table 7	Determinants of access to institutional credit	273
Table 8	Institutional credit, net farm income and household consumption expenditure	274
Table 9	Impact of institutional credit on net farm income	276
Table 10	Impact of institutional credit on household consumption expenditure	279
Table 11	Hausman's test for endogeneity for net farm income and household consumption expenditure	282

Regional Pattern of Industrialisation and Urbanisation

Table 1	Region-wise trends in rural and urban population in Uttar Pradesh	294
Table 2	Region-wise number of working factories per hundred thousand population in Uttar Pradesh	297
Table 3	Region-wise number of small scale industries per hundred thousand population in Uttar Pradesh	298
Table 4	Correlation matrix of dependent and explanatory variables	301
Table 5	Regression results of the first model	302
Table 6	Regression results of the second model	303
Table 7	District-wise socio-economic indicators of Uttar Pradesh	306

Employment and Livelihood Potential of Rural Non-farm Informal Enterprises

Table 1	Growth rate of enterprise by size and region, 1999–2000 to 2010–11 (% per annum).	318
Table 2	Profile of enterprise owners.	321
Table 3	Employment growth and labour productivity: growth by broad industry group and size of enterprises in U.P., 1999–2000 to 2010–11 (% per annum)	322
Table 4	Employment growth and labour productivity growth by NIC category and size of enterprises, 1999–2000 to 2010–11 (% per annum).	324
Table 5	Reasons for starting up of RNFI enterprises (in percent)	327
Table 6	Contribution of enterprise profit in household income	328
Table 7	Percentage of enterprises having GVA per worker below notional income, U.P.	330
Table 8	Number of rural enterprises per 10,000 rural population.	333
Table 9	Employment growth and labour productivity growth in regions of U.P. by broad industry group and size of enterprises, 1999–2000 to 2010–11 (% per annum)	334
Table 10	Percentage of enterprises having GVA per worker below notional income by region	336
Table 11	Percentage of enterprises having GVA per worker below notional income by sub-industry category.	337

Trends in Private and Public Schooling

Table 1	Percentage of children studying in 'private schools', Rural India and Rural Uttar Pradesh, 2006–2014	346
Table 2	Percentage of children in private-unaided schools, by state, 2014–15	347
Table 3	Change in the number of government and private schools, by state (2010–11 to 2014–15).	347
Table 4	Change in student enrolment in government and private schools, by state (2010–11 to 2014–15)	348
Table 5	Emptying of government schools over time of India (the phenomenon of small and tiny government schools, and changes in it, over time).	350
Table 6	Speed of emptying of government schools, by state (or the speed of growth of 'tiny' and 'small' government schools, by state).	352

Table 7	Mean and median fee levels in private-unaided schools for children aged 6–14, by state, 2014–15	353
Table 8	Percent of 6–14-year-old private-unaided school attendees who pay fee below given thresholds, select states, 2014–15	356
Table 9	Benchmarking private schools' fee levels against (1) state per capita income, (2) government-funded schools' PPE and (3) minimum wages	357
Table 10	Private schools' fee compared with government-funded schools' per-pupil expenditure (PPE)—2014–15	359
Table 11	Learning achievement levels of children of class V in public and private schools	361
Table 12	Value for money from public expenditure on education in India	363
Table 13	Starting salary of primary and junior teachers in government schools, Uttar Pradesh	366

Health Status: Progress and Challenges

Table 1	Summary statistics of LEB among the districts of Uttar Pradesh, 2001–2011	380
Table 2	Absolute and relative inequality measures of health status across the districts by gender, 2001–11	383
Table 3	Absolute β-convergence estimates based on Barro regression model for LEB across the districts of Uttar Pradesh, 2001–2011	385
Table 4	Sigma convergence in gendered average LEB across the districts of Uttar Pradesh, 2001–2011	386
Table 5	Results from panel data regression model (random effects)	388

Burden of Private Healthcare Expenditure: A Study of Three Districts

Table 1	Demographic profile of Uttar Pradesh	395
Table 2	Demographic profile of the sample households	397
Table 3	Ailment-wise utilization of health facilities for ambulatory care in the study area	398
Table 4	Pattern of utilization of healthcare facilities for ambulatory care	399
Table 5	Expenditure under various heads on OOP payments by type of healthcare facilities for outpatient care (in Rs.)	401
Table 6	Out-of-pocket expenditure on ambulatory care by household characteristics	402

Table 7	Mean expenditure under various heads on OOP payments by type of healthcare facilities for inpatient care (in Rs.)	403
Table 8	Average total medical expenditure per hospitalization case at inpatient care (in Rs.)	404
Table 9	District-wise mean OOP expenditure on inpatient care (Rs.)	404
Table 10	Income-group-wise OOP for inpatient care in public versus private healthcare	405
Table 11	Insurance coverage under different schemes in the project area	406

Growth, Disparities and Inclusive Development: An Introduction and Overview

Rajendra P. Mamgain

Abstract India's high economic growth trajectory along with substantial reduction in poverty over the last two and half decades has been widely appreciated and analysed. The growth process, however, has not percolated evenly to all sections and all regions of the country. The process, in fact, has been marked by rising economic and social inequalities along with unequal access to opportunities. The pursuit of 'inclusive growth', defined as economic growth with equality of opportunity, faster increase in income levels and overall well-being of the poor and other deprived social groups and regions, has emerged as a vital element of the development agenda. The policies and programmes initiated in the Eleventh Plan towards achieving such 'inclusive growth' and their renewed continuation in the Twelfth Plan onwards only indicate the commitment of the government to promote inclusive growth. Such policies and programmes are not only introduced by the centre, but the states also have a measure of autonomy in initiating them to impact on the social and economic goals of inclusive development.

Keywords Growth · Employment · Regional disparities · Inclusive development

1 Regional Disparities in India

The available evidence suggests a mixed response of such policies and programmes initiated and strengthened during the recent years. While economic inequalities tended to rise, there has been a marked improvement in several social indicators of development (Thorat and Dubey 2012; GoI-MoF-Economic Survey 2017). With a per capita income of Rs. 24,572 in 2015–16 (at 2011–12 prices), Bihar remains at the bottom among Indian states. Bihar's per capita income is almost eleven times lower than that in Goa—a highest per capita income state. Uttar Pradesh ranks just

R. P. Mamgain (✉)
Giri Institute of Development Studies, Sector-O, Aliganj, Lucknow 226024,
Uttar Pradesh, India
e-mail: mamgain.rp@gmail.com

© Springer Nature Singapore Pte Ltd. 2019
R. P. Mamgain (ed.), *Growth, Disparities and Inclusive Development in India*,
India Studies in Business and Economics,
https://doi.org/10.1007/978-981-13-6443-3_1

above Bihar with a per capita income of Rs. 36,850. The convergence in economic growth across states in India is rather weak, thereby fuelling inequality as reflected in rising value of Gini index in recent years. The less developed states such as Bihar, Madhya Pradesh and Chhattisgarh though improved their relative performance, but such trends were neither strong nor durable enough to change the underlying picture of divergence or growing inequality (GoI-MoF-Economic Survey 2017). The relative performance of Uttar Pradesh tended to deteriorate as the gap in per capita income of the state as compared to that of national per capita income widened over the years (Mamgain and Verick 2017; Srivastava and Ranjan 2017). Similar divergent tends are seen in the levels as well as rate of reduction in poverty across Indian states. Chhattisgarh stands as most impoverished state with its 39.9% population being poor in 2011–12. Jammu and Kashmir and Maharashtra are next most impoverished states with about 37% of poor population therein. With its 29.4% population remaining poor in 2011–12, Uttar Pradesh ranked at ninth poorest states among 29 Indian states. The percentage decline in poverty was also low in Chhattisgarh (21.6%) between 1993–94 and 2011–12. So was the case of Madhya Pradesh (28.9) and Uttar Pradesh (39.1%). The corresponding decline at national level was higher at 51.7% and much higher in states like Karnataka (57.8%) and Maharashtra (63.6%). These figures again show the divergence in poverty reduction in India and question the inclusiveness of growth process, particularly in poorer states like Uttar Pradesh. Agriculture sector, which still remains a major source of employment for over half of Indian workforce, has huge regional diversities in its productivity (Singh 2018). Such diversities were significant in case of irrigation facilities and input use—the factors that influence productivity of the sector.

Unlike the economic progress, there has been convergence in social indicators such as life expectancy and infant mortality rates in India over a period of time (GoI-MoF-Economic Survey 2017). The rate of decline in infant mortality rate was almost similar to the national average in less developed states such as Uttar Pradesh and Madhya Pradesh over a period of 22 years, i.e. 1994 to 2016. However, economically better -off states such as Karnataka and Maharashtra had better performance in reducing their IMRs. UP's dismal record on human development over several decades has been pointed out in several studies (Dreze and Sen 1995, 1997, 2013; Dreze and Gazdar 1997; GoUP 2003, 2007; Planning Commission 2007; IAMR 2011). UP ranked the lowest in terms of combined gross attendance rate (GAR) in 2014–15 among 21 major states (with a GAR of 83). The state ranked 19th among 20 states in per capita income (2014–15), 17th among 20 states in infant mortality rate (IMR) (2014) and 14th among 16 states in life expectancy at birth (LEB) for the period 2009–13.

Alongside inter-state regional disparities in India, there exist significant gaps in different indicators of development across various social/religious groups, gender and regions, more so in states like Uttar Pradesh (Mamgain and Verick 2017). Being the most populous state in the country, Uttar Pradesh has been the bedrock of the country's economic, social and political development for long. Available statistics show significant achievements that the state has made in the spheres of economic, social and cultural well-being, particularly since the early 1990s. It achieved reasonably high economic growth in the last decade, supported by higher growth in agriculture, resulting in faster decline in poverty. However, the pace of catch up process is less than desired (GoUP 2017). The per capita income of the state still remains less than half of the Indian average. It ranks ninth among 29 states in the incidence of poverty. The health indicators continue to lag behind all-India outcomes and are very slow to change. In almost all development indicators, the state remains among those at the bottom (RBI 2015; Diwakar 2009) in the country. Nearly 55% of workers are dependent on agriculture for their livelihoods, whereas the sector contributes only 27.5% to the state's GDP. Although there has been a substantive shift of workers from agriculture and allied activities to other areas, yet most of such opportunities are casual in nature and fetch low income to a large majority of workers. The economy of Uttar Pradesh has lagged far behind other states in generating adequate quantity of good quality jobs (Mamgain and Verick 2017). The incidence of distress-induced migration also has tended to increase over the years and is a major issue that could be addressed simply by improving employment opportunities in the state.

Another major challenge is the growing mismatch in the demand and supply of education and skills that affect the overall employability of youth in the state, as well as the country (World Bank 2010). While employers complain against shortage of skilled manpower that poses hurdles in their growth on the one hand, there is a very high rate of unemployment among educated youth, particularly women, on the other. Employers find a large number of job-seekers unemployable due to insufficient exposure of the latter to practical aspects of education (FICCI 2010; Assocham 2017).

According to available statistics, Uttar Pradesh and few other states are way behind others in effective delivery of anti-poverty programmes, provision of institutional support systems including developing quality livelihoods, education and health infrastructure. The major concerns regarding poor implementation of development programmes largely are attributed to weak governance, lack of political will and weakening of economic, social and political institutions in the state (Srivastava and Ranjan 2017).

There persist huge inter-regional disparities in various indicators of development within Uttar Pradesh that consists of four economic regions: Western, Central, Eastern and Bundelkhand region. The per capita income in the Eastern region of the state is almost half of its Western region. There are striking differences in the development outcomes among various social and religious groups even within the regions, which are yet to disappear. About 56% of districts in the state have low levels of development. Another 30% have medium levels of development (Diwakar 2009). Like the national pattern, Scheduled Castes (SCs), Muslims and Other Backward Classes (OBCs) lag behind other castes in Uttar Pradesh. The pace of progress in case of SCs and Muslims in UP is far behind than in several other states, resulting in increasing inequality among these groups at the national as well as sub-national level. Such disparities in development among various social/religious groups assume importance due to the fact that there is a strong, avowed concern for social inclusion at the state level, which has arisen from the political formations that have governed the state for over nearly two and half decades drawing their political mobilization around social identity from social groups such as OBCs, SCs and Muslims (Srivastava 2012).

Statistics show how Uttar Pradesh could not step up the rate of inclusive growth above the rest of the Indian economy despite being governed by social identity-based political parties for a fairly long period (Srivastava and Ranjan 2017). In fact, the general slipping of the state in various spheres of development has also affected the relative status of deprived groups, more so the Muslims. This may well be due to three reasons: first, the affirmative action policies and programmes have helped SCs gain better access to education and to a limited extent to other resources and assets. Second, declining employment opportunities in agriculture and rising employment opportunities in construction have shifted significant numbers out of agriculture and increased their wages and income. Third, a large proportion of Muslims have been struck in low productivity, petty manufacturing jobs where returns are very low and pro-active state policies virtually absent (Srivastava 2012).

In brief, promoting inclusive development is a pre-requisite for achieving the well-being of everyone. Like any other less developed states, Uttar Pradesh faces three major challenges in redressing poverty and expanding inclusive growth—first to expand economic opportunities, second to ensure that the poor and marginalized groups are empowered to take advantage of new opportunities in a rapidly changing world, and third to ensure that an effective safety net is in place to reduce vulnerability and protect the very poor and destitute. Strategies suggested for inclusive development have three important pillars containing various sub-sets of policies and actions. These pillars are:

(i) promoting high and sustained economic growth,
(ii) broadening social inclusiveness through greater access to economic and social opportunities at a faster pace, and
(iii) strengthening social protection through social safety nets for the chronically poor and mitigate their risks and vulnerabilities by good governance and institutions. The existing policies and programmes for the development of Uttar Pradesh need introspection from the perspective of these three pillars of inclusive development.

This volume, consisting of selected papers on the broad theme of growth, disparities and inclusive development in Uttar Pradesh, provides a holistic assessment of economic and social development achieved by the state in specific areas, viz. employment, agriculture, industry, education, health and related reduction in poverty and inequalities. These issues assume critical importance as the nature and pace of development of Uttar Pradesh would significantly shape the overall development of the country. The papers in this volume are categorized into the following five thematic sections.

(i) Growth, employment and inequality;
(ii) Poverty, vulnerability and inclusion;
(iii) Agriculture development;
(iv) Industrial development and informality; and
(v) Human development concerns.

What follows is a summary as also a commentary on the relevance and findings of the papers with a view to introduce them in as succinct a manner as possible to the readers so as to provide an overview on their rich content.

2 Growth, Employment and Inequality

The onset of economic reforms was expected to propel employment and thereby transfer some of the benefits of economic growth to labour via employment avenues with relatively better remuneration, and, hopefully, social protection measures as well. Economic growth did occur but sans the expected employment growth. The manner in which the growth–employment relationship indeed pans out over the last few decades, and the analysis of why employment generation did not occur as expected in spite of growth has been discussed in this section by Ravi Srivastava and Rahul Ranjan and Rajendra P. Mamgain in the context of Uttar Pradesh and by Rizwanul Islam in the context of South Asian region.

Ravi Srivastava and Rahul Ranjan in their paper on 'Deciphering growth and development: Past and present' argue that despite the initial favourable conditions such as Uttar Pradesh's location in the fertile Indo–Gangetic belt, implementation of land reforms, a legacy of a unified administration under British India, a diversified base of traditional and modern industries and a political leadership which carried weight in the national political establishment after independence, the state could not build up the momentum of growth and development, thus continued to remain as laggard state. The gap between state's per capita income and national income widened over the years. Various political regimes in Uttar Pradesh could hardly make any significant dent on accelerating the growth and development process despite their agenda of social development. UP's comparatively better growth story in the 1970s and 1980s can broadly be understood in terms of a spread of agricultural growth to the agriculturally poor regions, which was supported by public policy, along with higher industrial growth, the concentration of which in the Western region was sustained partly by higher levels of agricultural development in that region and in other regions by public investment and industrial incentives. But in later years, the state could not accelerate agricultural growth to higher levels and failed to bring about more dispersed and accelerated non-farm growth despite avowed focus on such growth. The regional disparities within the state tended to widen with concentration of poverty in Eastern and Central regions. Per capita domestic product in Eastern region was lowest by 42% as compared to Western region of the state. The performance of the state on human development front was less than satisfactory.

The authors argue that successive governments of various political parties in Uttar Pradesh could hardly step up the rate of inclusive growth over and above the rest of the country. The industrial development of the state tended to concentrate in few regions along with languishing micro- and small enterprises in the state. Agriculture continued to suffer with lacklustre policy approach, particularly in Eastern and Bundelkhand regions, thereby affecting the livelihoods of those depending on this sector. The special development package for Bundelkhand region could not make the desired impact on the development of the region. In terms of social policy, the Bahujan Samaj Party (BSP) and the Samajwadi Party (SP) have followed an agenda which has purportedly been more tilted in favour of Dalits and Muslims or Muslims and OBCs. But small-scale production, which forms the economic basis of livelihoods of Muslims and OBCs, has languished in the state. Large-scale corruption and inefficient implementation have limited the benefits of social protection programmes. This has prevented UP's growth from being inclusive, even by the lacklustre national standards. Overall, UP's position among Indian states in terms of human development indicators remains virtually unchanged.

The relationship between growth and employment is an inextricable part of development economics. After all, the argument for growth in a poor economy rests largely, if not only, on its ability to help workers in the backward or stagnant sector (agricultural and allied activities) to come out of their low productivity-low earnings syndrome by moving to the growing modern sectors of the economy with higher productivity and earnings (Lewis 1954). Lewis's development path provides the framework for the paper of Rajendra P. Mamgain on 'Employment, its quality and inequality' towards explaining the slower pace of structural change in employment in Uttar Pradesh. He questions employment and its quality in one of the least developed states in India with a focus on gender and social groups. Despite a reasonable growth in Uttar Pradesh, the per capita income in the state is almost half of the national average, and such gap tended to increase over the years. Along with a slow pace of structural transformation, most of the growth in employment opportunities was in the form of casual wage works, mainly in the construction sector of the state. Such high pace of casualization was widespread in all regions of the state except the Eastern region where dependence on agriculture did not reduce due to lack of such opportunities. The growth rate in regular employment opportunities in the state was almost three times lower than that at the national level.

Uttar Pradesh suffers from a huge deficit of remunerative employment opportunities. A large proportion of those working as casual wage labour and those self-employed in agriculture are located at the bottom 20% quintile of income distribution in the state, and the proportion of such workers in the bottom quintile significantly increased since the early 1990s. The state faces relatively higher challenge of poor employability of its labour force mainly due to low levels of education and poor formal skill training along with slow growth in employment opportunities. Though the state has enormous potential to shift to a development path characterized by remunerative jobs for its increasing labour force both within farm and non-farm sectors, it would require substantial investment supported by active public policy support towards improved access to credit, technology, skill training and market. In brief, the success of a future inclusive growth agenda for Uttar Pradesh would depend on its strategy of promoting investment in employment potential sectors and ensuring equal participation of its people belonging to various regions, gender and social groups.

What lessons can be learnt from other parts of the world for the expansion of employment and income opportunities forms the theme of Rizwanul Islam's paper on 'Labour market outcomes and inclusive development'. He examines whether labour market outcomes like employment, wages, returns to self-employment and social protection are contributing to make economic growth inclusive in the context of South Asian countries with a purpose to draw lessons for states like Uttar Pradesh. He finds labour market outcomes of direct relevance towards achieving inclusive growth in South Asian countries. Due to declining labour absorptive capacity of the countries in the sub-continent, the process of transformation of the structure of employment has been slow, and as a result, the informal economy has remained the predominant source of jobs for the growing labour force. That, in turn, has meant limited access to social protection because there is a negative relationship between the proportion of employment in the informal economy and access to social protection. Furthermore, the relationship between access to social protection and economic growth has not been linear, thus indicating that growth alone cannot be relied upon to address the issue. Public policy is also important. On the positive side, in some countries, real wages have registered increases in some sectors, especially in agriculture—showing the potential for making contribution to poverty reduction. But the rise in real wages has not been sustained in recent years and has lagged labour productivity. As a result, there has not been much impact on growing income inequality. Gender differences in wages have also persisted. On the whole, Islam argues that labour market outcomes in South Asia have not moved in the direction needed to make economic growth more inclusive. This contrasts with the experience of countries of East and South East Asia, such as the Republic of Korea (South Korea), Malaysia and Taiwan that have been successful in attaining economic growth with productive employment and rapid rate of poverty reduction.

Islam argues that for gearing labour market outcomes towards attaining the goal of inclusive development, actions are required on a number of fronts. These include re-thinking the development strategy and policies that could not deliver the desired employment outcomes, public policy support towards broadening social protection coverage, improving labour productivity and devising innovative mechanisms for redistribution of income. The employment policy has to be broad-based, and a combination of economic and labour market policies will be needed to address the various factors responsible for growth not leading to desired job creation.

Along with the deficit of productive employment opportunities, Uttar Pradesh is also characterized with significant regional disparities and inequality in various socio-economic indicators of development. In the recent period, both the central and state governments have made sizeable investment in the backward regions of the state for their overall development. However, the achievements are disproportionately low. This situation questions the very progress of several developmental programmes and policies for their less than desired impact on improving development and reducing regional disparities and inequality. The paper on 'Intra-state disparities in economic and social development' by Nomita P. Kumar analyses the pattern and trends in inter-district disparities in the levels of development particularly in levels of income and physical and social infrastructure by using multivariate analysis. There exist wide regional disparities across districts in the availability of social and economic infrastructure which have persisted and prolonged over time. Among the four broader economic regions, the districts of Western region continued to occupy top ranks in economic infrastructure as compared to other three regions, viz. Central, Eastern and Bundelkhand. Bundelkhand region presents the grim scenario with almost six out of seven districts falling in the category of backward districts in India. The Central and Eastern regions have almost mediocre status. Such a pattern provides a strong justification for the recent policy initiatives of the state government for improving the economic infrastructure especially banking services, industrialization and agricultural infrastructure to facilitate production and sale of outputs and social infrastructure for building human capital. However, budgetary support for such initiatives and weak implementation are major concerns for any meaningful results, particularly in backward districts. The paper advocates more rigorous efforts towards developing economic and social infrastructure, particularly in laggard districts. This would also help in accelerating the pace of economic growth and employment opportunities and reducing regional disparities in development in Uttar Pradesh.

3 Poverty, Vulnerability and Inclusion

In the last decade, extreme poverty in India has declined at a relatively faster rate and has achieved the Millennium Development Goals (MDG) target of reducing extreme poverty to half by 2015. However, regional progress in reducing poverty has been mixed. The highest number of 59.82 million poor populations in Uttar Pradesh in 2011–12 accounted for over 22.2% total poor population in the country and 29.43% population of the state itself. Apart from extreme poverty, a very high proportion of population suffers with various kinds of vulnerabilities, such as food insecurity, low levels of consumption, distress-driven migration, poor quality of assets, seasonality in income opportunities and caste-related atrocities. Papers in this section focus on issues of poverty and inequality, food security, migration and violation of civil rights.

Among the 29 states in India, Uttar Pradesh ranked nine in the percentage share of poor population. The state of Chhattisgarh was on top with the highest percentage of poor population (39.93%) in 2011–12. The state has higher incidence of poverty (29.43%) than the national average. In their paper 'Poverty and inequality,' Dubey and Tiwari show an appreciable rate of reduction in poverty at about 1.6% annually between 2004–05 and 2011–12 in the state. This has been largely in rural areas and that too among SCs and Others and across economic regions. In contrast, the incidence of poverty increased in urban areas of the state by 1.32% during 2004–05 to 2011–12, showing the urbanization of rural poverty due to lack of remunerative employment opportunities and social security measures. However, poverty in the state is predominantly rural. In 2011–12, around 48 million out of 60 million poor people in the state were living in rural area.

The incidence of poverty also varies significantly across different regions of the state. The Eastern region has the highest poverty incidence while Western region has the lowest, the latter being the most developed relatively among the four regions. Along with the absolute levels of deprivations, there is huge inequality in distribution of income and consumption expenditure particularly in urban areas that severely hampers the pace of poverty reduction. In 2011–12, Gini coefficient of consumption expenditure distribution was 43 and 27%, respectively, for urban and rural areas in the state. Dubey and Tiwari further provide detailed estimates of poverty and inequality at the more disaggregated level of 17 administrative divisions (ADs) of the state with an objective to suggest effective policy interventions and make a concerted dent on poverty. The ADs with high incidence of poverty are Basti, Chitrakoot, Devipatan and Lucknow in the Eastern and Central economic region, which are highly deprived and need to be targeted for poverty reduction. It is found that regions and divisions with high urbanization level and better rural connectivity have lower poverty incidence. Thus, given the large share of rural population, improving agricultural productivity and subsequently developing vibrant and integrated urban centres would be a highly effective strategy to achieve the target of eradicating extreme poverty from the state.

The role of food security is well recognized in eradicating hunger, malnutrition and poverty. The Food Security Act is being implemented in Uttar Pradesh, which is supposed to benefit more than 152.1 million people in the state. Using a rigorous conceptual framework, the paper on 'Inclusion and marginalisation: Economic and food security dimensions in Uttar Pradesh' by M. S. Suryanarayana examines the extent of inclusion and marginalization of different social groups in rural and urban areas and across different National Sample Survey (NSS) regions of Uttar Pradesh as compared to the country. The paper quantifies the extent of inclusion, mainstreaming and marginalization of different social groups in a plural society. Further, it examines the extent of inclusion and marginalization across social groups with respect to both food consumption and total consumer expenditure. Based on these two relative profiles, it defines rules for identification of vulnerable groups and calls for targeted food policy intervention. It finds evidence of marginalization of the third degree suggesting that marginalization is essentially a question pertaining to distribution of resources and not disparities across social groups. Examining the inclusion and marginalization profiles of different social groups in terms of food and total consumer expenditure shows that the SCs and OBCs deserve special attention to promote food security. In the Northern Upper Ganga Plains, both the SCs and OBCs call for targeted intervention in the rural sector but only OBCs need intervention in the urban sector. Another novel feature of the paper is its verification of food insecurity status in terms of incidence of outlier food consumption, that is, proportion of poorest outliers. Empirical profiles for UP show that the rural area of Eastern region is the most deprived, followed by Northern Upper Ganga plains, Central, Southern Upper Ganga plains and the Southern region. As regards urban UP, the incidence of outlier food insecurity is the highest in the Northern Upper Ganga Plains, followed by Eastern and Southern NSS regions; the incidence is nil in the Central and Southern Upper Ganga Plains. As regards the profiles across social groups, the findings show the poorest rural food consumption in the Eastern region among the OBCs; the richest among the poorest food consuming sample households also happen to be among the OBCs from the Southern region. As regards urban UP, the poorest food consuming sample household is from the Eastern region among the OBCs; the richest of the poorest food consuming households are also from OBCs in Southern UP. It is contrary to the general perception about the relative economic and food security status of different social groups in Uttar Pradesh.

Lack of remunerative employment opportunities is one of the major reasons for out-migration from the region. However, the role of migration and remittances sent by migrants is a matter of debate in the existing literature on migration research. It is argued that migration helps in reducing poverty and vulnerability and promotes development. The paper on 'Migration, remittances, and poverty reduction in Uttar Pradesh and Bihar' by Imtiyaz Ali, Abdul Jaleel C. P, and R. B. Bhagat contributes to the debate on the impact of internal and international remittances on poverty reduction by using the nationally representative household data from the 64th round of National Sample Survey. Uttar Pradesh and Bihar often top the list of Indian states for their high out-migration rates and low progress in social and economic indicators. Migration is mainly a phenomenon in eastern Uttar Pradesh and northern Bihar. Remittances play a critical role which not only reshape the life chances of the remittance-receiving households, but also help in diversifying the economy of the states that witness migration. However, a huge diversity exists in the utilization of internal and international remittances in the areas of origin.

The results from the multivariate logistic analysis show that households from rural areas received higher remittances compared to urban areas. A significant number of Muslim households remain economically dependent on remittances, particularly in case of Uttar Pradesh. They are more likely to spend on food consumption and less likely to spend on education than Hindus in Uttar Pradesh. Similarly, SCs/STs are more likely to spend remittances for meeting their food requirements and less on education as compared to other social groups. Thus, remittances give strength to rural households to absorb the risks and shocks of catastrophic health, marriage expenditure and incidence of crop failures. The findings of the paper show that migration-based remittances enhance the socio-economic status and reduce poverty of migrant households. Based on the propensity score matching technique, the results also show that the impact of international remittances on reducing household poverty out-weigh that of the internal (intra-country) remittances in Uttar Pradesh, but in Bihar, domestic remittances play a significant role in reducing poverty at the household level than international remittances. The state governments need to make a strong migration and remittance management policy to get the maximum benefit out of it.

Another dimension of vulnerability which is quite common yet generally neglected in academic and policy analyses relates to denial of basic rights and atrocities against Scheduled Castes (SCs) on account of their low caste identity, and the prejudices and discrimination associated with it. It clearly exposes the convoluted connection between social identities and social relations. Some states have the dubious distinction of registering a very high number of such human rights violations. Given the sociopolitical context and caste dynamics of UP, over the last two decades the violation of civil rights and perpetration of caste-based atrocities against SCs have raised question marks on the role of the state machinery. While it is important to promote an understanding of the linkages between sociopolitical conditions and enforcement of the laws on the issue of human rights in the state, it is also critical to explore the implications of human rights violations on the overall development of lower caste people.

The paper 'Violation of civil rights, atrocities and deprivation' by G.C. Pal reflects on the patterns of violation of civil rights and atrocities against SCs in Uttar Pradesh with a focus on the responses of state administration and its potential impact on socio-economic conditions of lower caste groups. Evidence is drawn from various sources that include data of the National Crime Record Bureau (NCRB), fact-finding reports of civil society organizations, media reports, state-level official documents, experiential account of human rights activists in the state and case studies. The results reveal a disturbing trend of commission of certain atrocities against SCs like physical assault due to petty issues, sexual assault against women and girls, and perpetration of atrocities in a collective and organized manner. Another critical issue is that the political role of caste identity continues to define the social relationship among social groups in the state, and this very often creates a ground for confrontations between caste groups. As SCs start utilizing public space due to their increasing social and political participation, it results in hostile attitudes among dominant caste groups towards them. The socio-economic power of dominant castes and their ability to provide employment opportunities to SCs in the agricultural sector offer a disproportionate scope for perpetrating atrocities against them with impunity. Moreover, with the emergence of a few lower caste groups as assertive groups, SCs with poor socio-economic conditions also remain more vulnerable to atrocities. Violation of civil rights and atrocities directly or indirectly restricts their opportunities for social and work participation. All these increase the feeling of social insecurity among SCs, making it difficult for them to realize their dreams. The paper suggests an effective support mechanism to strengthen the process of implementation of laws and respond to the violation of civil rights and atrocities on a priority basis.

4 Agriculture Development: Challenges and Opportunities

The economy of Uttar Pradesh is predominantly agrarian, and performance of agriculture and allied activities such as horticulture, animal husbandry, dairy farming and fisheries are critical in determining the growth rate of the state. The dependence on agriculture is much higher in Uttar Pradesh as compared to many other states. The state is endowed with favourable factors for agriculture in terms of vast fertile plains laden with alluvial soil, good rainfall, plentiful surface and ground water, temperate climate and sunshine. It is characterized by rich diversity in natural resources and suitable climate. In spite of these favourable conditions, yields of major food grain crops are much lower than the neighbouring states of Punjab and Haryana, indicating the unexploited development potential of agriculture in the state. Three papers in this section discuss the challenges of agriculture development for accelerating growth and inclusive development in the state.

The paper titled 'Agricultural growth in Uttar Pradesh: performance, constraints and strategy for future development' by Ajit Kumar Singh argues that agricultural growth was reasonably high during the 1970s and 1980s in the wake of green revolution in the state. Thereafter, the agricultural economy of the state registered a severe setback since the early nineties as growth rates of nearly all crops plummeted sharply, adversely affecting the income of agricultural households. Further, agriculture growth varies significantly across various geographic regions of the state with Bundelkhand witnessing the highest growth rate of food grain output during the period 2000–2013, yet with low levels of productivity, while the Western region witnessed the lowest growth rate of 1.02% per annum and the Central and Eastern regions registered a growth rate of around two per cent per annum.

Land, irrigation, fertilizer consumption, access to credit, market and price incentives are regarded as major determinants of agricultural growth. Agricultural growth in UP, however, is constrained by a number of factors which include small and declining size of land holdings making them economically non-viable, poor rural infrastructure, weak reach and poor quality of public support systems for agriculture in terms of input supply, credit and marketing support, and non-conducive policy environment with severe restrictions on land and lease markets in the state. This calls for an integrated strategy for agricultural development with particular focus on the small farmers and lagging districts.

The lack of capital formation too has hindered the development of agriculture in the state. This issue has been dealt in detail by Seema Bathla and Shiv Jee in their paper, 'Public and private capital formation in agriculture and contribution of institutional credit in Uttar Pradesh'. They have estimated the magnitude of public and private capital formation in agriculture in the state with an aim to analyse its contribution in accelerating agricultural growth rate and the role of institutional credit in raising investment of rural households. It has been observed that both public and private capital formation in agriculture have scaled up to reach Rs. 18 billion and Rs. 47.2 billion, respectively, by 2013 at 2004–05 prices. However, the quantum of investment seems to be critically low in view of the existing low rate of agricultural growth and sizeable population dependent on it. Investment must increase by 2.76 times from 2015 to 2016 level to achieve the targeted 5.1% rate of growth set by the state government. While the required rate of increase in private investment (mainly by rural households) is estimated at 6.2% per annum, the same by the respective state government in agriculture as well as rural infrastructure is estimated at 3.1% per annum. Private investment is mainly done through borrowings—52.8% from non-institutional sources and 47.2% from institutional sources with little disparity across the land size holdings. Farmers borrowing from institutional sources tend to make relatively higher investments, which suggest improving the outreach of institutional agencies to small land holders across poorer regions. The estimated elasticity of institutional credit with respect to private investment in agriculture is reasonably high at 0.26. The analysis suggests increasing institutional credit together with public investments in irrigation and rural infrastructure to facilitate higher rate of growth in agriculture in the state. A growing investment preference of rural households in non-farm business activities is identified for which a favourable credit policy should be in place.

The challenges of access to credit for improving farm incomes and eradication of poverty are equally important in the quest to promote inclusive growth. As is well known, access to credit (especially formal) and the incidence of indebtedness among rural households has been a matter of intense policy debate in India. It is, therefore, important to empirically understand and feel the pulse of changing rural credit markets and their implications on farmers' economic welfare. The paper 'Access to credit and indebtedness among rural households: implications for farm income and poverty' by Anjani Kumar and Sunil Saroj analyses the changes in the structure of rural credit delivery in Uttar Pradesh. It identifies factors that influence the choice of credit sources in the state and also assesses the impact of access to credit on farmers' welfare. The structure of credit system has been assessed in terms of access of rural households to different credit outlets, share of formal credit institutions, availability of credit and interest rate.

It is observed that the structure of credit market has changed with times and the share of institutional credit has increased. The initiatives taken by government have paid off and the flow of institutional credit to rural areas has increased significantly in real terms. The indicators of financial inclusion have shown a sign of improvement. However, the presence of informal agencies in the disbursement of rural credit in Uttar Pradesh is still intact. Rural households' access to institutional credit is influenced by a number of socio-economic, institutional and policy factors. The role of education, caste affiliation, gender and assets ownership is found to influence the access of rural households to institutional credit significantly. Conditioned on participation, the access to formal agricultural credit has a significant positive impact on the economic welfare of farming households. It is in this milieu that a concerted effort and appropriate policy reform are required to make rural households' access to institutional credit neutral to caste, class and regions to realize the potential impact of agricultural credit on farmers' economic welfare in the state.

5 Industrial Development and Informality

In economic theory, the role of urbanization and industrial development is regarded as critical for promoting economic development. Cities are regarded as the centres of knowledge, innovation and new ideas. They have the advantage of having better physical, socio-economic and business infrastructure than villages and consequently attract high-value manufacturing and services activities. It is also argued that along with economic development, informal enterprises grow into formal ones with well-defined job contracts and social security for workers. However, the development dilemma of many developing countries like India is the very high presence of informal enterprises and informal employment with abysmally low levels of productivity, and resultant low income and weak social security of workers. India is yet far behind in reaching the 'Lewesian turning point' despite a high growth for a reasonably long period of over two and half decades. Two papers discuss the issues of urbanization, industrialization and informal enterprises in Uttar Pradesh.

The paper on 'Regional pattern of industrialization and urbanization in Uttar Pradesh' by S.P. Singh and Divyanshu Kumar Dixit examines the district-wise and region-wise pattern in the levels of urbanization and industrialization in the state. In order to study the regional pattern, the state is divided into five NSS regions, namely Northern Upper Ganga Plains (NUGP), Southern Upper Ganga Plains (SUGP), Central Region (CR), Bundelkhand Region (BR) and Eastern Region (ER). The level of urbanization in the state significantly varies between the highest of 38.2% in NUGP and the lowest 12.2% in ER. The number of registered factories per hundred thousand of population is observed to be the highest in NUGP (25.06) and lowest in SR and ER (less than 2.0). The per capita gross value added (GVA) in the industries has been highest in NUGP, distantly followed by CR and SUGP. It is found to be the lowest in SR, followed by ER. The number of employees in registered factories is highest in NUGP and lowest in SR. It is observed that the 10 districts in NUGP have the highest level of urbanization and industrialization, while ER as a whole is lagging behind the other regions. Regression analysis shows a significant positive impact of urbanization and industrialization on the economic development, measured in terms of composite index of development (CID) and per capita net state domestic product (NSDP). The value of coefficient of dummy for ER indicates that the level of CID and per capita NSDP in ER is much lower than that of other regions of the state. The paper concludes with the observation that there exist inter-region and intra-region disparities in the level of urbanization and industrialization and consequently in the level economic development of the state. The policy implication is that to accelerate the pace of economic development, the focus must be on addressing the issues related to urbanization and industrialization of ER and SR. Also, there is a need to create new manufacturing towns in these regions. Amritsar-Kolkata Industrial Corridor (AKIC), proposed to be set up alongside of Eastern Dedicated Freight Corridor (EDFC), covering 18 districts of the state and the Delhi-Agra-Lucknow expressway have high potential to transform the economy of the state.

Rural non-farm informal enterprises (RNFIEs) are important sources of livelihood for a sizeable population both in Uttar Pradesh as also India as a whole. These enterprises are predominantly informal. However, there are two diametrically opposite views about RNFIEs. While the first view considers RNFIEs a low productivity sector producing low-quality goods and services, the second one recognizes it as dynamic, flexible, and innovative sector that contributes significantly to economic development. This is examined in detail by Nripendra Kishore Mishra in his paper, 'Employment and livelihood potential of rural non-farm informal enterprises in Uttar Pradesh'. Based on the National Sample Survey unit-level data (1999–2000 and 2010–11) and village-level household enterprise data, this paper examines the employment and livelihood potential of RNFIEs in the state. Even though a high percentage of informal enterprises have reported expansion, still more than half of RNFIEs are stagnant. These enterprises are essentially owned by illiterate, landless and SCs/STs who have nothing else to do. Almost three-fourths of own account enterprises (OAEs) and more than half of the establishments have GVA per worker below national income which is a matter of major policy concern. Nevertheless, this study confirms that enterprise profit contributes significantly to household income;

whereas in its absence, a household takes recourse to casual wage income to support its earnings. It also shows the precarious nature of most RNFIEs. The study has also questioned the aggregative method of studying RNFIEs.

6 Human Development Concerns

Human development in itself is a goal and engine of overall development of any economy and society. This has been widely recognized and popularized as a strategy of development since the publication of first human development report by UNDP in 1990. It is argued that although high economic growth is necessary, yet it is not a sufficient condition for human development. Education and health are important components of human development besides income levels. Several state governments in India have been periodically publishing their human development reports to monitor their progress on this count. Now the indicators of human development have assumed centre stage in the sustainable development approach of monitoring development. Uttar Pradesh faces the challenge of its lower human development levels including educational and health development as compared to many other Indian states. The lower outcomes in human development are both 'cause and effect' of lower income levels in the state. Two papers in this section exclusively focus on education and health concerns in Uttar Pradesh.

The paper on 'Trends in private and public schooling in Uttar Pradesh' by Geeta Gandhi Kingdon raises concerns over growth and access of school education in the state. The growth in school enrolment in the state is largely led by private schools, whereas government schools have been rapidly getting emptied during the second decade of the new millennium (2010–11 to 2014–15). Such decline in government school enrolment comes in the face of a 7.7% increase in the child population of primary-school age group in UP over the same period. A declining enrolment in government schools alongside increased salaries and increased teacher numbers therein only shows the rising per pupil expenditure in the government school system and consequent drop in value-for-money from public expenditure on government schools. The value-for-money from government schools was found to be 29 times lower than that from private schools in Uttar Pradesh and that the state was an outlier in terms of its low value-for-money from public expenditure on education. Contrary to popular perception, a very high proportion of private schools cater to the poor in Uttar Pradesh as has emerged from the analysis of fee data from the National Sample Survey 2014–15—32% of private school students pay monthly fee of less than Rs. 100, and 84% pay fee less than Rs. 500 per month. In contrast, at the national level only 11% pay less than Rs. 100 per month while only 57% private school students pay less than Rs. 500 a month! The median fee of private schools in UP is only 6.5% of the government schools' per pupil expenditure, which means much of private schooling is provided at very low cost in the state, by far the lowest among all states in India. The evidence suggests that a very high percentage of private schools in Uttar Pradesh and even in India can be considered 'low fee' in the sense that their fee is below the government's per pupil expenditure in its own schools. This evidence explodes the myth that much of private schooling in India is elite and exclusive.

The chapter also raises a pertinent question as to how can private schools (without any state subsidy) with fee levels far lower than government schools' per pupil expenditure, comply with the infrastructure norms of the Right to Education (RTE) Act 2009 when a high proportion of well-funded government schools cannot do so? It also draws the policy maker's attention to the fact that majority of the private schools in the Uttar Pradesh are running on a small fraction of the unit cost of government schools. The kind of data presented in this study to benchmark private school fee levels can help decision-makers formulate a more 'evidence-informed' education policy that is more realistic and less wishful, and avoid counter-productive effects such as closure of low-fee private schools which may be successfully imparting learning but lack the resources to fulfil the demanding infrastructure and other stipulated norms for private sector schools. The data showing low and falling learning achievement levels of children in government schools and their rapid emptying at the cost of growth and preference for private schools also has policy implications such as the pay commission process through which across-the-board hike in teachers' salaries are decided and where the narrative and justifications are decided on whether and how much pay of particular public sector workers should be raised. It would also have implications for government negotiations with teacher unions at the state level, before deciding whether and to what extent to apply the Central Pay Commission's recommendations in the state, on the basis of pay for productivity.

India is often described as a country with substantial progress in average health status in spite of sizable geographical, rural-urban, social, economic and bio-demographic disparities. Lack of equitable progress in the health status of the population in laggard states such as UP is one of the key features in its growth story. In this backdrop, the paper 'Health status in Uttar Pradesh' by Goli et al. examines the conversion/diversion hypothesis across the districts of the state for one indicator of health outcome, i.e. life expectancy at birth (LEB) from the Census 2001 and 2011 data. Further, for assessing the determinants, multiple data sources are used for various indicators which are considered as predictors of LEB in literature. The convergence process is found to be underway both regarding absolute and relative inequality in LEB across the districts, during 2001–2011. Similarly, the findings based on catching-up plots, absolute β and sigma convergence measures affirm the convergence across districts of the state. Presence of a strong evidence of convergence clubs indicates that the growth process is not inclusive and is limited to a few district clusters in the state. LEB growth process has favoured some districts compared to others. Further, findings of determinants of health status suggest that decrease in infant mortality, progress in income level, improvement in literacy rate, full immunization of children and health infrastructure in laggard districts would help in convergence of the health status across the geographical space in the state. In other words, achieving health targets of sustainable development goals (SDGs) in Uttar Pradesh will not be possible unless acceleration in the speed of convergence is achieved equitably. The state should prioritize the agenda for reduction of its infant mortality rate (IMR), a substantial increase in literacy rate and major investment in healthcare infrastructure availability and accessibility, universal access to immunization services, especially in the laggard districts.

One of the major concerns from the perspective of public health policy is providing health security to all. However, with dwindling public health infrastructure and increasing privatization and commercialization of health services, particularly in the post-liberalization era has put a question mark on the very role of the 'welfare state' in providing health security to its citizens. As a result of increasing cost of health care and resultant severe impact on households, particularly poor and low-income categories, many households are trapped in a vicious cycle of poverty. The paper 'Burden of private healthcare expenditure in Uttar Pradesh' by C. S. Verma and Shivani Singh assesses the pattern of healthcare expenditure in public and private healthcare sector in the state and argue how the private healthcare market is flourishing at the cost of public healthcare sector. For this, out-of-pocket expenditure (OOPE) on ambulatory care and in-patient care in public and private sector has been assessed across a sample of 3338 households spread across 47 villages and 13 wards in three districts of Uttar Pradesh.

The findings from the study suggest that although a majority of the people prefer private health care, the choice of private healthcare provider largely depends on their economic status. People from lower economic groups seek care from Registered Medical Practitioners (RMPs), unregistered and informal providers, while people from higher income groups seek care from high-end private facilities. The out-of-pocket expenditure (OOPE) is high in both public as well as private facilities, but certainly more so in private sector. Lack of trained personnel, drugs and equipment in public healthcare sector is the cause of high OOPE there. The high costs of good quality private healthcare services further deprive people of lower economic strata from seeking proper healthcare services because of their lack of affordability. Low coverage under health insurance schemes like *Rashtriya Swasthya Bima Yojana* (RSBY) and dominance of private hospitals in providing treatment under the schemes has also resulted in the failure of health insurance in reducing OOPE. Lack of proper regulatory and monitoring authority and legal provisions further leads to exorbitant prices and corrupt practices in private sector. In order to provide universal health coverage and ensure health care for all, it is the need of the hour to promote private healthcare sector, but at the same time, it needs to be properly regulated and monitored. The government should strengthen public health system by increasing public expenditure on preventive and primary health care in order to reduce the OOPE on health.

7 Conclusion

The high growth trajectory in India is marked with increasing inequality (Oxfam 2018). The low-income states such as Uttar Pradesh are on the catching-up process in different indicators of development. However, the pace of such catching-up process is less than desired due to a variety of reasons including its historical disadvantages, thereby resulting in widening disparities over a period of time. Further, the rising intra-state disparities in socio-economic development in the state are a cause of concern for achieving inclusive development agenda. Given its geographical size and diversity, as also demographic diversity, the state has an advanced industrial Western region with high economic progress along with a predominantly poor agrarian Eastern region. The present book clearly identifies three major challenges that Uttar Pradesh faces in redressing poverty and expanding inclusive growth. These are expanding economic opportunities, ensuring that the poor and marginalized groups are empowered to take advantage of the new opportunities available in a rapidly changing world and ensuring an effective safety net to reduce vulnerability and protect the very poor and destitute people. The strategies, therefore, must focus on the following:

(i) Promoting high and sustained economic growth,
(ii) Broadening social inclusiveness through greater access to economic and social opportunities at a faster pace, and
(iii) Strengthening social protection through social safety nets to protect the chronically poor and to mitigate the risks and vulnerabilities of people, supported by good governance and institutions.

The existing policies and programmes for the development of Uttar Pradesh need introspection from the perspective of these three pillars of inclusive development. The focus on the aforementioned pillars of inclusive development strategy is again reiterated in the following message by the state Chief Minister, Shri Yogi Aditya Nath, in Sustainable Development Goals-Vision 2030 document of the government of Uttar Pradesh:

> Balanced, inclusive and sustainable development together with the socio-economic progress of all individuals is the vision of the Government of Uttar Pradesh. The Sustainable Development Goals (SDG), articulated by the global community, reinforce and commit us to continue our efforts with a goal-oriented approach. (GoUP 2017)

The papers in the present volume provide a holistic yet critical analysis of the achievements made by the state so far in a comparative manner with other states in the country and identify challenges and suggest measures for accelerating the inclusive development process in the country's most populated state.

References

Assochem. (2017). *Uttar Pradesh—Economic growth and investment performance, 2012–2017*. Economic Research Bureau, New Delhi: The Associated Chambers of Commerce and Industry.

Diwakar, D. M. (2009). Intra-Regional disparities, inequality and poverty in Uttar Pradesh. *Economic and Political Weekly, 44*(26 & 27), 264–273.

Dreze, J., & Sen, A. K. (1995). *India: Economic development and social opportunity*. Delhi and Oxford: Oxford University Press.

Dreze, J., & Sen, A. K. (Eds.), (1997). *Indian development: Selected regional perspectives*. Delhi: Oxford University Press.

Dreze, J., & Sen, A. K. (2013). *An uncertain glory: India and its contradictions*. Delhi and London: Penguin.

Dreze, J., & Gazdar, H. (1997). Uttar Pradesh: The burden of inertia. In J. Dreze & A. Sen (Eds.), *Indian development: Selected regional perspectives*. Delhi: Oxford University Press.

FICCI. (2010). *The skill development landscape in India and implementing quality skills training*. New Delhi: Federation of Indian Chambers of Commerce and Industry.

GoI-MoF. (2017). *Economic Survey, 2016–2017*. New Delhi: Government of India, Ministry of Finance.

GoUP. (2003). *First human development report of Uttar Pradesh*. Lucknow: Planning Department, Government of Uttar Pradesh.

GoUP. (2007). *Uttar Pradesh human development report 2003*. Lucknow: Planning Department.

GoUP. (2017). *Uttar Pradesh vision document, 2030*. Lucknow: Department of Planning, Government of Uttar Pradesh.

IAMR. (2011). *India human development report 2011: Towards social inclusion*. New Delhi: Institute of Applied Manpower Research.

Lewis, A. W. (1954). Economic development with unlimited supply of labour. *The Manchester School, 22*(2), 139–191.

Mamgain, R. P., & Verick, Sher. (2017). *The state of employment in Uttar Pradesh: Unleashing the potential for inclusive growth*. New Delhi: International Labour Organisation.

Oxfam. (2018). *The widening gaps: India inequality report 2018*. New Delhi: Oxfam India.

Planning Commission. (2007). *Uttar Pradesh development report* (Vols. 1 & 2). Government of India, New Delhi: Academic Foundation.

RBI. (2015). *Report of the committee for evolving a composite development index of states*, Government of India, Ministry of Finance, New Delhi: Chairman Raghuram Rajan.

Singh, A. K. (2018). *Patterns of development*. New Delhi: APH Publishing Corpn.

Srivastava, R. (2012). Economic change and social inclusion in Uttar Pradesh, 1983–2010. Revised Presidential Lecture. In *Seventh Annual Conference of the Uttar Pradesh and Uttarakhand Economics Association, October 2011, UPEA Journal, 5*(5), (pp. 3–25).

Srivastava, R., & Ranjan, R. (2017). Deciphering growth and development: Past and present. *Economic and Political Weekly, 51*(53), 32–43.

Thorat, S., & Dubey, A. (2012, March 10). Has growth been socially inclusive during 1993–94/2009–10? *Economic and Political Weekly*.

World Bank. (2010). India living conditions and human development in Uttar Pradesh: A regional perspective. *Poverty reduction and economic management South Asia report No 43573–IN*. Washington DC: World Bank.

Rajendra P. Mamgain is a Development Economist from India. With more than three decades of research experience, he is currently a Professor at Giri Institue of Development Studies, Lucknow, India. He is also an Adjucnct Professor in Doon University, and a Visiting professor and former Director of Indian Institute of Dalit Studies (IIDS), New Delhi. In addition he was a Senior Academic Consultant at the Indian Council of Social Science Research from 2012–13, a Senior Fellow at the Institute for Human Development, New Delhi and a member of the faculty at the Institute of Applied Manpower Research. He obtained PhD in Economics from the Jawaharlal Nehru University, New Delhi, and specialises in the areas of labour, employment, migration, skill development, human poverty, inclusive development and impact evaluation of government programmes. He has considerable expertise in large field-based research and has authored/co-authored nine books and more than 65 research papers in various respected national and international journals. He serves on the editorial boards of numerous journals and has been the Managing Editor of the Indian Journal of Labour Economics(published by Springer since 2015) for more than twenty five years. He has been a consultant to various national and international organizations. Dr. Mamgain has been a member of various policy advisory bodies of leading institutions in India and abroad.

Part I
Growth, Employment and Inequality

Deciphering Growth and Development: Past and Present

Ravi Srivastava and Rahul Ranjan

Abstract This paper argues that despite the initial favourable conditions such as Uttar Pradesh's location in the fertile Indo-Gangetic belt, implementation of land reforms, a legacy of a unified administration under British India, a diversified base of traditional and modern industries and a political leadership which carried weight in the national political establishment after independence, the state could not build up the momentum of growth and development and thus continued to remain as laggard state. The gap between state's per capita income and national income widened over the years. Various political regimes in Uttar Pradesh could hardly make any significant dent on accelerating the growth and development process despite their agenda of social development. UP's comparatively better growth story in the 1970s and 1980s can broadly be understood in terms of a spread of agricultural growth to the agriculturally poor regions, which was supported by public policy, along with higher industrial growth, the concentration of which in the western region was sustained partly by higher levels of agricultural development in that region and in other regions by public investment and industrial incentives. But in later years, the state could not accelerate agricultural growth to higher levels and failed to bring about more dispersed and accelerated non-farm growth despite avowed focus on such growth. The regional disparities within the state tended to widen with concentration of poverty in eastern and central regions. The performance of the state on human development front was less than satisfactory. The authors argue that successive governments of various political parties in Uttar Pradesh could hardly step up the rate of inclusive growth over and above the rest of the country. The industrial development of the state tended to concentrate in few regions along with languishing micro and small enterprises in the state. Agriculture continued to suffer from lacklustre policy approach, particularly in eastern and Bundelkhand regions, thereby affecting the livelihoods

---

This paper is published earlier in *Economic and Political Weekly*, Vol. LI, No. 53, 2016, pp. 32–43. The editor of this book is thankful to Economic and Political Weekly for permitting him to reprint the paper in this volume.

R. Srivastava (✉) · R. Ranjan
Centre for the Study of Regional Development, Jawaharlal Nehru University, New Delhi 110067, India
e-mail: ravisriv@gmail.com

of those depending on this sector. The special development package for Bundelkhand region could not make the desired impact on the development of the region. In terms of social policy, the Bahujan Samaj Party (BSP) and the Samajwadi Party (SP) have followed an agenda which has purportedly been more tilted in favour of Dalits and Muslims or Muslims and OBCs. But small-scale production, which forms the economic basis of livelihoods of Muslims and OBCs, has languished in the state. Large-scale corruption and inefficient implementation have limited the benefits of social protection programmes. This has prevented UP's growth from being inclusive, even by the lacklustre national standards. Overall, UP's position among Indian states in terms of human development indicators remains virtually unchanged.

Keywords Economic growth · Human development · Industrial development · Social protection · Inclusive development

Uttar Pradesh's growth and development are increasingly becoming a part of the political discourse as the countdown to the 2019 Lok Sabha elections gets underway. Given that UP is the most populous state with maximum representation in parliament to decide its course of progress, growth and development are issues no political party can afford to ignore. Since all the political parties in the reckoning have been in power in the state at some point of time or another, this paper analyses UP's record of growth and development over the long run and over specific periods linked to various political regimes. It specifically examines how growth strategies, focused on industrial and infrastructure growth, have evolved since the early 1990s, and poor governance has influenced the general development scenario and the impact of 'social justice'-oriented governments on socially inclusive development. The paper focuses on the signal failure of successive governments to accelerate growth, build on the productive potential, improve the rule of law and to provide the benefits of development to marginalized social groups who have been the core support groups of the parties in power in recent years.

1 Economic Growth

UP possessed some initial advantage in terms of its location in the fertile Indo-Gangetic plains, implementation of land reforms, a legacy of a unified administration under British India, reasonably good physical and social infrastructure, a diversified base of traditional and modern industries and a political leadership which had a large clout in the national political establishment after independence. But the state was not able to build a momentum of growth and has steadily slipped back. The state's per capita income was 97% of the national per capita income in 1951. It gradually fell to 68% of this average in 1971–72, remained close to this level till 1991–92 (67.5%), and then gradually fell to 50.5% in 2001–02 and to a further low of 40.5%

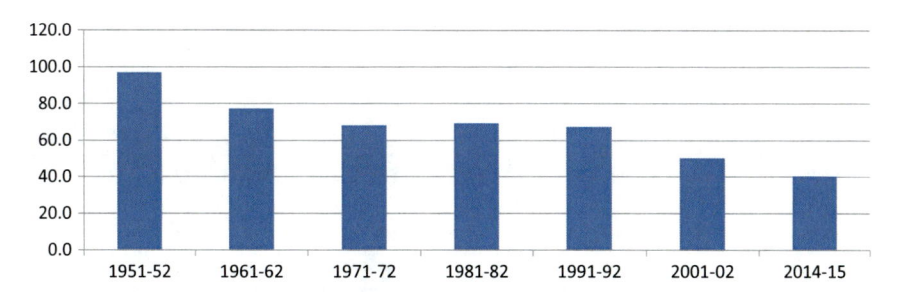

Fig. 1 UP per capita income as percentage of India. *Source* Computed from UP state plans, National Account Statistics (CSO) and EPW Research Foundation

in 2014–15 (Fig. 1). This shows that UP's aggregate growth performance remained close to the national level only during the 1970s and 1980s.

Given the periodic and multiple regime changes, UP's lacklustre growth performance cannot be attributed to a single political party or even to the political instability that it experienced over long periods. It might be interesting to compare the state's relative performance over five periods—1950–51 to 1966–67 (Congress rule); 1967–68 to 1979–80 (non-Congress and mixed regimes); 1980–81 to 1988–89 (second and last spell of Congress rule); 1989–90 to 2002–03 (mixed regimes, but with six years of BJP rule); 2003–04 till 2016 (stable governments of the Samajwadi Party (SP) or the Bahujan Samaj Party (BSP) followed by the present BJP regime of Yogi Adityanath.[1] Comparative trends (UP and all India) for sectoral and aggregate net domestic product, as well as those for two major industry groups (agriculture and manufacturing), is presented in Table 1 for the five different sub-periods (the first sub-period is truncated for lack of data). Aggregate growth figures for the years since 2011–12 (with 2011–12 as the new base year), which also relate to the period of the SP government under Mr. Akhilesh Yadav, have been presented separately in Fig. 1.

UP's aggregate growth performance remained close to the national level in the second period and outperformed that of the country in the third sub-period during the 1980s, when the state also did better in both agriculture and manufacturing. In all other sub-periods, UP's growth performance lagged behind the national growth performance. In the most recent period (2003–04 to 2014–15), UP's economy grew

---

[1] UP experienced unbroken Congress rule for the first fifteen years (1952–1967) under five of its Chief Ministers. The spell of Congress rule was broken in 1967 by the Bharatiya Kranti Dal, and between 1967 and 1980, the state oscillated between non-Congress and Congress governments, and President's rule and saw nine Chief Ministers. The state reverted to Congress rule between 1982 and 1989. Between 1989 and 1997, the state again oscillated between four unstable non-congress government formations and two spells of President's rule. The Thirteenth Assembly (1997–2002) saw a fragile alliance between the BSP and the BJP, with the BJP taking reigns for most of the period (four and a half years). The fourteenth Assembly first saw the BSP assume power, but the SP then engineered a majority and formed government from 2003 to 2007 for a period of about 3 years and 9 months. Since 2007, the state has seen two stable majority governments, first by the BSP and then by the SP.

Table 1 Growth across different periods—Uttar Pradesh and India

Sector	1961–62 to 1966–67		1967–68 to 1979–80		1980–81 to 1988–89		1989–90 to 2002–03		2003–04 to 2015–16	
	UP	India	UP	India	UP	India	UP	India	UP	India
Agriculture and allied	−2.41	1.92	2.18	1.32	7.52	4.16	2.05	2.27	2.15	3.54
Primary	1.19	2.07	1.16	1.42	2.40	4.51	1.62	2.54	2.03	3.59
Manufacturing	5.58	4.90	4.85	4.95	11.26	5.43	2.43	5.98	5.23	7.35
Secondary	6.04	5.93	5.36	4.07	8.60	5.36	2.84	5.95	6.63	7.41
Tertiary	1.63	4.75	3.35	4.63	5.83	6.32	4.14	7.40	8.23	8.13
NDP/NSDP	−0.13	3.34	3.02	3.21	7.20	5.52	3.27	5.57	6.56	7.52

Source Computed from National Account Statistics (CSO), and EPW Research Foundation
Note Data is available at different base years. To make it comparable, all data has been converted to 2004–05 base year

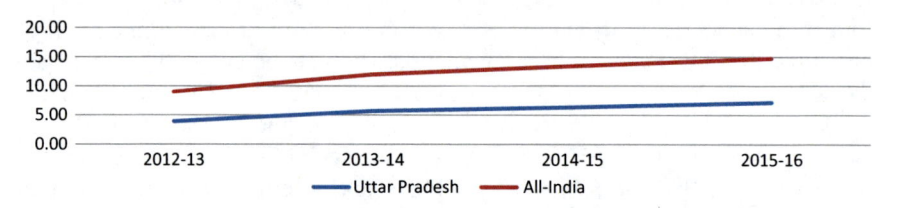

Fig. 2 Percentage growth in income: UP and India. *Source* National Account Statistics

at a good rate of 6.56% annually, but the national economy grew at a still higher rate of 7.52%. During this period, while the tertiary sector growth rate was comparable, both agriculture and manufacturing and the broader sectors (primary and secondary) registered lower growth rates in the state. Since 2011–12, Fig. 2 shows that UP has been consistently outperformed by the national growth performance.

UP's comparatively better growth story in the 1970s and 1980s can broadly be understood in terms of a spread of agricultural growth to the agriculturally poor regions, which was supported by public policy, along with higher industrial growth, the concentration of which in the Western region was sustained partly by higher levels of agricultural development in that region, and in other regions, by public investment and industrial incentives. But in later years, the state could not accelerate agricultural growth to higher levels and failed to bring about more dispersed and accelerated non-farm growth despite avowed focus on such growth.

2 Human Development

UP's dismal record in human development over several years has been analysed in a number of studies and reports (Dreze and Sen 1995, 1997, 2013; Dreze and Gazdar

1997; GoUP 2003, 2007; Planning Commission 2002; IAMR 2011). There has been virtually no improvement in the state's relative performance over several decades. According to GoUP (2007), UP ranked second lowest and third lowest in terms of a composite HDI indicator in 1991 and 2001. The most recent figures also reveal a similar picture. UP was the lowest in terms of combined gross attendance rate (GAR) in 2014–15 among 21 major states (with a GAR of 83). The state ranked 19th among 20 states in per capita income (2014–15), 17th among 20 states in infant mortality rate (IMR) (2014) and 14th among 16 states in Life Expectancy at Birth (LEB) for the period 2009–2013.[2]

3 Regional Concentration of Growth and Development Disparities

Uttar Pradesh is a large state with several regions with distinct features, background and growth trajectories. Apart from the hill region which is now a part of Uttarakhand, the state has four other regions, viz. western, central, eastern, and Bundelkhand (south-western). The National Sample Survey Organization has now further divided the western region into the northern and southern upper Ganga Plains.

The western and the eastern regions have a share of about 37 and 40%, respectively, in the state population while about one-fifth of the population lives in the central region, and only five per cent lives in Bundelkhand. The density of population in the Bundelkhand region is less than half of the population density of the state, whereas the eastern region has the highest population density with the lowest per capita availability of land.

The economic disparity between the different regions in UP has influenced both politics and policy in UP. The western region is relatively the most developed region of the state in terms of economic prosperity and leads in terms of agricultural and industrial performance. East U.P. and Bundelkhand are officially designated as backward regions. The characteristics of these regions in terms of development and poverty have been analysed at the district and region level in the two State Human Development Reports (GoUP 2003, 2007) and by the World Bank (2010).

The regions have largely retained their share of net domestic product since the 1980s (Table 2). The share of the western region in net domestic product declined in the 1980s but again picked up and was 46.4% of the state domestic product in 2013–14.

In terms of per capita net product, the eastern region shows the largest gap with the western region, while the central and Bundelkhand regions appear on par (Table 3).

Monthly per capita consumption expenditure (MPCE), which is also based on household incomes originating outside the regions, again reflects the higher level

---

[2]Gross attendance rate (GAR) is estimated from NSSO, Education in India, round data for 2014. Infant mortality rate (IMR) and Life Expectancy at Birth (LEB) are estimates as provided by the Census of India.

Table 2 Region-wise share in net state domestic product

Region	1980–81	1990–91	1999–00	2013–14
Western region	47.0	44.9	47.7	46.4
Bundelkhand region	5.2	5.5	5.1	5.1
Central region	16.4	18.2	16.0	17.8
Eastern region	31.4	31.5	31.1	30.6

Source Statistical abstract of Uttar Pradesh and planning commission of India

Table 3 Per capita net domestic product as percentage of western region

Region	1980–81	1990–91	1999–00	2013–14
Western region	100	100	100	100
Central region	78	81	75	86
Bundelkhand region	80	88	80	85
Eastern region	60	66	57	58

Source Statistical abstract of Uttar Pradesh and planning commission of India

Table 4 Regions' MPCE as percentage of MPCE in western UP

Region	1983	1987–88	1993–94	1999–00	2011–12
Central	79.8	89.3	80.3	83.4	83.8
Eastern	76.2	79.1	76.4	76.3	76.7
Southern	67.5	71.6	65.3	87.8	79

Source Estimated from various NSSO consumption expenditure quinquennial rounds

of living in the western region, but with a smaller disparity between the other three regions. The MPCE of the central region was about 80% of the MPCE in western UP in 1983 and 1993–94 but 83.8% of that level in 2011–12. Bundelkhand's MPCE was about two-third that of western UP in 1983 and 1993–94 but nearly four-fifth that level in 2011–12. However, eastern UP's MPCE has remained at just over three-quarter of the level of western UP throughout these years (Table 4).

Analysis by broad sectors shows that tertiary sector growth is the most evenly spread between the regions, while secondary sector growth is the most spatially concentrated. In 2013–14, the western region's share in secondary, primary and tertiary sector net domestic product was 52.2, 48.8 and 43.5%, respectively. Regional growth rates by sectors in between 1980–81 and 2013–14 also does not show wide differential between the regions. The high growth of the tertiary sector in all regions, with its large share in SDP, and relatively even spread has probably prevented regional disparities from becoming more explosive.

However, regions are less significant signifiers of development differentials in the state now with increasing differences between districts, both at the state level and within regions, for the secondary and tertiary sectors. Intra-regional differences have become particularly sharp in the western region. The first and the second Human Development Reports of UP which have mapped human development at the district level have further shown how districts at the lowest end of the HDI are spread across the regions (GoUP 2003, 2007).

3.1 Tenuous Link Between the Existing Pattern of Growth and Good Jobs

There is a strong recognition in state policy that rapid growth in industries and services in the state is required to create jobs for the new entrants into the workforce. UP's level and pace of employment diversification are lower than the country with agriculture's share in total employment being 51.9, compared to 47.8 in the country. Moreover, although the share of employment in manufacturing is almost the same, the share of service sector employment is 6.1% lower than the country. However, the stark difference is in the quality of employment that UP's growth has generated or failed to generate—jobs which are good and could be attractive to young, educated people.

Even though the national economy in itself is not creating enough good jobs, the gap between UP and the country is simply huge. This is seen in Table 5. Only 10.79% workers in UP have a regular wage or salaried employment in any sector of the economy, compared to 18.45% workers in the country. This is more than a reflection of the agrarian nature of UP's economy. Even within manufacturing and services, UP generates far fewer regular wage/salaried jobs. The formal sector is also much smaller in UP. Only 8.52% workers in UP are employed in the formal/organized sector, compared to 13.4% workers in the country. Further, the percentage of formal sector workers is smaller in both manufacturing and services.

Using a minimalist definition of a formal worker as a worker with any kind of written contract, we find that only 4.17% workers in UP had formal employment, compared to 6.7% workers in India. Only 3.11% workers employed in manufacturing in the state were formal workers, and 8.65% workers were formally employed in services. Finally, only 3.72% of all workers also employed in the organized sector were formally employed.

The structure of employment is poor in the country. But there is a greater concern in UP. The state economy is simply not generating enough good jobs, and this is getting reflected in higher levels of employment among the youth with tertiary levels of education. The unemployment rate among tertiary-educated young men was as high as 23.6% in 2011–12, compared to 19.2% in India. The unemployment rate among young women was higher still at 32.7% in UP, compared to 29.4% in India.

Table 5 Quality of employment, UP and India (2011–12)

(%)		Manufacturing	Services	Total employment
Regular workers	UP	23.15	22.16	10.79
	India	35.22	34.59	18.45
Formal sector workers	UP	20.65	17.68	8.52
	India	29.36	25.44	13.40
All formal workers to total workers	UP	3.11	8.65	4.17
	India	7.89	12.77	6.70
Formal workers in formal sector to total workers	UP	2.64	7.75	3.72
	India	6.41	10.80	5.67

Source Estimated from NSSO employment and unemployment round data for 2011–12

3.2 Agricultural Growth: Why Extremes Become Political Foci

UP, like most other states, is still an agrarian state, with 43.6% cultivating households and 11.7% agricultural labour households in rural areas in 2011–12. Given the large variations across regions and subregions in UP, agricultural growth in the state has to be understood both in terms of factors which affect both aggregate and regional/subregional performance. Large parts of the western, central and eastern regions are in the alluvial Indo-Gangetic belt, whereas Bundelkhand is in the central plateau region and has rocky terrain and low rainfall. These regions are also distinguished by revenue settlement arrangements during the colonial period (Mahalwari, Talukdari, Permanent Settlement and Bhaichara), histories of public investment in irrigation, agro-ecological and social features, land holding structure and population density.

Variations in the agro-ecological characteristics along with variations in agrarian and social structure and population density persist across the regions and must figure in any explanation of current economic and political trajectories. Computations based on the NSS 70th round show that the average size of operational holding varied from 1.53 ha in Bundelkhand to 0.83 and 0.67 ha in the northern and southern upper Ganga Plains, and 0.58 and 0.53 ha, respectively, in central and eastern regions. Further, as much as 21.47% of operated area in Bundelkhand and 9.65 and 6.26% area in the northern and southern upper Ganga Plains was concentrated in medium and large holdings, compared to only 3.86 and 3.76% operated area in these size of holdings in Central and eastern UP.

Overall agricultural growth was highest in the state during the 1970s and 1980s but has decelerated since then. The period of high growth was also marked by higher growth in area under public and private irrigation, growth in productivity made possible by use of HYV (high yield varieties) and fertilizers, and phases of land consolidation (Bhalla and Singh 2012; Singh 1997; Lieten and Srivastava 1999) (Table 6).

Table 6 Period-wise and region-wise growth rate of agricultural output value in UP

Compound average growth rate (CAGR) of output value					
Region	1962–1973	1973–1983	1983–1993	1993–2006	1962–2006
Western region	2.16	3.82	3.62	1.46	2.66
Central region	1.43	2.59	3.71	1.85	2.33
Bundelkhand region	2.80	1.14	2.43	1.79	2.04
Eastern region	0.93	3.54	4.20	0.97	2.27
Total	1.70	3.33	3.74	1.40	2.44

Source Computed from Bhalla and Singh (2012)

The western region has maintained an overall edge in growth, but there were phases, especially during the 1980s when the other regions showed higher growth in performance over the western region. The western region's early lead in agriculture occurred because its agrarian structure and infrastructure made it the springboard of the green revolution in Uttar Pradesh, which was initially biased towards crops such as wheat and sugarcane, already favoured in the west. As land consolidation progressed, investment in private tubewells also increased, giving farmers greater access to assured irrigation which sustained high rates of agricultural growth in the region. But by the end of the 1970s, agriculture in the rice-based eastern region began to show an upturn and was faster than the western region during the 1980s (Lieten and Srivastava 1999).

By the beginning of this decade, all regions in the state saw more than a doubling of the percentage of the cropped area under irrigation, with close to 90% of the cropped area in the western region being irrigated, compared to only about 44% of the cropped area in Bundelkhand.[3] It should be noted that the sources of increased irrigation came both from public and private sources and that particularly during the period 1970s–1990s, canal irrigation expanded significantly in the poorer agrarian regions of UP.

The cropping pattern that has emerged in the state shows a high dominance of rice–wheat in the central and eastern regions with every small percentage of area under high-value crops. On the other hand, the western region, and in particular the northern upper Ganga Plains, has shown a steady increase in sugar cane area and the area under other high-value crops. At the turn of this decade, the northern upper Ganga Plains had close to 40% of its area was under sugarcane and other high-value crops. The Bundelkhand region also shows a diversification away from cereals, but this has been in favour of the less irrigated/rain-fed oilseeds and pulses (ibid).

The resultant changes in UP's regions in land and worker productivity in terms of value of output vis a vis the western region are shown in Table 7. In terms of both indicators, the western region has been able to maintain its lead over the other regions.

---

[3]District-level data provided by the Directorate of Agricultural Statistics, UP.

Table 7 Value of output per cropped hectare and per agricultural worker as per cent of western UP

Region	1962–65	1970–73	1980–83	1990–93	2003–06
Per cropped hectare					
Central	84.96	84.01	77.36	79.95	79.05
Bundelkhand	65.88	71.79	59.65	54.25	49.79
Eastern	74.04	69.70	68.61	73.81	70.89
Per agricultural worker					
Central	61.12	70.00	58.29	60.31	59.30
Bundelkhand	77.66	116.63	69.88	55.85	54.71
Eastern	41.33	56.03	46.74	47.67	39.90

Source Computed from district-level data compiled by Bhalla and Singh (2012)

Given the vastly different trajectories of these regions, it is interesting that the focus of political interest in UP has been, for completely different reasons, on farmers in two very differently placed regions—western UP and Bundelkhand and the state's responses to it too have been very different.

In the western region, particularly in the districts comprising the northern upper Ganga Plains, there is a recurrent crisis for farmers associated with the non-realization of the value of the sugarcane crop, which comprises the main source of income for these farmer households. It may be pointed out that the farming community in this region is dominated by peasant castes, among whom Jats are the most numerous. The non-realization of cane dues is due to multiple factors, including the liberalization of the sugar industry due to which there is greater fluctuation in sugar prices, the lower efficiency of sugar factories in UP and the errant behaviour of these factories which use cane arrears to bargain with the central and state government for greater subsidies even in years when the market conditions are good. The political support of the peasantry, as well as the mills, is important for all major parties. Thus, both the central and state governments take steps to support industry and to reduce distress among farmers by dealing with the payment arrears. The central government, which has been announcing a Fair and Remunerative Price for cane since 2009, has for some years been extending interest-free loans to the factory owners and giving export subsidies to boost sugar exports and support sugar prices. The state government announces support prices for cane but has frozen these since 2013–14. In the past, it was providing subsidies to mills to meet cane arrears. But since last year, it has used the DBT route to meet cane arrears. The 2016–17 state budget makes a provision of Rs. 139 crore towards these arrears. Nevertheless, cane farmers have to cope with arrears over long periods of time, impacting unevenly across factory areas and size classes. With the decline in associations such as the Bharatiya Kisan Union (BKU), it becomes easier for organizations and political parties to organize them around issues of identity politics and culture.

The Bundelkhand region, as we have shown earlier, has also seen some increase in irrigation and a diversification of agriculture away from coarse grain, towards wheat, oilseeds, chickpea and pulses. But most agriculture is still rain-fed. Any crisis in this region has also to be understood in terms of its fairly in-egalitarian agrarian structure, as large landowners tend to control access to public irrigation as well as sources of private irrigation. Nonetheless, smaller farmers have also attempted to invest in irrigation and diversify their production base, often at very significant risks.

Long-term neglect of traditional forms of irrigation and drought proofing has exacerbated drought-related risks. This, as a recent study (Gupta et al. 2014) has pointed out, has broken the sequence between meteorological drought, hydrological drought and agricultural drought even creating drought conditions in rain surplus years. The droughts have had a dramatic effect on marginal and small farmers and labourers. Lack of a diversified economy in this region means migration becomes virtually the only coping mechanism for poorer households. The region faced drought conditions for almost half the years in the last decade, and for successive years, this decade with horrendous consequences, documented by a recent survey (Abhiyan 2015).

The 'backwardness' of the region prompted Mayawati to seek a special Rs. 80,000 crore package for Bundelkhand, along with eastern Uttar Pradesh, when she became Chief Minister in 2007. The Planning Commission instituted a committee under Mr. B. K. Chaturvedi to consider her demands. But after Rahul Gandhi took up the demand for a package for drought-hit Bundelkhand, the UPA government at the Centre instituted an inter-Ministerial Committee which awarded a Bundelkhand 'package' of Rs. 7466 crore in 2009, with about 58% of the package allocated to UP. Till March 31, 2015, UP had not utilized 47.4% of the award (http://agricoop.nic.in/imagedefault1/Bundelkhand_Package.pdf).[4] Moreover, the quality of expenditure has been very poor under the two successive governments over this period. While these governments also instituted some measures for Bundelkhand at the state level, these also have had little impact on the region. Political parties, especially the Congress, have tried to drum up political support on the basis of the continued vulnerability of the small farmers and labourers in this region, which contrasts with the clout of the dominant peasant castes in western UP and hence has been able to provide limited currency till date.

4 Elusive Industrial Growth

The successive governments in UP have focused on a strategy of rapid industrialization as a way of creating growth, good quality jobs and development. Industrialization is seen as encompassing both manufacturing and services, and the growth of infrastructure is seen as a precondition to industrial growth. The aim of the liberalization initiated in the 1990s was to unleash the growth potential of the Indian economy, and the industrial sector was considered central to these reforms. However, as pointed out earlier, UP's industrial growth has been significantly lower than the national econ-

---

[4] Accessed on 25 September 2016 http://agricoop.nic.in/imagedefault1/Bundelkhand_Package.pdf.

omy since the 1990s. The state's share in manufacturing income had increased from about 5.6% in the early 1960s to about nine per cent in the late 1980s and has fallen to about five per cent currently. The share of manufacturing income in state income also more than doubled from about seven per cent in the early 1960s to about 15% in the late 1980s but is currently only at about nine per cent.

The state's industrial economy in the organized sector is predominantly agro-processing based with significant strengths in the chemicals and engineering sector. The small industrial units in the state range from family-run enterprises (own account units) to small units working with a few hired workers. Typically, these units are in the handloom/handicraft sector or are unregistered modern small-scale units. The state had about 22.34 lakh unregistered units with a gross output of Rs. 37,024 crore (10% of the national output) employing about 51.76 lakh persons (12.66% of persons employed nationally) in this segment in 2006–07 (Fourth Report of All-India Census of Medium, Small and Micro Enterprises, 2006–07: Unregistered Sector). The SSI units are prominent in the agro-processing (sugar and vegetable oil), brassware, glassware and cotton yarn sectors. 67% of these enterprises were in manufacturing.

A major distinguishing feature of the industrial economy of Uttar Pradesh is a massive presence of a large number of skill-intensive traditional industries. These include handloom, zardosi, chikan work, perfume industry, brassware, pottery, glassware, lock-making, leatherwork, wooden toys and furniture carving. UP is estimated to have about 1.1 lakh handloom worker households and about 2.2 lakh workers of whom one lakh were full time. 42% weaver households were located in urban areas. More than 90% of the workers belong to OBC category. Nearly three-quarter weavers work with master weavers, while a quarter are independent weavers. The cooperative sector covers a negligible proportion of units in the state (Census of Handlooms, 2009–10). The element of art and crafts present in the Uttar Pradesh handloom sector makes it a potential sector for upper segments of the market both in India as well as globally (GoI 2007).

The total unregistered manufacturing sector retains an important place in UP, not only in employment and its contribution to exports but also in its share in manufacturing income (SDP). Its share in the manufacturing sector was about 58% in the early 1960s but fell to about 37% in the early 1990s after a period of fairly brisk growth of registered manufacturing and currently stands at about 49% of manufacturing SDP.

The high industrial growth in the 1980s, referred to earlier, was driven by large doses of public investment (both central and state) and stimulation of private sector participation in the state's industrial growth in a period when industrial policy instruments were more state-driven; there were Congress governments in the state and at the centre. Industrial investments were especially directed to certain areas which were constituencies of important leaders such as Indira Gandhi and Rajiv Gandhi. This pattern of industrialization was neither feasible nor sustainable with the economic reforms of 1991.

The reforms set the stage for a more liberal economic environment and competition among states to attract private investment. Struggling with relative backwardness, infrastructural, fiscal and governance constraints in the 1990s, UP tried to fall in line with the changed environment. The Mulayam Singh government of 1994 initiated some policy changes which were followed by comprehensive policy statement by the BJP government under Kalyan Singh in 1998 (Pai 2005). Since then, there have been two other industrial policies for the state in 2004 and 2012. Each of these aimed at making UP a more attractive destination for Indian and foreign capital and promoting more rapid growth of the different segments of industry, services and infrastructure. There were also industrial policy-related decisions by governments led by Mayawati in 2002 (alliance government with BJP) and in 2008.

The 1998 industrial policy (under the BJP government of Kalyan Singh) recognized the need to allay apprehensions regarding UP's security environment. It also proposed the development of six industrial corridors. The government under Mulayam Singh (2003–2007), made a slew of policy announcements to promote the growth of industry and modern services. The basic edifice of policy was elaborated in the 'U.P. Industrial and Services Sector Investment Policy 2004.' The policy aimed at an industrial growth rate of 12.4%. It proposed four special economic zones in Greater Noida, Kanpur, Bhadohi and Moradabad, and one more SEZ was proposed in Noida by the Handicrafts Export Promotion Council. Like its predecessor policy, it also aimed to 'ensure creation of an atmosphere of security to develop confidence in the entrepreneurs' because of UP's stereotypical image, although the crime data facts 'speak otherwise'. It proposed financial concessions to industry and laid emphasis on 'deregulation' of labour laws and other laws, such as pollution laws. It also proposed a 'single-table scheme' for web-based registration of firms.

The Samajwadi Party government of Akhilesh Yadav again laid stress on deepening market-based industrial policies to make UP an attractive destination for domestic/foreign capital. At the core of the strategy was a renewed focus on infrastructure-led development in the industries and services sector. The earlier policy was replaced with the 'Infrastructure and Industrial Development Policy 2012'. As in 2004, several other sectors and industry-specific policies have also been announced. The new policy highlighted the role of infrastructure development through public–private partnerships and spoke of the State Industrial Development Corporation building a land bank. It continued the cluster development policies, SEZ and other policies announced earlier. It also offered further simplification of procedures in clearances, registration, tax payments and labour laws, and time-bound land acquisition in addition to fiscal incentives (graded regionally, industry and sector-wise) and slabs of investment with case-specific incentives for mega projects. The fiscal incentives ranged from Investment Promotion Scheme (interest-free loan as working capital), Capital Interest Subsidy Scheme, infrastructure interest subsidy scheme, EPF reimbursement scheme, industrial quality development subsidy scheme and special facilities for mega projects (with an investment of more than Rs. 200 crore), among others.

We saw in Table 1 that UP's manufacturing growth was close to the all-India growth rate in the second period (late 1960s to late 1970s) and higher than the all-India growth in the 80s, but in the two subsequent periods, it remained well below the

Table 8 Annual average growth rate of manufacturing in UP in different sub-periods

Sector	1961–62 to 1966–67	1967–68 to 1979–80	1980–81 to 1988–89	1989–90 to 2002–03	2003–04 to 2014–15
Manufacturing	5.58	4.85	11.26	2.43	5.23
Registered	7.77	5.57	15.21	1.99	6.43
Unregistered	3.99	4.93	7.14	3.54	4.40

Source Computed from National Account Statistics (CSO) and EPW Research Foundation

all-India growth rate.[5] Growth rates of registered and unregistered manufacturing in UP, disaggregated by sub-periods, are given in Table 8. Compared to the high growth rates in the 1980s, both registered and unregistered manufacturing growth rates in UP decelerated during 1980–90 to 2002–03. During 2002–03 to 2014–15, registered manufacturing picked up, but unregistered manufacturing grew at a slower rate.

In terms of the regional pattern of industrialization, there has been a steady growth in industrial concentration, which has shown an accelerated tendency in recent decades. We have compared trends in organized manufacturing across districts and regions at three points of time (1986–87, 2000–01 and 2010–11). Between 1986–87 and 2010–11, persons employed in organized manufacturing declined in a majority of districts in eastern and central UP, half the districts in Bundelkhand and 30% of the districts even in western UP. Employment declined in all the major industrial centres in eastern and central UP, including Kanpur, Lucknow, Varanasi, Allahabad, Gorakhpur, Raebareli–Sultanpur.

But at the regional level, there is increased concentration of organized manufacturing in western UP in terms of total investment, persons employed, and net value added (Table 9). Between 1987–88 and 2010–11, the share of the eastern, central and Bundelkhand regions in total persons employed declined from 25.5, 20.1 and 2.1% to 10.1, 14.2 and 2.0%, respectively, while the share of the western region increased from 52.2 to 73.7%. It is noteworthy that in the last region, NOIDA and Ghaziabad districts alone accounted for about 36% of value added in registered manufacturing in 2013–14.

For unregistered manufacturing, we have compared district-level data for two years, viz. 1998–99 and 2013–14. Due to disparate district-level growth performances, there has been a sharp increase in concentration in unregistered manufacturing. At the state level, the Gini coefficient for NVA from unregistered manufacturing increased from 0.46 to 0.69. The concentration of unregistered manufacturing also increased within each region (except eastern region) with the sharpest increase occurring in the western region—from a Gini of 0.31 to 0.82. This points towards the decline of many of the industrial clusters in UP, something which is well documented in several case studies.

---

[5]Between 1970–71 and 1985–86, the growth rate of the manufacturing sector in the state was higher than of several industrialised states such as Maharashtra, Gujarat and Punjab. In particular, the growth of the unregistered manufacturing sector was truly spectacular at 7.6% annually.

Table 9 Percentage share of regions in total invested capital (TIC), net value added (NVA) and total persons engaged (TPE)

Region	1987–88			2000–01			2010–11		
	TIC	NVA	TPE	TIC	NVA	TPE	TIC	NVA	TPE
Eastern	36.99	24.42	25.49	23.6	19.95	20.09	13.5	16.47	10.06
Western	45.96	60.97	52.24	65.94	62.61	63.16	72.2	62.15	73.71
Bundelkhand	1.52	2.4	2.14	0.93	1.37	1.37	0.73	1.5	2.04
Central	15.54	12.21	20.12	9.53	16.07	15.38	13.58	19.88	14.19
Total	100	100	100	100	100	100	100	100	100

Source Various years, Statistical Abstract of Uttar Pradesh

It is also clear that the measures taken by the Akhilesh Yadav government did not bear results in terms of the objective of attracting large-scale investments. Between 2010 and 2015, the Indian Entrepreneur Memorandum (IEM) filed for investment in UP averaged Rs. 21,524 crore, which was just 2.1% of the IEMs filed for the country as a whole. Between 2010 and March 2016, the actual investment was only Rs. 8800 crore (less than an average annual investment of Rs. 1500 crore) and only 2.2% of the national figure (Ministry of Commerce and Industry).

Thus, successive governments in UP have neither been able to build on the strengths on the state's industrial base in the handicraft/handloom sector, nor build the modern small-/medium-/large-scale sector.

5 Some Elements of the Political Economy of UP's Industrial Development

Although the state has not been short on policy statements, its record in terms of transforming the industrial sector (broadly defined) has left a growing gap with other states and even with a number of poorer states. The constraints on this growth come from a number of sources, the main being the state's failure to respond adequately to existing opportunities as an issue of poor 'governance'. This can mean several things (Weiss 2000) but the allusion is usually to the inability of successive governments to provide a coherent policy direction; lack of transparency in decision-making, along with inefficiency, lack of responsiveness and accountability; high levels of corruption; poor rule of law (weak law and order, lack of communal peace, and influence of criminal mafia) (Centre for Policy Dialogue 2003; GoUP 2003).These elements can be distinguished from the need to provide a good business environment (in central government metrics, UP currently ranks fourteenth), although there is an overlap in some of the elements.

The Bharatiya Janata Party (BJP) gained ascendancy in UP after the communal polarization following its sustained mobilization on the issue of a Ram temple at the site of 'the Babri mosque. The BJP was also part of two subsequent alliance governments. Communal peace in the state remains tentative with an escalation in the occurrences of communal riots/incidents in the state. These particularly affect large numbers of direct producers in the urban informal manufacturing sector. Weak rule of law in the state has been of concern for several decades. As pointed out earlier, two successive industrial policies of the state government also acknowledged the need to address security concerns. Further, the change in government in 2007 is also mainly attributed to the poor law and order situation under the then SP government.

Cronyism, lack of transparency and ad hocism have characterized a number of decisions. The SP government under Mulayam Singh formulated industrial policies in 2004, but its major decision to attract investors was to put together a 'Development Council' comprising a number of well-known industrialists at the national level and a famous film star, headed by a political figure very close to the Chief Minister and also to two of the industrialists nominated to the Council. Detailed analysis of the work of this Council has not been undertaken, but some of the decisions taken by the then government appeared to bypass competitive bidding procedures and amounted to passing benefits to some of the industrial groups considered close to the government (Tripathi 2004). In some cases, as in power and housing, policies formulated by the government appeared to benefit these industrialists at the cost of the public exchequer. The Council, a clear manifestation of crony capitalism, was disbanded on the first day that the new BSP government assumed office in 2012, also, however, jeopardising the investments promised by these industrial houses.

When, after languishing for decades, the sugar industry in UP surged ahead during 2002–04 on the basis of high demand and decline in domestic production, the government's Sugar Investment Promotion Policy announced in 2004 allowed for a major expansion in sugar production capacity through setting up of new sugar plants, The main beneficiaries of the move, however, turned out to be a few big private sector groups in UP. Simultaneously, the government in a more controversial decision also decided to lease out 24 state-run sugar factories to a leading industrial house making it the largest sugar producer in UP, again raising apprehensions of crony capitalism and lack of transparency in its decision-making. The latter move was reversed by the new BSP government which also seized (in October 2007) sugar stocks of 63 factories to pay price arrears to growers in a move to placate almost seven million cane growers in the state.

Mayawati's government was itself open to the charge of cronyism due to its alleged proximity to single industrial house and non-transparent procedures that were followed in contracts that were set up in this period. The government also announced 30% reservations in private sector companies which had dealings with government through partnerships or outsourcing, but the decision was withdrawn in the face of opposition from private investors.

The knee-jerk reactions of state governments and their failure to evolve transparent rules seem to point to discretionary control and rent-seeking without systematically seeking to overcome barriers to growth. Successive governments have taken on board the interests of industrialists only through discretionary policies rather than address systemic issues.

Similar failure also extends to the governments' lacklustre approach towards the small sector and traditional industries. As discussed earlier, these industries involve a very large number of workers, mainly belonging to the 'backward castes' among both Hindus and Muslims. The actual producers in these industries live in very poor conditions, and these industries face very real problems. It is a moot question why successive governments, which swear by the social base to which these small producers belong, have failed to take significant steps to transform their condition. One answer perhaps lies in the fact that these small producers are part of a production chain dominated by merchant capitalists who are themselves quite content in extracting absolute surpluses from the poor producers, and the politically dominant class find it easier to accommodate the interests of the merchant capitalists, who are powerful locally, and whose demands on the economic system do not extend to radical transformation of the production base.

Another reason why policies have not yielded the desired results is the state's initial backwardness and lack of proper infrastructure that makes it difficult for it to compete with more developed states to attract investment, both foreign and domestic. The development of physical infrastructure has been a priority for successive state governments for some decades, but the path adopted for infrastructure development has often been both contentious and controversial.

5.1 Highways to Growth? Land Acquisition and Infrastructure Creation

Agra-Lucknow Expressway and Samajwadi Purvanchal Expressway will prove to be growth highways for the state: Chief Minister'. (Press Information Bureau. Lucknow. Sept. 2, 2016)

The state has sought to overcome its infrastructural constraints with a much larger focus on physical infrastructure in recent years, especially on roads and electricity.[6] However, decisions on investors/developers have again been open to charges of non-transparency and cronyism and conflicts related to land acquisition. Most of the large-scale developments have been in the public–private partnership mode, except recently when the state government stepped in with direct investments for the Agra-Lucknow Expressway.

Infrastructure development involves multiple types of investments, including investment on roads, energy, telecommunication, storage and marketing infrastructure for agriculture, industrial estates and common facility centres for industrial clusters. Expressways and power plants represent two types of large-scale invest-

---

[6]In 2013-14, UP spent 6.2 and 6.8% of its aggregate expenditure on physical expenditure and energy, respectively, compared to 6.3 and 6.5%, respectively, for all low-income (category C) states taken together (RBI State Finances: A Study of Budgets, and UP Budget, Various years). However, capital outlay has been rising steadily since 2013–14—from 3.81% of SDP in 2013–14 in 2013–14 to 5.65% in 2014–15, 7.23% in 2015–16 (RE) and an estimated 6.13% in 2016–17 (UP Budget documents).

ments which also require land acquisition. It was the BJP government in UP, which in 2002, had first embarked on ambitious plans to build expressways and plants. The succeeding Mulayam Singh government went all out to woo a small band of investors to the state, who also announced ambitious plans. Many of these plans did not fructify due to irregularities of various kinds, including the manner in which the colonial Land Acquisition Act of 1896 was used to forcibly acquire land from farmers.

Many of the recent conflicts have their genesis in the implementation of the provisions of the 1896 Land Acquisition Act. For instance, the Anil Ambani group (ADAG) offered to set up a 7480 MW gas-fired power plant at Dadri (In 2007, after the company's dispute with the Mukesh Ambani group, the company examined the prospect of setting up a 1320 MW thermal power plant at the site) (Shrivastava 2009). The plant was inaugurated by Mulayam Singh Yadav in 2004. However, the acquisition was set aside by the High Court in 2009 which upheld the plea of the farmers that provisions of the Land Acquisition Act had not been followed and their consent was not obtained. The petitioners had alleged that cultivable land had been acquired for the project and that the compensation at the rate of Rs. $120/m^2$ paid to the farmers was much below the market rate of Rs. $15,000/m^2$. About 2500 acres had been acquired for the power plant (Khan 2009). Protests were also held against land acquisition and setting up of three thermal power plants by the Mayawati government in 2007 in Karchhana and Bara in Allahabad. Two plants are being set up by the JP Group, and the third by NTPC and the UP Power Corporation. The Karchhana site, in particular, has been the site of intense protests, and here, too, the court has struck down the acquisition and allowed the farmers to reclaim their land and return the compensation to the government (Rashid 2013).

The decision to construct the 165 km. Yamuna Expressway connecting NOIDA to Agra was approved by the Uttar Pradesh state government in 2001 when Rajnath Singh was Chief Minister, as part of a plan of building an expressway from NOIDA to Ballia. The tender for the Yamuna Expressway was awarded to Jai Prakash Associates in February 2003 under a thirty-six-year BOT agreement. The same group was also given the contract for executing the construction of Ganga Expressway. Construction of the Expressway began in 2007. However, land was acquired not only for the construction of the expressway but for giving the JP group exclusive rights for real estate development over large tracts of land near the expressway and making this land available to other private developers. The Mayawati government acquired about 6500 hectares of land under Section 17 of the Acquisition Act, in over 1300 villages, for the expressway development, sparking off farmer's unrest and a major protest in Bhatta and Parsaul villages near Dadri in 2011. Both the High Court and the Supreme Court struck down a number of land acquisitions although the acquisition of land for the expressway was upheld by the courts (Mehra 2011; Parashar 2011; Sood 2011).

In response to the agitations, the Uttar Pradesh government under Mayawati announced a new Rehabilitation and Resettlement Policy on September 3, 2010, which was further modified in June 2011. The policy was converted into a law in 2013 with additional modifications under the Akhilesh Yadav government. The Right to Fair Compensation and Transparency in Land Acquisition, Rehabilitation and Resettlement Act 2013 (in force from 2014) has put forth a more restricted definition of public purpose, as land required for strategic purpose or infrastructure (includes transport, energy, telecom, water and sanitation, and social and commercial infrastructure) and for certain other categories of projects. A consent clause will be operational if land is acquired for transfer to PPP or private projects. In case of urban land acquisition, there is a provision of sharing of appreciated value (40%). The final value of compensation is based on a new and more liberal formula, which further offered an annuity/job/lump sum; or 20% of the land acquired for urbanization may be offered to affected families

The Akhilesh government claimed that it acquired 5000 acres of land for the Agra-Lucknow Expressway, and 70% of it was acquired only in six months (June–Nov 2014). The government also claimed to have adopted modified and more transparent bidding procedures with seemingly better outcomes. The expressway has been built with state budget through five developers for different sections.

6 Social Protection Schemes

Successive regimes in Uttar Pradesh have avowedly focused on new or existing social protection schemes in order to provide benefits to different sections. The SP's announcement regarding an employment benefit scheme for the youth and a laptop distribution programme during its election campaign in 2012 created quite a buzz and is considered to have contributed to Akhilesh's popularity. In its pre-election budget in 2016, his government upscaled allocations to several programmes, especially in pensions and housing.[7] It raised the target for pensions to the old and disabled under the Samajwadi Pension Programme from Rs. forty-five to fifty-five lakh. The farmers' accident and life insurance scheme Rs. with five lakh life cover and Rs. 2.5 lakh accident cover (rechristened as Samajwadi Sarvhit Bima Yojana) was provided an additional Rs. 240 crore budgetary support, while the state rural housing scheme (Lohia Grameen Awas) was provided with Rs. 1779 crore. Free smart phones were to be provided under the Samajwadi Smartphone Yojana to those with higher secondary education and an annual income of less than Rs. two lakh.

The BSP which has been in power in UP five times since 1993, in alliances, or on its own had also launched some programmes. It had initiated the Ambedkar Village Programme (AVP) in 1995 through which it converged development schemes to develop localities/villages with a large Dalit population.[8] The other important programme, with mildly redistributive overtones, was Mayawati's emphasis on distribution of

---

[7] As a percentage of total aggregate expenditure, UP's social sector expenditure (excluding education and health) does not show a distinct trend. Reserve Bank of India (RBI), budget documents of the state governments. It increased from 16.5% in 2012–13 to 17.5% in 2013–13 and further to 19.1% in 2014–15, but is estimated at 17.3% in 2016–17 (BE). (RBI State Finances: A Study of Budgets, and UP Budget, Various years).

[8] However, despite claims to the contrary (Chatterjee 2003; Kumar 2003), some studies claimed that its impact was lacklustre (Pai 2002, 2004).

patta land, ensuring possession of lands already distributed and regularization of de facto possessions and encroachments. The programme was more successful in awarding possession than in fresh land allotments and was modest in relation to patta land distribution programmes undertaken earlier under Congress governments (Pai 2005). At the very end of its last tenure, the BSP government also introduced a scheme to provide financial assistance to poor non-SC families under the Mahamaya Garib Arthik Madad Yojana, pledging support to 25 lakh poor families with financial assistance of Rs. 400 per month, with a proposed budget of Rs. 1080 crore budgeted in 2011–12.

However, in the past, many of the schemes—both central and state—have been mired in corruption, and there is little evidence to suggest that their effectiveness improved under successive governments.

In the last two decades, a number of scams have come to light in UP. Some of these relate to issues such as recruitments, postings and transfers, land acquisitions and sweet deals with developers,[9] but a number of scams relate to the implementation of programmes primarily intended for the poor.

Large-scale scams in the distribution of food grains meant for government programmes such as the JRY, Sampoorna Grameen Rozgar Yojana, the Antyodaya Anna Yojana (AAY), Midday Meal Scheme and the TPDS occurred in the state between 2000 and 2007, under which food grains were sold in the open market or smuggled to neighbouring countries (Bangladesh, Nepal). The scams were considered to be worth Rs. 35,000 crore.[10] There were allegations that the scam involved parties across the political spectrum as well as senior leaders and the Food and Civil Supplies Minister in the Mulayam Singh government (Khetan 2012).

In 2009, a pension scam relating to old age pensions, involving the forging of age certificates and false BPL certificates was uncovered in several districts of the state (Srivastava 2009). Similar scams have also been reported in the Widows Pension Scheme and the National Family Benefit Scheme. In Muzaffarnagar district alone, the scam was estimated to be to the tune of about Rs. 30 crore.[11]

The biggest scam which came to light during the Mayawati government related to the National Rural Health Mission (NRHM) and reportedly involved an amount of Rs. 9400 crore. The Health Minister, Health Secretary, and scores of health department

---

[9]The Mayawati government ordered a high-level probe into a police recruitment scam alleged to have taken place in UP during the previous Mulayam Singh government. Later, the High Court ordered a CBI enquiry in the scam, but this was stayed by the Supreme Court in 2008.

The arrest of Yadav Singh, an engineer, posted with the NOIDA authority has again brought to light large-scale irregularities and scams related to land acquisitions and deals with developers in NOIDA and Greater NOIDA areas of the state. These deals are also said to implicate Mayawati's own brother, as well as other officials and political figures (Vivek Awasthi. 'CBI knocks on the doors of NOIDA and seeks details of property owned by Mayawati's brother', First Post, September 28).

[10]Mr. Mulayam Singh Yadav set up a SIT in 2006 to investigate the scam which filed 5000 cases. The government under Mayawati transferred the investigation to the CBI in 2007, and later, under the instruction of the High Court, the CBI was asked to enquire into all ramifications of the scam and conclude the investigations in within six months.

[11]Patrika, Dec 15, 2015http://www.patrika.com/news/muzaffernagar/widow-pension-scam-in-muzaffarnagar-1-4032/.

officials were arrested for their alleged roles in the scam.[12] A huge scam involving payment of crore of scholarship to SC students was uncovered in 2010.[13] These scams raise serious concerns about the quality of governance of social protection programmes in the state.

We reviewed the performance of several programmes (public employment programmes, TPDS, ICDS, Midday Meal and programmes relating to reproductive and child health) for 2004–05, across major states, ranking their performance using specific indicators (Srivastava 2012). For some indicators, the analysis was updated till 2009–10 (ibid.). UP was a consistently poor performer in all the programmes reviewed, unlike several other low-income states, such as Odisha, Chhattisgarh or Madhya Pradesh which showed silver linings in terms of good performance in some of the programmes.

More recent performance also continues to underscore the state's abysmally poor record. The Mahatma Gandhi National Rural Employment Guarantee Act or MGNREGA, the national flagship programme for ensuring employment to the poorest of poor, which has the potential of being an important safety net in drought years, is a case in point. The performance of UP in this scheme has been comparatively poor throughout, and its recent performance shows a downward trend. An analysis of the NSS employment–unemployment round survey data for 2009–10 shows that in that year only 16.24 % rural households in UP participated in MGNREGA. Among the low-income states, this was the second lowest after Bihar. The person-days of employment generated was only 34, higher than 23 days in Bihar, but lower than Odisha's 37 days, 63 days in Madhya Pradesh and 76 days in Rajasthan. The national average is 43 days.

The performance of MGNREGA has continued to show a steady worsening in the state after the first year of its universalization. The official MIS data shows that although the households receiving employment and person-days of employment generated rose in the 2015–16 drought year compared to the preceding year, it remained lower than the years 2009–10 to 2011–12. Moreover, there was no increase in the days of employment provided per household, which remained at a low 33.5.

The National Food Security Act (NFSA) has started being implemented by the state only in March 2016. It replaces the TPDS which has shown poor performance. An National Council for Applied Economic Research (NCAER) survey carried out between October and December 2014 in six states found that the programme functioned poorly in three states—Assam, UP and West Bengal—with the highest leak-

---

[12] Venkitesh Ramakrishnan, 'Blatant in Uttar Pradesh', Frontline, Vol. 28, Issue 17, August 13–26, 2011 Venkitesh (2011). First Post, 'NRHM scam: CBI filed charge sheet against Kushwaha, 5 others', December 7, 2012, First Post, 'Former UP Health Secy arrested in NRHM proble', May 10, 2012.

[13] Umesh Raghuvanshi, 'UP changes rules to check scholarship frauds', Hindustan Times, Lucknow. Oct 14, 2010. Umesh (2010). http://www.hindustantimes.com/lucknow/up-changes-rules-to-check-scholarship-frauds/story-8LQq9NsStad925oLHAJvdI.html

Indian Express, "UP govt probing multi-crore scam in SC scholarship funds", June 7, 2012. http://archive.indianexpress.com/news/up-govt-probing-multicrore-scam-in-sc-scholarship-funds/959045.

ages (NCAER 2015). Leakage as a percentage of BPL entitlement was found to be 35.29% in UP, compared to 16.28% in Bihar. Exclusion errors were the highest/second highest in UP among the six states, depending on the criteria used (ibid).

The Public Evaluation of Entitlement Programmes (PEEP) survey (Dreze and Khera 2014) assessed five entitlement programmes: the Integrated Child Development Services, midday meals, the Public Distribution System, the National Rural Employment Guarantee Act and social security pensions across ten states. UP was assessed to be one of the laggard states in all five programmes.

7 Did Successive Governments Make Growth in UP Being Socially Inclusive?

Has UP has experienced socially inclusive growth in the last several years? An earlier paper (Srivastava 2012) examined relevant trends in employment, consumption, education and land ownership between 1999–00 and 2004–05 for SCs and Muslims and concluded that although improvement had taken place in some of the indicators, 'Overall UP has not been able to step up the rate of inclusive growth over and above the rest of the country' (ibid., p. 25).

We have now analysed trends in the performance of the three social categories (Hindu SC and OBC, and Muslim) over a longer time period—1983 to 2011–12, based on NSS data on different rounds of survey of consumption and employment/unemployment.[14] But we focus on changes in the more recent period, when 'social justice' parties have been in government in UP.

7.1 Education

Our analysis of educational attainment across social groups has been undertaken at two levels of attainment—at least middle school attainment and at least secondary school attainment. We find that the OBC has been able to bridge the gap with the state average for middle school-level education and have been also able to almost close the gap at secondary school-level attainment. The gap with the state average remains large for SCs, but was marginally reduced for middle school attainment after 1993–94, while it has continued to grow for high school achievers. Muslims,

---

[14] All results in this section are based on estimates made from the NSS employment–unemployment and consumption rounds. Corrections have been made for changes in the geographical boundary of the state and the industrial and occupational categories used have been concorded. The data for OBCs is only available from 1999–00, but a significant percentage of OBCs appear to have misreported as General castes, so for OBCs, comparison is only possible between 2004–05 and 2011–12. The results are presented for rural and urban locations taken together, and hence do not control for locational characteristics. This is important since urban-rural location matters and some groups are overrepresented (Muslim, Upper Caste) or underrepresented (SC, OBC) in urban areas.

however, face a growing gap with the state averages at both education levels, with a larger deficit compared to SCs.

There is also a growing gap between SC and Muslim educational attainments at the state level and at the national level. For OBCs, this gap is much smaller, although it increased marginally between 2004–05 and 2011–12. With upper caste Hindus, it is the other way around, with their attainment levels in the state outperforming the national levels with increasing levels of margin.

7.2 Consumption

The distributional change in consumption appears to reflect somewhat greater differentiation among SCs and Muslims in recent years, but with a worsening at the bottom. For example, SCs formed 27.7% of persons in the bottom 40% in terms of MPCE in 1983 and 30.2% in 1993–94. This share was above 31% both in 2004–05 and 2011–12. The Muslim share in the bottom 40% rose systematically from 14.5% in 1983 to 16.6% in 1993–94, 19.2% in 2004–05 and 20.6% in 2011–12. OBC share in this group also increased from 41.4% in 2004–05 to 42.2% in 2011–12. Upper caste Hindus comprised only 5.1% of the bottom group in 2011–12.

In the top quintile, the percentage of SCs fell from 13.8 in 1983 to 9.2 in 1993–94, but this rose to 11.4% in 2004–05 and 12.1% in 2011–12—still below their share in 1983. Muslims formed 11.3% of the top group in 1983, 13.1% in 1993–94, 16.7% in 2004–05 and 14.7% in 2011–12. OBC (Hindus) formed 39.3% of the top group in 2004–05, but this share fell to 36.1% in 2011–12.

7.3 Social Categories and Jobs

We have used two indicators to assess labour market inclusion, viz. access to regular jobs and access to white collar jobs (NCO 1–5).

The absolute gap in the percentage of members of the major social groups with regular wage/salaried jobs has increased; the absolute gap is very large and has grown, over the years. In 2011–12, eight per cent SCs, 7.3% OBCs and 12.5% Muslims held regular jobs in UP, compared to 23.5% from upper castes. Moreover, since the shift towards regular jobs was higher at the national level, there was a growing gap between the percentage of SCs and OBCs holding regular jobs in UP and in India (while for Muslims this gap remained constant). However, as a share of all regular jobs in the state, although the share of SCs declined from 20% in 1983 to 14.6% in 1993, but between 2004–05 and 2011–12, SCs share in total regular jobs increased to 18.4%. Muslim share in regular jobs in the state has also increased from 14.9% in 1983 and 14.6% in 1999–00, to 20.2% in 2011–12.

The percentage share of SCs in NCO 1 to 5 (predominantly white collar jobs) has increased in UP from 7.9% in 1983 to 11.2% in 1999–00 and further to 13.8%

in 2011–12. But the share of Muslims in white collar jobs has remained stagnant, while the share of non-SC/ST Hindus has dipped marginally from 69.8% in 1983 and 69.3% in 1999–00 to 66.6% in 2011–12.

7.4 Land

Changes in land ownership are more likely to be a result of autonomous economic processes and land sales, but land transfer via distribution and repossession of *pattas* was also a policy objective of the Mayawati government. Data from the NSSO employment–unemployment round shows that OBC and general categories own more land than their share in population, whereas the reverse holds for SCs and Muslims. However, there has been some accretion of land by SCs whose share in land owned was 8.2% in 1993 and 10.4% in 2011–12 (this is also confirmed by the land holding surveys and microstudies), whereas the data is less unambiguous for Muslims since estimates how fluctuations between rounds and the trend is also less clear for other groups because of lack of long-term data. As pointed out, this could be attributed to autonomous processes, as SCs who accumulate small surpluses through outmigration invest in land purchase, but a small part of this accretion may also be attributable to policies of the successive BSP governments.

Thus, it is noted that the progress which SCs, Muslims and OBCs have made in UP in matters of education and consumption has, in general, not closed the gap with upper castes on most indicators. In terms of jobs and land ownership, there is a small shift, particularly for SCs. But changes in the state have generally been smaller than the changes that have occurred at the national level.

8 Conclusion

Since 1989, the three major parties (BJP, SP and BSP) have participated in governments in UP, either on their own, or as coalition partners. In matters of economic policy, there has been a great deal of continuity in the state. This continuity has not rewarded the state in terms of accelerated growth or development with an increasing gap observed between the centre and the state and large persistent difference between various regions in the state.

In terms of social policy, the BSP and the SP have followed an agenda which has purportedly been more tilted in favour of Dalits and Muslims or Muslim/OBC. But small-scale production, which forms the economic basis for the livelihoods of Muslims and OBCs, has languished in the state. Large-scale corruption and inefficient implementation have limited the benefits of social protection programmes. This has prevented UP's growth from being inclusive, even by the lacklustre national standards. Overall, UP's position among Indian states in terms of human development indicators remains virtually unchanged.

The Akhilesh government belatedly stepped up its focus on infrastructure-led growth and on social protection programmes, which was reflected in his pre-election budget for the state. However, the basic strategy is itself open to question. The Akhilesh government appeared to have learnt from the mistakes of its predecessor governments in matters of land acquisition and cronyism. His successor Yogi Adityanath has also emphasised on infrastructure-led growth. How much progress he is able to achieve with his party in power at the centre too remains to be seen. As of now, there is no evidence that these changes have translated into higher growth or more broad-based development in the state.

References

Abhiyan, S. (2015). Bundelkhand drought impact assessment survey 2015. Retrieved on September 6, 2016 from https://static.swarajabhiyan.org/content/news/prod/145/bundelkhand%20survey%202015_v05.pdf.

Bhalla, G. S., & Singh, G. (2012). *Economic liberalisation and Indian agriculture: A district-level study*. Delhi: Sage.

Centre for Policy Dialogue. (1998). *Crisis in governance*. Dhaka: The University Press.

Chatterjee, M. (2003). Maya's gone but in these dalit homes the change's for real. *The Indian Express*, September 1, New Delhi.

Dreze, J., & Sen, A. K. (Eds.) (1997). *Indian development: Selected regional perspectives*. Delhi: Oxford University Press.

Dreze, J., & Gazdar, H. (1997). Uttar Pradesh: The burden of inertia. In J. Dreze & A. Sen (Eds.), *Indian development: Selected regional perspectives*. Delhi: Oxford University Press.

Dreze, J., Khera, R., & PEEP Team. (2014). *A peep at another India*. Retrieved on November 5, 2016 from http://gap2015.org/downloads/A_peep_at_another_India.pdf.

Dreze, J., & Sen, A. K. (1995). *India: Economic development and social opportunity*. Delhi and Oxford: Oxford University Press.

Dreze, J., & Sen, A. (2013). *An uncertain glory, India and its contradictions*. Delhi and London: Penguin.

Government of India, Planning Commission. (2002). *National human development report 2001*. New Delhi: Planning Commission.

Government of India, Planning Commission. (2007).*Uttar Pradesh development report* (Vol. 1 & 2). New Delhi: Academic Foundation.

Government of Uttar Pradesh. (2003). *First human developmentr of Uttar Pradesh*. Lucknow: Government of Uttar Pradesh, Planning Department.

Government of Uttar Pradesh, Planning Department. (2007). *Uttar Pradesh human development Report 2003*. Lucknow: Government of Uttar Pradesh, Planning Department.

Gupta, A. K., et al. (2014). *Bundelkhand drought: Retrospective analysis and way ahead*. New Delhi: National Institute of Disaster Management.

Institute of Applied Manpower Research. (2011). *India human development Report 2011: Towards social inclusion*. New Delhi: Institute of Applied Manpower Research (IAMR).

Khan, A. (2009, September 5). Reliance power's Dadri project hits road block. *The Hindu*.

Khetan, A (2012, April 21). The Raja who stole from the poor. *Tehelka Magazine*, 9(16).

Kumar, V. (2003). Uttar Pradesh: Politics of change. *Economic and Political Weekly, 38*(37), 3869–3871.

Lieten, G. K., & Srivastava, R. (1999). *Unequal partners: Power relations, devolution and development in Uttar Pradesh*. Delhi: Sage.

Mehra, P. (2011, August 7). No man's land. *Tehelka*.

NCAER. (2015). *Evaluation study of targeted public distribution system in selected states*. New Delhi: National Council for Applied Economics Research.
Pai, S. (2002). *Dalit assertion and the unfinished democratic revolution: The Bahujan samaj Party in Uttar Pradesh*. Delhi: Sage.
Pai, S. (2004). Dalit question and political response: Comparative study of Uttar Pradesh and Madhya Pradesh. *Economic Political Weekly, 39*(11), 1141–1150.
Pai, S. (2005). Populism and economic reform: The BJP Experiment in Uttar Pradesh. In J. Mooij (Ed.), *Politics of economic reform in India*. Delhi: Sage.
Parashar, A. (2011, May 14). Farmers versus investment: The conflict unfolds in UP. *Tehelka*.
Rashid, O. (2013, November 14). Karchana power plant: Farmers to take a decision. *The Hindu*.
Shrivastava, B. (2009, September 19). The curious case of the Dadri power plant. *Mint*.
Singh, A. K. (1997). *Socio-economic status at the district level in Uttar Pradesh, A Report*. Lucknow: Giri Institute of Development Studies.
Sood, J. (2011, June 15). Road to disaster. *Down to Earth*.
Srivastava, P. (2009, August 17). Pension scam storm hits UP. *Mail Today*.
Srivastava, R. (2012). Economic change and social inclusion in Uttar Pradesh, 1983–2010. *UPEA Journal*, 5(5), 3–25 (Revised Presidential Lecture, *Seventh Annual conference of the Uttar Pradesh and Uttarakhand Economics Association*, October 2011).
Tripathi, P. (2004, February 14–27). Industry and concerns. *Frontline*.
Umesh, R. (2010, October 14). UP changes rules to check scholarship frauds. *Hindustan Times*, Lucknow.
Venkitesh, R. (2011, August 13–26). Blatant in Uttar Pradesh. *Frontline, 28*(17).
Weiss, T. G. (2000). Governance, good governance and global governance: Conceptual and actual challenges. *Third World Quarterly, 21*(5), 795–814. https://doi.org/10.1080/713701075.
World Bank. (2010, April 30). *India living conditions and human development in Uttar Pradesh: A regional perspective, poverty reduction and economic management*. South Asia Report No. 43573-IN. April 30, Washington DC: The World Bank.

Ravi Srivastava is Director, Centre for Employment Studies, Institute for Human Development, Delhi. He is a former Professor of Economics, Centre for the Study of Regional Development (CSRD), Jawaharlal Nehru University, New Delhi and a full-time member of the erstwhile National Commission for Enterprises in the Unorganised Sector. He has published several books and more than one hundred papers in national and international journals in the areas of agriculture, rural development and rural poverty, the informal sector, regional development, decentralization, human development, land reforms, social protection, labour and employment, and migration. He has been involved with extensive research on Uttar Pradesh over several decades. He was the principal author of the first Human Development Report of Uttar Pradesh and one of the authors of the World Bank's report on poverty in Uttar Pradesh. His book (with G. K. Lieten) on decentralisation and development in UP ("Unequal Partners", Sage Publications, New Delhi, 1999) has been widely acclaimed. He has co-authored a book (*"Uncaging the Tiger: Costs and Financing of Elementary Education in India"*, Oxford University Press, New Delhi) on access and financing of Elementary Education in UP and India.

Rahul Ranjan is a Ph.D. research scholar in the CSRD, Jawaharlal Nehru University, New Delhi, and working on "Cooking Energy Consumption and Women's Health in Rural India". His research interests include poverty, inequality, human development, energy and environmental economics. He has jointly published four papers in his areas of research interest in reputed journals.

Employment, Its Quality and Inequality

Rajendra P. Mamgain

Abstract The article questions employment and its quality in one of the least developed states in India, namely Uttar Pradesh, with a focus on gender and social groups. Despite a reasonable growth in Uttar Pradesh, the per capita income in the state is almost half of the national average, and such gap tended to increase over the years. Along with a slow pace of structural transformation, most of the growth in employment opportunities was in the form of casual wage works, mainly in the construction sector of the state. Such high pace of casualization was widespread in all regions of the state except the eastern region where dependence on agriculture did not reduce due to lack of such opportunities. The growth rate in regular employment opportunities in the state was almost three times lower than that at the national level. Uttar Pradesh suffers from a huge deficit of remunerative employment opportunities. A large proportion of those working as casual wage labour and those self-employed in agriculture are located at the bottom 20% quintile of income distribution in the state, and the proportion of such workers in the bottom quintile significantly increased since the early 1990s. The state faces relatively higher challenge of poor employability of its labour force mainly due to low levels of education and poor formal skill training along with slow growth in employment opportunities. Though the state has enormous potential to shift to a development path characterised by remunerative jobs for its increasing labour force both within farm and non-farm sectors, it would require substantial investment supported by active public policy support towards improved access to credit, technology, skill training and market. In brief, the success of a future inclusive growth agenda for Uttar Pradesh would depend on its strategy of promoting investment in employment potential sectors and ensuring equal participation of its people belonging to various regions, gender and social groups.

Keywords Employment growth · Quality of employment · Income inequality · Demand-side concerns of employment

---

R. P. Mamgain (✉)
Giri Institute of Development Studies, Sector-O,
Aliganj, Lucknow 226024, Uttar Pradesh, India
e-mail: mamgain.rp@gmail.com

© Springer Nature Singapore Pte Ltd. 2019
R. P. Mamgain (ed.), *Growth, Disparities and Inclusive Development in India*,
India Studies in Business and Economics,
https://doi.org/10.1007/978-981-13-6443-3_3

1 Introduction

Eradication of poverty and expansion of productive employment to ensure work for all have been important concerns of development policy throughout the past six decades of development planning in India. However, while the country has made several significant strides since Independence, the problems of widespread poverty, unemployment and underemployment still persist. In recent years, the process of globalisation has also resulted in certain trends in labour markets putting the employment issue at centre stage. While the Indian economy has grown at an average rate of more than 6.5% since the 1990s and new avenues of employment opportunities have opened up, there is also evidence of deteriorating job conditions and declining social security arrangements (GoI-MoF 2015). The prevalent policies and programmes have achieved limited success in shifting labour from the less remunerative agriculture sector to other sectors ensuring decent employment. There are striking regional inequalities in employment and income-generating opportunities. This is also true across gender and socio-religious groups of population.

Uttar Pradesh—the most populous state in the country—has long been the bedrock of India's economic, social and political development. The available statistics show significant achievements that Uttar Pradesh has made in the spheres of economic, social and cultural well-being, particularly since the early 1990s. However, in almost all development indicators, the state remains among the bottom states with significant regional inequalities (Diwakar 2009; CSO 2015; Mathew et al. 2016). Nearly 55% of workers are dependent on agriculture for their livelihood, whereas the sector contributes only 27.5% to gross state domestic product (GSDP). Though there has been a substantive shift of workers from agriculture and allied activities, most of such opportunities are casual in nature and fetch low income to a large majority of workers in the state. The economy of Uttar Pradesh lags behind in generating an adequate quantity of good quality jobs. The incidence of distress-induced migration has increased over the years, which is yet another major issue that could be addressed simply by improving employment opportunities. Uttar Pradesh faces three major challenges in redressing poverty and expanding inclusive growth: first, expanding economic opportunities for employment generation; second, ensuring that the poor and marginalised groups are empowered to take advantage of new opportunities in a rapidly changing world; and third, ensuring an effective safety net to reduce vulnerability of the very poor and destitute and protect them.

This paper examines in detail the nature, quality and growth in employment in the state with a focus on gender and social groups. By using the monthly per capita consumption expenditure (MPCE) of households as a proxy of income, it presents the magnitude of income inequalities among various categories of workers in the state. The demand-side concerns of labour market are examined by highlighting low enterprise development in the state and related problems faced by entrepreneurs in operating their enterprises. The concluding section summarises the major findings of the chapter. NSSO rounds on employment and unemployment are used as a main source of data for our analysis with a focus on workers in 15–59 years age group.

The other data used include Sixth Economic Census, 2013, and Micro, Small and Medium Enterprises (MSME) Census.

2 Employment and Its Quality

2.1 The Employment Challenge

With a population of 199.58 million in 2011, Uttar Pradesh is the most populous state of the India, accounting for 16.5% the country's population. Women constitute about 47.6% of population in the state. Scheduled Caste constitutes 21.15%, while Muslims comprise 18.6% of the state population. An overwhelming majority of 80.6% of the state population is Hindu. There were about 66.5 million workers in Uttar Pradesh constituting about one-third of total population of the state. According to National Sample Survey Organisation's (NSSO) 68th Round, nearly 53.3% of population in the age group of 15–59 years constitute the workforce in Uttar Pradesh in 2011–12. Over 80% of men and nearly one-fourth women in this age group were working in the state during 2011–12. The patterns in workforce participation rates (WPRs) for men do not vary substantially across rural and urban areas in Uttar Pradesh and in the rest of the country. However, the WPRs vary significantly in case of women. In urban areas, only 14.5% of women are working as compared to over 28% in rural areas of Uttar Pradesh. The proportion of women as workers is also substantially lower in Uttar Pradesh as compared to the national average (Table 1). Among social groups, while WPR of men is almost similar for SC/ST and Others (general, higher caste), it is higher for SC/ST women as compared to 'Other' women in the state (Table 2). The WPR of SC/ST women is much lower in Uttar Pradesh than their counterparts at national level, while such differences are marginal for men. Explanations for significantly low WPRs of women in the state as compared to the national level figure are indicative of lesser employment opportunities for women in the state.

It is also interesting to see how the WPRs of men and women have changed over the past three decades, across rural and urban areas and different regions of Uttar Pradesh. In tandem with the national pattern, there has been a declining trend in WPRs of both men and women in the state between 2004–05 and 2011–12. Female WPRs declined by a highest of ten percentage points while that of males by about four percentage points between 2004–05 and 2011–12. During the earlier period, 1993–94 to 2004–05, WPRs did not change substantially for men but increased by about five percentage points for women. The highest decline in women WPRs is seen in rural areas, which declined from over 40.5% in 2004–05 to 28.1% in 2011–12. A similar pattern in the WPRs for men and women can be seen at all-India level as well (Annexure Tables 14 and 15).

The pace of decline in WPRs, however, significantly varies between SC/ST and Others for their men and women in Uttar Pradesh. For example, while WPRs of SC/ST

Table 1 Workforce participation rates (15–59 years), 2011–12

	Male	Female	Person
Uttar Pradesh			
Rural	81.60	28.14	55.28
Urban	77.05	14.50	47.17
Total	80.44	24.82	53.25
India			
Rural	81.98	36.97	59.71
Urban	78.38	20.90	50.56
Total	80.76	31.70	56.67

Source NSSO unit level data, 68th round

Table 2 Workforce participation rates (15–59 years), 2011–12 by social groups

	Male	Female	Person
Uttar Pradesh			
SC/ST	81.82	30.78	57.54
Others	80.00	23.02	51.92
Total	80.44	24.82	53.25
India			
SC/ST	82.62	40.77	61.99
Others	80.08	28.34	54.70
Total	80.76	31.70	56.67

Source Computed from NSSO unit level data, 68th round
Note Others include Other Backward Classes and general category of population

men declined by six percentage points, it declined by three percentage points for men of the Others category between 2004–05 and 2011–12. The highest decline of about sixteen percentage points in WPRs is observed among SC/ST women during the period 2004–05/2011–12. The corresponding decline for women in Others category was much less, by about nine percentage points (Annexure Tables 16 and 17).

In brief, the decline in WPRs among women has been steeper in rural areas and among those belonging to SC/ST social groups. Thus, the overall decline in the WPRs of women in Uttar Pradesh, as well as in India, can be explained to some extent by the rising enrolment/retention in the spheres of secondary and tertiary education. Also, an improvement in household income along with lack of remunerative employment opportunities is leading to lowering of female labour force participation rate (LFPRs) (Neff et al. 2012; Rangarajan et al. 2011). The interplay of various sociocultural, economic and religious factors also resulted in their overall low participation in the labour market (Verick and Choudhary 2016). The non-recording of women's work in recent years has also been cited as yet another reason for low LFPR among them (Hirway 2014). Neff et al. (2012) argue that while education can be an explanatory factor in rural areas for the decline in women's WPRs), it does not hold true for urban areas. Rather, they found a significant evidence of the decline in women WPR due to improvement in household incomes, suggesting reduction in distress-induced WPRs.

2.2 Quality of Employment

Regular salaried employment is generally regarded as a more stable form of employment over casual or self-employed mode of employment due to its tenurial nature and social security to workers. The incidence of poverty is observed to be the highest among casual wage labour, followed by self-employed, and is least among regular salaried workers. However, a large part of available regular employment does not meet the quality of 'decent employment' as it did not provide any tenurial and social security to workers, indicating its precarious nature like other modes of employment (Mamgain and Tiwari 2015). Nearly 48% of regular employees were working in informal enterprises in India during 2011–12 and that too without any tenurial and social security. Even those working in public sector, nearly one-third were not covered by any tenurial and social security. In private organised sector, only one-fourth of regular workers had such security. The situation in UP was worse than many states and the national average (Mamgain and Tiwari 2015). In Uttar Pradesh, about 62.2% of the workforce was self-employed in various economic activities in 2011–12. Over one-fourth workers were engaged in casual wage work while the remaining had regular salaried jobs (Table 3). A comparatively higher share of self-employment, casual employment and poor quality of regular jobs in the state indicates the higher incidence of precarious nature of employment and is also reflected in higher incidence of poverty compared to many other states in India.

Table 3 Share of workers by employment status, (15–59 years) (%)

Type of employment	1993–94	2004–05	2011–12
Uttar Pradesh			
Self-employed	69.36	71.15	62.24
Regular salaried	9.34	10.98	11.71
Casual labour	21.31	17.87	26.05
Total	100	100	100
India			
Self-employed	52.9	54.91	50.72
Regular salaried	14.72	16.22	19.63
Casual labour	32.38	28.87	29.65
Total	100	100	100

Source Computed from NSSO unit level data, various rounds

Table 4 Gender-wise trends in share of workers by employment status (15–59 years) (%)

Year	Male			Female		
	SE	REG	CL	SE	REG	CL
Uttar Pradesh						
1993–94	67.47	11.32	21.21	75.27	3.12	21.61
2004–05	66.69	13.72	19.59	82.75	3.85	13.4
2011–12	57.58	13.13	29.28	78.03	6.88	15.09
India						
1993–94	51.29	18.57	30.14	56.23	6.74	37.03
2004–05	52.33	19.46	28.20	60.25	9.49	30.26
2011–12	48.78	21.77	29.45	55.83	13.97	30.20

Source Computed from NSSO unit level data, various rounds
Note SE self-employed, REG regular salaried workers, CL casual wage labour

How does the nature of employment differ between male and female workers in the state? Among the female workforce, the highest share was of self-employed (78.0%) women, followed by those engaged in casual wage labour, while the least number was engaged in regular salaried employment. However, the proportion of women working as self-employed was substantially higher as compared to men—78% for women as against 58% for men—in Uttar Pradesh (Table 4). Most of the self-employed female workforce was employed as unpaid household workers in agriculture. Thus, the proportionate share of women in regular as well as casual work is almost half than that of their male counterparts.

The status of employment of workers varies significantly across NSSO regions in the state. In the eastern region, over 68% of workers were self-employed, largely in agriculture and allied activities. Dependence on such employment is comparatively much less in the western and the southern regions. Around 30% of workers were casual wage labourers in all regions except the eastern region, where about 23% of workers were engaged in casual wage work. This is mainly due to overdependence of workers in this region on farm-based livelihood options. Thus, almost all regions of the state are facing the deficit of regular wage employment opportunities. The western region is relatively better off in this regard since it is a highly industrialised zone offering a comparatively higher scope for regular wage work to about 15% of workers. The share of regular workers in other regions was about one-tenth of their workforce in 2011–12 (Table 5).

The trends in the employment status of workers over the past 18 years, since 1993–94, show a slow pace of change—a decline of about seven percentage points in the share of self-employment. The corresponding increase was largely seen in casual wage work in the state. The share of regular employment hovered between nine to ten per cent during the entire period since 1993–94. If we look at the changes in employment in the recent period, between 2004–05 and 2011–12, the share of self-employed people in Uttar Pradesh declined remarkably, by about eleven percentage

Table 5 Region-wise trends in share of workers by employment status in Uttar Pradesh (15–59 years) (%)

NSSO region[a]	SE	REG	CL	Total
1993–94				
Western	70.46	11.60	17.94	100
Central	68.71	11.42	19.87	100
Eastern	68.26	6.85	24.89	100
Southern	71.57	5.38	23.05	100
All	69.36	9.34	21.31	100
2004–05				
Western	68.38	14.70	16.91	100
Central	70.40	12.56	17.04	100
Eastern	73.48	7.22	19.30	100
Southern	76.43	6.14	17.43	100
All	71.15	10.98	17.87	100
2011–12				
Western	57.25	14.95	27.80	100
Central	62.38	9.69	27.92	100
Eastern	67.99	9.44	22.56	100
Southern	58.81	10.10	31.09	100
All	62.24	11.71	26.05	100

Source Computed from NSSO unit level data, various rounds
Note SE self-employed, REG regular salaried jobs, CL casual wage labour
[a]NSSO regions generally represent geographical agglomeration of districts in a given state

points. The southern region witnessed a highest decline of about seventeen percentage points in the share of self-employed workers, whereas the least decline of about five percentage points was seen in the eastern region of the state. Such shift was largely into casual wage work in the state (Table 5). Contrary to this trend, the share of self-employment at the national level declined only by 4.2% points, from 54.9% in 2004–05 to 50.7% in 2011–12. This shift has largely been in favour of regular salaried employment (Table 3).

The share of self-employed among women declined from nearly 83% in 2004–05 to 78% in 2011–12. The corresponding increase in their share has been seen mainly in regular employment and to some extent casual wage employment in the state. In case of men, the share of self-employment declined by almost ten percentage points, and the shift has been entirely in favour of casual wage work in the state between 2004–05 and 2011–12 (Table 4).

Thus, the period of high growth in Uttar Pradesh witnessed a significant casualization of employment with important implications for earnings of people employed in such jobs. Such a high pace of casualization was widespread in all regions of the

Table 6 Quality of employment, 2010–11 (%)

Type of worker/employment	Men	Women	Total
Casual	25.8	21.4	25.4
Contractual	29.4	43.0	30.3
Regular	43.7	33.6	42.9
Unspecified[a]	1.2	4.5	1.5
Total	100	100	100
Number	20,972	1609	22,581

Source Mehta (2015)
[a]Includes family workers, ad hoc workers, etc

state except eastern region. In these regions, the proportionate share of casual labour increased by about eight to ten percentage points between 1993–94 and 2011–12 (Table 5). In the eastern region, the dependence on agriculture did not reduce due to lack of casual wage opportunities outside the farm sector and substantial migration of male workers outside the state (World Bank 2010). When juxtaposed with numbers at the national level, such pace of casualization is neither seen among men nor women as most of the shift from self-employment took place in favour of regular salaried jobs. The slow pace of decline in poverty in urban areas of the state indicates the lowering of income of workers and their increasing vulnerability due to lack of social security provisions. This deserves policy attention in order to take measures to redress the comparatively higher incidence of poverty in urban areas of the state.

In a similar vein, a survey on the quality of jobs in 550 small and medium enterprises in organised sector in Uttar Pradesh indicates the precarious nature of employment. About one-quarter of workers were casual; another 30% contractual. Thus, less than 43% of industrial employment was of regular nature during the period of 2011–12 (Mehta 2015) (Table 6). In other words, due to the very nature of casual and contractual employment, more than half of the workers do not have any written contracts and lack any kind of social security benefits. Though an overwhelming majority of enterprises reported providing social security benefits to their workers, experience shows how casual and contractual workers are bereft of any such benefits, thereby seriously eroding their income levels and leaving them vulnerable to risks of all kinds including loss in income levels.

2.3 Growth in Employment

Similar to the all-India trend, the growth of employment in Uttar Pradesh decelerated from 2.4 per cent per annum between 1993–94 and 2004–05 to 0.7% during the succeeding periods, namely 2004–05 and 2011–12. Such deceleration has been more pronounced in the case of women employment. The number of women workers sub-

Employment, Its Quality and Inequality 57

Table 7 Growth rate (%) in employment in Uttar Pradesh and India

Type of employment	1994–2005			2005–2012		
	Male	Female	Person	Male	Female	Person
Uttar Pradesh						
SE	1.88	4.65	2.68	−0.42	−2.88	−1.17
REG	3.79	5.76	3.96	1.06	6.39	1.66
CL	1.25	−0.66	0.82	7.71	−0.38	6.31
Total	1.99	3.75	2.44	1.69	−2.06	0.74
India						
SE	2.21	2.68	2.38	0.64	−2.86	−0.53
REG	2.46	5.26	2.93	3.30	3.78	3.39
CL	1.41	0.18	0.97	2.28	−1.83	0.99
Total	2.02	2.04	2.03	1.66	−1.80	0.61

Source NSSO unit level data, various rounds
Note SE self-employed, REG regular salaried employment, CL casual wage labour

stantially declined in absolute numbers between 2004–05 and 2011–12, registering a negative annual growth of around two per cent in Uttar Pradesh as well as in India. This decline in overall growth in women employment has been largely due to their withdrawal from unpaid family labour, generally categorised as self-employment, and also from casual wage work in Uttar Pradesh. In fact, women started withdrawing from casual wage work in the state since 1993–94 and continued to do so till 2011–12 (Table 7).

Women's employment in regular salaried jobs maintained a very high growth of about six per cent during 1994–2005 and 2005–12 (Table 7). Although it is a positive development, such employment too is of precarious nature, mostly in informal work and menial domestic services in the unorganised sector (IHD 2014). Women withdrew themselves mostly from self-employment as unpaid family workers. This may be due to an improvement in their family income, or due to their larger participation in education—in Uttar Pradesh and in India as a whole.

The growth scenario of male employment in Uttar Pradesh is significantly different from that of females. There has been a sharp increase in their casualization process in more recent period (2004–05 and 2011–12). Their annual growth in casual wage work jumped from just 1.3% between 1993–94 and 2004–05 to 7.7 per cent per annum between 2004–05 and 2011–12. There has been a sharp dip in regular salaried jobs for male workers in the state as their annual growth rate decelerated from 3.8% between 1993–94 and 2004–05 to 1.1 per cent per annum during 2004–05 and 2011–12. At the national level, this trend in regular employment of male workers was more favourable than in Uttar Pradesh, with a growth acceleration from 2.6% between 1993–94 and 2004–05 to about 3.3 per cent per annum between 2004–05 and 2011–12 (Table 7).

Employment growth varied for workers belonging to different social groups in Uttar Pradesh. While deceleration in job opportunities was witnessed by SC/ST as

Table 8 Growth rate in employment in Uttar Pradesh and India by social group of workers

Type of employment	1994–2005			2005–2012		
	SC/ST	Others	Total	SC/ST	Others	Total
Uttar Pradesh						
SE	4.07	2.34	2.66	−2.21	−0.88	−1.14
REG	3.70	4.00	3.95	5.85	0.83	1.68
CL	−0.26	2.09	0.82	4.59	7.91	6.31
Total	2.22	2.50	2.43	1.14	0.63	0.76
India						
SE	2.86	2.22	2.37	0.03	−0.69	−0.52
REG	4.81	2.47	2.93	3.17	3.45	3.39
CL	0.92	1.01	0.97	0.11	1.73	1.00
Total	2.12	1.98	2.02	0.47	0.68	0.62

Source NSSO unit level data, various rounds
Note SE self-employed, REG regular salaried employment, CL casual wage labour. (This should be mentioned in tables mentioned earlier as well)

well as Others, the pace of deceleration was more sharp for Others. This has been perhaps due to faster withdrawal of females from workforce belonging to Other castes/social groups. While SC/STs experienced a steep decline in self-employment, such decline was not that rapid in case of Others (Table 8). In regular jobs, SC/STs experienced an accelerated pace of growth (3.7% between 1993–94 and 2004–05 to 5.9 per cent per annum during 2004–05 to 2011–12), whereas Others experienced rapid deceleration in such jobs. In fact, Others suffered from overall slow growth in their employment accompanied by faster casualization of employment opportunities.

This higher increase in the number of casual wage labourers indicates the lack of regular and secure employment opportunities in the state, which has therefore accelerated the pace of male-specific migration from the state to seek livelihoods outside (Bhagat et al. chapter in this book).

2.3.1 Industrial Structure of Employment

Although there has been a significant shift of the Indian workforce from agriculture to the industry and services sectors over the past two or three decades (Papola and Sahu 2012), nearly half of the workers are still engaged in agriculture and allied activities. This share of agriculture in employment is comparatively more in Uttar Pradesh as compared to the Indian average (Table 9). After agriculture, the other important industrial sectors in terms of employment are manufacturing and construction, each employing about 13.2 and 13.6% of the workforce, respectively, in 2011–12. Over one-tenth of the workers were employed in trade in Uttar Pradesh (Table 9). Though this broad structure of employment across various industrial sectors in the state is

Table 9 Industrial structure of employment, 2011–12

Industry	Rural		Urban		Total	
	UP	India	UP	India	UP	India
Agriculture	61.61	63.17	7.85	6.10	49.73	46.20
Mining and quarrying	0.50	0.50	0.85	0.80	0.58	0.59
Manufacturing	8.71	8.62	28.94	23.33	13.18	13.00
Electricity, water, etc.	0.23	0.25	1.33	1.32	0.47	0.57
Construction	14.55	11.61	10.32	9.57	13.62	11.00
Trade, hotels and restaurants	6.25	6.51	23.82	23.17	10.13	11.46
Transport, storage and communication	2.93	3.14	5.96	10.25	3.60	5.26
Other services	5.22	6.19	20.92	25.46	8.69	11.92
Total	100	100	100	100	100	100

Source NSSO unit level data, 68th round

similar to the national pattern, the dependence on agriculture is relatively higher in Uttar Pradesh than the Indian average.

Workers in rural areas, understandably, are largely dependent on agriculture for their livelihood. In terms of numbers, 61.61% of workers in rural Uttar Pradesh were engaged in agriculture. Another 14.6% were employed in the construction sector. Manufacturing and trade were next two important activities providing employment to 8.7 and 6.25% of rural workers, respectively, during 2011–12. In all, non-farm sector provided employment to 38.39% of the rural workforce in Uttar Pradesh (Table 9). In urban areas, the highest 28.94% of workers were employed in manufacturing. This share is relatively much higher than the national average (23.3%). Other major employing sectors in the urban areas included trade (23.82%) and other services (20.92%).

2.4 Industry-wise Growth in Employment

Growth in employment in agriculture declined in absolute terms for the first time both in Uttar Pradesh and India between 2004–05 and 2011–12. Some scholars term it as the 'Lewisian Turning Point', which, however, is rejected by others. Even then, about half of Uttar Pradesh's workforce is dependent on agriculture and allied activities. Construction emerged as the major growth driver in employment in the state, registering a CAGR of about 12% since 1993–94. Although mining and quarrying, and electricity sectors have a very small share in total employment, they witnessed a fairly high CAGR of about 16% in the period between 2004–05 and 2011–12. Although growth of employment in sectors like trade and transport witnessed a sizeable growth of 5.6% in the period between 1993–94 and 2004–05, it decelerated at a faster rate in the next period, between 2004–05 and 2011–12 (Table 10).

Table 10 Industry-wise growth in employment (compound annual growth rates)

Industry	Uttar Pradesh		India	
	1993–94/2004–05	2004–05/2011–12	1993–94/2004–05	2004–05/2011–12
Agriculture	1.2	−1.6	0.9	−1.9
Mining and quarrying	4.9	16.0	−0.1	0.0
Manufacturing	4.9	1.0	3.5	1.2
Electricity, water, etc.	−2.6	15.9	−0.7	9.7
Construction	12.1	12.5	7.4	9.8
Trade, hotels and restaurants	5.7	0.2	5.4	1.2
Transport, storage and Communication	5.6	−0.1	5.2	3.6
Other services	0.0	3.1	1.3	2.8
Total	2.5	0.7	2.1	0.6

Source Computed from NSSO unit level data, various rounds

Employment grew over three per cent per annum in Other services between 2004–05 and 2011–12 after a negligible growth in the earlier period. This was mainly due to faster growth in public sector jobs both in Uttar Pradesh and in India as a whole, mostly in the banking and financial services' sector. The manufacturing sector lagged far behind in job creation in recent years after a sizeable growth of about five per cent in the period between 1993–94 and 2004–05. The reasons for such slow growth (about one per cent only) in non-farm jobs, particularly in manufacturing, in the country are linked to weak demand for products by a large segment of workers dependent on informal jobs, rapid pace of capital deepening in Indian organized manufacturing sector, and sluggish growth in export of goods and services due to recessionary condition in major economies of the world (IHD 2014).

3 Income Inequality Across Types of Employment

For evaluating the quality of available employment with respect to its contribution to household income, we have juxtaposed the type of employment across income quintiles by using NSSO data on employment. Due to lack of data on income, monthly per capita expenditure or MPCE of each household is considered as a proxy of income. High-income inequality emerges as an important feature of the labour market in Uttar Pradesh. Since a large majority of workers in the state are self-employed and another one-fourth work as casual wage labourers, inequality in income distribution is prominent. Over 42% of workers in Uttar Pradesh fall in the lowest 20% MPCE

Employment, Its Quality and Inequality

Table 11 Distribution of workers across MPCE quintiles

MPCE quintile	SEA	SENA	REG	CAS	ALL
1993–94					
1	29.31	24.41	10.86	49.53	30.97
2	24.18	22.89	13.50	23.71	22.84
3	20.07	21.06	18.93	15.51	19.18
4	15.85	17.77	24.07	7.91	15.29
5	10.60	13.88	32.65	3.34	11.72
All	100.00	100.00	100.00	100.00	100.00
2011–12					
1	40.95	36.33	20.39	55.81	42.14
2	28.12	25.63	18.74	25.43	25.95
3	16.58	15.37	20.33	10.21	14.92
4	11.26	13.85	17.45	6.18	10.97
5	3.10	8.82	23.10	2.38	6.01
All	100.00	100.00	100.00	100.00	100.00

Source Computed from NSSO unit level data
Note MPCE monthly per capita consumption expenditure class, SEA self-employed in agriculture, SENA self-employed in non-agriculture works, REG regular salaried workers, CAS casual labourers. 1–5 MPCE quintiles correspond from the lowest to highest

quintile. Only six per cent workers could be categorised in the top 20% income quintile in 2011–12. The highest 56% of casual wage labourers belong to the lowest 20% income quintile. Similarly, over 41% of self-employed workers in agriculture belong to the lowest MPCE quintile. The situation of self-employed people in non-farm sector is comparatively better than their counterparts in agriculture in terms of income distribution. Only one-fifth of regular salaried workers were found in lowest income quintile (Table 11). Moreover, income inequality is comparatively much less among regular workers.

Inequality in income distribution increased rapidly in Uttar Pradesh between 1993–94 and 2011–12. This can be seen in the increased concentration of workers in lower-income quintiles in 2011–12 as compared to 1993–94 (Fig. 1). Such an increase in concentration at low-income quintiles is seen across all types of employment (Table 11 and Fig. 2). This should be a matter of serious concern for policy-makers.

Region-wise, over half of workers in Eastern region were in lowest 20% income quintile in 2011–12. The situation of central and eastern regions was similar with a very high proportion of workers belonging to lowest income quintiles. In contrast, the proportion of workers belonging to bottom income quintile was much less in western region (Fig. 3). Understandably, this region has comparatively better agriculture productivity and non-farm employment opportunities as compared to other regions.

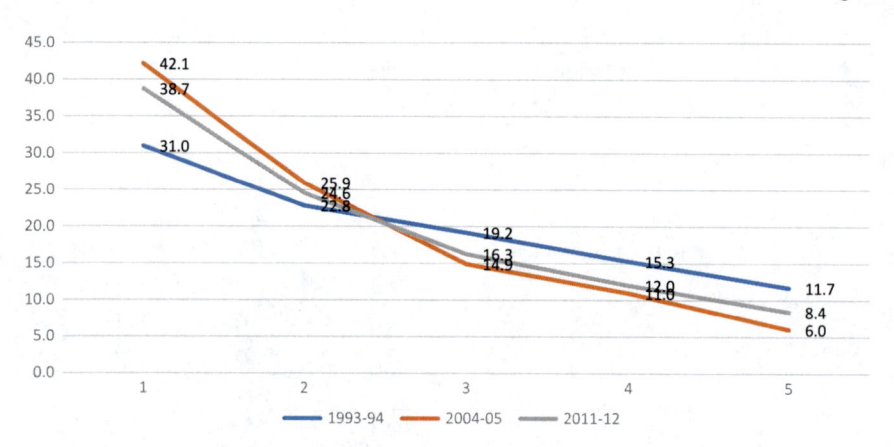

Fig. 1 Trends in income inequality in Uttar Pradesh (Share of workers by MPCE Quintiles). 1993–94, 2004–05 and 2011–12. *Note* MPCE monthly per capita consumption expenditure class; *Y*-axis and *X*-axis indicate share of workers and MPCE quintile, respectively. *Source* Computed from NSSO unit level data

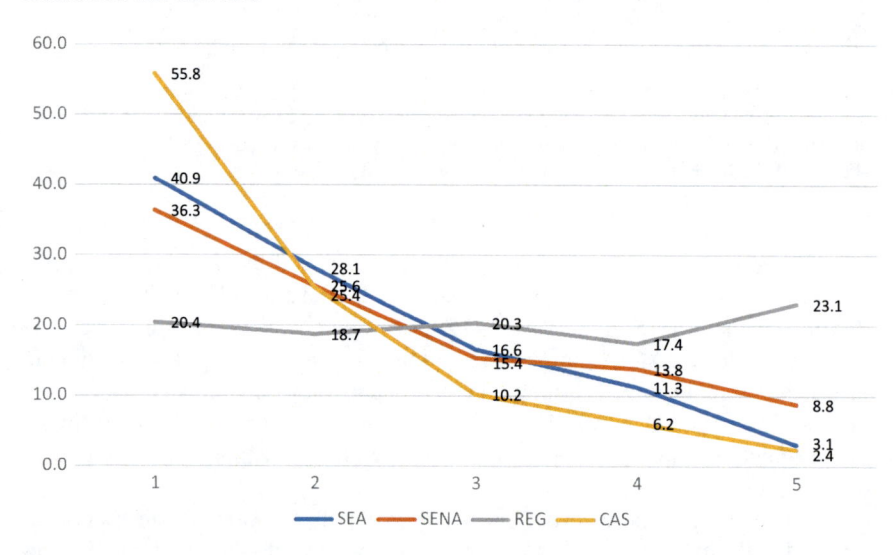

Fig. 2 Income inequality across types of employment in Uttar Pradesh (share of workers by MPCE quintiles). 2011–12. *Note* MPCE monthly per capita consumption expenditure class, SEA self-employed in agriculture, SENA self-employed in non-agriculture, REG regular salaried workers, CAS casual labourers; *Y*-axis and *X*-axis indicate share of workers and MPCE quintiles, respectively. *Source* Computed from NSSO unit level data

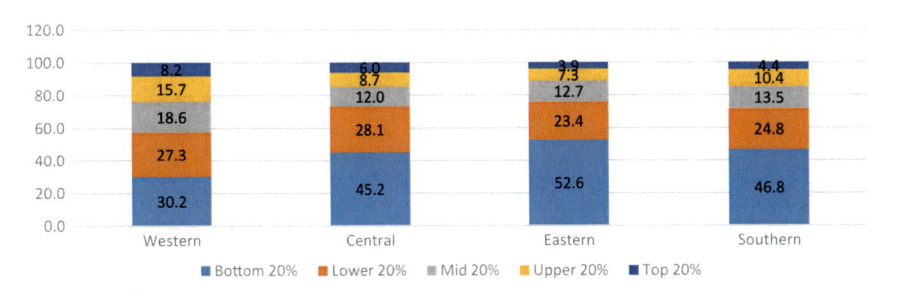

Fig. 3 Region-wise income inequality in Uttar Pradesh, 2011–12

This also explains the comparatively higher income of population residing in western region in the state (Table 2).

In other words, Uttar Pradesh suffers with a huge deficit of remunerative employment opportunities. The situation is rather worrisome particularly for those working in agriculture and casual wage works at low levels of earnings with their increasing concentration in lowest 20% income quintile of income distribution in the state. Such poor income levels along with rising inequality have far-reaching implications for the overall well-being of households at bottom income quintiles. The challenge, therefore, is to create employment opportunities outside the farm sector by promoting MSMEs and reducing the overdependence on agriculture. At the same time, productivity levels need to be improved at a much higher pace through measures of improved access to credit, technology, skill training and market. This would help the state catch up with other states in the country.

4 Demand-Side Concerns of Labour Market

Before commenting on the demand-side concerns of employment, it would be useful to look at enterprise development in Uttar Pradesh for understanding employment opportunities outside agriculture. According to the latest Sixth Economic Census, there were 6.7 million enterprises in Uttar Pradesh, accounting for about 11.5% of total enterprises in the country in 2013. These enterprises provided employment to 13.75 million people in the state. Over 60% of the enterprises were located in rural areas of the state; the share of rural areas in total employment stood at about 43.7%. At the all-India level, this share has been much higher, at 48.1% (GoUP 2015).

The number of enterprises and employment generated therein witnessed a phenomenal growth between 2005 and 2013 in Uttar Pradesh as compared to India (Table 12). This high growth has been largely due to growth witnessed in rural Uttar Pradesh. However, the figures for such high growth in rural areas are not corroborated by NSSO data on self-employment. In fact, NSSO data show an absolute decline in the number of self-employed persons in the state between 2004–05 and 2011–12 (Table 7). The jump in high growth may be partly explained in the creation

Table 12 Average annual growth of establishments and employment between the fifth (2005) and sixth (2013) Economic Census (%)

Area	Uttar Pradesh	India
Enterprise		
Rural	10.9	4.91
Urban	5.01	5.70
Both	8.24	5.22
Employment		
Rural	10.8	3.95
Urban	7.15	4.68
Both	9.41	4.29

Source Sixth Economic Census, MoSPI, New Delhi
Note Due to exclusion of Public Administration, Defence and Compulsory Social Security Services Activities in the Sixth Economic Census from the count, the growth rates between Fifth and Sixth Economic Censuses are not strictly comparable

of additional 2.43 hundred thousand micro and small registered units in the state during the period 2007–08 and 2013–14) which have been financed by the state government through its network of district industries centres (Department of MSME, GoUP 2015). However, given the population size of Uttar Pradesh, the all-India share of the state in enterprises is quite small, at about 12% (Table 12).

Over one-third of enterprises in rural Uttar Pradesh and about half of those in the urban areas operate from fixed premises, while 15% operate without any fixed premises. Another 44.5% of enterprises operate from inside households—these are largely informal enterprises. The proportion of enterprises operating from homes is comparatively higher in Uttar Pradesh than the Indian average (38.4%). Thus, an overwhelming majority of enterprises are informal enterprises in the state. The opportunities for hired wage employment in such enterprises were comparatively far less in Uttar Pradesh (34.5%) than the national average (45.6% of total workers). Similarly, women constitute about one-fifth of the total workers in the enterprises in Uttar Pradesh—their share being comparatively higher, at 26%, than in India.

Industrial development in Uttar Pradesh is highly skewed. It is concentrated in the western region of the state, accounting for over 68% of industries. The next important region for industrial activity is the central region, while the least significant region on this count is Bundelkhand. The western region remains on the top and Bundelkhand at the bottom in terms of number of industries and employment per hundred thousand population (Mamgain and Verick 2017). This huge locational disparity in industrial development in the state adversely affects the employment prospects for the labour force living in industrially backward regions.

In brief, enterprises in Uttar Pradesh are predominantly rural based with lesser opportunities for wage employment and women employment as compared to several other states in India. Per worker productivity in micro and small enterprises

Table 13 Per worker market value of fixed capital (INR'000) during 2006–07

State	SC	OBC	Others	Total
Uttar Pradesh	663	261	2781	1787
Gujarat	4974	5085	6785	6608
Tamil Nadu	2663	1598	2612	1842
Maharashtra	3860	1921	7031	6264
Bihar	346	777	835	726
West Bengal	1018	288	3083	2624
India	1423	1095	4390	2863

Source Calculated from Fourth MSME Census, 2006–07, Registered Sector

in the state is significantly lower, mainly due to lack of capital and infrastructure (Mamgain 2016). Per worker fixed capital in Uttar Pradesh in registered MSMEs was substantially lower in comparison to many other Indian states (Table 13). In this, the availability of fixed capital was lowest for OBCs, followed by SCs. The latest Annual Survey of Industries (ASI) data for registered manufacturing industries for the year 2013–14 show per unit invested capital in the state at INR 11.72 million for its 14,463 units. This figure is considerably lower than the national average of INR 15.07 million. Similarly, per worker annual wages in Uttar Pradesh was lower, at INR 1,13,500, than the Indian average of INR 1,21,100 during the year 2013–14.

5 Understanding Slow Growth in Non-farm Employment

While large industries tended to deepen their capital intensity by using labour-replacing technologies, micro and small enterprises—considered to be the growth engines—still suffer due to lack of capital and technology. As is well-known, these enterprises make significant contribution to income and employment generation. However, these enterprises are facing several difficulties in their operation and expansion, thereby hindering the prospects of employment and growth. A recent study of micro and small enterprises in Uttar Pradesh (Mamgain 2016) shows how entrepreneurs face a variety of problems. The most severe problems include lack of working capital, insufficient space to efficiently operate the enterprise, inadequate raw material, power shortages and shortage of skilled labour (Fig. 4). Such problems are common to entrepreneurs belonging to SC and Other social groups in Uttar Pradesh, but the intensity is comparatively more severe in case of the former group of entrepreneurs (Fig. 4). The persistence of such problems over the years despite several policy initiatives needs serious retrospection and more curative approach particularly when focus is increasing on enterprise development. This would require review of trade and investment policies for labour-intensive enterprise development in manufacturing as well as service sectors in the country.

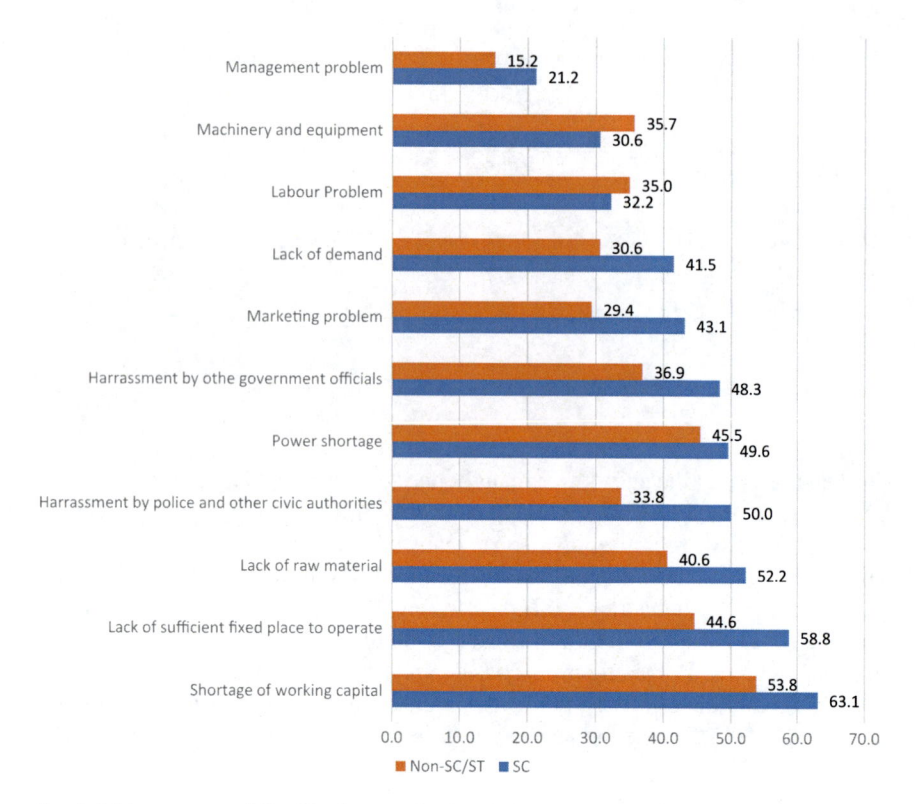

Fig. 4 Major or severe difficulties in operating business enterprises in UP, 2015. *Source* Mamgain (2016). Private enterprise development among scheduled castes in Uttar Pradesh (mimeograph)

6 Conclusion

While analysing the nature and trends in employment in Uttar Pradesh, this paper brings out several interesting features regarding employment in the state. It shows how, despite a reasonably higher annual growth of over six per cent during last decade, growth in employment opportunities was abysmally low. This trend was similar to the pattern observed at national level. However, Uttar Pradesh had few distinct features of employment as compared to several other states. Most of the growth in employment opportunities was in the form of casual wage works, mainly in construction sector of the state. Such high pace of casualization was widespread in all regions of the state except the eastern region. The growth rate in regular employment opportunities in Uttar Pradesh was almost three times lower than that at the national level. The faster deceleration in employment growth in manufacturing, trade and transport industries could hardly reduce the overdependence of workforce on agriculture sector and self-employment mode of employment in the state; more so in eastern region where dependence on agriculture did not reduce due to lack of casual wage opportunities outside the farm sector and large out-of-state migration of males. Among social groups, SC/ST benefitted more as compared to Others in the recent period with a substantial rise in their number in regular employment in the state.

In sum, Uttar Pradesh suffers from a huge deficit in remunerative employment opportunities. A large proportion of those working as casual wage labour and those self-employed in agriculture are located at the bottom 20% quintile of income distribution in the state. Such deficit of quality employment has grown over the years as the proportion of workers in bottom quintile significantly increased since the early 1990s. A disproportionately larger concentration of workers in lowest income decile and its rising tendency over the years pose a serious challenge for improving their incomes, social security and well-being.

Much of the problems of the labour force and its employability in Uttar Pradesh pertain to its low levels of education and poor skill training. The challenge of developing skill training for its population, particularly those in the age group of 18–24 years, will remain a critical priority in the coming years. The low proportion of technically trained persons in Uttar Pradesh can be traced to the historically inadequate infrastructure for technical and vocational education in the state. The skill development programmes under the Uttar Pradesh Skill Development Mission (UPSDM) are expected to have a major impact in the years to come in addressing these challenges.

Another major issue that needs to be addressed is the extremely low participation of women in labour force in India, more so in Uttar Pradesh. Studies show how the present per capita income in India can increase by 33% by closing the gender gap in economic participation. These gains would come from two sources—about two-thirds from closing the gap in their participation in labour market and the remaining from eliminating barriers to entrepreneurship (Cuberes and Teignwer 2015). India ranks 70th out of 77 countries surveyed in Female Entrepreneurship Index in 2015, suggesting ample room for improvement. Bringing more women into the labour market requires more investment in girls' education, better child care options and their safety (World Bank 2016).

For promoting employment through industrial development, the Government of Uttar Pradesh has several policies and programmes, such as concessional finance, subsidies on use of infrastructure, mainly power and transportation of goods and materials, and R&D among others. However, the industrial development in Uttar Pradesh has been highly skewed, with the highest concentration in the western region. Manufacturing particularly MSMEs is being visualised as a major driver of economic growth and employment generation across different regions of the state. However, MSMEs face several problems such as lack of working capital, insufficient space to efficiently operate the enterprise, inadequate raw materials, power shortages and shortage of skilled labour. To further assist SMEs, sector-specific promotional policies for enterprise development are needed. Dedicated efforts are needed to unleash the entrepreneurial spirit and business activity in all parts of the state.

In brief, the state has enormous potential to shift to a development path characterised by remunerative jobs for its increasing labour force, both within farm and non-farm sectors. The strategy therefore should focus on creating employment opportunities outside the farm sector by promoting MSMEs and reducing the overdepen-

Table 14 Trends in workforce participation rates (15–59 years) in Uttar Pradesh

Area	Male	Female	Person
1993–94			
Rural	89.48	33.78	62.59
Urban	79.07	16.52	50.33
Total	87.21	30.28	60
2004–05			
Rural	86.39	40.47	63.99
Urban	80.21	17.34	51.54
Total	84.85	35.25	61.03
2011–12			
Rural	81.6	28.14	55.28
Urban	77.05	14.5	47.17
Total	80.44	24.82	53.25

Source NSSO unit level data, various rounds

dence on agriculture. At the same time, productivity levels need to be improved at a much higher pace in agriculture as well as MSME sector through measures like improved access to credit, technology, skill training and market. Upscaling the current social security measures such as minimum income support to distressed households and provisioning of quality education and health security needs to be pegged with better provisioning of public resources in the state. The strategy of doubling farmers' income by 2020 is in the desired direction, but much would depend on its effective implementation to achieve the desired goal. The experience of implementation of development programmes including those aimed at creating employment opportunities in the country including in Uttar Pradesh has been less than satisfactory. These require time-bound implementation through improved governance and strengthening of service delivery institutions. These measures would help the state in the catch-up process with other states in the country. Equally important would be to overcome gender and social gaps in employment opportunities and earnings, while reducing the pace of distress migration. Thus, the success of a future inclusive growth agenda for Uttar Pradesh would depend on its strategy of promoting investment in employment potential sectors and ensuring equal participation of its people belonging to various regions, gender and social groups.

Annexure

See Annexure Tables 14, 15, 16, 17, 18 and 19.

Table 15 Trends in workforce participation rates (15–59 years) in India

Area	Male	Female	Person
1993–94			
Rural	88.27	51.15	69.96
Urban	79.60	23.17	53.12
Total	85.77	43.63	65.27
2004–05			
Rural	87.11	51.20	69.34
Urban	80.10	24.22	53.71
Total	84.84	43.00	64.43
2011–12			
Rural	81.98	36.97	59.71
Urban	78.38	20.90	50.56
Total	80.76	31.70	56.67

Source NSSO unit level data, various rounds

Table 16 Workforce participation rates (15–59 years) by social groups—Uttar Pradesh

Gender	SC/ST	Others	All
1993–94			
Male	91.73	85.93	87.21
Female	45.07	26.02	30.28
Person	69.22	57.38	60.00
2004–05			
Male	88.27	83.9	84.88
Female	46.46	31.98	35.23
Person	68.15	58.99	61.04
2011–12			
Male	81.82	80.00	80.44
Female	30.78	23.02	24.82
Person	57.54	51.92	53.25

Source NSSO unit level data, various rounds

Table 17 Workforce participation rates (15–59 years) by social groups—India

Gender	SC/ST	Others	All
1993–94			
Male	89.32	84.53	85.77
Female	57.95	38.56	43.63
Person	73.99	62.20	65.27
2004–05			
Male	86.86	84.10	84.84
Female	54.58	38.74	43.01
Person	71.14	61.96	64.44
2011–12			
Male	82.62	80.08	80.76
Female	40.77	28.34	31.7
Person	61.99	54.7	56.67

Source NSSO unit level data, various rounds

Table 18 Trends in nature of employment—Uttar Pradesh (%)

Type of employment	Male	Female	Person
1993–94			
Self-employed	67.47	75.27	69.36
Regular salaried	11.32	3.12	9.34
Casual labour	21.21	21.61	21.31
Total	100	100	100
2004–05			
Self-employed	66.69	82.75	71.15
Regular salaried	13.72	3.85	10.98
Casual labour	19.59	13.40	17.87
Total	100	100	100
2011–12			
Self-employed	57.58	78.03	62.24
Regular salaried	13.13	6.88	11.71
Casual labour	29.28	15.09	26.05
Total	100	100	100

Source NSSO unit level data, various rounds

Table 19 Trends in nature of employment—India (%)

Type of employment	Male	Female	Person
1993–94			
Self-employed	51.29	56.23	52.90
Regular salaried	18.57	6.74	14.72
Casual labour	30.14	37.03	32.38
Total	100	100	100
2004–05			
Self-employed	52.33	60.25	54.91
Regular salaried	19.46	9.49	16.22
Casual labour	28.20	30.26	28.87
Total	100	100	100
2011–12			
Self-employed	48.78	55.83	50.72
Regular salaried	21.77	13.97	19.63
Casual labour	29.45	30.2	29.65
Total	100	100	100

Source NSSO unit level data, various rounds

References

Central Statistical Organisation (CSO). (2015). *Millennium development goals: India Country report 2015*. New Delhi: Government of India, Ministry of Statistics and Programme Implementation.

Cuberes, D., & Teignwer, M. (2015). *Aggregate effects of gender gaps in the labour market: A quantitative estimate* (mimeo). Retrieved on May 5, 2016 from www.marcteignier.com/research_files/GGLMAP_CT.pdf.

Diwakar, D. M. (2009). Intra-regional disparities, inequality and poverty in Uttar Pradesh. *Economic and Political Weekly, 44*(26/27), 264–273.

GoI-MoF. (2015). *Economic survey 2014–15*. New Delhi: Government of India, Ministry of Finance.

GOI-RGI. (2011). *Primary census abstract of India 2011*. New Delhi: Government of India, Registrar General of India, Ministry of Home Affairs.

GoUP-DES. (2015). *Sixth economic census, Uttar Pradesh*. Lucknow: Provisional Results, Directorate of Economics and Statistics, Government of Uttar Pradesh.

GoUP-Department of MSME. (2015). *Data on MSMEs in Uttar Pradesh*. Kanpur: Department of Micro, Small and Medium Enterprises.

GoUP-UPSDM. (2016). *Uttar Pradesh skill development mission* (p. 18). Government of Uttar Pradesh, April 2016.

Hirway, I. (2014). Unpaid work and the economy: Linkages and their implications. In *Presidential Address at the 56th Annual Conference of the Indian Society of Labour Economics*, Ranchi, December.

Institute for Human Development (IHD). (2014). *India labour and employment report 2014: Works in the era of globalisation.*. New Delhi: Academic Foundation, Institute for Human Development and The Indian Society of Labour Economics.

Mamgain, R. P. (2016). *Private enterprise development among scheduled castes in Uttar Pradesh*. Lucknow (mimeo): Giri Institute of Development Studies.

Mamgain, R. P., & Verick, Sher. (2017). *The state of employment in Uttar Pradesh: Unleashing the potential of inclusive growth*. New Delhi: ILO.

Mamgain, R. P., & Tiwari, S. (2015). Regular salaried employment opportunities in India: Nature, access and inclusiveness. *The Indian Journal of Labour Economics, 60*(3), 415–436. https://doi.org/10.1007/s41027-018-0101-z.

Mathew, C. K., Mukunthan, A., & Divekar, V. (2016). *Public affairs index: Governance in the states of India*. Bengaluru: Public Affairs Centre.

Mehta, G. S. (2015). *Factors impacting growth of employment*. New Delhi: Abhijeet Publications.

Neff, D., Sen, K., & Kling, V. (2012). *The puzzling decline in rural women's labour force participation in India: A Re-examination*. GIGA Research Unit: Institute of Asian Studies, No. 196, May.

Papola, T. S., & Sahu, P. P. (2012). *Growth and structure of employment: Long-term and post-reform performance and emerging challenges*. Occasional Paper Series, 2012/1, ISID, Institute for Studies in Industrial Development, New Delhi.

Rangarajan, C., Kaul, P. I., & Seema, S. (2011, September 24). Where is the missing labour force? *Economic and Political Weekly, 46*(39).

Verick, S., & Chaoudhary, R. (2016). The participation of women in the labour force in India and beyond. In K. P. Kannan, R. P. Mamgain, & P. Rustagi (Eds.), *Labour and development—Essays in honour of Professor T. S. Papola*. New Delhi: Academic Foundation.

World Bank. (2010). *Living conditions and human development in Uttar Pradesh: A regional perspective* (India Report No. 43573-IN). Washington DC, April 30.

World Bank. (2012). *World development report 2013: Jobs*. Washington DC: World Bank.

World Bank. (2016). *The World Bank in India* (Vol. 14, no. 5, p. 9), March 2016.

Rajendra P. Mamgain is Professor at Giri Institute of Development Studies, Lucknow, India. Earlier he has been Director and Professor of Economics with Indian Institute of Dalit Studies (IIDS), New Delhi. He served Indian Council of Social Science Research (ICSSR) as a Senior Academic Consultant (in the rank of Professor) for a brief period. Dr. Mamgain has worked as Senior Fellow in Institute for Human Development and faculty at Institute of Applied Manpower Research. He has a doctoral degree in Economics from Jawaharlal Nehru University with an experience of over 30 years in the areas of labour, employment, migration, skill development, human poverty, inclusive development and impact evaluation of government programmes. He specializes in undertaking large field based research in his areas of interest. He has completed 25 research studies in his areas of interest. He has nine books to his credit and has published more than 65 research papers in various national and internationals journals of repute.

He also worked as the Managing Editor of the Indian Journal of Labour Economics for 25 years and transformed the journal into a quality product with world-wide dissemination. The journal is published by Springer Publications. At present Prof. Mamgain is Editor of Journal of Social Inclusion Studies and Associate Editor of Indian Economic Journal. Both the journals are being published by Sage International.

Prof. Mamgain has been a consultant to various national and international organizations. He has been a member of various policy advisory bodies of reputed institutions in India and abroad including Minimum Wage Board, Government of Uttar Pradesh; High Level Rapid Appraisal Committee on Social Exclusion and Discrimination in Health and Nutrition Programme, Planning Commission, Government of India; Performance Budget Committee, Ministry of Social Justice and Empowerment, Government of India; International Planning Committee of IDRC Think Tanks Global Meet; Indian Society of Labour Economics R&D Trust; G20 Summit on Skill Development; and Oxfam India. Prof. Mamgain is a recipient of ILO bursary to visit Lima, ICSSR-Science de Humane fellowship programme, Adjunct Professor to Doon University and Visiting Professor to IIDS.

Prof. Mamgain's recent jointly written/edited books are The State of Employment in Uttar Pradesh-Unleashing the potential for inclusive growth, Labour and Development: Essays in Honour of Professor T.S. Papola and Mizoram Human Development Report 2013. His forthcoming book on Formal Labour Market in Urban India: Job Search, Hiring Practices and Discrimination is being published by Sage Publications. His recent work on youth and challenge of decent employment is widely acclaimed by academia. Prof. Mamgain has been actively engaged in research and policy advocacy and delivered more than 35 special lectures and keynote addresses in various seminars and workshops. He also organised over 25 national as well as international seminars/workshops/conferences.

Labour Market Outcomes and Inclusive Development: Experiences of South Asian Countries

Rizwanul Islam

Abstract The article examines whether labour market outcomes like employment, wages, returns to self-employment and social protection are contributing to make economic growth inclusive in countries of South Asia. Although the term inclusion may be conceptualized in different ways, it is important to focus on both the process and outcome. While the process of inclusion can be captured through measures relating to employment, the outcomes can be assessed in terms of poverty, inequality or other dimensions of human development like education and health. Another important element of inclusion is the degree of social protection provided by a society. Characterized this way, labour market outcomes are of direct relevance for inclusive growth. A number of questions may be raised in this context: (a) Is economic growth leading to the growth of productive employment that is needed for absorbing the new members of the labour force and for transferring workers from sectors characterized by low productivity to those with higher productivity? (b) Is sector composition of employment changing in a way that contributes to poverty reduction (through higher incomes of workers)? (c) Is access to social protection expanding along with economic growth? (d) Is economic growth associated with the growth of labour productivity and rise in real wages? and (e) Are real wages rising to contribute to reduction in poverty and inequality? The present paper attempts to address some of the above questions with a particular focus on the experience of the countries of South Asia. Using the concept of employment elasticity with respect to output growth, it shows that the labour absorptive capacity of the countries of the region has been low and has declined. The process of transformation of the structure of employment has been slow, and as a result, the informal economy has remained the predominant source of jobs for the growing labour force. That, in turn, has meant limited access to social protection because there is a negative relationship between the proportion of employment in the informal economy and access to social protection. Furthermore, the relationship between access to social protection and economic growth has not been linear, thus indicating that growth alone cannot be relied upon to address the issue. Public policy is also important. On the positive side, in some countries, real

R. Islam (✉)
Formerly of Employment Sector, International Labour Office, Geneva, Switzerland
e-mail: rizwanul.islam49@gmail.com

© Springer Nature Singapore Pte Ltd. 2019
R. P. Mamgain (ed.), *Growth, Disparities and Inclusive Development in India*,
India Studies in Business and Economics,
https://doi.org/10.1007/978-981-13-6443-3_4

wages have registered increases in some sectors, especially in agriculture—showing potential for making contribution to poverty reduction. But the rise in real wages has not been sustained in recent years and has lagged behind that of labour productivity. As a result, there has not been much impact on growing income inequality. Gender differences in wages have also persisted. On the whole, it seems that labour market outcomes in South Asia have not moved in a direction needed to make economic growth more inclusive. This contrasts with the experience of countries of East and South-East Asia, e.g. Republic of Korea, Malaysia and Taiwan (China), that have been successful in attaining economic growth with productive employment and rapid rate of poverty reduction. The findings of this paper could be useful to India and more specifically to the state of Uttar Pradesh in accelerating inclusive growth.

Keywords South Asian economies · Structural transformation · Social protection · Wage inequality · Inclusive development

1 Introduction

During the second half of the twentieth century and the first decade of the current millennium, development paradigm has undergone several shifts in focus. The journey that started with trickle down approach and passed through redistribution with growth, structural adjustment and pro-poor growth is now docked at inclusive growth. Although the term inclusion may be conceptualized in different ways, it is important to focus on both the process and outcome. While the process of inclusion can be captured through measures relating to employment, the outcomes can be assessed in terms of income relative to some benchmark of poverty, inequality or other dimensions of human development like education and health. Another important element of inclusion is the degree of social protection provided by a society. Characterized this way, labour market outcomes like employment, wages, returns to self-employment and social protection are of direct relevance for inclusive growth. A number of questions may be raised in this context.

(a) Is economic growth leading to the growth of productive employment that is needed for absorbing the new members of the labour force and for transferring workers from sectors characterized by low productivity to those with higher productivity?
(b) Is sector composition of employment changing in a way that is contributing to poverty reduction (through higher incomes of workers)?
(c) Is access to social protection expanding along with economic growth?
(d) Is economic growth associated with the growth of labour productivity and rise in real wages?
(e) Are real wages rising to contribute to reduction in poverty and inequality?
(f) What is happening to the share of wages in national income and in terms of value added?

The experience of countries that have been successful in their development effort, e.g. Republic of Korea (South), Malaysia and Taiwan, shows that economic growth was associated with high rate of labour absorption in modern sectors and a corresponding reduction in the share of jobs in the informal economy leading to an increase in social protection for the labour force. Also, employment growth was not achieved at the cost of labour productivity. In fact, labour productivity increased and real wages also rose!

This paper attempts to address some of the above questions with a particular focus on the experience of the countries in South Asia. Using the concept of employment elasticity with respect to output growth, it shows that the labour absorption capacity of the countries in the sub-continent has not only been low but has also declined. The process of transformation of the structure of employment has been slow, and as a result, the informal economy has remained the predominant source of jobs for the growing labour force. That, in turn, has meant limited access to social protection because there is a negative relationship between the proportion of employment and the informal economy, and access to social protection. On the positive side, real wages have registered increases in some sectors—showing potential for contributing to poverty reduction. But that has not been enough to make any impact on inequality.

The paper is organised as follows. Section 2 presents some basic information such as per capita income, GDP growth and the structure of output in South Asian countries. Section 3 looks at the nexus between economic growth and employment and examines the outcome of economic growth in terms of employment. Section 4 deals with another important labour market outcome, viz. structural transformation while Sect. 5 dwells on the challenge of social protection. Section 6 examines what has happened to the wages of workers, with particular focus on gender difference. Some concluding observations are made in Sect. 7.

2 Economic Growth and Structure of South Asian Economies: A Brief Overview

Although there is a general perception that the economies of the countries of South Asia are quite similar, there is a good degree of difference in terms of the level of per capita income, their structure as well as their performance in terms of economic growth. As for per capita income (Atlas method), the range is from US dollars (USD) 680 in Afghanistan to 7290 in the Maldives. The application of PPP (purchasing power parity) method does not change the variation and ranking (Table 1). It may, however, be noted at the outset that this paper does not cover Afghanistan, Bhutan and Maldives—the countries that lie at two extremes of the income spectrum. Amongst the countries covered in this study, Nepal is the poorest while Sri Lanka is the richest, therein between are countries like Bangladesh, India and Pakistan whose per capita incomes range between one and two thousand US Dollars.

Table 1 Per capita (2014) income in South Asian Countries

Country	Gross national income per capita (US Dollars, Atlas method)	Gross national income per capita (US Dollars PPP method)
Afghanistan	680	1980
Bangladesh	1080	3340
Bhutan	2390	7560
India	1610	5760
Maldives	7290	12,770
Nepal	730	2420
Pakistan	1410	5100
Sri Lanka	3400	10,270

Source World Bank: World Development Indicators 2015

In terms of economic growth also, the performance of the countries varies considerably. Focusing on the five countries covered by this paper, the following observations may be made on the basis of data presented in Table 2. First, India, Sri Lanka and Bangladesh have done better than Nepal and Pakistan, especially during the post-2000 period. Second, all countries except Nepal have done better during that period compared to the 1990s. In that sense, there is something positive in the growth experience of the region. In fact, India witnessed substantial acceleration in economic growth while Bangladesh and Sri Lanka have also done quite well.

Third, the above observation applies more strongly for the growth of manufacturing industries in India and Pakistan. Bangladesh and Sri Lanka have also attained notable acceleration in the growth of manufacturing industries. While these performances may appear very positive, one qualifying remark needs to be made at this stage. When compared to GDP growth, such growth rates in manufacturing may not appear very impressive. In India, for example, the growth of manufacturing sector was just 1.09 times that of overall GDP growth. The ratios are slightly higher for Bangladesh and Pakistan, but still below 1.5. If manufacturing were to act as the real engine of economic growth, and if the experience of successful developers like South Korea is any indicator, the ratio has to be much higher.[1]

That the growth in manufacturing attained so far is not adequate for attaining a real structural change in the economy is reflected in the data on the sector composition of GDP (Table 3). As expected, the share of agriculture has declined in most South Asian countries, but the share of manufacturing has not risen correspondingly. One extreme case is Sri Lanka where the share of agriculture halved during 2000–2014 but that of manufacturing increased by just one percentage point. In Nepal and Pakistan, the share actually declined. And in Pakistan, the share of agriculture increased. In all the countries, the share of the service sector increased—and in some cases like

---

[1] During the early stages of economic growth in South Korea, the ratio (GDP growth: growth of manufacturing sector) was over 2 during the 1960s, 1.8 during 1970–80 and 1.4 during 1980–90. In Malaysia, the corresponding figures were between 1.5 and 1.8 during 1970–1996 (Islam 2008).

Table 2 Growth of output in South Asian countries, 1990–2014 (% per annum)

Country	GDP		Agriculture		Industry		Manufacturing		Services	
	1990–2000	2000–2014	1990–2000	2000–2014	1990–2000	2000–2014	1990–2000	2000–2014	1990–2000	2000–2014
Afghanistan	n.a.	8.9	n.a.	3.3	n.a.	8.4	n.a.	3.7	n.a.	n.a.
Bangladesh	4.7	5.9	2.6	4.4	7.3	8.0	7.2	8.3	4.2	5.8
Bhutan	5.2	8.0	1.7	1.9	6.6	9.8	8.9	9.3	7.2	8.8
India	6.0	7.6	3.2	3.3	6.1	7.7	6.9	8.3	7.8	9.2
Maldives	n.a.	7.0	n.a.	−0.2	n.a.	6.6	n.a.	1.4	n.a.	7.0
Nepal	4.9	4.1	2.5	3.3	7.1	2.7	8.9	1.5	6.0	4.7
Pakistan	3.8	4.2	4.4	3.0	4.1	5.3	3.8	6.0	4.4	4.9
Sri Lanka	5.3	6.1	1.9	3.6	6.9	6.9	8.1	5.3	6.0	6.3

Source World Bank: World Development Indicators 2015

Table 3 Structure of output of South Asian countries, 2000 and 2014 (in %)

Country	Agriculture		Industry		Manufacturing		Services	
	2000	2014	2000	2014	2000	2014	2000	2014
Afghanistan	38	24	24	21	19	12	38	55
Bangladesh	24	16	23	28	15	17	53	56
Bhutan	27	17	36	42	8	8	37	41
India	23	17	26	30	15	17	51	53
Maldives	9	4	15	19	8	5	76	77
Nepal	41	34	22	15	9	6	37	50
Pakistan	26	25	23	21	15	14	51	54
Sri Lanka	20	10	27	34	17	18	53	56

Source World Bank: World Development Indicators 2015

Nepal, very substantially. These experiences may be variously interpreted as cases of growth led by service sector or cases of premature de-industrialization.

3 The Nexus Between Economic Growth and Employment[2]

High rate of economic growth is an objective that countries at all levels of development aim to attain. However, this cannot be a goal by itself, especially for developing countries of South Asia where, despite notable progress, the incidence of poverty remains high. High rate of economic growth is, of course, a necessary condition for poverty reduction, but a number of studies have demonstrated that this is not sufficient; the pattern and sources of growth and the manner in which its benefits are distributed are critical from the point of view of achieving the goal of poverty reduction (Islam 2006a; Khan 2006). There are country experiences demonstrating that the relationship between economic growth and poverty reduction is not invariant, and that variables relating to employment and labour market are critical in determining the poverty-reducing outcome of growth.[3] Empirical exercise based on cross-country data (Islam 2006a) demonstrates that the employment intensity of economic growth has a significant influence on the rate of poverty reduction.

There are different ways of looking at the relationship between economic growth and employment. One that is commonly employed is to estimate the elasticity of employment growth with respect to output growth and see its level and trend. But employment elasticity reflects the inverse of labour productivity: while an elasticity higher than unity implies a decline in productivity, elasticity lower than unity means

---

[2]This section draws on the author's earlier work on the subject, especially Islam (2006a, b, 2010a, b).

[3]See, for example, the country studies in Islam (2006b) and the chapter in that book summarizing those experiences.

that employment expansion is taking place alongside an increase in productivity. A rise in productivity would lead to a reduction in employment elasticity. However, this measure of employment intensity of growth is not without its limitations.

One limitation that is obvious is that for many developing countries, overall employment growth cannot be taken as a reflection of labour demand alone for a variety of reasons. Employment growth may not correctly reflect the demand for labour. However, for organized sectors like manufacturing, employment would perhaps reflect demand side more closely than overall employment, and hence, it may be more meaningful to look at the relationship between employment and output growth of such sectors.

Another limitation of employment elasticity as a measure of employment intensity of growth is that the estimated value could be high with a combination of low output growth and high employment growth. This cannot be a desirable outcome especially if productive employment is the goal and is looked at as a mechanism for poverty reduction. It would, therefore, be important to look at the underlying figures of output and employment growth in order to have a clear understanding of the real nature of economic growth that is taking place.[4]

Studies on employment intensity of economic growth in developing countries date back to the early 2000s when a number of country studies as well as a cross-country study were published (Islam 2006b). Another study (Khan 2007) covered countries of South Asia as well as of East and South-East Asia, thus providing a comparative perspective of the experiences of the sub-regions.[5] Subsequently, a study focusing on manufacturing industries in a larger set of developing countries was undertaken in order to examine what has happened to the employment intensity of growth within that sector (Islam 2010b; Islam and Islam 2015, Chap. 2). Studies carried out under the South Asia Research Network (SARNET) on labour market project of the Institute for Human Development, Delhi, covering five countries of South Asia, viz. Bangladesh, India, Nepal, Pakistan and Sri Lanka, provide updates and extensions to the earlier studies. These studies provide useful and interesting data for analysing the nexus between economic growth, employment and poverty reduction. To begin with, a few major findings from the earlier set of studies may be highlighted.

First, there is no invariant relationship either between economic growth and employment or between economic growth and poverty reduction. While high rate of economic growth is a necessary condition for generating productive employment and for achieving poverty reduction on a sustained basis, it is not a sufficient condition. Much depends on the pattern and sources of growth and to what extent the poor benefit from it. Second, one variable that has a significant impact on the rate of poverty reduction in relation to economic growth is employment intensity of economic growth. In other words, what happens to employment and labour markets is important for translating the benefits of economic growth into poverty reduction.

---

[4]For a detailed discussion of this aspect of employment intensive growth, see Islam and Islam (2015), Chap. 2.
[5]A synthetic analysis of the results of those studies can be found in Khan (2007).

Third, what happens to the structure of the economy as a result of economic growth is also important from the point of view of poverty reduction. Transfer of workers from sectors characterized by low labour productivity (e.g. agriculture and other traditional economic activities) to those with higher productivity (e.g. manufacturing and modern services) helps increase incomes of the poor. Fourth, education and skills make a contribution to poverty reduction from the supply side of the equation by enabling labour to benefit from productive employment that may be created through growth of output (Islam 2006a).

A comparison between the 1980s and 1990s shows that employment intensity of economic growth (measured through the elasticity of employment growth with respect to output growth) as a whole and for major sectors, by and large, declined during the latter period (Islam 2010b, 2014a; Khan 2007). Data for the 2000s indicate that this trend continued after the 1990s (Islam 2010b). This is an important finding indicating that the employment generating ability of economic growth has been declining over time. A comparison between countries of South Asia and East and South-East Asia shows that the latter groups of countries, during their early stages of economic development, were characterized by higher degrees of employment intensity of growth. In fact, growth in some of them, especially Malaysia, has remained more employment intensive compared to some countries of South Asia. This is contrary to what one would expect if levels of development and relative factor endowments were to be taken into account.

Studies carried out under the SARNET project covering Bangladesh, India, Nepal, Pakistan and Sri Lanka provide useful extensions to the data and analysis presented in the studies mentioned above. First, it has been possible to compile estimates of elasticity of employment for the economies as a whole and the broad sectors for different sub-periods extending up to the first decade of the new millennium.[6] Second, it is also possible to examine what has been happening to labour productivity (which, of course, is the mirror image of employment elasticity) and whether there has been a trade-off between growth of employment and improvement in labour productivity. The relevant data are presented in Tables 4 and 5.

Data presented in Table 4 indicate, by and large, a continuation of the trend observed in earlier studies (aforementioned)—i.e. of a decline in the employment intensity of economic growth. The decline (during the 2000s) in employment intensity for the economy as a whole and for the manufacturing sector is quite striking for India, Nepal and Sri Lanka. This has happened in India despite high economic growth attained during that period. Likewise, the growth in Sri Lanka has also been respectable during that period, and yet, employment intensity of growth has declined sharply. In Nepal, this has happened during a period of declining economic growth. So, while one can ascribe the decline in India and Sri Lanka to the pattern of economic growth, for Nepal, the problem is both low output and employment growth.

Bangladesh presents a mixed picture. Employment elasticity for the economy as a whole registered a small increase during the first half of the 2000s compared to

---

[6]The study on Pakistan (Amjad and Yusuf 2014) does not provide such figures. But it was possible to estimate them by using the figures for growth of output and employment available in the paper.

Table 4 Elasticity of employment with respect to output, select South Asian countries

Country and periods	GDP	Agriculture	Manufacturing	Construction	Services
Bangladesh					
1995–96 to 1999–2000	0.54	0.73	0.26	0.27	0.21
1999–2000 to 2005–06	0.59	0.82	0.78	0.63	0.69
2005–06 to 2010	0.55	0.71	0.87	2.42	0.27
2010 to 2013	0.39	0.20	1.28	−0.77	0.21
India					
1983–84 to 1993–94	0.42	0.49	0.41	1.16	0.39 to 0.67[a]
1993–94 to 2004–05	0.29	0.26	0.47	0.94	0.06 to 0.99[a]
2004–05 to 2011–12	0.04	−0.42	0.13	1.15	0.12 to 0.59[a]
Nepal					
1991–2001	0.64	0.32	2.15	3.76	1.55 to 2.60[a]
2001–2011	0.18	0.25	−4.85	0.47	−1.43 to 0.74[a]
Pakistan[b]					
1981–90	0.30	0.45	0.26[c]	n.a.	0.42
1991–2000	0.55	0.36	0.24[c]	n.a.	0.82
2001–2010	0.79	1.19	0.82[c]	n.a.	0.80
Pakistan[b]					
1992–98	0.81	n.a	n.a.	n.a.	n.a.
1998–2001	0.50	n.a.	n.a.	n.a.	n.a.
2001–2005	0.43	n.a.	n.a.	n.a.	n.a.
Sri Lanka					
1981–94	0.44	0.38	1.28	n.a.	0.25
1994–2005	0.52	0.18	1.31	n.a.	0.57
2005–2012	0.085	0.67	0.06	n.a.	0.03

Sources For Bangladesh, Rahman (2014), and Islam (2015b); for India, IHD (2014); for Nepal, Khannal (2014); for Pakistan, Amjad and Yusuf (2014), and Arif and Farooq (2011); for Sri Lanka, Chandrasiri (2014)

Notes [a]In these cases, data are available for sub-sectors of the service sector, e.g. trade, transport, finance and real estate and community, social and personal services. The figures mentioned here are the lowest and the highest of those figures

[b]The figures for Pakistan have been estimated by the present author from data on output and employment growth that are available in the sources cited

[c]These figures are for industry as a whole not for manufacturing

n.a. denotes not available

Table 5 Growth of labour productivity (% per annum)

Country and period	GDP	Agriculture	Industry	Services
Bangladesh				
1995–96 to 2006	0.16	−1.80	1.25	0.23
2006 to 2010	2.65	2.03	−1.08	5.13
India				
1993–94 to 2004–05	4.11	1.64	1.55	4.82
2004–05 to 2011–12	7.09	4.67	4.96	6.82
Nepal				
1991 to 1998–99	0.66	−2.33	−10.76	9.10
1998–99 to 2008	1.22	1.31	−0.19	−1.59
Pakistan				
1996 to 2005–06	0.72	0	0.59	0.31
2005–06 to 2010–11	0.28	−1.79	−0.06	2.07
Sri Lanka				
1997 to 2006	2.00	−3.63	1.18	3.59
2006 to 2011	3.52	1.01	2.66	2.71

Sources Employment data from national labour force surveys and output data from the national accounts statistics of the respective countries have been used to calculate output per worker at constant prices

the second half of the 1990s. That was the result of increases in employment elasticity of all sectors—agriculture, manufacturing, construction and services. However, there was a reversal in this trend during the second half of the 2000s when overall employment elasticity declined somewhat. At the sector level, employment elasticity increased in manufacturing and construction, but declined in agriculture and services (the latter quite sharply). During 2010–2013, overall employment elasticity declined further, and that happened despite manufacturing becoming more employment intensive. Employment elasticity declined sharply in agriculture and construction, and the declining trend in services continued. Several things seem to be happening. On the one hand, the manufacturing sector which is dominated by the labour-intensive ready-made garment industry, continued to be employment intensive to the extent that employment growth exceeded that of output growth. On the other hand, the ability of agriculture to absorb additional labour declined sharply. And, after a high rate of growth of employment in the construction sector during 2005–2010, there was a reversal in the subsequent years. The net result was that overall employment elasticity registered a decline.

Several points may be worth noting in the case of Bangladesh. First, for a variety of reasons, agriculture can no longer be counted on as a source of much additional employment. Second, growth in the construction sector appears to have slowed down after several years of high growth and job creation. Likewise, the service sector does not seem to be very labour-intensive any more. Third, the weight of the manufacturing sector in total GDP is still rather low, and hence, even a high degree of employment intensity in the sector is unable to offset the low labour absorption in other sectors. In fact, higher than one employment elasticity in the sector is indicative of declining labour productivity which is not desirable from the point of view of competitiveness and future growth of the sector.

It thus seems that maintaining a desirable degree of employment intensity of growth would depend on a variety of factors including attaining higher growth, especially of manufacturing and construction, and higher growth of those segments of the service sector that combine growth potential with the ability to create productive employment.

Pakistan's experience appears to be less straightforward compared to the trend in the other countries considered in the paper. Data provided by Amjad and Yusuf (2014) indicate a rise in employment elasticity during 2001–2010 compared to the 1990s and 1980s—overall as well as for manufacturing. On the other hand, Arif and Farooq (2011), who provide data up to 2005, show that overall employment elasticity during 2001–2005 was lower than during 1998–2001 and 1992–98. A closer look at the data for the 2000s shows that while the first half of the decade was a period of rising growth, the second half saw the opposite.[7] Unlike in developed countries, in developing countries with large informal sector, a decline in economic growth does not automatically lead to a decline in employment (except in the formal segments of the economy). This may have happened in the case of Pakistan during the 2005–2010 period and may have resulted in high employment elasticity for the decade as a whole. This, however, is merely a conjecture, and with conflicting sets of data, it is not possible to be more confident.

As expected, data on labour productivity (Table 5) are consistent with the estimates of employment elasticity. When the latter increases, labour productivity declines and vice versa. Particularly notable are:

- Bangladesh, 2005–06 to 2010 compared to 1995–96 to 2005–06: decline in the growth of labour productivity in industry, while labour productivity growth as a whole increased.
- India, 2004–05 to 2011–12 compared to 1993–94 to 2004–05: increase in the growth of labour productivity as a whole as well as in all sectors.
- Nepal, 2000s compared to the 1990s: increase in the growth of overall labour productivity as well as for agriculture and industry.
- Pakistan, 2005–06 to 2010–11 compared to 1996 to 2005–06: decline in labour productivity growth—overall as well as for agriculture and industry.
- Sri Lanka, 2006 to 2011 compared 1997 to 2006: increase in the growth of labour productivity—overall as well as in agriculture and industry.

The conclusion that one may reach is that with the exception of Pakistan, economic growth in South Asian countries during the 2000s has been associated with increases in the growth of labour productivity and declines in employment elasticity—overall

---

[7] Amjad and Yusuf (2014) call the former a period of "high growth" and the second half a period of "low growth".

as well as in major sectors. These countries thus faced a trade-off between growth of employment and labour productivity.

4 Structural Transformation[8]

An important aspect of the relationship between poverty reduction and employment and labour market variables is the sector composition of employment. The transfer of workers from low productivity sectors like agriculture to modern sectors with higher productivity such as manufacturing and modern services is an important mechanism for improving the employment outcome of growth as well as for poverty reduction. That is why structural transformation is regarded as key to inclusive growth that can result in high rates of both productive employment and poverty reduction. However, there can be a debate on what is meant by this and whether there could be alternative pathways to such changes. In fact, there are differences in the experiences of developing countries in this regard—countries of East and South-East Asia following the traditional path of growth of manufacturing industries at the initial stages of growth followed by services while countries of South Asia showing no such clear pattern. This can be seen from data presented in Tables 6 and 7.

Data on changes in sector composition of output (Table 6) show that a few countries in East and South-East Asia, especially South Korea, Indonesia, Malaysia and Thailand, have undergone structural transformation similar to that experienced by

Table 6 Change in the sector composition of GDP in select developing countries, 1960–2010

Country	Agriculture (%)		Industry (%)		Services (%)	
	1960	2010	1960	2010	1960	2010
Bangladesh	53	19	11	28	36	53
China	22	10	45	47	33	43
India	43	19	20	26	38	55
Indonesia	51	15	15	47	33	38
Malaysia	34	11	19	44	46	45
Nepal	65	36	11	15	23	48
Pakistan	46	21	16	25	38	53
Philippines	26	12	28	33	47	55
Republic of Korea	38	3	18	39	43	58
Sri Lanka	28	13	21	29	51	58
Thailand	36	12	19	45	45	43

Source World Bank: World Development Indicators 2004 (CD-ROM), World Development Report 1990 and World Development Indicators 2012

---

[8] This section draws on Islam (2015a) which has subsequently appeared in Reddy and Sarap (2017).

Table 7 Sector composition of employment in South Asia (% of total employment)

Country and period	Agriculture	Industry	Manufacturing	Construction	Services
Bangladesh					
1999–2000	50.7	12.3	9.5	2.8	36.1
2005–06	48.1	14.5	11.0	3.2	37.5
2010	47.6	17.7	12.5	4.8	35.3
India					
1993–94	64.8	14.7	10.5	3.1	20.5
2004–05	58.5	18.1	12.0	5.6	23.4
2011–12	48.9	24.4	12.9	10.6	26.7
Nepal					
1998–99	78.2	10.5	5.8	3.6	11.3
2008–09	73.9	10.8	6.6	3.1	15.3
Pakistan					
2005–06	42.3	20.7	13.8	6.1	37.0
2010–11	44.2	21.3	13.7	7.0	34.4
Sri Lanka					
2004	33.5	24.1	n.a.	n.a.	42.4
2011	33.0	24.0	n.a.	n.a.	42.8

Source Labour force surveys of different countries

developed countries during the earlier stages of their development. In these countries, the decline in the share of agriculture and increase in that of industries have been notable. Clearly, manufacturing in these countries has acted as the engine of growth. But the experience of the countries in South Asia has been different. In Bangladesh and India, for example, the decline in the share of agriculture has not been followed by a similar increase in the share of industry; the increase has been more than proportionate in services. This is particularly the case when one looks at the structure of employment (Table 7).

In order to understand the pattern of structural change in South Asian countries (and their contrast with countries of East and South-East Asia), it would be useful to look more closely at their growth rates and pattern. In Bangladesh, there has been a steady acceleration in economic growth since the 1990s: from an annual GDP growth of less than five per cent, the country achieved a six per cent GDP growth in a decade. In 2003–04, growth rate exceeded six per cent, and since then, it has hovered around that mark. Although GDP growth appears to have plateaued in recent years, it has remained over six per cent per annum. Economic growth in India has been more impressive, especially since the mid-1990s. GDP growth rate started accelerating since 1994–95 and ranged between six and nine per cent per annum in most years after that. The annual average GDP growth in India has increased from six per cent during the 1990s to 7.6% during 2000–2014 (Table 2). Sri Lanka also witnessed acceleration in GDP growth from 5.3% during the 1990s to 6.1% per annum during 2000–2014. However, Nepal and Pakistan's growth record is not as impressive, although Pakistan was able to raise its economic growth during the first half of the 2000s (Amjad and Yusuf 2014).

Despite such impressive rates of GDP growth, the slow rate of structural transformation in employment observed from Tables 6 and 7 is something to take note of. In order to understand this, one has to look at the pattern of growth and its drivers. One particular element in that is whether manufacturing has acted as the driver of growth.

In Bangladesh, there has been very little difference between overall GDP growth and growth in manufacturing during 1995–96 and 1999–2000. The ratio increased to about 1.5 during 1999–2000 to 2005–06, but then declined to 1.23 during 2005–2010.[9] In India also, industry has not emerged as the driver/engine of economic growth. The elasticity of manufacturing growth with respect to GDP growth has actually declined from 1.14 during 1990–2000 to 1.09 during 2000–2010.[10] In Nepal, this elasticity has been declining steadily since mid-1990s and was negative after 2005 (Islam 2014b). In Pakistan, the figure has fluctuated—declining from 1.34 during the 1980s to 1.04 during the 1990s and then rising to 1.54 during the 2000s.[11] In Sri Lanka, the elasticity varied from 1.6 during the 1980s to 0.7 during 2000–05 (Islam 2008).

In Republic of Korea (South Korea), the corresponding figure was over 2 during the 1960s, 1.8 during 1970–80 and 1.4 during 1980–90. In Malaysia also, the figure was between 1.5 and 1.8 during the 1970–96 (Islam 2008).

The conclusion that follows from the figures mentioned above is that manufacturing has not been the driver of economic growth in the same way as it has been in countries like South Korea and Malaysia during the early stages of their growth. One important outcome of this difference in the pattern of economic growth is the preponderance of employment in the informal economy in South Asia compared to South Korea and Malaysia (Table 8). And that has implications for a country's ability to provide social protection to its citizens, especially to the working people.

---

[9]These figures have been calculated from data presented in Islam (2014a).

[10]These figures have been calculated by using data from the World Bank: *World Development Indicators* (various years).

[11]These figures have been calculated by the author using data available in Government of Pakistan: Pakistan Economic Survey 2010–11, Table 1.2.

Table 8 Share (%) of informal employment in total non-agricultural employment

Country	The share of informal employment (%) and year
Bangladesh	87.1 (2013)
Cambodia	90.0 (2012)
China	32.6 (2010)
India	83.6 (2009/10)
Indonesia	72.6 (2009)
South Korea	25.8 (2005)
Malaysia	11.4 (2015)
Mongolia	15.6 (2007/08)
Nepal	96.2 (2008)
Pakistan	78.4 (2009/10)
Philippines	70.1 (2008)
Sri Lanka	62.1 (2009)
Thailand	42.3 (2010)
Vietnam	68.2 (2009)

Source ILO (2012) except for Bangladesh, Cambodia, Korea, and Malaysia and Mongolia which are from national labour force/household surveys. For Bangladesh, BBS (2015); for Cambodia, ILO-GOC (2013); for South Korea, OECD (2008); for Malaysia, Department of Statistics Malaysia (2016); and for Mongolia, Heintz (2010). For Bangladesh, Cambodia and Mongolia, the sources are labour force surveys. For South Korea, the source is the Korea Labour and Income Panel Study. For Malaysia, it is Informal Sector Workforce Survey

5 The Challenge of Social Protection

5.1 Economic Growth and Social Protection

Till about the end of the twentieth century, social protection was not very high on the agenda either in the developed or developing countries. There was even a tendency to invoke the debate between the 'growth first model' versus the 'European social model' and the perceived superiority of the former as a justification for relegating the importance of social protection. Indeed, in the developed world, countries that achieved high economic and employment growth appear to be the ones characterized by lower unemployment rates as well as lower levels of unemployment benefits. Amongst the OECD countries, for example, USA is known to have been able to achieve higher economic growth (in terms of GDP growth) than, for example, the countries in Western Europe—at least during the two decades before the global economic crisis of 2008–09.[12] And the duration of unemployment benefit as well

---

[12]For example, according to data presented in OECD Employment Outlook 2006, GDP growth in USA during 1993–2003 was 3.2% per annum compared to 2.3% for the 15 EU countries and the OECD average of 2.7% per annum. During 2004–07, also growth in USA has been higher than that

as expenditure on unemployment compensation has been consistently lower in USA compared to the latter.[13]

Countries in the developing world generally did not have any unemployment benefits, and social protection in them—covering mainly the formal sector workers—basically was in the form of severance benefits (of varying duration), pensions and provident fund, and programmes of social assistance. For workers outside the formal sector, there was virtually no social protection except for some programmes of social assistance and labour market programmes targeted at specific groups. Even in countries that had achieved high rates of economic growth on a sustained basis for some time, such as those in East and South-East Asia, there was not much thinking about unemployment benefits until they were hit by a severe economic crisis in 1997–98. High rates of output growth were generally associated with high rates of employment growth in higher productivity activities like manufacturing, construction and services, and some increases in real wages appeared to have made it possible for policy-makers in those countries to postpone thinking about social protection for workers.

The experiences mentioned above perhaps gave rise to the question whether high rates of economic and employment growth could obviate the need for social protection or at least make its case somewhat weaker. Even apart from the normative issue of the desirability of social protection, two points need to be considered in this context. The first relates to economic growth itself: what has been the experience with respect to growth—both in terms of rates and stability. The second point relates to the outcome of economic growth in terms of employment growth. Let us look at both points briefly.

As for economic growth, market-based economies of the present-day world face uncertainties of different kinds, the result of which is frequent fluctuations in growth and occasional recessions. Developing countries don't remain immune from such instability in growth and recessions. The impact of economic downturns and recessions on employment and labour market is usually negative, and recovery in labour markets often takes longer than economic recovery. In such situations, it is the general people, especially those dependent on their own labour, who are the ultimate sufferers. Measures are needed to provide them with protection and ability to cope with such an environment.

As for the employment outcome of economic growth, it has already been shown above that the employment intensity of economic growth in South Asia has been low and declining in recent years. Growth of employment in the formal sector has been rather low, and much of the employment growth takes place in the informal segments of the economy. In this kind of a situation, the prospects of high rates of employment-

---

achieved by EU-15. Unemployment rate in USA has been much lower (5.3% on an average during 1993–2003) than in EU-15 (8.8% during the same period).

[13] In 2004, according to OECD (2006), the duration of unemployment benefit was 6 months in USA compared to 30 and 12 months, respectively, in France and Germany and an average of 34 months in Nordic countries (Denmark, Finland, Norway and Sweden). Likewise, public expenditure as percentage of GDP was much lower in the USA (0.55% in 2002) compared to 1.39 and 2.1% in France and Germany, respectively (Auer et al. 2005).

intensive growth of the kind achieved by the East and South-East Asian countries during the past few decades do not appear to be bright.[14] Unless there is willingness on the part of policy-makers to re-think and re-orient development strategies, economic growth may not become significantly more employment-intensive than at present. Hence, it would be important to develop a strategy for social protection alongside the growth strategy.

5.2 The Challenge Posed by a Large Informal Sector

In the context of developing countries, an important aspect of the structure of labour markets is the duality that characterizes them—a small formal sector coexisting with a large informal sector. This has important implications for the coverage and type of social protection. For example, higher employment growth in the formal sector can facilitate a greater coverage of workers through various social insurance schemes. If, on the contrary, a high proportion of the labour force is engaged in the informal economy, alternative mechanisms for providing social protection are required. The high proportion of the employed labour force in self-employment and in informal employment does pose an additional challenge for developing countries in this respect. For those who are self-employed, it is not so easy to arrange for insurance against ill health and inability to work due to unforeseen contingencies and make provision for incomes during old age.[15] The same applies to those who are in informal employment, because it is difficult to use formal mechanisms of social protection, especially those based on insurance, in such cases. Conventional mechanisms of social protection, e.g. unemployment allowance, pensions, may not be applicable to the vast number of people in these categories. But rather than overlooking and ignoring the need for social protection for them, it is essential to identify alternative measures, and if necessary, innovative mechanisms for providing social protection.

The challenge posed for social protection by the high proportion of employment in the informal economy is illustrated by Fig. 1 where social protection index[16] for select countries of Asia has been plotted against data on the share of informal employment in total non-agricultural employment. This plotting shows a negative correlation between the two variables—indicating that improvements in the coverage of social protection come with increase in the share of formal sector employment.

The conventional wisdom in development discourse is that high and sustained economic growth should result in more formal sector employment. And given the negative relationship between informal employment and social protection, higher

---

[14]For a more detailed analysis of this aspect, see Islam (2008).

[15]This, of course, is not to say that it is impossible for the self-employed to organize social protection for themselves. For a description of some such efforts, see ILO (2014).

[16]The idea of Social Protection Index has been developed by the Asian Development Bank and is defined as the ratio of total social protection expenditure and total intended beneficiaries. Three categories of social protection expenditures have been included: (i) social insurance, (ii) social assistance and (iii) labour market programmes. For further details, see (ADB 2013).

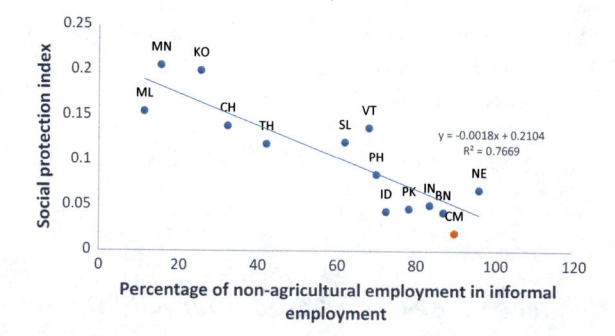

Fig. 1 Social protection index and informal employment in select countries of South Asia. *Note* BN = Bangladesh, BH = Bhutan, CM = Cambodia, CH = China, IN = India, ID = Indonesia, SKO = S.Korea, ML = Malaysia, NE = Nepal, PK = Pakistan, PH = Philippines, SL = Sri Lanka, TH = Thailand, VT = Vietnam. *Source* Constructed by the author using figures for Social Protection Index from ADB (2013) and figures for informal employment from Table 8

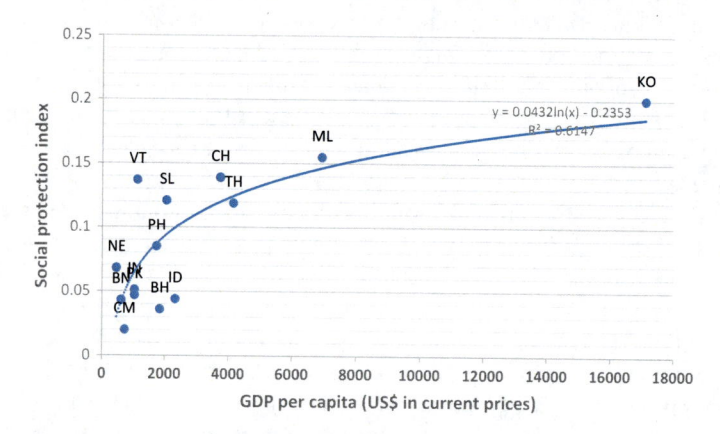

Fig. 2 Social protection index and GDP per capita at current prices, 2009. *Note* BN = Bangladesh, BH = Bhutan, CM = Cambodia, CH = China, IN = India, ID = Indonesia, SKO = Korea, ML = Malaysia, NE = Nepal, PK = Pakistan, PH = Philippines, SL = Sri Lanka, TH = Thailand, VT = Vietnam. *Source* Constructed by the author using data from ADB (2013)

levels of income should lead to an improvement in social protection. Indeed, data from select Asian developing countries on GDP per capita and social protection do point towards this possibility (Fig. 2). However, it needs to be noted that although the relationship between these two variables is positive, it is not linear. The rate of improvement in social protection index declines at higher levels of income—indicating that the relationship between economic growth and social protection should not be taken for granted. Public policy has an important role to play in that regard.

In situations where the social protection system is weak or inadequate, the poor usually depends on traditional support systems based on family and community. For example, during the Asian economic crisis of 1997–98, many workers who lost jobs in Indonesia and Thailand had to return to their rural households and rely on support from their families. At that time, there was a good deal of talk about so-called Asian values. But what happened in reality was sharing of family income, and the creation of a new class of poor. On the other hand, in the Republic of Korea (South Korea), the social protection system was strengthened at that time by increasing the number of people covered by unemployment insurance. In addition, attempt was made to prevent increase in the rate of unemployment by introducing public works' programmes. In Thailand as well, debates and discussion on the possibility of introducing unemployment insurance started at that time.

While conventional thinking is that social protection may not be economically feasible in developing countries, empirical exercises show that it should be possible to introduce at least some basic social protection measures, like old-age allowance and unemployment benefits, in such countries. One exercise (Lee 1998) showed that in Indonesia and Thailand, the expenditure that would be needed to replace half of the regular incomes for unemployment for a period of six months can be feasibly shared between the government, employers and workers.

A good example of what can be done to provide social protection for those engaged in the unorganised sector is demonstrated by the adoption, in India in 2008, of the Unorganized Workers' Social Security Bill. Under this Act, provision was made to bring 340 million people (out of a total labour force of 458 million) under the cover of pension, basic health, life and disability insurance as well as group accident insurance within a period of five years. This shows that it is not unpractical or a luxury to think of providing social protection to those who are engaged in the informal economy. What is important is the political will and the adoption of innovative approaches.[17]

6 Real Wages and Inclusive Development

Wage is a key labour market outcome and has important implications for inclusive development. Increases in real wages and earnings can play an important role not only in reducing poverty, but also in reducing inequality in the distribution of income. It needs to be noted, however, that a rise in real wages may not necessarily help poverty reduction, especially if it is associated with a decline in the quantity of employment (e.g. the number of days for which employment is available in a year for an agricultural labourer). The latter may actually neutralize the positive effect of the rise in real wages and prevent total earnings from increasing.

Likewise, a rise in real wages may not help improve income distribution if labour productivity increases at a faster rate than real wages. The gains from productivity

---

[17]It may be noted in this context that in India, the 2006 report of National Commission for Enterprises in the Unorganized Sector (NCEUS) had made a set of recommendations social security for unorganized workers. Researchers are of the view that the Unorganized Workers' Social Security Act of 2008 does not adequately reflect the recommendations of the NCEUS. On this and the implementation of various programmes of social security for the poor in India, see Kannan and Breman (editors) (2013).

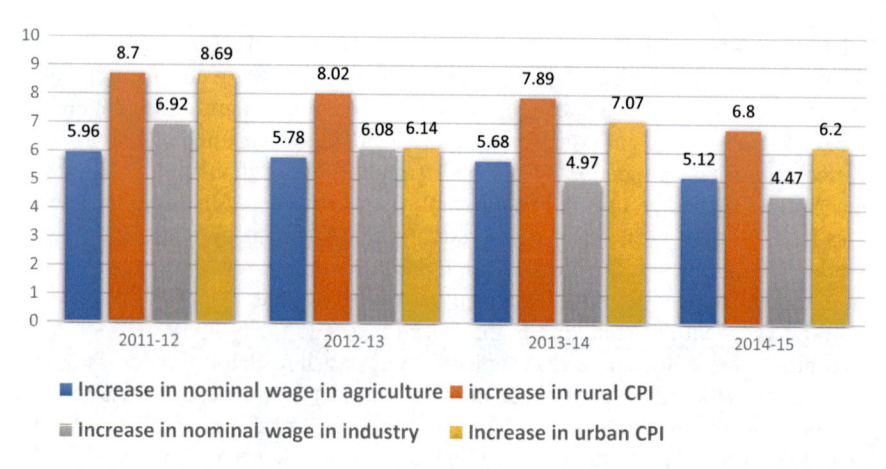

Fig. 3 Bangladesh—Increase (%) in nominal wages and consumer price index. *Source* Constructed by the author using data from GOB (2016)

increase may be unevenly shared by the factors of production, and the share of labour in the value added may even decline. That, in turn, may have an adverse effect on personal income distribution.

If one looks at the data on trends in real wages in South Asian countries, a somewhat mixed picture emerges. First, let us look at the wages of agricultural labourers—a category on which studies and data are more easily available. Although several countries, especially India and Bangladesh, witnessed acceleration in economic growth since the mid-1990s, real wages of such workers started to rise significantly only after the mid-2000s (Table 9).[18]

In Nepal and Sri Lanka also, real wages of agricultural workers registered healthy growth during the second half of the 2000s. Pakistan appears to be an exception to this trend where real wages in agriculture declined between 2007 and 2012.

An important question is whether the rise in real wages is sustained over a period of time or represents short-term changes. An example is provided by the trends in wages in Bangladesh agriculture. Data on real wages in agriculture for recent years are not available from official sources. What is available are data on changes in nominal wages and in consumer prices (see Fig. 3). In all the four years from 2011–12, increases in rural consumer price index (CPI) exceeded those of nominal wages—thus indicating that real wages in agriculture most likely declined during those years.

What has happened to wages in urban areas (or in sectors like manufacturing and construction) is less clear. In Bangladesh, for example, real wages in manufacturing did register healthy increases for a few years after 2008. But the trend was not sustained in subsequent years (Islam 2015b). Data on nominal wages in industry and

---

[18]On India, there are studies that show real wages in rural areas rising consistently since the 1980s, although the rate of increase varied between sub-periods and for different categories of workers, e.g. regular and casual workers. See, for example, Jose (2013) and IHD (2014).

Table 9 Real wages of agricultural workers in countries of South Asia

Country and category	Real daily wages (US$, constant 2010)			Percentage change		
Bangladesh	*2000*	*2005*	*2010*	*2000–2005*	*2005–2010*	*2000–2010*
National peak season, male	1.92	1.92	2.78	0	45	44
National lean season, male	1.53	1.52	2.21	−1	46	45
National peak season, female	1.32	1.22	2.02	−8	66	53
National lean season, female	1.10	1.02	1.62	−7	58	48
India	*2000/01*	*2005/06*	*2012/13*	*2000–05*	*2005–12*	*2010–12*
National agricultural labour, male	2.13	2.15	2.91	1	35	36
National agricultural labour, female	1.59	1.61	2.21	1	37	38
Pakistan		*2007*	*2012*			*2007–12*
National agricultural worker, male		3.36	2.97			−12
National agricultural worker, female		1.68	1.46			−13
Nepal		*2003/04*	*2010/11*			*2003/04 to 2010/11*
National agricultural worker		1.73	2.22			29
Sri Lanka		*2007*	*2012*			*2007–12*
National agricultural daily work		2.24	3.08			38

Source Wiggins and Keats (2014)

urban CPI presented in Fig. 3 actually indicate a decline in real wages in the sector from 2011–12.

What happened to real wages in urban areas and in industry in India is not so clear. One study, using data from the National Sample Survey organization (NSSO), shows that urban wages also increased (from 1983 to 2011/12), but at a lower rate compared to rural wages. Within urban areas, the rate of growth of wages in the secondary sector has been lower than in the primary sector (IHD 2014).[19] But another study, using data from the Annual Survey of Industries, points out that real wages in registered manufacturing declined during the second half of the 1990s and remained stagnant after that (Chandrasekhar and Ghosh 2015).[20]

From the data and analysis of trends in real wages presented above, it appears that the picture in this regard is somewhat mixed. While there have been periods during which real wages in some sectors have increased in some countries, it cannot be said confidently that real wages have been rising on a sustained basis.

Moreover, as mentioned already, even a rise in real wages can be consistent with a decline in the share of labour in total factor income. As a result, the rise in real wages can be associated with a rise in the degree of inequality in the distribution of income. This appears to have happened in the case of both Bangladesh and India.

In India, during 1983 to 2011, real wages on the whole rose 3.1% per annum while value added per worker rose 4.8% per annum.[21] The gap between the increases in labour productivity and real wages is indicative of the decline in the share of wages in value added. Data on manufacturing industries provide some corroboration to this hypothesis.[22] Data from the Annual Survey of Industries show that the share of wages in value added declined from about 45% in the early 1980s to about 25% in 2010–11. During that period, the share of profit rose from 20 to 58%. Hence, it should not be a surprise that the distribution of income has worsened during that period. Indeed, the estimated Gini coefficients of earnings show a rise from 0.483 in 1983 to 0.542 in 2004–05. Although the figure went down to 0.510 in 2011–12, it is clear that inequality has increased during the 2000s compared to the 1980s and 1990s.

On Bangladesh, calculations made by the author (using data from the Survey of Manufacturing Industries of various years)[23] show that the rise in real wages fell short of the increase in labour productivity. In the manufacturing sector, for example, growth of employment cost per worker (a proxy for wages) during the entire period of 2001–02 to 2012 fell short of the growth of value added per worker (proxy for labour productivity). The share of employment cost in total value added stagnated around 25% during 2000 to 2005 and then increased to thirty-six per cent in 2012.

An important aspect of inclusive development is how women fare in the employment field, and one indication of that is provided by the male–female differences in wage rates. Data presented in Table 10 may be used to throw some light on that aspect—although this set of data is limited to rural workers only. Figures in Table 10 show a few interesting patterns and trends. First, irrespective of the season (i.e. peak

---

[19] Studies that cover up to 2004–05 show an acceleration in the growth of urban wages during 1993–94 and 1999–90 (compared to the period of 1983 to 1993–94), but the rate of increase declined after that (ILO 2009).

[20] It may be mentioned in this context that data presented in that study (in Fig. 8) seem to show that real wages in 2010–11 and 2011–12 were higher than that of 2009–10. But the key question is whether that represented the beginning of a rising trend in subsequent years.

[21] These and other data presented in this paragraph are from IHD (2014).

[22] Despite high growth of real wage rates (6–7% per annum during the 2000s), the share of wages in value added has declined in China as well. See ILO (2015).

[23] Data are from BBS (2013, 2014).

Table 10 Gender difference in real wages in select countries of South Asia

Country and category	Ratio of female to male wages		
Bangladesh	2000	2005	2010
National Peak	0.69	0.64	0.73
National Lean	0.72	0.67	0.73
India	2000/01	2005/06	2012/13
National Agriculture	0.75	0.75	0.76
Pakistan		2007	2012
National Agriculture		0.50	0.49

Source Calculated from data in Table 8

Table 11 India: average daily wages of male and females, 1983 to 2011–12 (wages in Rs.)

Category	1983		1993–4		2004–5		2011–12	
	Male	Female	Male	Female	Male	Female	Male	Female
RR	17.6	12.8	58.5	34.9	144.9	85.3	320.2	202.8
RC	7.8	4.9	23.2	15.3	55.1	34.9	150.4	104.6
UR	25.7	19.5	78.1	63.3	203.3	153.2	462.8	368.8
UC	11.1	5.6	32.4	18.5	75.1	43.9	185.0	114.9

Source IHD (2014)
Note RR rural regular, RC rural casual, UR urban regular, UC urban casual

or lean), the male–female differences are of the same order of magnitude. Second, the data indicate a stubborn persistence, over time, of the gender gap in wages. And that applies to all the three countries of South Asia (viz. Bangladesh, India and Pakistan) for which data are presented in Tables 9 and 10. This shows that despite sustained economic growth (at least in Bangladesh and India) and an overall rise in real wages, the male–female difference in wages has not only remained but there are no signs of any convergence.

Data on wages of workers as a whole (as opposed to rural or agricultural workers) presented in Tables 11 and 12 are generally in line with the data on rural/agricultural workers presented earlier—with some differences. As for trends, there was some worsening of the gap for rural regular workers between 1983 and 2004–05. Although there was a recovery after that year, the gap remained worse in 2011–12 compared to 1983. Looking at the differences between different categories of workers, one finds that the situation is worst for urban casual female workers. They earned about half of what their male counterparts got in 1983. In 2011–12, their situation improved somewhat, but they still earned less than two-thirds of their male counterparts.

The main points emerging from the data presented in this section may be summarized as follows. One good news about the trends in real wages of workers is that except in the case of rural workers of Pakistan, there has been a rise in the wages of workers over time. This could have a positive impact on the incidence of poverty

Table 12 India: ratio of female wage to male wage

Category	1983	1993–94	2004–05	2011–12
RR	0.73	0.60	0.59	0.63
RC	0.63	0.66	0.63	0.70
UR	0.76	0.81	0.75	0.80
UC	0.50	0.57	0.58	0.62

Source Calculated from data in Table 11
Note RR rural regular, RC rural casual, UR urban regular, UC urban casual

because labour income is a major source of income of the low-income households. Moreover, as the incidence of poverty is generally higher in rural areas, a rise in wages of rural workers may have made a positive contribution to poverty reduction. However, the good news almost ends there—especially if the contribution of wages to inclusive development is considered in a broader framework to include inequality in the distribution of household incomes and gender inequality. Since wages have not moved in tandem with increases in labour productivity, and since the share of wages in value added has declined, the rise in real wages failed to make any contribution to improving the distribution of income. In fact, inequality in income has risen in the countries of South Asia. Likewise, there has been very little impact of rising wages on the gender gap in wages.

7 Concluding Observations

The present paper has looked at a number of labour market outcomes that have a bearing on inclusive development. They include employment intensity of economic growth, social protection and real wages. Using data on countries of South Asia (and comparing with countries of East and South-East Asia), the paper has pointed out the following.

- In South Asia, employment intensity of economic growth has generally been low and has declined over time. Of course, there have been exceptions like the manufacturing sector of Bangladesh.
- Although there has been some degree of structural transformation of employment, the pace has been slow, and the share of manufacturing has not increased to the extent expected, especially given the success achieved in accelerating GDP growth.
- As a result, despite sustained and high growth of output (especially in India and Bangladesh) growth of formal sector employment has been rather low and the share of informal employment in total employment continues to remain high.
- That, in turn, poses a challenge for social protection, and the level of coverage of social protection is generally rather low.

- While the level of social protection is positively correlated with the level of income, the relationship is not linear—indicating that high income or economic growth is not a sufficient condition for expansion of social protection.
- A positive labour market outcome witnessed in some countries (except Pakistan) is the rise in real wages, especially in agriculture and in rural areas. But the rise has not been sustained in recent years. Moreover, growth of wages has lagged behind that of labour productivity. As a result, the rise in real wages has not been able to make an impact on growing income inequality. Gender differences in wages have also persisted.
- On the whole, it seems that labour market outcomes in South Asia have not moved in the direction needed to make economic growth more inclusive.

In order to gear labour market outcomes towards attaining the goal of inclusive development, action will be required on a number of fronts. Consider the issue relating to employment, especially the growth of productive and remunerative jobs. It is clear that economic growth attained during the past two decades has not delivered the desired employment outcome. And that shows that conventional policies are not working. A re-thinking of development strategy and policies is required in order to pursue this goal. A major issue in this regard is to get out of the conventional approach of treating employment policy as synonymous with labour market policies. There is a typical argument that labour market rigidities are responsible for low employment growth, and hence, higher employment growth can be achieved by making labour markets more flexible. This approach is too narrow and does not recognize the importance of economic policies in promoting a pattern of growth that would be more conducive to employment expansion. The employment policy has to be broad-based, and a combination of economic and labour market policies will be needed to address the various factors that are responsible for growth not leading to desired job creation.

As for social protection, an easy option may be to take the view that with economic growth, the coverage of social protection will also expand. This does happen to some extent, but the relationship is not linear. Hence, the expansion of the coverage of social protection cannot be expected to continue automatically. Public policy including legislation would be necessary to achieve real continuous progress in this respect.

A major challenge in the area of social protection is that economic growth has not led to an increase in the growth of formal employment at the desired rate. Given the persistence of high proportion of informal employment, it is necessary to consider ways and means of extending social protection to workers in the informal economy. India's Unorganized Sector Workers' Social Security Act of 2008 provides a good example of moving in that direction.

The experience of East and South-East Asian countries during their period of high growth shows that formal sector employment may not be a guarantee to access to social protection. Some of those countries started to look at it seriously only in the wake of the economic crisis that hit the region in 1997–98. In the countries of South Asia also, social protection is not universal for workers in the formal sector. Rather than waiting for a crisis, a better way would be to develop strategies and plan of action for extending social protection to all workers.

Improvements have happened with regard to wages of workers. However, since the rate of increase has not matched that of labour productivity, the share of wages in output has declined. As a result, the rise in wages has not been able to stem the rise in income inequality. In order to address these challenges, action would be needed on several fronts. First, since one of the variables influencing real wages is labour productivity, efforts to raise productivity continuously would be important. However, as growth in real wages has fallen short of growth in productivity, public policy and legislation would be necessary to address the issue. Although the debate on the impact of minimum wage legislation on employment and poverty is a continuous one, there is no convincing evidence to point to a negative impact on employment. Apart from legislation, there may be other ways of supporting the growth of real wages. The experience of India shows that employment guarantee programmes like Mahatma Gandhi National Rural Employment Guarantee Programme (MGNREGP), by providing alternative sources of employment, could improve the supply price of labour and thereby have a positive impact on wages.

References

Amjad, R., & Yusuf, A. (2014). *More and better jobs for Pakistan: Can the manufacturing sector play a greater role?* Monograph Series, Graduate School of Development Studies, Lahore School of Economics, Lahore.

Arif, G. M., & Farooq, S. (2011). *Poverty, inequality and unemployment in Pakistan*. Background paper prepared for the IDB group MCPS Document for Pakistan. PIDE and IDB.

Asian Development Bank. (2013). *The social protection index: Assessing results for Asia and the Pacific*. Manila: ADB.

Auer, P., Efendioglu, U., & Leschke, J. (2005). *Active labour market policies around the world*. Geneva: ILO.

BBS (Bangladesh Bureau of Statistics). (2014). *Statistical Yearbook of Bangladesh 2013*. Dhaka: BBS.

BBS. (2015). *Report of labour force survey 2013*. Dhaka.

BBS. (2013). *Survey of manufacturing industries 2012*. Dhaka: BBS.

Chandrasekhar, C. P., & Ghosh, J. (2015). *Growth, employment patterns and inequality in Asia: A case study of India*. ILO Asia-Pacific Working Paper Series, Bangkok.

Chandrasiri, S. (2014). *Towards inclusive growth through more and better jobs: Can the manufacturing sector play a greater role in Sri Lanka?* Paper prepared for SARNET project, IHD, Delhi.

Department of Statistics Malaysia. (2016). *Informal sector workforce survey report, Malaysia, 2015*. Kuala Lumpur.

GOB. (2016). *Bangladesh economic review 2015–16 (in Bengali)*. Government of Bangladesh: Ministry of Finance.

Heintz, J. (2010). *Defining and measuring informal employment and the informal sector in the Philippines, Mongolia, and Sri Lanka*. ESCAP Working Paper No. 3. ESCAP, Bangkok.

ILO (International Labour Organization). (2009). *Towards and employment strategy for India*. Report prepared for the Government of India. ILO, Delhi.

ILO. (2012). *Statistical update on employment in the informal economy*. Geneva: ILO.

ILO. (2014). *World of work report 2014: Developing with jobs*. Geneva: ILO.
ILO. (2015). *Global wage report 2014/2015: Wages and income inequality*. Geneva: ILO.
ILO-GOC. (2013). *Cambodia labour force and child labour survey 2012, Labour Force Report*. ILO and National Institute of Statistics, Cambodia, Geneva and Phnom Penh.
Institute for Human Development. (2014). *Growth, labour markets and employment: India*. New Delhi: IHD.
Islam, R. (2006a). The nexus of economic growth, employment and poverty reduction: An empirical analysis. In Islam (Ed.), *Fighting poverty: The development-employment link*. Lynn Rienner, Boulder, and London.
Islam, R. (Ed.) (2006b). *Fighting poverty: The development-employment link*. Lynn Rienner, Boulder, and London.
Islam, R. (2008). Has development and employment through labour-intensive industrialization become history? In K. Basu & R. Kanbur (Eds.), *Arguments for a better World: Essays in honour of Amartya Sen*. Oxford: Oxford University Press.
Islam, R. (2010a). Pattern of economic growth and its implication for employment. In L. Banerjee, A. Dasgupta, & R. Islam (Eds.) *Development, equity and poverty: Essays in honour of Azizur Rahman Khan*. Macmillan India and UNDP, Delhi and New York.
Islam, R. (2010b). *Addressing the challenge of jobless growth in developing countries: an analysis with cross-country data*. Occasional Paper Series No. 01. Bangladesh Institute of Development Studies, Dhaka.
Islam, R. (2014a). The employment challenge faced by Bangladesh: How far is the Lewis turning point? *The Indian Journal of Labour Economics, 57*(2), 201–225.
Islam, R. (2014b). *Nepal: Addressing the employment challenge through the sectoral pattern of growth*. Kathmandu: ILO Country Office.
Islam, R. (2015a). *Structural transformation and alternative pathways to the Lewis Turning Point*. Paper presented at the International Seminar on Labour and Employment Issues in the Emerging Rural-Urban Continuum: Dimensions, Processes and Policies, March 12–14, 2015, National Institute of Rural Development, Hyderabad, Hyderabad.
Islam, R. (2015b). *Employment and labour market in Bangladesh: An overview of trends and challenges*. Paper prepared for the ILO and ADB.
Islam, R., & Islam, I. (2015). *Employment and inclusive development*. London: Routledge.
Jose, A. V. (2013). Changes in wages and earnings of rural labourers. *Economic and Political Weekly, 48*(26 & 27), 107–114.
Kannan, K. P., & Breman, Jan (Eds.). (2013). *The long road to social security: Assessing the implementation of national social security initiatives for the working poor in India*. Delhi: Oxford University Press.
Khan, A. R. (2006). Employment policies for poverty reduction. In R. Islam (Ed.), *Fighting poverty: The development-employment link*. Boulder and London: Lynn Rienner.
Khan, A. R. (2007). *Asian experience on growth, employment and poverty: An overview with special reference to the findings of some recent case studies*. Geneva and UNDP, Colombo: ILO.
Khannal, D. R. (2014). *Employment challenges in Nepal: Trends, characteristics and policy options for inclusive growth and development*. Paper prepared for the SARNET project, IHD, New Delhi.
Lee, E. (1998). *The Asian financial crisis: The challenge for social policy*. Geneva: ILO.
OECD. (2006). *OECD employment outlook 2006*. Retrieved from www.oecd.org/employment/emp/oecdemploymentoutlook2006.htm.
OECD. (2008). *OECD employment outlook 2008*. Retrieved from www.oecd.org/employment/emp/oecdemploymentoutlook2008.htm.
Rahman, R. I. (2014). *Employment for inclusive growth and development in Bangladesh*. Paper prepared for the SARNET project, IHD, New Delhi.
Reddy, D. N., Sarap, K. (Eds.). (2017). *Rural labour mobility in times of structural transformation: Dynamics and perspectives from asian economies*. Palgrave Macmillan, Singapore.
Wiggins, S., & Keats, S. (2014). *Rural wages in Asia*. London: Overseas Development Institute.
World Bank. (various years). *World development indicators*.

Rizwanul Islam is former Special Adviser, Employment Sector, International Labour Office, Geneva. He has held various directorial positions at the ILO during his career with the organization. Prior to joining the ILO, he was an Associate Professor of Economics at Dhaka University. Currently, he is Visiting Professor at the Institute for Human Development, Delhi, India, and a Senior Visiting Fellow at the Centre for Development and Employment Research, Bangladesh.

Dr. Islam has been a Visiting Professor at BRAC University, Dhaka, and Guest Lecturer at various universities including New School University, New York, Institute of Social Studies at the Hague, and South Asian University in New Delhi. He has held visiting positions at the Bangladesh Institute of Development Studies, Dhaka, and the Institute of Research for Development (REPOA), Dar Es Salaam, Tanzania.

He did his Ph.D. in Economics from London School of Economics and Political Science, 1976. He received Commonwealth Scholarship for Ph.D. degree during 1973–76. Dr. Islam specializes in development economics with a particular focus on employment, poverty and income distribution, and has published a number of books and articles in peer-reviewed journals and edited volumes. His most recent book titled Employment and Inclusive Development (written jointly with Iyanatul Islam) was published by Routledge, London, in 2015. Other recent publications include (i) two books in Bengali—one on Development Economics and another on Employment and Labour Market Issues in a Development Perspective (published by the University Press Limited, Dhaka), (ii) Development, Equity and Poverty: Essays in Honour of Azizur Rahman Khan, edited jointly with Lopamudra Banerjee and Anirban Dasgupta, Macmillan Publishers India Ltd., 2010, (iii) an edited book titled Fighting Poverty: The Development-Employment Link, Lynn Rienner, Boulder and London, 2006, and (iv) an edited volume (edited jointly with Gordon Betcherman of the World Bank) titled East Asian Labour Markets and the Economic Crisis: Impacts, Responses and Lessons, 2001.

The areas of Dr. Islam's current research include (i) The challenge of jobless growth, employment intensity of economic growth and poverty reduction, (ii) Economic growth and structural transformation for absorbing surplus labour, and (iii) The challenge of full employment in the context of Sustainable Development Goals.

His current work includes writing a book titled Full and Productive Employment in Developing Economies: Towards Sustainable Development Goals to be published by Routledge, London, in 2019.

Regional Disparities in Economic and Social Development

Nomita P. Kumar

Abstract This article analyses the pattern and trends in inter-district disparities in the levels of development particularly in levels of income, and physical and social infrastructure by using multivariate analysis. It finds wide regional disparities across districts in the availability of social and economic infrastructure which have persisted and prolonged over time. Amongst the four broader economic regions, the districts of western region continued to occupy top ranks in economic infrastructure as compared to other three regions, viz. central, eastern and Bundelkhand. Bundelkhand region presents the grim scenario with almost six out of seven districts falling in the category of backward districts in India. The central and eastern regions have almost mediocre status. Such a pattern provides a strong justification for the recent policy initiatives of the state government for improving the economic infrastructure especially banking services, industrialization and agricultural infrastructure to facilitate production and sale of outputs and social infrastructure for building human capital. However, budgetary support for such initiatives and weak implementation are major concerns for any meaningful results, particularly in backward districts. The article advocates more rigorous efforts towards developing economic and social infrastructure, particularly in laggard districts of the state. This would also help in accelerating the pace of economic growth and employment opportunities, and reducing regional disparities in development in Uttar Pradesh.

Keywords Regional disparities · Infrastructure development

1 Introduction

The corridors of academia resound with the rhetoric that development is bound to be 'in-egalitarian' because it does not occur simultaneously in every part of the economy. Many studies have tried to investigate the path of development with thrust on

---

N. P. Kumar (✉)
Giri Institute of Development Studies, Lucknow, India
e-mail: nomita.kumar36@gmail.com

© Springer Nature Singapore Pte Ltd. 2019
R. P. Mamgain (ed.), *Growth, Disparities and Inclusive Development in India*,
India Studies in Business and Economics,
https://doi.org/10.1007/978-981-13-6443-3_5

its regional pattern. Mostly states have been used as the unit of region and studied for cross-sectional disparity in development over a period of time. A large body of literature contains issues on inter-regional disparity in India but there is very little literature on intra-regional disparities. The main reason for it could be availability of macro-data at the provincial level or, as put by Chakraborthy (2009) that sub-provincial level, as a unit of analysis for examining intra-regional disparities. The issue that needs attention is the studies that ignore the causal factors responsible for inter-district or intra-regional variations in per capita state domestic product (Raychaudhary and Haldar 2009). Unfortunately, very few studies are available which unfold district-level movement of inequality indices and the possible reasons for that in terms of two very powerful factors, namely economic and social infrastructure. The goals are intended to advance sustainable development through greater integration of its three pillars: economic, social and environmental (Kapoor 2013). This paper tries to guide and contribute to transformative change in the pattern of movement of income inequality amongst the districts of Uttar Pradesh as well as changes registered in terms of rankings with regard to economic and social infrastructure.

Infrastructure is presumed to be the base upon which economic growth is built. It covers supporting services helping in the growth of directly productive activities like agriculture/industry and thus, economic development. These services may include economic and social infrastructural provisions like health, education, supply of power, irrigation, transport and communications amongst others. In fact, infrastructure has a two-way relationship with economic growth. First, infrastructure promotes economic growth; second, economic growth brings about changes in infrastructure. According to renowned economist Dr. V.K.R.V. Rao, *'the link between infrastructure and development is not a once for all affair. It is a continuous process and progress in development has to be preceded, accompanied, and followed by progress in infrastructure, if we are to fulfill our declared objectives of a self-accelerating process of economic development* (Rao 1980, pp. 10–11).

The forward linkage, between infrastructure and economic growth, derives from the fact that output of infrastructure sectors such as power, water, transport and so on are used as inputs for production in the directly productive sectors, viz. agriculture and manufacturing. Therefore, insufficient availability of the former results in sub-optimal utilisation of assets in the latter. Association between infrastructure and GDP growth as observed in many studies indicates that one per cent growth in the infrastructure stock is associated with one per cent growth in per capita GDP (Rao 1980; Bery et al. 2004). Further, the backward linkage between economic growth and infrastructure derives from growth, in turn making demands on infrastructure. With the increase in income levels, the composition of infrastructure also changes. Due to such linkages between infrastructure and the rest of the economy, efficiency, competitiveness, and growth of an economy significantly depends upon the development of infrastructure.

> Studies have indicated that with a 20% sustained increase in public investment in infrastructure the government can accelerate real growth by 1.8% points in the medium to long term, that is six to ten years. This is further estimated to accompany a 0.2% decline in the rate of inflation with the increase in resulting income leading to a 0.7% point annual reduction

in poverty in rural India. This shows the potential for achieving the much-debated 8–9% aggregate real GDP growth in the Indian economy (Mondal 2000, pp.).

In the development literature, infrastructure or social overhead capital, as it is often referred to, is recognized as a necessary pre-condition for economic development. Regional disparities in economic development can be explained in terms of varying levels of infrastructural services available to people in different regions (Thakur and Chauhan 2010, pp. 329). It is observed that public investment in various socio-economic activities not only determines the rate of overall development in the economy but also distributes the gains of development by making variations of infrastructural facilities available in different regions/districts of the state. It is these variations in the levels of socio-economic infrastructural facilities that lie at the root of overall imbalance and regional disparities in the development of the state's economy.

Given this brief background, the paper aims to (a) measure the extent of inter-district disparities in income, physical and social infrastructure, and (b) examine the relationship between infrastructure and economic developments in Uttar Pradesh with a view to strengthen the policies for promoting regional development. The paper is based on secondary sources of data collated by the economic and statistics division of government of Uttar Pradesh. By using multivariate analysis, the analysis has been carried out separately for economic and social infrastructure at two points of time, i.e. 2000–01 and 2011–12 to measure inter-district inequality. The years have been chosen to observe the decennial variations, which is a reasonable time frame for policy to get translated into actual plans and observe its consequent impact on different indicators of development.

As infrastructural variable consists of a large number of variables pertaining to social and economic infrastructure, we have reduced the variable to an aggregate index for better understanding. Principal component analyses (PCA) technique with some innovation to calculate weights as done by Raychoudhary and Haldar (2009) has been followed to derive the composite index of development.

2 Inter-district Disparities in Infrastructure

We may first look at the inter-district disparities in the availability of economic and social infrastructure in Uttar Pradesh in Table 1. Extreme disparities continue to prevail with respect to different economic and social variables in the state. The coefficient of variation (CV) for selected 13 indicators of economic infrastructure varied substantively in both years, i.e. 2001 and 2011. The value of CV is observed to decline in seven out of thirteen selected indicators of economic infrastructure in the state between 2001 and 2011. However, in case of some economic facilities, such as post and telegraph offices, and number of banks, intra-state disparities have actually increased during the period under study. Thus, we may say that the development

Table 1 Inter-district disparities in the availability of social infrastructure

Variable	Indicators of infrastructure	Value of coefficient of variation		Per cent change 2011–12 over 2000–01
	Social infrastructure indicators	CV 2001	CV 2011	
SOC1	No. medical institutions per hundred thousand population	29.50	26.98	−8.55
SOC2	No. medical bed per hundred thousand population	72.33	25.96	−64.10
SOC3	No. of MCH per hundred thousand of population	25.21	22.14	−12.19
SOC4	Number of institutions (JBS) per hundred thousand population	30.68	23.23	−24.27
SOC5	Number of institutions (SBS) per hundred thousand population	37.10	25.90	−30.18
SOC6	Number of institutions (HSS) per hundred thousand population	38.19	41.90	9.73
SOC7	Pupil teacher ratio (JBS)	19.54	31.48	61.10
SOC8	Pupil teacher ratio (SBS)	26.44	36.21	36.96
SOC9	Pupil teacher ratio (HSS)	23.33	27.31	17.06
SOC10	Enrolment ratio JBS	27.11	19.23	−29.02
SOC11	Enrolment ratio SBS	40.74	23.61	−42.04
SOC12	Literacy per cent	16.22	10.78	−33.55
Economic infrastructure indicators				
ECO1	Percentage of irrigated area to gross area sown	25.88	25.77	−0.40
ECO2	Availability of gross area sown per tractor	120.95	99.74	−17.53
ECO3	Road length per 1000 km^2	63.42	52.75	−16.83
ECO4	Post and telegraph offices per hundred thousand population	31.78	88.42	178.24
ECO5	Number of banks per hundred thousand population	20.85	39.08	87.42
ECO6	Percentage of villages electrified	20.49	26.94	31.48
ECO7	Number of registered factories per hundred thousand population	289.77	255.98	−11.66

(continued)

Table 1 (continued)

Variable	Indicators of infrastructure	Value of coefficient of variation		Per cent change 2011–12 over 2000–01
	Social infrastructure indicators	CV 2001	CV 2011	
ECO8	Number of primary agricultural societies per hundred thousand population	36.76	19.75	−46.27
ECO9	No. of agricultural marketing centres per hundred thousand hect. net area sown	62.84	58.13	−7.49
ECO10	Agricultural loans per rural person in Rs. {at current prices}	42.07	49.46	17.58
ECO11	Gross value of agricultural produce per hect. of net area sown in Rs. {at current prices}	41.06	41.39	0.80
ECO12	No. of cooperative agricultural marketing centres per hundred thousand of population	70.82	54.65	−22.84
ECO13	Percentage of electricity consumption in agriculture sector to total consumption	42.02	60.77	44.61

Source Author's calculation; based on data drawn from District-wise Development Indicators, Directorate of Economic and Statistics, Govt. of Uttar Pradesh for different years

efforts of the past decade have been far less than desired to address inter-regional disparities in the availability of economic infrastructure.

In case of most of social infrastructure, indicators the value of CV falls between 20 and 40% in 2001 and above ten per cent in 2011–12. The value of CV declined in eight out of twelve indicators of selected social infrastructure, indicating reasonably satisfactory progress in the reduction of regional disparities in the state. In brief, the issue of inter-district inequality in the availability of economic and social infrastructure seems to be at the root of inter-district inequality in the state. This has been further examined in the following sections.

There appears a strong association between variables across two components of infrastructure (Annexures Tables 9 and 10). A strong correlation between irrigated area, tractor usage, roads, gross agricultural produce, etc., shows their complementarity in nature. For instance, the increase in agriculture produces in irrigated areas led to the growth of marketing centres. Similarly, agricultural loans are related to agriculture produce. Also, a strong correlation is observed between the availability of banks and registered factories, cooperative societies and electricity consumption in agriculture.

Similarly, in case of social infrastructure variables a strong correlation is found between medical beds and availability of medical institutions, mother and child health (MCH) centres. Literacy levels, educational institutions and enrolment levels are found to be positively related.

3 Composite Indices of Infrastructure Development

For avoiding high correlation while selecting variables for constructing the composite index of development, the reductionist method such as principal component analysis (PCA) is generally used. Infrastructural inequality derived from the PCA analysis for economic and social infrastructure is analysed in this section. Before elaborating on the issue, it is pertinent to highlight the social and economic infrastructural variables and weights assigned to them for estimating disparity in Uttar Pradesh (Table 2).

Table 2 Weights of the economic infrastructure indicators in Uttar Pradesh

Indicators	Code	2000–01	2011–12
Percentage of irrigated area to gross area sown	ECO1	3.678	2.818
Availability of gross area (in Hac) sown per tractor	ECO2	2.097	2.376
Road length per 1000 km^2	ECO3	3.321	2.886
Post and telegraph offices per hundred thousand population	ECO4	2.274	2.927
Number of banks per hundred thousand population	ECO5	2.887	3.263
Percentage villages electrified	ECO6	3.590	2.735
Number of registered factories per hundred thousand population	ECO7	2.117	2.696
Number of primary agricultural societies per hundred thousand population	ECO8	2.313	1.235
No. of agricultural marketing centres per hundred thousand hect. net area sown	ECO9	2.868	2.978
Gross value of agricultural produce per rural person in Rs. {at current prices}	ECO10	3.327	1.722
Gross value of agricultural produce per hect. of net area sown in Rs. {at current prices}	ECO11	3.960	2.818
No. of cooperative agricultural marketing centres per hundred thousand population	ECO12	2.468	2.697
Percentage of electricity consumption in agriculture sector to total consumption	ECO13	2.644	2.818

Source Author's calculation; based on data drawn from District-wise Development Indicators, Directorate of Economic and Statistics, Govt. of Uttar Pradesh for different years

Table 3 Weights of the social infrastructure indicators in Uttar Pradesh

Indicator	Code	2000–01	2011–12
No. of medical institutions per hundred thousand population	SOC1	1.592	3.620
No. medical beds per hundred thousand population	SOC2	3.233	3.590
No. of MCH per hundred thousand of population	SOC3	3.168	3.217
Number of institutions (JBS) per hundred thousand population	SOC4	2.246	3.597
Number of institutions (SBS) per hundred thousand population	SOC5	2.746	3.982
Number of institutions (HSS) per hundred thousand population	SOC6	3.367	2.083
Pupil teacher ratio (JBS)	SOC7	1.293	1.797
Pupil teacher ratio (SBS)	SOC8	2.712	2.629
Pupil teacher ratio (HSS)	SOC9	2.072	2.365
Enrolment ratio JBS	SOC10	3.319	2.582
Enrolment ratio SBS	SOC11	1.620	2.518
Literacy rate (per cent)	SOC12	3.072	2.526

Source Author's calculation

In case of economic variables, focus on the component score matrix for the first factor reveals that five variables, viz. irrigated area, gross agricultural produce per hectare, gross agricultural produce per rural population, agricultural markets, villages electrified, and cooperative societies were the dominant economic factors which loaded heavily on economic growth for both years, i.e. 2000–01 and 2011–12.

In case of social infrastructure variables, the factors that loaded heavily were availability of medical institutions, educational institutions, teachers and enrolment ratio, and the literacy rate. In case of 2011–12, the first factor shows strong association with health services and weights of literacy, while availability of educational institutions showed improved situation at junior basic school (JBS) and senior basic school (SBS) levels. Enrolment in JBS and SBS has improved over the decades, as shown in reduced weights (Table 3).

In case of social infrastructural variables MI (medical institution), MB (medical bed), MCH (mother and child health centre), JBS and SBS have played a significant role over the years in causing disparity amongst the districts of Uttar Pradesh (Table 3). On the other hand considering the weights assigned for economic infrastructure index, we find that road length per sq. km, number of bank per hundred thousand of population, number of registered factories per hundred thousand of population and percentage of net irrigated area to net sown area play a crucial role in deciding disparity amongst the districts in Uttar Pradesh. Thus, for growth to trickle down policy formulators need to pay attention to policies which determine devolutions of investment keeping these factors in mind.

Table 4 Number of principal components with variance explained in each infrastructure sub-groups

Dimensions of infrastructure	Name of the indicators	Number of principal components	Percentage of variance explained
Social infrastructure (health and education)	SOC1, SOC2, SOC3, SOC4, SOC5, SOC6, SOC7, SOC8, SOC9, SOC10, SOC11, SOC12, SOC13	2000–01 = 4	64.90
		2011–12 = 4	72.25
Economic infrastructure (including financial)	ECO1, ECO2, ECO3, ECO4, ECO5, ECO6, ECO7, ECO8, ECO9, ECO10, ECO11, ECO12, ECO13	2000–01 = 4	68.84
		2011–12 = 5	72.76

Source Author's calculation

The above exercise might create an impression that other variables like medical beds in case of social variables, and irrigation and banks in the case of economic variables are not important for district-level economic well-being (Raychoudhary and Haldar 2009). This is not the truth as the above data reflects upon variables which are most important in causing inter-district disparity and not the ones which primarily determine growth in the districts. We are concerned here with the issue of disparity; thus, medical beds or minor irrigation projects are not the variables which are available in significantly different quantities across districts. They may be important determinants for the growth of district income but are not that significant in causing income disparity amongst the districts. The explanatory power of the principal components through the PCA taken to calculate the economic and social infrastructure indices for the two selected years is given in Table 4.

The districts were ranked according to the level of economic and social infrastructural indicators for the two points of time under consideration. Table 5 gives the ranks along with the infrastructure index thus calculated. Economic development is a highly dynamic phenomenon that is observed to vary year after year and is highly dependent on infrastructure. Though the composite indices and their ranking speak eloquently about relative position of the districts on the developmental scale, it does not indicate that particular stage of economic development in a particular district. Therefore, an attempt is made to divide the districts of Uttar Pradesh into four groups, using the principal component method and rank different districts from 1 to 70. Rank 1 is for highest factor scores and rank 70 for the lowest. Then different districts can be classified into four development categories according to their rank in composite index of development in the following manner:

Table 5 Region-wise ranks of districts for economic and social infrastructure in Uttar Pradesh

Western region	Economic infrastructure				Social infrastructure			
	2000–01		2011–12		2000–01		2011–12	
Developed	Meerut	1	Etawah	1	Etawah	1	Etawah	1
	Bulandshahr	2	Hathras	4	Agra	8	Mainpuri	5
	G.B. Nagar	3	Meerut	5	Mathura	10	Auraiya	7
	Ghaziabad	4	Saharanpur	6	Farrukhabad	11	Kannauj	14
	Rampur	5	Farrukhabad	7	Etah	14	Baghpat	15
	Muzaffarnagar	7	Baghpat	9			Etah	17
	Pilibhit	8	Auraiya	11				
	Budaun	9	Budaun	12				
	Baghpat	11	Bulandshahr	14				
	Mainpuri	12	Pilibhit	15				
	Aligarh	13						
	Mathura	14						
	Saharanpur	15						
	Jyotiba Phule Nagar (Amroha)	16						
Moderately developed	Farrukhabad	18	Shahjahanpur	18	Saharanpur	18	Firozabad	24
	Kannauj	20	G.B. Nagar	20	Mainpuri	21	G.B. Nagar	25
	Etah	21	Ghaziabad	23	Pilibhit	23	Hathras	26
	Hathras	22	Mainpuri	26	Bulandshahr	25	Mathura	27
	Bijnor	24	Muzaffarnagar	28	Auraiya	28	Ghaziabad	28
	Moradabad	25	Rampur	29	Shahjahanpur	29	Farrukhabad	29
	Shahjahanpur	26	Aligarh	34	Aligarh	31	Meerut	34
	Auraiya	29			Meerut	33		
	Firozabad	33						
	Agra	34						

(continued)

Table 5 (continued)

Western region	Economic infrastructure				Social infrastructure			
	2000–01		2011–12		2000–01		2011–12	
Less developed	Bareilly	37	Firozabad	36	Firozabad	36	Bulandshahr	35
	Etawah	45	Jyotiba Phule Nagar (Amroha)	37	Hathras	38	Agra	37
			Bijnor	38	Bijnor	39	Saharanpur	38
			Bareilly	40	Kannauj	45	Bijnor	42
			Moradabad	41	Rampur	46	Aligarh	45
			Kannauj	42	Moradabad	48	Muzaffarnagar	46
			Mathura	43	Bareilly	51	Jyotiba Phule Nagar (Amroha)	51
			Etah	47				
Least developed district			Agra	53	Muzaffarnagar	54	Pilibhit	56
					Budaun	55	Shahjahanpur	60
					G.B.Nagar	57	Moradabad	64
					Baghpat	58	Bareilly	65
					Ghaziabad	63	Rampur	66
					Jyotiba Phule Nagar (Amroha)	64	Badaun	68

Central region	Economic infrastructure				Social infrastructure			
	2000–01		2011–12		2000–01		2011–12	
Developed	Lucknow	6	Lucknow	2	Kanpur Dehat	2	Lucknow	3
	Kanpur Dehat	10	Barabanki	10	Fatehpur	13	Kanpur Dehat	4
			Kheri	17	Kanpur Nagar	16	Kanpur Nagar	9
Moderately developed	Rae Bareli	27	Sitapur	19	Hardoi	19	Fatehpur	40
			Kanpur Dehat	21	Rae Bareli	24	Hardoi	47
			Rae Bareli	24	Lucknow	32	Unnao	48
Less developed	Barabanki	39	Fatehpur	35	Sitapur	41		
	Kheri	42	Hardoi	51	Barabanki	43		
	Fatehpur	44			Unnao	47		

(continued)

Table 5 (continued)

Central region	Economic infrastructure		Social infrastructure	
	2000–01	2011–12	2000–01	2011–12
	Kanpur Nagar 46			
	Unnao 51			
Least developed district	Hardoi 52	Kanpur Nagar 55		Rae Bareli 52
	Sitapur 60	Unnao 57		Barabanki 58
			Kheri 49	Sitapur 61
				Kheri 62

Eastern region	Economic infrastructure		Social infrastructure	
	2000–01	2011–12	2000–01	2011–12
Developed	Ballia 17	Deoria 3	Faizabad 3	Ghazipur 10
		Kaushambi 8	Varanasi 7	Sultanpur 11
		Jaunpur 13	Ballia 12	Pratapgarh 12
		Faizabad 16	Pratapgarh 15	Jaunpur 13
			Basti 17	Deoria 16
Moderately developed	Mau 19	Azamgarh 22	Ghazipur 20	Ballia 19
	Azamgarh 28	Pratapgarh 25	Jaunpur 26	Mau 20
	Jaunpur 30	Ballia 27	Sonbhadra 27	Varanasi 21
	Ghazipur 31	Sultanpur 30	Sultanpur 30	Allahabad 22
	Mahrajganj 32	Ghazipur 31	Mau 34	Azamgarh 23
		Gorakhpur 32		Basti 30
		Mau 33		Faizabad 31
				Mirzapur 32
Less developed	Ambedkar Nagar 35	Mahrajganj 39	Allahabad 35	Gorakhpur 39
	Faizabad 36	Chandauli 44	Deoria 37	Chandauli 41
	Pratapgarh 38	Basti 45	Azamgarh 42	Ambedkar Nagar 43

(continued)

Table 5 (continued)

Eastern region	Economic infrastructure				Social infrastructure			
	2000–01		2011–12		2000–01		2011–12	
	Deoria	40	Sant Kabir Nagar	48	Gorakhpur	44	Sonbhadra	49
	Sultanpur	41			Mirzapur	50	Sant Ravidas Nagar (Bhadoi)	50
	Varanasi	43						
	Basti	47						
	Chandauli	48						
	Kaushambi	49						
	Gorakhpur	50						
Least developed district	Bahraich	53	Gonda	54	Kaushambi	52	Sant Kabir Nagar	53
	Allahabad	55	Allahabad	56	Chandauli	53	Mahrajganj	54
	Sant Kabir Nagar	56	Ambedkar Nagar	58	Mahrajganj	59	Kaushambi	55
	Kushinagar	57	Kushinagar	59	Siddharth Nagar	60	Siddharth Nagar	57
	Gonda	58	Varanasi	60	Gonda	61	Kushinagar	59
	Sant Ravidas Nagar	59	Balrampur	62	Bahraich	62	Gonda	63
	Mirzapur	62	Siddharth Nagar	64	Balrampur	65	Bahraich	67
	Siddharth Nagar	64	Mirzapur	65	Shrawasti	66	Balrampur	69
	Balrampur	66	Bahraich	67	Sant Kabir Nagar	67	Shrawasti	70
	Shrawasti	69	Sant Ravidas Nagar	68	Sant Ravidas Nagar	68		
	Sonbhadra	70	Shrawasti	69	Kushinagar	69		
			Sonbhadra	70	Ambedkar Nagar	70		

(continued)

Table 5 (continued)

Bundelkhand region	Economic infrastructure				Social infrastructure			
	2000–01		2011–12		2000–01		2011–12	
Developed	Jalaun	23			Lalitpur	4	Jalaun	2
					Jhansi	5	Jhansi	6
					Hamirpur	6	Hamirpur	8
					Jalaun	9	Banda	18
Moderately developed					Banda	22	Lalitpur	33
Less developed			Jalaun	46	Chitrakoot	40	Mahoba	36
			Jhansi	49			Chitrakoot	44
			Chitrakoot	50				
			Hamirpur	52				
Least developed district	Hamirpur	54	Banda	61	Mahoba	56		
	Banda	61	Lalitpur	63				
	Jhansi	63	Mahoba	66				
	Lalitpur	65						
	Mahoba	67						
	Chitrakoot	68						

Source Author's calculation

Table 6 Correlation matrix between the ranks in composite indices of economic and social infrastructure

	ecorank2001	ecorank2012	socrank2001	socrank2012
ecorank2001	1			
ecorank2012	0.665**	1		
socrank12001	0.517**	0.413**	1	
socrank12012	−0.380**	−0.384**	−0.203*	1

Source Authors calculation
**Correlation is significant at the 0.01 level (one-tailed); *Correlation is significant at the 0.05 level (one-tailed)

Developed districts: Rank 1–17
Moderately developed districts: Rank 18–34
Less Developed districts: Rank 35–51 and
Least Developed districts: Rank 52–70.

The correlation matrix in Table 6 shows that the ranking pattern of districts in composite index of economic and social infrastructure has remained broadly the same as depicted by significant value of correlation coefficient for the two points of time. There is also a strong correlation between the ranks of districts in economic and social infrastructure. Following are important observations emanating for our analysis:

- The quanta of disparity in economic infrastructure in the state found in both the extreme ends are 0.139 for Sonbhadra district, and 0.597 for Meerut during the year 2000–01. However in 2011–12, it is found to be −0.048 for Sonbhadra and 0.544 for Etawah. In case of social infrastructure, we have Etawah on the highest rung of the ladder with 0.495 index value in 2000–01 and 0.895 in 2011–12 and Ambedkar Nagar and Shrawasti were on the lower rung of the ladder in both the years as depicted in Table 11. It is also observed from the data based on the value of index that the ranks of the districts vary at these two points of time indicating more variation in the indices during 2000–01 compared to 2011–12 (as indicated by the value of CV). Further, the ranks of almost all the districts are found changing in the year 2011–12 as compared to 2000–01.
- Since Uttar Pradesh comprises 70 districts and it is difficult to describe the status on one to one basis, the data has been classified on the basis of regions to make it more understandable. Broadly speaking, we find that mostly districts of western region fall in the category of developed districts, followed by few in the category of moderately and less developed and only one district, i.e. Agra, is designated as backward district in economic infrastructure for the year 2011–12. None of the districts could be seen in the least developed category in economic infrastructure in 2000–01 in the western region. The situation for social infrastructure, however, is in contrast to economic infrastructure. Many districts fall in the category of moderately, less developed and many still as backward districts.

- Table 11 evaluating development based on the indicators of economic infrastructure shows developed districts in descending order in 2000–01 as: Meerut, Bulandshahar, Gautam Buddha Nagar, Ghaziabad, Rampur, Muzzafarnagar, Pilibhit, Badaun Baghpat, Mainpuri, Aligarh, Mathura, Saharanpur and Jyotiba Phule Nagar (Amroha). The story is all the more similar for 2011–12, except that Etawaha has taken the lead depending on the focus conferred by then ruling Samajwadi Party government. Hathras, Farrukhabad and Auraiya shifted to developed category in 2011–12.
- On the other hand, twelve most backward districts in terms of economic infrastructure are: Bahraich, Allahabad, Sant Kabir Nagar, Kushinagar, Gonda, Sant Ravidas Nagar (Bhadoi), Mirzapur, Siddhartha Nagar, Balrampur, Shrawasthi and Sonbhadra in 2000–01. Gonda, Allahabad, Ambedkar Nagar, Kushinagar, Varanasi, Balrampur, Siddhartha Nagar, Mirzapur, Bahraich, Sant Ravidas Nagar, Shrawasthi and Sonbhadra were the districts which are indexed as least developed districts of eastern region in 2011–12. Mostly, districts of eastern and Bundelkhand fall in the least developed category. What is interesting to note is that the districts of Bundelkhand region do not fall into developed and moderately developed category for economic infrastructure, whereas social infrastructure is being delivered to this region, perhaps after the focus of planning on the backwardness of the region only after 2009–10. The state government has made huge investments in backward regions so as to reduce regional disparities but the achievements are disproportionately low. In the Eleventh Plan period, the state government adopted 'inclusive growth' agenda and gave special emphasis to the schemes meant for reducing regional disparities and backwardness especially through the mechanism of decentralized planning. Similar tones could be deciphered in the Twelfth Plan regime also.

4 Inter-district Income Inequality

In this section, we shall look at the district income and population profile of Uttar Pradesh. District income is taken as net district domestic product (NDDP). At present, the state comprises 75 districts. Due to division of districts, comparison of data regarding population and per capita income is a real problem and to meet this issue we have clubbed the new districts to their parent districts and have limited ourselves to 70 districts in the study. The population data is interpolated to seek comparison using decadal growth rates thus derived.

As far as income is concerned (economic development) inter-district inequality did decline in Uttar Pradesh but the basic cause of decline is mooted in the growth of central region as it is the only region where Gini index showed a decline during the period. Rest of the regions, i.e. western, eastern and Bundelkhand all experienced rising inter-district inequality in terms of Gini index as shown in Table 7.

All the districts have shown a decline in inequalities over the decade, and this decline could be attributed to central region's decline whether we calculate Gini

Table 7 Region-wise Gini index and CV for per capita income

Region	Gini index		Coefficient of variation	
	2000–01	2011–12	2000–01	2011–12
Western	0.1748	0.1788	39.72	45.40
Central	0.1718	0.1654	28.89	24.06
Eastern	0.1224	0.1269	33.02	37.86
Bundelkhand	0.1207	0.1218	23.68	27.02
UP	0.2058	0.2034	46.32	43.63

Source Authors calculation

indices or coefficient of variation—both measures bring out the same results. The rise in coefficient of variation measures clearly exhibits more volatility in income distribution amongst the districts—some of the richer districts seem to have acquired wealth and became wealthier while the poor have increasingly fallen behind to be more precise. This asymmetric distribution of inter-district inequality in Uttar Pradesh speaks volumes about slack planning process.

Next, we have examined the reasons behind such inequalities in terms of economic and social infrastructure. As is well known, economic infrastructure helps in overcoming the obstacle of development by utilising existing resources while social infrastructure helps in human capital formation. Together, economic and social infrastructure optimizes the level of economic development. We have managed to understand the movement of ranking of the districts in terms of economic and social infrastructure indices and also correlated them with the rankings of the districts in terms of district per capita income (indicator of economic development). Inequality indices of social and economic infrastructure indices have also been computed, and their ranks are compared with the ranks of district incomes for our understanding.

5 Impact of Infrastructure on Income

As expected, economic and social infrastructure had a strong positive effect on income levels in Uttar Pradesh. The value of R^2 is fair enough to understand the association as depicted in the two separate Figs. 1 and 2.

To examine the relationship between combined infrastructure and economic development, we fitted multiple regression analysis of the form

$$Y = a + b_1 X_1 + b_2 X_2 + b_3 X_3 + b_4 X_4 + b_5 X_5 + b_6 X_6 + U$$

where Y represents per capita income and X represents the variables of infrastructure (economic and social infrastructure). The specification of the model presented some problem as many of the infrastructure indicators depicted high multi-collinearity as

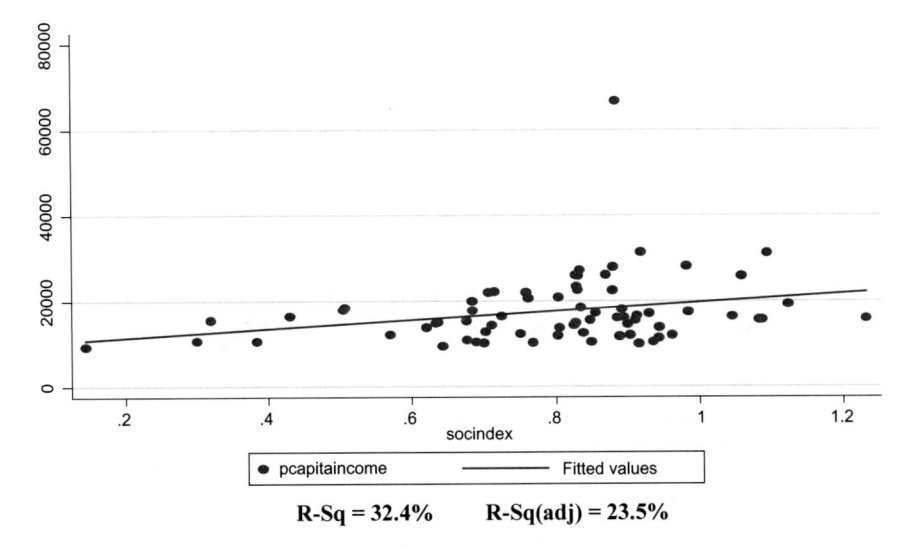

Fig. 1 Impact of social infrastructure on economic development (income)

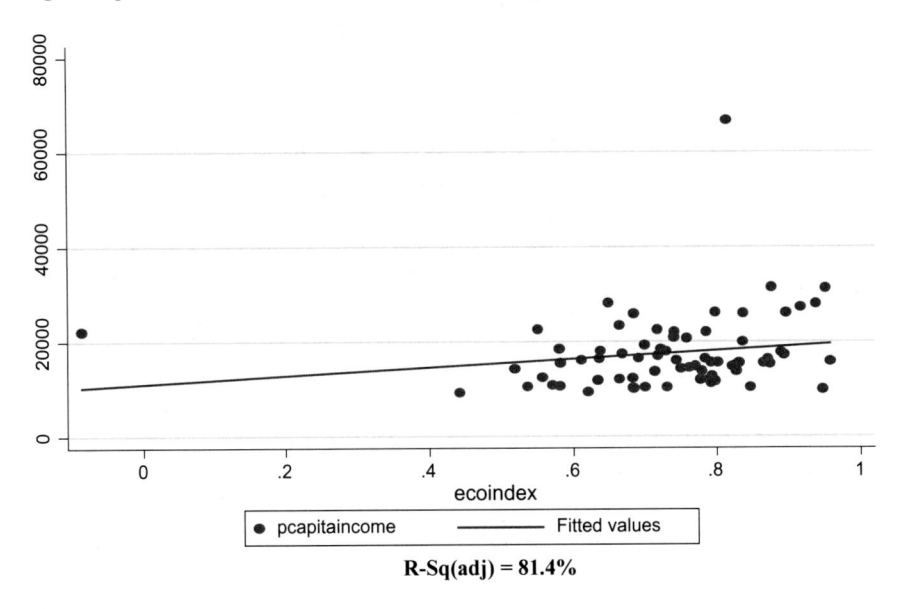

Fig. 2 Impact of economic infrastructure on income levels

shown in the aforementioned tables. We applied stepwise regression, and it turned out to select variables accordingly. Six models were tabulated with additional variables in each model.

The explanatory power of the regression is very high (R^2 89.5%), and the signs of coefficients are in the expected direction. Economic development in terms of levels of per capita income is understood to be stimulated by the number of bank branches followed by industrialization (number of registered factories) and also agricultural produce. In all the six models derived, these economic indicators have been taken one by one along with variables of social indicators in terms of availability of medical facility (bed) and MCH centres that are governing the social infrastructure of the state.

Table 8 Stepwise regression estimates of determinants of per capita income in Uttar Pradesh—2011–12

Model summary coefficients[a]							
Model		Unstandardized coefficients		Standardized coefficients	t	Sig.	R^2
		B	Std. error	Beta			
1	(Constant)	−318.522	1400.935		−0.227	0.821	0.733
	eco5 (banks)	3180.221	232.584	0.856	13.673	0.000	
2	(Constant)	5265.394	1659.490		3.173	0.002	0.804
	eco5 (banks)	1944.375	321.776	0.524	6.043	0.000	
	eco7	261.184	53.127	0.426	4.916	0.000	
3	(Constant)	2405.136	1481.483		1.623	0.109	0.865
	eco5 (banks)	1685.997	272.928	0.454	6.177	0.000	
	eco7 (registered factories)	294.175	44.790	0.480	6.568	0.000	
	eco10 (agricultural produce)	0.369	0.067	0.251	5.477	0.000	
4	(Constant)	4336.133	1701.782		2.548	0.013	0.874
	eco5 (banks)	1954.570	293.952	0.526	6.649	0.000	
	eco7 (registered factories)	245.401	49.218	0.400	4.986	0.000	
	eco10 (agricultural produce)	0.390	0.066	0.265	5.874	0.000	
	soc2 (medical bed)	−79.713	37.249	−0.109	−2.140	0.036	

(continued)

Table 8 (continued)

Model summary coefficients[a]							
Model		Unstandardized coefficients		Standardized coefficients	t	Sig.	R^2
		B	Std. error	Beta			
5	(Constant)	764.244	2136.967		0.358	0.722	0.886
	eco5 (banks)	2137.220	290.550	0.575	7.356	0.000	
	eco7 (registered factories)	241.070	47.222	0.393	5.105	0.000	
	eco10 (agricultural produce	0.352	0.065	0.240	5.400	0.000	
	soc2 (medical bed)	−124.409	39.670	−0.170	−3.136	0.003	
	soc3 (MCH centres)	460.025	177.716	0.133	2.589	0.012	
6	(Constant)	−144.280	2104.567		−0.069	0.946	0.895
	eco5 (banks)	1984.658	288.746	0.534	6.873	0.000	
	eco7 (registered factories)	256.222	46.157	0.418	5.551	0.000	
	eco10 (agricultural produce)	0.359	0.063	0.244	5.681	0.000	
	soc2 (medical bed)	−135.174	38.664	−0.185	−3.496	0.001	
	soc3 (MCH centres)	471.168	172.020	0.136	2.739	0.008	
	soc6 (HSS)	203.196	87.753	0.100	2.316	0.024	

[a]Dependent variable: p capita

The coefficients are less significant in case of agricultural produce and negative in terms of medical beds availability (Table 8).

6 Conclusion

This paper finds wide regional disparities in the availability of social and economic infrastructure across districts in Uttar Pradesh, which have persisted and prolonged over time along with some changes in the ranks of the districts. The western region enjoys comparatively better status in the field of economic infrastructure than other three regions, viz. central, eastern and Bundelkhand. Bundelkhand region presents a grim scenario with almost six out of seven districts falling in the backward category. Central and eastern regions are almost in mediocre status.

Having gained insight into the level of economic development at the district level, and keeping in mind the interventions mentioned in Twelfth Five-Year Plan to achieve the envisaged growth rate, we propose the following:

- A majority of the less developed districts suffering from overall backwardness are generally found to be at the low level of economic infrastructure, whereas those placed in category of high level of overall development are found to be posted with the high level of economic infrastructure. Based on the closer association between the two, the role of economic infrastructure in development appears to be the most crucial and its inadequacy in less developed districts seems to be one of the factors primarily responsible for low levels of both agricultural and industrial development. Therefore, development of economic infrastructure in less developed districts is deemed to be imperatively a pre-condition for accelerated balanced development (Tiwari 1983). Regionally differentiated strategies should be followed keeping the tact of economic infrastructure so as to achieve the full growth potential of every region of the state.
- Agriculture being the backbone of the state, it has to be delicately handled with timely supply of inputs such as seed, planting material, fertilizer, machinery, credit and insurance. Marking the lagging regions in terms of different indicators efforts should be made to reduce the cost of cultivation through enhancing input use efficiency and popularizing indigenous, cost-effective and location-specific technologies. For planned development of agriculture sector, development of marketing infrastructure should be emphasized along with setting up of processing units in the producing areas to avoid wastage, especially of perishable produce and create off-farm employment opportunities in rural areas (Govt. of Uttar Pradesh 2013).
- The subject of inequality appears in the present 2030 Agenda for Sustainable Development Goals (SDG), both directly and indirectly (Strategy of Annual Plan 2014–15, Department of Planning, Uttar Pradesh). When examined across four different angles of inequality—access, gender, opportunity and outcomes—many goals and targets of SDGs are clearly linked to inequality. These goals are intended to advance sustainable development through greater integration of its three pillars: economic, social and environment, and we here are covering economic and social aspects to chalk policies accordingly. Social services are positively associated with the level of overall development. The lopsided development of social infrastructure suggests that probably the norms prescribed under different programmes for providing education and health services in different districts were not strictly

adhered to in actual practice. An effective development of the social infrastructure would require a more vigorous and coordinated action to determine realistic physical targets and make rational distribution of financial resources amongst the less developed districts for achieving the set objective. Development of social infrastructure in terms of educational institutions, teacher pupil ratio and enrolment stability has to be maintained for proper development of the state. Medical institutions and delivery of medical services in terms of mother and child health centres need proper monitoring to enhance the proper development of the state through good health, educated masses and skilled manpower leading to increased employment and finally a developed state.
- Our analysis provides a strong justification for the recent policy initiative of the UP state government for improving economic infrastructure especially banking services, industrialization and agricultural produce to facilitate production and sale of output, and social infrastructure for building human capital. For this plan, funds have to be envisaged. There is a particular need in this context to pay heed to laggard districts and regions in terms of economic and social infrastructure with a view to removing regional imbalances for the development of the state as a whole.

Annexure

See Annexure Tables 9, 10, 11, 12 and 13.

Table 9 Correlation matrix for indicators of economic infrastructure: 2011–12

	Irrigated area	GSA tractor	Road length	Post office	Banks	Villages electrified	Registered factories	Primary agricultural societies	Agricultural marketing centres	Agricultural loans per rural population Produce	Gross agricultural produce	Cooperative societies	Electricity in agriculture
Irrigated area	1	−0.317**	0.492**	0.119	0.218	−0.039	0.175	0.109	0.128	0.097	0.545**	−0.065	−0.135
GSA tractor		1	−0.216	−0.154	−0.103	−0.079	−0.116	0.053	−0.083	−0.155	−0.324**	−0.027	0.184
Road length			1	0.074	0.212	−0.038	0.240*	−0.013	0.044	−0.173	0.255*	−0.245*	−0.234
Post office				1	−0.009	0.164	−0.137	0.008	−0.123	−0.19	−0.064	−0.125	0.126
Banks					1	−0.12	0.781**	0.138	−0.157	0.11	0.195	−0.365**	−0.340**
Villages electrified						1	−0.364**	−0.005	−0.21	0.273*	0.08	−0.093	−0.103
Registered factories							1	0.063	−0.001	0.402**	0.114	−0.199	−0.281*
Primary agricultural societies								1	0.184	−0.145	−0.12	0.072	−0.233

(continued)

Table 9 (continued)

	Irrigated area	GSA tractor	Road length	Post office	Banks	Villages electrified	Registered factories	Primary agricultural societies	Agricultural marketing centres	Agricultural loans per rural population Produce	Gross agricultural produce	Cooperative societies	Electricity in agriculture
Agricultural marketing centres									1	−0.306*	−0.042	0.807**	−0.314**
Agricultural loans per rural population										1	0.676**	−0.064	0.084
Gross agricultural produce											1	−0.149	0.004
Cooperative societies												1	−0.118
Electricity in Agriculture													1

**Correlation is significant at the 0.01 level (two-tailed); *Correlation is significant at the 0.05 level (two-tailed)
Source Author's Calculation

Table 10 Correlation matrix for indicators of social infrastructure: 2011–12

	Med Inst	Medical bed	MCH	JBS school	SBS school	HSS school	PT ratio JBS	PT ratio SBS	PT ratio HSS	Enrol JBS	Enrol SBS	Literacy
Med Inst	1	0.493**	0.718**	0.609**	0.583**	0.052	−0.106	−0.073	0.096	0.131	0.418**	0.002
Medical bed		1	0.445**	0.286*	0.361**	0.219	0.069	0.026	−0.196	0.382	0.225	0.094
MCH			1	0.441**	0.544**	−0.002	−0.025	−0.091	−0.032	0.240	0.432**	−0.004
JBS school				1	0.790**	0.122	−0.094	−0.098	0.113	0.369**	0.508**	−0.087
SBS school					1	0.280*	−0.198	−0.388*	−0.032	0.344	0.588**	0.050
HSS school						1	−0.166	−0.265*	−0.143	0.184	0.191	0.552**
PT ratio JBS							1	0.723**	−0.133	0.249	−0.130	−0.285*
PT ratio SBS								1	0.022	0.139	−0.258	−0.350*
PT ratio HSS									1	−0.070	0.250	−0.205
Enrol JBS										1	0.532**	0.064
Enrol SBS											1	0.187
Literacy												1

**Correlation is significant at the 0.01 level (two-tailed); *Correlation is significant at the 0.05 level (two-tailed)
Source Author's Calculation

Table 11 Factor scores for economic and social infrastructure

	District	Social infrastructure				Economic infrastructure			
		Final index	Rank	Final index	Rank	Final index	Rank	Final index	Rank
		2000–01	2000–01	2011–12	2011–12	2000–01	2000–01	2011–12	2011–12
1	Saharanpur	0.391	18	0.601	38	0.493	15	0.508	6
2	Muzaffarnagar	0.283	54	0.551	46	0.530	7	0.445	28
3	Bijnor	0.344	39	0.584	42	0.453	24	0.420	38
4	Moradabad	0.310	48	0.369	64	0.451	25	0.410	41
5	Rampur	0.328	46	0.313	66	0.555	5	0.445	29
6	Jyotiba Phule Nagar	0.226	64	0.514	51	0.490	16	0.421	37
7	Meerut	0.359	33	0.605	34	0.597	1	0.520	5
8	Baghpat	0.270	58	0.667	15	0.513	11	0.497	9
9	Ghaziabad	0.234	63	0.632	28	0.569	4	0.453	23
10	G.B.Nagar	0.270	57	0.642	25	0.583	3	0.463	20
11	Bulandshahr	0.371	25	0.603	35	0.589	2	0.475	14
12	Aligarh	0.362	31	0.553	45	0.503	13	0.430	34
13	Hathras	0.345	38	0.639	26	0.457	22	0.532	4
14	Mathura	0.421	10	0.639	27	0.495	14	0.407	43
15	Agra	0.430	8	0.602	37	0.425	34	0.377	53
16	Firozabad	0.345	36	0.644	24	0.431	33	0.422	36
17	Etah	0.399	14	0.664	17	0.458	21	0.392	47
18	Mainpuri	0.385	21	0.787	5	0.504	12	0.449	26
19	Budaun	0.278	55	0.233	68	0.521	9	0.491	12
20	Bareilly	0.301	51	0.367	65	0.414	37	0.414	40
21	Pilibhit	0.379	23	0.497	56	0.529	8	0.474	15
22	Shahjahanpur	0.363	29	0.462	60	0.448	26	0.469	18
23	Farrukhabad	0.414	11	0.621	29	0.470	18	0.507	7
24	Kannauj	0.329	45	0.676	14	0.458	20	0.407	42
25	Etawah	0.495	1	0.895	1	0.401	45	0.544	1
26	Auraiya	0.365	28	0.760	7	0.442	29	0.495	11
27	Kheri	0.308	49	0.451	62	0.406	42	0.469	17
28	Sitapur	0.337	41	0.461	61	0.303	60	0.466	19
29	Hardoi	0.391	19	0.546	47	0.330	52	0.387	51
30	Unnao	0.313	47	0.526	48	0.351	51	0.361	57
31	Lucknow	0.361	32	0.795	3	0.530	6	0.540	2
32	Rae Bareli	0.371	24	0.511	52	0.444	27	0.451	24

(continued)

Table 11 (continued)

	District	Social infrastructure				Economic infrastructure			
		Final index	Rank	Final index	Rank	Final index	Rank	Final index	Rank
		2000–01	2000–01	2011–12	2011–12	2000–01	2000–01	2011–12	2011–12
33	Kanpur Dehat	0.476	2	0.790	4	0.517	10	0.455	21
34	Kanpur Nagar	0.398	16	0.713	9	0.395	46	0.369	55
35	Fatehpur	0.401	13	0.599	40	0.402	44	0.426	35
36	Barabanki	0.334	43	0.491	58	0.411	39	0.496	10
37	Jalaun	0.428	9	0.816	2	0.453	23	0.397	46
38	Jhansi	0.453	5	0.769	6	0.298	63	0.388	49
39	Lalitpur	0.459	4	0.607	33	0.244	65	0.329	63
40	Hamirpur	0.447	6	0.715	8	0.323	54	0.379	52
41	Mahoba	0.274	56	0.603	36	0.211	67	0.313	66
42	Banda	0.383	22	0.662	18	0.302	61	0.330	61
43	Chitrakoot	0.342	40	0.558	44	0.174	68	0.388	50
44	Pratapgarh	0.398	15	0.685	12	0.412	38	0.450	25
45	Kaushambi	0.286	52	0.498	55	0.386	49	0.505	8
46	Allahabad	0.349	35	0.648	22	0.320	55	0.362	56
47	Faizabad	0.463	3	0.616	31	0.418	36	0.472	16
48	Ambedkar Nagar	0.143	70	0.583	43	0.423	35	0.360	58
49	Sultanpur	0.362	30	0.686	11	0.407	41	0.442	30
50	Bahraich	0.243	62	0.280	67	0.323	53	0.304	67
51	Shrawasti	0.215	66	0.105	70	0.150	69	0.251	69
52	Balrampur	0.221	65	0.218	69	0.234	66	0.330	62
53	Gonda	0.248	61	0.415	63	0.308	58	0.377	54
54	Siddharth Nagar	0.259	60	0.492	57	0.248	64	0.324	64
55	Basti	0.394	17	0.617	30	0.394	47	0.397	45
56	Sant Kabir Nagar	0.214	67	0.509	53	0.315	56	0.388	48
57	Mahrajganj	0.266	59	0.501	54	0.433	32	0.415	39
58	Gorakhpur	0.330	44	0.601	39	0.358	50	0.437	32
59	Kushinagar	0.184	69	0.467	59	0.311	57	0.352	59
60	Deoria	0.345	37	0.665	16	0.410	40	0.537	3

(continued)

Table 11 (continued)

	District	Social infrastructure				Economic infrastructure			
		Final index	Rank	Final index	Rank	Final index	Rank	Final index	Rank
		2000–01	2000–01	2011–12	2011–12	2000–01	2000–01	2011–12	2011–12
61	Azamgarh	0.334	42	0.646	23	0.442	28	0.453	22
62	Mau	0.353	34	0.654	20	0.465	19	0.432	33
63	Ballia	0.403	12	0.656	19	0.470	17	0.448	27
64	Jaunpur	0.370	26	0.680	13	0.440	30	0.481	13
65	Ghazipur	0.391	20	0.699	10	0.438	31	0.441	31
66	Chandauli	0.284	53	0.585	41	0.394	48	0.405	44
67	Varanasi	0.440	7	0.650	21	0.403	43	0.347	60
68	Sant Ravidas Nagar	0.210	68	0.517	50	0.306	59	0.294	68
69	Mirzapur	0.307	50	0.608	32	0.300	62	0.316	65
70	Sonbhadra	0.366	27	0.520	49	0.139	70	−0.048	70

Source Author's calculation

Table 12 Inequality indices (Gini index) for infrastructure indices

	Social infrastructure		Economic infrastructure	
	2000–01	2011–12	2000–01	2011–12
Western	0.107	0.193	0.096	0.124
Central	0.089	0.116	0.154	0.079
Eastern	0.123	0.129	0.183	0.166
Bundelkhand	0.067	0.094	0.12	0.177

Source Author's calculation

Table 13 Value of correlation coefficient between factor scores of economic and social infrastructure and per capita income

Rank correlations between Pc income and Soc and Eco index				
	Ecofac2000–01	Ecofac2011–12	Socfac2000–01	Socfac2011–12
Pc income2001	0.421**	0.149	0.444**	−0.099

**Correlation is significant at the 0.01 level (one-tailed)
Source Author's calculation

References

Bery, S., Gupta, D. B., Krishna, R., & Mitra, S. (2004). *The nature of rural infrastructure: Problems and prospects*. NCAER, Working Paper No. 94, National Council of Applied Economic Research, New Delhi.

Chakraborthy, A. (2009). Some normative relevant aspects of inter-state and intra-state disparities. *Economic and Political Weekly, 46*(26–27), 179–184.

Department of Planning, Uttar Pradesh. (as per Annual Plan 2014–15). *Strategy of Annual Plan 2014–15*. Available on http://upenvis.nic.in/Database/Strategy_836.aspx.

Government of Uttar Pradesh. (2013). *Uttar Pradesh agriculture policy, 2013: Roadmap for progress and prosperity*.

Kapoor, S. (2013). *India and sustainable development goals (SDGs)*. November 12, on http://www.teriin.org/policy-brief/india-and-sustainable-development-goals-sdgs.

Mondal, P. (2000). Relationship between infrastructure and economic growth in www.yourarticlelibrary.com/ visited on August 6, 2016.

Raychaudhary, A., & Haldar, S. K. (2009, June 27). An investigation into the inter-district disparities in West Bengal, 1991–2005. *Economic and Political Weekly, 44*(26–27), 258–263.

Rao, V. K. R. V. (1980). Infrastructure and economic development. *Commerce, Annual Number, 141*, 10–11.

Thakur, A. K., & Chauhan, S. S. S. (2010). *Inter regional disparities in India*. Indian Economic Association, Annual Conference, Deep and Deep Publications, India.

Tiwari, R. T. (1983). *Economic infrastructure and regional development in India*. Working Paper No. 67, Giri Institute of Development Studies, Lucknow.

Nomita P. Kumar holds Post Graduate Degree in Economics from Lucknow University. Having received a Ph.D. Degree in Economics, she has been actively engaged in research for over 30 years. She was awarded ICSSR Doctoral Fellowship at Giri Institute of Development Studies from 1989–1993 for her PhD. For her Post-Doctoral research she was awarded UGC Fellowship during 2003–2006. Her major areas of research are Women Issues and Economic Development, Issues related to Labour Market and Employment, Issues related to Family Planning and Family Welfare Program and Health Policies, Gender and Health Inequality in Women, Labour Economics, Agriculture Economics, Social Sector Development and Small Scale Industries and Development. In the initial phase of her career she joined as a part-time lecturer in Economics Department, University of Lucknow. She was Senior Research Fellow to Second State Finance Commission, Government of Uttar Pradesh. Besides research experience she also earned teaching experience at the graduation and post -graduation level. She has three books to her credit and has published extensively in various refereed journals of national repute. She has also completed large number of research projects sponsored by national and international organisations. She is also the Joint Editor of UPUEA Journal of Economics. She has been a member of Board of Management of State Resource Centre (Educational and Social Research), India Literacy Board, Government of Uttar Pradesh. She is also the member of various academic associations.

Part II
Poverty, Vulnerability and Inclusion

Poverty and Inequality: A Disaggregated Analysis

Amaresh Dubey and Shivakar Tiwari

Abstract This article finds an appreciable rate of reduction in poverty at about 1.6% annually between 2004–05 and 2011–12 in the state of Uttar Pradesh, which has been largely in rural areas and that too among SCs and Others and across economic regions. In contrast, the incidence of poverty increased in urban areas of the state by 1.32% during 2004–05 to 2011–12, showing the urbanisation of rural poverty due to lack of remunerative employment opportunities and social security measures. However, poverty in the state is predominantly rural. In 2011–12, around 48 million out of 60 million poor people in the state were living in its rural area. The article estimates the poverty in the state at more disaggregated level of 17 administrative divisions (ADs) with an objective to suggest effective policy interventions and make a concerted dent on poverty. The incidence of poverty varies significantly across different regions and ADs of the state. The Eastern region has the highest poverty incidence, while Western region has the lowest, the latter being the most developed relatively among the four regions. The ADs with high incidence of poverty are Basti, Chitrakoot, Devipatan and Lucknow in the Eastern and Central economic regions, which are highly deprived and need to be targeted for poverty reduction. Along with the absolute levels of deprivations, there is huge inequality in distribution of income and consumption expenditure particularly in urban areas that severely hampers the pace of poverty reduction. In 2011–12, Gini coefficient of consumption expenditure distribution was 43 and 27%, respectively, for urban and rural areas in the state. It is found that regions and divisions with high urbanisation level and better rural connectivity have lower poverty incidence. Thus, given the large share of rural population, improving agricultural productivity and subsequently developing vibrant and integrated urban centres would be a highly effective strategy to achieve the target of eradicating extreme poverty from the state.

A. Dubey · S. Tiwari (✉)
Centre for the Study of Regional Development, Jawaharlal Nehru University, New Delhi, India
e-mail: shivakar1984@gmail.com

A. Dubey
e-mail: amaresh.dubey@gmail.com

Keywords Growth and redistribution · Poverty · Urbanisation · Administrative divisions · Inequality

1 Introduction

Sustainable Development Goals (SDGs) aim at eradicating poverty by 2030 (UN 2015). The progress of India is highly crucial in achieving the global goals given the size of its poor population. In fact, the Millennium Development Goals (MDGs) which targeted to reduce the number of poor in the world by half by 2015 could be made possible due to appreciable performance of India and China. India on its part cannot imagine at targeting poverty elimination without lifting millions of people living below the poverty level in Uttar Pradesh, its most populous state. The state lags behind other states because of its slow economic growth, low level of human capital and high concentration of poor (World Bank 2016).

As per Census 2011, the population of Uttar Pradesh (UP) is 199 million of which 78% lives in rural area. In 2011–12, as per official poverty line (GoI 2009) the poverty incidence measured by head count ratio (HCR) in the state was 29.4%. In absolute terms, there are 60 million individuals living below poverty line in UP. Among them, around 48 million are in rural area, constituting about 30% of total rural population. The cause of relatively higher poverty incidence has been both low level of economic development and inequity in distribution of resources.

In 2011–12, per capita income of UP was Rs. 18,099, which was 40% of the all India per capita income of Rs. 43,624. Even at this low level of income, the distribution is highly uneven. Among four agro-climatic regions of the state, per capita State Domestic Product (SDP) in Eastern region is just half of the Western region, and there has been a huge gap between rural and urban areas. In 2011–12, monthly per capita consumption expenditure (MPCE) was Rs. 1072 in rural area as against Rs. 1942 in urban area. Between the rural and urban areas separately, there was a huge gap. The Gini coefficient for urban area was 0.43 as against 0.27 for rural area.

The nature and determinants of poverty at the all India level and at sub-national level have been extensively studied (Himanshu 2007; Thorat and Dubey 2012), but there are very few studies that have focused on the development and poverty of Uttar Pradesh at more disaggregated level (Diwakar 2009; Ranjan 2009; Tiwari 2014). Given the large size of the state in terms of geographic area, administrative units and population, there exists huge intra-state disparity. In 2011, administratively the state included 71 districts, 17 administrative divisions (mandals) and 107,753 villages. Even though there has been attempt by Tiwari (2014) to analyse the poverty level at disaggregated agro-climatic regions of various states, yet a vacuum exists on detailed study for effective policy. In order to fill the gap of serious research for a concerted effort on poverty reduction in the state, this paper attempts to comprehensively analyse poverty incidence at the further disaggregated level.

The paper has been organised in six sections. Section 2 discusses the data source and methodology which is followed by Sect. 3 on stylised facts that show extensive intra-state variations in the level of development. Section 4 discusses the trends and change in poverty incidence in the state at further disaggregated level: regions and administrative divisions. Section 5 further discusses the broad pattern of inequality in consumption and income in the state. It is followed by the last section on conclusions and policy implications.

2 Data Source and Methodology

The main data source is quinquennial rounds of consumption expenditure survey (CES) of National Sample Survey Organisation (NSSO), Ministry of Statistics and Program Implementation (MoSPI). For this, CES data of three quinquennial rounds, viz. 50th (1993–94), 61st (2004–05) and 68th (2011–12), have been utilised. At the disaggregated level, NSSO collects and provides information at NSS regions and district level. However, the sample size is much small at district level which restricts the analysis only up to NSS region level. However given the size of the Uttar Pradesh state, some of the NSS regions that comprise many districts, for example, Eastern region, eclipse many facts at further micro-level. Thus, in this study information on NSS region level is utilised and district-level information on consumption expenditure has been aggregated at the administrative division level of the state. In 2011, there were 17 administrative divisions and 71 districts in Uttar Pradesh for which information is aggregated.

Apart from this, one more adjustment is done particularly in data of 50th NSS round. In 2000, the hilly region of Uttar Pradesh was carved out to form the Uttarakhand state. For comparable data, districts of Uttarakhand are excluded while that of Uttar Pradesh lying in Uttarakhand are included in the 50th rounds of CES data. Further, for estimating poverty incidence, benchmark poverty line recommended by task force (GoI 1979) and updated according to Lakdawala Committee (GoI 1997) has been utilised. For 1993–94 and 2004–05, poverty line calculated and published by Planning Commission has been used, and for 2011–12 the poverty line has been calculated as suggested by Lakdawala Committee for rural and urban areas. State-level poverty line has been used to estimate poverty at NSS regions and administrative division level.

3 Growth Performance

When compared to the indicators of economic development, Uttar Pradesh not only lags much behind to relatively developed and industrialised states like Gujarat and Maharashtra but also is behind the all India average (Tiwari 2014). Further, in the state among different economic regions, administrative divisions and districts there exists

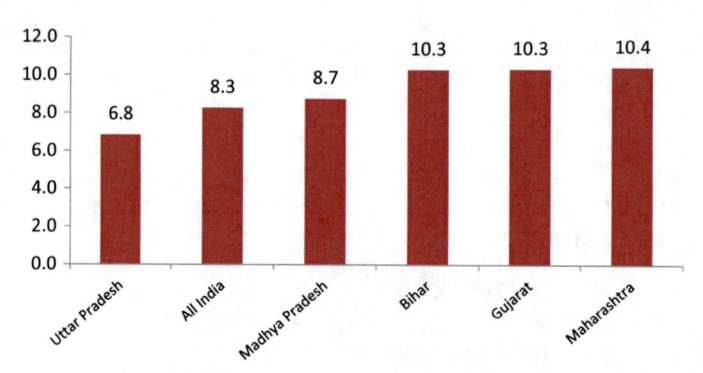

Source: Authors' calculation from CSO, MoSPI Data

Fig. 1 Average annual growth rate of GSDP; 2004–05 to 2011–12

a significant degree of variation. To highlight the inter-divisional and inter-regional variations in Uttar Pradesh in crucial economic indicators like per capita income, share of urbanisation rate, education level, workforce participation rate, etc., have been analysed. Further inequality in welfare has been measured in average monthly per capita expenditure (MPCE) through Gini coefficient.

3.1 Growth and Structure of Income

Higher and sustained economic growth is necessary for improvement in standard of living and poverty reduction (Thorat and Dubey 2012). But over the period, growth performance of Uttar Pradesh has remained relatively low as compared to all India average growth and other states as can be seen from Fig. 1. In the period during 2004–05 and 2011–12, compound annual growth rate (CAGR) of NSDP of the state was around 6.8% per annum, while the all India CAGR was 8.3%. Not only with all India, but the growth performance of UP was also below the achieved growth of similarly less developed states like Madhya Pradesh and Bihar whose growth rate was 8.7 and 10.3%, respectively, and relatively developed states like Gujarat and Maharashtra whose average growth was around 10.3 and 10.7%, respectively. The structure of NSDP in the state shows, as compared to all India, relatively higher share of primary sector and lower share of manufacturing and service sector. However, the trend has been similar as in the last two decades of reform period, and the share of primary sector particularly agriculture has declined drastically (Fig. 2). Subsequently, the share of service sector has increased with unchanged share of secondary sector.

At the disaggregated level, there is considerable degree of variation among district as well as economic regions. There are considerable variations in per capita net district domestic product (NDDP) among different agro-climatic regions, viz. Western, Central, Bundelkhand and Eastern regions which is shown in Fig. 3. The logarithmic

Poverty and Inequality: A Disaggregated Analysis

Source: Authors' calculation from CSO, MoSPI Data

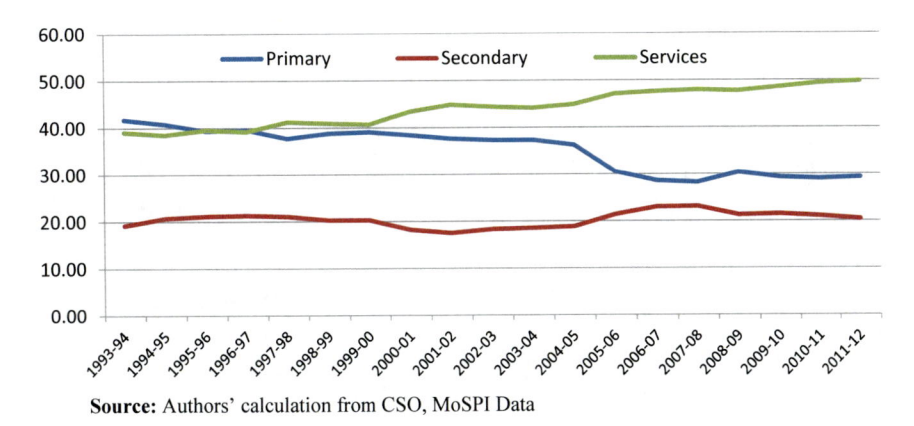

Fig. 2 Change in structure of SDP in two decades

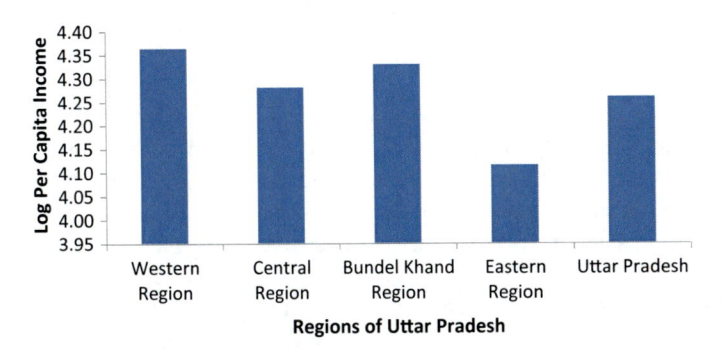

Source: *DES, Uttar Pradesh*

Fig. 3 Inter-regional variation in per capita income, 2011–12

value of per capita income in different regions is plotted in the figure; thus, actual difference is higher than is visible here.[1] It is evident from the figure that among four regions, per capita NDDP was the highest in Western region and lowest in Eastern region. The level of gap is substantial as the ratio of per capita income in Western region was three times to that of Eastern region. The gap in per capita income has severe impact on the state as Eastern region with lowest per capita income has largest share of population. In the total population of the state, as per Census 2011, the share of population in Eastern region was around 41% compared to around 37% in Western region and just 5% in Bundelkhand region which is sparsely populated.

At further disaggregated level, per capita income of different administrative divisions of the state is given in Fig. 4. In 2011–12, out of 17 administrative divisions,

---

[1] Since DES Uttar Pradesh does not provide separately the estimate for different regions, per capita NDDP of regions is calculated by dividing the total domestic product of all the districts in a region with the population size of the region as per Census 2011.

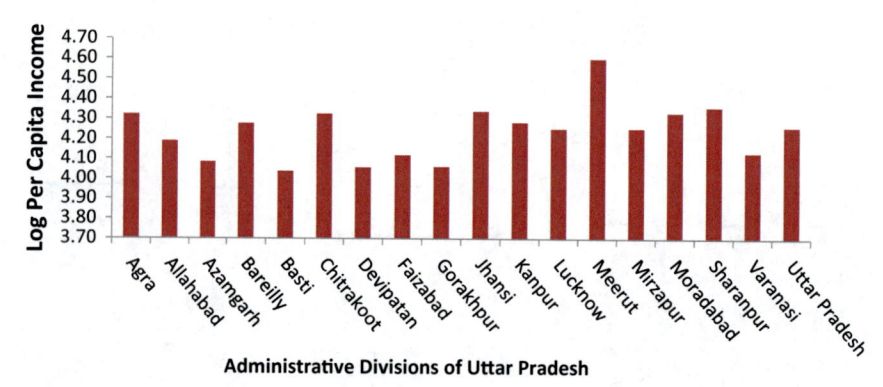

Fig. 4 Inter-divisional variations in per capita income, 2011–12. *Note* Average per capita income of administrative divisions has been calculated by taking simple arithmetic mean of per capita NDDP at 2004–05 prices and total population of particular division

per capita NDDP was highest in Meerut division followed by Saharanpur, both of which are in Western region of the state. It is not surprising that divisions which are at the lowest rank in per capita NDDP were Basti and Devipatan (Gonda) which come in Eastern region of the state. It reflects the clear divide in economic development of the state on two extremes. The level of disparity can be understood as there are nine administrative divisions whose per capita income level is lower than the state average. Administrative division-level analysis shows that variation in per capita income at division level was larger than the inter-regional variations. The per capita income in Basti, Devipatan and Gorakhpur divisions was around 28% that of Meerut division.

3.2 Variation in Urbanisation Level and Literacy Rate

Along with per capita income, the other indicators of development also include urbanisation level, female literacy, gender equality and social justice among others. Better market integration along with human capital contributes to higher level of productivity (Dubey et al. 2001; Macmillian and Rodrik 2011). Similarly, female literacy has larger impact on household welfare and social development.

Viewed from this perspective, Uttar Pradesh lags far behind in pace of urbanisation. As per Census 2011, percentage of population living in urban area was 22.3 as compared to the all India level of 31.2%. Across divisions, there is huge variation in urbanisation level (Fig. 5). Meerut is highly urbanised with its 48.3% of urban population followed by Kanpur and Agra. The lowest rate of urbanisation (6.3%) is in Basti division followed by Devipatan, and Faizabad division. Its merits mention here that all these four divisions, namely Basti, Devipatan, Faizabad and Gorakh-

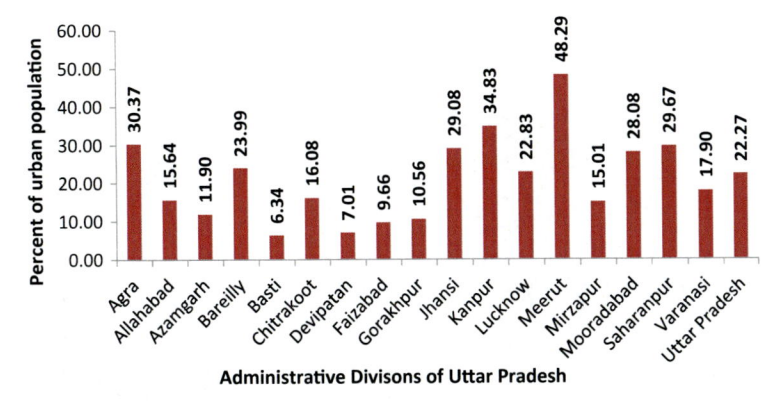

Fig. 5 Urbanisation level in different divisions of Uttar Pradesh, 2011

pur, are at the lowest level of urbanisation and are in the Eastern region which is economically the poorest region of Uttar Pradesh (Table 1).

The state is also lagging behind in educational development. In 2011, the share of literate population in total population above 6 years of age was 67.7% in the state against 74% at the all India level. Similarly, the gender gap in literacy level was higher in the state than the all India level.

At the division level, only Kanpur and Meerut divisions have literacy rate higher than the all India level of 74% and there are seven divisions which are lagging behind state average. Most poorly performing divisions of state in literacy are Devipatan and Bareilly. Thus, the gap in literacy level is substantial. This situation is more worrisome if one looks at female literacy in different divisions of the state. It is only Kanpur division that has female literacy higher than the all India average. In contrast, Devipatan division has lowest female literacy (41%) followed by Bareilly (46%). In fact, the disparity is much higher if one looks among the districts in the division except in the Western region and those divisions whose average literacy rate are higher; it is due to one or two districts.

4 Trends in Poverty Incidence

Uttar Pradesh along with Bihar and Orissa has one of the highest poverty incidences in the country (Table 2). The average HCR of the state varies significantly among agro-climatic regions and administrative division which is analysed in this section. It is further concentrated among certain deprived social groups.

Poverty incidence measured by head count ratio (HCR) has declined consistently along with higher state economic growth and improvement in level of per capita income. The HCR in UP has declined from 57% in 1973/74 to 21% in 2011/12.

Table 1 Gender-wise literacy rate in different divisions of Uttar Pradesh, 2011

State/divisions	All	Female	Male
Agra	70.3	58.9	80.3
Allahabad	69.5	58.1	80.2
Azamgarh	71.4	61.1	81.6
Bareilly	57.2	46.6	66.5
Basti	64.1	52.6	75.4
Chitrakoot	66.6	53.9	77.5
Devipatan	52.3	41.3	62.3
Faizabad	67.7	57.8	77.3
Gorakhpur	67.9	55.6	79.9
Jhansi	71.8	60.1	82.2
Kanpur	76.5	69.1	82.9
Lucknow	66.4	56.9	75.0
Meerut	74.3	64.2	83.3
Mirzapur	67.2	55.2	78.4
Moradabad	60.6	51.4	69.0
Saharanpur	69.7	60.1	78.4
Varanasi	72.7	61.8	83.2
Uttar Pradesh	*67.7*	*57.2*	*77.3*
All India	*74.0*	*65.5*	*82.1*

Source Census 2011

Table 2 States with lowest and highest level of poverty

States	1993–94	2004–05	2011–12
State with lowest poverty			
Punjab	11.3	8.1	1.7
Himachal Pradesh	28.6	9.8	3.8
Andhra Pradesh	21.9	14.8	5.9
Kerala	25.1	14.8	2.8
States with highest poverty			
Uttar Pradesh	40.8	32.7	21.4
Madhya Pradesh	42.5	38.2	31.6
Bihar (JHA)	55.1	42.0	34.2
Orissa	48.6	46.6	40.2
India	35.9	27.5	14.9

Source Planning Commission (1993–94 & 2004–05) and Authors' Calculation (2011–12)

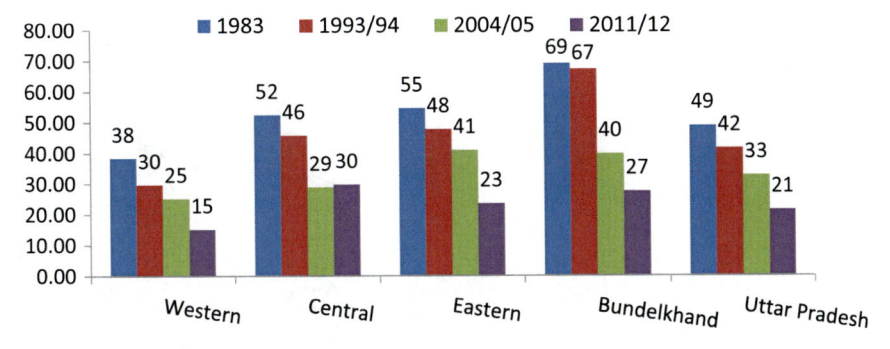

Source: Planning Commission (1993-94 & 2004-05) and Authors' Calculation (2011-12)

Fig. 6 Trends in HCR in Uttar Pradesh in different NSS regions

However, it is evident from Fig. 6 that the state still remains in the category of the states with high poverty incidence (Table 2). Relatively higher HCR in the state is a serious issue of concern as given the high level of population the state has largest size of poor population and this is prevalent across social groups. There is substantial variation in poverty level among different economic regions and divisions as well.

4.1 Economic Regions

Among the four economic regions as is given in Fig. 6, there is a significant variation in HCR. As similar to average state trend, HCR has declined in all the four regions during the period of study. The level of poverty incidence has been highest in Bundelkhand followed by Eastern region and lowest in the Western region.

In 1983, the gap in HCR between Bundelkhand and Western regions was 38%, and after a gap of three decades, in 2011–12, it has reduced to around 12%. Thus, disparity among regions in level of HCR has declined and the poorer regions seem to be catching up with the relatively better ones in terms of absolute deprivation (Fig. 6).

This variation in level of poverty incidence and its rate of decline also varies considerably if we look at rural and urban areas reported in Table 3. Rural poverty has declined consistently over the period, but urban poverty has shown a fluctuating trend. It has been mentioned earlier also that urbanisation in the state has been followed by increase in poverty incidence in the latest period for which data are available.

At the aggregate state level, poverty has declined in both rural and urban areas with the rate of decline being relatively faster in rural area. In the rural area, HCR was 48.1% in 1983. It declined to around 16.5% in 2011–12; but in urban area it was 39.4% in 2011–12 as compared to 52.4% in 1983, thus a decline of 13 percentage

Table 3 Change in HCR (% per annum) in Uttar Pradesh; NSS region and sectors

NSS regions	1993/94 to 2004/05	2004/05 to 2011/12
Rural		
Western	−0.42	−2.29
Central	−1.82	−0.75
Eastern	−0.67	−3.04
Bundelkhand	−2.59	−2.27
All	−0.88	−2.4
Urban		
Western	−0.39	0.88
Central	−0.43	2.67
Eastern	−0.24	1.31
Bundelkhand	−2.16	−0.03
All	−0.5	1.32
Total		
Western	−0.41	−1.42
Central	−1.54	0.12
Eastern	−0.62	−2.5
Bundelkhand	−2.5	−1.76
All	−0.81	−1.61

Source Authors' calculation from unit record data

points during the period. In fact, in comparison with 2004–05, HCR has gone up in urban area of the state. Further similar to the all India trend, rate of decline in HCR has been relatively faster in the reform period particularly in the period between 2004–05 and 2011–12. The rate of decline in this period was 1.6 percentage points per annum as compared to 0.8 percentage point per annum in the period between 1993/94 and 2004/05. Similarly, the rate of decline was 2.4 percentage points per annum in rural area as compared to 0.9 percentage point per annum during the period 1993–94 to 2004–05. However, in the urban area, the poverty incidence has gone up at the rate of 1.3 percentage points per annum.

At the level of NSS economic regions, rural poverty incidence has declined in all the four regions of the state, while urban poverty has gone up except in Bundelkhand. In fact, increase in urban HCR at state level is net result of increase in Central and Eastern regions. Higher increase in urban poverty in these regions may be the result of urbanisation of rural poverty as poor/weakened social security in urban areas. If we look at the share of urban population according to NSS figures, the urban population of Central and Eastern regions has increased by around 12.7 and 17.7% as compared to just 2.5 and 4.6% in Western and Bundelkhand regions of the state.

4.2 Social Groups

Similar to state level, social structure clearly shows disparity in terms of standard of living in society in both rural and urban areas as seen in Table 4. In 1993–94, in rural area, HCR for SCs was highest at around 61% as compared to HCR of 37% for STs and Others groups. After a period of 18 years in 2011–12, the HCR has declined by around 26 percentage points, and across social groups the decline has been higher for SCs followed by Others and STs. However, still the gap in HCR between SCs and Others was around 10 percentage points. 'Others' also includes OBC, or else the poverty incidence among 'Others' would have been much lower. In Uttar Pradesh, as discussed above, urban poverty trend has been highly unsatisfactory as between 1993–94 and 2011–12 the urban poverty has shown an increasing trend. In urban area, the rise in poverty incidence is true across social groups. In fact, poverty in 'Others' category has increased at relatively higher rate than STs and SCs. The variation in decline in poverty incidence across NSS regions and for different social groups has been presented in Table 5.

In the period between 1993–94 and 2004–05, the decline in poverty incidence across regions has been similar in both rural and urban areas. The decline in poverty incidence has been higher in Bundelkhand followed by Central region while relatively slow in Eastern region. Furthermore, there has been variation in poverty reduction across social groups. Between SCs and Others,[2] decline in poverty incidence is similar to both groups except in Central region where SCs have experienced relatively higher poverty reduction. Urban poverty incidence in Bundelkhand has declined at three times higher among SCs as compared to Others, whereas in Eastern region it has gone up slightly. During 2004–05 and 2011–12, as compared to previous period, the rate of decline in the HCR has increased in rural area; however, in urban area poverty incidence has gone up at the rate of around 1.3 percentage point per annum.

Table 4 Poverty incidence across social groups

Year	STs	SCs	Others	Total
Rural				
1993–94	37.84	60.49	37.47	43.00
2004–05	32.18	44.73	29.39	33.32
2011–12	14.91	23.95	13.80	16.51
Urban				
1993–94	25.56	50.67	33.39	35.60
2004–05	37.59	43.46	27.97	30.13
2011–12	35.17	51.36	37.51	39.37

Source Authors' calculation from unit record data

---

[2] Here, we have taken only SCs and Others for comparison as in Uttar Pradesh STs population is very less and sparsely distributed that too mostly in rural area. Also, the level of poverty incidence of STs and Others is similar.

Table 5 Change in HCR (% per annum); region and social groups

State regions	Rural			Urban		
	SC	Others	Total	SC	Others	Total
1993/94–2004/05						
Western	−0.54	−0.42	−0.42	0.32	−0.47	−0.39
Central	−2.65	−1.54	−1.82	−1.60	−0.23	−0.43
Eastern	−1.15	−0.52	−0.67	0.15	−0.40	−0.24
Bundelkhand	−2.69	−2.52	−2.59	−4.17	−1.43	−2.16
Uttar Pradesh	−1.43	−0.73	−0.88	−0.66	−0.49	−0.50
2004/05–2011/12						
Western	−3.26	−2.02	−2.29	0.04	0.91	0.88
Central	−0.44	−0.91	−0.75	2.79	2.96	2.67
Eastern	−3.85	−2.81	−3.04	2.19	1.24	1.31
Bundelkhand	−2.66	−2.46	−2.27	3.44	−1.20	−0.03
Uttar Pradesh	−2.97	−2.23	−2.40	1.13	1.36	1.32

Source Authors' calculation from unit record data

Across the regions in urban area, poverty incidence has increased at a higher rate in Central and Eastern regions while declining slightly in Bundelkhand. Also, across social groups poverty incidence has gone up except for Others in Bundelkhand. In Central and Eastern regions, HCR of both SCs and Others has witnessed increase in HCR significantly.

4.3 Administrative Divisions

In order to further decipher the variation in poverty incidence, it is imperative to analyse the poverty trend at a much disaggregated level. In the second stage of disaggregation, poverty incidence has been analysed at the administrative division level.

Similar to the variation in poverty reduction at NSS economic region level, the level of poverty incidence varies extensively among administrative divisions of the state. In 1993/94 when state HCR was 41.6%, in Chitrakoot, Jhansi and Devipatan divisions it was much higher. Further, in the duration of two decades, in 2011–12, when the state HCR was 21.4% it was significantly lower around six per cent in Meerut and Saharanpur divisions. This was similar to relatively developed states like Punjab. However, in Basti and Chitrakoot administrative divisions the HCR was around 32 and 38%, respectively, which is as high as in the states of Orissa and Bihar as shown in Tables 2 and 6.

Table 6 Level and trends of poverty incidence (HCR) in different divisions

Division	HCR			Change in HCR (%)	
	1993–94	2004–05	2011–12	1993/94 to 2004/05	2004/05 to 2011/12
Agra	28.3	29.1	18.2	0.07	−1.56
Allahabad	46.4	41.8	25.1	−0.42	−2.39
Azamgarh	53.5	37.1	20.9	−1.49	−2.31
Bareilly	26.7	30.2	19.4	0.32	−1.54
Basti	48.0	47.9	32.1	−0.01	−2.26
Chitrakoot	69.6	53.0	38.1	−1.51	−2.13
Devipatan	59.1	39.3	22.1	−1.80	−2.46
Faizabad	55.2	29.6	28.5	−2.33	−0.16
Gorakhpur	46.4	52.2	20.8	0.53	−4.49
Jhansi	64.9	28.0	17.1	−3.35	−1.56
Kanpur	34.6	28.4	18.1	−0.56	−1.47
Lucknow	48.3	31.3	31.9	−1.55	0.09
Meerut	17.3	16.3	5.5	−0.09	−1.54
Mirzapur	50.4	30.4	26.5	−1.82	−0.56
Moradabad	41.4	21.2	18.1	−1.84	−0.44
Saharanpur	36.7	23.5	6.0	−1.20	−2.50
Varanasi	35.8	35.7	22.0	−0.01	−1.96
Uttar Pradesh	41.6	32.7	21.4	−0.81	−1.61

Source Authors' calculation from unit record data

Not only the level but the rate of decline in poverty has also been varying. During 2004–05 and 2011–12 as similar to aggregate trend, poverty has declined at faster rate; however, in Faizabad, Jhansi, Lucknow, Mirzapur and Moradabad divisions the rate of decline in the poverty incidence has slowed down. In fact, Lucknow division has witnessed a slight increase in poverty incidence. Thus, administrative division-level analysis provides further evidence of rise in poverty incidence in Central region as Lucknow division is in Central region while Faizabad and Mirzapur lie in Eastern region.

Below administrative division-level disaggregation is not feasible due to very thin sample size. However, we have attempted to understand variation in district poverty by plotting the poverty incidence at administrative divisions on district-level map of Uttar Pradesh. To see some tentative trends, the exercise has been done at three points of time in post-reform period (Figs. 7, 8 and 9). The figures show poverty incidence in districts in five different categories from very low level of HCR to very high level. A glance of the figures shows concentration of poverty in different regions of the state. In 1993–94 (Fig. 7), the districts lying in Western region have very low-to-low HCR with some districts of Bundelkhand and Central Uttar Pradesh. The districts

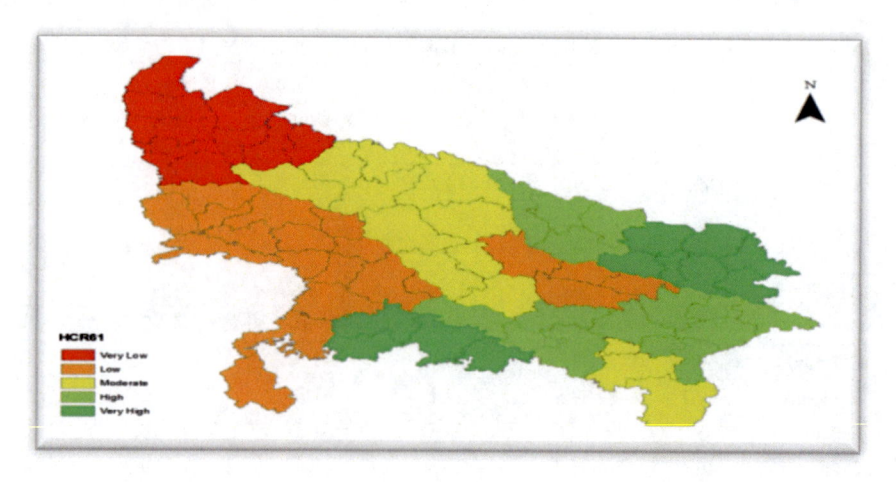

Fig. 7 HCR in different districts of Uttar Pradesh, 1993–94

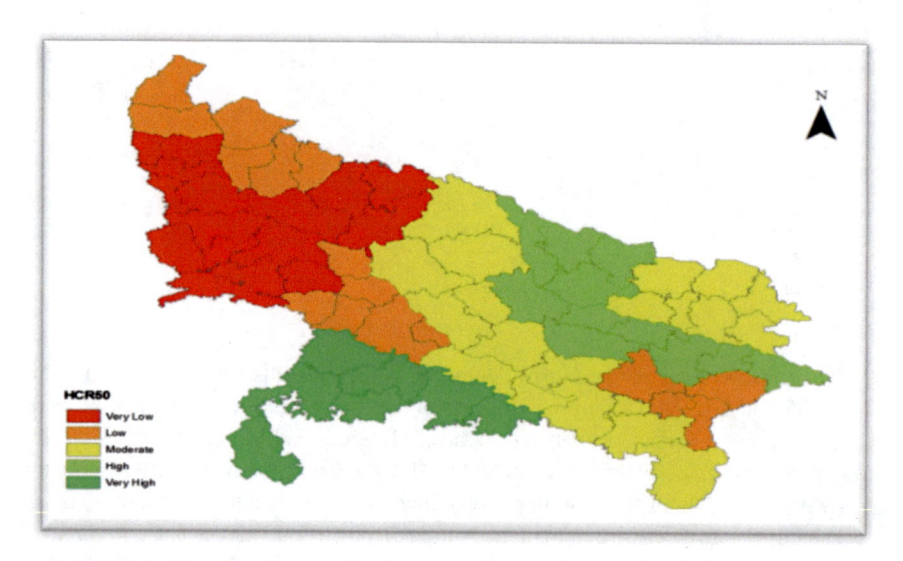

Fig. 8 HCR in different districts of Uttar Pradesh, 2004–05

in Eastern region and some districts of Bundelkhand have very high-to-high poverty incidence. Over the period (2004–05 and 2011–12), there has been a slight change in distribution of district with broad pattern remaining intact.

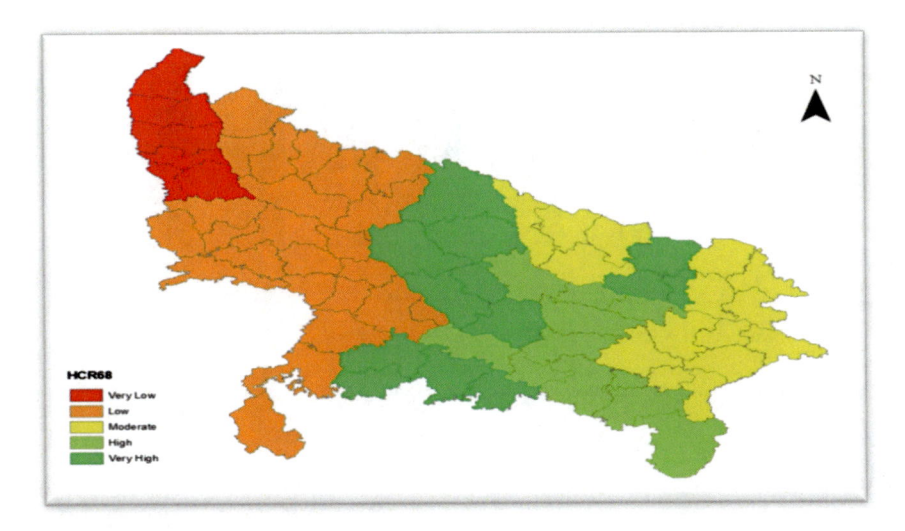

Fig. 9 HCR in different districts of Uttar Pradesh, 2011–12

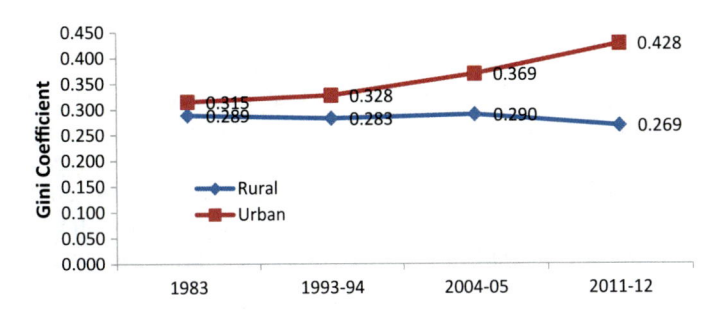

Fig. 10 Trend in consumption inequality (Gini)

5 Trends in Inequality

Given the average per capita income level and its improvement over the period, the impact on absolute poverty depends on distribution of income around the mean over the period. Uttar Pradesh has one of the lowest levels of per capita income in the country with high incidence of poverty. Thus, it is imperative to examine the trend in the distribution with such modest growth during the period of high growth. Inequality in both consumption and income as measured by Gini coefficient is shown in Figs. 10 and 11.

As evident in Fig. 10, the inequality trend across sectors shows completely opposite trend. The long-run trend in rural consumption inequality is declining, while it is increasing in urban area. In the period between 2004–05 and 2011–12, the consumption inequality has increased in urban area by around 16%, while it has declined in

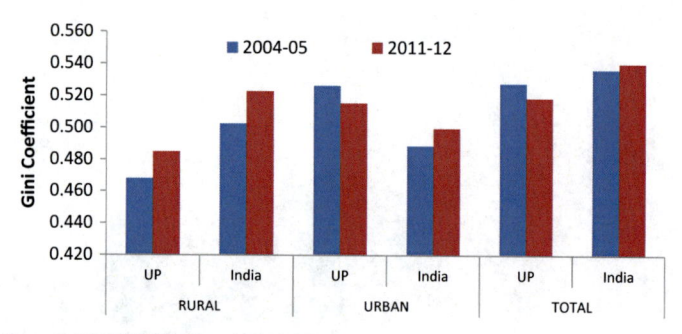

Fig. 11 Change in income inequality; UP and all India

rural area by around 7%. Against this, in 1983 distribution of consumption expenditure in rural and urban areas was almost same, and difference in Gini coefficient was of just three percentage points which has increased to around six percentages points in 2011–12. Given the relatively modest growth in Uttar Pradesh, this high increase in inequality is responsible for rise in HCR in urban area.

Inequality in consumption expenditure of households is somewhat smoother than income inequality. In this regard, income inequality (Gini) is calculated from IHDS data available for two points of time 2004–05 and 2011–12 as shown in Fig. 11 for rural and urban areas. Income inequality in both Uttar Pradesh and all India is higher than the consumption inequality. In 2004–05, the income inequality measured through Gini coefficient was 0.528 and 0.536 in Uttar Pradesh and all India, respectively, which was higher than consumption inequality. In the same period, income inequality in rural area of the state was lower than all India level, but it was higher in urban area by around four percentage points. Between 2004–05 and 2011–12, inequality in rural area has increased by around two percentage points, while in urban area it has declined slightly in Uttar Pradesh. Nonetheless, income inequality in urban Uttar Pradesh is higher than the all India level. During this period as compared to income inequality, consumption inequality has increased substantially in urban area of the state.

5.1 Role of Growth and Redistribution Effect

The decomposition result of change in HCR into growth and inequality effect for rural and urban areas is given in Tables 7 and 8. In rural area, the decline in poverty incidence has been predominantly due to growth effect, while inequality effect has either diluted growth effect or contributed slightly in poverty reduction. In the period between 1993–94 and 2004–05, growth effect has predominantly contributed to poverty reduction in all the regions, while inequality effect has contributed slightly in

Table 7 Decomposition results of the per annum change in HCR (rural)

State/regions	ΔH	Growth effect	Inequality effect
Between 1993–94 and 2004–05			
Western	−0.45	−0.53	0.09
Central	−1.90	−2.03	0.13
Eastern	−0.75	−0.96	0.21
Bundelkhand	−2.68	−2.60	−0.08
Uttar Pradesh	−0.90	−1.04	0.14
Between 2004–05 and 2011–12			
Western	−2.07	−1.53	−0.54
Central	−0.70	0.18	−0.88
Eastern	−2.61	−2.68	0.07
Bundelkhand	−2.24	−0.53	−1.71
Uttar Pradesh	−2.09	−1.66	−0.44

Source Authors' Calculation

Table 8 Decomposition results of the per annum change in HCR (urban)

State/regions	ΔH	Growth effect	Redistribution effect
Between 1993–94 and 2004–05			
Western	−0.36	−0.58	0.22
Central	−0.66	−1.79	1.13
Eastern	−0.06	−0.50	0.44
Bundelkhand	−2.03	−1.43	−0.61
Uttar Pradesh	−0.47	−0.99	0.52
Between 2004–05 and 2011–12			
Western	0.84	−1.41	2.25
Central	2.27	1.59	0.67
Eastern	0.90	−0.97	1.87
Bundelkhand	−0.78	−2.54	1.76
Uttar Pradesh	1.13	−0.6	1.74

Source Authors' Calculation

Bundelkhand region. Further in the period between 2004–05 and 2011–12, the magnitude of growth effect has increased leading to higher poverty reduction in Western and Eastern regions. Inequality effect has also contributed to reduction of poverty in these regions. In Bundelkhand, even though growth effect contribution has declined, yet higher contribution of inequality effect has led to faster reduction in HCR.

In urban area, growth effect has been the dominant factor in poverty reduction. In the periods 1993–94 and 2004–05, growth effect remained dominant and contribution of inequality effect remained adverse except in Bundelkhand. Further in the period

Table 9 Correlation matrix, 2011–12

	hcr	bank off	u.lev.	gini	mwal	mwcl	f.lit.
hcr	1.000						
bank off	−0.236	1.000					
u.lev.	−0.692	0.558	1.000				
gini	−0.154	0.314	0.154	1.000			
mwal	−0.483	0.090	0.517	0.097	1.000		
mwcl	−0.722	0.223	0.685	0.329	0.817	1.000	
f.lit.	−0.329	0.372	0.524	0.485	−0.007	0.231	1.000

Source Authors' Calculation

between 2004–05 and 2011–12, even though growth effect has been effective in reducing poverty in all regions except the Central region, yet higher magnitude of adverse inequality effect has led to either an increase in HCR or slight decline in Bundelkhand.

Nonetheless, decomposition exercise cannot be done at further disaggregated administrative division level. However, the implication of the pattern is similar, higher growth effect is poverty reducing and its effect can be enhanced by inequality-reducing policies.

In order to tackle poverty, the important determinants of poverty that may contribute to higher growth and lower or positive inequality effect are discussed here. There have been insightful studies into the aggregate all India level which have analysed the factors explaining uneven poverty reduction among different states which include land distribution, agricultural productivity, infrastructure facilities, urbanisation, credit market or financial penetration, industrialisation and education level and its quality.

Table 9 depicts a correlation matrix showing the level of association between poverty incidence measured by HCR and different determinants for Uttar Pradesh. Among various factors, the most important is urbanisation level, the correlation coefficient of which is around 0.7 and negative. It shows that divisions which are urbanised have less poor people. For 2004–5, infrastructure measured in terms of 'village connected with *pucca* road' (vcpr) shows correlation coefficient of around 0.7 which is significant. It implies that divisions which are largely rural can make substantial dent on poverty by increasing rural connectivity. Further, vcpr is strongly related to urbanisation level which means increasing connectivity and mobility leads to expansion of urban gradation.

Consumption inequality always has a dragging effect on growth poverty relationship. Here, correlation coefficient of HCR with inequality in MPCE measured by Gini coefficient has been negative although not very strong. As Gini coefficient is associated with all the indicators of development like urbanisation level, literacy rate, financial inclusion and infrastructure like road connectivity, the effect of inequality on poverty reduction can only be understood through decomposition of poverty incidence into growth and inequality effect.

Educational level is measured by the adult female literacy rate although negatively related to HCR, but its magnitude seems to be weak. Weak association of literacy rate can be understood in terms of gainful employment. Lack of employment opportunities for educated population is high, especially for youth. Mostly, those who are poor are either illiterate or having lower educational level along with high-educated unemployed particularly youth. However, given the large rural population that is dependent on agriculture for livelihood, agricultural productivity is strongly related to lower poverty incidence. As can be seen from the correlation matrix in Table 9, male agriculture labourer wage (mwal) and male casual labourer wage (mwcl) are negatively and strongly correlated with HCR. There has been strong positive association between mwal and mwcl with correlation coefficient of 0.8, and its improvement in agricultural productivity can affect wages of both agricultural and non-agricultural labourers.

6 Conclusion and Policy Implications

Uttar Pradesh, as similar to all India, experienced sustained decline in poverty incidence over the period under study. However, still it has relatively high level of poverty incidence that has declined at a slower rate when compared to the all India average and many other states. Not only is its size of poor population very high but there has been a huge degree of intra-state unevenness in the development of the state. It is reflected in the poverty trend analysed at the disaggregated level which includes four NSS economic regions and 17 administrative divisions. The paper has been unique in the sense that it has attempted to analyse for the first time progress in poverty reduction at the administrative division levels in the state against the four NSS regions by Tiwari (2014).

The variations in the levels of poverty and its reduction among four economic regions are further reflected among divisions of the same regions. In the Eastern and Central regions, the variation in poverty levels has been much higher than the Western region. Disaggregation at the administrative division level shows that divisions like Basti, Chitrakoot, Devipatan and Lucknow in the Eastern and Central regions are among the most deprived and economically the most poor in the state. In fact, poverty incidence in these and some other divisions is higher than the state and national average, and compares with less developed states like Bihar and Orissa. The graph plot of HCR at district level shows concentration of poverty in certain pockets which is yet maintained over the last two decades in reform period despite a relatively higher growth.

Decomposition results of change in HCR for different economic regions show dominant role of growth effect as well as adverse impact of inequality effect. Thus, policies promoting growth and smooth distribution of income should be promoted for inclusive development of the state. Some determinants of such policy mix are analysed that include urbanisation level, inequality measured by Gini coefficient, infrastructure, wages of agriculture and casual wage labourers, and literacy rate. Correlation analysis shows that regions and divisions with high urbanisation level and better rural connectivity have lower poverty incidence. Given the large share of rural population, increasing agricultural productivity would be a more effective way to reduce poverty which has been argued long ago by Ahluwalia (1978). The improvement in agricultural productivity through increased marginal product of labour may be the most effective way to reduce poverty. Lack of non-farm employment opportunities as well as poor/weakened social security system seems to be aggravating urban poverty which needs to be looked into greater detail.

References

Ahluwalia, M. S. (1978). Rural poverty and agriculture performance in India. *Journal of Development Studies, 14*(3), 298–323.
Diwakar, D. M. (2009). Intra-regional disparities, inequality and poverty in Uttar Pradesh. *Economic and Political Weekly, 44*(26 & 27), 264–273.
Dubey, A., Gangopadhyay, S., & Wadhwa, W. (2001). Occupational structure and incidence of poverty in Indian towns of different sizes. *Review of Development Economics, 5*(1), 49–59.
GOI. (1979). The report of the task force on projections of minimum needs and effective consumption demand, perspective planning division, planning commission, New Delhi.
GOI. (1997). The report of the expert group on estimation of proportion and number of poor, perspective planning division, planning commission, New Delhi.
GOI. (2009). The report of the expert group to review the methodology for estimation of poverty, perspective planning division, planning commission, New Delhi.
Himanshu. (2007). Recent trends in poverty and inequality: some preliminary results. *Economic and Political Weekly, 42*(5), 497–508.
India Human Development Surveys (IHDS) 2004–05 and 2011–12, National Council of Applied Economic Research, New Delhi and University of Maryland, USA.
Macmillian, M. S., & Rodrik, D. (2011). *Globalisation, structural change and productivity growth*. Working Paper 17143, National bureau of Economic Research.
Ranjan, S. (2009). Growth of rural non-farm employment in Uttar Pradesh: Reflections from recent data. *Economic and Political Weekly, 44*(4), 63–70.
Thorat, S., & Dubey, A. (2012). Has growth been socially inclusive in the period between 1993-94-2009-10? *Economic and Political Weekly, 47*(10), 43–53.
Tiwari, S. (2014). Assessment of growth, poverty, and inequality in Uttar Pradesh: A long term analysis. *Journal of Economic and Social Development, 10*(1), 31–44.
United Nations. (2015). Transforming the world: The 2030 agenda for sustainable development, Retrieved on July 25th, 2017 from https://sustainabledevelopment.un.org/content/documents/21252030%20Agenda%20for%20Sustainable%20Development%20web.pdf.
World Bank. (2016). Uttar Pradesh: poverty, growth and inequality, Retrieved on July 26th, 2017 from http://documents.worldbank.org/curated/en/187721467995647501/pdf/105884-BRI-P157572-ADD-SERIES-India-state-briefs-PUBLIC-UttarPradesh-Proverty.pdf.

Amaresh Dubey is Professor of Economics at the Centre for the Study of Regional Development, Jawaharlal Nehru University (JNU) since 2008. Before moving to JNU he taught Economics at North-Eastern Hill University (NEHU) Shillong (1987–2005) and worked at the National Council of Applied Economic Research (NCAER), New Delhi (2005–2007). His publications include five coauthored and co-edited books, over seventy five articles and papers in international and national refereed journals and edited volumes, thirty-four research project reports and commissioned policy papers for the Government of India, World Bank, DFID, UNDP, Asian Development Bank, etc. and about a dozen opinion pieces in the national newspapers. Besides these, he is Editor of the Indian Economic Journal since 2016. His ongoing collaborative research include projects with University of Maryland (College Park) and NCAER (New Delhi), Manchester University, University of East Anglia and University of Tokyo.

Dr. Shivakar Tiwari is Ph.D. in Economics from Centre for the Study of Regional Development Jawaharlal Nehru University, New Delhi. His research interests are related to poverty and inequality in India and its states. Apart from this he has also worked on issues of labour market particularly youth employment and education in India. He has worked with reputed institution like Giri Institute of Development Studies, Lucknow and Indian Institute of Dalit Studies, New Delhi. He has published in national and international journals.

Inclusion and Marginalization: Economic and Food Security Dimensions

M. H. Suryanarayana

Abstract This article seeks to examine the extent of inclusion and marginalization of different social groups in the rural and urban sectors of Uttar Pradesh (UP) (by different NSS regions) and all-India (by rural/urban sectors) using a rigorous conceptual framework. Using this framework, the article quantifies the extent of inclusion, mainstreaming and marginalization of different social groups in a plural society. Further, it examines the extent of inclusion and marginalization across social groups with respect to both food consumption and total consumer expenditure. Based on these two relative profiles, it defines rules for identification of vulnerable groups calling for targeted food policy intervention. It finds evidence of marginalization of the third degree suggesting that marginalization is essentially a question pertaining to distribution and not disparities across social groups. Examining the inclusive and marginalization profiles of different social groups in terms of food and total consumer expenditure, it shows that the Scheduled Castes and the OBCs deserve special attention to promote food security. In the Northern Upper Ganga Plains, both the SCs and the OBCs call for targeted intervention in the rural sector but only the OBCs in the urban sector. Another novel feature of the article consists in its verification of food insecurity status in terms of incidence of outlier food consumption, that is, proportion of poorest outliers. Such empirical profiles for UP show the Eastern region of rural Uttar Pradesh to be the most deprived followed by Northern Upper Ganga Plains, Central, Sothern Upper Ganga Plains and the Southern region. As regards Urban UP, the incidence of outlier food insecurity is the highest in the Northern Upper Ganga Plains, followed by Eastern and Southern NSS regions; the incidence is nil in the Central and Southern Upper Ganga Plains. As regards the profiles across social groups, the findings show the poorest rural food consumption in the Easter region of Uttar Pradesh among the OBCs; the richest among the poorest food consuming sample households also happens to be among the OBCs from the Southern region. As regards urban UP, the poorest food consuming sample household is from the Eastern region among the OBCs; the richest of the poorest food consuming households is also from the OBCs in Southern UP. This is in contrast with the general perception

M. H. Suryanarayana (✉)
Indira Gandhi Institute of Development Research, Goregaon East, Mumbai 400065, India
e-mail: surya.igidr@gmail.com

© Springer Nature Singapore Pte Ltd. 2019
R. P. Mamgain (ed.), *Growth, Disparities and Inclusive Development in India*,
India Studies in Business and Economics,
https://doi.org/10.1007/978-981-13-6443-3_7

about the relative economic and food security status of different social groups in Uttar Pradesh.

Keywords Economic security · Food security · Marginlaisation · Inter-group disparity · Inclusion

1 Introduction

The state of Uttar Pradesh has begun implementing the Food Security Act, which is going to benefit more than 152.1 million people in the state. The Act would be implemented in three phases. In the first phase, the scheme will be implemented in 24 districts; the second phase would cover 26 districts and the final phase would cover 25 more districts. Since January 2016, the Act is already being implemented in 28 districts, namely Etawah, Mainpuri, Amroha, Agra, Auraiyya, Baghpat, Basti, Bijnor, Bulandshahr, Farrukhabad, Firozabad, Noida, Ghaziabad, Jalaun, Hapur, Jhansi, Kannauj, Kanpur city, Kanpur rural, Lucknow, Mathura, Lalitpur, Meerut, Sant kabir nagar, Siddharth Nagar, Mahoba, Amirpur and Chitrakoot. It is not really clear how the districts have been identified and listed under different categories for the implementation of the Act. Similar questions apply to the concept underlying the Food Security Act itself (Suryanarayana 2013).

Given the contextual emphasis of this book on inclusive development involving inclusion and mainstreaming, this paper examines the following questions:

(i) *What is the extent of inclusion and marginalization of different social groups in Uttar Pradesh?*
(ii) *What is the profile of consumer expenditure and food consumption distribution by social group across regions in rural and urban UP?*
(iii) *What is the relative food consumption status of the poorest by social groups across regions in rural and urban UP?*

An empirical verification of these questions would presuppose a well-defined concept and measure of these two oft-repeated terms in development policy literature and their measures. However, despite its wide common usage, there is no well-defined concept of inclusion. There is a school of thought which says that everyone knows what is meant by 'inclusion,' thus there is no need for such a concept and its measurement.[1] However, going by the Indian Twelfth Five-Year Plan document (Government of India (GoI) 2013a),[2] 'inclusion' means 'desirable outcome'.

---

[1] Of course, this school misses out on the fundamental task, and hence, prerequisite of a policy-maker, namely, assess the magnitude of the problem with reference to its estimate.

[2] The *Twelfth Five-Year Plan (2012–2017)* defines inclusive growth from multiple perspectives in terms of 'poverty reduction, group equality, regional balance, inequality reduction, empowerment and employment generation'. It lists inclusive achievements of the Eleventh Five-Year Plan in terms of conventional development outcome evaluation indicators such as gross domestic product (GDP)

As regards marginalization too, its meaning is taken for granted in many policy discussions and documents.[3] Marginalization refers to a process which involves exclusive benefits, rights and resources to the mainstream population and their denial to certain select social groups/subgroups. Such exclusion restricts the integration of the latter into the former involving in the limit two distinct distributions of the variable of public policy interest. While the underlying notion is simple and clear, how do we measure and quantify the extent of marginalization? This is a moot question which is not addressed in the literature.

This paper uses the concepts of inclusion (Suryanarayana 2008) and marginalization proposed in (Suryanarayana 2015) and illustrates them for four select years between 1993/94 and 2011/12 with reference to the rural and urban sectors of Uttar Pradesh and five regions of the state. It examines the issue of inclusion and marginalization from the perspective of access to income and its benefits as reflected in estimates of consumption. The paper is organized as follows: Sect. 2 explains the concepts of inclusion and marginalization. Section 3 presents empirical illustrations based on comparable Indian National Sample Survey data on household consumption distribution for the post-reform period. The final section concludes the paper.

2 Inclusion/Exclusion and Mainstreaming/Marginalization

This study extends the concept of 'inclusion' defined and measured for a single-group/multi-group society in Suryanarayana (2008). Since marginalization essentially refers to a process in a multi-group context, it is important to distinguish between inclusion/exclusion and mainstreaming/marginalization with reference to single homogenous social group/region and stratified social/regional contexts.

2.1 Inclusion/Exclusion: Single Social/Regional Context

Following conventional approaches, let us measure and evaluate economic performance of a country/region in terms of an outcome measure of economic activity, that is, income generated or a welfare measure like consumption, which is very positively correlated with the former.[4] Income/consumption is generally skewed in distribution across households/persons. Hence, we cannot follow convention and measure the mainstream with reference to a measure of location like mean or per

---

growth, poverty reduction, growth of real consumption, unemployment, real wages, immunization rate and school enrolment rates (GoI 2013a).

[3] See for instance GoI (2013b, p. 169).

[4] Of course, one has to be aware of the limitations of such an analysis due to saving and dissaving at either end of the distribution. However, in a poor economy, such limitations are unlikely to affect the discussion of issues related to the bottom sections.

capita income/consumption. We may opt for order-based averages like the median which provide robust estimates of changes in the location of the distribution. Mainstream may be defined with reference to an interval specified by a fraction, say, from 60% of the median up to its 140%. Since median is an order-based average and is the 50th percentile of the variable under review, the focus may be on the bottom half of the population. Hence, one may define an inclusion coefficient as 'bottom half of the population falling in the mainstream interval'. Thus, we have a relative perspective on deprivation, that is, anyone whose income is less than the threshold, that is, 60 per of the median is considered excluded and if their income exceeds this threshold, they are considered included in the mainstream.[5] An improvement in the fraction of the bottom half of the population in the mainstream band would indicate progressive inclusion in the mainstream economic activity and vice versa. The complement of the inclusion coefficient would provide an estimate of the extent of exclusion for a homogenous society. Symbolically, we have an 'Inclusive **Coefficient**' (IC) denoted by 'ψ', which is given by

$$\psi = 1 - 2 \int_0^{\delta \xi_{.50}} f(x) dx \qquad (1)$$

Where $0 < \delta < 1$ ($\delta = 0.60$ in this study) and $\xi_{0.50}$ such that

$$\int_0^{\xi_{.50}} f(x) dx = \frac{1}{2} = \int_{\xi_{.50}}^{\infty} f(x) dx$$

where $0 \le \psi \le 1$

a. Mainstreaming/Marginalization: Stratified Social/Regional Context

It would be pertinent to examine inclusive/exclusive profiles with reference to different social/regional strata in a country like India. How do we define progress and inclusion in a plural society characterized by social/regional stratification? When there are different social groups/regions, and welfare schemes exclusively meant for some select social groups/regions are pursued, it would be worthwhile to examine (i) the extent of progress of each group/region as a whole in an absolute sense as well as relative to the mainstream; and (ii) verify how far such programmes have enabled the deprived in these groups/regions to catch up with better off in their own strata as well as with those in the mainstream.

To address these dual objectives, we examine (1) average progress, absolute as well as relative, made by each social group/region, (2) mainstreaming/marginalization of the deprived in each of the social groups independently and also in a collective sense. This would call for defining measures of strata (sub-stream)-specific as well as overall

---

[5]For further details, see Suryanarayana (2008).

(mainstream) progress; this may be done in terms of estimates of the group (sub-stream)-specific as well as overall (mainstream)-specific median. In a similar way, one may measure inclusion/exclusion of the poorest in each social group in its own progress as well as that of the mainstream by estimating the inclusion coefficients proposed in Eq. (1) with reference to mainstream and sub-stream medians, respectively. The measures corresponding to these two concepts and their implications are as follows.

2.1.1 Measure of Inter-group Disparity (Inclusion/Exclusion)

Methodologically, verification of absolute progress would involve review of status/improvement in median income/consumption of the specific social group only. Assessment of inclusion or improvement relative to the mainstream would involve estimates of inter-group median disparities. For the latter, one may define the following measures.

Let μ_m denote mainstream (overall) median and μ_s sub-stream median. Disparity between the subgroup and the mainstream could be examined by comparing the median estimates. The following results would be obtained:

(1) $\mu_s < \alpha \mu_m$ implies exclusion of the subgroup.
(2) $\mu_s > \alpha \mu_m$ implies inclusion of the subgroup.

Let us define a measure of inclusion (η_{inter}) as follows:

$$\eta_{inter} = [(\mu_s/\alpha\mu_m) - 1] \qquad (2)$$

where $0 < \alpha < 1$; (0.6 in this study)

$\eta_{inter} > 0 \Rightarrow$ Inter-group inclusion and $\eta_{inter} < 0 \Rightarrow$ Inter-group exclusion

2.1.2 Measure of Mainstreaming/Marginalization

One may examine income/consumption of the bottom rungs of a given social group relative to its own median (one aspect of the intra-group dimension, that is, inclusion in the subgroup progress, namely, IC-subgroup) as well as the mainstream median (another aspect of the intra-group dimension, that is, inclusion in the mainstream progress, namely, IC-mainstream). These estimates may be worked out by defining the estimator (1) with respect to sub-stream and mainstream median, respectively. The former would give us a measure of participation of the bottom rungs of the social group concerned in its own (group-specific) progress, while the latter with respect to mainstream progress.

It could so happen that there is some progress in terms of inclusion of the deprived section of a given social subgroup in its own progress (median), but the progress is quite unsatisfactory when measured with reference to the community as a whole.

Such differences in progress could be measured by taking the ratio (ω) of IC-mainstream to IC-Subgroup, which may be called Inclusive Coefficient in a Plural society (ICP). ICP would take the value 'one' when the extent of inclusion is the same with respect to both subgroup and mainstream median; a value less than one would imply that the extent of inclusion in the mainstream is less than the extent of inclusion in the subgroup's own progress; it would be an indication of marginalization. If one could consider IC-subgroup as a measure of inherent potential of the social group under review, the extent of its marginalization in the economy could be defined with reference to ICP (ω). A given social group is marginalized if its $\omega < 1$ and the extent of marginalization is given by ($\omega - 1$). If $\omega > 1$, ($\omega - 1$) would be >0, which would indicate mainstreaming of the social group in the economy.

The estimators would be as follows:

Define inclusion coefficient (1) with respect to both mainstream median (ψ_m) and sub-stream median (ψ_s); their ratio ω would provide a measure of subgroup inclusion from its distributional perspective.

$$\text{Define } \eta_{\text{intra}} = (\omega - 1) \qquad (3)$$

We have $\eta_{\text{intra}} > 0 \Rightarrow$ mainstreaming and $\eta_{\text{intra}} < 0 \Rightarrow$ marginalization

2.2 Marginalization: First, Second and Third Degree

Marginalization: First Degree
When the distribution for a certain social group, say SG1, lies entirely to the left of the distribution corresponding to the rest of the population (RoP) such that the following conditions hold:

(i) $P_{99}(\text{SG}_r) < P_1(\text{SG}_{\text{rop}})$ where $P_{99}(\text{SG}_r) = $ 99th income/consumption percentile of the social group under review (SG_r) and $P_1(\text{SG}_{\text{rop}}) = $ 1st income/consumption percentile of the rest of the population (SG_{rop})
(ii) $\eta_{\text{intra}} = (-) 1$

Marginalization: Second Degree

- $\eta_{\text{inter}} < 0$
- $\eta_{\text{intra}} < 0$

Marginalization: Third Degree

- $\eta_{\text{inter}} > 0$
- $\eta_{\text{intra}} < 0$

Given this framework, estimates of median across different social groups could be worked out using the latest available National Sample Survey data sets on consumption distribution for the years (Tables 1 and 3). For this purpose, the following social groups (for which data are available) are considered: Scheduled Tribes (STs),

Scheduled Castes (SCs), Other Backward Castes (OBCs) and Others, of whom the first three are generally considered to be marginalized.

3 Empirical Evidence: Inclusion versus Marginalization—Uttar Pradesh versus All India

This study presents the salient profiles for the five NSS regions of Uttar Pradesh by rural and urban sectors, respectively. The NSS regions and their district-wise composition are as follows:

(i) **Northern Upper Ganga Plains (091)**[6]: Saharanpur (01), Muzaffarnagar (02), Bijnor (03), Moradabad (04), Rampur (05), Jyotirao Phule Nagar (06), Meerut (07), Baghpat (08), Ghaziabad (09) and Gautam Buddha Nagar (10)

(ii) **Central (092)**: Sitapur (24), Hardoi (25), Unnao (26), Lucknow (27), Rae Bareli (28), Kanpur Dehat (33), Kanpur Nagar (34), Fatehpur (42), and Barabanki (46).

(iii) **Eastern (093)**: Pratapgarh (43), Kaushambi (44), Allahabad (45), Faizabad (47), Ambedkar Nagar, (48), Sultanpur (49), Bahraich (50), Shrawasti (51), Balrampur (52), Gonda (53), Siddharthnagar (54), Basti (55) S. Kabir Nagar (56), Maharajganj (57), Gorakhpur (58), Kushinagar (59), Deoria (60), Azamgarh (61), Mau (62), Ballia (63), Jaunpur (64), Ghazipur (65), Chandauli (66), Varanasi (67), S. R. Nagar (Bhadohi) (68), Mirzapur (69) and Sonbhadra (70)

(iv) **Southern (094)**: Jalaun (35), Jhansi (36), Lalitpur (37), Hamirpur (38), Mahoba (39), Banda (40) and Chitrakoot (41).

(v) **Southern Upper Ganga Plains (095)**: Bulandshahr (11), Upper Aligarh (12), Ganga Hathras (13), Plains Mathura (14), Agra (15), Firozabad (16), Etah (17) Mainpuri (18), Badaun (19), Bareilly (20), Pilibhit (21), Shahjahanpur (22), Kheri (23), Farrukhabad (29), Kannauj (30), Etawah (31) and Auraiya (32).

It may be noted that the NSS reported estimates of monthly per capita consumer expenditure only for a threefold classification of social groups (STs, SCs and OSGs) for the agriculture year 1993–94 and for a fourfold classification (STs, SCs, OBCs and OSGs) thereafter. Hence, a comparable profile is available only for the agricultural years from 2004/05.

---

[6]Figures in parentheses refer to NSS codes.

3.1 Social Group Inclusion Profiles

To facilitate an appreciation of the UP profile in the national context, this section would begin with the results for all India.

Rural All India: The extent of subgroup inclusion in terms of median per capita consumer expenditure is the maximum for OSGs; it was 100% in 2004/05. The estimates for the STs, SCs and the OBCs for the same year are 34, 49 and 67%, respectively (Table 1). This is consistent with the general perception about the relative economic status of different social groups in rural India. The estimates of measures of inter-group inclusion for rural all India for the years 2004/05, 2009/10 and 2011/12 show a marginal improvement for STs, SCs and the OBCs. However, the OSGs suffered a perceptible reduction in the extent of inclusion from 100 to 95% between 2004/05 and 2011/12.

Urban All India: The extent of inclusion (109%) of the OSGs in the mainstream was the highest in urban all India; this was higher in urban India than that in the rural. Contrary to the rural profile, the STs (52%) enjoyed higher extent of mainstream inclusion than the SCs (28.5%) and even the OBCs (44%) in urban India in 2004/05. The STs and the OSGs suffered a reduction in the extent of inclusion while the SCs and the OBCs enjoyed an increase between 2004/2005 and 2011/2012. On the urban front, while the (percentage points) improvement/reduction in the extent of inclusion was perceptible and similar (around 10) for the STs/SCs, the magnitude was similar (around five percentage points) for the OBCs/OSGs (Table 1).

How does Uttar Pradesh fare as compared to all India? The extent of different social groups' inclusion is almost similar for both rural and urban sectors in UP and All India. Rural Uttar Pradesh has a slightly different tale to report (Table 3). Results are not reported for the STs because of the small population share and issues related to robustness of estimates.[7] The SCs experienced a marginal improvement while the OBCs suffered a marginal reduction in the extent of inter-group inclusion in rural UP. However, the OSGs enjoyed perceptible improvement (about 11 percentage points). Urban UP has a different profile to report. The SCs and the OSGs experienced substantial improvement (about 12 and 38 percentage points, respectively) while the OBCs suffered a marginal reduction. Thus, the UP profile of inclusion/exclusion of different social groups is different from that of the nation.

3.2 Social Group Marginalization

Rural All India: The STs and SCs are the two marginalized social groups. Between them, the extent of marginalization of the STs is almost three times than that of SCs in 2004/05 (Table 2). The extent of marginalization has virtually remained unchanged for these two social groups between 2004/05 and 2011/12. The OBCs are marginally

---

[7]The proportion of ST population is less than one per cent in Uttar Pradesh; hence, sample estimates are unlikely to be robust.

mainstreamed, while the OSGs are mainstreamed to the extent of about 18% which has remained stable in the new millennium.

Urban All India: The urban profile is different from the rural one: The SCs were the most marginalized in 2004/05. The extent of marginalization of STs worsened by nine percentage points between 2004/05 and 2011/12. The SCs and the OBCS experienced an improvement as reflected in the reduction of marginalization by 23 and six percentage points respectively. The OSGs experienced deterioration in their status as reflected in the reduction in the extent of mainstreaming by six percentage points.

Rural Uttar Pradesh: The SCs are the only marginalized social group in rural UP. They experienced a reduction in the extent of marginalization by about four percentage points between 2004/05 and 2011/12. The OBCs got marginalized by about three percentage points by the year 2011/12. The OSGs too experienced deterioration in their mainstream status by about two percentage points during the period.

Urban Uttar Pradesh: The SCs are the most marginalized. The extent of their marginalization in the urban sector is nearly three times that in rural UP in 2004/05 (Table 4). They experienced an improvement in their status between 2004/05 and 2011/12. The OBCs experienced a worsening of their status by about two percentage points, while the OSG enjoyed an improvement by about 14 percentage points between the same two years.

India: Marginalization—3rd Degree

Table 1 Estimates of median consumption per person and measures of inclusion/exclusion: all India

Survey period	1993–94	2004–05	2009–10	2011–12	1993–94	2004–05	2009–10	2011–12
	All India rural				All India Urban			
	Median				Median			
STs	202	366.5	664	848.17	312.68	721.2	1236.13	1508.17
SCs	209.72	406.33	687.7	938	281.93	610.83	1019.25	1457.2
OBCs	–	457.88	770.14	1054.36	–	685.67	1143.8	1581
OSGs	253.24	547.6	896.5	1210	374.77	992.83	1640.12	2157.2
All	237.1	455.8	765.17	1035.5	358.6	792.25	1307.2	1758
Extent of inclusion/exclusion: η_{inter} for $\alpha = 0.6$								
STs	41.99	34.01	44.63	36.52	45.32	51.72	57.61	42.98
SCs	47.42	48.58	49.79	50.97	31.03	28.5	29.95	38.15
OBCs	–	67.43	67.75	69.7	–	44.24	45.83	49.89
OSGs	78.01	100.23	95.27	94.75	74.18	108.86	109.11	104.51

Source Author's estimates based on the NSS unit record data

Table 2 Mainstreaming/marginalization: all India

Survey period	Rural				Urban			
	AY 1993–94	AY 2004–05	AY 2009–10	AY 2011–12	AY 1993–94	AY 2004–05	AY 2009–10	AY 2011–12
Inclusive coefficient—mainstream for $\delta = 0.6$								
All groups	0.788	0.793	0.782	0.768	0.695	0.625	0.621	0.629
STs	0.632	0.523	0.607	0.509	0.571	0.449	0.448	0.412
SCs	0.682	0.726	0.699	0.686	0.452	0.386	0.413	0.449
OBCs	–	0.820	0.804	0.797	–	0.543	0.536	0.561
OSGs	0.842	0.911	0.896	0.910	0.734	0.781	0.784	0.784
Inclusive coefficient—subgroup for $\delta = 0.6$								
All groups	0.788	0.793	0.782	0.768	0.695	0.625	0.621	0.629
STs	0.804	0.792	0.778	0.777	0.722	0.548	0.514	0.562
SCs	0.815	0.841	0.819	0.798	0.748	0.731	0.707	0.590
OBCs	–	0.818	0.797	0.785	–	0.707	0.684	0.678
OSGs	0.785	0.776	0.779	0.772	0.686	0.590	0.593	0.622
Extent of marginalization: η_{intra} (%)								
STs	(−)21.39	(−)33.96	(−)21.98	(−)34.49	(−)20.91	(−)18.07	(−)12.84	(−)26.69
SCs	(−)16.32	(−)13.67	(−)14.65	(−)14.04	(−)39.57	(−)47.20	(−)41.58	(−)23.90
OBCs		0.24	0.88	1.53		(−)23.20	(−)21.64	(−)17.26
OSGs	7.26	17.40	15.02	17.88	7.00	32.37	32.21	26.05

Source Author's estimates based on the NSS unit record data

STs and SCs (Uttar Pradesh): Marginalization– 3rd Degree

Table 3 Estimates of median consumption per person and measures of inclusion/exclusion: Uttar Pradesh

Social group	Rural				Urban			
	AY 1993–94	AY 2004–05	AY 2009–10	AY 2011–12	AY 1993–94	AY 2004–05	AY 2009–10	AY 2011–12
Median								
SC	192.75	385.75	613.50	804.67	235.75	512.98	844.40	1052.43
OBC		440.33	693.42	874.50		567.52	853.75	1063.80
Others	247.75	513.79	826.25	1107.70	331.40	794.80	1371.31	1777.00
All	232.63	437.00	693.42	891.60	316.85	636.50	1019.12	1200.56
Extent of inclusion/exclusion: η_{inter} for $\alpha = 0.6$								
SC	38.09	47.12	47.46	50.42	24.01	34.32	38.09	46.10
OBC	NA	67.94	66.67	63.47	NA	48.60	39.62	47.68
Others	77.50	95.95	98.59	107.06	74.32	108.12	124.26	146.69

Source Author's estimates based on the NSS unit record data

Table 4 Mainstreaming/marginalization: Uttar Pradesh

Social group	Rural				Urban			
	AY 1993–94	AY 2004–05	AY 2009–10	AY 2011–12	AY 1993–94	AY 2004–05	AY 2009–10	AY 2011–12
IC-mainstream for δ = 0.6								
SC	0.597	0.760	0.755	0.767	0.432	0.480	0.566	0.609
OBC		0.840	0.872	0.836		0.620	0.575	0.677
Others	0.834	0.910	0.963	0.938	0.723	0.840	0.783	0.867
IC-subgroup for δ = 0.6								
SC	0.834	0.890	0.903	0.862	0.835	0.800	0.762	0.798
OBC		0.830	0.872	0.849		0.740	0.768	0.829
Others	0.765	0.800	0.877	0.839	0.675	0.630	0.580	0.588
Extent of mainstreaming/marginalization: η_{intra} (%)								
SC	(−)28.36	(−)14.61	(−)16.30	(−)10.98	(−)48.30	(−)40.00	(−)25.68	(−)23.70
OBC	NA	1.20	0.00	(−)1.51	NA	(−)16.22	(−)25.09	(−)18.27
Others	9.00	13.75	9.80	11.84	7.18	33.33	35.13	47.38

Source Author's estimates based on the NSS unit record data

3.3 Food Security: Dimensions of Inclusion

How far would the state succeed in ensuring inclusion of the deprived groups in the mainstream of the society would depend upon their ability to participate in the production process, earn income, and enjoy consumption which in turn critically depends upon the status of food security and human development. Hence, it would be pertinent to examine the status of food security from the inclusive and marginalization perspectives.

The conventional approach to issues related to food security is to assess the status of an individual or macroeconomy with reference to exogenous subsistence standards. It is well known that household food consumption depends upon income and awareness about choice and preferences. Hence, this section proposes to examine the inclusive and marginalization dimensions of food consumption across social groups and by different NSS regions in Uttar Pradesh and its comparative profile with respect to all India for the year 2011/12 (Tables 5 and 6).

Rural All India: The extent of subgroup inclusion is higher for food consumption than for total expenditure for the STs and SCs and vice versa for the OBCs and the OSGs in rural India. While the extent of inclusion is the highest for the OSGs followed by the OBCs, SCs and the STs for consumer expenditure, the profile across social groups is just the reverse for food consumption.

Urban All India: Food inclusion is higher than that for total expenditure for the STs, SCs and the OBCs only in urban India. As between the four social groups, food inclusion is the highest for the STs followed by the OBCs, SCs and the OSGs.

Table 5 Estimates of median consumption per person and measures of inclusion/exclusion: all India and Uttar Pradesh (NSS region-wise) 2011/12

Social group	All India				Uttar Pradesh			
	Median MPCE		Median food consumption		Median MPCE		Median food consumption	
	Rural	Urban	Rural	Urban	Rural	Urban	Rural	Urban
ST	848.17	1508.17	12.00	10.75	–	–	–	–
SC	938	1457.2	11.83	10.29	804.67	1052.43	12.06	10.51
OBC	1054.36	1581	11.78	10.36	874.5	1063.8	12.19	10.75
Others	1210	2157.2	11.67	9.92	1107.7	1777	11.9	10.33
All	1035.5	1758	11.8	10.2	891.6	1200.56	12.1	10.57
	Extent of inclusion/exclusion: η_{inter} for $\alpha = 0.6$				Extent of inclusion/exclusion: η_{inter} for $\alpha = 0.6$			
ST	36.52	42.98	69.49	75.65	–	–	–	–
SC	50.97	38.15	67.09	68.17	50.42	46.10	66.12	65.84
OBC	69.70	49.89	66.38	69.40	63.47	47.68	67.91	69.48
Others	94.75	104.51	64.90	62.17	107.06	146.69	63.91	62.94
Social group	Rural		Urban		Rural		Urban	
	Median	Inclusion	Median	Inclusion	Median	Inclusion	Median	Inclusion
	UP-NSS region (091) MPCE				UP-NSS Region (091) food consumption			
SC	944.6	45.68	1696.4	79.15	11.03	65.50	10.67	65.89
OBC	1034	59.46	1318.7	39.26	11.11	66.70	10.40	61.80
Others	1261.8	94.60	2329	145.96	11.25	68.80	10.79	67.73
All	1080.7		1578.2		11.10		10.72	
	UP-NSS region (092) MPCE				UP-NSS region (092) food consumption			
SC	783.33	59.92	949	38.56	12.88	69.36	10.83	82.84
OBC	783.2	59.89	956.5	39.66	12.67	66.67	10.30	73.84
Others	1012.6	106.72	1587.2	131.74	12.04	58.38	9.17	54.72
All	816.4		1141.5		12.67		9.88	
	UP-NSS region (093) MPCE				UP-NSS region (093) food consumption			
SC	741.5	46.84	778.4	17.25	12.08	63.86	11.10	56.71
OBC	846.47	67.63	1020.2	53.68	12.42	68.54	12.07	70.40
Others	1104	118.62	1962.7	195.65	12.14	64.69	11.43	61.38
All	841.63		1106.4		12.29		11.81	
	UP-NSS region (094) MPCE				UP-NSS region (094) food consumption			
SC	736.00	41.61	1003.6	44.16	13.25	65.54	11.56	67.64
OBC	866.25	66.67	1068.5	53.48	13.34	66.72	10.75	55.80
Others	1000	92.40	1797.4	158.18	13.55	69.29	12.05	74.64
All	866.25		1160.3		13.34		11.5	
	UP-NSS region (095) MPCE				UP-NSS region (095) food consumption			
SC	866.17	53.94	1013	52.10	11.62	65.40	9.18	56.42
OBC	944.71	67.89	1063.8	59.73	11.75	67.17	10.35	76.36
Others	1107.7	96.86	1388.9	108.54	11.71	66.67	8.93	52.26
All	937.8		1110		11.71		9.78	

Source Author's estimates based on NSS unit record data sets

Table 6 Mainstreaming/marginalization: all India and Uttar Pradesh (region-wise)

Social group	MPCE		Food consumption	
	Rural	Urban	Rural	Urban
Mainstreaming/marginalization: all India (2011/12)				
	IC-mainstream for $\delta = 0.6$			
ST	0.768	0.768	0.926	0.926
SC	0.509	0.509	0.937	0.937
OBC	0.686	0.686	0.922	0.922
Others	0.797	0.797	0.933	0.933
Total	0.910	0.910	0.928	0.928
	IC-subgroup for $\delta = 0.6$			
ST	0.768	0.562	0.915	0.942
SC	0.777	0.590	0.935	0.927
OBC	0.798	0.678	0.922	0.936
Others	0.772	0.622	0.935	0.912
	Extent of mainstreaming/marginalization: η_{intra} (%)			
ST	−34.49	(−)26.69	1.25	1.29
SC	−14.04	−23.90	0.23	0.79
OBC	1.53	−17.26	(−)0.12	0.50
Others	17.88	26.05	(−)0.26	(−)1.30
Mainstreaming/marginalization: Uttar Pradesh (2011/12)				
	IC-mainstream for $\delta = 0.6$			
SC	0.767	0.609	0.96	0.929
OBC	0.836	0.677	0.95	0.942
Others	0.938	0.867	0.96	0.869
Total	0.834	0.736	0.96	0.914
	IC-subgroup for $\delta = 0.6$			
SC	0.862	0.798	0.96	0.929
OBC	0.849	0.829	0.95	0.940
Others	0.839	0.588	0.97	0.889
	Extent of mainstreaming/marginalization: η_{intra} (%)			
SC	−10.98	−23.70	0.000	0.000
OBC	−1.51	−18.27	0.26	0.25
Others	11.84	47.38	−0.41	−2.25

(continued)

Table 6 (continued)

Social group	MPCE		Food consumption	
	Rural	Urban	Rural	Urban
Mainstreaming/marginalization: Uttar Pradesh—NSS Region (091)				
	IC-mainstream for δ = 0.6			
SC	0.793	0.708	0.958	0.995
OBC	0.841	0.372	0.925	0.946
Others	0.922	0.920	0.995	0.899
Total	0.856	0.667	0.952	0.930
	IC-subgroup for δ = 0.6			
SC	0.912	0.708	0.969	0.995
OBC	0.868	0.629	0.925	0.958
Others	0.840	0.485	0.995	0.899
	Mainstreaming/marginalization: Uttar Pradesh			
SC	−13.05	0.000	−1.13	0.00
OBC	−3.11	−40.860	0.00	−1.19
Others	9.73	89.739	0.00	0.00
Mainstreaming/marginalization: Uttar Pradesh—NSS region (092)				
	IC-mainstream for δ = 0.6			
SC	0.840	0.671	0.964	1.000
OBC	0.859	0.683	0.973	0.963
Others	0.912	0.939	0.902	0.937
Total	0.858	0.793	0.957	0.955
	IC-subgroup for δ = 0.6			
SC	0.851	0.971	0.964	1.000
OBC	0.913	0.869	0.973	0.963
Others	0.657	0.668	0.91	0.938
	Extent of mainstreaming/marginalization: η_{intra} (%)			
SC	−1.23	−30.903	0.00	0.00
OBC	−5.89	−21.424	0.00	0.000
Others	38.96	40.573	−0.88	- 0.10
Mainstreaming/marginalization: Uttar Pradesh—NSS region (093)				
	IC-mainstream for δ = 0.6			
SC	0.731	0.276	0.961	0.923
OBC	0.843	0.755	0.961	0.932
Others	0.994	0.923	0.956	0.949
Total	0.836	0.740	0.960	0.934

(continued)

Table 6 (continued)

Social group	MPCE		Food consumption	
	Rural	Urban	Rural	Urban
	IC-subgroup for δ = 0.6			
SC	0.839	0.968	0.966	0.979
OBC	0.840	0.815	0.961	0.919
Others	0.871	0.645	0.956	0.960
	Extent of mainstreaming/marginalization: η_{intra} (%)			
SC	−12.91	−71.512	−0.52	−5.79
OBC	0.27	−7.310	0.000	1.42
Others	14.07	43.147	0.000	−1.15
Mainstreaming/marginalization: Uttar Pradesh—NSS Region (094)				
	IC-mainstream for δ = 0.6			
SC	0.734	0.697	0.996	1.000
OBC	0.870	0.691	0.995	0.992
Others	0.956	0.982	1.000	1.000
Total	0.841	0.767	0.996	0.996
	IC-subgroup for δ = 0.6			
SC	0.821	0.835	0.998	1.000
OBC	0.870	0.784	0.995	0.992
Others	0.956	0.723	1.000	1.000
	Extent of mainstreaming/marginalization: η_{intra} (%)			
SC	−10.54	−16.479	−0.20	0.000
OBC	0.00	−11.862	0.000	0.000
Others	0.00	35.834	0.000	0.000
Mainstreaming/marginalization: Uttar Pradesh—NSS region (095)				
	IC-mainstream for δ = 0.6			
SC	0.826	0.863	0.940	0.963
OBC	0.860	0.830	0.960	0.901
Others	0.986	0.865	0.991	0.899
Total	0.871	0.848	0.959	0.912
	IC-subgroup for δ = 0.6			
SC	0.954	0.915	0.941	0.963
OBC	0.860	0.841	0.960	0.896
Others	0.874	0.614	0.991	0.967
	Extent of mainstreaming/marginalization: η_{intra} (%)			
SC	−13.44	−5.777	−0.15	0.000
OBC	0.01	−1.272	0.000	0.57
Others	12.77	40.729	0.000	−7.021

Source Author's estimates based on NSS unit record data

The observation that extent of food inclusion is higher than that for total expenditure for the relatively deprived social groups could be consistent with Engel's law which predicts a decline in the proportion of income spent on food as income increases. In other words, if this relation were to be used for identifying the social groups for targeted food security interventions, then it would follow that the STs and SCs, in rural India and the STs, SCs and OBCs in urban India call for targeted intervention to promote food security. This result validates the policy of the Government of India which assigns special weights to these social groups in targeted food intervention programmes.

Uttar Pradesh: The profile of total expenditure inclusion across social groups in rural and urban Uttar Pradesh is similar. The SCs are the least included, followed by OBCs and the OSGs. Food consumption inclusion is lower than that for total expenditure for the SCs and the OBCs in both rural and urban UP. Hence, at the state level, these two social groups deserve special attention to promote food security.

Uttar Pradesh regional profiles of inclusion: The aggregate UP profile across social groups generally holds well across regions but for the following differences. The OBC inclusion in the mainstream is the least in urban Northern Upper Ganga Plains. In this region, both the SCs and the OBCs call for targeted intervention in the rural sector but only the OBCs in the urban sector. The general profiles are the same across rural and urban sectors of the remaining regions. Hence, the SCs and the OBCs remain the two social groups that need attention in targeted policy interventions to promote food security.

3.4 Food Security: Marginalization

The estimates of marginalization in total expenditure provide clear evidence on the extent of inclusion of different social groups in a society. However, the same interpretation cannot be extended to these measures on estimates of food consumption for reasons like the Engel law. For instance, Table 6 shows that the OSGs are marginalized in food consumption in both rural and urban India and the OBCs are the marginalized group in rural India. Are they? Definitely, they are not. On the other hand, the evidence on the mainstreaming of the STs and the SCs in food consumption would suggest their relative deprivation and, hence, priority to food consumption. Still there are some glaring features. Even the SCs are food marginalized in rural sectors of the following regions in UP: Northern Upper Ganga Plains, Eastern, Southern and, Southern Upper Ganga Plains. They are marginalized only in the urban sector of Eastern UP. Hence, it would follow that the SCs in these regions need special policy attention to promote their food security.

One may also verify the extent of food deprivation in different regions of Uttar Pradesh with reference to estimates of incidence of 'Outlier Food Insecurity'. We define this incidence as the percentage of population with food consumption less than the lower inner fence in a box plot of the relevant consumption distribution. The estimates show the incidence to be the highest in the Eastern region of rural Uttar

Table 7 Estimates of incidence of outlier food insecurity across NSS regions by sector: Uttar Pradesh (2011/12)

NSS region	Rural		Urban	
	Threshold (Kg/capita/month)	Incidence (%)	Threshold (Kg/capita/month)	Incidence (%)
Northern upper ganga plains (NSS region: 091)	5.14	0.38	6.13	2.54
Central (NSS region: 092)	5.08	0.32	3.45	0.00
Eastern (NSS region: 093)	6.18	0.64	5.57	0.79
Sothern (NSS region: 094)	7.41	0.07	5.74	0.22
Southern upper ganga plains (NSS region: 095)	5.08	0.15	2.44	0.00
Sector total	5.66	0.46	3.89	0.07

Note The thresholds for measuring food deprivation outliers are measured by estimates of lower inner fence in a Box–whisker plot for personal consumption distribution in a given region, where the lower inner fence = First quartile—1.5* Inter-quartile range

Pradesh followed by Northern Upper Ganga Plains, Central, Sothern Upper Ganga Plains and the Southern region. As regards Urban UP, the incidence of outlier food insecurity is the highest in the Northern Upper Ganga Plains, followed by Eastern and Southern NSS regions; the incidence is nil in the Central and Southern Upper Ganga Plains (Table 7).

Finally, the NSS findings show the poorest rural food consumption in the Eastern region of the state among OBCs; the richest among the poorest food consuming sample households happens to be among the OBCs from the Southern region. As regards urban UP, the poorest food consuming sample household is from the Eastern region among the OBCs; the richest of the poorest food consuming households is also from the OBCs in Southern UP (Table 8) (Figs. 1 and 2).

4 Conclusion

Inclusive growth and marginalization are oft-repeated terms in contemporary policy literature. However, they are neither well-defined nor empirically measured and estimated. This paper examines the extent of inclusion and marginalization of different social groups in the rural and urban sectors of Uttar Pradesh by different NSS regions.

Table 8 Per capita food consumption of the poorest across social groups by NSS regions: Uttar Pradesh (2011/12) (kg/capita/month)

Social group	Northern upper ganga plains	Central	Eastern	Southern	Southern upper ganga plains	Uttar Pradesh
Rural sector						
STs	7.38	9.38	7.13	9.13	7.39	7.13
SCs	2.25	4.38	3.42	6.75	4.50	2.25
OBCs	4.78	4.21	2.13	6.25	5.17	2.13
Others	5.95	5.43	2.50	8.75	5.50	2.50
Total	2.25	4.21	2.13	6.25	4.50	2.13
Urban sector						
STs	5.57	8.30	6.17	9.80	8.26	5.57
SCs	5.00	6.70	4.42	7.80	3.93	3.93
OBCs	4.00	4.53	3.43	4.83	4.48	3.43
Others	3.96	3.75	4.31	7.63	4.00	3.75
Total	3.96	3.75	3.43	4.83	3.93	3.43

Source Author's estimates based on NSS unit record data

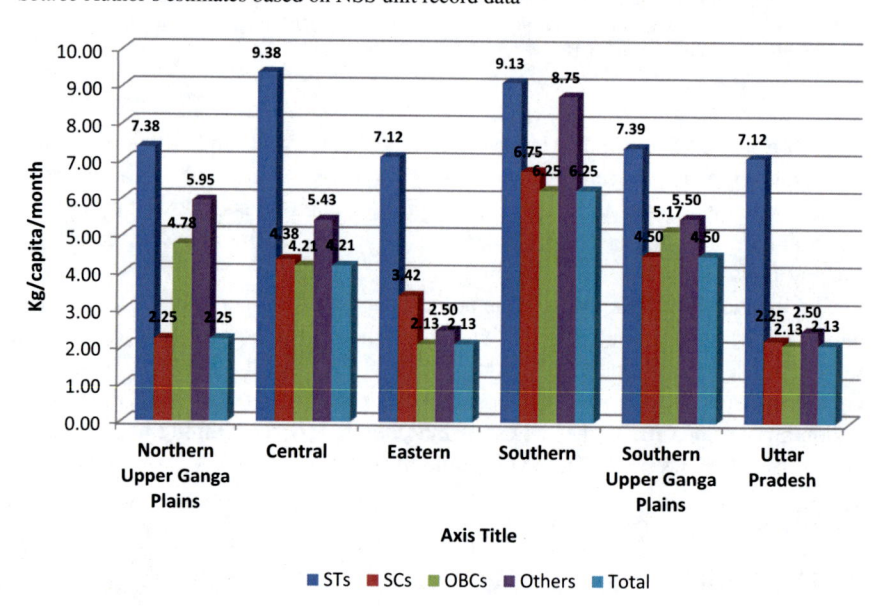

Fig. 1 Monthly per capita food of the poorest sample household: rural Uttar Pradesh (2011/12). *Source* NSS Unit record data

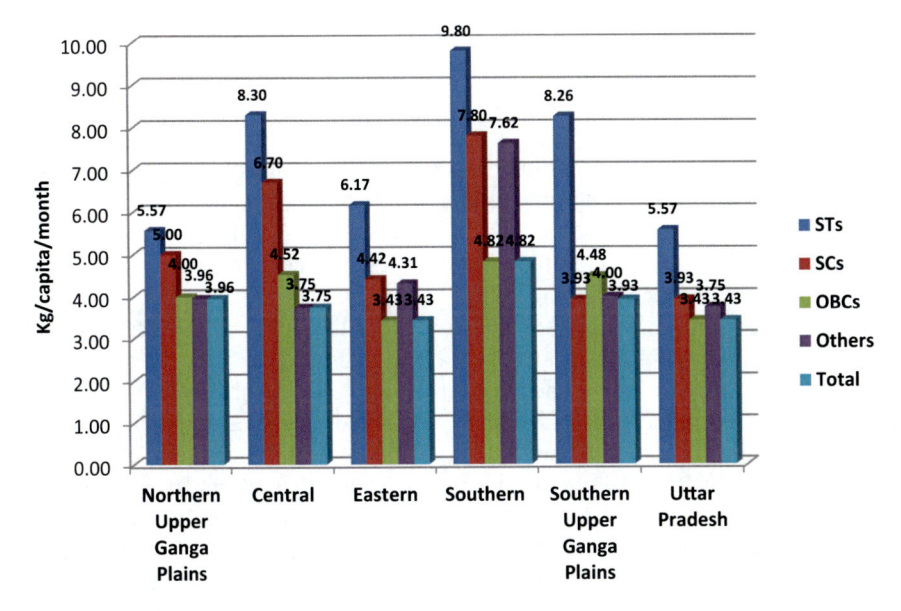

Fig. 2 Monthly per capita food of the poorest sample household: urban Uttar Pradesh (2011/12). *Source* NSS unit record data

In this pursuit, it has examined the dimensions of inclusion and marginalization with respect to total consumer expenditure and food consumption. In order to highlight the UP experience, the results are juxtaposed with those for all India.

As regards rural all India, the study finds that the STs and SCs are the two marginalized social groups. Between them, the extent of marginalization of STs is almost three times than that of the SCs. The extent of marginalization has virtually remained unchanged for these two social groups between 2004/05 and 2011/12. The OBCs are marginally mainstreamed while the OSGs are mainstreamed to the extent of about 18% which has remained stable in the new millennium. In urban all India, the SCs were the most marginalized in 2004/05. The extent of marginalization of the STs worsened since then. The SCs and the OBCs have experienced an improvement as reflected in the reduction of marginalization by 23 and six percentage points, respectively. The OSGs have experienced deterioration in their status as reflected in the reduction in the extent of mainstreaming by six percentage points.

In rural Uttar Pradesh as a whole, the SCs are the only marginalized social group. They have experienced a reduction in the extent of marginalization since 2004/05. The OBCs have got marginalized and the OSGs too experienced deterioration in their mainstream status. In urban Uttar Pradesh, the SCs are the most marginalized and the extent of their marginalization in the urban sector is more than three times that in rural UP in 2004/05. They experience an improvement in their status since then. The OBCs experienced a marginal worsening of their status, while the OSG enjoyed an improvement.

As regards the food security dimensions of inclusion, the study finds that in rural all India, the extent of subgroup inclusion is higher for food consumption than for total expenditure for the STs and SCs and vice versa for the OBCs and the OSGs in rural India. While the extent of inclusion is the highest for the OSGs followed by the OBCs, SCs and the STs for consumer expenditure, the profile across social groups is just the reverse for food consumption. In urban India, food inclusion is higher than that for total expenditure for the STs, SCs and the OBCs only in urban India. As between the four social groups, food inclusion is the highest for the STs followed by the OBCs, SCs and the OSGs.

This study proposes to use the relation between the extent of food inclusion and total expenditure inclusion to identify the social groups that need special policy attention for food security. It finds that for targeted food security interventions, the STs and the SCs in rural India and the STs, SCs and the OBCs in urban India need special attention. As regards Uttar Pradesh, food consumption inclusion is lower than that for total expenditure for the SCs and the OBCs in both rural and urban UP. Hence, at the state level, these two social groups deserve special attention to promote food security. The aggregate UP profile across social groups generally holds well across regions but for the following differences. The OBC inclusion in the mainstream is the least in urban Northern Upper Ganga Plains. In this region, both the SCs and the OBCs call for targeted intervention in the rural sector but only the OBCs in the urban sector. The general profiles across rural and urban sectors of the remaining regions are similar. Hence, the SCs and the OBCs are the two social groups that need attention in targeted policy interventions to promote food security.

The study also examines the extent of food deprivation in different regions of Uttar Pradesh with reference to the box plots of food consumption in different regions. The profile of the incidence of outlier food insecurity across regions shows the Eastern region of rural Uttar Pradesh to be the most deprived followed by Northern Upper Ganga Plains, Central, Southern Upper Ganga Plains and the Southern region. As regards Urban UP, the incidence of outlier food insecurity is the highest in the Northern Upper Ganga Plains, followed by Eastern and Southern NSS regions; the incidence is nil in the Central and Southern Upper Ganga Plains.

Finally, the NSS findings show the poorest rural food consumption in the Eastern region of Uttar Pradesh among the OBCs; the richest among the poorest food consuming sample households also happens to be among the OBCs from the Southern region. As regards urban UP, the poorest food consuming sample household is from the Eastern region among the OBCs; the richest of the poorest food consuming households is also from the OBCs in Southern UP. This is in contrast with the general perception about the relative economic and food security status of different social groups in Uttar Pradesh.

References

Government of India. (2013a). *Twelfth Five Year Plan (2012–2017): Faster, More Inclusive and Sustainable Growth* (Vol. I). New Delhi: Sage Publications India Pvt Ltd.

Government of India. (2013b). *Twelfth Five Year Plan (2012–2017): Twelfth Five Year Plan 2012–2017 Social Sectors,* (Vol. III). New Delhi: Sage Publications India Pvt Ltd.

Suryanarayana, M. H. (2008). What is exclusive about 'inclusive growth?'. *Economic and Political Weekly, XLIII*(43), 91–101.

Suryanarayana, M. H. (2013). *The Pursuit of Food Security in India: Policies sans Concept and Commitment? One Pager No 207*. Brasilia: International Policy Centre for Inclusive Growth.

Suryanarayana. (2015). Marginalization: A Concept, Measure and Estimates, Paper presented at the seminar on '*Poverty and Deprivation in South Asia*' organised by the Department of Economics and the Centre for Study of Nepal, Banaras Hindu University, Varanasi; 9–11 March 20–15.

M. H. Suryanarayana working as Professor in Indira Gandhi Institute of Development Research, Mumbai, is development economist with experience in providing technical assistance in the preparation of human development reports, poverty reduction strategy papers and tracking of MDGs. As a 'Senior Trainer', he designed, developed and conducted a month-long workshop on 'Food Policy Analysis' sponsored by the FAO, IFPRI and the Government of Bangladesh for academicians and policy makers in Bangladesh. Prof. Suryanarayana formulated and taught a course on Food Policy at the Maastricht Graduate School of Governance.

He designed an empirical methodology corresponding to the one in Human Development Report 2011 and estimated Inequality Adjusted Human Development Indices for states in India. Prof. Suryanarayana drafted and finalized a Poverty Monitoring and Analysis System for the three administrations of Somalia.

In addition to teaching and research experience (Econometrics, Development Economics, Food Policy Analysis, Human Development and Indian Economy) for over 30 years, Prof. Suryanarayana served as consultant for ADB, OECD, UNDP, World Bank, and provided technical assistance to developing country governments including Bangladesh, Botswana, Brunei Darussalam, India, Nepal, Somalia and Vietnam.

Migration, Remittances and Poverty Reduction

Imtiyaz Ali, Abdul C. P. Jaleel and R. B. Bhagat

Abstract The role of migration and remittances sent by the migrants is a matter of debate in the existing literature on migration research. Using the nationally representative data from the 64th round of National Sample Survey, this paper contributes to the debate about the impact of internal and international remittances on poverty reduction in Uttar Pradesh and Bihar. In the list of states in India, these two states are often placed at the top, for their high out-migration rates and low progress in social and economic indicators. This paper begins with a discussion of migration, remittances and poverty at the household level. A huge diversity exists in the utilisation of internal and international remittances in the areas of origin. The estimate reveals that internal and international remittances not only reshape the life chances of remittances receiving households but also fulfil the diverse non-food necessities. The result from the multivariate logistic analysis shows that households from rural areas received higher remittances compared to urban area. Thus, it gives strength to absorb the risks and shocks of catastrophic health, marriage expenditure and incidence of crop failures to the rural households. In line with an optimistic view, the findings of the present study show that remittances based migration enhances the socio-economic status and reduces poverty of migrant households. Based on propensity score matching technique, the results also show that the impact of international remittances on reducing household poverty out-weigh that of the internal remittances in Uttar Pradesh, but in Bihar, domestic remittances play a significant role in reducing poverty at the household level than international remittances.

Keywords Migration · Remittances · Poverty · Propensity score matching

---

I. Ali · A. C. P. Jaleel
International Institute for Population Sciences, Mumbai, India
e-mail: aliimtiyaz09@gmail.com

A. C. P. Jaleel
e-mail: cpjaleel@gmail.com

R. B. Bhagat (✉)
Department of Migration and Urban Studies, International Institute for Population Sciences, Mumbai, India
e-mail: rbbhagat@iips.net

© Springer Nature Singapore Pte Ltd. 2019
R. P. Mamgain (ed.), *Growth, Disparities and Inclusive Development in India*,
India Studies in Business and Economics,
https://doi.org/10.1007/978-981-13-6443-3_8

1 Introduction

Migration is a form of spatial mobility that denotes a change in the usual place of residence. Economic necessities or aspirations dominate migration as many people migrate for accumulating wealth whereas others migrate for just survival. Most of the people in India resort to migration to earn relatively more than what they actually get in their place of origin. Migrants in India are not a homogenous category; many are working abroad (international migrants), whereas many move within the boundaries of the country (internal migrants). As per National Sample Survey, the overall out-migration rate from Uttar Pradesh was 13 per thousand in the year 1993, and it is more than doubled (29 per 1000 population) in the year 2007–08. In Bihar, it increased from 28 per thousand in the year 1993 to 35 in the year 2007–08.[1] According to the Tendulkar Committee estimates, about 34% population in Bihar and 29% in Uttar Pradesh was poor in 2011–12. These are two comparable states in India where high level of poverty and migration coexists. Remittances sent by migrants form a major source of household income in these two states. This chapter estimates the impact of remittances on poverty reduction in these states. It also examines the utilization of remittances received internally or internationally in these states. The chapter demonstrates that the migrant's remittances contribute significantly to the poverty reduction in Bihar and Uttar Pradesh.

The available literature shows how several push factors shape the rural out-migration; among them poverty and environmental degradation are most critical. There is also a new explanatory framework known as new economics of labour migration (NELM) which explains migration as a part of household's strategy to mitigate rural distress and risks. The migrant's remittances sent to their households are considered to be an important means to diversify and improve the household income and meet the consumption needs. Migration is considered as a new form of insurance in the context of market failure and climate change risks. Research findings from many developing countries show that households which receive remittances are financially better off than those that do not receive remittances (Adams 1991; Stark and Bloom 1986; Stark et al. 1988; Adams and Page 2005; Gupta et al. 2009). Studies have also highlighted that the international remittances sent back to home countries have profound impact on the household's well-being in various parts of Asia, Africa, Latin America and the Middle East. International remittances are also found to be the second most important source of external funding in developing countries (World Bank 2004, 2011).

The scholars and policy makers have been debating the impact of migration and remittances at the place of origin, but it is not clear how its impact varies in varied regional contexts. The impact of remittances on productive investment and non-productive consumption, poverty and labour force participation is often either diverse or inconclusive due to lack of data. Furthermore, the existing studies can be categorized into three schools of thought, i.e. some studies show that migration has negative impact on left-behind families; it has positive impact, and there is no impact at all.

---

[1] See "Appendix".

Although it is true that migration is not a panacea for development yet its role in reshaping life of people and society cannot be ignored (de Haan 1999; de Haas 2007; Jimenez-Soto and Brown 2012; Tumbe 2012; Sikder and Ballis 2013; Adams and Cuecuecha 2013; Fransen and Mazzucato 2014; Dey 2014; López-Videla and Machuca 2014; Ali and Bhagat 2016).

We first document the link between remittances receiving households and non-remittances receiving households with non-migrant, internal out-migrant and emigrant households' conditions. Furthermore, this chapter explains the socio-economic determinants of remittances received both from within the country and abroad and also explains the impact of remittances on the poverty level of households. In order to assess the impact of remittances on poverty level, we use propensity score matching technique that makes comparisons of outcomes between those households who had received remittances from internal and international sources and those who had not received any remittances.

2 Data and Empirical Strategy

The data on migration and related information was taken from unit level data of the 49th (1993) and 64th (2007–2008) Rounds of National Sample Survey (NSS). The NSS is a nationally representative sample survey carried out by the National Sample Survey Organization (NSSO), a wing in the Ministry of Statistics and Programme Implementation, Government of India. The 49th NSS Round conducted in 1993 collected information on migration from all the states/union territories of India as part of survey on 'Housing condition and migration in India'. This survey covered a sample of 14,130 households in Uttar Pradesh (9764 in rural areas and 4336 in urban areas) and a population of 79,789 persons (56,916 in rural areas and 27,873 in urban areas). It covered a sample of 8839 households (6859 in rural areas and 1980 in urban areas) and a population of 45,800 persons in Bihar (35,857 in rural areas and 9943 in urban areas). Out-migrants were defined as a former member of the household who had migrated out of the village/town in the last five years and was alive on the date of survey. Similarly, an out-migrant household is defined as one, if at least any member of this household has out-migrated within and outside India provided the migrant was alive on the date of survey. There are some limitations to compare out-migration rates on the basis of the two survey rounds because the 49th round captured an out-migrant in last 5 years whereas the 64th round determined out-migration from the household at any time in the past. Further, in both rounds of the surveys they asked the same question about out-migrant households receiving remittances keeping the reference period as the last one year. In the 64th round, NSSO survey also added some additional questions regarding remittances, such as utilization of remittances by the receiving households on priority basis.

2.1 Multivariate Analysis

In order to examine the association between households' socio-economic condition with migration status, we have used a binary logistic regression. Migration status of the household was considered as dependent variable and gender, the place of residence, social groups, religion, household size, land possession, monthly per capita consumer expenditure (MPCE) and region are taken as independent variables. The equation of logistic regression for multiple predictors is defined as:

$$\text{Logit}(Y) = \ln\left(\frac{p}{1-p}\right) = \alpha + \beta_1 x_1 + \beta_2 x_2 + \in$$

where p is the probability of the event and α is an intercept β is regression coefficient, x_1 is set of predictors and $\in$ is an error term.

2.2 Propensity Score Matching (PSM)

In the absence of randomized trials, PSM is an innovative statistical method to evaluate the treatment effects for cross-sectional/observational/non-experimental data (Rosenbaum and Rubin 1983). The main aim of this chapter is to make comparisons of outcomes between those households who had received remittances from all sources (domestic as well as international), and those who had not received remittances from any sources. However, such a comparison assumes that the selection of household which received remittances is random, and the selection process is not correlated with the outcome variable. In PSM, the average outcome of households which have received remittances is simply compared with the average outcome for those which have not received remittances. It is the probability that a household had received remittances from all sources, given various background characteristics.

The evaluation seeks to estimate the mean impact of utilization of remittances on those who had received remittances, obtained by averaging the impact across all the households who had received remittances or not in the sample. This parameter is known as average exposure effect (AEE) (for details of PSM, see Rosenbaum and Rubin 1983).

The matching variables for PSM include place of residence, sex of the head of the household, educational attainment, marital status, religion and social group. These variables cover the most important determinants of migration and remittances identified in the literature that play a role in understanding the relationship between remittances and poverty.

We use nearest neighbour matching with replacement, i.e. household receives remittances from all sources versus not-receiving remittances, the household receives international remittances versus household receives internal remittances, and household receives internal remittances versus households receive no remittances.

Table 1 Out-migrants and remittances receiving households in Uttar Pradesh and Bihar, 2007–08

NSS regions	Proportion of households having out-migrants	Proportion of households receiving remittances
Eastern Uttar Pradesh	43.4	25.6
Southern Uttar Pradesh	44.4	7.4
Central Uttar Pradesh	33.3	10.6
Southern Upper Ganga Plains	28.4	9.4
Northern Upper Ganga Plains	27.8	6.0
Uttar Pradesh	**34.7**	**14.6**
Northern Bihar	24.8	19.5
Central Bihar	24.6	15.4
Bihar	**24.7**	**18.3**

Notes Proportion is taken as percentage of households having out-migrants or receiving remittances to the total households in the region

3 Results and Discussion

Table 1 presents region-wise proportion of migrant households (a household with at least one out-migrant for employment) and proportion of households receiving remittances in Uttar Pradesh and Bihar. In Uttar Pradesh, out-migration was higher in regions, namely Southern and Eastern Uttar Pradesh. The state of Uttar Pradesh as a whole had 35% migrant households. Proportion of such households was 44.4% in Southern Uttar Pradesh and 43.4% in Eastern Uttar Pradesh, followed by 33.3% in Central Uttar Pradesh, 28.4% in Southern Upper Ganga Plains and 27.8% in North Upper Ganga Plains. In the state of Bihar, 24.7% of the total households were migrant households. Proportions of migrant households were 24.8% in Northern Bihar and 24.6% in Central Bihar.

Table 1 also shows region-wise proportion of households who have received remittances in the states of Uttar Pradesh and Bihar. In Uttar Pradesh, 14.6% households received remittances. Region-wise the proportion of remittances receiving households was: 25.5 in Eastern Uttar Pradesh, 10.5% in Central Uttar Pradesh, 9.3% in Southern Upper Ganga Plains, 7.4% in Southern Uttar Pradesh and 6.0% in North Upper Ganga Plains. The proportion of remittances receiving households in Uttar Pradesh increased by more than three times from 4.3 to 14.6% between 1993 and 2007–08.[2] On the other side, 18.3% of the total households in Bihar received remittances—19.5% in Northern Bihar and 15.4% in Central Bihar. The increase in remittances receiving households has been impressive with likely impact on poverty reduction and investment in education and health.

Table 2 presents the proportion of households that received remittances and poverty status by their migration status. Of all households, 22% were identified as

---

[2] See "Appendix".

Table 2 Composition of households in Uttar Pradesh and Bihar by remittances and poverty status (in %)

	Non-migrant HH	Intra-state migrant HH	Interstate migrant HH	Emigrant HH	Total
Uttar Pradesh					
RRHH	0.1	2.9	10.9	0.1	14.6
NRRHH	64.5	17.6	3.2	0.7	85.4
Total	64.6	20.5	14.1	0.8	100
Poor	15.2	4.0	2.8	0.1	22.1
Non-poor HH	49.3	16.6	11.2	0.7	77.9
Total	64.5	20.5	14.1	0.8	100
Bihar					
RRHH	0.0	2.0	15.7	0.5	18.3
NRRHH	75.1	4.3	2.1	0.0	81.6
Total	75.1	6.3	17.8	0.5	100
Poor	24.6	1.1	5.0	0.0	30.8
Non-Poor HH	50.5	5.2	12.8	0.5	69.1
Total	75.1	6.3	17.8	0.5	100

Source Estimation based on NSS, 2007–08
RRHH Remittance receiving households; *NRRHH* Non-remittances receiving households

poor[3] in Uttar Pradesh including 15% those belonging to non-migrant households. In the case of Bihar, 18.3% households in the state received remittances which comprised 15.7% from interstate migrants and two per cent from intra-state migrants. The share of households receiving international remittances is only 0.5% in Bihar. Of all households in the state, 31% were identified as poor households whereas 25% belonged to non-migrant households. More than 95% of remittance receiving households both in Uttar Pradesh and Bihar received it from internal out-migrants. Another important finding is that, among the all poor households, a majority have no out-migrating member.

To understand the relationship between households' socio-economic characteristics with remittance status, a multivariate binary logistic regression analysis is used (where dependent variable is dichotomous namely 'households received remittances' is coded as '1' and 'household received no remittances' is coded as '0'). In Model I and Model II, we have considered households with at least one migrant received remittances as dependent variable, whereas sex of the head of household, rural–urban residence, MPCE (monthly per capita consumer expenditure), social groups,

---

[3]The paper defines the poor and non-poor households based on the official measure of poverty line defined as the value of a set of household consumer expenditure. Thus, if per capita household expenditure is below the poverty line the household is poor.

religion, land possession, household size and region are taken as independent (predictor) variables (Table 3).

The results of odds ratio show that even controlling the place of residence, social status, household size, land possessed and economic status (based on MPCE), probability of receiving remittances is one and half times higher for Muslim households compared to Hindu households in Uttar Pradesh. This further shows that a significant number of Muslim households are economically dependent on remittances. No significant association is found between remittances receiving households and religion in Bihar. Furthermore, we note that, in Bihar and Uttar Pradesh, urban households received lesser remittances as compared to rural households. This indicates that labour out-migration in the states of Uttar Pradesh and Bihar is largely from rural households.

3.1 Utilization of Remittances in Uttar Pradesh and Bihar

Table 4 shows the utilization of remittances as a first and second priority by remittance receiving households. The results show that both in Uttar Pradesh and Bihar a large part of remittances was directly going to household's food consumption. Purchasing of food for household consumption was found as the first priority for 63% of the remittance receiving households in Uttar Pradesh and 69% in Bihar. Education was second priority expenditure for remittances receiving households in Uttar Pradesh (41%), followed by health care (22%) and purchasing of household durables (15%). In the case of Bihar, the second priority in the use of remittance receiving households was purchasing of household durables (25%), followed by purchasing of consumer durables (24%) and spending on education (24%). Overall, it emerges that both in Uttar Pradesh and Bihar a large share of remittances received were directly spent on attaining basic needs.

Table 5 shows the results of a logistic regression describing the determinants of the utilization of remittances (as first priority) by the remittance receiving households in Uttar Pradesh and Bihar. Dependency on remittances for purchasing of food items reduces constantly for households climbing the ladder of MPCE. Households falling under rich quintile category were found spending more on non-food items like education, saving and buying of other assets. Among different social groups, the likelihood of spending more on health and less on food was higher for 'other castes' compared to the SC/ST households. Further in different religious groups, it has been noticed that Muslims are more likely to spend on food items and less likely to spend on education than Hindus. It is clear from the analysis that the first priority of use of remittances both in Uttar Pradesh and Bihar is on food consumption. This indicates that a large proportion of migrants from Uttar Pradesh and Bihar belong to those population groups merely surviving on subsistence at the place of origin.

Table 3 Determinants of remittances in Uttar Pradesh and Bihar, India, 2007–08

Covariates	Uttar Pradesh	Bihar
	Model I	Model II
Head of household		
Male®	1.00	1.00
Female	9.71*	10.06*
Place of residence		
Rural®	1.00	1.00
Urban	0.71*	0.80*
MPCE		
Lowest®	1.00	1.00
Lower	1.21*	1.44*
Medium	1.68*	1.71*
Higher	1.99*	2.26*
Highest	2.65*	2.41*
Social group		
Scheduled caste/tribe®	1.00	1.00
Others backward classes	1.06	0.93
Others	1.24*	1.07
Religion		
Hindu®	1.00	1.00
Muslim	1.52***	1.04
Others	1.13	0.96
Land possession		
Less than 1 ha®	1.00	1.00
1–4 ha	1.42*	1.17***
More than 4 ha	1.02	1.82
Household size		
Less than 5®	1.00	1.00
5 and More than 5	1.40*	1.34*
Region		
North Upper Ganga Plains®	1.00	–
Central Uttar Pradesh	0.9	–
Eastern Uttar Pradesh	1.30*	–
Southern Uttar Pradesh	0.84	–
Southern Upper Ganga Plains	0.89	–
Northern Bihar®	–	1.00
Central Bihar	–	0.96*
Pseudo R2	0.1319	0.1287
Log Likelihood	−6236.8814	−4443.073
N	12,602	8764

Notes Significance level—*$p < 0.01$, **$p < 0.05$, ***$p < 0.1$, ®Reference category, Model I (dependent variable: HH received remittances = 1, HH received not remittances = 0

Table 4 Utilization of remittances by remittances receiving household in Uttar Pradesh and Bihar, 2007–08

	Uttar Pradesh		Bihar	
	First priority	Second priority	First priority	Second priority
Food	62.6	4.6	69.3	2.0
Education	2.7	41.1	0.4	24.3
Household durable	0.8	14.5	0.8	24.6
Marriage	2.8	1.0	2.3	1.0
Health	10.2	21.9	6.5	15.4
Other consumer durables	13.7	10.5	9.9	24.4
Improving housing condition	2.4	2.7	3.1	3.3
Repayment of debt	2.1	1.8	0.9	2.2
Financing capital	0.4	0.5	0.3	0.7
Entrepreneurial activity	0.0	0.1	0.1	0.1
Saving	0.7	0.9	0.4	1.7
Other	1.6	0.5	6.0	0.4
Total	100	100	100	100

Source Authors' own calculation based on NSS, 2007–08

3.2 Remittances and Poverty

Table 6 presents an estimated propensity score for all cases (households). The mean propensity score was 0.25 and 0.26 with standard deviation of 0.17 and 0.18 for Uttar Pradesh and Bihar, respectively. The range of common support between the remittance receiving households and non-receiving households was high which ranged from 0.06 to 0.80 for Uttar Pradesh and Bihar, respectively. Remittance receiving and non-receiving households with propensity scores outside the common support were not considered for the analysis. The balancing property of propensity score matching is satisfied at the significance level 0.03 for both states.

The average exposure effect (AEE) of remittances on poverty reduction is given by exposure coefficient in Table 7. The results show a significant positive exposure effect (AEE) of -0.062 and -0.11 respectively for Uttar Pradesh and Bihar, i.e. 6.2 and 11.0% lower poverty level among remittances receiving households from all sources (i.e. domestic as well as international remittances) than that of matched control group households respectively in both Uttar Pradesh and Bihar. Nevertheless, there seems to be no effect of remittances from all sources (domestic as well as international remittances) in poverty level when the sample is restricted to urban areas in Bihar. Further, result also shows that domestic remittances compared to international remittances play a significant role in reducing poverty at the household level in Uttar Pradesh compared to Bihar. However, on the whole the result confirms

Table 5 Determinants of utilization of remittances (as first priority) by remittance receiving households, 2007–08

Covariates	Uttar Pradesh		Bihar	
	Food	Health	Food	Health
	Model I	Model II	Model III	Model IV
Head of household				
Male®	1.00	1.00	1.00	1.00
Female	2.35*	0.43*	4.24*	0.46*
Place of residence				
Rural®	1.00	1.00	1.00	1.00
Urban	1.17	0.52*	1.07	0.83
MPCE				
Lowest®	1.00	1.00	1.00	1.00
Lower	0.86	1.10	1.03	1.17
Medium	0.88	1.13	0.93	1.27
Higher	0.84	1.39	0.64**	1.58
Highest	0.48*	1.83**	0.34*	2.43**
Social group				
Scheduled caste/tribe®	1.00	1.00	1.00	1.00
Others backward classes	0.77**	1.40***	0.66*	1.50€
Others	0.56*	1.95*	0.57*	1.33
Religion				
Hindu®	1.00	1.00	1.00	1.00
Muslim	1.66*	1.08	1.21	0.86
Others	0.61	1.66	1.50	5.36
Land possession				
Less than 1 ha®	1.00	1.00	1.00	1.00
1–4 ha €	0.61*	1.13	0.39*	1.55 €
More than 4 ha	0.24*	0.97	0.05*	6.70*
Household size				
Less than 5®	1.00	1.00	1.00	1.00
5 and more than 5	0.75*	1.04	0.75**	1.57**
Pseudo R2	0.0707	0.0381	0.1197	0.0486
Log likelihood	−1930.8272	−954.92123	−1324.5892	−580.82326
N	3241		2354	

Notes Significance level—*$p < 0.01$, **$p < 0.05$, ***$p < 0.1$, ®Reference category, Model I and III (dependent variable: utilization of remittances by remittances receiving HH as food = 1, non-food = 0), Model II and IV (dependent variable: utilization of remittances by remittances receiving HH as Health = 1, Non-health = 0)

Table 6 Description of propensity scores in Uttar Pradesh and Bihar

	Uttar Pradesh	Bihar
Range of common support	[0.06–0.80]	[0.06, 0.80]
Mean of propensity score	0.25	0.26
Standard deviation	0.17	0.18
Significance of balancing property	0.03	0.03

Source Estimation based on NSS, 2007–08

Table 7 Propensity score matching estimators in Uttar Pradesh and Bihar

	Remittance receiving versus non-receiving			International remittances versus internal remittances			Internal remittances versus no-remittances receiving		
	Overall	Rural	Urban	Overall	Rural	Urban	Overall	Rural	Urban
Uttar Pradesh									
AEE	−0.062*	−0.068*	−0.048**	−0.046*	−0.058*	0.057	−0.052*	−0.059*	−0.035**
	(0.01)	(0.01)	(0.02)	(0.06)	(0.08)	(0.13)	(0.01)	(0.01)	(0.02)
Bihar									
AEE	−0.11*	−0.11*	−0.09	−0.06	−0.11	NA	−0.10*	−0.11*	−0.08*
	(0.01)	(0.01)	(0.03)	(0.06)	(0.06)	–	(0.01)	(0.01)	(0.03)

Notes Significance level—*$p < 0.01$, **$p < 0.05$, ***$p < 0.1$, bootstrapped standard error in parentheses; *NA* Number of cases not sufficient for propensity score matching

that the utilization of internal remittances has a significant impact in reducing poverty among both rural and urban households in the states of Uttar Pradesh and Bihar

4 Conclusion

The study shows that the utilization of remittances has significant impact on poverty reduction. The internal remittances sent by internal migrants are more effective in reducing poverty in relatively poor states like Uttar Pradesh and Bihar. An examination of the regional pattern of out-migration suggests that it is mainly a phenomenon in Eastern Uttar Pradesh and Northern Bihar. The results also show that internal and international remittances not only reshape the life chances of remittances receiving households, but also help in diversifying the economy. An examination of remittance receiving households by rural and urban residence suggests that rural area households received higher remittances compared to an urban area. Remittances income gives rural households the strength to absorb risks and shocks of catastrophic health, marriage expenditure and incidence of crop failures. In Bihar, higher use of remittances in a household for consumer durables and other durables may encourage rural industrialization through demand-side increase in local economy.

The logistic analysis shows that a significant number of Muslim households are economically dependent on remittances in Uttar Pradesh. However, there is no significant difference in remittances receiving households by religion in Bihar. The results of logistic regression on the utilization of remittances show that among the different social groups, there is higher likelihood of spending on health for 'other castes' compared to SC/ST groups. Further in different religious groups, it has been noticed that Muslims are more likely to spend on food consumption and less likely to spend on education than Hindus. The main priority of the utilization of remittances both in Uttar Pradesh and Bihar is household food consumption, and thus, it is imperative to say that large portions of migration from Uttar Pradesh and Bihar are of subsistence type.

The propensity score matching technique shows a positive role of remittances in poverty reduction and development at the household level. It also shows a positive effect on reducing poverty in both rural and urban areas. As international migration largely belongs to the comparatively better-off households, the role of international remittances in poverty reduction is expected to be ineffective as compared to internal remittances reaching to more poorer households. However, the role of international remittances in meeting higher order needs of households like education and healthcare expenditure cannot be denied. A suitable policy and programme leveraging remittances at the household level would be helpful in promoting development. It is up to the government to make a strong migration and remittance management policy to get the maximum benefit out of it.

Appendix

Out-migration rate (per 1000 population) and remittances receiving households in Uttar Pradesh and Bihar, India

		Interstate out Migration rate	Emigration rate	% of remittances receiving HH (last one year)
		Migration rate per 1000 population*		
India	1992–93	8.3	1.4	2.8
	2007–08	15.3	2.3	9.2
Uttar Pradesh	1992–93	12.6	0.5	4.3
	2007–08	28.3	1.5	14.3
Bihar	1992–93	27.7	1.0	9.7
	2007–08	35.3	1.1	18.3

Source Estimated based on NSS 1993 and NSS 2007–08
Notes *Migration rate in the last 5 years at that time of survey

References

Adams, R. H. (1991). *The effects of international remittances on poverty, inequality, and development in rural Egypt* (Vol. 86). Washington: International Food Policy Research Institute.

Adams, R. H., & Cuecuecha, A. (2013). The impact of remittances on investment and poverty in Ghana. *World Development, 50,* 24–40.

Adams Jr, R. H., Cuecuecha, A., & Page, J. (2008). The impact of remittances on poverty and inequality in Ghana. In *World Bank Policy Research Working Paper Series, Vol 2008.*

Adams, R. H., & Page, J. (2005). Do international migration and remittances reduce poverty in developing countries? *World Development, 33*(10), 1645–1669.

Ali, I., & Bhagat, R. B. (2016). Emigration and impact of utilisation of remittances at household level in India: A propensity score matching approach. *Social Science Spectrum, 2*(1), 8–19.

de Haan, A. (1999). Livelihoods and poverty: The role of migration-a critical review of the migration literature. *The Journal of Development Studies, 36*(2), 1–47.

De Haas, H. (2007). *Remittances, migration and social development: A conceptual review of the literature.* Social Policy and Programme Development Paper No. 34, United Nations Research Institute for Social Development, Geneva.

Dey, S. (2014). Impact of remittances on poverty at origin: A study on rural households in India using covariate balancing propensity score matching. *Migration and Development.* https://doi.org/10.1080/21632324.2014.979022.

Fransen, S., & Mazzucato, V. (2014). Remittances and household wealth after conflict: A case study on urban Burundi. *World Development, 60,* 57–68.

Gupta, S., Pattillo, C. A., & Wagh, S. (2009). Effect of remittances on poverty and financial development in Sub-Saharan Africa. *World Development, 37*(1), 104–115.

Gustafsson, B., & Makonnen, N. (1993). Poverty remittances in Lesotho. *Journal of African Economies, 2*(1), 49–73.

Jimenez-Soto, E. V., & Brown, R. P. (2012). Assessing the poverty impacts of migrants' remittances using propensity score matching: The case of Tonga*. *Economic Record, 88*(282), 425–439.

Lachaud, J. P. (2007). HIV prevalence and poverty in Africa: Micro-and macro-econometric evidences applied to Burkina Faso. *Journal of Health Economics, 26*(3), 483–504.

López-Videla, B., & Machuca, C. E. (2014). The effects of remittances on poverty at the household level in Bolivia: a propensity score matching approach. *Políticas Públicas, 2*(1), 7–22.

National Sample Survey Organisation (NSSO). (1993). In *Housing condition and migration survey. 49th round.* New Delhi: Ministry of Statistics and Programme Implementation, Government of India.

National Sample Survey Organisation (NSSO). (2008). *Migration in India* (Report No. 533(64/10.2/2), 2007–08). New Delhi: National Sample Survey Organization, Ministry of Statistics and Programme Implementation, Government of India, Retrieved March 2011 from http://www.mospi.gov.in/mospi_nsso_report_pubn.htm.

Rosenbaum, P. R., & Rubin, D. B. (1983). The central role of the propensity score in observational studies for causal effects. *Biometrika, 70*(1), 41–55.

Spatafora, N. (2005). Two current issues facing developing countries. In *World economic outlook* A Survey by the Staff of the International Monetary Fund.

Stark, O., & Bloom, D. E. (1986). The new economics of labor migration. *The American Economic Review, 75*(2), 173–178.

Stark, O., Taylor, J. E., & Yitzhaki, S. (1988). Migration, remittances and inequality: A sensitivity analysis using the extended Gini index. *Journal of Development Economics, 28*(3), 309–322.

Sikder, M. J. U., & Ballis, P. H. (2013). Remittances and life chances: A study of migrant households in rural Bangladesh. *Migration and Development, 2*(2), 261–285.

Tumbe, C. (2012). Migration persistence across the twentieth century India. *Migration and Development, 1,* 87–112.

World Bank. (2004). *Global development finance.* Washington: The World Bank.

World Bank. (2008). *Migration and remittances fact book 2008.* Washington, DC: The World Bank.

World Bank. (2011). *Migration and remittances factbook*. Washington: The World Bank.
World Bank. (2014). *Migration and remittances data*. Washington: The World Bank.

Imtiyaz Ali Ph.D. research scholar from International Institute from International Population Sciences and, Public health Consultant, IQVIA Consulting and Information Services Pvt. Ltd., Delhi. His research interest include international migration, remittances and development, demography and public health. He has served as consultant to the IQVIA India in various projects. He is well versed with working on large scale data handling, sampling, quantitative methods, statistical software and analysis.

R. B. Bhagat is working as Professor and Head, Department of Migration and Urban Studies, International Institute for Population Sciences (Deemed to be University), Mumbai, India. His research areas include—migration, urbanization and environment; Demography, ethnicity and politics. He has published 5 books and 55 research articles in the leading international and national journals like GENUS, Asian Population Studies, Population and Environment; Singapore Journal of Tropical Geography, Asian Profile, International Journal of Anthropology, Asia Pacific Population Journal, Asian and Pacific Migration Journal and about a dozen of articles in Economic and Political Weekly. He has been associated with the IUSSP Working Group on Urbanisation during 2001-2003. He has been a member on the IUSSP panel on Demography of Armed Conflict, 2006-10. He was Co-ordinator of the Centre for Environmental Information System (ENVIS Centre) on Population and Environment at IIPS funded by the Ministry of Environment and Forests, Government of India. He has been consultant and expert invited by UNESCO, UNICEF, Ministry of Human Resources, International Organisation of Migration (IOM), United Nations (Population Division) and other national/international organizations. Currently, he is a co-ordinating lead author of migration chapter of Hindukush Himalayan Monitoring Programme (HIMAP) under the aegis of International Centre for Integrated Mountain Development (ICIMOD), Kathmandu. His recent book entitled "Climate change, vulnerability and migration" is published by Rutledge 2018 (jointly with Irudaya Rajan). Apart from research work, he is engaged in teaching and guiding research work of students doing M.Phil and Ph.D. in population studies related to the areas of migration, urbanization and environment.

Violation of Civil Rights, Atrocities and Deprivation

G. C. Pal

Abstract The incidence of denial of basic rights to and atrocities against Scheduled Castes (SCs) on account of the low caste identity has been a common phenomenon across the country. This clearly reflects on the convoluted connection between social identities and social relations. There are certain States that have a dubious distinction of being home to the highest number of such human rights violations. Given the changed socio-political context and caste dynamics of the State of Uttar Pradesh (U.P.), over last two decades, the violation of civil rights and perpetration of caste-based atrocities against SCs have raised many questions on the role of state machinery. While it is important to promote an understanding of the linkages between sociopolitical conditions and enforcement of the laws on the issue of human rights in the state, it is also critical to explore the implications of human rights violations on the overall development of the SCs or lower caste groups. This article reflects on the patterns of violation of civil rights and atrocities against SCs in U.P. with a focus on the responses of state administration and its potential impact on socio-economic conditions of the groups. Evidence is drawn from various sources that include data of the National Crime Record Bureau (NCRB), fact-finding reports of civil society organizations, media reports, state-level official documents, experiential account of human rights activists in the state and case studies. Results reveal a disturbing trend of commission of certain atrocities against SCs and perpetration of atrocities in a collective and organized manner. Another critical issue is that the political role of caste identity continues to define the social relationship amongst social groups in the state, and this very often creates a ground for confrontations between caste groups. While SCs start utilizing the public space due to the increasing social and political participation, these result in hostile attitudes amongst dominant caste groups towards them. The socio-economic power of dominant caste coupled with higher economic dependence among SC on them offer a disproportionate scope for perpetrating atrocities with impunity. Violation of civil rights and atrocities directly or indirectly restrict

G. C. Pal (✉)
Indian Institute of Dalit Studies, D-11/1, Road no. 4,
Andrews Ganj, New Delhi 110049, India
e-mail: gcpal@dalitstudies.org.in

© Springer Nature Singapore Pte Ltd. 2019
R. P. Mamgain (ed.), *Growth, Disparities and Inclusive Development in India*,
India Studies in Business and Economics,
https://doi.org/10.1007/978-981-13-6443-3_9

the opportunities for social and work participation. All these increase the feeling of social insecurity amongst SCs, making it difficult to realize many of their hopes.

Keywords Civil rights · Crimes · Atrocities · Deprivation · PoA act · Access to justice

1 Introduction

In India, the issue of lack of access to civil rights amongst the historically marginalized sections like Scheduled Castes (SCs) and Scheduled Tribes (STs) has been a major concern, especially in the context of the national agenda on inclusive development. Despite the presence of a wide array of human rights laws and institutions, human rights abuses in the form of discrimination, violence, and atrocities against them based on their group identities continue unabated, and even are on the rise in many parts of the country. More specifically, although comprehensive legislations such as the Protection of Civil Rights (PCR) Act, 1976, and the Scheduled Castes and Scheduled Tribes (Prevention of Atrocities) (PoA) Act, 1989, later on amended as the PoA Amendment Act, 2015 enunciate strategies and punishments to counter civil rights violations, these socially marginalized groups still remain vulnerable to various forms of discrimination and atrocities. It often accentuates deprivation of public resources and services to them having significant consequences on their socioeconomic development. Given the fact that atrocities in rural areas have strong roots in the age-old practice of caste-based discrimination, failure of the state machinery to effectively implement the laws for curbing these atrocities cannot be ignored.

Although many factors are attributed for the atrocities, in recent years, greater consciousness amongst SCs in particular about their rights due to the changed sociopolitical scenario have, ironically, created more social conditions for such atrocities. Still the norms of the traditional caste system continue to govern the thought process and behaviour of the dominant caste groups; and the SCs continue to be at the receiving end of socio-economic discrimination and atrocities. The complex sociopolitical dynamics occurring at the state/local level also play a significant role in such actions. The problem of violation of rights and atrocities against SCs therefore also needs to be situated in a specific sociopolitical context, for specific interventions.

This paper examines the overall patterns and trends of caste-based atrocities in the state of Uttar Pradesh (U.P.), the linkage between sociopolitical conditions and the implementation of the legislation on atrocities, the responses of the administration and judicial in the state, and the functioning of monitoring bodies and other key stakeholders dealing with caste atrocities and other human rights violations. The approach to understand various aspects of caste-based atrocities has been both quantitative and qualitative in nature. Evidence is drawn from various sources that include data on crimes provided by the National Crime Record Bureau (NCRB) for the period from 2002 (in view of the division of the erstwhile state of Uttar Pradesh in 2000, and assuming a clear-cut database on crimes for the new state from 2002 onwards) to 2015, around 450 media reports (both national and regional) on caste atrocities that occurred in the state in the years 2011 and 2012, over 45 fact-finding reports of various human rights organizations in the state, experiential accounts of about 40 human rights activists from 30 organizations in the state working on the issues of atrocities, a dozen of case studies based on field study, and other official documents obtained through the filing of RTIs. Some indicators for analysis included the nature and forms of atrocities, causes of the atrocities, gender dimension of the victims, the sub-castes of the victims and accused, sociopolitical context of the incidence of atrocities, responses of the state machinery, problem areas in the implementation of the laws on atrocities. The challenges faced by the victims in the process of justice delivery, and the larger impact of atrocities on the 'well-being' of the victim survivors, and their families and communities were also explored. Thus, evidence froms a wide range of sources provided insights into various critical issues related to violation of civil rights and atrocities in U.P. that have larger policy implications.

2 The Sociopolitical Context

The state of U.P. has the largest SC population in the country. Although the Other Backword Class (OBC), as a social group constitutes the highest proportion of the state's total population, the proportion of SCs is higher than other major socio-religious groups. The existence of caste complexities in the state can further be understood from the very fact that apart from the upper castes, there are as many as 66 subgroups belonging to the SCs and another 79 subgroups designated as OBC groups (Srivastava 2012). Although there has been a major improvement in the social status of the SCs in the state (Prasad et al. 2010), development amongst the SCs has, however, been lopsided. 'Over the past one decade, the *Jatavs*, who have become economically well-off as compared to most of the other sub-caste groups, are emerging as an assertive caste, and have stood up to the oppressive forces in the state' (Parashar 2011). With the presence of several caste groups in mainstream society, a strong caste tradition especially in the rural areas is deeply embedded in the social fabric of the state. Caste-based hierarchy also largely governs the social relationships between various caste groups in the state. Amongst other states, U.P. has the dubious distinction of being home to the highest incidence of atrocities against SCs, and it substantially contributes to the national atrocity rates.

Another precarious issue is that caste has also been a dominant factor in the state politics. Unlike many other states, caste-identity-based politics is more explicit. The political role of caste identity also continues to define the social relationship amongst social groups. As Srivastava (2012) observes, 'In U.P., people don't cast their vote, they vote their caste'. The leaders representing the interests of different caste groups also symbolize their aspirations. This sometimes permeates enough confidence amongst the suppressed caste groups to assert their identity. While the support base of caste groups plays an important role in terms of political power in the state, it also creates the grounds for further dividing of the people a caste configuration.

A matter of serious concern is that the persistent use of caste in different political categories not only serves to exacerbate tensions between various caste groups but also forces one group to see another as nothing more than a competitor for patronage and resources (Mahmudabad 2012). This results in increasing resentment and alienation amongst different caste groups. The manipulation of caste identities for political agenda sometimes also fuels inter-community antagonism. With caste politics trying to capitalize on the support of different caste groups, there has been an increasing trend of caste groups asserting themselves in various spheres of life and harbouring hostile attitudes towards other caste groups. All these lead to increasing violations of civil rights and atrocities against the lower castes (Kumar 2008; Rawat 2011). Thus, with the issue of caste domination prevailing both in social and political life in U.P., conflicts between social groups continue to be on the rise.

Nonetheless, the rise in caste-based atrocities in the state reflects negatively not only on the effectiveness of the existing legislations but also on the accountability of the state machinery to protect basic rights of all sections of population and to promote social security. In last two decades, the increase in caste atrocities in the state in relation to its sociopolitical contexts has raised many questions regarding the role of the leadership and state machinery to deal with atrocities. Therefore, it remains critical to understand the patterns of civil rights violations and atrocities against SCs in the state, and the responses of the state machinery in dealing with them.

3 Crimes and Atrocities: Patterns and Trends

The incidents of atrocities against SCs are officially registered in all states and reported regularly. The official figures, for many valid reasons, are however believed to be an underestimation of the actual magnitude of the atrocities. Notwithstanding the limitation, official data available from the NCRB helps in promoting an understanding of the patterns and potential trends of the atrocities. The analysis considers the data spanning 14 years (i.e. during the period 2002–2015) on the incidence of overall crimes against SCs, crimes registered under the PCR Act (indicating violation of civil rights) and the PoA Act (referred as 'atrocities'), rates (indicating incidence per lakh SC population) of overall crimes and PoA crimes, the various forms of crimes committed against SCs, and the disposal of crimes by the police and the courts. The analysis of patterns and trends of crimes and atrocities against SCs in U.P. is situated on the corresponding scenario observed at the national level.

3.1 Overall Patterns of the Total Crimes and Atrocities

Data reveals that, during the period 2002–15, on an average, more than six thousand crimes were annually registered in U.P. This constituted about one-fifth of the total crimes recorded in India during the corresponding period. The number of registered crimes in U.P. showed an increase in recent years, a trend similar to the national crime figures (Fig. 1a, b). Despite the enactment of the PCR and PoA Acts to curb the denial of civil rights to SCs through discriminatory practices and atrocities against them, the perpetration of several forms of discrimination and atrocities continues to persist.

But the registered PCR crimes do not provide a correct reflection of the actual discriminatory practices, which is normally attributed to the enactment of the PoA Act, following which many cases of atrocities on SCs are being increasingly booked under this Act. Notably, no case was registered under the PCR Act from 2010 onwards although there were 61 registered cases in 2009. This raises question on the relevance of the PCR Act in the present context. However, during 2002–15, of the total number of registered PCR crimes in India, on an average, about 13% was registered in U.P. The percentage share of PoA crimes in U.P. to the total number of PoA crimes in India indicated that on an average, about one-fifth of the PoA crimes in India were registered in U.P. annually during the period 2002–15. This was similar to that of the percentage share for the total crimes.

While the PCR and PoA crimes together constituted on an average 44.5% of the total crime in India during the period 2002–15, they constituted 45.6% of the total crimes in U.P. during the corresponding period, showing almost a similar pattern (Fig. 2). But during 2002–09, the percentage share of the PCR and PoA crimes to the total crimes in U.P. was relatively higher as compared to the all-India figure. Although the trends of the registered PCR and PoA crimes in U.P did not show a definite pattern, there has been a surprising upsurge during 2014 and 2015. Almost

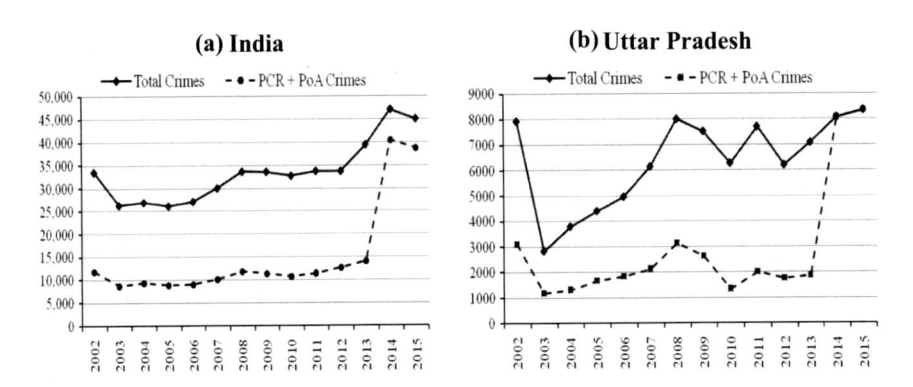

Fig. 1 Patterns and trends of the total crimes and PCR and PoA crimes together against SCs in India and U.P. during 2002–15. **a** India, **b** Uttar Pradesh. *Note* Given the non-registration of PCR crimes in recent years, PCR and PoA crimes are combined. *Source* Based on data, 'Crime in India', National Crime Record Bureau, Government of India

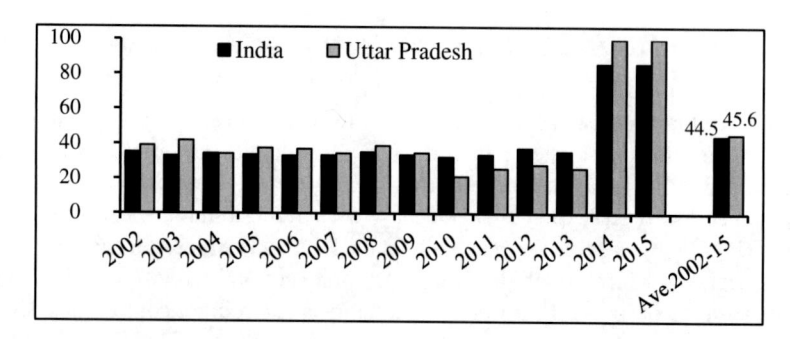

Fig. 2 Percentage share of PCR and PoA crimes together to the total crimes against SCs in India and U.P. *Source* Based on data, 'Crime in India', National Crime Record Bureau, Government of India

all the crimes against SCs were registered under the PCR and PoA Act (Fig. 1b). While it was lower than the national average during 2010–13, it was considerably higher in the year 2014 and 2015 (Fig. 2).

It might be noted that in some states with higher concentration of SC population such as U.P., Rajasthan, Andhra Pradesh, Bihar, Madhya Pradesh, Karnataka and Orissa; the percentage share of the total crimes to that of the all-India crimes had been higher than the percentage share of the state population. Further, like U.P., states such as Bihar, Karnataka, Orissa and Himachal Pradesh had higher percentage share of registered PoA crimes than the national average, whereas it was found to be lower in Tamil Nadu, Gujarat and Maharashtra, Haryana, Punjab and West Bengal.

The number of registered crimes might not reflect realistically on the magnitude of crimes against SCs across states. An analysis of the rate of crimes against SCs across states indicates that the rate of crimes in U.P. was slightly less than the national rate for the overall crimes against SCs, but there was not much difference in the PoA crimes, particularly in 2014 and 2015 (Table 1). However, there are other states such as Andhra Pradesh, Bihar, Gujarat, Madhya Pradesh, Odisha and Rajasthan, which had considerably higher crime rate against SCs than the national crime rate. However, it is not the actual magnitude of crime but the nature of crimes committed and the access of victims to justice that have greater implications on the life of the victims.

3.2 Forms of Crimes

There are some major crimes listed under the Indian Penal Code (IPC) such as murder, rape, kidnapping and abduction, dacoity, robbery, arson, and physical hurt. The incidence of such crimes against SCs is, however, not uniform. According to the NCRB data, at all-India level, on an average, 3791 cases of physical hurt/assault, 1543 cases of rape, 673 cases of murder, 475 cases of kidnapping and abduction, and 212 cases of arson against the SCs were registered annually during the period

Table 1 Rate of registered crimes against Scheduled Castes in select states, 2012–15

States	Total crimes against SCs				PoA crimes against SCs			
	2012	2013	2014	2015	2012	2013	2014	2015
Andhra Pradesh	22.0	23.6	48.7	52.3	5.8	5.0	24.9	26.8
Bihar	29.1	40.6	47.6	38.9	26.8	33.7	47.5	38.0
Gujarat	25.2	29.2	27.7	25.7	5.3	5.2	26.4	24.8
Haryana	4.9	9.6	16.2	16.3	0.3	0.3	8.7	10.0
H Pradesh	7.5	8.6	7.1	5.5	4.8	4.7	6.5	5.3
Jharkhand	17.5	24.5	22.7	18.5	8.4	12.0	22.7	18.5
Karnataka	24.9	24.5	20.4	19.0	12.7	13.2	17.8	17.6
Kerala	26.7	24.9	26.8	24.7	2.2	2.4	23.4	22.9
Madhya Pradesh	25.4	26.0	36.6	36.9	0.0	0.0	29.0	31.3
Maharashtra	8.2	12.6	13.3	13.7	2.0	2.1	13.3	13.5
Orissa	31.5	36.1	31.5	32.1	27.0	24.8	23.1	25.3
Punjab	0.8	1.4	1.4	1.7	0.1	0.2	1.4	1.7
Rajasthan	45.5	53.0	65.7	57.3	0.9	0.9	55.1	48.4
Tamil Nadu	11.4	12.8	10.7	12.3	7.9	9.2	10.3	12.0
Uttar Pradesh	15.0	17.1	19.5	20.2	4.2	4.5	19.5	20.2
All India	16.7	19.6	23.4	22.3	6.2	6.9	20.0	19.2

Note The rate of crimes indicates incidence per lakh SC population based on Actual Census, 2011
Source 'Crime in India', National Crime Record Bureau, Government of India

2002–15. But the number of registered economic crimes against SCs like dacoity and robbery were relatively less.

In U.P. alone, the average numbers of physical hurt, rape, murder, kidnapping and abduction, arson, and dacoity and robbery cases were found to be 363, 322, 269, 222, 45 and 13, respectively. Over the period 2002–2015, changes in the various registered crimes have not been uniform. The numbers of rape and kidnapping and abduction cases indicated a significant increase, whereas the number of murder, arson, dacoity and robbery cases declined, particularly after 2007. The number of registered rape, kidnapping and abduction and physical assault cases in recent years has increased considerably.

The percentage share of various crimes in U.P. to the total number of crimes against SCs in India widely varied (Fig. 3). During the period 2002–15, on an average, about 47% of the total registered kidnapping and abduction cases against SCs in India, occurred in U.P. The percentage share of murder cases was also considerably high (at 40%). Amongst other crimes, the percentage share of rape and arson cases constituted about 21% each, whereas share of economic crimes such as dacoity and robbery, and physical hurt constituted relatively lower percentages (at about 12% and 10%, respectively).

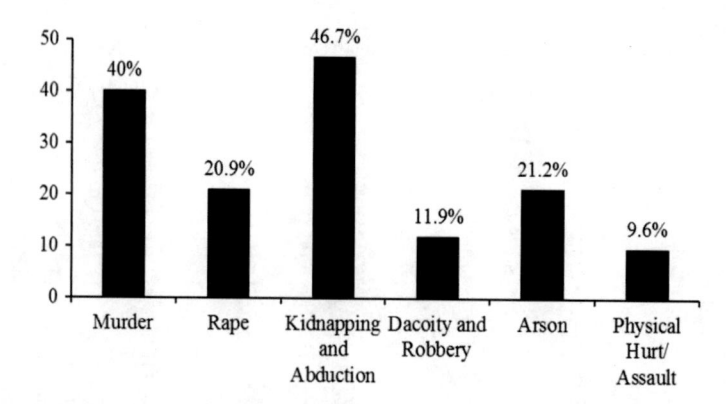

Fig. 3 Annual percentage share of various registered crimes against SCs in U.P. to total crimes in India during 2002–15. *Source* Based on data, 'Crime in India', National Crime Record Bureau, Government of India

The changes in the percentage share of various crimes against SCs in U.P. to the total crimes against SCs in India, however, showed a declining trend in murder, dacoity and robbery and arson cases. But for the kidnapping and abduction, it increased considerably while there was remarkable change in case of rape and physical assault. Thus, the matter of concern is that the state significantly contributed to the overall registered kidnapping and murder cases. Amongst the states, in recent years, U.P., Madhya Pradesh, Rajasthan and Bihar accounted for most of the serious crimes like murder, rape and kidnapping and abduction against SCs.

3.3 Disposal of Atrocity Cases and Delivery of Justice

The PoA Act Rule, 1995 and the PoA Amendment Act Rule, 2016 underlie specific provisions for the speedy disposal of crimes against SCs and ensuring justice to the victims. The disposal of cases in fact indicates the efficiency of state machinery in dealing with the crime cases. It mainly takes place at two levels—police and court. The state-level disposal rates available for the period 2002–13 along with the national rate are shown in Fig. 4. The national scenario on the disposal of crimes indicates that on an average, about one-fourth of the registered crimes against SCs remained pending for investigation in the police station at the end of each year over the period 2002–13. On an average, about 91% of the total valid cases in India were chargesheeted during the same period. In U.P., the average pendency rate at police stations was found to be less than half of the national figure. However, the pendency rate was higher for the PoA crimes than the overall crimes against SCs. The chargesheet rate in U.P. was lower than the national average, and showed a decline after 2005.

Unlike the pendency rate in the investigation by the police, the pendency rate in the courts was quite high. At the national level, on an average, 81% of the cases remained pending for trial annually, and there has been no significant improvement in the pendency rate in the court over the years. In fact, in 2014 and 2015, it was higher than in all the previous years. The conviction rate, the key reflection on the delivery of social justice, on an average, was found to be about 29% for all the crimes against SCs. It was found to be lower in recent years (2012–15) as compared to the previous years (2007–11). In 2015, the conviction rate at the national level was recorded at 27.6%, which was less than the annual average over last 14 years.

The disposal rate by the court in U.P. indicated that the average pendency rate in the courts was found almost similar to that of the national rate. However, the pendency rate for the PoA crimes as compared to the overall crimes was higher across states, and it was distinctly higher in U.P. along with Madhya Pradesh and Rajasthan. Although the average charge-sheet rate in U.P. during 2002–13 was lower than the national charge-sheet rate, in U.P., the disposal rate by the court in terms of conviction rate indicated a better picture. In contrast to the national conviction rate for overall crimes against SCs, which was less than one-third of cases, it was found to be striking in U.P. During the period 2002–13, on an average, the accused were convicted in more than half of the cases that underwent trial. Notably, the conviction rate in the state increased in recent years. It reached the highest point of about 65% in 2010, though it slightly decreased in the following years. It is worth mentioning here that having recorded the highest number of cases of atrocities against SCs, the state of U.P. has also had the highest conviction rate over the years, remarkably higher than almost all the states in the country (Fig. 4).

The above analysis of overall crimes and atrocities against SCs in U.P. at macro-level indicates that over the years, the state has witnessed an increase in atrocities against SCs despite the enforcement of the laws for the protection of their rights. For this, the state also remains in the limelight on the issue of atrocities against SCs. Despite changes occurring in the sociopolitical sphere in the state, the persistence of atrocities against SCs shows the continued vulnerability of SCs to the oppressive behaviour of 'other' castes in the state. This calls for understanding the structural roots of caste-based atrocities and also the process of implementation of protective laws as well as the functioning of the implementing and monitoring agencies. In the following sections, the prominent causes of caste atrocities and the responses of the

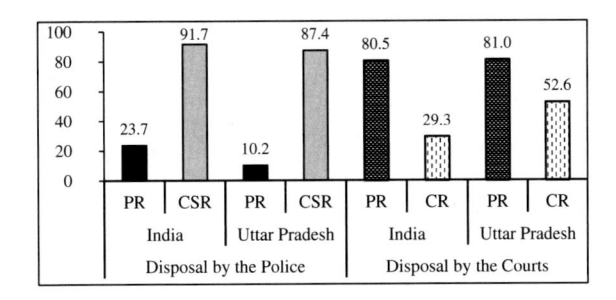

Fig. 4 Disposal of crimes against SCs by the police and courts. *Notes* PR = Pendency Rate, CSR = Charge-sheet Rate; CR = Conviction Rate. *Source* Based on data, 'Crime in India', National Crime Record Bureau, Government of India

state machinery to such human rights violations are examined based on field-level data collected from multiple sources. While an attempt is made to cross-examine the patterns of atrocities against SCs as reflected through the official data using the field data, the critical issues pertaining to the implementation of laws, monitoring of atrocity cases and overall impact of caste atrocities on the socio-economic development of SC victims are also highlighted for policy considerations at the state level.

4 Caste Atrocities: An Analysis at Micro-Level

This section delineates the major observations from around 450 cases of caste atrocities perpetrated against SCs in U.P. as reported by the national- and state-level print media pertaining to the years 2011 and 2012. The analysis revealed that nearly half of the reported cases were from 11 districts. Notwithstanding other limitations in the media reports, the predisposition of these districts to caste atrocities might not be contested. But the critical issue is that of the districts with a higher proportion of reported cases, a majority of them fall under the 20 atrocity-prone districts identified by the state government. These districts still witness a large number of atrocity cases despite the fact that special precautionary and preventive measures as per the PoA Act Rules 1995 have been implemented in these districts to ensure the effective implementation of the Act.

Another regional dimension is that some regions in the state exhibit the occurrence of a particular type of atrocity more frequently than others. As one senior human rights activist from U.P. says:

> In the state, land issues and damage of properties are common in [the] eastern part, murder and attempt to murder in [the] central part, physical assault in Bundelkhand and [the] western parts; whereas rape comes as the common form across [the] state. (Field Notes)

An analysis of the distribution of major atrocities across 11 districts with a higher number of reported cases indicated that in ten districts, rape and gang-rape were the most common forms of atrocities, besides physical assault. A higher number of murder cases were reported from six of these eleven districts, whereas kidnapping and abduction from two districts and caste slurs (harassment and humiliation) from four districts. The data also points out that the gender-specific atrocities in the form of rape, gang-rape and sexual harassment together constituted more than one-third of the total number of reported cases. In line with this, as reported:

> 45% of rape cases in U.P. in 2010 were against SCs. The rape cases accounted for about one-fifth of total number of rape cases over 2007–09. Although there was decline in the total number of rape cases in the state in 2010 as compared to 2009, the number of rape cases against Dalit (SC) women jumped to 54%. (Hindustan Times 2011)

Consistent with this, the analysis also showed that amongst the total number of victims of atrocities, only females were victims in 61% of the cases while only males were the victims in 30% of the cases, and in the remaining nine per cent of the cases, both males and females were victims. The data suggests that SC women are more vulnerable to caste atrocities. Moreover, the intersection of factors such as gender, class and age make the young (minor) SC girls the soft target of many atrocities, and they have to live under intense insecurity. Notwithstanding the fact that the causes behind the atrocities are normally understood properly only after the investigation, yet first-hand reports indicate that many of the accused committed sexual assault while taking advantage of the fact that the victim was alone at the time of the incident. The other major causes of the atrocities were related to caste discrimination, revenge and retaliation. Structural and cultural violence also continues to haunt illiterate women in a tradition-ridden society.

The ratio of victims and accused indicates that in a vast majority of cases individuals were the victims. Although the exact number of accused could not be identified in several media reports, still, a rough estimate from many cases indicated that the number of accused was higher than the victims. There are some sub-castes within the SCs that are more prone to atrocities than others, as reported, because of their awareness and assertion of rights. Amongst the accused, a larger proportion belonged to OBC. However, it might be mentioned that at the physical level a specific social group might be identified as accused but in many cases the real perpetrators of atrocities are 'others' (high castes) who with their strong social positions and power, use members of other groups to commit the crime, and later, play a role in getting the accused get scot-free.

The data also showed that many of the atrocities were committed in combination. Atrocities such as rape, murder, kidnapping and abduction were associated with other forms of atrocities either as antecedents or as consequents. For instance, 90% of the rape and gang-rape cases were associated with other forms of crime. Similar was the situation regarding cases of kidnapping, and abduction and murder. Very often, indirect violence is tacitly perpetrated on the victims in the form of harassment, humiliation, and mental torture, amongst other atrocities. These combined forms of atrocities often, in fact, complicate the process of justice delivery. Another critical issue is that atrocities against SCs have increasingly been collective, or organized in nature. For instance, in more than two-third cases more than one accused were involved in atrocities against either a single or more than one SC victim. In all such cases, any resistance from SCs is dealt with the perpetration of inhuman behaviour against them.

According to the NCRB data, U.P. has registered a steep rise in political murders in recent years. The analysis also highlights one of the most disturbing aspects of cases of atrocities, wherein people's elected representatives have been directly or indirectly involved in the perpetration of several heinous atrocities. In many cases, these people also thwart justice through manipulations and intimidation, often foisting false police cases against the victim survivors. There are also many horrifying stories of police atrocities, which have also been proved by competent authorities. Atrocities by persons in public services, as brought to the attention through the PoA Amendment Act 2015, also remain other critical issue, given their larger responsibilities towards society. Some of the cases of shameful instances of atrocities committed by people employed in public services include sexual assault by schoolteachers and officials in hospitals, caste abuse by government officials, amongst others. The matter of serious concern is that any sort of repressive behaviour by these perpetrators under the power nexus creates a sense of helplessness amongst SCs, and they are always at the risk of being the sufferers of atrocities committed by others.

5 Implementation of the Laws in the State: Gaps and Concerns

Given the overall scenario on the patterns of atrocities against SCs in U.P., it is important to understand whether the PoA Act has been enforced in true spirit by the state government, whether state machinery has implemented the law efficiently and effectively, and whether monitoring bodies have performed their duties properly. This section largely focuses on these issues through an analysis of official documents, fact-finding reports, experiential accounts of human rights activists working at grassroots level and a few case studies, and attempts to highlight the gaps in implementation of legislation and major concerns that would have immediate policy implications in the state. These issues are discussed in the following sections.

5.1 Diluting the Purpose of the PoA Act

An examination of the manner in which the implementation of the Act has been undertaken, since its inception, by the state government given the changes in the political scenario in U.P., clearly point that government actions on the implementation of law from time to time, have been dubious. For instance, despite the significance of the PoA Act (1989) for a caste-ridden state like U.P., it was adopted in the state only in 1995. Following the enactment of the Act, there were political parties who openly opposed the law. As a result, its implementation was kept in abeyance even though it had been formally adopted by the state government. In early 2000, although there was a shifting of political power, the situation became quite complex because of the coalition government. On account of a political compulsion, an attempt was made to dilute the proposed Act. This was evident from the declaration that any complaints lodged by SCs/STs would be considered only after verification of the facts, and cases of petty litigation would not be covered under the PoA Act, but would be dealt with under ordinary laws. This in fact provided a ground for the officials to reject many complaints. Despite the fact that the government had knowledge of atrocities against SCs, it still struggled to make any headway.

With the fall of government before completing its tenure due to political compulsions of coalition partners, the next stopgap government formed by the main opposition party moved one step further to kill the spirit of the Act. A circular against the PoA Act was issued outlining the misuse of the Act, and the need for careful preliminary investigation and examination of atrocity cases. With the end of term of that stopgap government, when the political party of the previous regime returned to power with full majority with an agenda of 'welfare for all', it proceeded to dilute the scope of the Act by declaring that the Act need not be imposed without investigation in crimes barring in the cases of murder and rape, reportedly to avoid social disharmony. But, the larger discontent amongst SCs against the leadership subsequently forced the government realize the consequences of the dilution of this Act, and the order issued earlier was withdrawn. As a result, many cases of atrocities got registered. This, however, did not go well with the high castes, who expressed their resentment as the party in power went against its earlier declared principle of 'society for all people'. The opposition party at that time made it an election plank and sought a review of this Act. In fact, it had a wide impact on the election campaign as it provided hope for the withdrawal of registered cases. On assuming power, that political party attempted to fulfil its promise related to atrocity cases. The same party went on to govern the state for a longer term.

Thus, if we look at the history of implementation of the PoA Act in 2000s, in particular it is clear that the purported implementation of the PoA Act unleashed a type of warfare in the state as conflicting views on the Act could not get it implemented in its true spirit.

5.2 *Responses of Implementing Agencies*

This section discusses the responses of various implementing agencies towards caste atrocities that play a vital role in the process of justice delivery based on the evidence derived from various sources—fact-finding reports, case studies, experiential accounts of human rights activists in the state, and other official documents obtained through RTIs. The analysis revolves around the issues of the registration of complaints, carrying out of the investigation, filing of charge sheets, court trials and monitoring related to atrocity cases. The data clearly revealed the carelessness and insensitive behaviour of law enforcement officials. In a vast majority of cases of atrocities, the police did not heed the requests of the victim(s) and also refused to accept the complaints written by the victims on one pretext or the other, rather forced them to compromise with the accused against their wishes. This is substantiated by the approach of many victims to higher authorities in the administration, human rights commissions and civil society organizations in the response to the refusal of the police to file FIRs. In many cases, the victims decided to highlight their plight in the media to get their FIRs registered. It nevertheless causes a lot of mental agony, financial loss, and hardship to the victims and their families. The available data from the cases dealt by human rights activists revealed that the problem pertaining to the 'refusal of the police to record the FIR' was reported by two-thirds of respondents. An equal proportion of respondents also claimed that the police exert undue pressure on the victim(s) to refrain from filing FIRs.

Following the registration of the FIRs, under some circumstances, attempt is made to dilute the evidence, either by registering under incorrect sections of the Act or through improper investigation. The officials in charge of registering cases tend to display a consistent unwillingness to register offences under the PoA Act. The responses of the human rights activists indicated that the investigating officer as per the PoA Act rule also fails to conduct the investigation; they rather send a lower-ranked officer to do so. Moreover, the investigation too is conducted as per whims and fancies of investigating officer, and the statements of the victims are hardly taken into account, the activists alleged. Victims encounter various problems such as non-receipt of a copy of FIR, dilution of charge sheet, incitement of the accused to harass the victims, attempts to change the statements of witnesses, deliberately delaying the completion of formalities, exertion of pressure to enter into a compromise, and refusing to record the statements of victims. As claimed by 48% of the respondents, the accused are given undue advantage by the submission of the charge sheets in an inordinately delayed manner. Such a situation approach inevitably creates a sense of insecurity and mistrust amongst the SCs in the legal and judicial system.

Following the submission of charge sheet at the court, the role of prosecutors becomes important in providing speedy justice to the victims. However, evidence from the macro-level data shows that in majority of cases, the cases are made to linger on, rendering the pendency rate in the courts significantly high. The micro-level evidence also substantiates this. This denies quick delivery of justice to the victims who suffer a lot both economically and psychologically. The responses of human rights activists showed that inordinate delay in settlement of case(s) was the main problem area during the court trial, in addition to the indifference of public prosecutors, intimidation by the accused, financial burden on the victims, and loss of livelihood due to repeated visits to the court.

The above evidence points that atrocity cases can be settled speedily and the victims ensured of justice only if the police personnel and public prosecutors work in close cooperation and coordination with the courts, and bring the perpetrators of crimes against the hapless SC victims to timely and effective justice. The sufferings of the victims thus do not end with the administrative dealings and but are extended to court. All these factors deprive many victims of atrocities of their rights to justice and also affect their livelihood pattern.

5.3 *Implementation Gaps*

The PoA Act Rules (1995) prescribe specific provisions and time frames for the effective implementation of the law under the criminal justice system, particularly at the administrative level. However, these provisions are not enforced due to the insensitive attitude and negligence of the law-implementing agencies. This often results in the delay of the delivery of justice, and persistent suffering and harassment for the victims. It is not that the FIR is not registered immediately, the arrest of the accused is delayed and the investigation is either delayed or is not conducted properly as per the law. An analysis of about 45 fact-finding reports and a dozen of case studies indicated that in 15% of cases there was a delay in registration of cases within the stipulated time. In 11% of the cases, this was done after two days of the occurrence of the incident. The data of course suggests that there is 'not much delay' in registering of a formal complaint in the police station. But the critical question is whether, as per the law, all the FIRs are registered immediately after the complaints are made. The gap between the incident and the FIR showed that in about half of the total cases, the FIR was registered within 24 hours of the occurrence of the incident while in another 25% of the cases, it was registered within two-to-four days, and in the remaining one-fourth of the cases, it was after four days. Even in five per cent of the cases, the FIR was registered after ten days of the incident whereas in eight per cent of the cases, it was registered after fifteen days.

Similarly, the data on the gap between FIR and arrest of accused indicated that in less than one-third of the cases, the offender was arrested immediately after the FIR. Even in 64% of cases, the offender was arrested after two days. Amongst the delayed cases of arrest, while in 36% of the cases, the arrest of offender was made after five days, in about 30% of the cases, the arrest was made after ten days and in 15% of the cases, the arrest was made after twenty days, while in nine per cent of the cases, the arrest was made after one month. Another issue is the time of the investigation. Data obtained from fact findings and cases studies revealed that while in about half the cases, the investigation started immediately after the FIR, in 22% of the cases, it started after two weeks of filing of the FIR. This inordinate delay in investigation has larger implications not only for the submission of investigation reports and further charge sheets but also for the victims who face relentless pressure from the accused to compromise before the charge sheet is filed.

5.4 Responses of District- and State-Level Monitoring Bodies

As per the PoA Act Rules, different committees constituted at district and state levels should review the status of the atrocities and monitor the functioning of the state machinery periodically. The functioning and performance of these committees are also reviewed by a high-powered vigilance and monitoring committee constituted by the state government. At the district level, the District Vigilance and Monitoring Committee (DVMC) through quarterly meetings, is to review the implementation of the provisions of the Act and ensure that the relief and rehabilitation measures are provided to the victims. An examination of the functioning of these committees using the minutes of proceedings of 24 such meetings held during the year 2011 (received from several districts through the filing of RTIs), clearly showed that majority of the DVMC meetings are not held regularly (quarterly). While in many cases, two meetings appeared to be held during the same quarter; in few other cases, two meetings were held during two different halves of the year. Further, the attendance of the members, the agenda of the discussions, and the outcomes of the meetings indicated a lot of discrepancies. For instance, in a majority of the cases, there was a huge discrepancy between the actual members in the committee and the members who attended. Similarly, all the meetings did not focus on the critical issues pertaining to the district-level atrocities. For instance, in one-third of the meetings, issues related to overall district welfare programmes and development work (for example, MNERGS, BPL, drinking water projects, TSC, road repairing, PHC and school building construction, utilization of MP fund, etc.) were taken up for discussion. While there were only two meetings, which dealt with the achievements and shortfalls pertaining to the implementation of the PoA Act, there are some others where there was a discussion on compensations given to the victims of atrocities. Thus, with a few exceptions, the DVMC meetings, by and large, do not focus on the critical issues that need to be addressed urgently, leaving aside the fact that in many districts, the DVMC meetings are not organized for the purpose as per the law.

Like the DVMC, the State Vigilance and Monitoring Committee (SVMC), as per the rules, is supposed to review the status of atrocities in the state periodically. But, with many loopholes at district-level monitoring, expectedly, the outcome of the SVMC remains far from satisfactory. This was reflected from the discussions in one state-level meeting convened by the Director General Prosecution (official data obtained through filing of RTIs), indicating several gaps in the implementation of the law in various districts. A review by the DGP pointed out that the implementation of various provisions under the law is not taken seriously by officials at the district level; hence, there is the poor implementation of the provisions under the PoA Act.

The above discussion indicates that given the intensity of the atrocity cases in U.P., loopholes in the implementation of the laws on atrocities, the SCs are left with very little choices for self-protection. Their social and economic disabilities further add to their oppression. Keeping in mind the basic rights of the victims, it is important that the state authority periodically and critically reviews the procedural defects that defeat the purpose of enactment of the law.

6 Civil Rights Violation, Atrocities and Development

Is there any link between increased civil rights violations and atrocities, and socio-economic conditions of lower castes? Theoretically, there could be two schools of thought. First, historically marginalized groups like SCs hold a lower economic position. They are more likely to increase their economic dependence on dominant caste groups, and in turn, the vulnerability to oppression, exploitation and violence. On the contrary, an increase in their socio-economic position may reduce such behaviour as a result of an increased ability to defend themselves against any offences by the high castes with greater confidence, improved bargaining power and investment in better security measures. At the same time, there could be an increase in the incidence of caste-based atrocities with increased assertions by lower castes on their rights, and simultaneously perceived threat by high caste groups to their established caste-based social positions. The question therefore remains, 'which of these conjectures dominate in the context of caste atrocities in U.P.?' It is a fact that the relationship of civil rights violations and atrocities against lower castes and socio-economic development remain under-researched though there is a numerous literature on these human rights violations.

However, a limited number of studies in recent time have looked into this issue and given some explanations. At the practical level, the violation of civil rights and atrocities can directly or indirectly limit the opportunities for social and economic participation, depriving SCs their rights to public resources, resulting in adverse consequences at social, economic, and psychological levels. In the cases of heinous crimes like murder or an assault leading to the physical disability of an earning member of a Dalit family, the family also has to overcome the huge challenge of economic loss. The socio-economic impact of human rights violations against SC women could be higher. This is likely to not only increase their vulnerability to such acts outside the home but also deny their rights to freedom and security of life (Aloysius et al. 2006), thereby hampering their social and work-related participation. Given that the higher proportion of victims of atrocities in U.P. are SC women, and SCs have high economic dependence on high-caste employers, lack of women participation in outside work due to social insecurity and fear of exploitation is more likely to limit the means of livelihood.

Another serious social impact of incidence of heinous atrocities, particularly cases of rape, is manifested in the form of prolonged social tension and disharmony within the community. Often, the social boycott of families of SC victims and their communities have had a tremendous adverse impact on their lives. As Human Rights Watch Report (1999) observes, '…SC community is collectively penalized for individual transgressions through social boycotts. For most SCs in rural India who earn less than a subsistence living as agricultural labourers, a social boycott may mean destitution and starvation.'

There are many recorded instances of abuse and assault of SCs by the high castes when the former dare to challenge the social order. The manifestations of ruined relationships are seen in the denial of or restricted access to the opportunities and resources to the assertive groups. Protest against oppressive behaviour is often thwarted through increasing social boycotts from social and economic life. Thus, due to the interface of social structure and economic development, it has greater implications for social life and human development. The frosty social relationship, or social boycott, or forced migration, impinge upon daily lives of the targeted group mainly in economic spheres. There is a definite cyclic relationship between caste atrocities, social exclusion and development (Pal 2015). Caste atrocities deprive SC victims of fulfilling their basic needs and affect their morale, which in turn trap them into social exclusion having a bearing on poor socio-economic conditions; and accentuating the conditions for vulnerability to exploitation and further atrocities.

It is not that atrocities have implications on development of victims, the sociology of crimes suggests that with the changes in social structure the rate of atrocities at the local level can be an outcome in relation to other socio-economic and developmental indicators of the population in the area. A few studies have touched on this issue. In the early 1990s, the study by Oldenburg (1992) using the district-level data for U.P. to show that there is a negative correlation between the incidence of murders and the female–male ratio in the population. Similarly, Dreze and Khera (2000) examined the relation between crime rates (murder) and the social composition of the population, and indicated that districts with a higher proportion of SC or ST population register higher rate of murder cases. Literacy was also found to have a significant negative correlation with violence, lending support to the hypothesis that education exercises a moderating influence on criminal violence (Dreze and Khera 2000; Bhatnagar 1990). In a recent study, Sharma (2015) used official district-level crime data in U.P. to show a positive association between crimes and expenditure of SCs/STs vis-à-vis the upper castes. In specific terms, a widening gap in expenditures between lower and upper castes is associated with a decrease in crimes, particularly the violent crimes. Moreover, this relationship was on account of changes in the upper castes' economic well-being rather than changes in the economic position of the SCs/STs. The relative position of SCs in economic position thus not only reflects on inter-caste equality, but also has consequences on inter-group relationships to cause deprivation.

7 Conclusions and Policy Implications

What makes the state of U.P. distinct with regard to the issues of civil rights violations and atrocities against SCs? It is clear that despite significant social, economic and political transformation, caste hierarchies continue to remain deeply entrenched in the state, and fraught caste relations often result in atrocities against SCs. Although the overall registered crimes against SCs in the state have come down in recent years, still, the state exhibits a higher percentage of PoA crimes than the national average. A higher incidence of atrocities is reported from a majority of the identified atrocity-prone districts of the state, despite special measures implemented over the years.

The issue of concern is that in recent years, the state still accounts for a large proportion of serious crimes like murder, rape and kidnapping and abduction against the SCs. Further, SC women, particularly girls are more vulnerable to sexual abuse, and multiple forms of atrocities. Although, the 'vulnerability' to atrocities increases with lower representation of SC population in the locality/village, in many cases SCs also suffer from the oppressive behaviour of the high-caste groups despite their higher representation.

The evident gaps in the implementation of the SC/ST (PoA) Act in U.P. call for specific attention. The changes in the state's political scenario over the years have not led to enforcement of the Act in true spirit. The political dimensions of the implementation of the Act could be understood from the changes in the state leadership, and the rule of a coalition government and its political compulsions. Because of the constant review of the Act, it has failed to act as a forceful deterrent to curb atrocities. There has also been a wide range of gaps in the functioning of the criminal justice system, despite specific rules laid down for the effective implementation of the Act. The sloppiness of law enforcement agencies causes victims mental agony and other hardships in the process of seeking justice. Evidence also indicates gaps in the monitoring of the implementation of laws. Although the conviction rate in the state has been impressive, yet the state machinery has failed to prevent the occurrence of atrocities.

Given the scenario of civil rights violations and caste atrocities in the state and the wide range of gaps in the implementation of laws, a strong monitoring mechanism needs to be instituted to ensure that officials respond to the cases of atrocities on a priority basis. The state government also needs to launch a regular special drive against such incidents of atrocities with the help of district-level officials. The police and investigation team also need to be sensitized to the victim's plight. The issuance of regular reminders from the higher authorities to the concerned officers against whom complaints are received may act as deterrents for indulging in unlawful activities. Since the public prosecutor is the lifeline for the victims to provide justice, the appointment of public prosecutors, should be rigorously undertaken to ensure that they are sensitive towards the issue of caste discrimination, and understand the gravity of the human rights violations against lower caste groups and its larger consequences on overall well-being of the victims in particular and the society at large.

Since the interference by the socio-economically powerful accused in the investigation process remains a critical issue, it is essential to ensure that rules related to arrests of the accused are strictly adhered to prevent dilution of evidence which has a large impact on the final outcome of the cases. In view of delayed judgment on many atrocity cases, there is a need to ensure that the existing special courts, many of which have not been functional, work properly; and more special courts are set up as per the PoA Act Rules, especially in the districts witnessing more atrocities. With the human rights violations against lower caste groups attaining disturbingly high levels in U.P., there is an urgent need for preventing them, for which the state government should initiate strategic planning to ensure that the district-level authorities and committees assess the situation periodically, and make special interventions to prevent occurrence of such atrocities rather than acting after they take place. In this regard, the networking and collaborative efforts of the government with other human rights organizations would constitute an effective supporting mechanism for strengthening the process of implementation of laws. It is significant that the law enforcement machinery is sensitized in the most serious areas of concern regarding the enforcement of the laws, and response of judiciary system is strengthened to establish a broader anti-discriminatory and anti-oppressive climate in the state.

Acknowledgements The author would like to thank the DFID and Christian-Aid UK for the support to undertake the study on 'Mapping Caste-based Atrocities in U.P.'. Thanks are also due to Sukhadeo Thorat, R.P. Mamgain, Anand Kumar, Sirivella Prasad, Ram Kumar, Ram Dular, and Abirami, and other officials and members of different organizations in U.P. who provided support in innumerable ways towards completion of the study.

References

Aloysius, I. S. J., Mangubhai, J. P., & Lee, J. G. (2006). *Dalit Women speak out: Violence against Dalit Women in India* (Vols. I & II). Chennai and New Delhi: IDEAS, NCDHR and NFDW.

Bhatnagar, R. R. (1990). *Crimes in India: Problems and Policy*. New Delhi: Ashish Publishing.

Drez, J., & Khera, R. (2000). Crime, gender, and society in India: Insights from homicide data. *Population and Development Review, 26*(2), 335–352.

Hindustan Times. (2011, June 26). Forty five per cent of rape cases in U.P. in 2010 were of SCs. *Hindustan Times*. Indore.

Human Rights Watch (HRW). (1999). *Broken people: Caste violence against untouchables*. New York: HRW.

Kumar, V. (2008). Changing trajectory of Dalit assertion in U.P. In N. Ram (Ed.) *SCs in contemporary India: Discrimination and discontent* (Vol. 1). New Delhi: Siddhant Publications.

Mahmudabad, A. K. (2012, March 5). UP's caste of characters. *The Times of India*. New Delhi.

National Crime Record Bureau (NCRB). (2002–2015). *Crimes in India*. National Crime Record Bureau (NCRB), Ministry of Home Affairs, Government of India, New Delhi.

Oldenburg, P. (1992). Sex ratio, son preferences and violence in India: A research note. *Economic & Political Weekly*, 2657–2662.

Pal, G. C. (2015). Social exclusion and mental health: The unexplored aftermath of caste-based discrimination and violence. *Psychology & Developing Societies, 27*(2), 189–213.

Parashar, A. (2011, May 4). One more party for SCs in U.P. *Current Affairs*, New Delhi. Retrieved from www.tehelka.com/story_main49.asp.

Prasad, C. B., Shyam Babu, D., Kapur, D., & Pritchett, L. (2010). Rethinking inequality: SCs in U.P. in the. *Economic and Political Weekly, XLV*(35), 39–49.

Rawat, R. S. (2011). *Reconsidering untouchability: Chamars and Dalit history in North India*. USA: Indiana University Press.

Sharma, S. (2015). Caste-based crimes and economic status: Evidence from India. *Journal of Comparative Economics, 43*, 204–226.

Srivastava, T. (2012, February 1). Caste-ing the Vote in U.P. *SIFY*. New Delhi.

The Protection of Civil Rights (PCR) Act. (1976). Act No. BC.12013/2/76-SCT-V, 15 September 1977. *Ministry of Social Welfare and Empowerment*. New Delhi: Government of India.

The Scheduled Castes and Scheduled Tribes (Prevention of Atrocities) Act. (1989). Act No. 33, 11 September 1989. *Ministry of Social Welfare and Empowerment*. New Delhi: Government of India.

G. C. Pal is Associate Professor and Director at Indian Institute of Dalit Studies (IIDS), New Delhi. He was ICSSR Senior Fellow during 2016–18, and Post-Doctoral Visiting Fellow for three years at Tata Institute of Fundamental Research (TIFR), Mumbai. He has M.Phil. and Ph.D. in Social Psychology. He has teaching experiences of five years at university level, and research experiences of more than twenty years.

He specializes in interdisciplinary research to understand development issues from socio-psychological perspectives, with a special focus on marginalized groups such as scheduled castes, scheduled tribes, persons with disabilities and urban poor; and explore research methodology. In addition to his doctoral work on social psychology of unemployment, he has completed over fifteen major research projects in the areas of human cognition and education, identity-based social exclusion, discrimination and violence, inter-sectionality and deprivation, disability, impact evaluation and inclusive policies.

To his credit, he has a book titled 'Unemployment: A socio-psychological perspective', over forty research papers published in edited books and journals; besides the publication of ten book reviews in academic journals, and several synthesis/discussion/ occasional/working papers and policy briefs. He has presented over sixty research papers in national and international conferences/seminars besides delivering over eighty invited lectures/talks on research work and methodological issues in various in academic forums and capacity development programmes.

Part III
Agriculture Development: Challenges and Opportunities

Agricultural Growth: Performance, Constraints and Strategy for Future Development

Ajit Kumar Singh

Abstract The article examines the performance of the agricultural sector in the state of UP in recent years. The analysis reveals that UP registered high agricultural growth during the 1970s and 1980s in the wake of green revolution, but the agricultural economy of the state registered a severe setback since the early 1990s. The yield growth of all the cereal crops has sharply declined since the beginning of the 1990s. There is also evidence that there has been a significant decline in total productivity growth (TFP) in UP agriculture after 1993–94. Agricultural growth has been marked by sharp variations in growth rates at the regional and the district level. Analysis of major determinants of agricultural growth revealed that the growth rate of irrigated area and fertilizer consumption, which were the main sources of agricultural growth during the 1979s and the 1980s, has significantly slowed down after 1990–91. The role of price incentive in agricultural development has been nominal in Uttar Pradesh. The paper highlights the major constraints on agricultural development in the state like the small and declining size of holding, poor rural infrastructure, unsatisfactory condition of the public support systems to agriculture in terms of input supply, credit and marketing and lack of a suitable policy environment in the state for agricultural growth. The paper suggests an integrated strategy for agricultural development is required for accelerating agricultural growth in the state with a particular focus on small farmers and lagging districts.

Keywords Agricultural growth · Factor productivity · Regional variations · Constraints on agricultural development · Strategy for accelerated agricultural development

---

A. K. Singh (✉)
Formerly of Giri Institute of Development Studies, Lucknow, India
e-mail: aksingh101@rediffmail.com

1 Introduction

The economy of Uttar Pradesh is predominantly agrarian. Around 60% of the total workers in the state are employed in agriculture, which contributes about one-fourth of the state's income. Uttar Pradesh (U.P.) is a major producer of diverse agricultural crops in the country. Among all Indian states, it is the largest producer of wheat, pulses, sugarcane, tobacco, potato and milk; the second largest producer of rice, fruits and vegetables; and the third largest producer of coarse grains among states in India. Clearly, agriculture in Uttar Pradesh is critical to food production and food security of the country (U.P. Development Report 2007, p. 27).

The state is well endowed with favourable factors for agricultural development in terms of vast tracts of fertile alluvial plains, good rainfall, plentiful surface and groundwater, temperate climate and sunshine. Although U.P. is characterized by rich diversity in natural resources and favourable climate, yet sharp differentials prevail in the levels of agricultural development and productivity in all the regions and even at district level in the state. Thus, we see the yield of food grain crops in the western region is distinctly higher than other regions. Bundelkhand, where irrigated area is relatively low, has the lowest level of yields (Table 1).

In spite of its favourable agro-climatic conditions, the growth rate of agriculture was much lower in U.P. than in the country as a whole during the entire planning period except during the fifth (1974–79) and the tenth plan (2002–2007) period. This paper looks at the performance of the agricultural sector in U.P. in recent years, identifies the major constraints on agricultural development and suggests strategy for accelerating agricultural growth in the state.

We have hypothesized that the major sources of agricultural growth are expansion in the irrigated area, and intensification of the new technology reflected in the use of major agricultural inputs like fertilizers. We have also examined the role of public and private investment in accelerating agricultural growth. The role of price incentive on private investment in agriculture has been examined by analysing trends in terms of trade for agriculture.

Table 1 Region-wise productivity of major crops in U.P. (2014–15) (Quintl./Ha.)

Crop	Western region	Central region	Eastern region	Bundelkhand	U.P.
Food grains	22.24	19.77	19.38	8.77	19.05
Wheat	22.38	20.13	19.94	13.53	20.27
Rice	24.40	23.25	21.50	16.56	22.56
Potato	240.81	176.75	199.92	225.20	225.20
Sugarcane	687.53	654.42	577.04	404.43	658.21
Oilseeds	9.68	5.13	6.03	3.54	8.75

Source District-wise development indicators, Uttar Pradesh 2016

Data on agricultural output and area and major agricultural inputs have been taken from various government publications of the U.P. Government like *The Statistical Abstract, Statistical Diary and Agricultural Statistics* of U.P. Compound growth rates of output, area and yield have been computed for three sub-periods, viz., 1969–1990 (the green revolution period), 1990–2001 (the post-liberalization period) and 2001–2015 (recent period) taking triennium averages at the beginning and the end of each period. In addition to examining the growth rates of agriculture for the state as a whole, the pattern of agricultural growth at the regional and district level has also been analysed.

2 Agricultural Performance

U.P. registered high agricultural growth during the 1970s and 1980s in the wake of the green revolution, which initially started from western region but gradually spread to other regions of the state. In the 1980s, growth rate of food grain output as well as that of gross value of agricultural output in U.P. was clearly above the national average growth. However, by the end of the 1980s the growth potential of the green revolution was almost fully exhausted. Agricultural economy of the state as well as that of the country registered a severe setback in the 1990s, and growth rates of nearly all crops, particularly the food grains, plummeted sharply and the output were adversely affected.

Appendices 1–3 show the trends in area, output and yield of major crops in U.P. Table 2 shows crop-wise compound growth rate of output, area and yield in U.P. during the different periods between 1969–70 and 2014–15 based on triennium averages. Food grain output had registered a high growth rate of 3.47 per cent per annum during the period 1969–1990. But the growth rates fell to 2.06% during 1990–2001 and further to 0.62% during 2001–2015. Decline in the growth rate of rice and wheat output was even sharper. Bajra showed an improved performance in the latter two periods, but other coarse grains showed a decline in output. Pulse output has registered a continuous decline throughout the period. Among oilseeds, groundnut output has showed a negative trend. Rapeseed and mustard, however, showed an impressive growth in output in the first period, but modest growth after that. Sugarcane and potato have shown high growth during the first period, but a modest growth in the last two periods under consideration.

It is noted from Table 2 that area of cultivation of rice, wheat and bajra has increased throughout the period. But area under coarse cereals and pulses has suffered a decline. Among non-food grain crops, groundnut shows a decline in area, but sugarcane and potato show a positive trend in all the sub-periods. What is more striking is that the yield growth of all the cereal crops has sharply declined since the beginning of the 1990s. Yield of pulses shows a modest growth in the first two sub-periods, but has shown a negative trend in recent sub-period. Among non-food grain crops, yield growth rates show decline in case of oilseeds and potato. Sugarcane yields were stagnant in the 1990s, but have shown a modest increase in the last period.

Table 2 Compound growth rate of output, area and yield of major crops in U.P. (% per annum)

Crops	1969–1990			1990–2001			2001–2015		
	Area	Output	Yield	Area	Output	Yield	Area	Output	Yield
Rice	1.16	5.67	4.46	0.42	2.23	1.81	0.42	1.40	0.98
Wheat	2.31	5.22	2.85	0.60	2.86	2.25	0.57	1.60	1.03
Jowar	−1.62	0.80	2.46	−5.00	−4.61	0.41	−5.05	−3.95	1.16
Bajra	−1.30	0.89	2.22	0.36	2.43	2.06	0.78	4.23	3.42
Maize	−1.30	0.00	1.31	−2.32	0.25	2.63	−1.64	−0.41	1.25
Barley	−5.45	−2.71	2.89	−5.14	−2.11	3.19	−4.01	−2.63	1.44
Total cereals	0.73	4.20	3.45	−0.08	2.27	2.35	0.29	0.81	0.52
Gram	−2.52	−2.02	0.52	−3.87	−3.12	0.78	−3.01	−5.00	−2.05
Arhar (pigeon pea)	−1.00	−0.58	0.43	−2.06	−1.78	0.29	−2.33	−4.69	−2.41
Total pulses	−1.60	−1.39	0.22	−0.99	−0.92	0.07	−1.11	−2.74	−1.65
Total food grains	0.31	3.47	3.16	−0.21	2.06	2.28	0.11	0.64	0.53
Groundnut	−4.22	−3.19	1.07	−3.27	−2.83	0.45	−0.39	−0.40	0.00
Rapeseed and mustard	6.01	8.85	2.68	−0.83	0.86	1.71	0.96	0.45	−0.51
Sugarcane	1.59	2.82	1.21	1.18	1.27	0.09	0.63	2.01	1.38
Potato	3.76	7.26	3.37	1.64	3.47	1.80	2.56	2.65	0.09

Note Growth rates are based on the triennium averages at the beginning and end of the period
Source Calculated from data given in *Statistical Diary U.P.* (*Annual*), Economics and Statistics Division, State Planning Institute, U.P.

In short, we observe that for over two decades, agriculture in U.P. has been showing a sluggish growth in output and yields. The decline in growth rates is seen in case of most of the food grains as well as non-food grain crops. The food grains output growth has in fact lagged behind the population growth in the state since 2000–01. There is also evidence that there has been a significant decline in total factor productivity (TFP) growth in U.P. agriculture after 1993–94. According to one study, TFP growth in U.P. sharply declined from 1.73 per cent per annum during the period 1984–85 to 1993–94 to −0.56 during the period 1994–95 to 2003–04 (Kumar and Taneja 2008). The negative trend in TFP is a cause of concern and calls for urgent measures to reverse it.

2.1 Regional Pattern of Growth

We have examined the regional pattern of growth in terms of trends in total food grains output and in terms of net district domestic product (NDDP) of agriculture and animal husbandry. Central region witnessed highest growth rate of food grain output during the period 2001–14 followed by eastern region (Table 3). On the other hand, the western region, agriculturally the most developed region of the state, witnessed the lowest growth rate of 0.95 per cent per annum. In terms of the agricultural and animal husbandry, net domestic product eastern region registered highest growth during the last decade (3.71 per cent per annum) followed by western region (3.00 per cent per annum). Animal husbandry makes a substantial contribution to growth of agricultural sector in these regions. But the growth rate in central region and Bundelkhand was much lower (Table 3).

At the district level growth rate of food grains, output shows sharp variations (Table 4) ranging from negative 3.3 to 4.9%. As many as twelve districts registered a growth rate of over 2.5 per cent per annum in food grain output over the period 2000–14. Most of the fast-growing districts belonged to western and central region. In fourteen districts, growth rate of food grain output was between 1.5 and 2.5 per cent per annum. These districts are located in all the regions of the state. Growth rates of food grain output ranged between 1.0 and 1.5% in twelve districts and U.P., and one per cent in fourteen districts. On the other hand, as many as fifteen districts registered negative growth rate of food grain output, with nine of them belonging to western region. Thus, more than half of the districts of the state have experienced sluggish or negative growth of food grains output indicating a general crisis in U.P. agriculture.

Table 3 Region-wise agricultural growth in U.P.: 2001–14

Region	Food grain output (hundred thousand tonnes)		CAGR (%)	NDDP agriculture and animal husbandry (Rs. crore)		CAGR (%)
	2000–01	2013–14		2004–05	2013–14	
Western region	176.00	198.93	0.95	31,885.21	41,592.33	3.00
Central region	70.41	92.24	2.10	12,146.21	13,829.25	1.45
Eastern region	146.27	185.40	1.84	16,045.82	22,270.42	3.71
Bundelkhand	23.86	28.44	1.36	3790.11	4189.34	1.12
Uttar Pradesh	427.36	505.02	1.29	63,867.35	81,881.34	2.80

Source Calculated from data in Statistical Abstract (Annual), Uttar Pradesh and State Domestic Product

Table 4 District-wise growth rate of food grains output during 2000–01 to 2013–14 (% per annum)

Above 2.50		1.50–2.50		1.00–1.50		0.00–1.00		Negative	
District	CAGR	District	CAGR	District	CAGR	District	CAGR	District	CAGR
Hardoi	2.50	Ballia	1.52	Gonda	1.03	Sonbhadra	0.23	G.B. Nagar	−3.30
Etah	2.52	Aligarh	1.52	Jaunpur	1.07	Bijnor	0.23	Jhansi	−1.74
Fatehpur	2.54	Bulandshahar	1.54	Pratapgarh	1.10	Lucknow	0.31	Hathras	−0.58
Auraiya	2.65	Raebareli	1.55	Kanpur	1.10	Chitrakoot	0.45	Muzaffarnagar	−0.52
Etawah	2.67	Jalaun	1.75	Basti	1.11	Kannauj	0.46	Mathura	−0.45
Sitapur	2.73	Agra	1.82	Balrampur	1.15	Kheri	0.58	Shrawasti	−0.43
Unnao	3.09	Ghaziabad	1.86	Ghazipur	1.16	Santravidas Nagar	0.61	Farrukhabad	−0.38
Lalitpur	3.52	Firozabad	1.96	Baghpat	1.22	Maharajganj	0.68	Mirzapur	−0.28
Barabanki	3.77	Moradabad	1.99	Kanpur	1.24	Pilibhit	0.78	Varanasi	−0.24
Siddharthnagar	3.83	Sant Kabir Nagar	2.00	Ambedkar Nagar	1.25	Faizabad	0.78	Meerut	−0.23
Bahraich	4.18	Hamirpur	2.03	Banda	1.28	Kaushambi	0.80	Allahabad	−0.17
J.B. Phule Nagar	4.89	Azamgarh	2.09	Mau	1.43	Bareilly	0.87	Rampur	−0.12
		Gorakhpur	2.13			Deoria	0.96	Badaun	−0.09
		Mahoba	2.16			Shahjahanpur	0.98	Kushinagar	−0.08
								Saharanpur	−0.02

Source Calculated from data given in *Statistical Abstract, Uttar Pradesh (Annual)*

Large variations in growth rate of agricultural NDDP were also observed at the district level (Table 5). In twelve districts, the growth rate of NDDP during 2004–05 and 2013–14 exceeded five per cent per annum, nine of which belonged to the eastern region, two to western and one to Bundelkhand region. In thirteen districts, the growth rate was between three and five per cent, seven of which belonged to the eastern and six to western region. Growth rate of agricultural NNDP varied between two and three per cent in nineteen districts and between zero and two per cent in eighteen districts. Eight districts experienced negative growth in agricultural NNDP. Four of these districts were in Bundelkhand, three in western and one in central region.

From the above discussion, the following conclusions may be made about the pattern of agricultural growth in U.P. over the last decade. First, the pattern of agricultural growth has been quite uneven across regions and districts. Central and eastern regions experienced higher growth in food grain output. The western and eastern regions registered higher growth in agricultural NDDP. Bundelkhand experienced low growth of agricultural NNDP. Second, in all the regions, there were sharp intra-regional disparities in agricultural growth at the district level. All regions had a mix of high and low growth districts. Thirdly, NDDP growth seems to be propelled by the growth in the non-food crops and animal husbandry. Fourthly, about half of the districts have experienced high agricultural growth, while the remaining are experiencing stagnation.

3 Trends in Use of Major Agricultural Inputs

Agricultural growth depends on a number of factors like introduction of new technology, increase in cropped area, expansion of irrigation facilities, increase in agricultural inputs and relative agricultural prices. There has been no significant new technological breakthrough since the introduction of the green revolution technology in the state. In this section, we look at the trends in the total and irrigated area, trends in use of major agricultural inputs like fertilizers and trends in relative agricultural prices. The analysis is done for three sub-periods, namely 1980–81 to 1990–91, 1991–92 to 2001–02 and 2002–03 to 2012–15. Appendix 4 shows the trends in agricultural output and inputs in U.P. over the period 1980–81 to 2012–13, while Table 6 shows the rates of growth in major agricultural inputs in different sub-periods.

Gross sown area increased at a moderate rate of 0.36 per cent per annum in 1981–91. It remained stagnant during 1992–2002, but showed higher growth during the period 2002–15. The growth rate of irrigated area shows a marked decline in the last period. Growth rate of fertilizer consumption also sharply declined after 1991. Thus, growth rates of irrigation and fertilizer consumption, which were the main sources of agricultural growth during the 1970s and the 1980s, have significantly slowed down after 1990–91 (Fig. 1).

Table 5 District-wise CAGR of NDDP (agriculture and animal husbandry) at 2004–05 prices during 2004–05 to 2013–14 (%)

Above 5%		3–5%		2–3%		0–2%		Negative	
District	CAGR	District	CAGR	District	CAGR	District	CAGR	District	CAGR
Sonbhadra	13.27	Gonda	4.75	Hardoi	2.99	Azamgarh	1.99	Jhansi	−0.13
Hamirpur	10.76	Auraiya	4.49	Ramabai Nagar (Kanpur Dehat)	2.93	Basti	1.83	Farrukhabad	−0.65
Bareilly	10.62	Fatehpur	4.48	Aligarh	2.90	Gorakhpur	1.77	Mahoba	−0.71
Etah	9.92	Mainpuri	4.14	Bulandshahar	2.88	Ambedkar Nagar	1.66	Bijnor	−0.99
Bhadohi	9.09	Moradabad	4.13	Pilibhit	2.82	Baghpat	1.54	Gautam Budh Nagar	−1.85
Faizabad	8.97	Varanasi	4.00	Maharajganj	2.82	Ghazipur	1.46	Chitrakoot	−3.12
Ballia	6.53	Kaushambi	3.92	Kheri	2.75	Kannauj	1.43	Barabanki	−5.09
Sultanpur	6.22	Badaun	3.55	Ghaziabad	2.75	Allahabad	1.40	Jalaun	−5.37
Shravasti	5.95	Shahjahanpur	3.54	Balrampur	2.68	Banda	1.09		
Deoria	5.86	St. Kabeer Nagar	3.46	Unnao	2.66	Lalitpur	1.04		
Siddharth	5.48	Bahraich	3.31	Sitapur	2.66	Etawah	0.85		
Mirzapur	5.23	Chandauli	3.17	Agra	2.47	Jyotiba Phule Nagar (Amroha)	0.74		
		Jaunpur	3.09	Mahamaya Nagar (Hathras)	2.46	Pratapgarh	0.69		
				Firozabad	2.28	Kanpur Nagar	0.49		
				Mathura	2.19	Saharanpur	0.45		
				Meerut	2.10	Rampur	0.31		
				Kushinagar	2.06	Rae Bareli	0.19		
				Mau	2.04	Lucknow	0.13		
				Muzaffarnagar	2.01				

Source Calculated from data in District Domestic Product, Economics and Statistics Division, State Planning Institute, U.P.

Table 6 CAGR of agricultural inputs since 1980–81 by sub-periods (per cent per annum)

Year	Food grain output	Area irrigated			Gross sown area (hundred thousand ha.)	Fertilizer distribution	
		Net area irrigated	Gross area irrigated	% of gross irrigated area to GSA		Total	Per ha. of GSA (kg)
1981–1991	3.60	1.10	2.65	2.28	0.36	6.89	6.51
1992–2002	2.19	1.50	1.68	1.61	0.07	3.78	3.71
2003–2015	0.14	0.95	1.38	0.77	0.61	2.33	1.71

Source Calculated from data in Statistical Abstract U.P. and Statistical Diary U.P.

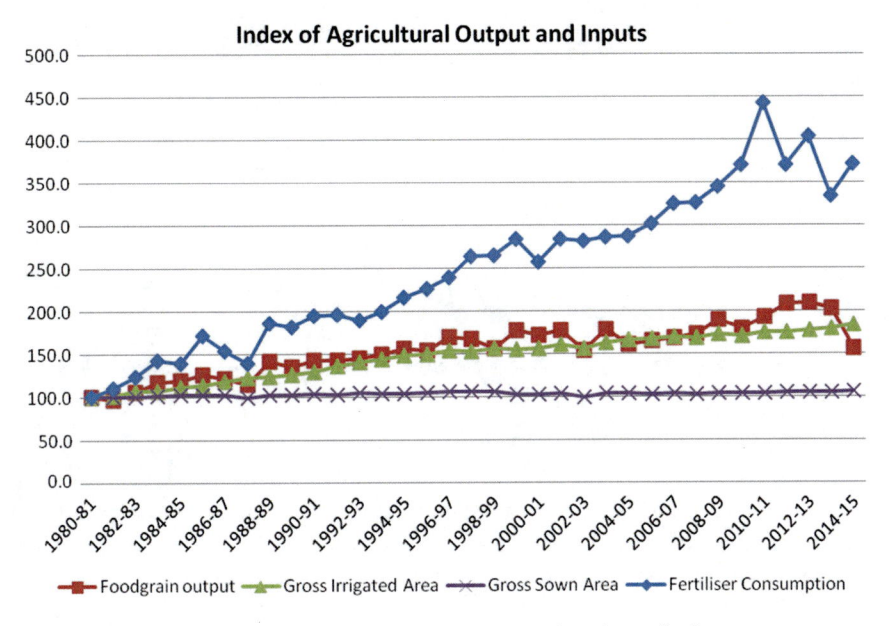

Fig. 1 Index of agricultural outputs and inputs. *Source* Based on Appendix 4

4 Trends in Agricultural Price Parity Index

Improvement in agricultural price parity index is expected to have a positive impact on agricultural investment and growth. Appendix 5 gives data on the trends in agricultural price parity index for the period 1980–81 to 2014–15, while Table 7 gives the CAGR of agricultural price parity index for the three sub-periods. As is observed from the table, agricultural price parity index was negative during the 1981–91 period. It improved at a modest growth rate of 0.21 per cent per annum during 1992–2002, which further improved to 0.55 per cent per annum during the period 2003–15. On the whole, there has been little change in the agricultural price parity index over the

Table 7 CAGR of agricultural parity prices 1981–2015 in U.P. (% per annum)

Year	Prices paid by farmers	Prices received by farmers	Agriculture prices parity index
1981–91	9.30	8.58	−0.67
1992–2002	6.70	6.91	0.21
2003–15	11.45	12.07	0.55

Source Calculated from data given in Statistical Diary U.P. Various years

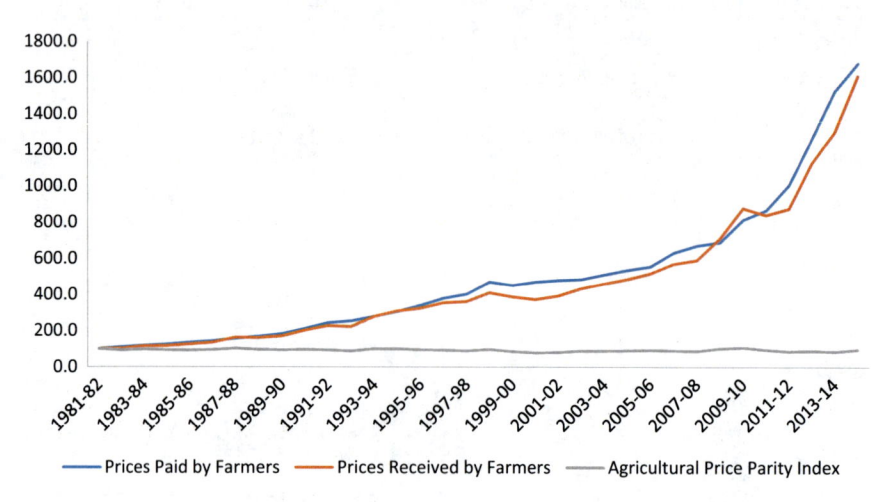

Fig. 2 Agricultural price parity index

entire period (Fig. 2). In fact, the agricultural price parity index has exceeded 100 only in three out of the last thirty years. In other words, prices received by farmers have lagged behind the prices paid by the farmers for the entire period. Thus, the role of price incentive in agricultural development has been nominal in Uttar Pradesh.

5 Investment in Agriculture

Estimates of private investment in agriculture are not available on a regular basis. Some indirect evidence of investment in agriculture can be gathered from investment in irrigation which is the major component of private investment in agriculture. Table 8 shows some indicators of private investment in irrigation in U.P. It is observed that the number of new pump sets installed was fairly high between 1981–91 and 1992–2002, but it declined very sharply after that. The loans distributed by the Primary Agricultural Credit Societies (PACs) also provide a rough indicator of the level of current investment in agriculture. The loans distributed by PACs have increased very sharply during the study period.

Table 8 Indicators of private investment in agriculture in U.P. 1981–2015

Year	No. of new pump sets installed (in '000)	Loans distributed by primary agricultural credit societies (Rs. in billion)
1981–91	1460.00	31.27
1992–02	1472.86	92.45
2003–13	549.96	237.21

Source Calculated from data given in Statistical Abstract U.P. and Statistical Diary U.P.

Table 9 CAGR of public investment in agriculture and GSDPAG (per cent)

Period	CAGR of public investment in agriculture	CAGR of GSDP agriculture	Investment as % of GSDP agriculture
1993–2002	22.02	8.80	2.07
2003–2010	19.06	16.59	2.90
2011–2014	12.88	12.63	1.32

Source Calculated from Budget Documents, U.P. Government, and State Domestic Product

5.1 Public Investment in Agriculture

Public investment in agriculture and irrigation plays an important role in agricultural development and also boosts private investment in agriculture. Appendix 6 shows year-wise trends in public investment in agriculture. Annual growth rate of public investment in agriculture and irrigation has been shown in Table 9. It shows that public investment in agriculture in nominal terms experienced a high growth of around twenty per cent per annum during the period 1993–2010. However, the growth rate declined after that. Growth Rate of Gross State Domestic Product-Agriculture (GSDPAG) also declined during the period 2011–14. Public investment as per cent of GSDPAG increased from 2.07% in the period 1993–2002 to 2.90% during the period 2003–2010, but declined to 1.32% during the period 2011–14. The decline in public investment has contributed to decline in the growth rate of agriculture during the recent period. It is observed in Graph 3 that the index of public investment in agriculture has exceeded the index of GSDPAG throughout the period except in the years from 2011–12 to 2013–14. This also indicates that the marginal productivity of public investment has been declining over the years.

To sum up the above discussion, several factors have contributed to the slowdown of agricultural growth in Uttar Pradesh. Agricultural prices have hardly kept pace with the increase in cost of cultivation. Thus, there is little incentive for the farmers to invest in agriculture. Private sector investment in agriculture has declined, so has public investment in agriculture and irrigation. As a result, growth in irrigated area

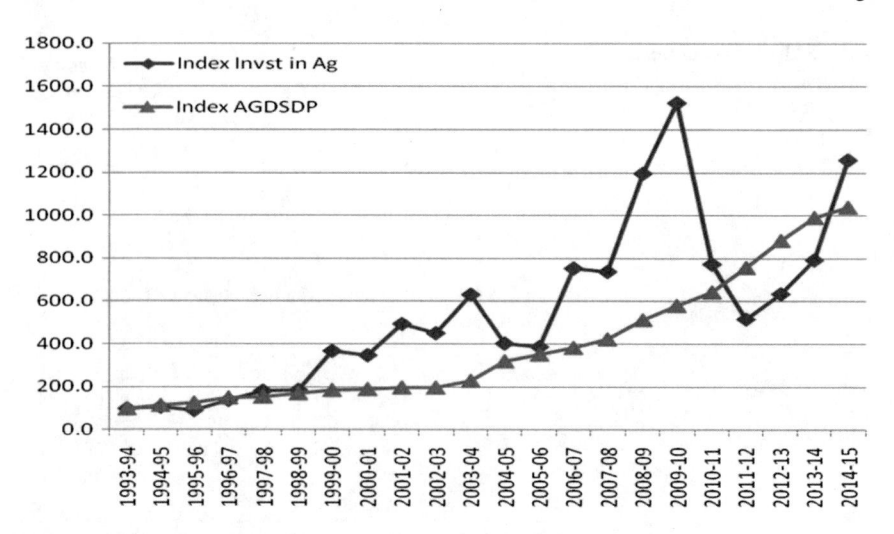

Fig. 3 Index of public investment in agriculture and irrigation and agricultural GSDP

and fertilizer consumption, which were the main sources of agricultural growth, have slowed down in recent years.

6 Major Constraints on Agriculture Development

Agricultural development in U.P. is constrained by a number of factors including structural, infrastructural and policy constraints (Planning Commission 2007, 2008). We briefly touch upon some of the major constraints on agricultural development in the state.

(i) *The predominance of marginal holdings*

A major factor in the deepening agrarian crisis in U.P. and in the country as a whole has been the continuous decline in the size of holdings and growing marginalization of holdings (Reddy and Mishra 2010; Singh 2012a). As per the National Sample Survey (NSS 71 round) on land holdings covering the year 2012–13, as many as 83.5% of farm holdings in U.P. are marginal (less than one hectare), while 8.36% are small (between one and two hectares). These account for 42.6 and 24.1% of the area owned (Table 10). Thus, two-thirds of the land in U.P. is now under marginal and small holdings. Medium holdings account for 12.1% of land and the large holdings for less than one per cent.

The small land base is not able to provide sustenance to the farm households or to generate any surplus for investment. As per the latest report on *Farmers Situation*

Table 10 Trends in distribution of land holdings by size in U.P.: 1971–2013

Year	Marginal	Small	Semi-medium	Medium	Large	All
Percentage of households						
1971–72	73.13	11.39	6.75	3.00	0.46	100.00
1982	81.85	10.89	4.95	2.16	0.16	100.00
1992	87.13	8.01	3.81	0.92	1.11	100.00
2003	81.00	12.30	4.80	1.60	0.10	100.00
2013	83.52	8.36	3.81	0.96	0.03	100.00
Percentage of area owned						
1971–72	20.23	21.84	25.21	22.97	9.75	100
1982	23.57	27.24	23.53	20.94	4.71	100
1992	33.28	26.24	24.15	12.15	4.18	100
2003	34.89	27.38	20.74	14.65	2.34	100
2013	42.61	24.07	20.37	12.16	0.78	100

Source NSS rounds on household ownership and operational holdings

in India 2014 (NSS 71 Round), a farm household earns only Rs. 2853 per month from cultivation. Majority of holdings in U.P. have become economically non-viable forcing farmers to seek non-agricultural occupations in increasing numbers. Scholars have noted a positive association between the size of holding and agricultural productivity at the district level (Singh 2014).

(ii) *Land degradation and poor soil health*

Another serious problem affecting agriculture in U.P. is the widespread land degradation and declining quality of soil. About two-thirds of land is suffering from land degradation of various types, and about one-fourth of land in U.P. is under wasteland. The soil health has been declining. There is a serious deficiency of micro-nutrients in the soil. Unbalanced use of chemical fertilizers has worsened the situation.

(iii) *Poor rural infrastructure*

A developed rural infrastructure is a necessary pre-condition of agricultural growth. U.P. is lagging behind in this respect (Planning Commission 2008). Nearly 40% of the villages in the state are still unconnected with all-weather roads. Power shortage is another major bottleneck. Similarly, agricultural infrastructure in terms of warehouses, cold storages and banking facilities suffers from serious deficiencies.

(iv) *Inadequate public support systems*

The reach and quality of public support systems to agriculture are far from satisfactory (Singh 2012b). The public extension system has almost collapsed. There are large scale vacancies in the positions in extension services at various levels. Farmers face the problem of poor quality and inefficient system of input supply. Often critical inputs like seeds and fertilizers are not available in time. Supply of spurious and adulterated fertilizers and pesticides is common. There are serious deficiencies in the credit system; particularly, the small farmers have limited access to institutional credit. The marketing system suffers from various inadequacies. Even the public procurement system is not free from corruption and malpractices. As a consequence, farmers are unable to get a fair price for their produce. Public agricultural research system is in a state of neglect and suffering from lack of funds and good quality researchers.

(v) *Policy and institutional issues*

The policy environment in the state is not conducive to rapid agricultural growth. U.P. is one of the few states which have not amended their Agricultural Produce Market Committee (APMC) Act. This has prevented entry of organized sector in agricultural marketing and processing. Land markets suffer from various restrictions. The Zamindari Abolition Act prohibits subletting and leasing of land, which restricts access of the poor to land and contract farming. Politicization of sugarcane prices has led to large state advised price (SAP) over the minimum support price (MSP) announced by the Central Government. This has created the problem of non-viability of sugar industry and piling up of dues to the farmers. Instead of dealing with the basic issues, the state government often resorts to short-term palliative measures like abolition of irrigation charges and waiving of farmers' debts.

7 Strategy for Doubling Farmers' Income

The government has adopted the goal of doubling farmers' income in five years. It is indeed a daunting challenge given the historical trends in agricultural growth and incomes. Estimates based upon NSS Farmers Situation Survey show that farmers' income in real terms in U.P. increased at the annual compound rate of 4.72% (Satyasai and Mehrotra 2016). At this rate, it will take fifteen years to double farmers' income in the state. To obtain the goal of doubling farmers' income, agricultural growth should be 12% in real terms. Pushing up the growth rate in real terms to that level seems to be clearly an impossible task. However, it should be possible to attain a growth rate of around 7.5% per year if concerted efforts are made. Several experts have given suggestions for attaining the goal (Chand 2017; Satyasai and Mehrotra 2016; Narayanmoorty 2017; Singh 2018). One must realize that there are several pathways for attaining the goal, and every state has to adopt its own approach in the context of existing situation. Some states like Madhya Pradesh and Chhattisgarh have already come out with strategy papers for doubling their farmers' incomes. Uttar Pradesh too has initiated efforts in this direction. In the context of U.P., the strategy of doubling farmers' income should have the following components.

7.1 Expansion of Area

The scope of extension of cultivated land in the state is limited. The area under cultivation has remained more or less constant around 16.6 million hectares. About one-fourth of area in the state is under various categories of wasteland. A significant part of it can be reclaimed for cultivation. About 1.8 million hectares, that is, over one-tenth of the cultivated area, is under fallow land. These can be brought under cultivation without much investment. Although irrigated area covers over 80% of the cultivated area in the state, the cropping intensity has remained static at about 150. Thus, only one crop is being cultivated on half of land in a year. Efforts should be made to increase cropping intensity on farms. Strengthening of the irrigation system can play a useful role in this direction. All these measures can enhance agricultural income by about 10%.

7.2 Filling the Yield Gap

Yield levels in U.P. are relatively low. The gap between the yields on experimental farms and farmers' field is about 50% in case of all crops. In comparison, the yield levels prevalent in agriculturally advanced states like Punjab and Haryana are higher. Wheat yields are more than 75% higher in these two states as compared to U.P. Rice yield is higher by about 50% in Haryana and 84% in Punjab. Sugarcane yield is also about 20% higher in these states as compared to U.P. Moreover, there are marked variations in the yield levels within U.P. at the regional and the district level. Thus, there is a huge potential of raising agricultural productivity in the state even with the existing technology. An integrated strategy for agricultural development is called for to tap this potential and accelerate agricultural growth in the state. Adoption of proper agronomic practices and reducing crop losses through integrated pest management can bring about substantial improvement in productivity of crops and output. The extension agencies and agricultural universities have to play an active role in this respect. Through adoption of scientific agricultural practices, it should be possible to raise the yield levels in the state by at least 25% over the next five years.

7.3 Reducing Cost of Production

A major reason for the squeeze in farmers' income has been the sharp increase in the cost of cultivation. Reduction in cost of cultivation will contribute to increase in farmers' income. The major components of farm costs are seeds, fertilizers, irrigation and hiring of machinery. There is good scope of improving efficiency in all these areas and bringing down expenses on them. The efficiency in input use needs to be promoted. Control on spurious and low quality of seeds, fertilizers and pesticides is strongly needed. A more optimum use of fertilizers and use of organic fertilizers will bring down the cost of cultivation. Overuse of chemical fertilizers, insecticides, pesticides and weedicides should be discouraged. The state should promote hiring services for tractors, threshers, cultivators and other agricultural machinery through own service centres, cooperatives societies and promoting young entrepreneurs in this area. New techniques of cultivation like precision cultivation and zero tilling need to be promoted. There is a large scope for improving efficiency in irrigation and bringing down its cost. Regular supply of power for irrigation will also cut down on cost of irrigation and reduce dependence on diesel pump sets. Promotion of conjunctive use of surface and groundwater should be promoted. Drip and sprinkler irrigation need to be promoted on a larger scale. These measures can bring down cost of cultivation by about 20% and increase farmers' income by 10%.

7.4 Diversification Towards High-Value Crops

Agriculture in U.P. largely remains subsistence oriented with over 80% area under food grain crops. There is a good scope for shifting towards cultivation of high value crops like vegetables, flowers and horticulture. Shift towards high value crops will not only raise income per acre by three to four times; it will also raise demand for labour and promote sustainability. An integrated strategy is required for promoting agricultural diversification including extension services, ensuring good quality seeds, plantation material, credit, cold storage facilities, agro-processing facilities and marketing. A 10% shift from food grains to high value crops can increase farmers' income by about 25%.

7.5 Marketing Reforms

Raising productivity and output will not be of much help in increasing farmers' income unless market reforms are instituted to ensure higher share for farmers in the consumers' price (Singh 2018; Narayanmoorty 2017). The agricultural marketing system suffers from serious deficiencies and is dominated by middlemen. The public procurement system covers only a few crops, and even there, its share in total sales remains low. As a result, the farmers do not get full MSP. The public procurement system needs to be expanded and strengthened. Mobile purchasing centres can bring the procurement machinery within the reach of small farmers.

The efforts towards reforming agricultural markets have not been very successful (Chand 2017). The model APMC Act needs to be adopted without delay. Promotion of e-market, strengthening of market intelligence system and greater involvement of farmers in managing the marketing institutions are urgently required. Opening up agriculture and removal of various restrictions on marketing and land lease and raising of forest species on farmland will enable farmers to receive higher prices for their produce and enhance economic activities (Chand 2017). Effective implementation of marketing reforms can add about 20% to farmers' income.

7.6 Institutional Reforms

Marginal and small farmers constitute the overwhelming majority of farmers in India. They suffer from various handicaps and cannot reap economies of scale. They are also disadvantageously placed in the input and the output markets and have limited access to institutional credit. Institutional reforms are needed to organize these farmers to enable them to reap the benefits of scale. Farmers' cooperatives and producer companies are advocated by many experts in this context (Singh 2018). There are many successful stories of such farmers produce organizations, but they have to be multiplied on a large scale. This will enable them to get involved in domestic and global value chains, which can help lowering the costs of production and marketing, and achieve scale economies to realize higher prices and surpluses (Singh 2018).

7.7 Development of Livestock and Allied Activities

Livestock constitutes an important source of farmers' income. With rising demand for milk products and meat, there is a good scope for promoting livestock and allied activities like piggery, goat keeping, fishery and sheep breeding. Farming systems approach needs to be promoted to enhance farmers' income. Various constraints like limitation of available production technologies, biophysical or geophysical constraints, labour and input market constraints, financial and credit constraints, social norms, inter-temporal trade-offs, policy constraints and constraints to knowledge or skills need to be removed to promote farming systems approach on a large scale (Satayasai and Mehrotra 2016).

7.8 Promotion of Non-farm Activities

Non-farm activities including wage and salary work constitute nearly half of farmers' income. Their importance is greater in case of the small and marginal farmers. Non-farm sector needs to be given a big push in the rural areas. Lack of skills is an important constraint in promoting decent jobs in non-farm sector. There is a great need for imparting training to the rural youth to take up jobs in the entire value chain from input supply channels, farm machinery sale, operation and repair, agro-processing, farm trade and so on (Satyasai and Mehrotra 2016). Public construction works provide an important avenue of employment to the poor agricultural labourers and small and marginal farmers. Investment in these programmes needs to be expanded substantially. Higher allocations for programmes like Mahatma Gandhi National Rural Employment Guarantee Act (MGNREGA) will generate higher income to these sections. The development of rural infrastructure will also encourage development of non-farm activities in these areas.

8 Conclusion

U.P. registered high agricultural growth during the 1970s and 1980s in the wake of green revolution, but the agricultural economy of the state registered a severe setback since the early 1990s and growth rates of output of nearly all crops plummeted sharply. The yield growth of all the cereal crops has sharply declined since the beginning of the 1990s. There is also evidence that there has been a significant decline in total factor productivity (TFP) growth in U.P. agriculture after 1993–94. Agricultural growth in U.P. has been marked by sharp variations in growth rates at the regional and the district level. There were sharp variations in growth rates in food grains output among districts. More than half of the districts of the state have experienced sluggish or negative growth of food grains output indicating a general crisis in U.P. agriculture. Growth performance was better in terms of agricultural NDP, which was propelled by the growth in the non-food crops and animal husbandry.

Analysis of major determinants of agricultural growth revealed that the growth rates of irrigated area and fertilizer consumption, which were the main sources of agricultural growth during the 1970s and the 1980s, have significantly slowed down after 1990–91. The role of price incentive in agricultural development has been nominal in Uttar Pradesh. The prices received by the farmers have just kept pace with the prices paid by the farmers. Public investment in agriculture has also been low.

Agricultural growth in the state is constrained by a number of factors. The foremost structural constraint on U.P. agriculture is the small and declining size of holdings. The majority of holdings in U.P. have become economically non-viable forcing farmers to seek non-agricultural occupations in increasing numbers. U.P. is also lagging behind in terms of the development of rural infrastructure. The reach and quality of public support systems to agriculture in terms of input supply, credit and marketing support are far from satisfactory. The policy environment in the state is not conducive to rapid agricultural growth with severe restrictions on the land and lease markets.

There is a significant gap between the potential and the actual yields of the crops. An integrated strategy for agricultural development is called for to accelerate agricultural growth in the state with particular focus on small farmers and lagging districts. There is need to push up public investment in agriculture and rural infrastructure. The public support systems for extension, marketing and credit need to be revamped. Investment in agricultural research and education should be stepped up sharply. A suitable policy environment for agricultural growth needs to be created. The APMC Act should be amended as has been done by many states. Various restrictions on the land and lease market should be removed. Finally, the potential of allied sectors like sheep rearing, goat keeping, fishery, poultry and dairying should be aggressively tapped. A push to non-agricultural sector is also needed to create additional opportunities for enhancing farmers' income. In the long run, a shift of agricultural workers to the non-agricultural sector is needed to tackle the problem of low income and poverty of farmers in the state.

Appendix 1: Trends in Output of Major Crops in U.P.: 1969–2013

Crops	Output in hundred thousand tonnes (triennium average centred round)			
	1969–70	1989–90	2001–02	2013–14
Rice	32.27	97.21	123.89	146.45
Wheat	67.32	186.31	254.06	307.47
Jowar	4.58	5.37	3.20	1.97
Bajra	7.31	8.73	11.37	18.68
Maize	14.16	14.15	14.54	13.85
Barley	13.61	7.85	6.21	4.51
Total cereals	141.79	322.96	413.48	455.43
Gram	16.32	10.86	7.66	4.14
Arhar (pigeon pea)	6.88	6.13	5.03	2.83
Total Pulses	34.61	26.16	23.62	16.92
Total food grains	176.4	349.13	437.11	472.00
Groundnut	2.45	1.28	0.93	0.89
Rapeseed and mustard	1.01	5.51	6.06	6.39
Sugarcane	552.99	965.02	1108.76	1408.24
Potato	15.55	63.18	91.94	125.82

Source Calculated from data in Statistical Abstract U.P.

Appendix 2: Trends in Area Under Major Crops in U.P.: 1969–2013

Crops	Area in '000 ha (triennium average centred round)			
	1969–70	1989–90	2001–02	2013–14
Rice	4347	5474	5730	6024
Wheat	5474	8636	9220	9867
Jowar	763	550	313	168
Bajra	1066	821	854	938
Maize	1475	1136	877	720
Barley	1431	467	261	160
Total cereals	15,084	17,434	17,284	17,886
Gram	2168	1301	843	584
Arhar (pigeon pea)	594	486	386	291
Total pulses	4122	2983	2673	2338
Total food grains	19,206	20,417	19,957	20,224
Groundnut	346	146	101	97
Rapeseed and mustard	190	611	557	625
Sugarcane	1308	1793	2041	2199
Potato	163	341	408	553

Source Calculated from data in Statistical Abstract U.P.

Appendix 3: Trends in Yield of Major Crops in U.P.: 1969–2013

Crops	Yield in quintal per hectare (triennium average centred around)			
	1969–70	1989–90	2001–02	2013–14
Rice	7.42	17.76	21.62	24.31
Wheat	12.30	21.57	27.56	31.16
Jowar	6.00	9.76	10.21	11.73
Bajra	6.86	10.63	13.30	19.91
Maize	9.60	12.46	16.58	19.25
Barley	9.51	16.81	23.75	28.19
Total cereals	9.40	18.52	23.92	25.46
Gram	7.53	8.35	9.09	7.09
Arhar (pigeon pea)	11.58	12.61	13.03	9.73
Total pulses	8.40	8.77	8.84	7.24
Total food grains	9.18	17.10	21.90	23.34
Groundnut	7.08	8.77	9.21	9.21
Rapeseed and mustard	5.32	9.02	10.87	10.22
Sugarcane	422.78	538.22	543.33	640.30
Potato	95.40	185.28	225.34	227.66

Source Calculated from data in Statistical Abstract U.P.

Appendix 4: Trends in Agriculture Output and Input in Uttar Pradesh: 1980–81 to 2013–14

Year	Food grain output (hundred thousand tonnes)	Area irrigated (lakh ha.)			Gross sown area (hundred thousand ha.)	Fertilizer distribution	
		Net	Gross	Gross irrigated area As % of GSA		Total hundred thousand tonnes	Per ha. GSA (kg)
1980–81	249.5	94.5	113.7	46.3	245.7	11.5	46.8
1981–82	242.9	95.4	116.2	46.9	247.7	12.7	51.3
1982–83	265	98.8	121.3	49.1	247	14.3	57.9
1983–84	292	98.8	122.5	48.9	250.6	16.4	65.4
1984–85	299.2	101.5	127.3	50.7	251.2	16.1	64.1
1985–86	314.3	101.3	129.1	51.0	252.9	19.7	77.9
1986–87	303	98.5	134.1	53.2	251.9	17.7	70.3
1987–88	287	100.4	139.2	57.0	244.2	16	65.5
1988–89	354.4	101.7	141.1	55.9	252.5	21.4	84.8
1989–90	337.9	102.3	143.8	56.7	253.4	20.9	82.5
1990–91	355.2	105.4	147.7	58.0	254.8	22.4	87.9
1991–92	355.3	110.5	154.3	61.0	252.8	22.5	89
1992–93	362.5	113.2	160	62.3	256.8	21.8	84.9
1993–94	372.1	114.6	163.6	64.4	254	22.9	90.2
1994–95	388.3	116.7	168.2	66.2	254.2	24.8	102.5
1995–96	383.5	117.5	169.7	65.8	257.9	26	100.8
1996–97	423.8	120	174.7	66.9	261.3	27.6	105.6
1997–98	416.8	120.1	173.2	66.5	260.5	30.3	116.3
1998–99	388.2	126.9	177	67.7	261.6	30.5	116.6
1999–00	442.6	124.7	175.8	70.0	251.2	32.7	130.2
2000–01	427.4	124	176.9	69.9	253	29.6	117
2001–02	441.4	128.3	182.2	71.6	254.5	32.6	128.1
2002–03	382.8	128.5	177.9	73.2	243.1	32.4	133.3
2003–04	444.6	132.3	185.2	72.9	254.2	32.95	129.6
2004–05	400.0	131.2	189.4	74.2	255.2	33.1	129.7
2005–06	410.9	130.7	189.7	75.0	253.1	34.64	136.9
2006–07	418.7	133.1	192.2	75.6	254.1	37.35	147.0
2007–08	430.3	130.8	191.4	75.6	253.2	37.56	148.3
2008–09	473.8	134.4	196.1	77.0	254.7	39.73	156.0

(continued)

(continued)

Year	Food grain output (hundred thousand tonnes)	Area irrigated (lakh ha.)			Gross sown area (hundred thousand ha.)	Fertilizer distribution	
		Net	Gross	Gross irrigated area As % of GSA		Total hundred thousand tonnes	Per ha. GSA (kg)
2009–10	446.6	133.8	193.5	76.1	254.4	42.61	167.5
2010–11	481.9	134.4	199.0	77.7	256.1	50.88	198.6
2011–12	520.6	138.1	199.0	77.4	257.3	42.58	165.5
2012–13	522.8	139.3	201.9	78.2	258.2	46.51	180.1
2013–14	505.0	140.3	204.0	78.8	259.0	38.42	148.3

Source Statistical Diary, Uttar Pradesh (Annual)

Appendix 5: Agriculture Price Parity Index in Uttar Pradesh (1970–71 = 100): 1981–82 to 2014–15

Year	Prices paid by farmers	Prices received by farmers	Agriculture prices parity index
1981–82	248.8	242.3	97.4
1982–83	272.4	246.3	90.4
1983–84	292.3	276.6	94.6
1984–85	307.3	280.4	91.2
1985–86	336.2	303.6	90.3
1986–87	355.8	327.6	92.1
1987–88	390.5	392.4	100.5
1988–89	416.1	388.5	93.4
1989–90	453.6	411.4	90.7
1990–91	524.1	489.6	93.4
1991–92	605.6	551.8	91.1
1992–93	629.3	538.2	85.5
1993–94	692.7	675.4	97.5

(continued)

(continued)

Year	Prices paid by farmers	Prices received by farmers	Agriculture prices parity index
1994–95	761.8	748.1	98.2
1995–96	845.8	784.1	92.7
1996–97	943.5	856.1	90.7
1997–98	998.6	873.5	87.5
1998–99	1166.5	992.6	95.1
1999–00	1122.0	937.6	83.6
2000–01	1165.3	901.9	77.4
2001–02	1190.6	950.0	79.8
2002–03	1202.6	1050.3	87.3
2002–03	1203.6	1050.3	87.3
2003–04	1267.8	1113.8	87.9
2004–05	1331.2	1174.7	88.2
2005–06	1382.2	1252.5	90.6
2006–07	1570.0	1381.0	88.0
2007–08	1671.0	1431.1	85.6
2008–09	1714.8	1723.7	100.5
2009–10	2026.0	2125.7	104.9
2010–11	2157.9	2035.8	94.3
2011–12	2500.4	2120.5	84.8
2012–13	3133.7	2724.7	86.9
2013–14	3799.2	3146.1	82.8
2014–15	4179.3	3900.6	93.3

Note Figures for 2010–11 to 2014–15 which are at 2004–05 prices have been converted into 1970–71 prices
Source Statistical Diary U.P. (Annual)

Appendix 6: Indicators of Private Investment in Agriculture in U.P.: 1980–81 to 2013–14

Year	No. of new pump sets installed (in '000)	Loans distributed by primary agricultural credit societies (in Rs. million) (Rs. in crore)
1980–81	108	1889.4
1981–82	101	2212.7
1982–83	107	2397.0
1983–84	111	2579.9
1984–85	118	2299.6
1985–86	114	2544.8
1986–87	115	2590.3
1987–88	123	3247.4
1988–89	126	3165.2
1989–90	179	3875.4
1990–91	258	4470.4
1991–92	165	6371.5
1992–93	121	7599.4
1993–94	169	7635.3
1994–95	192	8026.1
1995–96	112	8170.5
1996–97	55	7974.7
1997–98	58	7949.0
1998–99	25	9146.8
1999–00	434	9891.7
2000–01	67	8703.1
2001–02	75	10,989.6
2002–03	56	10,425.4
2003–04	62	11,562.0
2004–05	64	13,804.7
2005–06	60	15,649.2
2006–07	69	17,183.7
2007–08	51	20,249.7
2008–09	26	21,175.9
2009–10	42	24,673.2
2010–11	54	29,159.9

(continued)

(continued)

Year	No. of new pump sets installed (in '000)	Loans distributed by primary agricultural credit societies (in Rs. million) (Rs. in crore)
2011–12	42	34,482.8
2012–13	24	38,850.6
2013–14	18	58,003.7

Source Calculated from Statistical Diary U.P. (Annual)

Appendix 7: Public Sector Investment in Agriculture in U.P.

Year	Investment in agriculture (Rs. million)	Investment in agriculture %	GSDPAG (Rs. billion)	Index investment in Ag.	Index GSDPAG
1993–94	4373.1	1.43	305.27	100.0	100.0
1994–95	4712.5	1.35	349.10	107.8	114.4
1995–96	3927.5	1.03	380.30	89.8	124.6
1996–97	5949.4	1.29	460.29	136.0	150.8
1997–98	7902.9	1.68	469.69	180.7	153.9
1998–99	8059.8	1.55	518.45	184.3	169.8
1999–00	15,973.8	2.82	567.31	365.3	185.8
2000–01	15,123.5	2.62	578.31	345.8	189.4
2001–02	21,487.4	3.58	599.57	491.4	196.4
2002–03	19,652.7	3.25	605.00	449.4	198.2
2003–04	27,578.3	3.92	703.18	630.6	230.3
2004–05	17,660.9	1.81	975.86	403.9	319.7
2005–06	16,831.7	1.56	1076.23	384.9	352.6
2006–07	32,914.1	2.80	1173.93	752.6	384.6
2007–08	32,274.9	2.50	1292.41	738.0	423.4
2008–09	52,277.1	3.33	1571.47	1195.4	514.8
2009–10	66,664.9	3.76	1771.84	1524.4	580.4
2010–11	33,874.5	1.72	1968.88	774.6	645.0
2011–12	22,522.5	0.97	2310.90	515.0	757.0
2012–13	27,851.9	1.03	2703.41	636.9	885.6
2013–14	34,739.0	1.15	3027.75	794.4	991.8
2014–15	54,995.0	1.74	3167.88	1257.6	1037.7

Source Calculated from Budget Documents, U.P. Government, and State Domestic Product

References

Chand, R. (2017). *Doubling farmers income: Rationale, strategy, prospects and action plan*. NITI Ayog Policy Paper No. 1/2017, New Delhi.
Division of Economics and Statistics. (2016). *District wise development indicators 2015*. Lucknow: State Planning Institute, Planning Department, U.P. Government.
Kumar, S., & Taneja, N. K. (2008). Agricultural growth and performance of Uttar Pradesh: A total factor productivity analysis. *Agricultural Situation in India, LIV*(VII), 463–469.
Narayanamoorthy, A. (2017). Farm income in India: Myth and realities. *Indian Journal of Agricultural Economics, 72*(3).
NSSO. (2014). *Farmers situation in India 2014*, 71 NSS Round NSSO, New Delhi.
Planning Commission. (2007). *Uttar Pradesh Development Report*. New Delhi: Academic Foundation.
Planning Commission. (2008). *Roadmap for rapid development of Uttar Pradesh*. New Delhi: Government of India.
Reddy, D. N., & Mishra, S. (2010). Economic reforms, small farmer economy and agrarian crisis. In R. S. Deshpande, & S. Arora (Eds.), *Agrarian crisis and farmer suicides* (pp. 43–69). New Delhi: Sage.
Satyasai, K. J. S., & Mehrotra, N. (2016). *Enhancing farmers' income*. Mumbai: NABARD.
Singh, A. K. (2012a). Economic viability and sustainability of small scale farming: A study in the irrigated Gangetic plains of U.P. *Anveshak, 42*(1 & 2), 9–30.
Singh, A. K. (2012b). Deficiencies in agricultural marketing and input delivery system: A view from the field. *Agricultural Economics Research Review, 25*, Conference Number, pp. 421–426.
Singh, R. (2014). Agrarian structure and agricultural development: An inter-district analysis. In A. K. Singh, & S. Mehrotra (Eds.), *Land policies for growth and equity: Transforming the agrarian structure in Uttar Pradesh* (pp. 76–91). New Delhi: Sage Publications.
Singh, S. (2018). Doubling farmers' incomes: Mechanisms and challenges. *Economic and Political Weekly, 53*(7), 15–19.
U.P. Planning Department. (2015). *Annual Plan Uttar Pradesh 2014–15*. Lucknow: U.P. Government.
U.P. State Planning Institute (Annual). (2015). *State income estimates: 2004–05 to 2012–13*. Lucknow: State Planning Institute, Planning Department, U.P. Government.
U.P. State Planning Institute (Annual). *Statistical Abstract U.P.* Lucknow: State Planning Institute, Planning Department, U.P. Government, (various issues).
U.P. State Planning Institute (Annual). *Statistical Diary U.P.* Lucknow: State Planning Institute, Planning Department, U.P.Government, (various issues).

Professor Ajit Kumar Singh (born 1944) obtained his M.A. and Ph.D. degrees in Economics from the University of Lucknow, Lucknow. He also holds a PG Diploma in National and International Development from the Institute of Social Studies, The Hague, Netherlands. He has taught at the University of Lucknow and Ram Manohar Lal Avadh University, Faizabad. He joined the Giri Institute of Development Studies, Lucknow as Professor in 1987 and was Director of the Institute from 2004 to February 2013. Presently he is National Fellow, Indian Council of Social Science Research.

A reputed economist Professor Singh has been a member of various working groups of the Planning commission and committees of the government at the state and central level. He was member Taxation and Resource Mobilisation Committee, Government of U.P. (1995) and Second State Finance Commission, U.P. (2001–02). He was also member of the Agrarian Relations Committee appointed by the Government of India. He was member of the Study Group for Preparation of Roadmap for Rapid Development of UP appointed by the Planning Commission. He has been member of the academic bodies of several universities.

Prof. Singh has written extensively on different aspects of planning and development with particular focus on the state of U.P. He has over 100 published papers to his credit apart from a large number of seminar papers. He has also guided forty research projects for national and international organizations.

Prof. A. K. Singh has authored many books, which include *Patterns of Regional Development; Economic Development and Inequalities in China, Rural Poverty and Agricultural Development; Land Use, Environment and Economic Growth in India; and Uttar Pradesh Development Report 2000; and Socio-Economic Conditions of the Farming Communities in Northern India, Patterns of Development.* In addition, he has edited five books: *Economic Planning and Policy in India; Planning Strategy for a Developing Region; Twelfth Finance Commission Recommendations; Their Implications for the State Finances; and Land Policies for Agricultural Growth With Equity; and Transparency, Disclosure and Governance.*

Prof. A. K. Singh has been Vice President, Regional Science Association 1990, President UP and Uttarakhand Economic Association 2007 and Vice President, Indian Society of Labour Economics, 2009. In 2010 he was given the Kautilya award by the UP and Uttarakhand Economic Association for his contribution to teaching and research in economics.

Public and Private Capital Formation in Agriculture and Contribution of Institutional Credit to Private Investment

Seema Bathla and Shiv Jee

Abstract This article estimates the magnitude of public and private capital formation in agriculture in Uttar Pradesh with an aim to analyse its contribution in accelerating the rate of agricultural growth and the role of institutional credit in raising rural household's investment. It begins with the temporal patterns in the public and private investments in agriculture and allied activities in the state as well as in India from 1981–82 to 2013–14. This is followed by a comprehensive evaluation of the investment behaviour of the borrower and non-borrower rural households during the NSS 70th round carried out in 2012–13. Broad findings reveal that both public and private capital formation in agriculture have scaled up to reach Rs. 18 billion and Rs. 47.2 billion respectively by 2013 at 2004–05 prices. However, the quantum of investment seems to be critically low in view of the existing low rate of agricultural growth and sizeable population dependent on it. Investment must increase by 2.76 times from 2015–16 level to achieve the targeted 5.1% rate of growth set by the government. While the required rate of increase in private investment (mainly by rural households) is estimated at 6.2% per annum, the same by the respective state government in agriculture as well as rural infrastructure would be 3.1% per annum. Private investment is majorly done through borrowings—52.8% from non-institutional sources and 47.2% from institutional sources with little disparity across the land size holdings. Farmers borrowing from the institutional sources tend to make relatively higher investments, which suggest improving the outreach of institutional agencies to the small land size holders across the poorer regions. The estimated elasticity of institutional credit with respect to private investment in agriculture is reasonably high at 0.26. The analysis suggests increasing institutional credit together with public investments in irrigation and rural infrastructure to facilitate higher rate of growth in agriculture in the state. A growing investment preference of rural households in non-farm business activities is identified for which a favourable credit policy should be in place.

Keywords Capital formation in agriculture · Investment · Institutional credit

---

S. Bathla (✉) · S. Jee
Centre for the Study of Regional Development, Jawaharlal Nehru University, New Delhi 110067, India
e-mail: seema.bathla@gmail.com

© Springer Nature Singapore Pte Ltd. 2019
R. P. Mamgain (ed.), *Growth, Disparities and Inclusive Development in India*, India Studies in Business and Economics,
https://doi.org/10.1007/978-981-13-6443-3_11

1 Introduction

Uttar Pradesh is one of the largest and the least developed states in India in terms of per capita income and high incidence of rural poverty. Being an agrarian state, the dependency of population on agriculture is significantly high at nearly 62%. The gross domestic product from agriculture and allied activities (GSDPA) has increased manifold from Rs. 467 billion in triennium ending (TE) 1983 to Rs. 766 billion in TE 2003 and further to Rs. 1001 billion in TE 2013 at 2004–05 prices and contributes 22% to the national income. However, the rate of growth in agriculture has persistently hovered around 2.5% per annum, though a slight increase has been witnessed of late. The land productivity has also become double at Rs. 60,118 per ha in TE 2013 from TE 1983, but the rate of growth is way below at 3.13 per annum per cent compared to that for major states at 4.29% per annum during 2000–13. Furthermore, marked variations in the agricultural performance across the districts have been identified, with those situated in the Eastern and Bundelkhand regions suffering from low productivity and extreme backwardness (Srivastava and Ranjan 2016; Mamgain and Verick 2017).

Among various factors cited behind a sluggish growth performance of agriculture in the state, small and declining size of land holdings and inadequate public investments are foremost (Singh 2016). The new agricultural policy announced by the state government in 2013 (Annual Plan 2014–15) proposed several strategies to achieve a 5.1% rate of growth in agriculture during the Twelfth Five-Year Plan (2012–16). The key measures included an increase in the production and productivity through improvement in input use efficiency, soil health and development of sodic and waste lands and rural infrastructure. These initiatives, mainly through public support, were expected to induce farmers to undertake investments and accelerate production and productivity. This essentially indicates that farmers would require adequate credit for meeting short-term expenses as well as making long-term investments. However, the progress and the effectiveness of these policy interventions are not known with much certainty as an increase in the GSDPA turns out to be trivial.

Furthermore, going by the central government's mandate to alleviate agrarian distress across the country, the respective state governments are expected to act swiftly on the developmental programmes and rehabilitation packages in the affected areas. The broad aim is to build up strategies that can revitalise agricultural growth, develop off-farm activities and infrastructure that enable doubling of farmers' real income (DFI) by 2022–23. For this to be accomplished, the agriculture and allied sector has to grow at 10.41% per annum in the next seven years by 2022–23 (Chand 2017). The annual rate of growth in farmers' real net income per ha in Uttar Pradesh is estimated at 4.5% between 2002 and 2012, which has to increase at 9.16% to facilitate doubling by 2022–23 (NCAER 2017).[1] Needless to say that growth in agriculture assumes considerable significance in this pursuit and has to be facilitated through

---

[1]Based on the NSS 70th round (2012–13) (schedule 33), the estimated average per hectare net income earned by farmers in UP is Rs. 62,426 (Rs. 51,683 from crop cultivation and Rs. 10,743 from livestock).

consistent public policy and institutional support together with the development of rural infrastructure, marketing, food processing and retailing.

In this backdrop, this chapter examines the size and composition of public and private investment (synonymous with capital formation) in agriculture in Uttar Pradesh with an aim to analyse its contribution in accelerating the rate of agricultural growth and the role of institutional credit in raising rural households' (private) investment. It begins with the temporal trends in public investment in agriculture and irrigation to gauge the extent of government support in the rural areas. The time series on public expenditure (revenue and capital)[2] from 1981–82 to 2013–14 is taken from the Finance Accounts, GOI. Section 2 delves into the composition of private (rural household) investment in agriculture based on the decennial National Sample Survey All India Debt and Investment (schedule 18.2) viz. 1981–82 (37th round) 1991–92 (48th round), 2002–03 (59th round) and 2012–13 (70th round), respectively. The nominal values are converted into real prices at 2004–05 base using the GSDP deflator. This is followed by a detailed evaluation of the investment behaviour of the borrower and non-borrower rural households across various lands holding size based on the 70th round in Sect. 3. The impact of institutional credit and other key factors on HH investment in agriculture is gauged using ordinary least squares approach in double log functional form. Section 4 draws conclusions and implications. The analysis would add to the literature in understanding the existing status of public and private capital formation in agriculture in the state, along with the required rate as a prerequisite for achieving the targeted growth and providing insights into the investment behaviour of the borrower and non-borrower households for devising appropriate policies.

2 Magnitude of Public Capital Formation in Agriculture and Irrigation

The total expenditure incurred by the Uttar Pradesh government and the share of development (i.e. social and economic) expenditure and agriculture–irrigation expenditure within it[3] is provided in Table 1. The estimates for major 17 Indian states are also given for the purpose of comparison. Uttar Pradesh spent Rs. 136 billion during TE 1983–84 which increased to Rs. 473 billion in TE 2003–04 and then surged to Rs. 950 billion by TE 2013–14. The expenditure grew at an annual rate of almost eight per cent. The share of expenditure is close to 14% of the total expenditure incurred by all the states at Rs. 8258 billion in TE 2013. The development expenditure which is primarily utilised for various social and economic activities has increased five times in UP and nearly seven times across all the states. The real rate of growth in the

---

[2]Capital expenditure on agriculture and irrigation is taken to represent public investment in agriculture due to non-availability of official estimates. It may slightly be on the higher side due to inclusion of expenditure on financial assets.

[3]This expenditure excludes loans and advances and transfers from the central/union government as a maximum amount is routed through the respective state governments only.

development expenditure has been much higher at almost nine per cent per annum during 2000–13 compared to the preceding decade. The nineties, which coincide with economic reforms witnessed a steep fall in the rate of growth in public expenditure, indicating a narrowing of fiscal space in almost every state. The brunt of declining pace of expenditure is however borne by the social and economic services as their share in total expenditure steadily dwindled from 74.9% in TE 1983 to 59.49% in UP and to 66.63% for all states by TE 2013. Within the development expenditure, spending on agriculture–irrigation has increased at a much slower rate compared to other services.

Public spending on agriculture–irrigation increased from Rs. 29 billion in TE 1983 to Rs. 71 billion in TE 2003 which is far below compared to that in other states. Not only that, the share of agriculture–irrigation expenditure in development expenditure has consistently fallen in every state including UP, thereby suggesting a low priority being accorded to the agricultural sector (Bathla et al. 2017). The decline in the share of agriculture expenditure in development expenditure is much higher from 28.6 to 12.5% compared to 28.95 to 16.94% for all states together. Apparently, an increase in rate of resource allocation to this sector at 4.9% per annum during the 2000s has not been able to trigger growth, which remained low at 2.56% per annum. This may be explained by a low rate of annual investment at 2.82% compared to a 9.2% for all states together as shown in Table 1.

Further, out of total expenditure incurred on agriculture–irrigation in the state, only 40.41% got invested during TE 1983. This share of investment has further reduced to 25.04% (Rs. 17.75 billion) implying that in spite of an increased spending on agriculture–irrigation from Rs. 20 billion to Rs. 71 billion over the period, it has not translated into investment. In other words, government resources are being diverted towards day-to-day expenses and input subsidies, categorised under the revenue expenditure. Low capital intensity is further validated by an insignificant increase in net irrigated area in the state at 0.49% per annum during 2000–13 compared to 1.68% for all states together. At the same time, irrigation subsidy has surged from Rs. 3.1 billion to Rs. 27.5 billion in TE 2013. It has grown at a much higher rate at 8.5% compared to that at all India at 5.2% per annum and growth in investment at 2.82% (Table 1).

On per hectare basis also, the investment scenario is found to be dismal in UP. As shown in Table 2, the real public spending in agriculture and irrigation has increased from Rs. 1688 to Rs. 4237 which is again below the national average of Rs. 6745. However, out of this spending, per ha investment turned out to be abysmally low during the nineties at Rs. 311, increased to Rs. 808 in TE 2003 and then slightly increased to Rs. 932 in TE 2013. Clearly, UP is way behind the average national level public investment in agriculture–irrigation at Rs. 2328 per ha. The expenditure intensity, measured as share of agriculture–irrigation expenditure in GSDPA, has hardly changed over the years from 6.24 to 7.05%, implying a low priority accorded to this sector in the state with hardly two per cent diverted towards asset creation.

Given that UP has rich soil and water resources, and productivity is comparatively higher at Rs. 60,118 compared to many states witnessing below Rs. 50,000, the state must raise investment in agriculture R&D, irrigation and other rural infras-

Table 1 Public expenditure on agriculture-irrigation in UP and India; Rs. billion at 2004–05 prices

		GSDPA	Total		Development		Agri-irrigation		Per cent share of agri-irri. exp		Per cent share of investment in agri-irri. in
			Expenditure		Expenditure		Expenditure		In dev. exp.		Total agri-irri. exp.
Uttar Pradesh	TE 1983	467	136		102		29		28.61		40.41
	TE 1993	612	262		160		38		23.50		14.22
	TE 2003	766	473		273		45		16.44		31.94
	TE 2013	1001	950		565		71		12.49		25.04
Major states	TE 1983	2954	1109		834		241		28.95		40.65
	TE 1993	4020	2047		1402		343		24.49		27.87
	TE 2003	5141	3863		2251		423		18.78		34.55
	TE 2013	7578	8258		5502		932		16.94		37.50
Annual rate of growth (per cent)											
Uttar Pradesh	1980–89	2.67	8.45		6.96		5.32		–		0.37
	1990–99	2.32	3.81		1.70		0.32		–		2.07
	2000–13	2.56	7.88		9.04		4.90		–		2.82
Major states	1980–89	2.89	7.16		6.31		4.41		–		0.52
	1990–99	3.66	5.67		4.10		2.73		–		4.01
	2000–13	3.81	7.74		9.05		7.80		–		9.14

Source Based on finance accounts, GOI

Table 2 Per ha public investment in agriculture–irrigation in UP and India (Rs. at 2004–05 prices)

		Public expenditure	Public investment	Per cent share of agri–irri.	Land
		In agri–irri./ha	In agri–irri./ha	Expenditure in GSDPA	Productivity
Uttar Pradesh	TE 1983	1688	636	6.24	27,043
	TE 1993	2175	311	6.14	35,448
	TE 2003	2562	808	5.85	43,772
	TE 2013	4237	932	7.05	60,118
All major states	TE 1983	1713	653	8.17	20,956
	TE 1993	2442	644	8.54	28,590
	TE 2003	2949	986	8.22	35,820
	TE 2013	6745	2328	12.30	54,827

Source Based on finance accounts, GOI and agricultural statistics at a glance, GOI

tructure. The incremental capital-output ratio[4] (averaged 2007–12 and 2012–14) for public investment in agriculture, irrigation together with rural road-transport and rural energy infrastructure (weighted by the respective share of every expenditure in GSDP) is estimated to be 1.70. This may suggest that if agriculture has to grow at 5.1% per annum, the public investment rate in rural areas (including agriculture, irrigation, rural roads, transport and energy) must increase by 8.67% by 2022–23. However, if the aim is to double farmers' income, i.e. to achieve a targeted growth of 9.16, the public investment rate must increase at 15.57% per annum over seven-year period, starting from 2015–16. The state would require an additional capital of Rs. 300 billion by 2022–23 at base 2015–16. Out of this amount, additional investment in rural roads–transport would be the maximum at Rs. 146 billion, followed by irrigation at Rs. 80 billion, rural energy at Rs. 31 billion and agriculture and allied activities at Rs. 43 billion, respectively. Total public investment (initial plus additional required) in agriculture–irrigation-energy-roads–transport would be Rs. 410 billion by 2022–23 and must grow at 20% per annum (Bathla 2017). It is worth mentioning that these projected capital requirements can reduce if the state makes sincere efforts to improve efficiency in the use of capital.

---

[4]The ICOR estimates additional unit of capital (investment) needed to produce an additional unit of output for a particular period. It is taken as a measure of capital efficiency, estimated as: i/g where i = investment rate and g is incremental GSDPA.

2.1 Size and Composition of Private Investment in Agriculture and Allied Activities

The All India Debt Investment Survey (AIDIS) provides estimates on gross capital expenditure (GCE) and fixed capital expenditure (FCE) of both rural and agricultural households. These are further categorised into (a) residential land and buildings (RLB), (b) farm business (FB) and (c) non-farm business (NFB). GCE is a broader concept which is equal to FCE, purchase of land and normal repairs and maintenance. The FCE in farm business broadly refers to private capital formation or investment by farmers. It encompasses eight components, of which expenditure is relatively higher in land improvement, livestock, irrigation, transport and machinery and implements. The non-farm business covers expenditure on manufacturing and other activities, land improvement, purchase of equipment and other accessories.[5]

The details on the magnitude of private investment in agriculture, i.e. FCE FB and its relative position vis-a-vis other investment activities by the rural households during the four rounds surveyed between 1981–82 and 2012–13, are presented in Table 3. The total real investment has increased from Rs. 11.818 billion in 1981–82 to 17.653 billion in 2002–03 and then sharply rose to Rs. 47.207 billion in 2012–13. The annual rate of growth in private farm investment, which was at a lowly 1.21% during 1981–1991, increased to 2.59% during 1991–2002 and then jumped to 10.34% in the subsequent decade. In terms of per rural household, farm investment has increased marginally from Rs. 769.5 in 1981–82 to Rs. 831 in 2002–03 and then to Rs. 2253 by 2012–13. The annual rate of growth in private investment had been much higher in the preceding decade and was somewhat closer to the national average rate of growth at 9.31%.

The relative position of investment in agriculture vis-à-vis non-farm investments (FCEFB/FCE) has consistently declined from 34.49% in 1981–82 to 30.6% in 2002–03 and slightly improved to 37.29% in the subsequent decade. Similar to the national level scenario, agriculture investment in the state has lost priority among the rural households between 1991 and 2002 and subsequently recouped as seen from the share of FCE FB in GCE as well as of FCEFB in FCE. Notwithstanding this renewed interest, the household's investment preference is found to be switching towards non-farm business (NFB). The annual real rate of growth in investment in the NFB is much higher at 15.21% compared to FB at 10.49 and RLB at 6.25%, respectively, between 2002 and 2012. This finding is different from the national level picture and across many states where a growing share of investment in RLB is undertaken by the farmers at the expense of agriculture investment. The rate of growth in NFB investment is also low at 3.5% per year (Bathla and Kumari 2017).

Within agriculture activities, the households are inclined to spend more on implements–machinery and transport. As shown in Table 4, the composition of investment has changed over the period from 1981 to 2012–13. Its grouping into seven heads clearly shows a changing preference of farmers towards purchase of implements—

---

[5]The survey considers expenditure on land improvement, land rights as components of fixed capital formation and exclude value of land in the estimation of capital stock.

Table 3 Private investment in agriculture and allied activities (FCE FB) at 2004–05 prices

		FCE FB: Rs. million	Rs./ha	Rs./rural HH	FCEFB/GCE (per cent)	FCEFB/FCE (per cent)	FCE NFB (Rs./rural HH)
UP	1981–82	11,818	684	769	18.86	34.49	–
	1991–92	13,325	770	703	17.05	27.35	–
	2002–03	17,653	1015	831	19.63	30.60	142
	2012–13	47,207	2835	2253	29.82	37.29	586
India	1981–82	66,268	471	753	20.17	35.30	–
	1991–92	94,150	672	815	22.24	32.81	–
	2002–03	94,675	687	669	15.56	21.80	434
	2012–13	227,290	1645	1631	18.78	23.32	611
Annual rate of growth							
UP	1981–91	1.21	–	−0.90	–	–	–
	1991–02	2.59	–	1.53	–	–	–
	2002–12	10.34	–	10.49	–	–	15.21
India	1981–91	3.57	–	0.80	–	–	–
	1991–02	0.05	–	−1.77	–	–	–
	2002–12	9.15	–	9.31	–	–	3.50

Source NSS AIDIS (schedule 18.2); All India estimates may not be comparable with NAS, CSO as these refer to only agriculture activities by rural HH based on a sample

machinery and transport from irrigation and other assets. Spending on irrigation structures has lost importance over time as its share in total FCE FB has fallen from 13.35 to 3.26%. Since the National Sample Survey (NSS) added livestock investment only from 2002, a comparison of relative share of each investment during 2002 and 2012 is more meaningful. It shows an increase in investment in land improvement from 1.22 to 3.13%; livestock from 18.75 to 19.8%; implements–machinery from 61.28 to 73.37%, respectively. The trend is similar to the national level, except for livestock whose share in total investment has increased considerably by 10 percentage points from 13.8 to 23.1%.

A decline in the share of agriculture investment in total investment and a concomitant increase in the non-farm business, mainly in the informal enterprises in UP may be attributed to both push and pull factors. Evidence exists on the lowering of net returns from crop cultivation from 2004 to 2013, which is manifested in an agrarian distress across many states and regions (Kannan 2011; Haque 2016), social and demographic factors and also a growing size of the non-farm sector, especially the informal trading enterprises (Maithi and Mitra 2011; Mishra and Singh 2016). Further, a consistent decrease in the employment share in agriculture from 67.19% in 1993–94 to 49.73% in 2011–12 is reported with growing employment opportunities

Table 4 Per cent share of components of fixed capital expenditure in agriculture in rural households

Key components	1981–82	1991–92	2002–03	2012–13	1981–82	1991–92	2002–03	2012–13
	UP	UP	UP	UP	India	India	India	India
1. Land improvements	4.51	9.51	1.22	3.15	14.80	14.29	5.90	11.88
2. Orchards	0.65	–	–	0.15	3.42	1.85	1.52	1.46
3. Irrigation	13.35	10.12	9.10	3.26	25.36	31.75	33.05	22.55
4. Agricultural implements and transport	68.36	73.01	61.28	73.37	46.12	45.50	35.92	39.69
5. Farm buildings	11.94	5.83	8.56	–	6.95	4.23	8.26	–
6. Others	1.18	1.84	1.22	0.28	3.33	2.12	1.35	1.34
7. Livestock	–	–	18.75	19.80	–	–	13.83	23.08
FCE FB	100	100	100	100	100	100	100	100

Source NSS AIDIS (schedule 18.2)

in the construction and manufacturing sectors. Such employment is mostly casual in nature and fetches low income to a majority of workers (Mamgain and Verick 2017).

These findings have strong implications for the future growth of agriculture in the state. A big push in investment is therefore required to accelerate the agricultural sector's growth as envisaged in the state's Five-Year Plan. The estimated ICOR on private account is 1.22, which implies that in order to achieve the targeted 5.1% agricultural growth and 9.16% growth in farmers real income, private investment rate must increase at 6.23 and 11.20% over the stipulated period. Accordingly, an additional private capital of Rs. 216 billion (total Rs. 352 billion—initial plus additional investment) will be required by 2022–23 at 2015–16 prices (Bathla 2017).

3 Contribution of Institutional Credit to Private Investment in Agriculture

This section provides insights into the investment behaviour of rural households with an aim to understand their dependence on institutional credit for making investments. The analysis is carried out across various land holding sizes based on the NSS 70th round (2012–13). Table 5 highlights the general characteristics of rural households, bifurcated as per borrowers and non-borrowers. Nearly 3000 HH fall under the two categories having almost equal age of the head of the HH and family size. A higher percentage of institutional borrower HHs (99%) are engaged in agricultural activities compared to non-institutional borrower HHs having non-agriculture activities and labour as their main occupations. The average size of land is higher at 0.93 ha in the first category compared to 0.30 ha in the second. As per the size of land, more than 60% of HHs fall under the marginal category under both the groups.

The percentage of small farmers (having 1–2 ha of land) hold 16.5% share under the first group (institutional borrowing HH) compared to 4.1% in the second group (non-institutional borrowing HH). The number of large farmer HHs is more in the first category compared to the second category. The social structure is dominated by other backward classes, following Hinduism as the main religion in the state. The education level of the head of the HH is low as a majority have studied only up to the primary level. The HH falling under the institutional borrowing category is relatively better educated. The t-test shows difference between the two categories of HH for each characteristic to be statistically significant.

As regards private investment, i.e. fixed capital expenditure, institutional borrowers are better off as they invest relatively more (Rs. 20,143) as compared to the non-institutional borrowers (Rs. 11,573). This is identified across each activity, and the difference turns out to be statistically significant at five per cent level. Both categories of HHs spend a higher amount on RLB at Rs. 9501 and Rs. 6093 compared to that in farm business, i.e. agriculture at Rs. 7175 and Rs. 4765, respectively. As elicited above, this phenomenon has been identified across each of the Indian state over the period, thereby suggesting a change in the investment behaviour of HHs away from agriculture (Bathla and Kumari 2017). Interestingly, even among the landless, marginal and small land holders, expenditure on RLB is higher than that in agriculture as shown in Table 6. The marginal farmers having an overwhelming presence in the state tend to make smaller investments in agriculture at Rs. 3519/hh which is way below the amount spent by medium size land holders at Rs. 22,733/hh. Needless to say that investment in each activity by the landless HH is substantially lower by five to even times compared to that by the medium and large land size holders. Out of total farm investments made, the contribution of marginal and small farmers is hardly 12%. Such disparities can be addressed by effective targeting of institutional credit and improving its outreach to the marginal and small farmers.

Table 7 presents details on the dependence of small and marginal farmers on institutional credit and the extent of borrowing done for the purpose of investment. It shows that a major portion of investment is undertaken through borrowings by each household grouped as per the land size. The small and large farmers make sizeable investment through personal sources, maybe from savings at Rs. 4271 and Rs. 23,739 compared to the borrowed amount at Rs. 5308 and Rs. 14,766. The dependence of landless and marginal farmers on borrowings from formal as well as informal sources for investment is much higher compared to other categories. Between institutional and non-institutional sources of finance for agriculture investment, the medium and large farmers borrow more from the non-institutional sources (Rs. 75,900/hh and Rs. 19,202/hh) compared to that from the institutional sources at Rs. 15,490 and Rs. 14,513 per HH, respectively.

The distribution of FCE FB as per broad land classes and sources of finance are shown in Table 8. Farmers make investments primarily through the borrowed amount—44.2% from non-institutional and 39.5% from institutional sources and there is hardly any disparity across various land size holdings. On an average, 16.3% investment in agriculture is done from personal sources. The large farmers make higher investment (39.7%) through their own sources. Their dependence on infor-

Table 5 General characteristics of rural HHs as per institutional and non-institutional borrowings in Uttar Pradesh (nominal prices)

Particulars	Institutional	Non-institutional	t-test value
Sample size (No.)	3074	3304	
Age (years)	49.3	44.5	13.05***
Family size (No.)	6.0	5.5	6.63***
Households as per type of occupation (per cent)			
Self-employment in agriculture	79.1	51.0	19.83***
Self-employment in non-agriculture	5.7	12.4	−3.73***
Regular wage/salary earning	5.1	7.2	−7.28**
Agricultural labour	3.7	9.6	−11.56***
Non-agriculture labour	4.9	15.6	−12.33***
Other	1.4	4.1	−5.89***
Land size (ha)	0.93	0.30	21.04***
Household as per size of land (per cent)			
Landless	9.8	27.0	−15.81***
Marginal (<1 ha)	63.0	67.7	−3.91***
Small (1–2 ha)	16.5	4.1	14.63***
Medium (2–10 ha)	8.1	1.1	11.97***
Large (>10 ha)	2.6	0.1	8.00***
Social structure of HH as per caste (per cent)			
Schedule tribe	0.40	2.0	−1.69*
Schedule caste	21.1	28.8	−8.81***
Other backward castes	53.8	55.1	−2.85***
General caste	24.7	14.1	13.94***
Social structure of HH as per religion (per cent)			
Hindu	88.6	86.3	1.98**
Muslim	10.4	13.4	−3.27***
Christian	–	0.2	−1.36
Other	1.0	–	5.11***
Education level of the head of household (per cent)			
Illiterate	38.6	53.8	−12.95***
Primary	18.3	19.0	−0.07
Middle	16.6	13.2	4.70***
Secondary	10.9	6.5	5.88***
Higher secondary and above	15.6	7.5	9.42***

(continued)

Table 5 (continued)

Particulars	Institutional	Non-institutional	t-test value
Fixed Capital Expenditure (Rs./HH)			
Fixed Capital Expenditure (FCE)	20,143	11,573	2.77**
FCE Farm Business (Agriculture)	7175	4765	4.19***
FCE Non-Farm Business	3467	721	1.99**
FCE Residential Land Buildings	9501	6093	0.78

Note *** is significant at one per cent, ** is significant at five per cent and * is significant at 10%

Table 6 FCE of rural HH as per land size in Uttar Pradesh during 2012–13 (nominal prices)

	Landless	Marginal	Small	Medium	Large	All
Average land size (ha)	–	0.33	1.38	2.63	6.71	0.54
FCE (Rs./hh)	5072	10,272	17,675	42,604	31,836	10,534
FCE FB (Rs./hh)	343	3519	4876	22,733	17,364	3432
FCE NFB (Rs./hh)	576	592	3923	9551	20	1063
FCE RLB (Rs./hh)	4153	6160	8876	10,320	14,452	6040

Table 7 FCE FB (agriculture) and extent of borrowing (Rs./hh)

Land class	FCE FB	From personal sources	From borrowing	From institutional borrowing	From non-inst. borrowing	Difference in mean (t test)
Landless	344	93	682	2153	364	1.76
Marginal	3523	909	5956	6687	5553	0.79
Small	4876	4271	5308	6840	1653	1.93***
Medium	22,651	11,558	26,651	15,490	75,900	−0.80
Large	17,364	23,739	14,766	14,513	19,202	0.36
All	3432	1132	5669	7184	4770	4.19***

Note *** is significant at one per cent, ** is significant at five per cent and * is significant at 10%

mal sources for investment is only 4.2% while that on formal is 56.1%. The landless and small farmers depend more on the institutional sources such as cooperatives and commercial banks by 57.8 and 47.2%, respectively, which is a positive aspect in UP. Furthermore, of the total borrowings taken for investment, the share of institutional sources is much higher among all categories of farmers, except marginal. The dependence of marginal farmers for asset creation is more on the non-institutional sources at 52.6%. The state average shows that 47.2% of farm investments are done through institutional sources and 52.8% from non-institutional sources. This is in contrast to the all India scenarios where institutional sources dominate in FCEFB at 63.4%. A high dependence on informal sources reflects the demand for credit for short-term and long-term purposes. Recognising a changing composition of long-

Table 8 Share of borrowings and non-borrowings in private FCE FB (%)

Land size	Distribution of FCE FB as per borrowing in UP (per cent)			Share of institutional and non-institutional sources in total borrowings (per cent)			
	Non-borrower	From Institutional sources	From Non-institutional	Institutional sources in UP	Non-institutional sources in UP	Institutional sources in India	Non-institutional sources in India
Landless	15.6	47.2	37.1	55.9	44.1	59.4	40.6
Marginal	12.4	35.0	52.6	39.9	60.1	47.9	52.1
Small	36.4	57.8	5.90	90.8	9.20	69.2	30.8
Medium	13.4	41.2	45.7	47.5	52.5	67.9	32.1
Large	39.7	56.1	4.20	93.0	7.00	79.1	20.9
All	16.3	39.5	44.2	47.2	52.8	63.4	36.6

term investments towards implements–machinery, tractors and livestock and also a growing preference of farmers for non-farm business, a credit policy that is inclusive and effective in meeting their needs is imperative.

Turning to the impact of institutional credit and other factors on private investment in agriculture in UP, we find a significant positive effect of credit advanced by the cooperatives and banks. The OLS results presented in double log functional form in Table 9 show elasticity of institutional credit to be 0.26, which implies that a 10% increase in the same would result in 2.6% increase in farm investment by rural HHs. Among the other determinants of private investment, family size and age of the household (representing experience) are found o be positive and statistically significant. Results also show that investment in agriculture is adversely affected by HH's priority to invest in non-farm business and residential land and buildings. The elasticity estimate turns out to be low and significant at 0.009 at one per cent level of significance. Further, investments by landless, small and other categories are much lower compared to that undertaken by large farmers. This is validated by Kumar and Saroj (2016) who found that the formal lenders (banks and other agencies) are explicitly biased towards large farmers and as a consequence marginal and small farmers are left out. The poor farmers have to depend on informal lenders for their credit needs and have to pay exorbitant rate of interest up to 36% per annum, which adversely impinge upon their welfare (Kumar et al. 2017). Another expected finding is that the self-employed HH in agriculture activities makes higher investments compared to those engaged in non-farm activities and labour. Education of the head of the HH matters as investments are more among those with better education. In view of large regional variations in the state, district dummies are taken in the equation, which are found to have positive and significant effect on investment in agriculture.

Table 9 Impact of institutional credit on private investment in agriculture in UP

Dependent variable—log FCE FB		
Explanatory variable	Coefficient	Standard error
Log of institutional credit (Rs./hh)	0.263***	0.028
Age of HH head (years)	0.005**	0.002
Family size (No.)	0.06***	0.010
Share of residential exp. in total expenditure (per cent)	−0.009***	0.0012
Land class (Large farmer as base)		
(Landless—1, otherwise—0)	−1.73***	0.242
(Marginal—1, otherwise—0)	−1.53***	0.19
(Small—1, otherwise—0)	−1.17***	0.195
(Medium—1, otherwise—0)	−0.63***	0.21
Household type (self employment in agriculture as base)		
(Self employment in non agriculture—1, otherwise—0)	−0.39***	0.13
(Agricultural labour—1, otherwise—0)	−0.48***	0.176
(Non-agricultural labour—1, otherwise—0)	−0.46***	0.148
(Regular/salaried job—1, otherwise—0)	−0.15	0.158
Other—1, otherwise—0	−0.43	0.339
Education of head (higher secondary and above as base)		
Illiterate—1, otherwise—0	−0.15	0.096
Primary—1, otherwise—0	−0.11	0.101
Middle—1, otherwise—0	0.051	0.101
Secondary—1, otherwise—0	0.25**	0.111
Caste (forward caste as base)		
ST—1, otherwise—0	−0.63	0.432
SC—1, otherwise—0	−0.46***	0.094
OBC—1, otherwise—0	−0.12*	0.072
District effects (dummy)	Yes	
Constant	5.79***	0.488
No. of observations	2786	

(continued)

Table 9 (continued)

Dependent variable—log FCE FB		
Explanatory variable	Coefficient	Standard error
R-squared	0.31	
Adj R-squared	0.28	
Root MSE	1.47	
Chi-square	13.23	
Prob Chi-square	0.0003	

Note *** is significant at one per cent, ** is significant at five per cent and * is significant at 10%

4 Main Findings and Implications

Uttar Pradesh lags behind most of the Indian states in terms of key economic and social indicators. Agriculture continues to be marred with low productivity growth and urgently requires public support through adequate investments and credit to augment private investment. This paper has examined these aspects by looking at the temporal trends in capital formation on public account from 1981/82 to 2013/14 based on the Finance Accounts and on private (farm households) account from 1981–82 to 2012–13 based on four decennial NSS AIDIS (schedule 18.2). A detailed analysis of investment behaviour of the borrower and non-borrower households is carried out for the recent NSS 70th (2012–13) round. The impact of institutional credit on private investment in agriculture is empirically analysed using the unit level data and applying OLS in double log functional form. The analysis is carried out at 2004–05 prices.

Broad findings reveal that real public and private capital formation in agriculture have grown at a much higher rate of 2.82 and 10.49% per annum during 2000–2013 compared to the preceding decades. However, the quantum of investment reached by 2013 at Rs. 23.4 billion on public account and Rs. 47.2 billion on private account appears to be critically small given the low rate of agricultural growth at 2.5% rate and sizeable population dependent on this sector. While the state government has set a growth target of 5.1% for the sector, the central government has aimed at 9.16% growth in real agriculture income to enable doubling of farmers' income by 2022–23. Such ambitious goals can be achieved by massive increase in public and private investments, among other measures. The estimated incremental capital-output ratio, when multiplied with the targeted rate of agricultural growth as well as farm income suggests the required public investment rate at 8.67 and 15.57% and private investment rate at 6.22 and 11.2%, respectively, over the stipulated period. For doubling farmers' income by 2022–23, the required annual rate of growth in investment would be 20.7% on public account and 14.51% on private account, amounting to an additional investment of Rs. 300 billion and Rs. 216 billion on respective accounts by 2022–23 at 2015–16 prices. This may necessitate provision for a significant increase in the resource allocation towards agriculture and irrigation in the annual budget and further efforts by the state to divert resources towards investment. Currently close to 25% of total expenditure is devoted to agriculture and irrigation, which constitutes almost seven per cent share in GSDPA. However, the amount that goes into investment is hardly two per cent of GSDPA, which should be increased.

For accelerating private investment, the analysis reveals that since farm HHs dependence on borrowings is considerably high (52.8% from non-institutional sources and 47.2% from institutional sources), an increase in the outreach of institutional agencies is a must. The magnitude of investments along with other socio-economic characteristics of institutional borrower HHs significantly differs from those of non-institutional borrower HHs. As of now, there is little disparity in the use of institutional loans for investment across various farm size holders. But medium and large farmers certainly have an edge over marginal and small farmers in accessing institutional loans. The estimated elasticity of institutional credit with respect to private investment in agriculture is reasonably high at 0.26, which suggests that a 10% increase would result in 2.6% higher investment in agriculture. The analysis suggests stepping up institutional credit together with public investments in irrigation and rural infrastructure to facilitate higher rate of growth in agriculture in the state. Finally, a growing investment preference of rural households in long-term assets such as implements–machinery, tractors, livestock and non-farm business assets is identified for which a favourable credit policy should be in place.

References

Bathla, S. (2017). *Public and private capital formation in agriculture in India: Current status and futuristic requirements for doubling farm income* (Report submitted to NCAER as Chapter 3 in Report of Committee for Doubling Farmers' Income—Vol. II—*Status of farmers' income: Strategies for accelerated growth*), Department of Agriculture, Cooperation and Farmers Welfare, Ministry of Agriculture & Farmers Welfare.

Bathla, S., & Kumari, Y. (2017). Investment behaviour of farmers across Indian States: Determinants and impact on agriculture income. In S. Bathla & A. Dubey (Eds.), *Changing contours of Indian agriculture: Investments, agricultural growth and non-farm employment*. Singapore: Springer (under printing).

Bathla, S., Joshi, P. K., & Kumar, A. (2017). *Revisiting investments and subsidies to achieve higher and equitable income and poverty alleviation in rural areas across Indian states* (Report Unpublished), New Delhi: IFPRI.

Chand, R. (2017). Doubling farmers' income: Strategy and prospects. In *Presidential Address at 76th IJAE Annual Conference, Jan–March 2016* (Vol. 72, No. 1). Indian Journal of Agricultural Economics.

Haque T. (Ed.) (2016). *Agrarian distress in India: Causes and remedies*. New Delhi: Concept.

Kannan, E. (2011). *Determinants of stagnation in productivity of important crops* (Research Report: XI/ADRTC/127). Bengaluru: Agricultural Development and Rural Transformation Centre, Institute for Social and Economic Change (ISEC).

Kumar, A., Mishra, A. K., Saroj, S., & Joshi, P. K. (2017). *Institutional versus non-institutional credit to agricultural households in India: Evidence on impact from a National Farmers Survey*. IFPRI Discussion Paper 01614, March.

Kumar, A., & Saroj, S. (2016). *Access to credit and indebtedness among rural households in Uttar Pradesh: Implications for farm income and poverty*. Paper presented at an International Seminar on growth Disparities and Inclusive Development in Uttar Pradesh: Experiences, Challenges and Policy Options, 23–25 September 2016. Giri Institute of Development Studies, Lucknow.

Maithi, D., & Mitra, A. (2011). Informality, vulnerability and development. *Journal of Development Entrepreneurship, 16*(2), 199–211.

Mamgain, R. P., & Verick, S. (2017). *The state of employment in Uttar Pradesh—unleashing the potential for inclusive growth*. New Delhi Office: International Labour Organisation.

Mishra, N. K., & Singh, U. B. (2016). *Employment and livelihood potential of rural non-farm informal enterprises: A disaggregated analysis of Uttar Pradesh*. Paper Presented at an International Seminar on Growth Disparities and Inclusive Development in Uttar Pradesh: Experiences, Challenges and Policy Options, 23–25 September 2016, Lucknow: GIRI Institute of Development Studies.

NCAER. (2017). *Status of farmers' income: Strategies for accelerated growth* (Report of Committee for Doubling Farmers' Income—Vol. II). Submitted to Department of Agriculture, Cooperation and Farmers Welfare, Ministry of Agriculture & Farmers Welfare, July.

Singh, A. K. (2016). *Agricultural growth in UP: Performance, constraints and strategy for future development*. Paper presented at an International Seminar on Growth Disparities and Inclusive Development in Uttar Pradesh: Experiences, Challenges and Policy Options, 23–25 September 2016. Lucknow: GIRI Institute of Development Studies.

Srivastava, R., & Ranjan, R. (2016). Deciphering growth and development: past and present, *Economic and Political Weekly, LI*(53), 32–43.

Seema Bathla is Professor, Centre for the Study of Regional Development, Jawaharlal Nehru University, New Delhi. She has earlier worked in the Institute of Economic Growth, The Energy Research Institute and Delhi College of Arts and Commerce, Delhi. She was fellow under the International Visitors Program sponsored by the US government. She obtained her M.Phil. from Delhi School of Economics and Ph.D. from Jawaharlal Nehru University. Professor Bathla has to her credit four books (three co-authored) and more than 50 research articles in refereed national and international journals. She is on the editorial board of Agricultural Economics Research Review and Indian Journal of Economics and Development. She has undertaken several assignments for the World Bank, IFPRI, UNCTAD, WWF-India and IASRI. She was conferred Jawaharlal Nehru Award for Outstanding Post-Graduate Agricultural Research by the Indian Council of Agriculture Research, New Delhi in 2008. She is also the recipient of Dr. R.T. Doshi award for best paper published in Agricultural Economics Research Review in 2014 and 2015. During recent years, she has undertaken important research studies on public and private capital formation and subsidies in Indian agriculture, agrarian change and food security, growth performance of food processing industry, multilateral and regional trade agreements in agriculture.

Shiv Jee has done graduation in economics hons. and obtained masters in sociology. He has almost 12 years of work experience related to research on various aspects of agricultural economics. His research work has been in collaboration with several international organizations viz. International Food Policy Research Institute, National Institute of IFPRI, National Institute of Agriculture Economics and Policy, International Livestock Research Institute and Jawaharlal Nehru University. He has high proficiency in working on the NSS database and command over time series and panel data models. He has to his credit seven research publications in the national journals.

Access to Credit and Indebtedness Among Rural Households in Uttar Pradesh: Implications for Farm Income and Poverty

Anjani Kumar and Sunil Saroj

Abstract The access to credit (especially formal) and the incidence of indebtedness among rural households has been a matter of intense policy debate in India. A scientific and empirical understanding of changing rural credit markets and their implications on farmers' economic welfare is critical to harness the potential of rural credit delivery mechanisms. The understanding of such issues at decentralized level based on micro-level evidence will also be useful in reorienting the credit policies and programmes for a better impact. In this context, the present study was undertaken to (i) analyse the changes in the structure of rural credit delivery in Uttar Pradesh (UP), (ii) identify the factors that influence the choice of credit sources in UP and (iii) assess the impact of access to credit on farmers' welfare. The study is based on the unit level data of Debt and Investment Survey carried out by National Sample Survey Organisation (NSSO) during 1992 (48th round), 2003 (59th round) and 2013 (70th round) and the farmers' situation assessment survey carried out in 2013 (70th round). The structure of credit system has been assessed in terms of access of rural households to different credit outlets, share of formal credit institutions, availability of credit and interest rate. The determinants of rural households' choice for credit sources in UP were analysed by using Heckman selection model, and the impact of farmers' access to formal credit was examined by using instrumental variable model. The structure of credit market has changed overtime, and the share of institutional credit has increased. The initiatives taken by the government have paid off, and the flow of institutional credit to rural areas has increased significantly even in real terms. The indicators of financial inclusion have shown a sign of improvement. However,

---

Some sections of this chapter draw from the authors' previous works which was earlier published in 2017 as "Institutional versus non-institutional credit to agricultural households in India: Evidence on impact from a national farmers' survey", co-authored by Anjani Kumar, Ashok K. Mishra, Sunil Saroj and P. K. Joshi, in Vol. 41, issue 3, pp. 420–432 of Elsevier journal *Economic Systems*. The original study can be accessed at https://doi.org/10.1016/j.ecosys.2016.10.005.

A. Kumar (✉) · S. Saroj
International Food Policy Research Institute, South Asia Office, New Delhi, India
e-mail: Anjani.Kumar@cgiar.org

S. Saroj
e-mail: s.saroj@cgiar.org

© Springer Nature Singapore Pte Ltd. 2019
R. P. Mamgain (ed.), *Growth, Disparities and Inclusive Development in India*, India Studies in Business and Economics,
https://doi.org/10.1007/978-981-13-6443-3_12

the presence of informal agencies in the disbursement of rural credit in UP is still intact. Rural households' access to institutional credit is influenced by a number of socio-economic, institutional and policy factors. In our analysis, the education, caste affiliation, gender and assets ownership have been found to influence the rural households' access to institutional credit significantly. Conditioned on participation, the access to formal agricultural credit has a significant positive impact on farming households' economic welfare. A concerted effort and appropriate policy reform are required to make rural households' access to institutional credit neutral to caste, class and regions to realize the potential impact of agricultural credit on farmers' economic welfare.

Keywords Rural credit: access · Equity · Determinants · Impact

1 Introduction

Credit plays an important role in agricultural development. It enables farmers to undertake new investments and/or adopt new technologies. Indeed, access to credit enhances the risk bearing ability of the farmers and support them invest in some little risky ventures with higher potential returns (Diagne et al. 2000). It also acts as a catalyst to break the vicious circle of poverty in rural areas (Coleman 1999; Khandker and Faruqee 2003; Awotide et al. 2015). Realizing the importance of credit in promoting agricultural growth and development, the agricultural credit policy in India strived to build a strong structure to expand the outreach of institutional credit.

In pursuit of this endeavour, several schemes were launched in the country. The major milestones in improving the rural credit after independence in India include with the acceptance of Rural Credit Survey Committee Report (1954). Nationalization of major commercial banks (1969 and 1980), establishment of Regional Rural Banks (RRBs) (1975), establishment of National Bank for Agriculture and Rural Development (NABARD) (1982), the financial sector reforms (1991 onwards), Special Agricultural Credit Plan (1994–5), launching of Kisan Credit Cards (KCCs) (1998–9), Doubling Agricultural Credit within three years (2004), Agricultural Debt Waiver and Debt Relief Scheme (2008), Interest subvention scheme (2010–1) and the *Jan Dhan Yojana* (2014) (Kumar et al. 2015) were the major steps to boost the rural credit delivery system. These schemes had a positive impact on the flow of agricultural credit (Ghosh 2005; Golait 2007; Kumar et al. 2010, 2015, 2017; Mohan 2006; Hoda and Terway 2015). The increase in the agricultural credit flow in recent years has been remarkable. Since the launch of doubling agricultural credit in 2004, the actual credit flow has consistently surpassed the target and the ratio of agricultural credit to agricultural GDP has increased from 10% in 1999–2000 to around 38% by 2012–13 (Economic Survey 2015–16). Also, the agricultural credit accounted for about 85% of input costs in agriculture and allied sectors (Narayanan 2016).

However, the agricultural credit policy in India is often criticized for its failure to contain the exploitative informal credit. The presence of moneylenders in the Indian rural credit market has been a matter of concern in the main policy discourse. The efficacy and effectiveness of institutional credit to agriculture is often questioned. But, in spite of the significance and relevance of these issues, the implications of institutional credit on farmers' welfare received less attention in India. The empirical evidence on the effects of credit on farmers' income is thin (Kumar et al. 2017). The most popular studies of the impact of formal agricultural credit in India include Binswanger and Khandker (1995), Burgess and Pande (2005), Das et al. (2009) and Subbarao (2012). Recently, the productivity of agricultural credit in India was analysed by Narayanan (2016) and Kumar et al. (2017). However, none of these studies is state specific and thus do not capture the dynamics and implications of rural or agricultural credit in a state like Uttar Pradesh (UP). UP is the most populous state of India, and if it were a separate country, UP would be the world's fifth most populous nation, next only to China, India, the USA and Indonesia. Further, agriculture contributes about 22% gross state domestic product and provides employment to about 63% of its rural population. Understanding of agricultural credit and its implications for farmers' welfare is very important in such contexts.

In this backdrop, this chapter examines the changes in rural credit pattern in UP, understands factors which influence the choice of credit for agricultural households and assesses the contribution of formal credit in influencing the farm and household income with the help of representative households' survey carried out by National Sample Survey Office.

The chapter is organised as follows. Section 2 describes the data used for the study. Section 3 explains the approach and econometric models used to identify the determinants and assess the impact of institutional credit. Section 4 discusses the characteristics of rural and agricultural credit market in UP. Section 5 highlights the socio-economic characteristics of institutional and non-institutional borrowers. The determinants of access to institutional credit and its impact on farmers' economic welfare are discussed in Sects. 6 and 7. The concluding Sect. 8 summarizes the findings and discusses policy implications.

2 Data[1]

The study is based on the unit level data of Debt and Investment Surveys carried out by National Sample Survey Office (NSSO) during 1992 (48th round), 2003 (59th round) and 2013 (70th round) and the Situation Assessment Survey of Agricultural Households carried out in 2013. The Debt and Investment survey, generally carried out once in 10 years, provides information on different aspects of rural finance. These surveys are undertaken across India, and a sufficient number of samples from each state are incorporated to represent a particular state. The survey also provides information on several household characteristics such as ownership of assets, social and demographic variables, households' association with networks such as self-help

---

[1] This Section Draws from the Author's (Anjani Kumar) Previous Publication Kumar (2017).

groups and cooperatives. Further, this dataset allows analysis from the borrowers' side, and therefore, the analysis is more dependable. The structure of credit system has been examined to see the pattern of rural households' access to different credit outlets, share of formal credit institutions, availability of credit and interest rate. The determinants of agricultural households' access to institutional credit and its impact on farm households' economic welfare have been analysed by using 70th round NSSO data on Situation Assessment of Agricultural Households. The survey collects comprehensive information on the socio-economic welfare of agricultural households, borrowing, lending and indebtedness, their farming practices and preferences, resource availability, receipts and expenses of household's farm and non-farm businesses, their awareness of technological developments and access to modern technology in the field of agriculture.

3 Empirical Framework

Besides descriptive statistics, we attempted to demystify two specific research queries through econometric methods. The first is what characteristics of farm households are associated with their accessing the institutional credit that is the issue of participation. The second question is the impact of formal credit on the farmers' economic welfare in UP. We have taken farm income and household consumption expenditure as indicators of agricultural households.

Identification of the causal impact of formal credit on farm profits is one of the toughest issues in the literature. Several observed and unobserved factors that influence farmers' participation in institutional credit market may also influence farm profits. In fact, access to credit is usually not random but based on certain socio-economic and geographical characteristics. The likelihood of excluded variables suggests that simple linear estimates of the effect of credit can be biased.

The use of instrumental variable is the standard approach to get out of this quandary (Khandker and Faruqee 2003). We use a two-step procedure with instrumental variables to address the issue of endogeneity.

In the first stage, the dependent variable is binary (access to formal credit = 1, otherwise = 0), and the independent variables are a mix of qualitative and quantitative variables. We use a logit model to examine the impact of factors associated with a farmer's access to formal credit. Specifically, the logistic regression is given by

$$Y = \text{Ln}\left[\frac{p}{1-p}\right] = \beta_0 + \Sigma \beta_i X_i \qquad (1)$$

where p represents the probability that the farmer takes formal credit and β_{is} are regression coefficients estimated by the maximum likelihood method. X_i represents the vector of characteristics of farmer i including several socio-economic and demographic characteristics.

In the second stage, to assess the impact of formal credit on farmers' profits, the profit function can be represented as

$$\pi_i = \alpha + \delta d_i + \gamma X_i + \varepsilon_i, \tag{2}$$

In the case of per capita consumption expenditures, the dependent variable (left-hand side) in Eq. (2) is replaced with C_i. Specifically,

$$C_i = \alpha + \text{did} + \gamma X_i + \varepsilon_i \tag{3}$$

where π_i is net profit per ha received by a farm household from farming, d_i is a dummy variable (=1 if the farmer takes formal credit and 0 otherwise), X_i is a vector of observable farm and operator characteristics, and ε_i is an error term.

Estimation of Eqs. (2 and 3) using a simple ordinary least square (OLS) regression may give biased estimates of the impact of formal credit as farmers are not randomly selected in getting credit. Farmers are either selected for lending credit by the financial agency or they decide to avail credit at their own. Both of these probabilities indicate non-random selection. Hence, unobserved factors could be influencing farmers' decision to access the formal credit. Thus, d_i, the variable representing farmer's access to formal credit, is likely to be endogenous and could be correlated with the error term, ε_i. We conducted Hausman's test for endogeneity and found access to formal credit to be endogenous, which indicates non-randomness in the selection of farmers availing institutional credit.

We used instrumental variables (IV) techniques to try to get unbiased estimates of the impact of formal credit on farm profits and household monthly per capita expenditure. An ideal instrumental variable should not correlate with the dependent variable in Eq. (2); however, it should be correlated with d_i, the variable representing access to formal credit. Additionally, the variable should not be from the vector of farm and operator characteristics, X_i. It is difficult to get an ideal instrument in such a situation.

The price can be a good instrument for predicting the demand for a good credit. The interest rate is a price of institutional loan. However, the interest rate of an institutional loan does not vary. Hence, the interest rate cannot be a good instrument. We identified the proportion of farmers availing institutional credit in a village as the instrumental variable. We call this variable the network variable we hypothesize that as more of the farmers in a given geographical and social neighbourhood choose to avail formal credit, the likelihood of a farmer from that location will increase to take loan from institutional agencies.

We test the strength of the instrument in the first stage by including it determinants of access to institutional credit as an explanatory variable. If the network variable as constructed above is found strongly correlated with d_i, that is, availing formal credit and it is not systematically related to per-unit profit in farming and monthly per capita consumption expenditure and this satisfied the condition of being an appropriate instrument.

4 Characteristics of Credit Markets in Rural UP

4.1 Trends and Patterns of Rural Credit in UP

India has a huge set-up of financial institutions which are active in the rural credit market. Many formal (institutional) and informal agencies are engaged in meeting the short- and long-term credit requirements of the agricultural household. The formal agencies include Cooperatives, Regional Rural Banks (RRBs), Scheduled Commercial Banks (SCBs), Non-Banking Financial Institutions (NBFIs), and Self-help Groups (SHGs), Micro-financial institutions and other government agencies. The informal sources comprise moneylenders, friends, relatives, traders/shopkeepers, employers, etc. The 1970s and 1980s witnessed a fast growth of India's financial system in the rural areas and financial structure has been further strengthened subsequently. The same financial structure exists in UP, and similar trends were witnessed in the state. The share of institutional rural credit in UP has increased from 55% in 1991–92 to 61% in 2012–13, which is almost a replica of national trend (Table 1). However, the existence of an informal credit market along with a formal institutional credit market has been a salient feature of rural credit market in developing countries (Guirkinger 2008; Conning and Udry 2007; Hoff and Stieglitz 1990). In UP too, the informal credit, which is often exploitative, still persists. Informal credit accounted for about 40% of the total borrowing by the rural households. Its persistence despite vigorous efforts to increase the flow of institutional credit is mysterious and raises many questions on the effectiveness of institutional credit.

The borrowing in absolute terms by rural households in UP has increased from Rs. 721 in 1992 to Rs. 3814 in 2013, more than five times, registering an annual growth rate of 7.9% (Table 2). At national level, it has increased from Rs. 980 in 1991–92 to Rs. 4850 in 2012–13. Growth in rural credit at 7.9% is very high by any standard (Government of India 2014). However, the growth in credit is not uniform over time. Between 1991–92 and 2002–03, the growth in rural credit in UP was higher than during 2002–03 to 2012–13. The same trend was observed at national level also. The patterns of growth hold true for both types of credit, i.e. formal and informal.

Table 1 Share of institutional borrowings in UP: 1991–92, 2002–03 and 2013–14 (per cent)

Year	UP	India
1991–92	54.8	55.7
2002–03	53.6	57.1
2012–13	60.7	60.3

Source Unit level data on Debt and Investment Surveys, 48th (1992), 59th (2003) and 70th (2013) rounds. National Sample Survey Office, New Delhi

Table 2 Amount of institutional and non-institutional borrowings: 1991–92, 2002–03 and 2013–14 (Rs./ha at 1993–94 price)

Year	Institutional		Non-institutional		Total	
	UP	India	UP	India	UP	India
1991–1992	395	545	325	435	720	980
2002–2003	1164	1916	1007	1440	2171	3356
2013–2014	2313	2926	1501	1924	3814	4850
CAGR 1991–92 to 2002–03	10.32	12.11	10.83	11.50	10.54	11.84
CAGR 2002–03 to 2013–14	6.44	3.92	3.69	2.67	5.26	3.40
CAGR 1991–92 to 2013–14	8.36	7.94	7.20	6.99	7.87	7.54

Source Unit level data on Debt and Investment Surveys, 48th (1992), 59th (2003) and 70th (2013) rounds. National Sample Survey Office, New Delhi

4.2 Patterns of Credit for Agricultural Households in UP

This section is devoted to understanding the pattern of credit for agricultural households in UP. Our data show that informal sources account for 28.7% of the loan volume for agricultural households in rural UP and the rest 71.3% is provided by institutional sources. The commercial banks are the dominant source of formal credit, which provide 88.6% of the total institutional loans followed by cooperative societies (7.4%) and government sources (3.9%) (Table 3). Professional moneylenders, who usually charge high interest, are the largest source of informal credit. It accounts for 43.0% of the informal loan volume. Friends and relatives who do not usually charge any interest provide 39.2% of the informal loan. The shopkeepers and others account for 17.8% of the informal loan for the agricultural households. The share of employer and landlord is negligible in providing informal credit to the agricultural households.

The further details on pattern of borrowing for agricultural households are given in Tables 4 and 5. The agricultural households are grouped into four categories: a non-loanee, an exclusively informal sector borrower, an exclusively formal sector borrower, and a borrower from both formal and informal sectors. It is worth mentioning to note that more than half of the agricultural households (51%), they do not avail any loan (Table 4). However, the non-borrowing households consist of voluntary and non-voluntary borrowers. The direct relationship between borrowing and land size indicates the involuntary exclusion of agricultural households from the rural credit market. Large segments of agricultural households still remain outside the formal credit system. The poor are often denied formal credit due to lack of collaterals or guarantors (Ray 1998; Shoji et al. 2012). About 29% of the agricultural households avail credit exclusively from formal sources, 12% are exclusively informal borrowers and the remaining 8% take loan from both formal and informal sources.

The access to institutional and non-institutional credit displays a contrasting relation with land size. The access to formal credit is not neutral to scale. The relationship between landholding and access to formal credit is direct. The agricultural households with better resources find their access to formal credit system relatively easier. Our results show that large farm households, who are about 6% of agricultural households, consist of about 9% of all agricultural households borrowing exclusively from formal sources and account for 12% of the formal credit (Table 3). In contrast, marginal households who constitute about 41% of agricultural households account for 21.6% of exclusive borrowers of formal sources and avail only 9.7% of the credit. A contrasting scenario is observed in case of informal credit. Marginal farmers comprising 66.5% of the agricultural households that borrow exclusively from the informal sources, whereas the large households constitute only 2.0% of the households in the same category. While access to institutional credit increases with the land size, the credit from non-institutional sources declines with the increase in land size. The credit at unfavourable terms may cause further distress to weaker households.

Table 3 Distribution of loans by sources

Share of formal sources		Share of informal sources	
Type	Per cent	Type	Per cent
Government	4.0	Employer or landlord	0.5
Cooperative society	7.4	Agricultural professional or money lender	42.5
Bank	88.6	Shopkeeper	4.5
		Relatives or friends	39.2
		Others	13.4
Total	100.0	Total	100.0
Total share of formal sources	71.3	Total share of informal sources	28.7

Source Authors' calculations based on unit level data from Situation Assessment Survey of Agricultural Households, 2013, National Sample Survey Office (NSSO), Government of India (GoI)

Table 4 Farmers' access to credit from formal and informal sectors, 2012–13

Land class	Distribution of households by borrowing (per cent)				Share of formal and informal credit in borrowing of households	
	Non-borrower	Formal sources only	Informal sources only	Both simultaneously	Formal credit	Informal credit
Marginal	59.6	15.0	19.3	6.1	53.9	46.1
Small	48.5	33.6	8.4	9.5	75.8	24.2
Medium	41.5	44.0	5.3	9.3	91.7	8.3
Large	40.8	46.6	4.2	8.4	92.4	7.7
All	51.2	28.9	12.0	8.0	71.3	28.7

Source Authors' calculations based on unit level data from Situation Assessment Survey of Agricultural Households, 2013, NSSO, GoI

Table 5 Distribution of borrower households by operational holding, 2012–13

Land class	Share of HHs	Non-borrower	Source of borrowing			Share in credit	
			Formal credit	Informal credit	Both simultaneously	Formal credit	Informal credit
Marginal	41.4	48.2	21.6	66.5	31.7	9.7	37.0
Small	31.7	30.0	36.9	22.1	37.5	33.3	33.5
Medium	21.2	17.2	32.2	9.3	24.7	41.1	19.6
Large	5.8	4.6	9.3	2.0	6.1	16.0	9.9
All	100.0	100.0	100.0	100.0	100.0	100.0	100.0

Source Authors' calculations based on unit level data from Situation Assessment Survey of Agricultural Households, 2013, NSSO, GoI

5 Characteristics of Institutional and Non-institutional Borrowers

In this section, we try to find whether socio-economic characteristics of institutional borrowers are different those of non-institutional borrowers. Table 6 reveals significant differences in most of the characteristics. The average land size (owned) for formal borrowers in UP is significantly larger (1.3 ha) than the average land size (0.5 ha) for non-formal borrowers. The average age of household head of formal borrowers is 53 years, have 7.1 family members and 2.2% of them are formally trained in agriculture. In case of informal borrowers, the average age is about 50 years, with family size of 6.5 and 1.5% of them are trained formally in agriculture. Significant differences are observed in other variables also. More than half of the institutional borrowers are OBC households (55.6%) followed by general caste (32.5%) and scheduled caste (11.5%). Only 0.51% of the institutional borrowers are STs. Again, the main principal source of income is generated by agricultural activity for both categories of households (90 and 76%, respectively). There seems to be gender bias in access to institutional credit, as the proportion of male-headed households is higher among formal borrowers. The access to formal credit depicts a positive relationship with education. The difference in schooling of formal and informal borrowers of loan is more pronounced at higher levels of education. The religious distribution of formal and informal borrowers did not show significant differences. The agricultural households who are aware of the minimum support prices (MSP) of agricultural commodities have a greater probability to avail formal credit. Around 44% of the formal credit borrowing households are aware about the MSP, significantly higher than the informal borrowers (26%). About 16.1% of institutional borrowers have MGNREGA card as compared to 27.5% of non-institutional borrowers. Further, 91% of the institutional borrowers and 85% of the non-institutional borrowers are having PDS ration cards. The sources of technical advice are mixed. The mass media (Radio/TV/Newspaper/Internet) as a whole appear to be the most important source

Table 6 Socio-economic characteristics of institutional and non-institutional borrower

Particular	Institutional	Non-institutional	Difference in means/proportions (*t*-test)
Socio-demographic variables			
Age (years)	53.20	49.49	6.082***
Family size (no.)	7.12	6.51	3.684***
Land size (ha)	1.26	0.52	13.585***
Per capita monthly expenditure (Rs.)	1811.01	1088.39	2.720***
Male-headed households (per cent)	97.31	92.08	5.405***
Received formal training in agriculture (per cent)	2.19	1.46	1.175
Social structure by caste (per cent)			
Schedule tribe	0.51	1.34	−2.009**
Schedule caste	11.45	20.71	−5.720***
Other backward caste	55.56	57.49	−0.859
General caste	32.49	20.46	5.980***
Social structure by religion (per cent)			
Hindu	92.20	92.00	−0.164
Muslim	7.06	6.40	−0.589
Other	1.60	0.73	1.726*
Education level of the head of household (per cent)			
Illiterate	24.75	42.51	−8.535***
Primary	18.60	18.51	0.050
Middle	20.37	18.51	1.029
Secondary	14.39	9.38	3.367***
Higher secondary and above	21.89	11.08	6.326***
Structure of households by farm categories (per cent)			
Marginal	21.55	52.62	−15.229***
Small	36.87	28.26	4.038***
Medium	32.24	15.47	8.642***
Large	9.34	3.65	4.934***
Principal source of household income (per cent)			
Agricultural income	90.32	77.59	8.486***
Non-agri income	7.74	18.76	−8.204***
Pension	0.51	0.37	0.550
Remittance	1.26	2.56	−1.785*

(continued)

Table 6 (continued)

Particular	Institutional	Non-institutional	Difference in means/proportions (*t*-test)
Awareness and access to social safety nets (per cent)			
Minimum support price awareness	44.44	26.43	8.354***
Having MGNREGA job card	16.08	27.53	−6.278***
Have PDS ration card	90.82	85.26	3.862***
Source of technical advice			
Extension agent	2.53	2.19	0.480
KVK and SAU	3.62	1.95	2.181*
Pvt. commercial agents	11.28	6.09	3.977***
Progressive farmer	15.66	15.35	0.188
Radio/TV/Newspaper/Internet	20.88	15.96	2.774***
NGO	0.76	0.49	0.742

Source Authors' calculations based on unit level data from Situation Assessment Survey of Agricultural Households, 2013, NSSO, GoI

Note ***significant at the 1% level, **significant at the 5% level and *significant at the 10% level

of information which is accessed by 21% of the formal borrowers and 16% of the informal borrowers. The government information sources together (extension agent, KVKs, SAUs) provide information to 6% of the institutional and 4% of the non-institutional borrowers. 15.66% of the formal borrowers and 15.35% of the informal borrowers rely on fellow progressive farmers for their technical advice.

6 Determinants for Access to Formal Credit

The average rate of interest charged by non-institutional sources (25.1%) continued to be exploitative and about 2.5 times higher the rate of institutional credit (11%) (Kumar et al. 2015). Given the choice, every borrower would like to avail loan from the institutional sources. However, every agricultural household is not able to access the institutional loan. In this section, we try to identify the factors which affect agricultural households' access to institutional credit. Table 7 depicts the factors which determine agricultural households' access to formal credit in UP. The access to institutional credit is significantly influenced by age, education, gender, land size and sources of technical advice. The age of household head affects the access to formal credit sources positively as age denotes experience and better decision-making. The household headed by male is having more probability to avail the institutional credit. The access to institutional credit has been found to be positively influenced by the level of education. It is found to increase with the level of education as the educated households have better knowledge of the credit opportunities and as well as the formalities required to avail a formal credit. Similarly, the lending institutions may also have greater trust in educated households due to their higher potential to get employment in the non-farm sector and thus have additional income to repay the loan. This kind of relationship has been observed in earlier studies in the context of India (Kumar et al. 2007, 2015; Pal and Laha 2015).

However, caste, religion, economic variables and social safety nets of the household do not influence households' ability to avail formal credit. The farmers' awareness about the minimum support price also increases their probabilities to avail institutional credit. The source of information has mixed effect on the agricultural households' access to formal credit. Land size has significant effect on agricultural households' access to credit. The probability of availing institutional credit increases with land size (Table 7).

7 Impact of Institutional Credit on Farm Income and Household Consumption Expenditure

Table 8 compares average net returns per unit of cropped area for formal and informal borrowers by farm size. In calculating the net returns from farming, gross returns from different crops are estimated. Net returns are estimated by deducting expenses from the gross returns. The net returns are divided by the cropped area. Some very important observations emerge out from the summary comparison of farm incomes across formal and informal borrowers in UP. First, the access to institutional credit is associated with higher farm income. The net farm income of formal borrowers (Rs. 40,974/ha) is significantly higher than that of informal sector borrowers (Rs. 31,392/ha) in the state. Second, the relationship between farm size and net returns per ha is not explicit. The inverse relationship between farm size and productivity in India has been observed in some recent studies (e.g. Chand et al. 2011; Birthal et al. 2013) though other studies question the negative association between farm size and productivity in India in the present context. Finally, the difference in farm incomes of formal and informal buyers increases for marginal and large farm size, and the difference is statistically significant at 1%.

Table 8 also compares average monthly per capita consumption expenditures (MPCE) for formal and informal borrowers by farm size. The access to institutional credit is positively associated with higher per capita monthly expenditure. The MPCE of formal borrowers (1811) is significantly higher than that of informal sector borrowers (1088) in UP. Second, the relationship between farm size and MPCE among formal borrowers is negative, while the same is positive for informal borrowers. The difference between formal and informal borrowers' MPCE decreases with farm size and turned out to be negative in the case of large farm size.

Table 7 Determinants of access to institutional credit

Dependent variable: access to institutional credit[a]	Logit model		Marginal effect	
	Coefficient	Standard error	dy/dx	Standard error
Socio-demographic variables				
Age of the household head (Ln)	0.847***	(0.215)	0.171***	(0.043)
Household size (Ln)	−0.045	(0.138)	−0.009	(0.027)
Gender (Male = 1, otherwise = 0)	0.732**	(0.298)	0.153**	(0.062)
Education level (illiterate as a base)				
Primary[a]	0.482	(0.602)	0.102	(0.124)
Middle[a]	0.283	(0.194)	0.060	(0.041)
Higher secondary[a]	0.461***	(0.120)	0.097***	(0.026)
Graduate and above[a]	0.850***	(0.188)	0.174***	(0.038)
Caste (schedule caste as a base)				
Schedule tribe[a]	−0.838**	(0.394)	−0.175**	(0.081)
OBC[a]	−0.030	(0.185)	−0.006	(0.037)
Other[a]	0.116	(0.205)	0.023	(0.041)
Religion (Hindu as a base)				
Muslim[a]	0.104	(0.244)	0.020	(0.048)
Others religion[a]	0.308	(0.361)	0.060	(0.069)
Economic variables				
Agricultural income[a]	0.633	(0.483)	0.128	(0.097)
Non-agri. income[a]	0.216	(0.466)	0.043	(0.094)
Pension[a]	0.617	(1.135)	0.124	(0.229)
Remittance[a]	0.939	(0.708)	0.189	(0.142)
Log of per capita monthly expenditure (Rs.)	0.096	(0.126)	0.019	(0.025)
Land size (marginal as a base)				
Small[a]	0.760***	(0.125)	0.171***	(0.029)
Medium[a]	1.065***	(0.153)	0.234***	(0.034)
Large[a]	1.147***	(0.242)	0.250***	(0.049)
Social safety nets				
MGNREGA job card[a]	−0.168	(0.146)	−0.033	(0.029)
Have ration card[a]	0.205	(0.209)	0.041	(0.042)
Source of technical advice				
Extension agent[a]	−0.268	(0.330)	−0.054	(0.066)
KVK and SAU[a]	0.169	(0.303)	0.034	(0.061)
Pvt. commercial agents[a]	0.427	(0.314)	0.086	(0.063)

(continued)

Table 7 (continued)

Dependent variable: access to institutional credit[a]	Logit model		Marginal effect	
	Coefficient	Standard error	dy/dx	Standard error
Progressive farmer[a]	−0.304*	(0.180)	−0.061*	(0.036)
Radio/TV/Newspaper/Internet[a]	−0.118	(0.169)	−0.023	(0.033)
NGO[a]	0.208	(0.548)	0.041	(0.111)
Other variables				
Formal training[a]	−0.069	(0.290)	−0.014	(0.059)
Minimum support price awareness[a]	0.273*	(0.159)	0.055*	(0.031)
Share of food crop	−0.170	(0.145)	−0.034	(0.029)
Share of high value crops	0.440**	(0.202)	0.088**	(0.040)
Share of oilseeds	0.641	(0.527)	0.129	(0.106)
Share of other crops (non-food)	0.065	(0.364)	0.013	(0.073)
Constant	−6.011***	(1.412)		
Observations	2009		2009	
District fixed effect	Yes			
Log-pseudo likelihood	−1184.510			

Source Authors' calculations based on unit level data from Situation Assessment Survey of Agricultural Households, 2013, NSSO, GoI
Robust standard errors in parentheses ***$p < 0.01$, **$p < 0.05$, *$p < 0.1$; [a]denotes dummy variables

Table 8 Institutional credit, net farm income and household consumption expenditure

Farm category	Net farm income (Rs./ha)		Difference in means (t-statistic)	Consumption expenditure (Rs./month/person)		Difference in means (t-statistic)
	Formal borrower	Informal borrower		Formal borrower	Informal borrower	
Marginal	46,248	31,967	7.206***	1947	1048	2.510***
Small	29,202	28,282	0.740[ns]	1577	1168	1.723*
Medium	35,692	26,890	1.053[ns]	1743	1511	1.765*
Large	45,069	30,571	3.807***	1449	2569	−2.534**
All	40,974	31,392	4.888***	1811	1088	2.720***

Source Authors' calculations based on unit level data from Situation Assessment Survey of Agricultural Households, 2013, NSSO, GoI
***$p < 0.01$, **$p < 0.05$, *$p < 0.1$; *ns* stands for not significant

7.1 Impact of Institutional Credit on Farm Income

Table 9 reports the estimates for both the 2SLS and ordinary least square (OLS) regressions. The second column reports parameter estimates of the first stage similar to the coefficients reported in Table 7, except for the inclusion of the instrumental variables as regressor. All the regressions include district fixed effects, and standard errors are clustered at the district level. The third column in Table 9 shows that the formal credit has a significant positive impact on net farm income. The institutional borrowers earn 33% higher net farm return as compared to non-institutional borrowers. The estimates from the IV estimation show that simple OLS estimates are probably downward biased (column 6 of Table 9). Other variables that show a significant relationship with net farm income include household size, caste, religion, land size, social safety nets, source of information and awareness about MSP. The household size, a proxy of labour availability, has a significant positive impact on farm income.

The households with bigger family size are likely to be significantly increasing their farm income by using institutional credit. Again, the households belonging to OBC and general caste tend to get more benefited as compared to SCs and STs. Conditioned on participation in formal credit market, the households belonging to other religion have higher propensity to enhance their farm income. The source of information also has a significant influence on farm income. The formal borrowers soliciting technical advice from private commercial sources, progressive farmers and NGOs have a greater chance to increase their farm incomes with the use of institutional credit. The awareness about the minimum support price also increases the farmer's ability to enhance their farm income. The awareness about MSP equips farmers to optimize their resource allocation in advance.

Table 9 Impact of institutional credit on net farm income

Variables	2SLS				OLS	
	First stage		Second stage			
	Coefficient	Standard error	Coefficient	Standard error	Coefficient	Standard error
Institutional credit[a]			0.206*	(0.123)	0.187***	(0.044)
Socio-demographic variables						
Age of the household head (Ln)	0.131***	(0.045)	0.113	(0.071)	0.116	(0.072)
Household size (Ln)	−0.028	(0.026)	0.275***	(0.040)	0.275***	(0.040)
Gender (Male = 1, otherwise = 0)	0.153***	(0.052)	−0.013	(0.080)	−0.010	(0.077)
Education level (illiterate as a base)						
Primary[a]	0.013	(0.121)	−0.107	(0.194)	−0.105	(0.196)
Middle[a]	0.045	(0.041)	0.008	(0.057)	0.010	(0.056)
Higher secondary[a]	0.073***	(0.025)	0.077*	(0.046)	0.079*	(0.044)
Graduate and above[a]	0.119***	(0.037)	0.020	(0.065)	0.023	(0.067)
Caste (schedule caste as a base)						
Schedule tribe[a]	−0.127*	(0.074)	0.130	(0.148)	0.127	(0.150)
OBC[a]	0.007	(0.036)	0.159***	(0.058)	0.159***	(0.059)
Other caste[a]	0.026	(0.039)	0.183***	(0.058)	0.184***	(0.059)
Religion (Hindu as a base)						
Muslim[a]	−7.670	(0.048)	−0.135**	(0.062)	−0.135**	(0.063)
Others religion[a]	0.081	(0.062)	0.325	(0.214)	0.326	(0.218)
Economic variables						
Agricultural income[a]	0.188*	(0.104)	0.166	(0.218)	0.169	(0.223)
Non-agricultural income[a]	0.119	(0.104)	−0.480**	(0.202)	−0.479**	(0.206)

(continued)

Table 9 (continued)

Variables	2SLS				OLS	
	First stage		Second stage			
	Coefficient	Standard error	Coefficient	Standard error	Coefficient	Standard error
Pension[a]	0.214	(0.222)	−0.272	(0.335)	−0.269	(0.343)
Remittance[a]	0.270*	(0.140)	−0.504**	(0.251)	−0.501*	(0.255)
Log of per capita monthly expenditure (Rs.)	0.017	(0.022)	0.304***	(0.041)	0.305***	(0.042)
Land size (marginal as a base)						
Small[a]	0.147***	(0.027)	0.884***	(0.046)	0.887***	(0.044)
Medium[a]	0.186***	(0.032)	1.325***	(0.060)	1.329***	(0.056)
Large[a]	0.190***	(0.047)	1.847***	(0.083)	1.852***	(0.077)
Social safety nets						
MGNREGA job card[a]	−0.020	(0.029)	−0.067*	(0.039)	−0.068*	(0.040)
Have ration card[a]	0.042	(0.042)	0.076	(0.050)	0.077	(0.051)
Source of technical advice						
Extension agent[a]	−0.046	(0.067)	0.010	(0.098)	0.009	(0.099)
Krishi Vigyan Kendra & SAU[a]	0.046	(0.056)	−0.305	(0.214)	−0.304	(0.218)
Private commercial agents[a]	0.076	(0.060)	0.216***	(0.071)	0.218***	(0.071)
Progressive farmer[a]	−0.057	(0.036)	0.043	(0.041)	0.042	(0.042)
Radio/TV/Newspaper/Internet[a]	−0.030	(0.032)	0.010	(0.045)	0.010	(0.045)
NGO[a]	0.003	(0.089)	0.365**	(0.178)	0.366**	(0.182)
Other key variables						
Formal training[a]	−0.021	(0.052)	−0.015	(0.120)	−0.015	(0.123)

(continued)

Table 9 (continued)

Variables	2SLS				OLS	
	First stage		Second stage			
	Coefficient	Standard error	Coefficient	Standard error	Coefficient	Standard error
MSP awareness[a]	0.053*	(0.031)	0.228***	(0.042)	0.229***	(0.043)
Share of food crop	−0.031	(0.030)	0.530***	(0.050)	0.530***	(0.051)
Share of high value crops	0.098**	(0.040)	0.748***	(0.077)	0.749***	(0.076)
Share of oilseeds	0.125	(0.096)	0.424***	(0.121)	0.426***	(0.122)
Share of other crops (Non-food)	0.009	(0.070)	0.110	(0.124)	0.110	(0.126)
Instrumental variable						
Proportion of HHs availed institutional credit by village wise	0.452***	(0.037)				
Constant	−0.668**	(0.273)	6.380***	(0.411)	6.366***	(0.426)
Observations	2009		2009		2009	
District fixed effect	Yes		Yes		Yes	
R^2	0.225		0.705		0.706	

Source Authors' calculations based on unit level data from Situation Assessment Survey of Agricultural Households, 2013, NSSO, GoI

Robust standard errors in parentheses ***$p < 0.01$, **$p < 0.05$, *$p < 0.1$; [a]denotes dummy variables

7.2 Impact of Farm Credit on Household Consumption Expenditure

Table 10 provides the impact of institutional credit on household consumption. The effect of formal credit on household monthly per capita consumption expenditure (MPCE) is positive and significant. The household per capita consumption expenditure increases by about 6% with access to institutional credit as compared to those who do not have access to such credit. The household consumption expenditure is a proxy of household income, and thus, an increase in household expenditure reflects a decline in poverty. These findings are significant with other studies in the literature (Coleman 1999; Khandker and Faruqee 2003; Awotide et al. 2015; Kumar et al.

Table 10 Impact of institutional credit on household consumption expenditure

Variables	2SLS				OLS	
	First stage		Second stage			
	Coefficient	Standard error	Coefficient	Standard error	Coefficient	Standard error
Institutional credit[a]			0.030	(0.089)	0.019	(0.024)
Socio-demographic variables						
Age of the household head (Ln)	0.131***	(0.045)	0.000	(0.044)	0.002	(0.043)
Household size (Ln)	−0.036	(0.023)	−0.467***	(0.028)	−0.467***	(0.029)
Gender (Male = 1, otherwise = 0)	0.154***	(0.052)	0.014	(0.044)	0.016	(0.044)
Education level (illiterate as a base)						
Primary[a]	0.011	(0.120)	−0.093	(0.090)	−0.092	(0.089)
Middle[a]	0.045	(0.041)	−0.008	(0.033)	−0.007	(0.032)
Higher secondary[a]	0.074***	(0.025)	0.068**	(0.028)	0.069***	(0.025)
Graduate and above[a]	0.122***	(0.037)	0.148***	(0.034)	0.150***	(0.028)
Caste (schedule caste as a base)						
Schedule tribe[a]	−0.127*	(0.073)	−0.035	(0.069)	−0.037	(0.069)
OBC[a]	0.008	(0.036)	0.059*	(0.034)	0.059*	(0.034)
Other caste[a]	0.027	(0.039)	0.055	(0.041)	0.056	(0.043)
Religion (Hindu as a base)						
Muslim[a]	0.001	(0.048)	0.083**	(0.041)	0.084**	(0.041)
Others religion[a]	0.086	(0.061)	0.302**	(0.140)	0.303**	(0.142)
Economic variables						
Agricultural income[a]	0.191*	(0.103)	0.195	(0.148)	0.197	(0.153)
Non-agricultural income[a]	0.123	(0.103)	0.222	(0.153)	0.223	(0.157)
Pension[a]	0.217	(0.221)	0.175	(0.166)	0.177	(0.172)
Remittance[a]	0.275**	(0.138)	0.292*	(0.176)	0.294	(0.179)
Land size (marginal as a base)						
Small[a]	0.150***	(0.027)	0.165***	(0.040)	0.167***	(0.036)
Medium[a]	0.192***	(0.031)	0.310***	(0.044)	0.312***	(0.036)
Large[a]	0.197***	(0.044)	0.395***	(0.070)	0.397***	(0.064)

(continued)

Table 10 (continued)

Variables	2SLS				OLS	
	First stage		Second stage			
	Coefficient	Standard error	Coefficient	Standard error	Coefficient	Standard error
Social safety nets						
MGNREGA job card[a]	−0.023	(0.029)	−0.142***	(0.028)	−0.143***	(0.028)
Have ration card[a]	0.042	(0.041)	0.030	(0.041)	0.031	(0.041)
Source of technical advice						
Extension agent[a]	−0.046	(0.067)	0.007	(0.067)	0.006	(0.068)
Krishi Vigyan Kendra & SAU[a]	0.046	(0.056)	−0.008	(0.079)	−0.007	(0.080)
Private commercial agents[a]	0.077	(0.061)	0.011	(0.061)	0.012	(0.061)
Progressive farmer[a]	−0.056	(0.036)	0.061*	(0.035)	0.061*	(0.034)
Radio/TV/Newspaper/Internet[a]	−0.029	(0.032)	0.028	(0.033)	0.028	(0.034)
NGO[a]	0.001	(0.091)	−0.099	(0.165)	−0.099	(0.168)
Other key variables						
Formal training[a]	−0.019	(0.052)	0.148	(0.104)	0.148	(0.106)
MSP awareness[a]	0.055*	(0.031)	0.104***	(0.035)	0.105***	(0.035)
Share of food crop	−0.032	(0.030)	−0.036	(0.031)	−0.036	(0.031)
Share of high value crops	0.101**	(0.040)	0.120*	(0.064)	0.121*	(0.063)
Share of oilseeds	0.123	(0.095)	−0.159*	(0.089)	−0.158*	(0.087)
Share of other crops (Non-food)	0.010	(0.069)	0.042	(0.085)	0.042	(0.086)
Instrumental variable						
Proportion of HHs availed institutional credit by village wise	0.452***	(0.037)				
Constant	−0.540***	(0.199)	7.315***	(0.204)	7.308***	(0.215)
Observations	2009		2009		2009	
District fixed effect	Yes		Yes		Yes	
R^2	0.225		0.332		0.332	

Source Authors' calculations based on unit level data from Situation Assessment Survey of Agricultural Households, 2013, NSSO, GoI

Robust standard errors in parentheses ***$p < 0.01$, **$p < 0.05$, *$p < 0.1$; [a]denotes dummy variables

2017) that claim that access to credit could reduce poverty in rural areas. The other variables associated with increasing household consumption expenditures include household size, education of household head, caste, religion, land size, access to safety nets programmes, sources of technical advice for agricultural technologies and practices, MSP awareness and training in agriculture. Compared to uneducated farmers, farmers with higher secondary and above education are likely to increase MPCE in the presence of institutional credit. Household size has a negative impact on MPCE. Most of the factors affecting MPCE in general are similar to those influencing on net farm income. However, a few exceptions are evident; for instance, the farmers soliciting information from progressive farmers with access to institutional credit have higher probability to increase MPCE. Surprisingly to note that households having MGNREGA card decrease their consumption expenditure by 14%.

8 Conclusion and Policy Implications

The study provided a broad pattern of borrowing of agricultural households in UP. The drivers of farmers' access to institutional credit and the impact of institutional credit on farmers' income and expenditure were quantitatively assessed in this paper. The net farm income and household consumption expenditure were taken as indicators for assessing agricultural households' welfare. We find statistically significant positive effects of institutional credit not only on the farm income, but also on household consumption expenditure in UP. Conditioned on access, the formal credit is playing an important role in increasing the farm income and improving agricultural households' welfare.

However, our results provide evidence of poor access of small landowners to formal credit. The formal lenders seem to give more preference to large farmers, and as a consequence, marginal and small farmers are left out. This anomaly needs to be rectified, and efforts must be taken to improve smallholders' access to formal credit.

Annexure

See Annexure Table 11.

Table 11 Hausman's test for endogeneity for net farm income and household consumption expenditure

Variables	Net farm income		Household consumption expenditure	
	Coefficient	Standard error	Coefficient	Standard error
Institutional credit[a]	0.201**	(0.102)	0.0278	(0.062)
Socio-demographic variables				
Age of the household head (Ln)	0.115*	(0.064)	0.002	(0.039)
Household size (Ln)	0.275***	(0.038)	−0.467***	(0.021)
Gender (Male = 1, otherwise = 0)	−0.009	(0.085)	0.016	(0.052)
Education level (illiterate as a base)				
Primary[a]	−0.106	(0.200)	−0.093	(0.123)
Middle[a]	0.009	(0.064)	−0.007	(0.039)
Higher secondary[a]	0.078*	(0.042)	0.069***	(0.026)
Graduate and above[a]	0.022	(0.056)	0.149***	(0.034)
Caste (schedule caste as a base)				
Schedule tribe[a]	0.128	(0.185)	−0.036	(0.113)
OBC[a]	0.160***	(0.051)	0.059*	(0.031)
Other caste[a]	0.184***	(0.060)	0.056	(0.036)
Religion (Hindu as a base)				
Muslim[a]	−0.135**	(0.068)	0.083**	(0.041)
Others religion[a]	0.327**	(0.154)	0.303***	(0.094)
Economic variables				
Agricultural income[a]	0.170	(0.264)	0.198	(0.162)
Non-agricultural income[a]	−0.478*	(0.266)	0.224	(0.163)
Pension[a]	−0.268	(0.362)	0.178	(0.222)
Remittance[a]	−0.499*	(0.294)	0.295	(0.180)
Log of per capita monthly expenditure (Rs.)	0.305***	(0.036)		
Land size (marginal as a base)				
Small[a]	0.887***	(0.046)	0.167***	(0.028)
Medium[a]	1.329***	(0.053)	0.312***	(0.031)
Large[a]	1.851***	(0.079)	0.397***	(0.047)

(continued)

Table 11 (continued)

Variables	Net farm income		Household consumption expenditure	
	Coefficient	Standard error	Coefficient	Standard error
Social safety nets				
MGNREGA Job Card[a]	−0.067	(0.045)	−0.142***	(0.027)
Have ration card[a]	0.077	(0.053)	0.031	(0.032)
Source of technical advice				
Extension agent[a]	0.009	(0.112)	0.006	(0.068)
Krishi Vigyan Kendra & SAU[a]	−0.304***	(0.103)	−0.007	(0.062)
Private commercial agents[a]	0.218***	(0.058)	0.012	(0.036)
Progressive farmer[a]	0.042	(0.047)	0.061**	(0.029)
Radio/TV/Newspaper/Internet[a]	0.009	(0.044)	0.028	(0.027)
NGO[a]	0.365*	(0.207)	−0.099	(0.127)
Other key variables				
Formal training[a]	−0.015	(0.125)	0.148*	(0.076)
MSP awareness[a]	0.229***	(0.038)	0.105***	(0.023)
Share of food crop	0.530***	(0.040)	−0.036	(0.024)
Share of high value crops	0.750***	(0.049)	0.121***	(0.030)
Share of oilseeds	0.427***	(0.109)	−0.158**	(0.066)
Share of other crops (Non-food)	0.110	(0.128)	0.042	(0.078)
Ehat	−0.015	(0.105)	−0.009	(0.064)
Constant	6.360***	(0.450)	7.305***	(0.221)
Observations	2009		2009	
R^2	0.706		0.332	

Source Authors' calculations based on unit level data from Situation Assessment Survey of Agricultural Households
Robust standard errors in parentheses, ***$p < 0.01$, **$p < 0.05$, *$p < 0.1$; [a]denotes dummy variables

References

Awotide, B. A., Abdoulaye, T., Alena, A., & Manyong, V. M. (2015). Impact of access to credit on agricultural productivity: Evidence from smallholder cassava farmers in Nigeria. In *Paper Presented at the International Conference of Agricultural Economists (ICAE)*. Milan, Italy, August 9–14, 2015.

Binswanger, H. P., & Khandker, S. (1995). The impact of formal finance on rural economy of India. *The Journal of Development Studies, 32*(2), 234.

Birthal, P. S., Joshi, P. K., Roy, D., & Thorat, A. (2013). Diversification in Indian agriculture towards high-value crops: The role of smallholders. *Canadian Journal of Agricultural Economics, 61*(2013), 61–91.

Burgess, R., & Pande, R. (2005). Do rural banks matter? Evidence from the Indian social banking experiment. *American Economic Review, 95*(3), 780–795.

Chand, R., Prasanna, P. A. L., & Singh, A. (2011). Farm size and productivity: Understanding the strengths of smallholders and their livelihoods. *Economic and Political Weekly, 46*(26/27), 5–11.

Coleman, B. E. (1999). The impact of group lending in Northeast Thailand. *Journal of Development Economics, 60*(1), 105–141.

Conning, J., & Udry, C. (2007). Rural financial markets in developing countries. In R. Evenson & P. Pingali (Eds.), *Handbook of agricultural economics*. Amsterdam: Elsevier.

Das, A., Senapati, M., & John, J. (2009). Impact of agricultural credit on agriculture production: An empirical analysis in India. *Reserve Bank of India Occasional Papers, 30*(2) (Monsoon 2009).

Diagne, A., Zeller, M., & Sharma, M. (2000). *Empirical measurements of households' access to credit and credit constraints in developing countries: Methodological issues and evidence.* Food Consumption and Nutrition Division (FCND) Discussion Paper 90. Washington, DC: International Food Policy Research Institute (IFPRI).

Ghosh, D. N. (2005). A policy approach for agricultural lending. *Economic and Political Weekly, 40*(2), 93–96.

Golait, R. (2007). Current issues in agriculture credit in India: An assessment. *Reserve Bank of India Occasional Papers, 28*(1), 79–100.

Government of India. (2013). *Situation assessment survey of agricultural households.* Unit-level data from 70th Round of National Sample Survey. New Delhi: National Sample Survey Office, Ministry of Statistics and Programme Implementation.

Government of India. (2014). *Key indicators of situation of agricultural households in India.* Report of 70th Round of National Sample Survey, December, 2014. New Delhi: National Sample Survey Office, Ministry of Statistics and Programme Implementation.

Government of India. (2016). *Economic survey 2015–16*. New Delhi: Ministry of Finance.

Guirkinger, C. (2008). Understanding the co-existence of formal and informal credit markets in Piura, Peru. *World Development, 36*(8), 1436–1452.

Hoda, A., & Terway, P. (2015). *Credit policy for agriculture in India—An evaluation.* Working Paper 302, June 2015. New Delhi: Indian Council for Research on International Economic Relations.

Hoff, K., & Stieglitz, J. E. (1990). Imperfect information and rural credit markets—Puzzles and policy perspectives. *World Bank Economic Review, 4*(3), 235–250.

Khandker, S. R., & Faruqee, R. R. (2003). The impact of farm credit in Pakistan. *Agricultural Economics, 28*(2003), 197–213.

Kumar, A. (2017). Dynamics of access to rural credit in India: Patterns, determinants and implications. In S. Bathla & A. Dubey (Eds.), *Changing contours of Indian agriculture*. Singapore: Springer.

Kumar, A., Singh, D. K., & Kumar, P. (2007). Performance of rural credit and factors affecting the choice of credit sources. *Indian Journal of Agricultural Economics, 62*(3), 297–313.

Kumar, A., Singh, K. M., & Sinha, S. (2010). Institutional credit to agriculture sector in India: Status, performance and determinants. *Agricultural Economics Research Review, 23*(2), 253–264.

Kumar, A., Singh, R. K. P., Shivjee, J., Chand, S., Tripathi, G., & Saroj, S. (2015). Dynamics of access to rural credit in India: Patterns and determinants. *Agricultural Economics Research Review, 28*(Conf.), 151–166.

Kumar, A., Mishra, A. K., Saroj, S., & Joshi, P. K. (2017). Institutional versus non-institutional credit to agricultural households in India: Evidence on impact from a national farmers' survey. *Economic Systems, 41*(3), 420–432, https://doi.org/10.1016/j.ecosys.2016.10.005, ISSN 0939-3625.

Mohan, R. (2006). Agricultural credit in India status, issues and future agenda. *Economic and Political Weekly, 41*(11), 1013–1021.

Narayanan, S. (2016). The productivity of agricultural credit in India. *Agricultural Economics, 47*(2016), 1–11.

NSSO, Debt and Investment Surveys, 48th (1992). 59th (2003) and 70th (2013) rounds. National Sample Survey Office, New Delhi.

Pal, D., & Laha, A. K. (2015). Sectoral credit choice in rural India. *The Journal of Choice Modelling, 14*(2015), 1–16.
Ray, D. (1998). *Development economics*. Princeton: Princeton University Press.
Shoji, M., Aoyagi, K., Kasahara, R., Sawada, Y., & Ueyama, M. (2012). Social capital formation and credit access: Evidence from Sri Lanka. *World Development, 40*(12), 2522–2536.
Subbarao, D. (2012). Agricultural credit: Accomplishments and challenges. Speech delivered at NABARD, July 12, 2012.

Dr. Anjani Kumar is currently a Research Fellow at International Food Policy Research Institute (IFPRI), New Delhi. He received his Ph.D. (1999) and Masters (1992) in Dairy Economics from National Dairy Research Institute, Karnal, India. Before joining to IFPRI, he was Principal Scientist (Agricultural Economics) at the International Crops Research Institute for the Semi-Arid Tropics, Hyderabad. Earlier, he has served as Principal Scientist at National Centre for Agricultural Economics and Policy Research, New Delhi and as Senior Agricultural Economist in the Asia Office of International Livestock Research Institute, Nairobi. He has also worked as a Consultant for many national and international institutions including FAO and World Bank, He has made significant contributions to agricultural economics and policy research and wrote about 80 research papers in national and international research journals on various agricultural development issues. He has also contributed more than 50 papers/chapters to important books and proceedings. His contributions have been well recognized and he is a Fellow of the National Academy of Agricultural Sciences of India. He has won a number of awards from national and international institutions.

Sunil Saroj is working as research analyst with International Food Policy Research Institute (IFPRI). He has worked on various issues like food safety, climate change, agricultural credit, education, dairy cooperatives, micro insurance, and public health & nutrition etc. in last seven years of his career. Prior to IFPRI, he has worked with IPE Global Pvt. Ltd., Micro Insurance Academy (MIA) and Collaborative Research and Dissemination (CORD). He holds a master degree in economics from the Jawaharlal Nehru University. He has authored several publications in reputed national and international journals.

Part IV
Industrial Development and Informality

Regional Pattern of Industrialisation and Urbanisation

S. P. Singh and Divyanshu Kumar Dixit

Abstract This article examines the district-wise and region-wise pattern in the levels of urbanization and industrialization in the state. In order to study the regional pattern, the state is divided into five NSS regions, namely, Northern Upper Ganga Plains (NUGP), Southern Upper Ganga Plains (SUGP), Central Region (CR), Bundelkhand Region (BR) and Eastern Region (ER). The level of urbanization in the state significantly varies between the highest of 38.2% in NUGP and the lowest 12.2% in ER. The number of registered factories per hundred thousand of population is observed to be the highest in NUGP (25.06) and lowest in SR and ER (less than 2.0). The per capita GVA (Gross value added) in the industries has been highest in NUGP, distantly followed by CR and SUGP. It is found to be the lowest in SR, followed by ER. The number of employees in registered factories is highest in NUGP and lowest in SR. It is observed that the 10 districts in NUGP have the highest level of urbanization and industrialization, while ER as a whole is lagging behind the other regions. Regression analysis shows a significant positive impact of urbanization and industrialization on the economic development, measured in terms of composite index of development (CID) and per capita NSDP (net state domestic product). The value of coefficient of dummy for ER indicates that the level of CID and per capita NSDP in ER are much lower than that of other regions of the state. The paper concludes with the observation that there exist inter-region and intra-region disparities in the level of urbanization and industrialization and consequently in the level economic development of the state. The policy implication is that to accelerate the pace of economic development, the focus must be on addressing the issues related to urbanization and industrialization of ER and SR. Also, there is a need to create new manufacturing towns in these regions. Amritsar-Kolkata Industrial Corridor (AKIC), proposed to be set up alongside of Eastern Dedicated Freight Corridor (EDFC), covering 18 districts of the state and the Delhi-Agra-Lucknow expressway have high potential to transform the economy of the state.

S. P. Singh (✉) · D. K. Dixit
Department of Humanities & Social Sciences, IIT Roorkee, Roorkee, India
e-mail: singhfhs@iitr.ac.in

D. K. Dixit
e-mail: divyanshu.k.dixit13@gmail.com

Keywords Industrialisation · Urbanisation · Inequality · Economic development

1 Introduction

Economic development of a region is largely determined by the growth of cities and expansion of services and industrial activities. Cities are generally considered as centres of knowledge, innovation, and new ideas. They have the advantage of having relatively better physical, socio-economic, and business infrastructure, thus attracting high-value manufacturing and services activities. At present, about 50% of the world population lives in urban areas and generates more than 80% of global gross domestic product (GDP) (Dobbs et al. 2011); although percentages vary across countries and regions.

In India, only about 31.2% of the total population resides in urban areas, which generate about 60% of GDP. As per the Barclays' Report, by 2020, urban India could have 35% of the population and contribute 70–75% to GDP (Ranjan 2014). However, due to the high cost of land in big cities, stringent environmental regulations, and availability of improved transportation and communication technologies, companies may have an incentive to shift their establishments and production units to small towns and rural areas. Population Census 2011 shows that between 2001 and 2011, small cities and towns grew faster than the bigger ones. But, at the same time, big cities have created agglomerations, encompassing a large number of villages and small towns in their vicinity (Singh 2017). The Credit Suisse Report (2013) estimates that almost 75% of the new factories during the last decade came up in rural India, contributing to 70% of all new manufacturing jobs created. The Government of India envisages creating a hundred smart cities over a period of ten years in different parts of India, equipped with all modern infrastructure, including smart buildings, roads, sanitation, sewerage, power back up, information technology and responsive public and private institutions. This initiative would attract manufacturing and modern services and resultantly more flow of people and resources from villages to cities.

State-wise data on urbanisation and composition of GSDP show that states with high level of urbanisation have a relatively higher share of industrial and services activities in GDP and consequently achieve a higher level of economic development. States like Tamil Nadu, Maharashtra, and Gujarat have higher level of urbanisation (48.45, 45.23, and 42.58% respectively, Census of India 2011) as well as higher share of manufacturing in their GSDP (19.58, 18.61, 26.42% respectively); while, states like Bihar and Uttar Pradesh have lower level of urbanisation (11.3 and 22.0% respectively) and also lesser share of manufacturing in GSDP (4.48 and 12.64% respectively). A perusal of information on urbanisation and industrialisation reveals that there exists not only inter-region but also intra-region variations in their levels. It is in this context that this paper examines district-wise and region-wise urbanisation and industrialisation and their impact on economic development in the state of Uttar Pradesh. It also suggests policy measures to reduce the regional imbalances in the level of urbanisation and industrialisation in the state.

This paper is based on secondary data collected from various sources. The study area has been divided into five regions as North Upper Ganga Plains (NUGP) (ten districts), South Upper Ganga Plain (SUGP) (eighteen districts), Central Region (CR) (nine districts), Southern Region (SR) (seven districts) and Eastern Region (ER) (twenty seven districts). These regions differ significantly in terms of various socio-economic development indicators (Table 7 in Appendix). The analysis is based on seventy-one districts of Uttar Pradesh due to unavailability of data of newly formed districts. However, information of newly formed districts is also included in the 71 districts. The region-wise urbanisation, industrialisation, and economic development have been examined in Sects. 2 and 3. The impact of urbanisation and industrialisation on economic development has been ascertained in Sect. 4 by using regression analysis by taking the composite index of development (CID) and net state domestic product (NSDP) separately as dependent variables. District-wise variations have also been examined using graphs and maps with the help of ArcGIS 10 software. The last section dwells on conclusions and policy implications of the study.

Initially, we have selected the following explanatory variables to study their impact on economic development: Percentage of urbanisation; Number of working factories per hundred thousand population; number of small scale industry (SSI) units per hundred thousand population; per capita gross value of industrial production; number of employees in registered factories per hundred thousand population; per capita consumption of power; length of *pucca* road in kilometers per hundred thousand population; credit-deposit ratio; percentage distribution of registered factories; percentage share of power consumption in industry to total power consumption; dummies for NUGP and ER. However, some of the variables are found highly correlated to each other and create the problem of multi-collinearity. Therefore, we have to exclude them and finally select six variables, as shown in the regression model given as follows.

$$CID_i = \alpha + \beta_1 URB_i + \beta_2 NSSI_i + \beta_3 NWF_i + \beta_4 PCGVIP + D_1 NUGP + D_2 ER + \mu_i$$

where, CID is composite index of development for the year 2011–12; URB is urbanisation rate in the state for the year 2011 measured as percentage share of total population living in urban areas; NSSI is number of small scale industries per hundred thousand population in a particular district calculated for the year 2011–12; NWF is number of working factories per hundred thousand population in a district for the year 2011–12. To know the regional variation, two dummies D_1 and D_2 are taken for the North Upper Ganga Plain and Eastern Region respectively. Same variables have been regressed on per capita net state domestic product using the following model:

$$NSDP_i = \alpha + \beta_1 URB_i + \beta_2 NSSI_i + \beta_3 NWF_i + \beta_4 PCGVIP + D_1 NUGP + D_2 ER + \mu_i$$

where, NSDP is per capita net state domestic product for the year 2011–12.

2 Regional Pattern of Urbanisation

Urbanisation is not only about the proportion of the urban population, it also provides a general idea about the economic development and explains various aspects such as level of industrialisation, occupational structure, socio-economic and demographic pattern, educational status of the associated region (Bose 1969; Pandey 1977). The positive association between urbanisation and industrialisation is one of the most critical facts in the development process of any region (Bloom et al. 2008; Dobb et al. 2011; Roberts et al. 2017). The expansion of cities provides economies of scale and generates several positive externalities (such as skilled workers, cheap transport, social and cultural amenities) and thus becomes the key driving factor in the development of industries and services. Delhi NCR is a good example to demonstrate how the neighboring cities of Uttar Pradesh (Meerut, Ghaziabad, Noida and Greater Noida) have become centres of modern manufacturing, businesses and services, including education and health. The social and environmental costs of overloading of housing, social services, civic amenities and congestion in big cities like Delhi became the driving factor in the expansion of urban agglomeration and satellite cities. This fact is quite clear when we look at the regional pattern of urbanisation in Uttar Pradesh (Fig. 1). NUGP, which constitutes ten districts, including Meerut, Ghaziabad and Gautam Budh Nagar (Delhi NCR), has the highest level of urbanisation (38.2%), while Eastern Region, which comprises 28 districts of the state, has the lowest level (12.2%). It is significant to note that NUGP has only 15.7% share in the total population of the state but its share in total urban population is 26.9%. Contrary to this, ER has 40% share in the total population, while its share in the urban population of the state is only 21.9%. Similarly, the share of SUGP and CR in urban population is slightly higher than their share in the total population of the state. Western

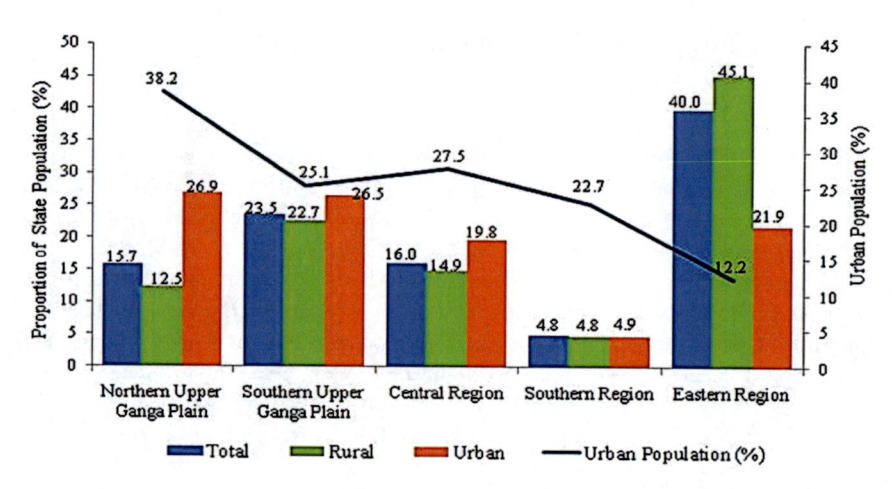

Fig. 1 Region-wise level of urbanisation in Uttar Pradesh (2011). *Source* Ganga River Basin Management Plan (2013)

Uttar Pradesh (NUGP + SUGP) and Eastern Uttar Pradesh (ER) are almost same in population and geographical area but there is a huge difference between them in the level of urbanisation. The level of urbanisation in the ER is less than one-third that of NUGP.

Table 1 shows the region-wise trends in rural and urban population in the state. As the table indicates, the rate of urbanisation in NUGP has increased from 31.76% in 1991 to 38.25% in 2011, thus registering a 6.49% point increase, while during the same period rate of urbanisation in the ER remained same (11.93). Between 1991 and 2011, SUGP, CR and SR observe 3.15, 2.03 and 1.75% point increase in the urbanisation respectively. Thus, NUGP registered the highest growth in the urbanisation, distantly followed by SUGP, CR and SR. ER did not achieve any change in the rate of urbanisation between 1991 and 2011. If we look at the decadal growth rates in the urban population, we observe that during 1991–2001 NUGP registered the highest growth (33.27%), followed by SUGP (32.47%) and CR (32.17%). The decadal growth in urban population was observed lowest in ER (24.05%). In the case of the rural population also, NUGP registered the highest growth (26.72%), followed by ER (25.79%). It was lowest in SR (20.36%).

The major difference in the urban growth across regions was noticed during the last decade (2001–11). NUGP achieved the highest growth (43.70%), distantly followed by SUGP (29.84%). The urban growth was lowest in SR (19.34%), followed by CR (21.59%) and ER (24.21%). Table 1 shows that decadal growth in rural population has declined in all the regions during 2001–11, with a sharp decline in NUGP. The trends in urban population growth indicate that urban centers in NUGP have become the attraction of a large number of migrants during the last decade, which significantly enhanced the share of urban population of the region. Comparing the urban growth pattern of two periods (1991–2001 and 2001–2011), we observe that the decadal growth of population in CR has significantly decelerated from 32.17% during 1991–2001 to 21.59% in 2001–11. It may be significant to note that the economic condition of CR vis-a-vis other regions of the state has deteriorated. Arora and Singh (2015) show that both urban and rural poverty between 2004–05 and 2011–12 increased in CR, while in other regions, it declined during the same period. As far as urban population growth in ER is concerned, it has remained almost same during both the periods. Bundelkhand (SR) also experienced the steep deceleration in the urban population growth during the last decade.

Besides the inter-regional differences in the context of urbanisation, the intra-regional variations also exist. Map 1 shows that most of the districts of ER are urbanized below 10%. Only Varanasi district (urbanisation: 43.43%) of this region comes under the highly urbanized district. It is notable that urban population of Varanasi and Allahabad districts is same but there is a huge difference in the percentage of urban population of both districts (Varanasi 43.43% and Allahabad 24.78%) due to the difference in the geographical area as Varanasi district is spread over 1535 km^2 while Allahabad district spans a geographical area of 5482 km^2. There are five districts in the neighbourhood of Varanasi; namely Mirzapur, Chandauli, Sant Ravidas Nagar, Jaunpur, and Ghazipur. Among them, first three are better urbanized, at 13.89, 12.55, and 14.73% respectively, while the rate of urbanisation in Ghazipur

Table 1 Region-wise trends in rural and urban population in Uttar Pradesh

Regions	1991			2001			2011		
	Total Urban Population	Total rural population	Urban population (per cent)	Total urban population	Total rural population	Urban population (per cent)	Total urban population	Total rural population	Urban Population (per cent)
NUGP	6,254,400	13,436,612	31.76	8,335,395 (33.27)	17,027,468 (26.72)	32.86	11,977,596 (43.70)	19,339,553 (13.58)	38.25
SUGP	6,849,645	23,297,642	22.72	9,073,790 (32.47)	28,737,199 (23.34)	24.00	11,780,622 (29.83)	35,193,228 (22.47)	25.87
CR	5,475,034	15,986,495	25.51	7,236,503 (32.17)	19,715,256 (23.32)	26.85	8,798,514 (21.59)	23,152,970 (17.44)	27.54
SR	1,409,713	5,307,306	20.99	1,845,043 (30.88)	6,387,803 (20.36)	22.41	2,201,881 (19.34)	7,479,670 (17.09)	22.74
ER	6,326,260	46,717,572	11.93	7,846,618 (24.03)	58,764,136 (25.79)	11.78	9,745,994 (24.21)	70,142,308 (19.36)	11.93

Note Figures in parentheses are decadal growth rates in the population
Source District-wise development indicators, UP (2006 and 2007) and Census of India, 2001 and 2011

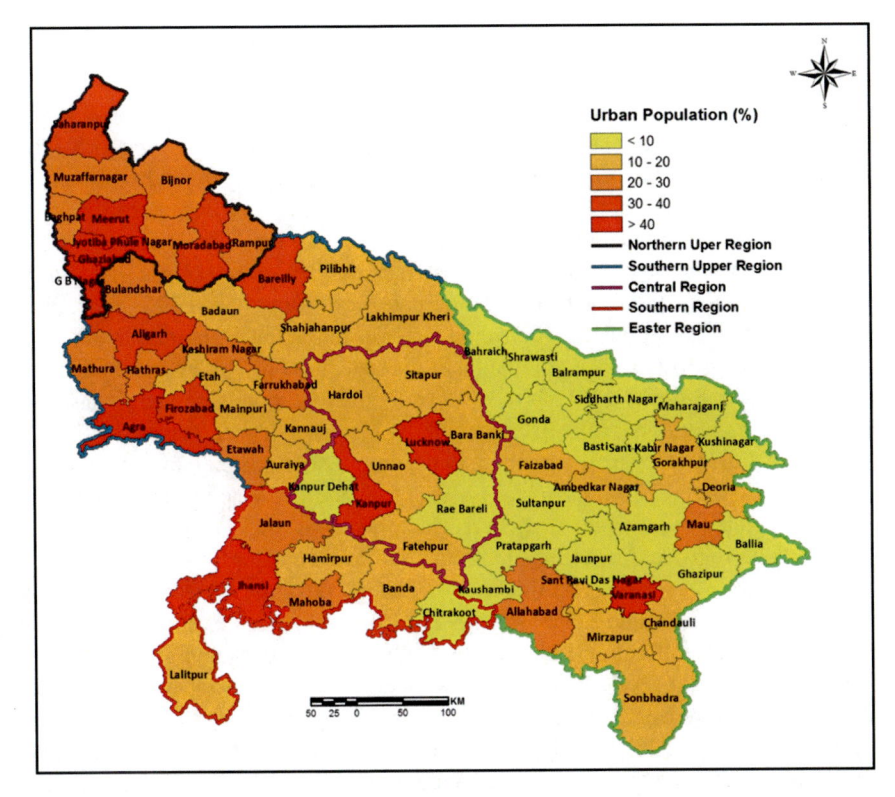

Map 1 District-wise urban population in Uttar Pradesh in 2011. *Source* Customised from the data of Census of India, 2011

and Jaunpur is only 7.56 and 7.45% respectively (Table 7 in Appendix). It seems that industrialisation in these districts (for example, the industrial area of Chandauli, and stone and coal mining in Mirzapur and Sonbhadra districts) have impacted the rate of urbanisation.

NUGP region too has intra-region variations but all the districts of this region are urbanized, at least, more than 20%. Five districts, namely Saharanpur, Meerut, Moradabad, Ghaziabad and Gautam Budh Nagar have urbanisation rate of more than 30% while the remaining districts are also urbanized more than the average state level urbanisation, except Baghpat district. In the CR, Jhansi district is highly urbanized with an urbanisation rate of 41.78%, while all the remaining districts, except Jalaun (25.06%), have urbanisation rate below the state average. It may also be noted that except Kanpur Dehat, Rae Bareli and Chitrakoot districts, all the districts of four regions (NUGP, SUGP, SR, and CR) are urbanized, at least, more than 10%.

3 Status of Industrialisation

In this section, inter-regional and intra-regional differences in the level of industrialisation are assessed on the basis of four indicators—percentage distribution of the number of registered factories, the number of working factories per hundred thousand population, the number of SSI per hundred thousand population and per capita gross value of industrial production. Figure 2 shows that there is a huge difference in the percentage distribution of a number of registered factories across regions. It is significant to note that NUGP (ten districts of the state) constitutes only 15.7% population of the state but it houses 48% of registered factories of the state. Contrary to this, ER, which is home to 40% of total population of the state, has only 11% registered factories of the state. Similarly, SR has 4.2% share in the total population but it has only 1.0% share in the number of registered working factories. It is clear from Fig. 2 that NUGP has the highest percentage share in the number of registered factories (48%), followed by SUGP (22%), CR (18%), ER (11%) and SR (one per cent). District-wise data related to number of registered factories show that Gautam Budh Nagar holds 19.59% registered factories of the state, followed by Ghaziabad (12.30%) and Meerut (4.43%) of NUGP. Agra district of SUGP constitutes 4.86%, followed by the Firozabad (2.96%) and Bulandshahar (2.76%). Remaining districts of this region fall in the category of below 1.0%, except Hathras, Aligarh, Mathura, and Bareilly. Thus, three districts of NUGP (Meerut, Ghaziabad and Gautam Budh Nagar) together share 36.32% of registered factories of the state. Kanpur Nagar (8.49%), Lucknow (3.96%), Unnao (1.32%) and Kanpur Dehat (1.0%) in CR are the major districts having relatively higher percentage distribution of registered working factories. All the districts of ER and SR, except Allahabad, Gorakhpur, and Varanasi, fall in the category of less than 1.0% of registered working factories (Table 7 in Appendix). District-wise and region-wise percentage distribution of number of registered factories indicates that there is a huge intra- and inter-region disparity in the distribution of a number of registered factories.

If we look at the number of working factories (NWF) per hundred thousand of population, the results are similar to what has been observed in the case of a number of registered factories. Table 2 shows that in the case of NWF per hundred thousand population also, NUGP stands first among all the regions. The NWF per hundred thousand population are the least in SR, followed by the ER. As against 25.7 working factories per hundred thousand of population, the corresponding figures in ER and SR are only 1.74 and 1.48 respectively. A perusal of Table 2 reveals that all the regions other than NUGP have NWF below the state average (6.64). It indicates that 10 districts of the state (NUGP) have the highest concentration of factories. NUGP is followed by CR and SUGP. Table 2 also shows that the number of working factories per hundred thousand population declined during the period 2004–05 to 2008–09, almost in every region. However, the number again went up in 2011–12 in all the regions.

District-wise data show that Gautam Budh Nagar of NUGP has the highest number of working factories (159.40) per hundred thousand population, distantly followed

Fig. 2 Region-wise percentage distribution of registered working factories in Uttar Pradesh. *Source* Compiled from the district wise development indicators of UP, 2015

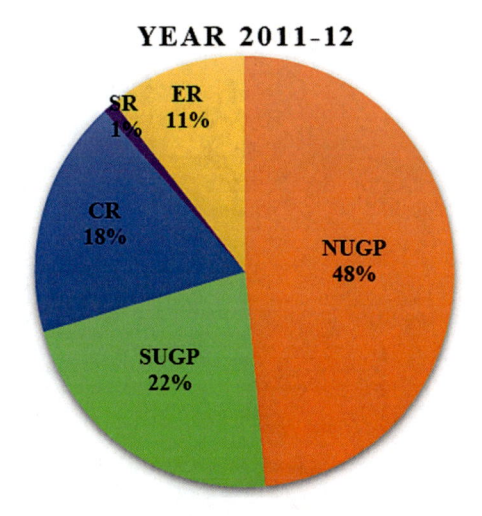

YEAR 2011-12

- NUGP 48%
- SUGP 22%
- CR 18%
- ER 11%
- SR 1%

Table 2 Region-wise number of working factories per hundred thousand population in Uttar Pradesh

Year	Northern Upper Ganga Plain	Southern Upper Ganga Plain	Central region	Southern region	Eastern region	Uttar Pradesh
2000–01	27.76	5.74	6.81	1.96	1.86	6.70
2004–05	21.87	5.61	6.13	1.53	1.87	5.90
2005–06	21.56	5.37	5.50	1.52	1.80	5.70
2006–07	25.06	5.42	5.51	1.53	1.89	6.09
2007–08	24.50	5.31	5.52	1.61	1.78	6.04
2008–09	19.60	4.88	5.17	1.47	1.61	6.40
2011–12	25.72	5.75	6.59	1.48	1.74	6.64

Source Compiled from the district-wise development indicators of UP, 2015

by Ghaziabad (34.14) and Meerut (16.59). Remaining districts of the NUGP have, almost, less than ten working factories per hundred thousand population. Maximum districts of ER have less than three working factories per hundred thousand population, except Chandauli (5.70), Sant Ravidas Nagar (5.59), Varanasi (5.16), Faizabad (3.8), Allahabad (3.76), and Gorakhpur (3.41) (Table 7 in Appendix). Intra-regional variation in the distribution of working factories is observed in almost all the regions. For example, districts like Etah, Mainpuri, Pilibhit of SUGP and Kanpur Dehat, Fatehpur and Unnao of CR consist of less than five working factories per hundred thousand population while districts like Hathras and Firozabad of SUGP and Lucknow and Kanpur Nagar of CR have, at least, more than ten working factories per hundred thousand population. As stated above, three districts of NUGP, which are close to Delhi, have outstanding performance in industrialisation as measured in

Table 3 Region-wise number of small scale industries per hundred thousand population in Uttar Pradesh

Year	Northern Upper Ganga Plain	Southern Upper Ganga Plain	Central region	Southern region	Eastern region	Uttar Pradesh
2000–01	28.07	18.25	17.86	23.67	11.41	17.4
2007–08	30.75	19.02	15.78	15.99	11.59	16.81
2008–09	30.66	19.25	16.87	23.56	11.68	17.32
2009–10	30.41	19.76	16.39	24.06	11.99	17.39
2010–11	29.79	19.01	16.11	23.69	11.78	17.09
2011–12	26.39	17.97	15.61	22.91	11.84	18.94
2014–15	39.06	34.48	21.98	26.63	13.92	24.14

Source Compiled from the district-wise development indictors of UP, 2015

terms of number of working factories. In general, urbanisation seems to be positively associated with industrialisation as the districts with a higher percentage of urban population also have higher number of working factories per hundred thousand population.

As far as the number of SSIs per hundred thousand population is concerned, we observe that there were 24.14 small scale industries (SSIs) per hundred thousand population in Uttar Pradesh but these numbers vary across regions (Table 3). Like other indicators of industrialisation, in the case of number of SSIs per hundred thousand population too, NUGP holds first rank among all the five regions. It had 39.06 SSI units per hundred thousand population in 2014–15. It is followed by SUGP (34.48), SR (26.63), CR (21.98) and ER (13.92).

Though NUGP is facing a gradual fall in the number of SSIs per hundred thousand population from 30.75 in 2008 to 26.39 in 2012; yet from the year 2011–12, there has been a remarkable increase in number of SSI (about 40.0%) as Table 3 shows the number of SSI increases from 26.39 in 2011–12 to 39.06 in 2014–15. A perusal of the table reveals that between 2011–12 and 2014–15, there has been a significant increase in the number of SSIs in all the regions, except ER. The highest increase is observed in SUGP, followed by NUGP and SR. The ER not only has the lowest number among all the regions but also shows a marginal decrease in the number between the period 2011–12 and 2014–15. Table 3 clearly depicts that ER, during all the years, and CR, during most of the years, have had less number of SSIs per hundred thousand population than the state average.

District-wise data show that Gautam Budh Nagar (103.68), Ghaziabad (51.86), Moradabad (51.37) and Rampur (46.43) are among the top ranking districts in the context of number of SSIs; on the other hand, Baghpat with 6.13 SSIs per hundred thousand population stands at the lowest position. This indicates the intra-regional disparity in the distribution of SSIs. In the ER, Balrampur (33.29), Sultanpur (28.03) and Allahabad (27.27) districts hold the top three ranks in number of SSIs per hundred

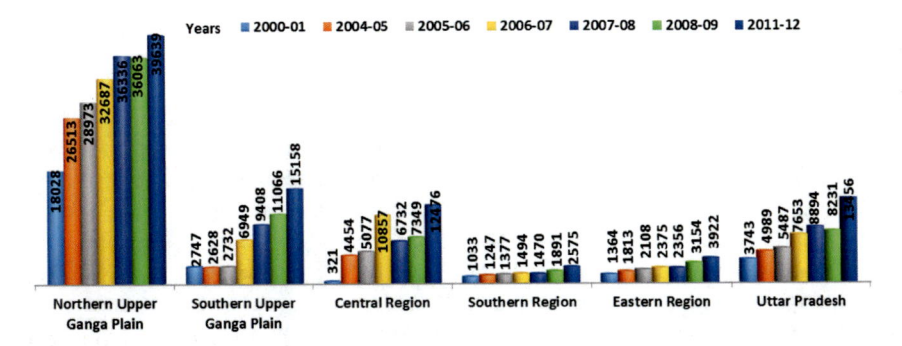

Fig. 3 Region-wise per capita gross value of industrial production (GVI) in Uttar Pradesh. *Source* Compiled from the district-wise development indicators of UP, 2015

thousand population. It is noteworthy to observe that 25 out of 28 districts of the ER have number of SSIs per hundred thousand population below the state average (24.14) and most of the districts have the number less than 15. There are only six out of 18 districts in SUGP (namely Etah, Auraiya, Badaun, Bulandshahar, Sahjahanpur, and Kheri), which have the number of SSI per hundred thousand population below the state average (Table 7 in Appendix).

We have also assessed the regional pattern of industrialisation in the state through per capita gross value of industrial production (GVI) as shown in Fig. 3. There is a continuous progress in per capita GVI after the year 2000 across all the regions of the state. The figure shows that per capita GVI in 2011–12 was highest in NUGP (Rs. 39,639). It is almost four times greater than that of the state average. CR is the only region that faces ups and downs in the per capita GVI during 2000–01 to 2008–09. Per capita GVI in SR and ER has been below the state average during the given period of twelve years. For example, in 2011–12, as against the state average GVI of Rs. 13,456, the average GVI in SR and ER were Rs. 2575 and Rs. 3922 respectively.

Very high intra-regional variation in terms of per capita GVI exists in all the regions of the state Uttar Pradesh as standard deviation in the NUGP is very high (Table 7 in Appendix). Per capita GVI of Gautam Budh Nagar and Ghaziabad districts are Rs. 337,425.83 and Rs. 62,208.02 respectively which are very high. Contrary to this, GVI in Baghpat district (Rs. 6888.48) is very low. Mathura and Bulandshahar of SUGP contain Rs. 150,277 and Rs. 23,295 GVI while districts like Etah (Rs. 417.27) and Mainpuri (Rs. 575.87) have very low per capita GVI. Figures 1 and 3 (region-wise urban population) express almost same pattern. In other words, the rate of urbanisation and per capita GVI were observed highest in NUGP, while both urbanisation and per capita GVI have lowest values in the ER. Thus, it can be concluded that the level of industrialisation and urbanisation in NUGP is much higher than that in other regions of the state.

4 Impact of Urbanisation and Industrialisation on Economic Development

In this section, we examine the impact of urbanisation and industrialisation on the economic development of the state. The impact is assessed through maps and regression analysis. Our concern is to know how the economic development is being affected by the industries and urban centers. We observe from Map 2 that urbanisation, per capita gross value of industrial production, composite index of development and per capita NSDP show almost similar patterns.

The districts having a higher level of urbanisation such as Gautam Budh Nagar, Meerut, Ghaziabad, Mathura, Bulandshahar, Lucknow, Agra, Kanpur Nagar, have also achieved a high level of GVI, NSDP, and CID. On the basis of Map 2, it can be concluded that urbanisation and industrialisation are positively correlated to each other.

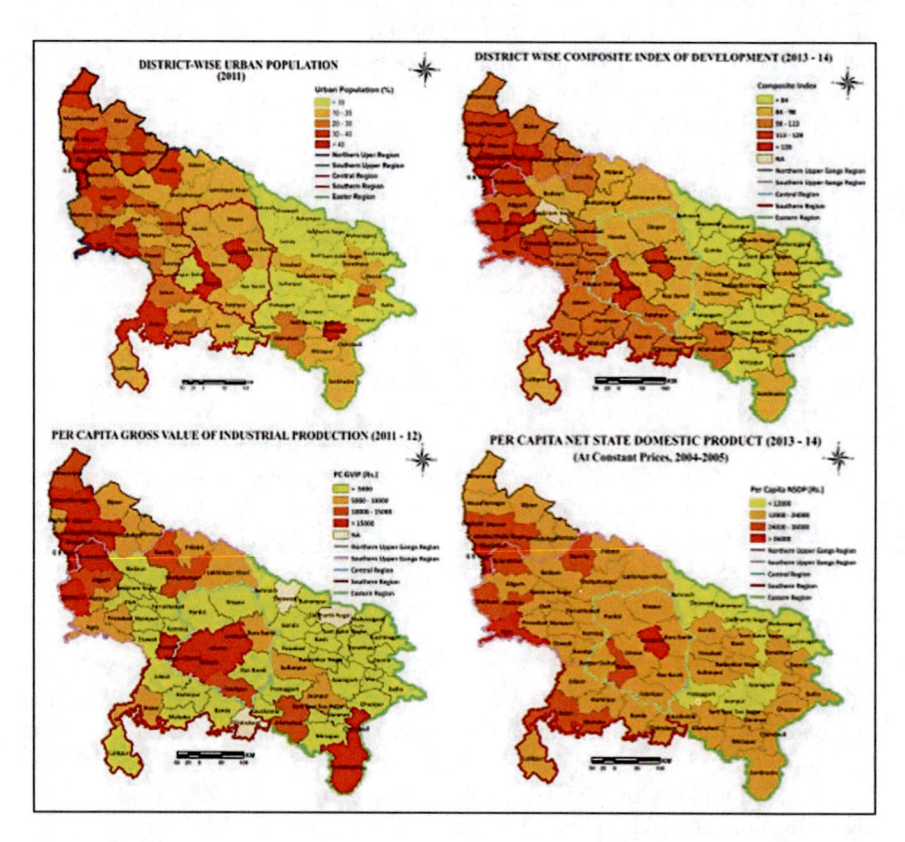

Map 2 District-wise urbanisation, per capita GVI, CID and per capita NSDP in Uttar Pradesh. *Source* Compiled from the district wise development indicators of UP, 2015, Niyojan Atlas, UP (2013–14), Census of India, 2011

Table 4 Correlation matrix of dependent and explanatory variables

Variables	CID (Y1)	NSDP (Y2)	URB (x1)	SSI (x2)	NWF (x3)	PCGVIP (x4)
CID (Y1)	1.00					
NSDP (Y2)	0.95	1.00				
URB (x1)	0.59	0.67	1.00			
SSI (x2)	0.68	0.70	0.61	1.00		
NWF (x3)	0.78	0.70	0.39	0.45	1.00	
PCGVIP (x4)	0.92	0.82	0.40	0.50	0.72	1.00

Source Authors' calculation

CID is one of the most significant indicators of socio-economic development. The CID constitutes thirty six development indicators out of which six pertain to industrial infrastructure, and ten to economic infrastructure, while the remaining twenty indicators pertain to agriculture and social infrastructure. Various variables like urban population, industrial production, working factories, small scale industries, and so on influence the magnitude of CID (Government of Uttar Pradesh, Annual Plan, 2016–17). In terms of CID, NUGP leads among all the regions followed by SUGP, CR, SR, and ER in the descending order. Those districts which have higher urbanisation rate, as well as higher NSDP like Gautam Budh Nagar, Ghaziabad, Agra, Hathras, Lucknow, Kanpur Nagar, also have a high score of CID; contrary to this, CID score is very low in the districts such as Kushinagar, Deoria, Mahrajganj, etc., which have lower rate of urbanisation (Table 7 in Appendix).

Table 7 in Appendix shows that ER has lowest per capita NSDP among all the regions. In 2013–14, NSDP in NUGP was highest (Rs. 30,750.04 in 2013–14), followed by SUGP, SR, CR and ER. Five regions of the state show the pattern of NSDP similar to CID (Table 7 in Appendix). Thus, we can say on the basis of general analysis of graphs and maps that CID and NSDP are following, region-wise as well as district-wise, similar pattern to that of urbanisation and industrialisation. However, it is not an intellectual decision to reach any conclusion only on the basis of graph and map analysis. For more comprehensive and statistical results, the impact of urbanisation and industrialisation has been assessed using regression analysis.

The CID and NSDP are taken separately as dependent variables. For better understanding, a correlation matrix of the dependent and independent variables is presented in Table 4. Per capita gross value of industrial production (PCGVI) has a high positive correlation with both the dependent variables (CID and NSDP). NWF is also found positively correlated with CID and NSDP. Remaining variables URB, SSI, have a moderate positive relationship with both the dependent variables. Among all the variables, urbanisation has moderate positive correlation with the explained variables. CID explains the status of development in any region. Here, our concern is to know the role of urbanisation and industrialisation in the development process.

Table 5 Regression results of the first model

Variables	Unstandardized coefficients		Standardized coefficients	t values	P value	Collinearity statistics	
	B	SE				Tolerance	VIF
Constant	78.975	4.146		19.048	0.000		
URB	0.264*	0.098	0.107	2.685	0.009	0.557	1.796
SSI	0.628*	0.217	0.13	2.889	0.005	0.439	2.28
NWF	0.432*	0.103	0.188	4.206	0.000	0.446	2.24
PCGVIP	0.001*	0.000	0.637	14.096	0.000	0.436	2.295
NUGP (D_1)	5.169	3.741	0.049	1.382	0.172	0.715	1.399
ER (D_2)	−8.132*	2.827	−0.107	−2.877	0.005	0.643	1.555

Dependent variable: CID $F = 176.37$ Adj. R^2 0.938 $N = 71$
*Significant at one per cent level of significance
Source Authors' calculation

Table 5 shows that urbanisation (URB), number of small scale industries per hundred thousand population (SSI), number of working factories per hundred thousand population (NWF), and per capita gross value of industrial production (PCGVIP) are found to have statistically significant positive impact on CID, while dummy for ER (D_2) shows the statistically significant negative impact on CID. The value of Adj. R^2 shows that the five explanatory variables together explain 94% variation in the CID. F-value is also significant and quite high. The coefficient of URB shows that if the level of urbanisation increases by one unit, it causes 0.264-unit increase in CID. Similarly, a unit increase in SSI would make a 0.628-unit increase in CID.

Districts having higher urbanisation rate generally also have a higher CID but it is not applicable to all the districts. Since CID is not the only result of urbanisation, it is affected by other factors like industrialisation that is why some districts are less urbanized but have higher CID e.g. Kanpur Dehat holds 115.58 score in CID while it is only 9.66% urbanized. The reason is that the industrial area of Kanpur is not only limited to Kanpur Nagar but a number of SSIs per hundred thousand population as well as a number of industrial area per hundred thousand population both figures are higher in Kanpur Dehat than Kanpur Nagar district. Results suggest that SSI has a significant influence on CID as an increase of 1 small scale industry per hundred thousand population makes an increase of 0.628 unit in CID. Variable NWF is also found positively affecting the CID as its value would increase by 0.432 unit with an increase of 1 working factory per hundred thousand population.

The coefficient of GVI suggests that if it increases by Rs. 1000, it leads to 0.001 unit increase in CID. Since the unit of measurement of explanatory variables is different, magnitudes of un-standardized coefficients cannot tell which variable is having how much contribution to the CID. For that we have to look at the standardized coefficients, which indicate that GVI has the highest impact on CID, distantly fol-

Table 6 Regression results of the second model

Variables	Un-standardized coefficients		Standardized Coefficients	t values	P value	Collinearity statistics	
	Coefficients	SE				Tolerance	VIF
Constant	11,034.14*	1750.01		6.31	0.000		
URB	161.00*	41.55	0.244	3.88	0.000	0.56	1.8
SSI	180.43**	91.77	0.14	1.97	0.050	0.44	2.28
NWF	90.10**	43.39	0.146	2.08	0.040	0.45	2.24
PCGVIP	0.15*	0.02	0.503	7.06	0.000	0.44	2.3
NUGP (D_1)	1457.59	1578.92	0.051	0.92	0.360	0.72	1.4
ER (D_2)	−2683.52**	1193.05	−0.132	−2.25	0.030	0.64	1.56

Dependent variable: PCNSDP $F = 64.56*$, Adj. R^2 0.845, $N = 71$
*Significant at one per cent level
**Significant five per cent level
Source Authors' calculation

lowed by NWF, SSI, and URB. Thus, GVI emerges as the highest contributor to the economic development of the state as measured in terms of CID.

Table 6 illustrates the results of model 2 in which per capita NSDP has been taken as dependent variable. Explanatory variables are same as in the first model. The regression results indicate that URB, SSI, NWF and GVI turn out to have a positive and statistically significant effect on the per capita NSDP, while Dummy for ER shows a negative impact on it. The value of Adj. R^2 indicates that 84.5% variations in the dependent variable are explained by the explanatory variables. Urban areas are the centre of various activities which are directly or indirectly linked with the development process and contribute to NSDP. An increase in urban population in total population leads to a positive impact on the economic development. This statement is supported by the regression results as urbanisation is found to have a statistically significant positive impact on per capita NSDP. The coefficient of SSI and NWF are significant at five per cent level of significance. We can say on the basis of the results that number of SSIs directly affects NSDP. If one small scale industry per hundred thousand population is set up, the per capita NSDP would increase by Rs. 180.43. Cheng (2012) also assesses the impact of urbanisation on economic growth by taking variables GDP and urbanisation, and finds a positive impact of urbanisation on GDP. In terms of NWF, if one working factory per hundred thousand population is increased, it would lead to an increase of Rs. 90.10 in the per capita NSDP.

Per capita GVI turns out to be one of the most significant factors in explaining the per capita NSDP. The values of coefficient of dummy for ER in both the models indicate that the level of economic development in the ER is much lower than that in other regions. The same has been observed from the figures and maps analysed in the preceding sections. On the basis of standardized coefficients, we can rank the contribution of individual factors to the per capita NSDP. As the magnitudes of standardized coefficients show, GVI occupies the first rank, followed by urbanisation, NWP and SSIs.

5 Conclusion and Policy Implications

This paper finds that urbanisation and industrialisation are growing together and both are significantly inter-related. The pace of urbanisation and industrialisation has impacted the economic development of Uttar Pradesh. Their differing levels together cause variations in the level of economic development across regions. For example, CID score in NUGP is very high (148.66) with a high urbanisation rate of 38.25% as well as high per capita NSDP (Rs. 37,050). Contrary to this, ER, with 109.43 CID score, not only has the lowest urbanisation rate of 11.93% but also has the lowest NSDP (Rs. 19,233) among all the five regions in the state. It is observed that all the ten districts of Western Uttar Pradesh located in NUGP have the highest level of urbanisation and industrialisation, while ER as a whole is lagging behind the other regions. Since urbanisation and industrialisation are highly inter-related issues, a high level of urbanisation in NUGP also has a high concentration of industries, thereby generating a high level of economic development. We have documented that industrialisation process is slow in ER and SR with low urbanisation rates; while NUGP and SUGP have faster development with high levels of urbanisation and industrialisation. Since region-wise and district-wise variations in urbanisation and industrialisation do exist; economic development also shows almost the similar pattern. Regression analysis indicates that urbanisation and industrialisation have a statistically significant positive impact on the economic development, measured in terms of CID and per capita NSDP. The value of the coefficient of dummy for ER indicates that the levels of CID and per capita NSDP in ER are much lower than that of other regions. The study concludes that inter-region and intra-region disparities in the state exist in the level of urbanisation and industrialisation and consequently in the level of economic development.

This study provides evidence of backwardness in terms of urbanisation, industrialisation and economic development of ER and SR of the state. Since these regions are most backward, to accelerate the pace of urbanisation and development, the focus must be on addressing the issues related to urbanisation and industrialisation of these regions. It is necessary to develop new cities and manufacturing towns as industrial clusters in ER and SR to improve the level of urbanisation and industrialisation. There is a need to identify the growth enablers and drivers of the economy of ER and SR and rework on them for accelerating the pace of economic development. Amritsar-Kolkata Industrial Corridor (AKIC), proposed to be set up alongside EDFC, covering 18 districts of the state, has high potential to transform the state economy. Similarly, the Delhi-Agra-Lucknow expressway can be an enabling factor in this context. Linkage of this highway with the districts of Bundelkhand (SR) and preparation of a prospective plan for making it a manufacturing hub of the state is the need of the hour, as development of agriculture in this region has limited scope due to water scarcity. Between 2011 and 2021, Uttar Pradesh is projected to share 21.9% of total addition to workforce, while it is expected to add only 5.6% to the total GDP of India, implying that the state has demographic advantage that can be converted into dividend by investing more in education and skill formation and creating employment opportunities in the manufacturing and services sectors. Emphasis on rural industrialisation like in China (Song et al. 2012) may be a better policy option for developing new industrial towns, specially, when our urban policies are looking towards smart cities, and distress migration from rural to urban areas has affected the carrying capacity of urban centres (megacities) in terms of civic amenities, availability of land and water, and environmental degradation.

Appendix

See Table 7.

Table 7 District-wise socio-economic indicators of Uttar Pradesh

Sr. No.	Districts	Urban population (per cent, 2011)	CID (2013–14)	Per capita gross value of industrial production (Rs.) at current prices (2011–12)	Per capita NSDP (Rs.) at constant prices (2004–2005)[a] 2013–14	No. of small scale industries per hundred thousand population (2014–15)	Percentage distribution of registered working factories (2011–12)	No. of registered working factories per hundred thousand population (2011–12)
1	Saharanpur	30.71	112.69	11,988.03	23,008.73	32.57	1.36	5.43
2	Muzaffarnagar	28.76	117.30	29,433.55[b]	22,922.04	38.71	3.18	10.05
3	Bijnor	25.13	104.28	8541.91	19,825.21	29.45	1.79	6.23
4	Moradabad	33.01	101.57	7665.21[b]	16,890.79	51.37	3.37	9.14
5	Rampur	25.21	102.01	8488.41	15,201.58	46.43	1.03	5.82
6	JyotibaPhule Nagar (Amroha)	24.83	139.14	23,245.40	28,841.81	30.03	0.80	6.74
7	Meerut	51.13	124.68	19,427.25	29,181.05	32.94	4.43	16.59
8	Baghpat	21.05	114.57	6888.48	27,540.47	6.13	0.34	3.67
9	Ghaziabad	67.46	165.59	62,208.02	27,434.84	51.86	12.30	34.14
10	G.B. Nagar	59.56	404.85	337,425.8[b]	86,960.58	103.68	19.95	159.4
NUGP (average)		38.25	148.668	39,639.39	37,050.04	39.06	48.55	25.72
Std. deviation		16.47	92.13	94,280.14	20,688.20	25.34	6.34	47.82
11	Bulandshahar	24.80	118.38	23,295.62	27,715.75	17.42	2.76	11.28
12	Aligarh	33.11	99.94	10,984.91	19,486.34	30.23	1.82	6.5

(continued)

Table 7 (continued)

Sr. No.	Districts	Urban population (per cent, 2011)	CID (2013–14)	Per capita gross value of industrial production (Rs.) at current prices (2011–12)	Per capita NSDP (Rs.) at constant prices (2004–2005)[a] 2013–14	No. of small scale industries per hundred thousand population (2014–15)	Percentage distribution of registered working factories (2011–12)	No. of registered working factories per hundred thousand population (2011–12)
13	Mahamaya Nagar (Hathras)	21.31	128.8	5338.84	24,992.75	48.28	1.18	12.26
14	Mathura	29.66	134.5	150,277.99	29,583.91	49.00	1.25	6.69
15	Agra	45.87	123.82	9619.01	36,187.61	40.28	4.82	14.00
16	Firozabad	33.33	113.81	6640.28	16,808.21	61.32	2.96	14.88
17	Etah	15.24	95.63	2188.78	22,427.60	22.73	0.12	0.89
18	Kanshiram Nagar (Kasganj)	20.05	NA	2966.52	20,338.43	27.85	0.07	0.65
19	Mainpuri	15.39	106.67	575.87	17,066.15	55.58	0.55	4.01
20	Badaun	17.37	91.84	3663.98	18,152.37	19.00	0.19	0.68
21	Bareilly	34.99	104.10	11,578.56	25,597.27	40.35	2.14	6.50
22	Pilibhit	17.43	95.70	5590.56	19,254.20	42.68	0.52	3.45
23	Shahjahanpur	19.70	95.15	12,741.64	17,581.89	9.84	0.92	3.89
24	Farrukhabad	22.00	99.48	787.47	14,792.74	26.24	0.43	3.11
25	Kannauj	16.92	110.82	1470.93	14,174.55	41.12	0.75	6.33
26	Etawah	23.20	109.82	417.27	19,348.60	58.52	0.45	4.02

(continued)

Table 7 (continued)

Sr. No.	Districts	Urban population (per cent, 2011)	CID (2013–14)	Per capita gross value of industrial production (Rs.) at current prices (2011–12)	Per capita NSDP (Rs.) at constant prices (2004–2005)[a] 2013–14	No. of small scale industries per hundred thousand population (2014–15)	Percentage distribution of registered working factories (2011–12)	No. of registered working factories per hundred thousand population (2011–12)
27	Auraiya	17.07	109.63	16,480.44	16,295.13	22.11	0.15	1.53
28	Kheri	11.49	89.07	8228.31	16,714.89	8.02	0.88	2.86
SUGP (average)		25.87	107.48	15,158.17	20,917.69	34.48	21.96	5.75
Std. deviation		8.85	28.38	34,276.88	5817.82	16.42	1.26	4.54
29	Sitapur	11.84	85.13	4258.19	16,038.54	7.39	0.90	2.72
30	Hardoi	13.22	84.19	2093.56	14,472.93	12.35	0.40	1.34
31	Unnao	17.14	90.83	15,764.00	18,330.75	7.36	1.32	5.58
32	Lucknow	66.20	127.44	25,628.29	33,633.03	28.36	3.96	11.07
33	Rae Bareli	9.05	94.52	2041.90	15,471.47	17.55	0.42	2.35
34	Ramabai Nagar (Kanpur Dehat)	9.66	111.79	28,787.07	16,536.92	20.66	1.00	7.33
35	Kanpur Nagar	65.93	128.4	16,698.05	30,090.86	49.55	8.49	22.39
36	Fatehpur	12.25	101.5	11,899.33	17,019.36	36.21	0.70	3.53
37	Barabanki	10.14	90.68	5117.73	13,955.71	18.39	0.74	3.06
CR (average)		27.54	101.60	12,476.46	19,505.51	21.98	17.93	6.59
Std. deviation		24.00	17.14	10,039.58	7180.10	13.95	2.67	6.65

(continued)

Table 7 (continued)

Sr. No.	Districts	Urban population (per cent, 2011)	CID (2013–14)	Per capita gross value of industrial production (Rs.) at current prices (2011–12)	Per capita NSDP (Rs.) at constant prices (2004–2005)[a] 2013–14	No. of small scale industries per hundred thousand population (2014–15)	Percentage distribution of registered working factories (2011–12)	No. of registered working factories per hundred thousand population (2011–12)
38	Jalaun	25.06	106.52	1716.55	17,369.06	14.39	0.18	1.46
39	Jhansi	41.78	111.1	7522.12	26,213.26	37.67	0.47	3.11
40	Lalitpur	14.38	95.35	41.37	14,891.11	46.22	0.02	0.23
41	Hamirpur	18.96	103.35	4929.03	18,354.25	12.60	0.10	1.16
42	Mahoba	21.19	110.13	215.71	25,120.32	46.26	0.17	2.80
43	Banda	15.35	98.61	1023.98	19,918.22	14.29	0.06	0.46
44	Chitrakoot	9.73	104.45	NA	21,014.48	14.99	c	NA
SR (average)		**10.45**	**5.75**	**2574.79**	**4090.72**	**15.94**	**0.16**	**1.23**
Std. deviation		**22.74**	**104.21**	**2910.50**	**20,411.53**	**26.63**	**1**	**1.48**
45	Pratapgarh	5.54	78.56	15.12	11,533.68	9.29	0.11	0.48
46	Kaushambi	7.79	96.2	306.19	17,297.18	1.77	0.20	1.99
47	Allahabad	24.78	100.57	11,058.90	19,647.81	27.27	1.77	3.76
48	Faizabad	13.89	93.26	4572.92	17,900.46	15.65	0.63	3.38
49	Ambedkar Nagar	11.74	87.77	2086.53	12,622.46	15.34	0.37	1.99
50	Sultanpur	5.28	94.53	6623.38	18,544.55	28.03	0.35	1.93

(continued)

Table 7 (continued)

Sr. No.	Districts	Urban population (per cent, 2011)	CID (2013–14)	Per capita gross value of industrial production (Rs.) at current prices (2011–12)	Per capita NSDP (Rs.) at constant prices (2004–2005)[a] 2013–14	No. of small scale industries per hundred thousand population (2014–15)	Percentage distribution of registered working factories (2011–12)	No. of registered working factories per hundred thousand population (2011–12)
51	Bahraich	8.26	75.44	2398.30	11,945.31	5.73	0.32	1.44
52	Shrawasti	3.45	76.25	NA	8795.23	10.92	NA	NA
53	Balrampur	7.74	79.68	4958.86	11,972.75	33.29	0.17	1.11
54	Gonda	6.56	78.85	2770.19	13,259.93	16.92	0.16	0.63
55	Siddharth Nagar	6.28	84.47	0.00	11,165.05	9.45	0	0
56	Basti	5.61	83.27	1395.05	13,083.40	10.36	0.14	0.74
57	SantKabir Nagar	7.47	77.63	1284.89	10,789.04	5.05	0.11	0.86
58	Mahrajganj	5.06	76.59	631.00	11,616.80	8.09	0.10	0.5
59	Gorakhpur	18.78	88.61	4625.04	16,746.10	12.7	1.14	3.41
60	Kushinagar	4.72	74.06	2283.59	10,754.76	10.92	0.08	0.29
61	Deoria	10.23	78.3	301.50	12,156.54	9.26	0.13	0.53
62	Azamgarh	8.52	76.35	11.82	10,774.92	4.45	0.11	0.3
63	Mau	22.66	87.93	438.10	14,646.29	18.45	0.14	0.84
64	Ballia	9.43	85.77	52.65	13,178.34	6.83	0.07	0.3
65	Jaunpur	7.45	79.39	5284.80	11,581.24	13.58	0.52	1.54

(continued)

Table 7 (continued)

Sr. No.	Districts	Urban population (per cent, 2011)	CID (2013–14)	Per capita gross value of industrial production (Rs.) at current prices (2011–12)	Per capita NSDP (Rs.) at constant prices (2004–2005)[a] 2013–14	No. of small scale industries per hundred thousand population (2014–15)	Percentage distribution of registered working factories (2011–12)	No. of registered working factories per hundred thousand population (2011–12)
66	Ghazipur	7.56	82.38	787.88	12,952.07	12.95	0.16	0.57
67	Chandauli	12.55	86.98	15,961.05	14,594.50	8.64	0.87	5.70
68	Varanasi	43.43	96.62	2506.06	19,079.69	22.27	1.46	5.16
69	Sant Ravidas Nagar	14.73	94.18	2025.16	16,225.88	23.65	0.68	5.59
70	Mirzapur	13.89	77.67	4266.57	14,346.70	13.54	0.47	2.43
71	Sonbhadra	16.86	97.74	28,435.70	21,655.87	19.94	0.13	0.88
	ER (average)	**11.93**	**84.77**	**3921.86**	**13,956.91**	**13.92**	**10.53**	**1.74**
	Std. deviation	**8.41**	**8.03**	**6114.12**	**3265.09**	**7.79**	**0.45**	**1.71**
	Uttar Pradesh	**22.28**	**109.43**	**13,456.43**	**19,232.84**	**24.14**	**100**	**6.64**

[a]Base year
[b]Muzaffar Nagar, Moradabad, Ghaziabad include information of Shamli, Sambhal and Hathras districts respectively
[c]Information of Chitrakoot district is included in Banda districts
Source District Wise Development Indicators, UP (2015)
Niyojan Atlas, UP—(2013–14)
Census of India, 2011

References

Arora, A., & Singh, S. P. (2015). Poverty across social and religious groups in Uttar Pradesh: An interregional analysis. *Economic and Political Weekly, L, L*(52), 100–109.

Bloom, D. E., Canning, D., & Fink, G. (2008). Urbanization and the Wealth of Nations. *Science, 319*(5864), 772–775.

Bose, D. K. (1969). Urbanisation, industrialisation and planning for regional development. *Economic & Political Weekly, 4*(28), 1171–1172.

Cheng, C. (2012). A study of dynamic econometric relationship between urbanisation and service industries growth in China. *Journal of Industrial Engineering and Management, 6*(1), 8–15.

Credit Suisse. (2013). Annual Report 2012. Retrieved May, 15, 2013 from https://www.credit-suisse.com/…/financial…/financial-reports/csgag-csag-ar-2012-en.p.

Dobbs, R., Smit, S., Remes, J., Manyika, J., Roxburgh, C., & Restrepo, A. (2011). Urban world: Mapping the economic power of cities. *McKinsey Global Institute*

Pandey, S. M. (1977). Nature and determinants of urbanisation in a developing economy: The case of India. *Economic Development and Cultural Change, 25*(2), 265–278.

Ranjan, N. A. (2014). *Urban India to contribute 75% of GDP by 2020*. Barclays. http://urbanupdate.in/in-depth/urban-india-contribute-75-gdp-2020-bracklays.

Roberts, M., Blankespoor, B., Deuskar, C., & Stewart, B. (2017). Urbanisation and development: Is Latin America and the Caribbean Different from the Rest of the World ? In *Policy Research working Paper 8019*. Washington DC: The World Bank.

Singh, S. P. (2017). Rural-urban divide in India. In K. N. Kabra & V. Upadhyay (Eds.), *Plutocracy, cronyism and populism: facets of neoliberalisation in India*. New Delhi: Vitasta Publishing Pvt. Ltd.

Song, H., Thisse, J.-F., & Zhu, X. (2012). Urbanisation and/or rural industrialisation in China. *Regional Science and Urban Economics, 42*(1), 126–134.

Dr. S. P. Singh has been engaging in teaching and research in economics for more than 25 years. He joined Department of Humanities & Social Sciences, Indian Institute of Technology Roorkee (erstwhile University of Roorkee) as Assistant Professor in 1996. Presently, he is professor of economics in the Department of Humanities and Social Sciences, IIT Roorkee. Besides having contributed more than 140 research papers and articles in national and international journals, he has written three books: Planning and Management for Rural Development; Growing Rural-Urban Disparity in Uttar Pradesh (co-author); Dynamics of Occupational and Educational Mobility in India (co-author) and one occasional paper: *Post* WTO Era: Impact on Export Prospects of Livestock Products, NABARD, Mumbai. Dr. Singh is actively engaging in guiding Ph.D. theses and conducting sponsored research projects in the field of efficiency and productivity analysis, rural development, agricultural economics, labour economics, and education and health. He has also organized several conferences, workshops and research methodology courses. He was a team leader for one of the thematic groups of the "Ganga River Basin Management Plan" project awarded to seven IITs by the Ministry of Environment and Forests, Government of India and also a member of Processional Institute Network (PIN) constituted by the MORD, Government of India to provide for steady and sustainable interventions to enhance the quality of the MGNREGS. Dr. Singh is life member of several professional societies, and also member of Board of Studies of several universities. He is member of reputed academic professional bodies wherein his contribution has been remarkable.

Divyanshu Dixit is a research scholar in the department of Humanities and Social Sciences, IIT Roorkee. His research interests are peri-urbanization, land-use and livelihood dynamics in the urban fringe of metropolitan cities. He holds a master's degree in Geography from the Banaras Hindu University. His research is supported by UGC under the JRF scheme

Employment and Livelihood Potential of Rural Non-farm Informal Enterprises

Nripendra Kishore Mishra

Abstract There are two quite opposite views about rural non-farm informal enterprises (RNFIEs). First, it is low productivity sector producing low-quality goods, and the second one recognizes it as dynamic, flexible, innovative and contributing significantly in economic development. Based on National Sample Survey unit-level data (1999–2000 and 2010–11) and village-level household enterprise data, this chapter examines the employment and livelihood potential of RNFIEs in Uttar Pradesh. Though a higher percentage of informal enterprises have reported expansion, still more than half of enterprises are stagnant. These enterprises are essentially owned by illiterate, landless and middle castes having nothing else to do. Almost three-fourths of OAEs and more than half of establishments have GVA per worker below notional income which is a matter of major policy concern. Nevertheless, this study confirms that enterprise profit contributes significantly in household income and in the absence of this, household takes recourse to wage income, suggesting that RNFIEs are replacing casual work in households with enterprises. This study also questions aggregative method of studying RNFIEs.

Keywords Employment and livelihoods · Rural non-farm informal enterprises · Gross value added

1 Introduction

It is a contemporary fact that the share of agriculture in output and employment generation has drastically declined in India. Still, there is acceleration in rural incomes and decline in rural poverty. In fact, growth in rural income has outpaced growth in urban income. In general, growth of rural economy of India has witnessed greater dynamism as compared to earlier times. Various explanations have been forwarded, like role of Mahatma Gandhi National Rural Employment Guarantee Scheme (MGNREGS),

N. K. Mishra (✉)
Department of Economics, Banaras Hindu University, Varanasi, India
e-mail: nripendra.mishra@gmail.com

remittance flows to rural economy, diversification of rural demand, changing power relations, changing land and resource ownership and urban spill over. However, the strongest driver of this change is expansion of rural non-farm sector. Decline in share of agriculture sector in rural GDP and employment and consequent rise in share of non-farm sector is a testimony to this. A large discussion is available on growth of rural non-farm employment (Srivastava 1996, 1999; Lerche 1995, 1999; Sharma and Poleman 1994; Dreze and Sharma 1998; Singh 2005; Ranjan 2009) assuming that employment is coterminous with output. These enterprises are generally smaller in size and are located either within the household or in the vicinity. However, there are enterprises which are larger in size. But those enterprises have a different character than that of the smaller ones. The smaller types of enterprises are closely associated with the livelihood of a large rural population and have altered the rural economy in a very significant way, at least in Uttar Pradesh. NCEUS (2007) has highlighted the importance of these enterprises in the context of poverty and vulnerability and has classified these non-agricultural (or non-farm) enterprises as rural informal enterprises, having less than 10 workers. The present study follows this convention and focuses on this kind of rural non-farm informal enterprises (RNFIEs) only. The primary motivation for taking up these enterprises is driven by Chen et al. (2006) and Kabeer (2012) formulation that these enterprises are at the bottom of pyramid and are survivalist in nature. A larger part of these survivalist enterprises are mainly own account enterprises (OAEs), which are family labour-intensive and therefore operate at low scale of production. This is automatically followed up by low capital intensity and low returns. Establishment is expected to be better-off type of enterprise. Hiring of labour is possible only at higher scale of production and with higher level of returns. It may be hypothesized that OAEs are primarily a supplementary source of income used as strategy of coping either with falling income or providing employment to family labour. These informal enterprises are a major source of livelihood for a large section of population. Ideally, the rate of return of these enterprises should be higher than market wage rate as these enterprises are using their own land and capital. But these enterprises are a classic case of self-exploitation of labour. However, there cannot be a simplistic view of these rural enterprises, as they are very sensitive to geographical space. They may appear to be a positive economic response in one region, but could be distress coping mechanism in another region. Therefore, it is also important to have a disaggregated view of these rural enterprises.

This becomes all the more important for a heterogeneous state like Uttar Pradesh (U.P.). Rural U.P. has gone through major changes in the last two decades. However, these changes are not uniform across all regions of state, depending upon rural dynamics. Basically, U.P. is divided into four well-defined economic regions: Western, Eastern, Central and Southern,[1] prosperous Western U.P. and relatively backward Eastern U.P. being two extremes. According to the fourth report on Poverty and Social Monitoring Survey (PSMS-IV, 2009–10) of U.P., per capita income is lowest in Eastern region (Rs. 11,392) and highest in Western region (Rs. 20,846). Almost 70.0% of

---

[1] These regions vary in size—area as well as population. Therefore, any comparison of these regions has to take this into account.

net state domestic product (NSDP) comes from non-farm sector (GoUP 2012–2013). Trade, transport, communication, and public and private services together contribute more than one-third of NSDP in non-farm activities. Though the poverty headcount ratio (HCR) has declined by 1.75% between 2004–05 and 2009–10 in rural U.P., still 42.5% population is below poverty line. Poverty ratio varies between 30.0% and 55.0% across regions. It is lowest in Western region and highest in Central region. Consumption inequality has also increased in all regions of state. It is highest in the Southern region and lowest in Western region.

Rural non-farm sector is a key for employment and output growth in rural U.P. as the employment share of this sector rose from 17.8% in 1987–88 to 27.2% in 2004–05 (Ranjan 2009). Role of agriculture, which is the first stimulator of rural enterprises, has been different in different regions. About 46.0% households each in Western and Eastern regions are found to be self-employed in agriculture as against 52.0% in Central and 56.0% in Southern regions. However, the percentage of households engaged as self-employed in non-farm sector is higher in Western and Eastern regions than other two regions. Unemployment rate was reported to be highest in the Eastern region, followed by Central region (GoUP 2009–2010a, b, 2011–2012). Besides, Eastern U.P. and Southern U.P. are characterized by large out migration compared to the other two regions, although urban influence is stronger in Western U.P.

It is observed that mainly landless and marginal farmers participate in non-farm activities for their survival. Therefore, land ownership pattern and consequent class/caste structure, which is quite different in regions of U.P., may also have a bearing on participation in RNFIE. Overall, regions of U.P. are very heterogeneous in nature and the aggregate level analysis of state could eclipse some important features of informal enterprises. So far, the examination of rural non-farm sector has been primarily in terms of employment, and that too has been examined generally at the national level and very rarely at state level. There is dearth of work/research on rural non-agricultural enterprise, and there is absolutely none in case of U.P. at the disaggregated level. The present study attempts to fill this gap in the available literature and mainly focus on employment and livelihood capacity of RNFIE in rural U.P.

Section 2 discusses the data and methodology used in the present study. Section 3 provides regional spread and growth dynamics of RNFIE in U.P. Section 4 attempts to profile participants of RNFIE. Growth rate of employment and labour productivity and implications of their interactions are examined in Sect. 5. It is often asked whether participation in RNFIE is a positive economic response or a coping-up strategy of households. This is answered in Sect. 6 by examining the choice or survival question. Section 7 concludes the whole discussion.

2 Data and Methodology

The National Sample Survey Organisation (NSSO) carries out enterprise surveys regularly. There are rounds specific to either manufacturing or services, or retail trade enterprises. However, there have been two enterprise rounds of NSS, wherein it has covered all informal non-agricultural enterprises. These are 55th round (1999–2000) and 67th round (2010–2011). These two rounds covered all non-agricultural enterprises. While the first one included construction and incorporated enterprises, the latter one excluded this. Despite of differences in sampling design, these two rounds can be made comparable. This paper uses unit data of these two rounds. Also, NSS 55th round includes Uttarakhand as part of U.P. which had become a separate state when the NSS 67th round was conducted. Nonetheless, necessary adjustments have been made to make the data from the two rounds comparable. Here, we are taking up only those non-agricultural enterprises which are located in rural U.P. and have less than 10 workers and name it as rural non-farm informal enterprises (RNFIEs). While NSS 67th round uses National Industrial Classification (NIC) 2008, the 55th round uses NIC 1998. We have constructed a concordance table to make sub-industries comparable. The sub-industry categories are as follows:

Manufacturing—M1: food products, beverages and tobacco products; M2: cotton ginning, cleaning and bailing, textiles, wearing apparel, leather and leather products; M3: wood and wood products, paper and paper products, printing, etc.; M4: petroleum products, chemicals, pharmaceuticals, rubber, plastics, metals, metal products, machinery and equipment, etc.

Trade—T6: commission agents for wholesale trade; T7: trade and repair of motor vehicles and motor cycles; T8: other wholesale trade; T9: other retail trade.

Services—S10: accommodation and food service activities; S11: transport, storage, information and communication; S12: financial and insurance activities; S13: real estate, professional, scientific and technical, rental and leasing activities; S14: education; S15: human health and social work; S16: other personal services.

Though the NSS enterprise surveys provide detailed information about informal enterprises, there are some issues lacking information. First, it provides information about enterprise only, independent of the household operating this enterprise. Thus, we do not get any information of the household where the enterprise is located or details of operator of the enterprise, though this is critical information impacting on success or failure of the enterprise. Second, it is too much focused on computation of gross value added (GVA) and in doing so neglects some other important dimensions like reasons of starting the RNFIE, role of working capital, problem faced by RNFIE, etc. Also, no questions are asked about initiation of non-agricultural enterprises. To overcome this problem, this study resorts to primary data collected from survey of rural non-agricultural enterprises of U.P., whenever the same information is not available in NSS enterprise survey. This primary state-level survey was carried out in the same year when NSS carried out 67th round. The carefully drawn sample[2] consists of enterprises selected from eight villages from four districts of U.P. representing four economic regions of state, i.e. Ambedkar Nagar (Eastern region), Kannuaj (Central

---

[2] A multistage sampling method has been used to select districts and villages. Districts have been chosen based on the highest percentage of rural non-farm employment in total rural employment. Then, we have selected two blocks based on distance from the district headquarter so as to capture rural and urban differences. Finally, based on information collected at the local level, one Panchayat each from every chosen block has been selected and from each Panchayat one village has been chosen for survey.

region), Saharanpur (Western region) and Hamirpur (Southern region). Finally, we have interviewed 890 households and 179 household enterprises across U.P. Note that we have taken information from all household enterprises that are currently under operation by members of sample households. One does not know whether GVA per worker generated by these enterprises is adequate or not for their survival. This requires obtaining some indicator of adequateness. Following NCEUS (2007), we have computed notional income[3] (minimum floor income) of a worker from the Employment and Unemployment Survey of NSS and used this as a benchmark to judge adequateness of GVA per workers of enterprises. While NCEUS (2007) used this for OAEs only, we extend this to establishments also, despite of the fact that it is not as appropriate in case of establishments as it is in OAEs.

3 Regional Spread and Status of Informal Enterprises

Almost half of rural non-farm informal enterprises of U.P. are located in Eastern region, and only one-third are located in Western region. There has been a growth in number of such enterprises in all regions of the state except Central region, where there has been a decline in absolute number. A marginal change has been observed in the share of other regions. Interestingly, the share of Western region, though lower than Eastern region, has increased during this period. The most significant change in estimated number of enterprises during 1999–2000 and 2010–11 is seen in Southern region, followed by Western region (Mishra and Singh 2015).

The percentage share of enterprises across the regions in state hides the fact that regions vary in size and that the geographically larger regions would have larger share. One needs to neutralize the size of regions. To do so, we have computed rural enterprise density of regions by computing number of enterprises per 10,000 of rural population of the region for the two reference periods of our analysis. Though the share of only Central region has gone down, but in general the enterprise density of rural U.P. has gone down in all regions (Table 8). This is a bit puzzling as rural non-farm employment has witnessed growth in all regions of U.P. Perhaps, the growth in employment has come through casual or wage employment in rural non-farm sector of state. However, the most plausible explanation is that the rate of growth in population has outpaced rate of growth in rural enterprises. Figure 1 shows this to be the reason for declining enterprise density. While enterprise growth is always lower than population growth for all regions, the former becomes negative in case of Central U.P.

Usually, the constraints faced by informal enterprises are often co-related with their size in terms of employment and assets (NCEUS, 2007). Informal enterprises

---

[3]Notional minimum income = minimum floor level wage × working days per year × earning units per family. Therefore, two notional incomes for two years 1999–2000 and 2010–11 were required to compare GVA per worker of two rounds of NSS enterprises. The notional income was Rs. 15,289 and Rs. 36,702 in 1999–2000 and 2010–11, respectively.

Fig. 1 CAGR of population and enterprises during 1999–2000 to 2010–11. *Source* Author computation based on Population Census 2001, 2011, and NSS 55th and 67th rounds unit-level data

Western: 1.50, 1.13
Central: 1.70, −0.43
Eastern: 1.78, 0.48
Southern: 2.50, 1.45
UP: 1.71, 0.57

■ Population ■ Enterprise

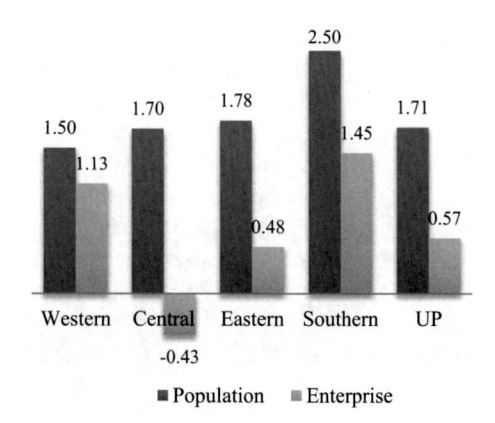

Table 1 Growth rate of enterprise by size and region, 1999–2000 to 2010–11 (% per annum)

Region	OAE owner operator	OAE Total	Est. 2–5 workers	Est. 6–9 workers	Total establishment	Total
Western	0.47	0.99	3.22	4.55	3.40	1.13
Central	−0.80	−0.69	6.53	0.43	5.64	−0.43
Eastern	0.79	0.50	−0.32	4.42	0.13	0.48
Southern	1.23	1.12	10.90	a	13.01	1.45
U.P.	0.43	0.47	2.08	4.27	2.33	0.57

Note [a] In Southern region, no observation is reported in establishment with 6–9 workers in 1999–2000
Source NSS 55th and 67th round unit record data

are broadly categorized into own account enterprises (OAE) and establishments. But this is too broad a category, and therefore, the present study considers the following categories of enterprises: owner operator (one worker enterprise), total OAE, establishment with 2–5 workers, establishment with 6–9 workers and total establishment.

Table 1 shows that the growth rate of enterprises has been sluggish (0.57%) in rural U.P. during 1999–2000 to 2010–11, especially in own account enterprises (OAEs). The growth rate of establishments has been much faster (2.33%) than OAEs growth rate (0.47%). Higher growth rate has been reported in relatively large enterprises, i.e. establishments with 6–9 workers. But, there are regional variations. The growth rates of enterprises (both OEAs and establishments) were highest in Southern region followed by Western region. Other two regions have reported lower growth rates, even being negative in Central region. In Western and Eastern regions, the highest growth rates have been reported in establishment with 6–9 workers. But in the Southern and Central regions, highest growth was reported in establishment with 2–5 workers. This may be an indication of conversion of OAEs into establishments across regions. While in Western and Eastern regions, OAEs have graduated into establishments with 6–9 workers, in Southern and Central regions they have converted into establishment with 2–5 workers. The larger trend in rural U.P. is increase in share of establishments

(Mishra and Singh 2015). This also suggests that something is wrong with OAEs as they have not shown as much growth as establishments.

Mishra and Singh (2015) show that more than ninety-four per cent of enterprises are perennial[4] and their share has increased between 1999–2000 and 2010–11. Among broad industry categories, trade appears to be much more perennial than manufacturing and services. In fact, these enterprises are the mainstay of illiterate and landless people. Therefore, they run their enterprises throughout the year for their basic livelihood. NSS 55th and 67th rounds record the status of enterprises during last three years (on the date of survey) as whether expanding, stagnant, or contracting. During periods 1999–2000 to 2010–11, there has been phenomenal growth in enterprises that reported to be expanding. This expansion is more pronounced in establishment than OAEs. Naturally, the percentage of enterprises reporting contraction has declined during this period. Interestingly, larger per cent of enterprises reported expansion during 1999–2000 to 2010–11 in Western region: this expansion is observed in all broad industry groups, viz. manufacturing, trade and services. But the other side of the growth story of the RNFIE sector is quite distressing. Almost more than half of such enterprises are stagnant. This pattern is common across the regions of U.P. and in all three industry categories. But the intensity of stagnant enterprises is highest in manufacturing enterprises especially in the Central region of U.P. Thus, it means that this period is characterized by expansion of RNFIE in all regions of U.P. and in all broad NIC categories along with substantial per cent of stagnant enterprises (Mishra et al. 2013).

4 Characteristics of Owners of Informal Enterprises

U.P. is marked as one of the laggard states in terms of growth rate of SDP and per capita income. In fact, there is a continuing divergence between growth rates of U.P. and other states of India. A better growth rate produces impacts on rural households in positive economic diversification. However, sluggishness in growth rate also impacts households albeit a different route; when there is a general unemployment, households do try to find out their own methods of coping up with distress, and engagement in household enterprises is one of them. The household enterprises are largely a product of households' attempt to create an alternative source of income or to diversify their income portfolio. Their location in rural area in itself is reason for their small size and their subsistence status. These enterprises are also set up almost on lines of caste occupations. Upper caste groups either did not venture out in establishing enterprises or even when they did so they preferred to move away from the rural area into urban areas or large enterprise size. Therefore, upper caste groups never

---

[4]Nature of operations of enterprises is of three kinds, i.e. perennial, seasonal and casual. Enterprises that are run more or less regularly throughout the year are called perennial enterprises. Seasonal enterprises are those that are usually run in a particular season or fixed months of a year, while causal enterprises are run occasionally, for a total of at least 30 days in the last 365 days.

fall into category of these occupational groups. At the same time, lower caste groups have had a subservient status and have been deprived of initial capital, so they did not find it possible to set up enterprises. As a result, enterprises are mainly owned by middle caste groups, that is OBCs in all four surveyed districts of our primary data.[5] Predominance of middle caste in ownership of enterprises has historical reasons also as these were associated with artisanal work in the *Varna system.* Moreover, growth of rural enterprises in U.P. got momentum in early 1990s and that is the period when middle caste assertion started and upper castes either vacated or were dislodged from power position. Lower caste groups were providers of manual labour, and even their later assertion could not catapult them to power position to have larger ownership of enterprises. While the OBCs had the necessary resource base, the SCs were lacking in this.

Three distinct forms of ownerships are evident in these rural enterprises, namely proprietary-male, proprietary-female and partnership within family. The most common form of ownership is proprietary-male. More than eighty-five per cent enterprises are run by males; women are generally missing from ownership of these enterprises. It is only in Western U.P. that some women are found to be proprietors of these enterprises[6] (Table 2).

Besides, about eighteen per cent enterprise owners are illiterate and almost forty-two per cent have completed middle-level schooling. Only fifteen per cent enterprise owners are graduates, which is a pointer that enterprises are the mainstay only for less educated persons who start enterprises to diversify the household risk. The literature also supports the same pattern of participation in household enterprises. Schultz (1988) explains that more educated farmers are more likely to supply labour off the farm. Similarly, Jolliffe (2004) found that there is higher return on education in farm work compared to non-farm activities and that affects the allocation of labour in rural households in Ghana. Besides, the average age of enterprise owner is between 38 and 45 years, suggesting that middle-aged people are operating these enterprises.

It is observed that the surplus income of agriculture leads the growth of non-agricultural enterprises to generate the supplementary income for household. It seems that large landholders are less likely to engage in informal enterprises. This study also found that about forty-one per cent enterprise owners are landless in rural U.P. This proportion is very high in Western region (eighty percent) and Southern region (fifty percent). However, households having less than one acre land are more likely to engage in non-farm household enterprises in Eastern region.

---

[5]NSS enterprise round does not provide information about operators of these enterprises. Therefore, this analysis uses primary data from our own survey, which did collect information about households. In fact, in this data, enterprises were tracked from household listing.

[6]Deshpande and Sharma (2013) found sharp gender disparity in ownership of firm.

Table 2 Profile of enterprise owners

Particulars	Western	Central	Eastern	Southern	U.P.
Ownership Type[a]					
Male	82.4	87.9	87.1	96.3	86.0
Female	17.6	12.1	12.9	3.7	14.0
Total	100	100	100	100	100
Average age of enterprise owner	44.5	40.8	41	38.6	41.3
Education					
Illiterate	19.5	16.7	23.4	6.3	17.9
Primary	43.9	16.7	18.8	28.1	25.7
Middle	9.8	16.7	20.3	15.6	16.2
10 + 2	17.1	35.7	25.0	25.0	25.7
Graduate	9.8	14.3	12.5	25.0	14.5
Total	100	100	100	100	100
Caste[a]					
SC/ST	17.7	17.1	20.7	24.4	19.2
OBC	61.3	65.2	65.6	58.5	63.8
Others	21.1	17.7	13.7	17.1	17.0
Total	100	100	100	100	100
Land ownership					
Landless	80.4	30.9	18.4	50	41.1
<1 acre	4.8	42.8	75.3	18.7	41.6
1.1–2.5 acre	7.3	14.2	6.1	12.5	9.4
>2.5 acre	7.3	11.9	0	18.7	7.7
Per cent of households owning a non-farm enterprise	17.7	16.2	27.1	19.1	20

Note [a]NSS 67th round
Sources Field survey and NSS 67th round unit record data

5 Employment and Labour Productivity

Employment growth in the formal sector has in fact been sluggish in Indian economy, and the challenge of employment is moderately met by the informal sector during the last couple of decades. The relative size of employment in informal sector is gradually increasing. It accounts for a substantial share of the total workforce in both the agriculture sector and non-agriculture sector (Papola 1981; Mitra and Pandey 2013; Bairagya 2012). This growing size of informal sector employment is due to the supply push component rather than demand-induced component (Maithi and Mitra 2011). Generally, employment growth in rural enterprises is considered to be a part of employment growth in rural non-farm sector and this has been captured by household

Table 3 Employment growth and labour productivity: growth by broad industry group and size of enterprises in U.P., 1999–2000 to 2010–11 (% per annum)

Enterprise type	Employment growth				Labour productivity growth			
	Manuf.	Trade	Services	Total	Manuf.	Trade	Services	Total
OAE owner operator	0.75	1.46	−0.73	0.47	1.57	1.09	3.1	1.92
OAE Total	−0.74	2.39	−0.88	0.38	1.93	0.33	3.11	1.75
Est. 2–5 workers	0.78	3.48	3.68	2.24	3.27	−1.8	−0.33	0.87
Est. 6–9 workers	2.48	2.61	7.39	4.76	3.9	10.66	2.91	3.66
Total Est.	1.21	3.38	4.82	2.89	3.45	−0.86	0.18	1.34
Total	−0.47	2.43	0	0.66	2.54	0.26	2.73	1.83

Source NSS 55th and 67th round unit record data

based Employment and Unemployment Survey (EUS) of NSS. There is no denying of the fact that employment growth is better captured by EUS. But our purpose here is to examine how far these rural enterprises have contributed in employment growth in rural U.P. We estimate the rate of growth of employment per annum (or labour absorption) in these enterprises during 1999–2000 to 2010–11. Establishments with 6–9 workers have recorded the highest (4.76%) employment growth, followed by establishments with 2–5 workers. This pattern continues in manufacturing and services, but is reversed in trade. OAEs have recorded only less than half per cent growth in employment. Employment growth is negative in manufacturing and the highest (2.43%) in trade. While OAEs have witnessed either negative or low employment growth in manufacturing and services, it is above 1.5% in trade. Trade in general has reported better employment growth across all enterprise types (Table 3).

Further disaggregation shows that employment growth is not uniform across regions (Table 9). While the Central and Eastern regions have recorded either negative or negligible employment growth during this period, the Southern and Western regions have recorded 2.15 and 1.67% employment growth, respectively. The dissimilarity of regions is also manifest from the fact that services have recorded either negative or negligible employment growth in all regions, except Southern where it has witnessed very high (6.02%) employment growth. The same picture is obtained in case of manufacturing. Only Western region reports high growth, and all other regions report negative or negligible growth. We pick up high (above three percent) and negative employment growth segments from our disaggregated (Table 9). Following results may be obtained (Box 1).

Employment and Livelihood Potential of Rural Non-farm …

Box 1

Regions	High growth in employment (above 3%)	Negative growth in employment
Western	1. Est., 2–5 workers, Manuf. 2. Est., 2–5 workers, Trade 3. Est., 6–9 workers, Services	1. OAE, Owner-operator, Services 2. OAE, Total, Services
Central	1. Est., 2–5 workers, Manuf. 2. Est., 2–5 workers, Trade 3. Est., 2–5 workers, Services 4. Est., 6–9 workers, Manuf.	1. OAE, Owner-operator, Manuf. 2. OAE, Owner-operator, Services 3. OAE, Total, Manuf. 4. OAE, Total, Services 5. Est., 6–9 workers, Trade 6. Est., 6–9 workers, Services
Eastern	1. OAE, Total, Trade 2. Est., 2–5 workers, Services 3. Est., 6–9 workers, Trade 4. Est., 6–9 workers, Services	1. OAE, Owner-operator, Services 2. OAE, Total, Manuf. 3. Est., 2–5 workers, Manuf. 4. Est., 2–5 workers, Trade
Southern	1. OAE, Owner-operator, Trade 2. OAE, Total, Services 3. Est., 2–5 workers, Manuf. 4. Est., 2–5 workers, Trade 5. Est., 2–5 workers, Services	1. OAE, Owner-operator, Manuf. 2. OAE, Total, Manuf.

Note Est. refers to establishment and manuf. refers to manufacturing
Source Based on Appendix Table 9

Two inferences can be made from Box 1. First, establishments are generally having high employment growth. Second, very rarely OAEs are reporting high growth. However, there are considerable regional variations and any one generalized conclusion for the whole of rural U.P. cannot be made.

Also employment growth has occurred in specific industry groups of trade and services during 1999–2000 to 2010–11 (Table 4). These groups are: repairing of motor vehicles and motor cycles in trade, financial and insurance activities, real estate, professional scientific and technical, rental and leasing activities, accommodation and food service activities, and more importantly education in services reported significant employment growth. Within the manufacturing sector, only wood and wood product, paper and paper products and printing establishments have reported significant employment growth. Overall employment growth is high in financial and insurance activities followed by real estate and repairing of motor vehicle and motor cycles and lowest in cotton ginning, cleaning and bailing, textiles, wearing apparel, leather and leather products.

Besides, some of the industries such as petroleum product, chemical, pharmaceutical, rubber, plastic, metal, machinery and equipments, other wholesale trade, transport, storage and communication, and other personal services have experienced negative employment growth. While it is true that employment growth in manufacturing is negative and is very low in services, but a further disaggregation by sub-industry shows that there is quite heterogeneity. Services in general have recorded very low employment growth; some sub-industry groups within services (financial and insurance activities and real estate, professional, scientific and technical, rental

Table 4 Employment growth and labour productivity growth by NIC category and size of enterprises, 1999–2000 to 2010–11 (% per annum)

Sub-industry group	Employment growth			Labour productivity growth		
	OAE	Est.	Total	OAE	Est.	Total
M1	−1.02	−0.08	−0.92	2.74	7.68	3.92
M2	−0.32	1.67	0.01	0.21	3.04	1.07
M3	0.69	3.91	1.04	2.49	3.08	3.00
M4	−3.48	−0.73	−3.01	3.87	1.09	3.34
Manuf.	−0.74	1.21	−0.47	1.93	3.45	2.54
T6	4.97	−11.38	0.75	10.44	2.71	6.32
T7	11.74	4.36	8.28	3.27	−4.85	−2.27
T8	−2.10	−1.47	−1.98	3.39	7.65	4.34
T9	2.56	6.24	2.65	0.10	−3.71	−0.02
Trade	2.39	3.38	2.43	0.33	−0.86	0.26
S10	4.74	11.21	5.25	−0.73	1.88	−0.27
S11	−2.19	1.20	−1.62	3.25	−0.55	2.53
S12	24.49	19.66	23.77	7.97	12.43	8.88
S13	14.24	11.68	13.66	0.57	0.87	0.66
S14	1.82	8.12	7.06	8.74	3.96	4.72
S15	0.14	2.77	0.52	3.28	3.08	3.24
S16	−3.78	−1.34	−3.65	2.78	1.88	2.75
Services	−0.88	4.82	0.00	3.11	0.18	2.73
Total	0.38	2.89	0.66	1.75	1.34	1.83

Sources NSS 55th and 67th round unit record data

and leasing activities) have exceedingly high employment growth for OAEs as well as establishments. While commission agents for wholesale trade has very negative employment growth for establishments, but high employment growth for OAEs.

Labour productivity has an important implication for livelihood dimension of these rural enterprises as it shows availability of output (GVA) per worker. Understandably, these enterprises are not characterized by high levels of labour productivity (GVA per worker) and that is why it becomes critical to know growth rate of labour productivity. While manufacturing and services have registered above 2.5% growth rate in labour productivity in rural enterprises of U.P., it is almost negligible in trade. Establishments with 6–9 workers have registered the highest labour productivity growth (Table 3). It is interesting to note that labour productivity growth is the highest in Sothern region, followed by Central region. There may be base effect also. But it is almost five times of growth rate of either Western or Eastern region. Labour productivity growth is always highest in services in all regions, except Southern region where it is the highest in manufacturing. Further, OAEs in Southern region have experienced higher labour productivity growth in comparison with their counterparts in other regions (Table 10). In fact, labour productivity growth is not uniform across sub-groups of industry (Table 4). Some groups have registered very high growth (up to 9.0%), and some groups have registered negative growth. Above 4.0% growth rate in labour productivity is recorded by commission agents for wholesale trade (6.32%), other wholesale trade (4.34%), financial and insurance activities (8.88%) and education (4.72%). It is also worth noting that out of sixteen sub-groups discussed here, growth of labour productivity is lower in 8 sub-groups in establishment in comparison with OAEs.

It may be discerned from Table 3 that growth rate of labour productivity (defined here as real gross value added per worker) in rural enterprises in U.P. has been much faster than the growth rate of number of workers working in these enterprises (defined here as employment growth) during 1999–2000 to 2010–11. But its further disaggregation shows that while it is so for OAEs only, establishments have just reverse picture. While growth rate of labour productivity is higher than employment growth in manufacturing and services, it is lower in trade-related activities. Growth rate of labour productivity is higher than growth rate of employment in Central, Eastern and Southern regions, but is lower in Western region. However, we observe that labour productivity growth is lower than employment growth in manufacturing in Western region and it is higher in trade in Central and Southern regions (Table 9).

Ideally, one expects that decline in employment should be accompanied by decline in GVA also and labour productivity is likely to decline, depending upon relative difference. This rests on the assumption that these enterprises are using labour-intensive techniques. If the number of workers is growing faster than GVA per worker, it means that over a period of time each worker is going to share lesser GVA. Growth in labour productivity might have occurred due to the retrenchment of redundant labourers, improvement in the definition of worker used in the survey. This may be a cause of decline in employment growth which has not been accompanied by decline in value-added growth (Mitra 2013). Another possibility could be growing sub-contracting in informal manufacturing sector and consequently substitution of large number of unskilled workers by small number of skilled workers, which raises GVA and reduces number of workers. Whatever is the reason, but lesser labour productivity is always a matter of concern. RNFIEs of U.P. are a mixed bag. While some industry groups have reported relatively higher growth in labour productivity in OAEs as well as establishments, in some cases it differs between OAEs and establishments.

It can be observed from Box 2 that all four sub-groups of manufacturing are reporting relatively higher growth in labour productivity in OAEs, but only three are reporting so in case of establishments. Out of four sub-groups of trade, commission agents for wholesale trade and other wholesale trade have reported relatively high labour productivity growth in both OAEs and establishments. It means rest two categories of trade have experienced relatively lower growth in labour productivity than employment growth. Besides, only two sub-groups of services such as human health and social work and other personal services in establishment show high labour productivity growth. It may be observed that labour productivity growth is higher than employment growth in OAEs in Central, Eastern and Southern regions and lower in Western region. Further, it is lower in establishments in Western, Eastern and Southern regions and higher in Central region (Table 9).

Box 2

Broad industry category	OAEs	Establishments
Manufacturing	1. Food products, beverages and tobacco products 2. Cotton ginning, cleaning and bailing, textiles, wearing apparel, leather and leather products 3. Wood and wood products, paper and paper products, printing, etc. 4. Petroleum products, chemicals, pharmaceuticals, rubber, plastics, metals, metal products, machinery and equipment, etc.	1. Food products, beverages and tobacco products 2. Cotton ginning, cleaning and bailing, textiles, wearing apparel, leather and leather products 3. Petroleum products, chemicals, pharmaceuticals, rubber, plastics, metals, metal products, machinery and equipment
Trade	1. Commission agents for wholesale trade 2. Other wholesale trade	1. Commission agents for wholesale trade 2. Other wholesale trade
Services	1. Transport, storage, information and communication 2. Education 3. Human health and social work, 4. Other personal services	1. Human health and social work 2. Other personal services

Source Based on Table 4

6 Choice or Survival

It is important to understand why people choose to start RNFIEs—whether it is a matter of choice or it is an outcome of their coping-up strategy by diversifying household income which is either squeezing or surrounded by risks and uncertainties. NSS data does not provide any information about this—partly due to the fact that household information is missing. Our survey data sheds some light on this by capturing reasons for starting up these enterprises (Table 5).

It seems that informal enterprises were started in a situation of distress as half of owners/proprietors had nothing else to do, while a substantial percentage is doing this as supplementary source of income. Besides, expectation of higher income is another important reason for starting up of enterprises in Western and Southern regions. However, almost one-fifth enterprises each in Eastern, Central and Southern

Table 5 Reasons for starting up of RNFI enterprises (in percent)

Reasons	Western	Central	Eastern	Southern	U.P.
Had nothing else to do	48.8	40.5	50.0	46.9	46.9
Higher income expectation	19.5	9.5	14.1	18.8	15.1
Supplementary income	2.4	19.1	18.8	21.9	15.6
Better future prospects	2.4	4.8	9.4	9.4	6.7
Social recognition	4.9	9.5	6.3	0.0	5.6
Had necessary skills	22.0	16.7	1.6	3.1	10.1
Total	100	100	100	100	100

Source Field survey

Table 6 Contribution of enterprise profit in household income

Sources of household income	Western	Central	Eastern	Southern	U.P.
Household having non-farm enterprise					
Ratio of non-farm income to total household income	95.5	84.4	92.5	88.0	90.5
Ratio of enterprise profits to household income	44.0	35.6	66.6	19.7	45.6
Ratio of enterprise profits to household non-farm income	46.5	43.6	72.9	23.9	51.3
Ratio of wage income to total household income	13.4	27.6	5.0	17.3	14.5
Household not having non-farm enterprise					
Ratio of farm income to total household income	12.1	32.5	17.2	18.7	20.7
Ratio of non-farm income to total household income	87.9	67.5	82.8	81.3	79.3
Ratio of wage income to total household income	57.4	44.5	33.2	58.6	47.9

Source Field survey

regions have been started to supplement income of households. Some of the enterprise owners in Central and Western regions acknowledge that they had the necessary skills to operate the particular enterprise that they set up. Social recognition was another important reason especially in Eastern and Central regions. It is observed that participation in a particular economic activity is restricted by caste system in a caste-divided society like U.P.

It is clear that majority of RNFIEs were started in distress situation when there were no other employment alternatives. In fact, these enterprises are the last resort for less educated, unskilled, landless and marginal famers. Now, can it be said that they start enterprises for their survival or to what extent non-farm enterprise profit contributes in household income? Whether profit of these enterprises is adequate to sustain their livelihood or is it only a marginal contributor in household income? Table 6 provides significant insight into this aspect. Households have been divided into two groups—households having RNFIE and not having RNFIE. More than ninety per cent household income comes from non-farm activities in households having non-farm enterprises. This share is almost eighty per cent in households not having non-farm enterprises. The ratio of enterprise profit to household income is forty-six percent, and it is almost fifty-one per cent in total non-farm income in household having enterprises, indicating that household enterprises are not only a mainstay for the uneducated and landless, but also significantly contribute to household income. The share of enterprise profit in households' total income and households' total non-farm income is not similar in all regions. About two-thirds of households' total incomes and almost three-fourths of households' non-farm incomes are contributed by enterprise profit in Eastern region. But forty-six per cent of household non-farm income in case of Western region and forty-four per cent of household non-farm income in Central region are contributed by enterprise profit. Though the share of enterprise profit is lowest in Southern region, it is almost one-fourth of non-farm income. Ratio of non-farm income to household total income is highest in Western region, but the share of enterprises profit in total income and even non-farm income is not as high as in Eastern region, indicating that other non-farm activities are contributing more in household income. Further, the share of wage income in total household income was almost fifteen per cent in households having RNFIE against forty-eight per cent of households not having RNFIE. It suggests that RNFIEs are replacing casual work in households with enterprises. This incidence is quite high in Eastern region than other regions of U.P.[7]

The NSS enterprise rounds provide information about gross value added (GVA) of these enterprises. But the question is whether GVA per worker is adequate to protect livelihood need of workers. One needs to set a benchmark for comparison of GVA. This is done by figuring out a notional income which is defined as minimum required income in a year for a worker to sustain livelihood (NCEUS 2007). Further analysis compares gross value addition (GVA) per worker to notional minimum income.

---

[7] Singh (2012) reports similar result in his study of Income and Consumption Level of Farmers in UP. He found that among non-farm sample households, 80% household income comes from non-farm activities in which share of wage income is almost 55%.

Table 7 Percentage of enterprises having GVA per worker below notional income, U.P.

Broad industry category	1999–2000			2010–11		
	OAEs	Establishment	Total	OAE	Establishment	Total
Manufacturing	82.42	50.38	80.16	87.37	60.3	85.15
Trade	61.91	41.09	61.48	69.72	38.45	68.99
Services	63.47	47.46	62.65	65.77	61.48	65.42
Total	69.04	47.96	68.05	73.87	57.2	72.91

Sources NSS 55th and 67th round unit record data

Table 7 confirms that GVA per worker is below notional income of a worker in three-fourths of OAEs and in almost fifty-seven per cent establishment in 2010–11 in rural U.P. This pattern is almost common across regions of U.P. for OAEs. The percentage of OAEs in manufacturing industry having GVA per worker below notional income is more than trade and service sector. However, in case of establishment, service sector reported highest percentage than manufacturing and trade sectors. It means that manufacturing OAEs are worse than other OAEs and service establishments are worse than other establishments. Since the growth rate of GVA per worker has been slower than notional income of workers during 1999–2000 to 2010–11,[8] the percentage of enterprises having GVA per worker below notional income has increased significantly in both OAEs and establishment across broad industry during the reference period. However, there are discordant notes also. Southern region has a different story. Here, the percentage of enterprises (OAEs as well as establishment) below notional income has gone down in 2010–11 as compared to 1999–2000, except for establishment in services. This decline is drastic in case of establishment in manufacturing and trading. The aggregate figure of both OAEs and establishment having GVA per worker below notional income is the highest in Eastern region followed by Central region and Southern region. Manufacturing sector is more vulnerable sector than trade and service sectors in all four regions and in both type of enterprises, i.e. OAEs and establishment (Table 10).

The above discussion is based on broad industry category, and these categories are quite heterogeneous. One needs to understand that RNFIEs have differential presence as well as performance within these broad categories. A further probing is required to know sites or sector/sub-groups of vulnerability and dynamism. These broad industry groups are disaggregated to identify sites of vulnerability and dynamism in these rural enterprises. This is all the more important because late rural enterprises have diversified in hitherto unchartered industry groups and a definite movement away from manufacturing is discernible. Therefore, sub-industry-wise comparison of GVA per worker and notional income is required. The two rounds of NSS enterprise data confirm that OAEs in all sub-groups of manufacturing accounts for the highest percentage of enterprises having GVA per worker below notional income than any

---

[8] In fact, due to the impact of MGNREGA, wage rate has significantly increased in rural UP.

other categories of OAEs. It is worth noting that OAE owner operator is better than total OAEs. It means that the latter is carrying the burden of family labour and consequently output (GVA) is being shared by more than one worker. This is quite likely to be the case in artisanal industrial groups in manufacturing. But the same pattern continues in trading and services also; suggesting that family labour-intensive enterprises are as vulnerable in manufacturing as in trade and services. The pattern observed earlier is evident here also. Generally, OAEs and establishments having experienced rise in number of enterprises below notional income have gone up in reference period. Some sub-industries in both OAEs and establishment have improved their GVA per worker during 1999–2000 to 2010–11; as a result, the percentage of enterprises having GVA per worker below notional income has declined (Table 11). Sub-industry groups T6 (commission agents for wholesale trade), T8 (other wholesale trade), S12 (financial and insurance activities) and S14 (education) have witnessed reduction in number of OAEs below notional income. Relatively better performance of establishments is evident here also. Decline in percentage of establishments below notional income is observed in M2 (cotton ginning, cleaning and bailing, textiles, wearing apparel, leather and leather products), all sub-groups of trading, S12 (financial and insurance activities) and S14 (education). It is to be noted that OAEs and establishments have done well in two sub-groups of services during this period. However, the larger story is that a very high percentage of enterprises is having GVA per worker lower than computed notional income. We try to locate vulnerable and relatively better industry sub-groups by listing industry sub-groups where percentage of enterprises below notional income is higher than three-fourths and less than one-fourth in year 2010–11 (Box 3).

Box 3

More than three-fourths of enterprises having GVA per labour below notional income		Less than one-fourth of enterprises having GVA per labour below notional income	
OAEs	Establishments	OAEs	Establishments
1. All manufacturing sub-groups 2. Accommodation and food service activities 3. Other personal services	1. Cotton ginning, cleaning and bailing, textiles, wearing apparel, leather and leather products 2. Financial and insurance activities 3. Education	1. Commission agents for wholesale trade	1. Other wholesale trade

Source Based on Appendix Table 11

7 Conclusion

Rural economy is generally characterized as going through a crisis, which is mainly agricultural in nature. However, a process of rural transformation is also evident in contemporary India. Rural non-farm employment and rural non-farm enterprises are the two central pillars of this transformation, having provided either some sort of relief from stress in agriculture or a supplementary source of income. However, this appears to be too narrow a characterization. A dynamic component is also present in the rural non-farm sector. It is well established that rural non-farm employment has been the principal source of employment in the rural economy in recent years, providing relief in a situation of stagnant or declining agricultural employment. However, the role of rural non-agricultural enterprises in generating employment and livelihood has not been properly investigated, especially in case of U.P. The issue gets further complicated by the fact that U.P. consists of four regions, quite different from each other resulting in different dynamics of rural non-agricultural enterprises in the regions. At times, these regions are diametrically opposed in outcomes. It is seen that enterprise density of rural U.P. has gone down during 1999–2000 to 2010–11 and the decline is very sharp in Central region. In general, rate of growth of rural enterprises has been sluggish in rural U.P. during this period, but establishments have experienced higher rate of growth than OAEs. This is important for the fact that OAEs constitute around two-thirds of RNFIEs and these are sites of poverty and vulnerability. A tendency of conversion of OAEs into establishment is also discernible. A higher percentage of these enterprises has reported expansion during 1999–2000 to 2010–11. But these enterprises are essentially owned by illiterate, landless or marginal holders and middle castes having nothing else to do. Income from these enterprises constitutes almost 90% of household income. However, GVA per worker for majority of these enterprises is below notional income, being three-fourths in OAEs and more than half in establishments. Manufacturing OAEs are in worst condition. The situation has further deteriorated from 1999–2000 to 2010–11, except in the case of Southern region. OAEs in commission agents for wholesale trade, other wholesale trade, financial and insurance activities and education and establishments in cotton ginning, cleaning and bailing, textiles, wearing apparel, leather and leather products, all sub-groups of trade, financial and insurance activities and education have recorded improvement during this period. This also reflects the fact that these are groups which have registered higher labour productivity growth than employment growth. In general, establishments have recorded higher employment growth than OAEs, but that does not reflect in higher labour productivity also; rather, the converse is true. OAEs have witnessed higher labour productivity growth than employment growth. This only shows that the conventional wisdom of branding OAEs as site of poverty and vulnerability and establishments as source of dynamism may not be correct. Further, the level of variations reported by regions also suggests that a generalization based at the level of state is always fraught with risks, especially in a heterogeneous state like U.P. These rural non-agricultural enterprises are a mixed bag, where some segments are a site of coping up with distress and some others

Table 8 Number of rural enterprises per 10,000 rural population

Region	No. of enterprises in 1999–2000	No. of enterprises in 2010–11
Western	313.8	309.6
Central	345.5	277.2
Eastern	351.7	312.1
Southern	230.6	214.2
Total	332.1	300.2

Source Author's computation based on U.P. Census 2001 and 2011, and NSS 55th and 67th round unit-level data

are providing dynamism to rural economy of U.P. However, the policy needs to be informed of tremendous regional variation within the state.

Appendix

See Tables 8, 9, 10 and 11.

Table 9 Employment growth and labour productivity growth in regions of U.P. by broad industry group and size of enterprises, 1999–2000 to 2010–11 (% per annum)

Type of enterprise	Employment Growth				Labour Productivity Growth			
	Manuf.	Trade	Services	Total	Manuf.	Trade	Services	Total
Western								
OAE owner operator	1.80	1.32	−1.07	0.51	0.95	−0.79	3.07	0.86
OAE Total	2.79	1.82	−1.49	1.34	0.92	−0.18	2.91	0.69
Est. 2–5 workers	3.02	4.79	2.87	3.32	1.62	6.64	−0.08	2.48
Est. 6–9 workers	1.35	1.67	10.07	5.21	6.83	14.88	0.92	4.37
Total Est.	2.50	4.50	5.42	3.88	3.45	7.26	0.43	3.10
Total	2.75	1.97	−0.26	1.67	1.56	0.44	2.49	1.19
Central								
OAE owner operator	−2.01	1.30	−2.55	−0.87	4.54	1.76	6.2	3.99
OAE Total	−1.68	1.65	−4.01	−0.94	2.85	1.74	6.88	3.60
Est. 2–5 workers	6.55	9.94	6.19	6.84	6.84	1.26	2.77	4.50
Est. 6–9 workers	6.2	−17.24	−2.91	0.11	6.17	16.63	10.2	8.84

(continued)

Table 9 (continued)

Type of enterprise	Employment Growth				Labour Productivity Growth			
	Manuf.	Trade	Services	Total	Manuf.	Trade	Services	Total
Total Est.	6.45	4.54	3.05	4.76	6.65	5.07	5.30	5.88
Total	−0.71	1.74	−2.92	−0.4	4.62	2.02	6.76	4.16
Eastern								
OAE owner operator	1.25	1.48	−0.04	0.86	0.61	2.61	2.02	1.91
OAE Total	−2.93	3.20	0.26	0.13	1.67	0.15	2.15	1.65
Est. 2–5 workers	−2.65	−0.49	3.16	−0.19	3.96	−6.21	−0.69	−0.32
Est. 6–9 workers	2.26	12.31	7.36	5.08	−2.61	0.08	2.57	0.01
Total Est.	−1.62	0.84	4.17	0.92	2.57	−5.99	−0.75	−0.7
Total	−2.74	3.11	0.81	0.22	1.99	−0.87	1.77	1.22
Southern								
OAE owner operator	−2.48	3.05	2.86	1.34	6.04	5.71	5.88	6.01
OAE Total	−0.39	1.73	3.43	1.19	5.74	5.21	5.87	5.71
Est. 2–5 workers	12.34	11.36	12.99	12.28	12.06	5.96	−5.55	2.26
Total Est.	13.16	13.77	22.94	17.44	13.24	7.79	−9.74	0.82
Total	0.24	2.14	6.02	2.15	7.19	6.10	3.49	6.03

Note [a]Zero reporting of enterprises under Est. 6–9 category in 55th round of NSS data
Sources NSS 55th and 67th round unit record data

Table 10 Percentage of enterprises having GVA per worker below notional income by region

Broad industry category	1999–2000			2010–11		
	OAEs	Establishment	Total	OAE	Establishment	Total
Western						
Manufacturing	74.36	46.4	72.04	84.15	58.87	81.9
Trading	48.58	47.22	48.55	59.51	37.17	58.76
Services	52.39	53.79	52.47	51.35	64.22	52.52
Total	57.25	49.15	56.83	65.61	56.64	65
Central						
Manufacturing	85.88	73.42	85.38	88.83	57.36	85.96
Trading	72.02	27.51	71.55	72.22	33.79	71.37
Services	74.99	70.8	74.82	69.36	59.68	68.48
Total	77.36	66.55	77.04	76.26	54.35	74.95
Eastern						
Manufacturing	84.97	48.09	82.08	90.02	64.51	88.13
Trading	65.9	36.91	65.26	75.63	43.58	75.10
Services	65.74	37.05	64.17	73.48	59.61	72.50
Total	72.43	42.87	70.88	78.95	59.60	77.98
Southern						
Manufacturing	90.55	100	90.68	82.46	37.97	79.92
Trading	82.12	73.63	82.04	72.67	32.93	71.56
Services	84.89	23.12	83.46	63.53	66.08	63.77
Total	85.95	68.40	85.70	73.51	48.73	72.21

Sources NSS 55th and 67th round unit record data

Table 11 Percentage of enterprises having GVA per worker below notional income by sub-industry category

Sub-industry group	1999–2000				2010–11			
	OAE owner operator	Total OAEs	Establishment	Total	OAE owner operator	Total OAEs	Establishment	Total
Manufacturing	76.18	82.42	50.38	80.16	83.82	87.37	60.3	85.15
M1	76.62	83.08	56.22	81.62	77.78	84.97	42.36	82.18
M2	78.46	83.73	67.36	82.36	90.83	92.97	76.23	91.29
M3	70.46	76.03	42.39	74.33	79.13	80.17	46.05	78.14
M4	79.42	87.01	10.19	79.48	84.65	89.64	49.46	85.48
Trading	57.08	61.91	41.09	61.48	62.04	69.72	38.45	68.99
T6	47.86	54.3	24.45	45.2	17.78	24.47	0	23.2
T7	47.38	48.29	64.41	54.49	47.31	57.79	63.41	59.04
T8	44.56	45.69	34.27	44.71	27.17	38.46	25.3	37.27
T9	57.96	63.03	38.51	62.75	63.78	71.28	35.28	70.68
Services	58.90	63.47	47.46	62.65	61.29	65.77	61.48	65.42
S10	39.93	53.84	57.2	53.96	70.72	82.83	64.29	81.7
S11	51.15	52.26	20.19	50.06	52.9	52.96	38.52	51.73
S12	65.42	64.78	100	66.57	51.93	56.65	75.56	57.61
S13	25.12	32.98	25.21	32.07	37.56	42.21	49.39	42.9
S14	70.82	75.34	86.96	81.35	68.41	71.49	83.5	78.86
S15	51.32	49.99	49.32	49.95	46.29	46.07	59.02	47.19
S16	69.30	75.28	70.63	75.19	76.10	79.93	73.51	79.76
Total	62.47	69.04	47.96	68.05	67.27	73.87	57.20	72.91

Sources NSS 55th and 67th round unit record data

References

Bairagya, I. (2012). Employment in India's informal sector: Size, pattern, growth and determinants. *Journal of the Asia Pacific Economy, 17*(4), 593–615.

Chen, M., Vanek, J., & Heintz, J. (2006). Informality, gender and poverty, a global picture. *Economic and Political Weekly, 41*(21), 2131–2139.

Deshpande, A., & Sharma, S. (2013). Entrepreneurship or survival? Caste and gender of small business in India. *Economic & Political Weekly, 28*(28), 38–49.

Dreze, J., & Sharma, N. (1998). Palanpur: Population, society economy. In P. Lanjouw & N. Stern (Eds.), *Economic development in Palanpur over five decades*. Oxford: Clarendon Press.

GoUP. (2009–2010a). Monitoring Poverty in Uttar Pradesh, A Report on the Fourth Poverty and Social Monitoring Survey (PSMS—IV), Government of Uttar Pradesh.

GoUP. (2009–2010b). Directorate of Economics and Statistics, Government of Uttar Pradesh (GoUP).

GoUP. (2011–2012). Directorate of Economics and Statistics, Government of Uttar Pradesh (GoUP).

GoUP. (2012–2013). Economic Survey, Directorate of Economics and Statistics, Government of Uttar Pradesh (GoUP).

Jolliffe, D. (2004). The impact of education in rural ghana: Examining household labor allocation and returns on and off the farm. *Journal of Development Economics, 73*(1), 287–314.

Kabeer, N. (2012). *Women's economic empowerment and inclusive growth: Labour markets and enterprise development*. SIG Working Paper 2012/1.

Lerche, J. (1995). Is bonded labour a bound category? Reconceptualising agrarian conflict in India. *Journal of Peasant Studies, 22*(3), 484–515.

Lerche, J. (1999). Politics of the poor: agricultural labourers and political transformation in Uttar Pradesh. *Journal of Peasant Studies, 26*(2–3), 182–241.

Maithi, D., & Mitra, A. (2011). Informality, vulnerability and development. *Journal of Developmental Entrepreneurship, 16*(2), 199–211.

Mishra, N. K., Raman, R., & Singh, U. B. (2013). Unpublished report on Dynamics of Growth of Rural Non-Farm Sector in Uttar Pradesh, Funded by University Grant Commission, submitted by Department of Economics, Banaras Hindu University, Varanasi.

Mishra, N. K., & Singh, U. B. (2015). Rural non-agricultural enterprises in Uttar Pradesh: Continuity and change. In S. Singh & D. Raina (Eds.), *Society and development: Regional perspective*. Jaipur: Rawat Publications.

Mitra, A. (2013). *Can industry be the key to pro-poor growth? An exploratory analysis for India*. ILO Asia Pacific Working Paper Series.

Mitra, A., & Pandey, A. (2013). Unorganized sector in India: Employment elasticity and wage-productivity nexus. *Journal of Development Entrepreneurship, 18*(4), 1350028 (1–19).

NCEUS. (2007). *Conditions of work and promotion of livelihoods in the unorganised sector*. National Commission for Enterprises in the Unorganized Sector (NCEUS), New Delhi: Government of India.

Papola, T. S. (1981). *Urban informal sector in a developing economy*. New Delhi: Vikas Publishing House.

Ranjan, S. (2009). Growth of rural nonfarm employment in Uttar Pradesh: Reflection from recent data. *Economic and Political Weekly, 44*(4), 63–70.

Schultz, T. P. (1988). Education investments and returns. In *Handbook of development economics* (Vol. 1). Elsevier.

Sharma, R., & Poleman, T. T. (1994). *The new economics of India's green revolution: Income and employment diffusion in Uttar Pradesh*. Delhi: Vikas Publishing House.

Singh, A. K. (2005). Role of rural non-farm sector in rural transformation: Evidences from Uttar Pradesh. In R. Nayyar & A. N. Sharma (Eds.), *Rural transformation in India: The role of non-farm sector*. Institute for Human Development.

Singh, A. K. (2012). *Income and consumption level of farmers in Uttar Pradesh*. Unpublished Project Report funded by Dept. of Planning Government of Uttar Pradesh submitted by Giri Institute of Development Studies, Luknow.

Srivastava, R. S. (1996). Agrarian change and the labour process. In P. Robb (Eds.), *Meanings of agriculture: Essays in South Asian history and economics*. Oxford University Press.

Srivastava, R. S. (1999). Rural labour in Uttar Pradesh: Emerging features of subsistence, contradiction and resistance. *Journal of Peasant Studies, 26*(2–3), 263–315.

Nripendra Kishore Mishra is Professor of Economics in Banaras Hindu University (BHU), Varanasi. He has more than 20 research papers in internationally and nationally acclaimed journals. He has carried out 12 research projects funded by national and international agencies, including USAID, ActionAID and the University of Wisconsin, Madison, USA. Prof Mishra has been associated with the exercise of identification of poor of erstwhile Planning Commission of India. He has been associated with National Commission for Enterprises in Unorganised Sector, Government of India. His research interest are poverty, unemployment, rural non-farm sector, rural transformation, women empowerment and home based workers. Uttar Pradesh (U.P) state in Indian is his main region of research.

Part V
Human Development Concerns

Trends in Private and Public Schooling

Geeta Gandhi Kingdon

Abstract Private fee-charging schools are a visibly ubiquitous phenomenon in both urban and rural Uttar Pradesh. Despite their preponderance and growth, and the public expectation of inclusivity from them, relatively little is known about the nature of private schools in the country, and much of the media and public discussion about them happens in a vacuum of hard facts. This review unravels the enigma by presenting evidence on several important facets of private schools and benchmarks these. It examines the size, growth, salaries, per-pupil costs, pupil achievement levels and cost-effectiveness of private schools in Uttar Pradesh and compares these with the government school sector. Official data presented here show a steep growth of private schooling and a corresponding rapid shrinkage in public schooling in UP, suggesting parental abandonment of government schools. Fee data from the National Sample Survey 2014–15 shows that, contrary to popular perception, a very high proportion of private schools in UP caters to the poor, where 32% of private school students pay fee less than Rs. 100 pm, and 84% pay fee less than Rs. 500 pm. Only 8% of private school-going children in UP pay fees of more than Rs. 1000 pm, and only 1.5% pay more than 2500 pm. In other words, the elite high-fee private schools visible in urban centres are a tiny proportion of the totality of private schools and are unrepresentative of private schooling in the state as a whole. A striking finding is that the median fee of private schools in UP is only 6.5% of the government schools' per-pupil expenditure. The evidence on fee levels thus suggests that affordability is an important factor behind the growth of private schools in UP. The main reasons for the low fee levels in private schools are firstly the competition they face from other private schools and, secondly, their low teacher salaries, which the data show to be a small fraction of the salaries paid in government schools. Low salaries are possible because private schools pay the market-clearing wage, which is depressed by a large

---

This chapter draws from the author's work "The Private Schooling Phenomenon in India: A Review" published in IZA Discussion Paper Series in 2017 and can be accessed at http://ftp.iza.org/dp10612.pdf. For more details, see Kingdon (2017a).

G. G. Kingdon (✉)
UCL Institute of Education,
University College London, London, UK
e-mail: g.kingdon@ucl.ac.uk

© Springer Nature Singapore Pte Ltd. 2019
R. P. Mamgain (ed.), *Growth, Disparities and Inclusive Development in India*,
India Studies in Business and Economics,
https://doi.org/10.1007/978-981-13-6443-3_15

supply of unemployed graduates, whereas government schools pay bureaucratically determined high minimum wages. Private schools' substantially lower per-student costs combined with their students' modestly higher learning achievement levels mean that they are significantly more cost-effective than government schools. The realisation that the bulk of private schooling in Uttar Pradesh is 'low fee' is significant because perceptions about the nature of private schools affect how they are judged in the media, in courts, and within government, e.g., with hostility or sympathy; as elitist or inclusive; as extractive/profiteering or as contributors to the educational effort; as lawbreakers (due to their inability to comply with all the stipulated infrastructure norms); or as budget schools that give poor people access to learning. The paper presents data that permits evidence-based judgments to be made about private schools, and it showcases how education policies can be flawed when made without seeking the evidence.

Keywords Government schools · Migration to private schools · Benchmarking of fee levels · Learning outcomes · Value of money from schools

1 Introduction

Private fee-charging schools are loved and loathed in equal measure in Uttar Pradesh: loved in the sense of being sought after by parents for quality education of their children and often criticised by the press/NGOs/authorities/for being profiteering commercialised 'teaching shops' that exploit parents with high fee levels and unjustifiable annual fee hikes. Despite their ubiquitous and growing presence, relatively little is known about these schools, largely because government statistics have tended to ignore them in data collection exercises, not just in the National Council for Educational Research and Training's (NCERT) National Achievement Surveys (NAS) of children's learning levels, but also in terms of collecting data on their teacher absence rates, salary levels, and pupil fee levels.

For sensible education policy-making, however, it is important to take account of the changing trends in the size of both the private and public schooling sectors in Uttar Pradesh. Ignoring these trends carries the risk of poor policies/legislation, with attendant adverse consequences for children's life chances. This study focuses on the temporal trends in the size of these two schooling sectors and spells out the risk of ignoring these trends.

There are several challenges in piecing together the picture on private-unaided schooling in Uttar Pradesh (and India), since there is no single comprehensive data source on private schooling. The official District Information System on Education (DISE), which is meant to be the annual census of all schools in the country, generally cannot collect data from most of the so-called non-recognised private-unaided schools[1] since such schools are not in the authorities' frame or list of schools. Moreover, DISE coverage of even the recognised private schools is thought to be incomplete. Finally, to compound matters, although the DISE questionnaire has a question on 'school type' which permits separately identifying and reporting on private-aided and private-unaided schools, in practice, in the DISE data report cards published annually by the official agency,[2] these two types of schools are mostly lumped together and treated as a single category 'private schools', though raw DISE data being publicly available enables one to overcome this shortcoming.

While the Annual Status of Education Report (ASER) published by NGO *Pratham* has been helpful in generating evidence on private as well as public schools across about 15,000 villages from all Indian districts annually, it is based only on rural survey and misses out urban areas altogether. Moreover, it also lumps together private-aided and private-unaided schools into a single category 'private'. While for some states, the distinction is unimportant because there are few aided private schools there, in other states, the distinction matters much.

Despite sharing the word 'private' in their names, private-unaided and aided schools differ fundamentally in their modes of operation, with aided schools lacking autonomy.[3] By contrast, private-unaided schools are autonomous fee-charging schools run by private managements which recruit/appoint their own teachers and pay them their own salary scales. Thus, we refer to private-aided schools simply as 'aided' schools and shall refer to private-unaided schools simply as 'private' schools. Thus, for the purpose of this study, all schools are categorised into three major types: government or 'public' schools, whether run by state, central or local government; 'aided' schools; and 'private' schools. At the elementary school level, aided schools constitute only a small proportion of all schools in the country and

---

[1] 'Recognition' is a government stamp of approval for a private school, to certify fitness to run as a school. The Right to Education Act 2009 obligates all private schools to be recognised, and it stipulates the conditions a private school must fulfil to be 'recognised'. Although state governments are clamping down on unrecognised private schools, surveys in various studies suggest that their numbers continue to be substantial, e.g. Muralidharan and Kremer (2008) find that in their national survey of 20 states, 51% of all private rural primary schools were unrecognised. Also, see evidence from individual states in five other studies which find that between 41 and 86% of all primary private schools were unrecognised (summarised in Kingdon 2007).

[2] The agency that collates the DISE data nationally from all the states is the National University of Educational Planning and Administration, NUEPA, in New Delhi.

[3] Centralising legislation in the early 1970s virtually nationalised the aided schools. Following extensive teacher union protests by the teachers of aided private schools, strikes and exam boycotts over a period of two years in the large north Indian state of Uttar Pradesh, the Salary Disbursement Act 1971 was passed by the UP Legislative Assembly and similar Acts were passed in other states, e.g. the Direct Payment Act of Kerala in 1972. These Acts virtually made aided schools like government schools; their teacher salaries are now paid at the same rate as government school teachers' and paid directly into their bank accounts from the government treasury, exactly as for government school teachers. Moreover, aided schools' teachers are recruited and appointed not by their respective managements but by a government-appointed state Education Service Commission, the same body that recruits and appoints teachers into the government schools. Finally, aided schools' fee is set by the government to be the same as in government schools, i.e. zero/nil.

we do not study them. We focus entirely on private schools, comparing them with government schools.

This study draws together evidence from a variety of sources, including raw National Sample Survey data for 2014–15 (71st Round NSS data), the ASER data, District Information System on Education (DISE) data, and data in studies carried out by individual scholars.

2 The Emptying of Government Schools and Growth of Private Schools in Uttar Pradesh

Table 1 shows a rapid growth of private schools at the elementary school age (6–14 years) in rural Uttar Pradesh and India, based on ASER data (ASER Trends 2015). In 2006, in India, 18.7% of rural children studied in private schools, and eight years later by 2014, their number had increased to 30.8%, an increase of 65%. In Uttar Pradesh, the utilisation of private education was already high in 2006, with 30.3% of U.P. children studying in private schools. By 2014, however, their number had risen to 51.7%. Thus, U.P saw an increase of 71% from a much higher base than in India. So by 2014, the majority of children in rural U.P. studied in private schools.

Table 2 shows the same trend again—the percentage of all elementary school children in the 6–14 years age group attending private schools—but using National Sample Survey data, only for the year 2014–15 for each of the 20 major states of India. The last row shows the weighted average for these 20 major states of India. It shows that in rural UP 40.5% of children were studying in private schools and in rural India, 20.8%. These are about 10 percentage points lower than in the ASER data. This is because, in the ASER data, no distinction is made between private-unaided and aided schools (the latter are government-funded/controlled).

Table 1 Percentage of children studying in 'private schools', Rural India and Rural Uttar Pradesh, 2006–2014

Year	Boys		Girls		All children	
	India	UP	India	UP	India	UP
2006	20.2	32.9	17.0	27.0	18.7	30.3
2008	24.6	39.6	20.3	31.2	22.6	35.9
2010	25.5	42.5	21.7	35.4	23.7	39.3
2012	31.5	53.1	25.2	43.2	28.3	48.5
2014	34.5	56.4	26.9	46.4	30.8	51.7

Note In the ASER data, no distinction is made between private-unaided and private-aided schools, so the above includes aided schools. Hence, the discrepancy with data in the rural columns in Table 2
Source ASER Trends (2015). Annual Status of Education Report, by Pratham

Table 2 Percentage of children in private-unaided schools, by state, 2014–15

	Age group (years)			
	6–10	11–14	15–18	Total
UP—rural	38.1	41.5	42.8	40.5
UP—urban	69.2	61.6	47.3	60.0
India—rural	20.8	17.5	24.5	20.8
India—urban	48.9	40.7	36.1	42.1

Source Author's calculations from the raw data of the National Sample Survey, 71st Round, 2014–15

Table 3 Change in the number of government and private schools, by state (2010–11 to 2014–15)

State	Government schools			Private schools		
	2010–11	2014–15	Change	2010–11	2014–15	Change
Uttar Pradesh	151,448	160,942	9494	41,961	73,157	31,196
India (20 states)	10,35,602	10,51,978	16,376	2,19,574	2,90,934	71,360

Source DISE raw data, from www.dise.in

Table 3 shows the temporal *change* in a number of government and private schools, and Table 4 shows the change in their enrolments, based on the author's analysis of raw DISE data on 20 major states of India, including Uttar Pradesh. Table 3 shows that, over the four-year period 2010–11 to 2014–15, the total stock of government schools in India (20 major states of India) rose by a mere 16,376 government schools. By contrast, the number of private schools rose by 71,360 schools. Despite the modest increase in the number of government schools, the total enrolment in government schools over this period actually fell by 1.11 million students, whereas total enrolment in private schools *rose* by 15.99 million students (Table 4).

In Uttar Pradesh, the growth of private schooling was very pronounced, with the number of private schools rising by 31,196 over this short four-year period, and private school enrolment rising by nearly seven million students even as government school enrolment fell by 2.6 million students during the same period. The abandonment of government schools and shift towards private schools is also visible when we examine how the number of government schools that are 'small' or 'tiny' has increased over time.

2.1 Abandonment of Government Schools, Migration to Private Schools

We define a 'small' school as one in which total enrolment (in the school as a whole) is fifty or fewer students, which means ten or fewer students per class, in a primary school, or it means six or fewer students per class, in an elementary school (which

Table 4 Change in student enrolment in government and private schools, by state (2010–11 to 2014–15)

	Government schools			Private schools		
	2010–11	2014–15	Change	2010–11	2014–15	Change
Total student enrolment						
Uttar Pradesh	19,688,240	17,059,852	−2,628,388	10,280,445	17,265,052	6,984,607
India (20 states)	12,62,02,002	11,50,62,064	−1,11,39,938	4,43,10,225	6,03,04,902	1,59,94,677
Average enrolment per school						
Uttar Pradesh	130	106	−24	245	236	−9
India (20 states)	122	109	−12	202	207	5

Note The increase in private school enrolments does not exactly mirror the decrease in government school enrolment because children may also shift to aided schools and because the child population of elementary school age increased in some states and fell in some states

Source DISE raw data, from www.dise.in

has classes 1–8), and we define a 'tiny' school as one in which total enrolment is twenty or fewer students, which means four or fewer students per class, in a primary school, or say three students per class in an elementary school.[4]

Table 4 illustrates the phenomenon of the abandonment and emptying of government schools by highlighting its manifestation in the rapid growth of 'small' and 'tiny' government schools in Uttar Pradesh and India. Firstly, the average size of government elementary schools in India fell from 122 students per school in 2010–11 to 109 students per school by 2014–15, a decline of twelve students per government school, or a decline of about 10% over a short four-year period. In Uttar Pradesh, the situation was more extreme: the average size of government schools fell steeply, from 130 in 2011 to a mere 106 pupils per government school four years later in 2015, a remarkable decline of twenty-four students (nearly 20% decline) in the short four-year span.

By contrast, private schools' mean size was much larger to start off with, and it also further rose in the four years to 2015. Nationally, in the baseline year 2011, the average size was 202 in private schools as compared to 122 in government schools, and by 2015, it further rose from 202 in 2010–11 to 207. In Uttar Pradesh, however, private schools' mean size fell by 4% from 245 to 236 per school, which was perhaps due to a great increase (of 31,200) in the number of private schools in this short period.

We can measure the emptying of government schools further by examining the small-school phenomenon, and asking whether the number of government schools that are small or tiny is growing with time. Table 5 shows that in the year 2010–11, India (20 major states) had 313,169 small government schools, i.e. those with a total enrolment of '50 or fewer' students. These constituted 30% of all government schools. By 2015–16, their number had increased to 418,825 small schools (40% of all government schools). This is indeed a marked increase and signifies rapid emptying of government schools in a short period. Moreover, the financial implications of this trend are also clear from the last few columns of Table 5: government schools' salary expenditure per pupil in these (40% of all) government schools rose to Rs. 3430 per month in 2015–16 from Rs. 1887 per month in 2010–11, an increase of 82%, signifying a marked deterioration in the cost-effectiveness of these schools, especially when one considers the decline in outputs as measured by student learning achievement levels (see Sect. 4).

Table 6 shows that in Uttar Pradesh, the number of 'small' schools (those with a total enrolment of 50 or fewer pupils) increased by 50%, from 22,438 in 2010–11 (14% of all government schools) to 33,651 in 2015–16 (20% of all government schools). It is clearly visible from Table 6 that Uttar Pradesh is among the states that have had the greatest emptying, in terms of absolute increase in the number of government schools that have become 'small'.

What has happened to the number of government schools that are 'tiny', i.e. with a total enrolment of 20 or fewer students? Here too, the number of such schools has increased over time, from 71,189 in 2010, to 95,637 in 2014, and further to 108,183

---

[4]If a school has both primary and junior sections, then the number of students per class will be even lower.

Table 5 Emptying of government schools over time of India (the phenomenon of small and tiny government schools, and changes in it, over time)

Total number of pupils in the school as a whole	Number of schools	Number of teachers	Total enrolment	Average pupils per school	Pupil teacher ratio	Teacher salary expenditure (Rs. Billion)	Government schools' annual per-pupil salary Exp. (Rupees)	Government schools' monthly per-pupil salary Exp. (Rupees)
2010–11								
Zero	4435	14,304	0	0	0	4.86	–	–
5 or less	8675	21,277	15,333	1.8	0.7	7.24	471,866	39,322
10 or less	21,008	42,843	118,166	5.6	2.8	14.57	123,288	10,274
20 or less	71,189	138,033	920,254	12.9	6.7	46.94	51,005	4250
50 or less	313,169	633,323	9,510,902	30.4	15.0	215.36	22,643	1887
2014–15								
Zero	3009	6063	0	0	0	2.91	–	–
5 or less	9333	17,328	23,195	2.5	1.3	8.32	358,693	29,891
10 or less	27,118	50,456	171,048	6.3	3.4	24.22	141,597	11,800
20 or less	95,637	187,399	1,256,183	13.1	6.7	94.40	75,148	6262
50 or less	372,163	838,385	10,872,610	29.2	13.0	416.30	38,289	3191

(continued)

Table 5 (continued)

Total number of pupils in the school as a whole	Number of schools	Number of teachers	Total enrolment	Average pupils per school	Pupil teacher ratio	Teacher salary expenditure (Rs. Billion)	Government schools' annual per-pupil salary Exp. (Rupees)	Government schools' monthly per-pupil salary Exp. (Rupees)
2015–16								
Zero	5044	6961	0	0	0		–	–
5 or less	12,196	19,419	26,186	2.1	1.3	10.16	387,992	32,333
10 or less	31,963	55,822	190,340	6.0	3.4	29.21	153,441	12,787
20 or less	108,183	208,534	1,394,126	12.9	6.7	109.10	78,260	6522
50 or less	418,825	923,929	11,743,182	28.0	12.7	483.40	41,164	3430

Note The total number of government schools in India (20 major states) in 2010–11 was 10,35,602; in 2014–15 was 10,51,978 (as seen in Table 4); and in 2015–16 was 10,46,500. Data on government school teachers' salary for 2014–15 is taken from NUEPA study (Ramachandran 2015), where mean government primary school teacher salary (averaged across new and experienced teachers) was 40,600 per month, but for the sake of simplicity, we took it as Rs. 40,000 per month. For 2015–16/2010–11, it has been inflated/deflated by 9%, assuming a salary inflation rate of 9% per annum. Thus, mean teacher salary is taken as Rs. 28,337 in 2010–11 and Rs. 43,600 in 2015–16. In Uttar Pradesh, DA has increased by 15% each year for the past at least 6 years

Source www.statereportcards/rawdata/201011. Data analysed here is for 20 major states in 2010–11 and (counting Telangana as a separate state) for 21 major states in 2014–15 onwards

Table 6 Speed of emptying of government schools, by state (or the speed of growth of 'tiny' and 'small' government schools, by state)

	No. of 'tiny' government schools (with 20 or fewer pupils)			
	2010–11	2015–16	Increase in number of 'tiny' government schools	
			Abs. increase	Percent increase
No. of 'tiny' government schools (with 20 or fewer pupils)				
Uttar Pradesh	4179	4789	610	14.6
India (20 major states)	71,189	108,183	36,994	52.0
No. of 'small' government schools (with 50 or fewer pupils)				
Uttar Pradesh	22,438	33,651	11,213	50.0
India (20 major states)	313,169	418,825	105,656	33.7

Source DISE raw data from www.dise.in. Analysis has been done for 20 major states of India

tiny government schools in 2015 in India. In Uttar Pradesh, the number of 'tiny' government schools rose from 4179 to 4789 between 2010 and 2015.

The emptying of government schools—and the resultant swelling number of government schools that have become 'tiny'—is largely the result of an exodus of students from government schools and migration towards private schools, since there has been no drop in the child population. On the contrary, over the period under consideration, there has been a substantial increase of 7.7% in the absolute primary-school-age population of 6–10 year olds in U.P., and of 4.3% in India, between 2009 and 2014 (IMRB Surveys 2009, 2014). The emptying of government schools at a time when the child population has been growing, and the implied bypassing of the free school option, is a sign of the perceived low quality of government schools, a perception supported by the observed sharp decline in the learning levels of students in government schools over the same period, as seen from the Annual Status of Education Report (ASER Trends 2015), shown in Table 11, and discussed later in Sect. 3.

3 Fee Levels of Private Schools

What are the fee levels of private schools, and can we benchmark them as 'high' or 'low'? Are private schools mostly of the high-fee variety or mostly low-fee, affordable schools?

While no official data is collected from private schools on fee levels, fortunately the questionnaire of the 71st Round National Sample Survey (NSS) of 2014–2015 included—in its Sect. 6—detailed questions on education expenditure on each individual person aged 5–29 years in the sample households. The variable we take as the measure of school fee is named in the survey as: 'course fee (including tuition fee, examination fee, development fee and other compulsory payments)'. The survey also asks separately for expenditure on 'books, stationery and uniform', on 'transport', and on 'private coaching', which we have not taken into account, as we were interested in isolating only the course fee including all compulsory payments that a school takes as 'fee'.

To find out the fee levels of private schools from this NSS data, we took the subset of children who reported studying in private-unaided schools and are aged between 6 and 14 years old, the elementary school age group. These children are of the age to which the Right to Education (RTE) Act 2009 applies and are meant to be in classes 1–8. The mean and median 'total course fee' in private-unaided schools, computed from the NSS data, are presented in Table 7.

Before turning to that, Fig. 1 shows that total course fee is very log-normally distributed, with a pronounced rightward skew, rather than normally distributed with the standard Gaussian bell shape. When a quantity is log-normally distributed, the median is a better measure of central tendency than the mean, since it down weights the undue importance of the few extremely high values; i.e., it does not permit undue influence of the extremely high fee levels of the few children who study in the very high-fee schools. Hence, in Table 7, although we present both private-unaided schools' mean and median fee levels, it is preferable to focus on the median fee levels.

Table 7 shows that median private-unaided school fee level in urban India was Rs. 500 per month and in rural India Rs. 275 per month. Taking all India (rural and urban), the median fee was Rs. 417 per month (or Rs. 5000 per annum). Uttar Pradesh is by far the lowest fee state among all the states of India (the full data for all states is not presented here for the sake of brevity—to see that, see Table 8 in Kingdon 2017a or Kingdon 2017b), which shows that there is a great deal of interstate variation in private school monthly fee levels, from Rs. 117 in rural Uttar Pradesh to Rs. 692 (six times higher) in rural Punjab; or from Rs. 250 in urban U.P. to Rs. 1800 (seven times higher), in urban Delhi. We examined the descriptive relationship between government school quality and the private school fee level in the state, across the

Table 7 Mean and median fee levels in private-unaided schools for children aged 6–14, by state, 2014–15

State	Mean			Median		
	Rural	Urban	Total	Rural	Urban	Total
Annual fee (Rs.)						
UP	2264	6303	4104	1400	3000	1800
India (weighted mean)	5396	9611	7959	3500	6500	5000
Monthly fee (Rs.)						
UP	189	525	342	117	250	150
India (weighted mean)	450	801	663	292	542	417

Source The author's own calculations on raw data from the National Sample Survey (71st Round)

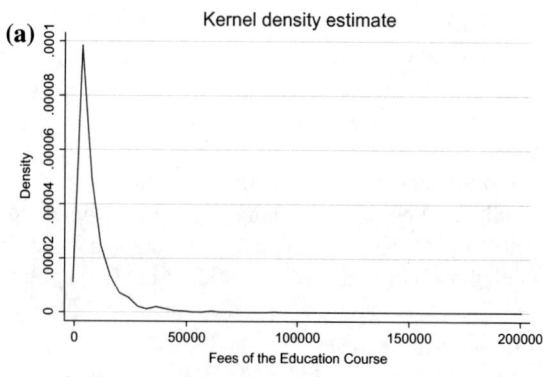

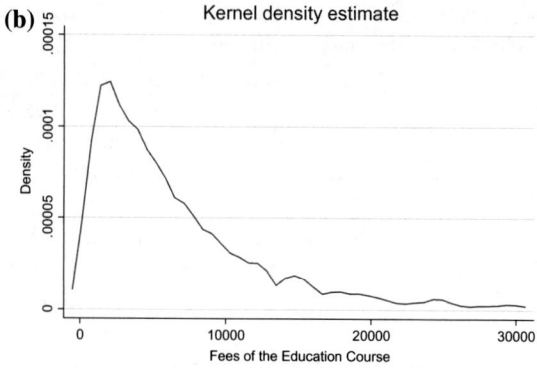

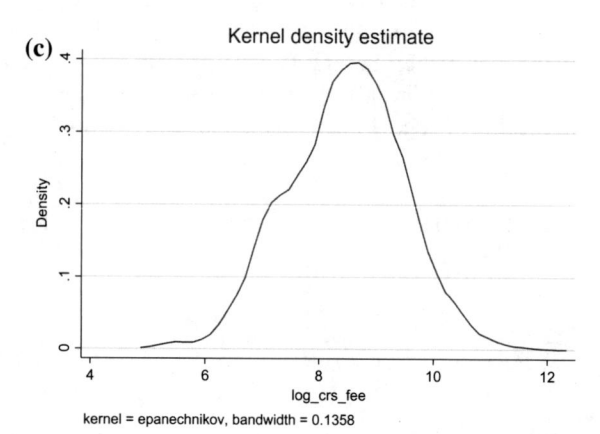

Fig. 1 Distribution of private-unaided schools' fee levels, age 6–14, India, 2014–15. a Distribution of (annual) fee level without constraining the fee values. Notice that a very tiny number of students report paying fee from Rupees 50,000 to Rupees 200,000 per annum (above about Rs. 4000 pm). **b** Distribution of (annual) fee level after constraining the fee values to be below Rs. 30,000 pa (Rs. 2500 pm). Even here, it is visible that only a very small number of students pay fees above around Rs. 12,000 pa or Rs. 1000 pm. **c** This shows the distribution of **log of course fee**, rather than of the course fee. It is apparent that this is much more normally distributed (much closer to the bell-shaped 'Gaussian' distribution) than graphs 1a and 1b. *Source* Kernel density distribution produced in STATA, using NSS data 2014–15

states of India in graphical form (see Kingdon 2017a, b) which showed that the lower the quality in government schools in a state (in terms of learning achievement levels of students measured in the ASER survey), the lower the private school fee levels on an average in that state.

3.1 Benchmarking Private School Fee Levels

Is the private-unaided schools' fee observed in Table 7 low or high? Before turning to that, we examine what percentage of private school students pay fee below given absolute threshold levels. This is presented in Table 8. To aid exposition, let us call the private schools that charge less than Rs. 100 per month as 'very low-fee schools' and those that charge less than Rs. 500 per month as 'low-fee schools'. Table 8 shows that in Uttar Pradesh 32% of all private school-going children attend private schools that charge only up to Rs. 100 per month. Nationally, this figure is 11% for India as a whole (20 major states). A few other states' data is also presented, and it shows that in Tamil Nadu, Haryana and Delhi, the proportion of very low-fee schools is only 0.6, 1.1 and 1.3%, respectively, and in Andhra, Himachal, Kashmir, Kerala, Punjab and Uttarakhand, it is less than three percent. When it comes to 'low-fee-charging schools', again, UP leads the way, with 84% of private school students paying less than Rs. 500 per month, compared to the national average of 57%. An interesting fact brought out in the last two columns of Table 8 is that the reimbursement level to be given to private schools, fixed by the state governments to implement section 12(1)(c) of the RTE Act 2009, is higher than the private school fee of the vast bulk of private schools in the state. Overall, the picture emerges that the bulk of private schools in India charged a total fee of less than Rs. 1000 pm (81.5% in India and 92.6% in UP) and that if 'high-fee school' is defined as a school that charges more than Rs. 2500 per month, only 3.6% of private schools in India and only 1.5% in UP are 'high-fee' schools. However, these thresholds are arbitrary. To see whether private school fee levels are 'low', we benchmark fee levels with respect to state per capita income, with respect to the prescribed 'minimum wages' and with respect to the per-pupil expenditure in government schools.

3.2 Benchmarking with Respect to State Per Capita Income

One way of benchmarking the size of the private school fee is to see its ratio with respect to the *state per capita income*. Here, since government reports mean (rather than median) per capita income, we use the mean private school fee level rather than the median. Table 9 shows that nationally, private schools' mean fee is around 9.2% of the state per capita income. In Uttar Pradesh, private schools' mean fee is 10.2% of the state per capita income.

Table 8 Percent of 6–14-year-old private-unaided school attendees who pay fee below given thresholds, select states, 2014–15

Fee level (Rs. per month)	Delhi	Himachal Pradesh	Karnataka	Rajasthan	Tamil Nadu	Uttar Pradesh	Uttarakhand	India
≤100	1.3	2	3.4	3.6	0.6	32.3	2.4	11.4
≤200	3.4	6.1	10	18	2.3	61.5	14.3	25.1
≤500	12.5	46.7	38.6	69.1	20.8	84	44.5	57.3
≤750	24.9	66.5	53.9	81.4	40.6	89.2	63.1	71.4
≤1000	33.5	78.2	71	89.6	60	92.6	82.1	81.5
≤1500	48.1	90.4	82.1	94.8	83.6	96.4	87.5	90.7
≤2000	58.8	97.5	90	97.2	93	97.7	92.9	94.2
≤2500	68.7	99	95.1	99	97	98.5	98.8	96.4
Government reimbursement amount to private schools (per month)	1190	1593	987	1383		450	860	
Percent pupils whose fee level is < RTE reimbursement level	35.2	91.9	66	92.8		80.6	71	

Source For fee information, National Sample Survey data

Table 9 Benchmarking private schools' fee levels against (1) state per capita income, (2) government-funded schools' PPE and (3) minimum wages

	Private school fee, annual (2014–15)		State per capita GDP (2014–15)	Ratio of private school fee to state per capita GDP	Per-pupil expense (PPE) in government-funded schools (2014–15)	PPE in government schools as a percent of state per capita income	Minimum daily wage 2014 (for MNREGA rural workers)	Annual private school median fee as a percent of the annual minimum wage[a]	Percent rural private school pupils whose *monthly* fee is below the minimum *daily* wage
	Mean (a)	Median (b)	(c)	(d) = (a/c) * 100	(e)	(f) = (e/c)*100	(g)	(h)	(i)
Tamil Nadu	12,197	10,800	128,366	9.5	14,229	11.1	167	21.6	1.6
Uttar Pradesh	4104	1800	40,373	10.2	13,102	32.5	156	3.8	66.8
India (weighted mean)	7671	5000	83,285	9.2	11,523	19.4	172.2	10.2	26.5

Source For columns (a) and (b), National Sample Survey or NSS data; for column (c) state per capita income (PCI), see http://pib.nic.in/newsite/PrintRelease.aspx?relid=123563. For column (e), Dongre and Kapur (2016) who report estimated per-pupil expenditure (PPE) in government and aided schools, based on state budget documents and DISE data, but their PPE figures are serious underestimates (Kingdon 2016). For column (g), Ministry of Rural Development eands.dacnet.nic.in/Graphs.xlsx (retrieved on 1.11.2016)

[a]We assume 300 days of work a year

3.3 Benchmarking with Respect to the Minimum Wage of Daily Wage Labourers

A second way of benchmarking private school fee is to see to what extent the poorest paid workers can afford private school fee. The last three columns of Table 9 attempt to do that. Srivastava (2013) suggests that a useful way of defining 'low-fee' schools is schools that can be afforded by the daily wage labourers, one of the lowest paid worker groups, who get the minimum daily wage as announced annually by the Ministry of Rural Development. Column (g) of Table 9 shows the officially mandated minimum daily wage of April 2014 for each state. We take it that daily wagers work 300 days a year and thus predict the annual wage for daily wagers. Expressing the median annual private school fee as a percentage of this annual minimum wage, column (h) shows that on an average, private schools' median annual fee is around 10.2% of the annual minimum wage of daily wagers. Uttar Pradesh is an outlier, in that private school annual fee is only 3.8% of the annual earning of daily wagers in the state, suggesting that even very poor people can access private schooling in Uttar Pradesh, and this is consistent with the high utilisation of private schooling in U.P. Another variant for benchmarking private schools' fee is to ask: for what percentage of rural private school pupils is their actual monthly fee below the daily minimum wage of their state. Column (i) shows that, on an average, 26% of rural private school pupils' monthly fee is below their state's daily minimum wage. While U.P. is again an outlier (with 67% rural private school pupils' monthly fee being below the minimum daily wage of U.P. in 2014), in states such as West Bengal, Odisha, Jharkhand and Chhattisgarh, the proportion is higher than one-third; it suggests that one-third or more of the private schools in these states are 'low-fee' schools by this definition, i.e. that educate the poorest children.

3.4 Benchmarking with Respect to the Per-Pupil Expenditure in Government Schools

A third way of benchmarking whether private school fee level in a state is 'high' or 'low' is to compare it with the state's per-pupil expenditure (PPE) in the government school system. The data on PPE in government schools is not reliably estimated, but we use the only published estimates available, namely by Dongre and Kapur (2016). Table 10 shows the private-unaided schools' median fee levels from NSS data for 2014–15 and also the per-pupil expenditure (PPE) in the government-funded school system, for U.P. and for India, again for 2014–15[5]; data for Tamil Nadu is also

---

[5]The weighted average across the states for which the PPE data is available. Since government provides free books and uniform to all children attending government schools, the estimate of government PPE on education includes government expenditure on books and uniforms, but our private school's per-pupil expenditure (proxied by the school's fee) does not include expenditure on books and uniforms, which undermines the ability to compare private and public schools' unit

Table 10 Private schools' fee compared with government-funded schools' per-pupil expenditure (PPE)—2014–15

	Median private school fee (Rs. per month)	Government-funded schools' PPE (Rs. per month)	Private schools' fee as a percent of government-funded schools' PPE	Percent private schools whose fee is lower than government-funded schools' PPE
	(a)	(b)	(c) = (a/b) * 100	(d)
Tamil Nadu	900	1186	75.9	70.0
Uttar Pradesh	150	1092	13.7	92.9
India (major states) weighted means	417	1091	47.4	79.4

Source NSS (2014–2015) data, for column (a) and Dongre and Kapur (2016) for column (b). Dongre and Kapur do not report government PPE for Delhi, Assam and Jammu and Kashmir. Columns (c) and (d) are calculated by the author. There is reason to believe that Dongre and Kapur's PPE figures are seriously underestimated; see Annex 1 and Kingdon (2017a, b)

presented to illustrate a point later. It shows that in India, nearly 80% of the private schools charge fee below the government PPE (or to phrase if more precisely) and 79% of private school-going children attend those private schools where the fee is below the government schools' per-pupil expenditure. In Uttar Pradesh, 92% of private schools' fee is lower than the government schools' PPE. In a large number of states other than U.P. also (Haryana, Himachal, Kerala, Rajasthan and Uttarakhand, not shown here; see Kingdon 2017a, b), more than 90% of private school students pay fees lower than the estimated PPE in the government-funded schools. The penultimate column (column c) in Table 10 shows that—averaging across the states—private school fee is only 47% of the PPE in government-funded schools.

While the data in Table 10 shows that private schools' mean fee is less than half the per-pupil expenditure of government schools estimated by Dongre and Kapur (2016), but, despite already being a surprisingly low number, this is still a serious overestimate because, as shown in Annex 1, Dongre and Kapur's calculations are great underestimates of the true government school PPE. For Uttar Pradesh, if we use Dongre and Kapur's estimate of government school PPE (Rs. 1092 pm), then the private schools' median fee of Rs. 150 pm is 13.7% of the government schools' PPE, and this is what is shown in Table 10. However, if we use the PPE figure of Rs. 2340 per month in 2014–15 calculated by Kingdon and Muzammil (2015) instead, then private school fee (Rs. 150 per month) is only 6.5% of the government schools' PPE, i.e. about half that shown in Table 10. To illustrate this from Tamil Nadu perhaps

costs of education. However, compared to the PPE estimates shown in Kingdon et al. (2015, 2016) and in Kingdon and Muzammil (2015), the PPE estimates for public schools presented here are likely to be serious underestimates of the true PPE of public schools.

even more convincingly, the PPE of government schools that the government of Tamil Nadu itself calculated and notified in its Gazette of 24th July 2017 is Rs. 28,206 for the whole year 2014–15 (or Rs. 2350 pm)—see Annex 1. And private schools' median fee in Tamil Nadu is Rs. 900 per month; thus, private school fee is 38% of government schools PPE in Tamil Nadu, i.e. half that when using Dongre and Kapur's PPE estimates, i.e. half of the figure of 76% seen in Table 10. Thus, if the pattern of U.P. and Tamil Nadu is applicable across all states, then nationally, private schools' median fee level as a percentage of the government schools true PPE is not 47% as shown in the last row of Table 10 but half that; i.e., it is of the order of 24%. Put another way, if the examples of Uttar Pradesh and Tamil Nadu can be extrapolated to all the states (i.e. if the true government school PPE nationally is roughly double that estimated by Dongre and Kapur), then median private school fee is only about a quarter of the government school PPE in the country; i.e., private schools' median fee levels are very significantly lower than—indeed a small fraction of—the government schools' per-pupil expenditure.

4 Learning Outcomes in Private and Public Schools

While the NCERT has been carrying out large-scale surveys of children's learning achievement levels using Item Response Theory since 2011, it conducts these only in public (government) schools. Fortunately, it is possible to compare achievement levels in government and private schools in the surveys carried out for the Annual Status of Education Report (ASER, various years). Table 11 based on ASER data shows that while children's raw learning levels in both private and public schools are low, they are very significantly higher in private than public schools.

The ASER data in Table 11 show that in 2014 in Uttar Pradesh, only 12% of government school children of grade five could do simple division, while in private schools 39% could. The upper part of Table 11 shows that 20.7% of rural government school children and 39% of private school children in India could do a simple division sum. The reading achievement data in the second main column shows a similar pattern of low achievement level in government schools and a better picture in the private schools, at least in raw data. Table 11 further shows that in Uttar Pradesh, over the four-year period from 2010 to 2014, learning levels fell sharply in government schools and rose in private schools, both in reading and in math. The public–private school learning achievement gap is smaller for India than U.P.

However, the ASER report presents only raw learning achievement data, and, since private school students typically come from better-off and more educated homes, their achievement levels would be expected to be higher even if private schools were of no better quality than public schools. Thus, comparing raw learning levels in private and public schools could lead to a potentially false inference that private schools are higher quality.

Luckily, there is more sophisticated evidence in India which compares learning levels in the two types of schools *after statistically controlling for the socio-economic*

Table 11 Learning achievement levels of children of class V in public and private schools

	Percent children in standard V who can do simple division			Percent children in standard V who can read a standard II-level text		
	Public	Private	Difference	Public	Private	Difference
Uttar Pradesh						
2010	18.7	36.3	17.6	36.0	58.4	22.4
2011	12.1	33.4	21.3	29.9	60.3	30.4
2012	9.1	33.3	24.2	25.6	59.6	34.0
2013	11.2	42.3	31.1	24.5	63.8	39.3
2014	12.1	38.7	26.6	26.8	61.4	34.6
Change 2010–2014	−6.6	2.4		−9.2	3.0	
India						
2010	33.9	44.2	10.3	50.7	64.2	13.5
2011	24.5	37.7	13.2	43.8	62.7	18.9
2012	20.3	37.8	17.5	41.7	61.2	19.5
2013	20.8	38.9	18.1	41.1	63.3	22.2
2014	20.7	39.3	18.6	42.2	62.5	20.3
Change 2010–2014	−13.2	−4.9		−8.5	−1.7	

Source ASER Trends over time. Pratham, 2015

background of the children studying in private and public schools. Different authors have used a variety of data sources, for example, the National Human Development Survey, the ASER survey, Young Lives survey, and field surveys conducted by authors themselves in various states or districts. The published literature uses either simple regression analysis (Tooley and Dixon 2005; Wadhwa 2009) or a variety of elaborate econometric techniques to correct for the problems of 'selectivity' and 'endogeneity', namely the problem that more able or more motivated students may self-select into private schools, using methods such as household fixed effects (where the learning levels of children from the same household going to private and public schools are compared), village fixed effects, propensity score matching methods, panel data approach and randomised control trials. These studies are by Kingdon (1996) with school survey data from Uttar Pradesh; Desai et al. (2008) and Chudgar and Quin (2012) with national data of Indian Human Development Survey (IHDS); Goyal (2009) with World Bank data from Odisha; French and Kingdon (2010) with national ASER data; Muralidharan and Sundararaman (2013) and Singh (2015) with Young Lives Project data for Andhra Pradesh; and Azam et al. (2016) with World Bank's school survey data from Rajasthan and Odisha.

This evidence shows that when students' home background is controlled for, the large raw learning gap between private and public schools falls substantially, but, in most econometric studies, it does not disappear: typically, an achievement advantage of 0.10–0.35 standard deviations remains. This literature indicates that children's learning levels in private schools are no worse than, and in many studies better than, those in government schools, after controlling rigorously for the home backgrounds of the children in these two types of school.

The next section puts this evidence (on the relative effectiveness of public and private schools) together with evidence on the unit costs of private and public schools, to examine the 'value for money' (VFM) offered to fee-paying parents by private schools and the VFM that accrues from public expenditure on education.

5 Value for Money from Public and Private Schools

A study by Kingdon et al. (2016) puts the ASER evidence on learning levels of students in public and private schools together with the evidence on per-pupil expenditure (PPE) in public and private schools for Uttar Pradesh and seven other major states of India, to examine the 'value for money' offered by public and private schools. Table 12 shows the value for money (VFM) calculation.[6] While there is much inter-state variation, we focus on Uttar Pradesh. Table 12 shows that in Uttar Pradesh in 2014–15, annual PPE in public schools was Rs. 23,012 and PPE in private schools was Rs. 1800 per annum, and thus, the public:private ratio of PPE was 12.8:1 (see row 'g'); i.e., public schools operated at nearly 13 times the per-pupil expenditure of private schools. It also shows that the ratio of public to private students' reading achievement levels was 0.44:1; i.e., public schools produced only 44% as much learning as private schools. Putting these two things together, we find that private schools offer 29 times the value for money (VFM) as public schools in Uttar Pradesh!

Table 12 shows that U.P. is an outlier in a league of its own, in terms of the very low VFM from government schools and with private schools offering 29 times as much VFM as public schools—which is largely due to the very low fee levels of private schools in Uttar Pradesh, as also seen earlier in Tables 7, 8, 9 and 10. While in Bihar, Tamil Nadu, Punjab and Odisha, private schools are roughly twice as cost-effective (offer twice as much VFM) as public schools, in Gujarat, private schools offer 12 times as much VFM as public schools, Kingdon et al. (2016) also present VFM calculations using numeracy achievement levels in private and public schools, and the results there are even starker, with private schools offering 41 times higher VFM than government schools, though they are not presented here.

Change over time in the 'cost per unit of learning' in government schools can also be seen in the last column of Table 13. The table shows how teacher salaries have risen in government schools of Uttar Pradesh between 2009 and 2017. The penultimate column also shows the change in the learning achievement level of children in government schools over the period 2010–2016. The last column shows

---

[6]The government school PPE calculated for these eight states differs from the estimates of Dongre and Kapur (2016), but the latter calculated PPE for government *and* aided schools. Also, see Annex 1 which discusses the reasons why Dongre and Kapur's PPE estimates are significantly lower than the true estimates.

Table 12 Value for money from public expenditure on education in India

S. No.	Variables	Uttar Pradesh	Bihar	Gujarat	Tamil Nadu	Madhya Pradesh	Kerala	Punjab	Odisha
a	Government per-pupil expenditure (rupees)	23,012	3105	47,044	33,126	9384	39,267	16,166	8897
b	Government achievement (reading)	27	45	45	50	28	61	61	50
c	Government expenditure per achievement unit (rupees) (c = a/b)	859	70	1055	664	338	641	265	178
d	Private per-pupil expenditure (rupees)	1800	4200	5400	10,800	3700	8400	7900	7150
e	Private achievement (reading)	61	88	64	40	58	71	74	77
f	Private expenditure per achievement unit (rupees) (f = d/e)	29	48	84	269	63	119	107	93

(continued)

Table 12 (continued)

S. No.	Variables	Uttar Pradesh	Bihar	Gujarat	Tamil Nadu	Madhya Pradesh	Kerala	Punjab	Odisha
g	Government/private per-pupil expenditure ratio (g = a/d)	12.8	0.7	8.7	3.1	2.5	4.7	2.0	1.2
h	Government/private numeracy ratio (g = b/e)	0.44	0.51	0.70	1.24	0.48	0.87	0.83	0.65
i	Private/government efficiency ratio (i = c/f)	29.3	1.5	12.5	2.5	5.3	5.4	2.5	1.9

Note PPE in public schools in each state is calculated by taking the total elementary education expenditure of the state plus central government's expenditure in the state on *Sarva Shiksha Abhiyan* (Total Literacy Campaign) inputs (such as free uniforms, textbooks, cash scholarships and school improvement grants but not on the mid-day meals) for 2014–15 and dividing this total public expenditure by the number of students enrolled in government elementary schools within the state, as taken from the District Information System on Education (DISE) data for 2014–15. These PPE estimates cannot be compared with those in Dongre and Kapur (2016) for a variety of reasons, several of which are set out in Annex 1

the salary cost per unit of learning in government schools. This shows that the salary cost per learning unit has roughly trebled in government schools in just the 6-year period between 2010 and 2016. This is a product of both falling learning achievement levels over time, and strongly rising teacher salaries in government schools, which the table shows, increased by over 15% per annum in the period 2008–2017 (the period from just before the Sixth Pay Commission to just after the Seventh Pay Commission) or increased by 8.5% per annum, if we take just the period from 2010 to 2016.

6 Conclusions and Policy Implications

Analysis of official DISE data in this paper demonstrates that despite the (anecdotal and circumstantial) evidence that government school enrolments are exaggerated in school returns data, government schools have been rapidly emptying and that private schools have been rapidly growing in Uttar Pradesh, over the period under study, namely 2010–11 to 2014–15. The fall in government school enrolment is despite a 7.7% increase in the child population of primary school age in U.P. over the same period. The average size of government schools fell significantly, and the number of government schools that have become 'small' (with 50 or fewer pupils) has dramatically risen from 22,438 to 33,651 in this short 4 year period, with these 33,000 government schools each having an average enrolment of only around 32 students.

The decline in government school enrolment—when taken together with increased salaries and increased teacher numbers—implies that per-pupil expenditure in the government school system has been rising, and thus, value for money from public expenditure on government schools has been falling. The analysis also showed that in Uttar Pradesh, value for money from government schools was 29 times lower than that from private schools and that U.P. was an outlier in terms of its low value for money from public expenditure on education.

Analysis of fee data from the National Sample Survey 2014–15 shows that, contrary to popular perception, a very high proportion of private schools caters to the poor in Uttar Pradesh, where 32% of private school students pay fee less than Rs. 100 pm, and 84% pay fee less than Rs. 500 per month (while in India as a whole, only 11% pay less than Rs. 100 pm and only 57% private school students pay less than Rs. 500 a month)! Only 8% of private school-going children in U.P. pay fees of more than Rs. 1000 pm, and only 1.5% pay more than 2500 pm. Median fee of private schools in U.P. is only 6.5% of the government schools' per-pupil expenditure; i.e., much of private schooling is provided at very low cost in U.P., by far the lowest among all the states of India. The evidence suggests that a very high percentage of private schools in Uttar Pradesh and even in India can be considered 'low fee' in the sense that their fee is below the government's per-pupil expenditure in its own schools. This evidence discredits the common perception that much of private schooling in India is elite and exclusive.

Table 13 Starting salary of primary and junior teachers in government schools, Uttar Pradesh

Year	Basic pay (a)	Dearness allowance (DA) (b)	House rent allowance (HRA) (c)	City compensatory allowance (CCA) (d)	Total pay (Rs. per month) (e)	Learning levels of pupils[b] (f)	Cost per learning unit (Rs.) (g) = e/f
Primary teachers							
2008	4500	5422	675	–	10,597	–	–
2009[a]	13,500	2970	2020	360	18,850	–	–
2010	13,500	4725	2020	360	20,605	18.7	1102
2011	13,500	7425	2020	360	23,305	12.1	1926
2012	13,500	9450	2020	360	25,330	9.1	2784
2013	13,500	11,475	2020	360	27,355	11.2	2442
2014	13,500	13,500	2020	360	29,380	12.1	2428
2015	13,500	15,525	2020	360	31,405	–	–
2016	13,500	17,550	2020	360	33,430	10.4	3214
2017+	35,400	708	2020	360	38,488	–	–
Annual salary growth rate 2008 to 2017 15.4%							
Annual salary growth rate 2009 to 2016 8.5%							
Junior teachers							
2008	5500	6627	825	–	12,952	–	–
2009[a]	17,140	3771	2760	360	24,031	–	–
2010	17,140	5999	2760	360	26,259	48.2	545
2011	17,140	9427	2760	360	29,687	–	–
2012	17,140	11,998	2760	360	32,258	24.4	1322
2013	17,140	14,569	2760	360	34,829	–	–
2014	17,140	17,140	2760	360	37,400	30.5	1226
2015	17,140	19,711	2760	360	39,971	–	–
2016	17,140	22,282	2760	360	42,542	25.5	1668
2017+	44,900	898	2760	360	48,918	–	–
Annual salary growth rate 2008 to 2017 15.9%							
Annual salary growth rate 2009 to 2016 8.5%							

Note [a]Sixth and seventh pay commission salaries were applied in 2009 and 2017, respectively. The dearness allowance (DA) is intended as inflation proofing. It is the annual increase in basic pay. The cumulative DA announced by the U.P. government was 22% (in 2009), 35% (2010), 55% (2011), 70% (2012), 85% (2013), 100% (2014), 115% (2015) and 130% (2016). That is, after 2009, DA increased by 15 percentage points every year

[b]This column shows the percentage of children in government schools of U.P. in class 5 (upper panel) and in class 8 (lower panel) who could do a three-digit by one-digit division sum. For example, in 2010, 18.7% of class 5 pupils and 48.2% of class 8 pupils could do division (ASER, various years)

Source Government Orders of the Government of Uttar Pradesh, various years

The data presented here has implications for the making of policy towards private schools. To take one example, the Right to Education (RTE) Act 2009 stipulates that no private-unaided school can be established or continue to function without obtaining a certificate of 'recognition' from the government, and Section 19 lays down the various penalties (including closure) for non-compliance with the given norms and conditions. NISA (2014) calculated that by March 2014, just over 15,000 private-unaided schools had received closure notices, due to not fulfilling infrastructure norms of the RTE Act. The realisation from this paper's evidence that, in the majority of private schools, fee levels are far lower than government schools' per-pupil expenditure, draws the education policy-maker's attention to the fact that when a high proportion of the well-funded government schools themselves cannot comply with the infrastructure norms of the Right to Education (RTE) Act 2009,[7] how can private schools do so (without public subsidy), since majority of them run on a small fraction of the unit cost of government schools. The kind of data presented here to benchmark private school fee levels can help decision-makers to make more evidence-informed education policy that is more realistic and less wishful and to avoid counter-productive effects such as the closure of the low-fee private schools which may be successfully imparting learning but which lack the resources to fulfil the demanding infrastructure and other stipulated norms for private schools.

The realisation that the bulk of private schooling in Uttar Pradesh, and indeed in the country, is 'low fee' is significant because perceptions about the nature of private schools have important implications for how private schools are seen and portrayed in the media, in courts and within government, i.e. with hostility or sympathy; as elitist/exclusivist or accessible/inclusive; as extractive/profiteering or as benign contributors to the educational effort of the country; as lawbreakers (due to their lack of compliance with all the infrastructure norms); or as budget schools that give the poor a chance to get better quality education than available in the free (government school) option. Data on private schools presented here, when disseminated through media, can help the public to see important aspects of the reality of private schools and to make evidence-based judgments about them.

The data showing that government school children's learning achievement levels are low and have been falling, and data showing that government schools have been emptying rapidly and private schools rapidly growing, could also have implications for policies such the pay commission process through which across the board increases in teacher salaries are decided, and where the narrative and justifications are decided for whether and how much the pay of particular public sector workers should be raised. They could also have implications for government negotiations with teacher unions at the state level, before deciding whether and to what extent to apply the Central Pay Commission's recommendations in the state, on the basis of pay for productivity.

---

[7] While section 8(g) of the Act specifies that government schools must also conform to the norms of the Act, there are no penalties if they do not, and thus, de facto, there is no momentum for government funded schools to comply. In a parliamentary question in August 2016, the then Education Minister replied that only 6.4% of government schools fulfil the recognition conditions of the RTE Act.

Annex 1: Reasons Why the Per-Pupil Expenditure (PPE) Estimates in Dongre and Kapur (2016) Are Serious Underestimates of the Actual PPE in the Government School System

Dongre and Kapur (2016) have made a pioneering contribution by estimating per-pupil expenditure in government-funded schools (government and aided schools) across the Indian states, and they have done it for two time periods, 2011–12 and 2014–15, so they are also able to show the temporal trends in government-funded schools' per-pupil expenditure (PPE). They have relied on state budget documents for getting information on public education expenditure and relied on the official District Information System on Education (DISE) for information on total elementary school enrolment in the different states. They have perforce had to live with the limitations of the state budget documents, in particular with the fact that different states follow somewhat different conventions, for example, whether to include in the state budget the *Sarva Shiksha Abhiyan* (Total Literacy Campaign) funds and the mid-day meal funds received from the central government.

The PPEs reported in Dongre and Kapur (2016) are likely to be great underestimates for reasons set out in detail in Kingdon (2017a, b).

To take one example, Dongre and Kapur estimate the 2014–15 PPE in the government-funded school system in Uttar Pradesh as Rs. 13,102 per annum (or Rs. 1092 per month), but the author's own estimate of the PPE in the government schools of U.P. for the same 2014–15 year (in Kingdon and Muzammil 2015) was Rs. 23,004 pa or Rs. 1917 pm, i.e. 75% higher than that estimated by Dongre and Kapur; after adjusting for inflated enrolment based on two different surveys of the extent of enrolment inflation, the estimated PPE in government schools of U.P. was Rs. 2320 per month or Rs. 27,840 pa. The true estimate of Rs. 27,840 is thus 112% higher than Dongre and Kapur's estimate.

Another example is that of Tamil Nadu. The Tamil Nadu state's PPE estimated by Dongre and Kapur (2016) is Rs. 1186 pm or Rs. 14,232 pa, but the Tamil Nadu Government Gazette Extraordinary No. 246 of 24 July 2017 publishes its estimate of the state PPE on government schools as Rs. 25,308 in primary classes 1 to 5 and Rs. 33,036 in upper primary classes. Giving a weight of 5 to primary classes and a weight of 3 to upper primary classes, the weighted mean per-pupil expenditure comes to Rs. 28,206 in 2016–17. Allowing for salary inflation of 8% each year implies that in 2014–15 it was Rs. 24,182 per child. Thus, the real PPE (Rs. 24,182) is 70% higher than the PPE estimated by Dongre and Kapur (Rs. 14,232).

References

ASER. (various years). *Annual Status of Education Report*, ASER Centre, Pratham, New Delhi.
ASER (ASER Trends). (2015). *Annual Status of Education Report*, ASER Centre, Pratham, New Delhi.
Azam, M., Kingdon, G. G., & Wu, K. B. (2016). The impact of private secondary schooling on cognitive skills: Evidence from India. *Education Economics, 24*(5), 465–480.
Chudgar, A., & Quin, E. (2012). Relationship between private schooling and achievement: Results from rural and urban India. *Economics of Education Review, 31,* 376–390.
Desai, S., Dubey, A., Vanneman, R., & Banerji, R. (2008). *Private schooling in India: A new educational landscape*. India Human Development Survey Working Paper No. 11.
Dongre, A., & Kapur, A. (2016, September 24). Trends in public expenditure on elementary education in India. *Economic and Political Weekly, 51*(39).
French, R., & Kingdon, G. G. (2010). *The relative effectiveness of private and government schools in Rural India: Evidence from ASER data*. Department of Quantitative Social Science, DQSS Working paper, 10-03, Institute of Education, University of London.
Goyal, S. (2009). Inside the house of learning: The relative performance of public and private schools in Odisha. *Education Economics, 17*(3), 315–327.
IMRB Surveys. (2009, 2014). Commissioned by the Ministry of Human Resource Development, Government of India.
Kingdon, G. G. (1996). The quality and efficiency of public and private education: A case study of urban India. *Oxford Bulletin of Economics and Statistics, 58*(1), 57–82.
Kingdon, G. G. (2007, Summer). The progress of school education in India. *Oxford Review of Economic Policy, 23*(2), 168–195.
Kingdon, G. G. (2017a). The private schooling phenomenon in India: A review. IZA Discussion Paper Series IZA DP No. 10612, IZA—Institute of Labor Economics, Bonn. Accessed at http://ftp.iza.org/dp10612.pdf.
Kingdon, G. G. (2017b). *The private schooling phenomenon in India: A review*. Working Paper No. 17-06, Department of Quantitative Social Science, UCL Institute of Education, University College London.
Kingdon, G. G., & Muzammil, M. (2015). *Government per pupil expenditure in Uttar Pradesh: Implications for the reimbursement of private schools under the RTE Act*. CSAE Working Paper WPS/2015-18-2, Department of Economics, University of Oxford. Also accessible at http://www.csae.ox.ac.uk/materials/papers/csae-wps-2015-18-2.pdf.
Kingdon, G. G., Sinha, S., Kaul, V., with Bhargava, G., & Pental, K. (2016, April). *Value for money from public education expenditure on elementary education in India*. Discussion Paper Series, Education Global Practice, South Asia Region, World Bank, New Delhi.
Muralidharan, K., & Kremer, M. (2008). Public and private schools in rural India. In R. Chakrabarti & P. Petersen (Eds.), *School choice international: Exploring public–private partnerships*. Boston, MA: MIT Press.
Muralidharan, K., & Sundararaman, V. (2013). *The aggregate effect of school choice: Evidence from a two-stage experiment in India*. NBER Working Paper, 19441.
NISA. (2014). National Sources on RTE, Reports and case studies, National Independent School Alliance, New Delhi.
NSS. (2014–2015). National Sample Survey, National Sample Survey Organization, New Delhi.
Ramachandran, V. (2015). *Teachers in the Indian education system: Synthesis of a nine-state study*. National University of Educational Planning and Administration, NUEPA, New Delhi.
Singh, A. (2015). Private school effects in urban and rural India: Panel estimates at primary and secondary school ages. *Journal of Development Economics, 113,* 16–32.
Srivastava, P. (2013). Low fee private schooling: Issues and evidence. In P. Srivastava (ed.), *Low-fee private schooling: Aggravating equity or mitigating disadvantage?* Oxford studies in comparative education series. Oxford: Symposium Books.

Tooley, J., & Dixon, P. (2005). An inspector calls: The regulation of 'budget' private schools in Hyderabad, Andhra Pradesh, India. *International Journal of Educational Development, 25*, 269–285.

Wadhwa, W. (2009). *Are private schools really performing better than government schools?* Annual Status of Education Report, Pratham, New Delhi.

Health Status: Progress and Challenges

Mohammad Zahid Siddiqui, Srinivas Goli, Md Juel Rana and Swastika Chakravorty

Abstract Achieving grand convergence in global health and bridging the gap between the countries, within country and between the states are important targets of ongoing SDGs. India is often described as a country with substantial progress in average health status alongside sizable geographical, rural–urban, social, economic and bio-demographic disparities. Although the country is witnessing a considerable improvement in health status across the states, alongside a steeper inter- and intra-state differentials in the speed of improvement coexist. Lack of equity with progress in the health status of the population in the laggard states of India is one of the key features in its growth story. In this backdrop, the paper examines the hypothesis that whether the districts of Uttar Pradesh are converging towards a homogenous state or diverging and explores its determinants. We have used the data from Census 2001 and 2011 published by Registrar General of India (RGI) for estimation of district-wise life expectancy for all persons, males and females separately. Further, for assessing the determinants, we have used multiple data sources for various indicators which are considered as predictors of Life Expectancy at Birth (LEB) in the previous literature. We have estimated LEB at the district level for all persons, males and females for the year 2001 and 2011 using the well-known Brass method for indirect estimation of IMR, child mortality rate (CMR) and corresponding LEB of different model life table parameters. We have adopted novel approaches to the objective of testing of convergence hypothesis in average health status and health inequalities across the districts. The inequality measures range from absolute inequality measured through Dispersion Measure of Mortality (DMM) to relative inequality measured through Gini index. The convergence in health status was examined by using the standard parametric models (absolute β- and σ-convergences). Further, non-parametric econometric models (kernel density estimates) have also been used to detect the presence of convergence clubs, and finally we have analysed the determinant of convergence through panel regression model. Findings revealed that the inequality-based measures of convergence suggest that convergence process is underway regarding both

---

M. Z. Siddiqui · S. Goli (✉) · M. J. Rana · S. Chakravorty
Centre for the Study of Regional Development,
Jawaharlal Nehru University, New Delhi, India
e-mail: sirispeaks2u@gmail.com

© Springer Nature Singapore Pte Ltd. 2019
R. P. Mamgain (ed.), *Growth, Disparities and Inclusive Development in India*,
India Studies in Business and Economics,
https://doi.org/10.1007/978-981-13-6443-3_16

absolute and relative inequalities in LEB across the districts, during 2001–2011. Similarly, the findings based on catching-up plots and absolute β-convergence and sigma convergence measures affirm the convergence across districts of Uttar Pradesh. The presence of a strong evidence of convergence clubs indicates that growth process is not inclusive and is skewed to few district clusters of the state. LEB growth process has favoured some districts compared to other. Further, findings of determinants of health status suggest that decrease in infant mortality, progress in income level, improvement in literacy rate, full immunisation of children and health infrastructure in laggard districts would help in convergence of the health status across the geographical space in the state of Uttar Pradesh. Achieving health goals of SDGs in Uttar Pradesh will not possible unless acceleration in the speed of the convergence is achieved with equity. The state should prioritise the agenda for reduction of IMR, a substantial increase in literacy rate and major investment in healthcare infrastructural availability and accessibility, universal access to immunisation services, especially in the laggard districts of the state.

Keywords Life expectancy at birth · Convergence · Determinants

1 Introduction

This chapter presents progress and challenges in the health status of people living in different regions of Uttar Pradesh. Along with economic and educational status, health status is a critical component of human well-being. It occupies an important place in contemporary development discourse worldwide. The United Nations bestowed a unique place to health in its previously adopted Millennium Development Goals (MDGs) and the ongoing Sustainable Development Goals (SDGs), set for the world countries to be achieved by 2030. The world has become a better place; people are living a longer and healthier life with greater access to modern healthcare technologies (Deaton 2013). However, the dark side of this intriguing success story is that the world has witnessed a '*great divide*' in health and well-being than ever before in human history (Stiglitz 2015; Mormot 2015; Piketty 2014; Oxfam 2017). The socio-economic gradient in health status had become more pronounced, and the increasing cost of socio-economic inequality is becoming unbearable (Marmot 2015; World Health Organisation [WHO] 2015; Milanovic 2016). When it comes to the regional difference in health status (Wagstaff 2002), the forerunners are almost all developed countries, where humans tend to live longer and healthier as compared to their counterparts in developing or underdeveloped regions. The gap in life expectancy between the countries had been evident in almost all developed and developing regions of the world (Global Health Observatory [GHO] 2017).

Similar is the case of India, which is often described as a country with substantial progress in average health status alongside sizable geographical, rural–urban, social, economic and bio-demographic disparities in it (Goli and Arokiasamy 2013). Health for all had been a priority of public health policy-makers since its inception at *Alma*

Ata Declaration which has been showing a notable impact on improvements in mortality and life expectancy of the Indian population. But, the country is also known for its peculiar characteristics of demographic, epidemiological and economic transition, increasing inequality in health and wealth with the most hierarchical healthcare system, meagre social safety nets and low level of human development which is commonly considered as an 'uncertain glory of India' (Drèze and Sen 2013; James and Goli 2016).

The gap in average life expectancy at birth (LEB) across states was 19.0 years in 1970 which reduced to 12.3 years in 2010 (Office of RGI 2014). Although the country is witnessing a considerable improvement in health status across the states, yet steeper inter- and intra-state differentials in the speed of improvement coexist (Goli and Arokiasamy 2013). Lack of equity with progress in the health status of the population in the laggard states of India is one of the key features in its growth story (Drèze and Sen 2013). Health and socio-demographic indicators of states such as Kerala are comparable with the most developed countries like Switzerland, whereas states such as Uttar Pradesh are comparable for a least underdeveloped country like Uganda. These stark differentials in socio-economic and health status across the Indian states seemed to suggest the presence of a 'tale of two worlds' (Goli and Arokiasamy 2013; Office of RGI 2016). The LEB in Uttar Pradesh remains lowest with the highest share of the country's population. The state is also lagging in many of the key socio-economic and health indicators: almost 50% of children are not fully immunised; 40% children are underweight; it stands second in maternal mortality, highest in maternal anaemia and highest one in infant mortality rate; and it ranked bottom in human development indicator (IIPS and MoHFW 2017). However, a significant issue which has not received necessary attention in the literature is the presence of stark intra-state differences in health status, which is the main focus of this study.

2 Background and Rationale

Achieving grand convergence in global health and bridging the gap between the countries, within the country and between the states are important targets of ongoing SDGs (Lim et al. 2016). There are efforts to investigate the progress in inter-country and interstate inequality in health status using convergence models (Smith et al. 2009; McMichael et al. 2004; Moser et al. 2005; Goli and Arokiasamy 2013, 2014a, b). Without acceleration of improvements among laggard states, convergence in LEB in India cannot be achieved. Moreover, laggard states suffer from huge intra-state inequalities (Goli et al. 2013). In spite of the fact that the improvement in the state average of LEB is not comparable to an earlier period, the literature showing whether such progress is leading to convergence or divergence across the smaller administrative units such as districts within the states is scant in India. In this backdrop, the paper examines the hypothesis whether the districts of Uttar Pradesh are converging towards a homogenous state or following a path towards a heterogeneous state in health and explores its determinants. The rationale of investigating the geographical differentials in LEB among the districts of Uttar Pradesh is: first, as pointed earlier, it is the biggest state regarding population and occupies a laggard position in many socio-economic and demographic indicators. Secondly, the regional convergence in LEB across the state is important for the future improvements in the LEB as it showed one of the lowest among other states.

Our approach is very similar to Goli and Arokiasamy (2014b), wherein they have assessed the transition in the health status of Indian states using different convergence metrics. They found that South Indian states with higher life expectancy are showing less gain as compared to North Indian states with lower life expectancy and higher gain which indicates that states are converging towards the homogenous state, but with the very slow speed of convergence. Here, we are interested in investigating whether the findings from Goli and Arokiasamy (2014b) still hold true in the recent period and across districts within states, especially in underperforming ones like Uttar Pradesh.

The anticipated fresh contribution of this study is that we have estimated the LEB at the district level and for all populations, including for males and females separately. Further, we have assessed the gender and geographical difference in health status and predicted their future trajectories to achieve the geographical convergence in health status by sex in order to achieve national and state health targets. We have arranged this paper in the order as follows: first, we describe the contextual importance of the present study. Second, we have explained data description and methodological approach. Third, the findings of the study start with trend analysis of life expectancy at birth among males and females over the years. This is followed by trends in dispersion measures of mortality (DMM) and Gini index of LEB, parametric and non-parametric convergence measures and determinants of convergence in health status across the districts of Uttar Pradesh. Finally, we discuss our empirical findings and suggest the policy implications for achieving progress in health status and thereby a convergence in LEB.

3 Methodology

3.1 Data Source

We have used the data from Census 2001 and 2011 published by Registrar General of India (RGI) for estimation of district-wise life expectancy for all people, males and females separately. Both the rounds of Census have asked the question to ever-married women about their total number of children surviving and dead and tabulated them according to the age of mother and sex of the children. This information is available for smaller units such as districts, by which we have estimated the life expectancy at birth of males, females and all people for the districts of Uttar Pradesh. Further, for assessing the determinants, we have used multiple data sources for various indicators

Box A Study variables and data sources

Variables	Data source
Children ever born and children surviving by the age of the mother and sex of the children	Office of RGI (Registrar General of India) and Census Commissioner (2001, 2011)
Population proportion	RGI and Census Commissioner (2001, 2011)
Full immunisation	National Family and Health Survey (NFHS) (1992–93, 1998–99, 2006–07) and Annual Health Survey (AHS) Report (2011–12)
Female literacy rate	Office of RGI (Registrar General of India) and Census Commissioner (2001, 2011)
Percentage of urbanisation	Office of RGI (Registrar General of India) and Census Commissioner (2001, 2011)
Log of NSDP per capita (Rs.)	Reserve Bank of India (RBI) Handbook (2004–05, 2011–12)
Index of health infrastructure	Rural Health Statistics, Health Management Information System (HMIS), 2011–12

Note NSDP Net state domestic product

which are considered as predictors of LEB in the previous literature. Data sources of various indicators are displayed in Box A.

3.2 Methods

3.2.1 Estimation of LEB

We have estimated LEB at the district level for all persons, males and females for the year 2001 and 2011 using the well-known Brass method and appropriate indirect estimation of IMR, child mortality rate (CMR) and corresponding LEB of different model life table parameters (Hill 2013). Thus, first, we estimated the IMR which has the estimates of corresponding LEB. For estimation of IMR, we need the average parity per woman which is estimated as:

$$P(i) = \text{CEB}(i)/W(i)$$

where $\text{CEB}(i)$ denotes the number of children ever born to women belonging to the age group i and $W(i)$ denotes the total number of women belonging to the age group i irrespective of their marital status (United Nations 1983). The proportion of children died for each age group of mothers is estimated by:

$$D(i) = \frac{\text{CEB}(i) - \text{CS}(i)}{\text{CEB}(i)} = \frac{\text{CD}(i)}{\text{CEB}(i)},$$

where CS(i) denotes the number of surviving children reported by mothers belonging to the age group i and CD(i) denotes the number of children died reported by mothers belonging to the age group i. The multipliers $K(i)$'s are calculated according to Trussell's variant of the original Brass method. The simplified equation is:

$$K(i) = \frac{a(i) + b(i)P(1)}{P(2)} + \frac{c(i)P(2)}{P(3)},$$

where $a(i)$, $b(i)$ and $c(i)$ are the coefficients for the estimation of child mortality multipliers.

Finally,

$$q(x) = K(i) * D(i)$$

The proportions of children surviving to the date of the survey are the net result of the mortality conditions in the past rather than the mortality conditions prevalent on the date of survey. However, since mortality is not constant and changes over different time periods, it is important to identify the period to which Brass-type estimates most closely pertain. Following on the work of Feeney (1980), Coale and Trussell (1977) developed formulae for the estimation of the reference period, $t(x)$ (number of years prior to the survey), to which the values of $q(x)$ refer. The equations have the same format as those for the estimation of the adjustment factors $K(i)$ (Preston et al. 2000). The equation to estimate $t(x)$ is

$$t(x) = \alpha(i) + \beta(i) * \frac{P(1)}{P(2)} + \gamma(i) * \frac{P(2)}{P(3)}$$

where $\alpha(i)$, $\beta(i)$ and $\gamma(i)$ are the coefficients for estimation of $t(x)$.

3.2.2 Choice of Model Life Table and Standardisation

For India, the most suitable choice in the different families of model life tables is *South Asian model life table* (United Nation model life table) for developing countries which seems to be reasonably valid assumptions of fertility and mortality in the population under study. We have standardised LEB estimates derived from Census information to pro rata with sample registration system state average values of LEB for males and females separately for both the corresponding years.

3.3 Measures of Convergence

At second stage, we have used various neoclassical and cutting-edge convergence models to assess the progress in average *vis-a-vis* progress in health inequality

Health Status: Progress and Challenges

between districts of Uttar Pradesh by males and females. We have also performed panel data regression with random effect model to assess the determinants of convergence in LEB across the district of Uttar Pradesh.

3.3.1 Absolute β-Convergence

Barro (1991) and Barro and Sala-I-Martin (1992, 1997) have proposed the growth regression approach for measuring progress and named it as absolute β-convergence. Theoretically, application of β-convergence is possible when the gap between laggard and advanced nations or states shrinks, especially due to faster progress in laggard states. Empirically, β-convergence can be seen as a negative association between the growth rate of an indicator and its initial value. This model can be represented by the following equation:

$$\ln\left[\frac{Y_{i,t+k}}{Y_{i,t}}\right] = \alpha + \beta * \ln(y_{i,t}) + \varepsilon_{i,t}$$

where $\ln\left[\frac{Y_{i,t+k}}{Y_{i,t}}\right]$ is the mean annualised growth rate of the variable Y in the state i in the period $(t, t + k)$, $Y_{i,t}$ is the value in the initial time t and ε_{it} are the corresponding stochastic terms. However, in order to assess the recent progress in LEB we have measured the rate of convergence. The speed of convergence in LEB will help to predict the expected time to converge to homogenous state with higher levels of health status. The speed of convergence has been estimated through the following equation

$$s = -[\ln(1 + T\beta)/T]$$

where s is the speed of convergence and $T\beta$ is the β-convergence in time period T.

3.3.2 Sigma Convergence

While estimates of β-convergence measure depict the catching-up process of laggard states to advance states, sigma convergence is about whether states are converging towards each other regarding LEB over time (rather than to their steady-state levels). The sigma convergence can be measured through the following equation

$$\sigma_t > \sigma_{t+T}$$

where σ_t is the standard deviation (or assimilated measure) of the LEB levels at initial time and T stands for current time. If the parameter σ_{t+T} declines over time, it implies convergence.

3.3.3 Convergence Clubs: Kernel Density Plots

The convergence estimates through β and sigma measures have some caveats as both assume certain assumption of nature of the data, i.e. LEB for this study, whereas non-parametric measure does not assume any assumption about nature of the data except smoothness (Quah 1993; Wang 2004). Gaussian kernel density estimate is the most used technique for measuring convergence through non-parametric approach (Romer 1986; Strulik and Vollmer 2015). The general kernel estimator is defined by

$$\widehat{f(x)} = \frac{1}{nh} \sum_{i=1}^{n} K\left(\frac{x_i - x}{h}\right) = \frac{1}{nh} \sum_{i=1}^{n} K(Yi)$$

where $Y_i = h^{-1}(x_i - x)$, n is the number of observations in the sample, h is the window width (bandwidth) which is a function of the sample size and goes to zero as $n \to$ to ∞.

3.3.4 Convergence in Averages and Inequalities in LEB

Dispersion Measures of Mortality

Through this method, one can quantify the degree of dispersion in mortality experience (measured in terms of LEB) of a particular population existing at any given point of time. It was calculated as the average of the absolute difference in mortality experience, weighted by its population size, between each pair of the district. The decrease in dispersion measures of mortality (DMM) indicates that mortality among the districts is becoming homogenous (convergence), and an increase indicates heterogeneous growth over time and refers to a divergence in mortality. The DMM for life expectancy at birth is measured in years of life (Shkolnikov et al. 2003; Moser et al. 2005). The mathematical equation of DMM is as follows:

$$\text{DMM} = \frac{1}{2(W_Z)^2} \sum_i \sum_J \left(|M_i - M_j| * W_I * W_J\right)$$

where i, j are districts, and one $\leq i, j \leq 75$, Z is equal to 1 and M is the mortality rate. Further, W is the weights and can be expressed as $\sum_i W_i = \sum_j W_j = W_z$.

3.3.5 Gini Coefficient

To assess relative inequality, we have used Gini coefficients. The estimation of Gini in the case of LEB is equal to DMM divided by the average life expectancy of the districts (Shkolnikov et al. 2003).

$$G = \frac{\text{DMM}}{\overline{e_0^0}}, \text{ where } \overline{e_0^0} = \left[\sum_1 \text{Pi } e_0^i\right]$$

where

G Gini index value,
DMM Dispersion measures of mortality
$\overline{e_0^0}$ is average life expectancy at birth adjusted by the population proportion of the district $i \ldots i_n$.

3.3.6 Determinants of LEB

We have also estimated the determinants of LEB through panel data regression using random effect model. To make a decision among fixed or random effects, we run a *Hausman test* where the null hypothesis is that the preferred model is random effect versus the alternative, i.e. fixed effects (see Torres-Reyna 2007). It essentially tests whether the unique errors (μ_{it}) are correlated with the regressors; the null hypothesis is they are not the results of *Hausman test* suggested performing random effect model for panel data regression. The equation can show the random effect panel regression:

$$Y_{it} = \alpha_{it} + \beta_i X_{it} + \mu_{it} + \varepsilon_{i,t}, \quad i = 1, \ldots, N, \ t = 1, \ldots, T,$$

where

$\alpha_i \ (i = 1, \ldots, n)$ is the unknown intercept for each entity (n entity-specific intercepts).
Y_{it} is the dependent variable where i = entity and t = time.
X_{it} represents one independent variable.
β_1 is the coefficient for that independent variable.
μ_{it} is between entity error.
$\varepsilon_{i,t}$ is within entity error.

4 Empirical Findings

4.1 Levels and Trends of District LEB

The chapter estimates the LEB by sex of the individuals for all districts of Uttar Pradesh for the year 2001 and 2011. Also, we have analysed convergence in absolute and relative inequality of LEB among all population, females and males and its determinants for districts of Uttar Pradesh during the year 2001–2011. The results of Table 1 summarise the descriptive district-wise statistics of LEB for the years 2001 and 2011. The average of LEB for all persons among the districts had increased

Table 1 Summary statistics of LEB among the districts of Uttar Pradesh, 2001–2011

Gender	Years	Observations	Mean	SD	Minimum	Maximum	Range
Persons	2001	70	60.47	1.32	57.83	63.50	5.68
	2011	71	63.00	1.07	61.05	65.16	4.11
Male	2001	70	60.85	1.27	58.45	63.85	5.40
	2011	71	62.11	1.04	59.95	64.13	4.18
Female	2001	70	60.07	1.41	57.00	63.10	6.10
	2011	71	63.95	1.16	61.71	66.22	4.51

Source Authors' estimates based on Census 2001 and Census 2011 (Office of RGI 2001, 2011)
Note SD standard deviation

from 60.5 years in 2001 to 63.0 years in 2011. Similar trends were observed for males (60.9 years in 2001 to 62.1 years in 2011) and females (60.1 years in 2001 to 64.0 years in 2011) LEB over the years. Moreover, the range of average LEB suggested that the gap across districts had narrowed down during the study period irrespective of sex but at a slower pace.

Further, results showed that the growth of LEB for females (3.9 years) outpaced the growth of males (1.3 years) during the last one decade. The male–female gap in LEB which was 0.8 years in 2001 has reversed in the year 2011 and shows a female–male gap of 1.8 years. For the year 2001, the lowest LEB formulae were observed in Pilibhit (58.4 years) and Balrampur (58.6 years) districts, whereas in the females, the lowest LEB was observed for Balrampur (57.0 years) and Shravasti (57.8 years). Similarly, for the year 2011, the lowest LEB for males and females was observed in Barabanki (59.9 years) and Badaun (61.7 years), respectively. Overall, it is evident from Figs. 1 and 2 that the LEB was skewed towards the males in 2001 but reversed in 2011 in almost all the districts of Uttar Pradesh. Similarly, the cluster of districts with a low level of LEB, often categorised as eastern or north-eastern districts of Uttar Pradesh, showed a consistent pattern. Despite several government policies and programmes implemented in these districts, health status had not shown any significant improvement.

We have also measured the convergence in mortality inequalities over the decade. In order to do so, we have used DMM, average inter-district difference (AID) and Gini index, while DMM and AID measure absolute inequality and Gini measures relative inequality. Table 2 presents the estimates of DMM, AID and Gini indices in LEB among the districts of Uttar Pradesh during 2001–2011. The results reveal that the decline in DMM of males is slightly higher than their female counterparts. Similar trends were also observed for AID in LEB of males and females. However, the result of relative inequality measured through Gini index shows a higher decline in females as compared to males. Thus, the estimates of absolute and relative inequality in LEB of males and females showed a declining trend which means the districts are moving towards the steady state.

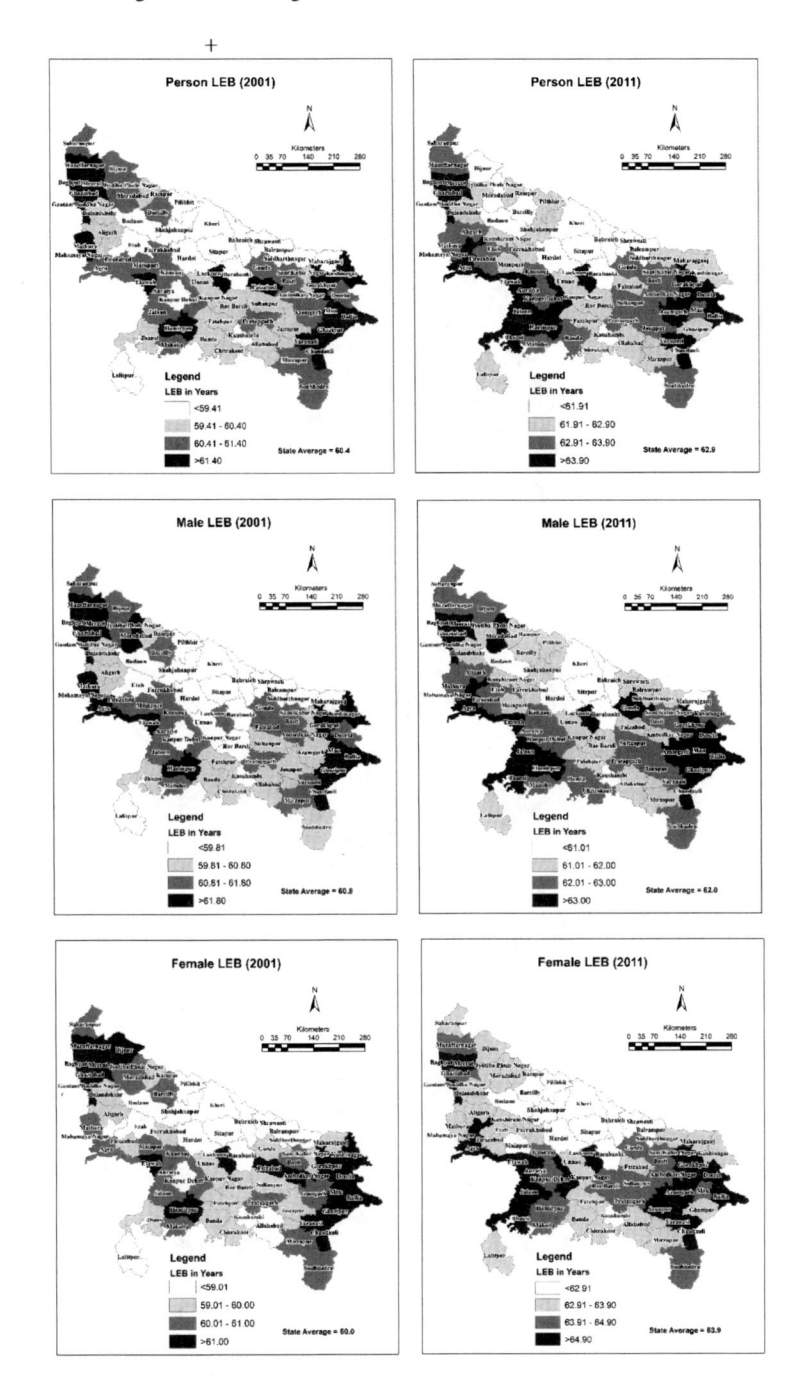

Health Status: Progress and Challenges

Fig. 1 Life expectancy at birth (LEB) for all persons, males and females in the districts of Uttar Pradesh during 2001 and 2011

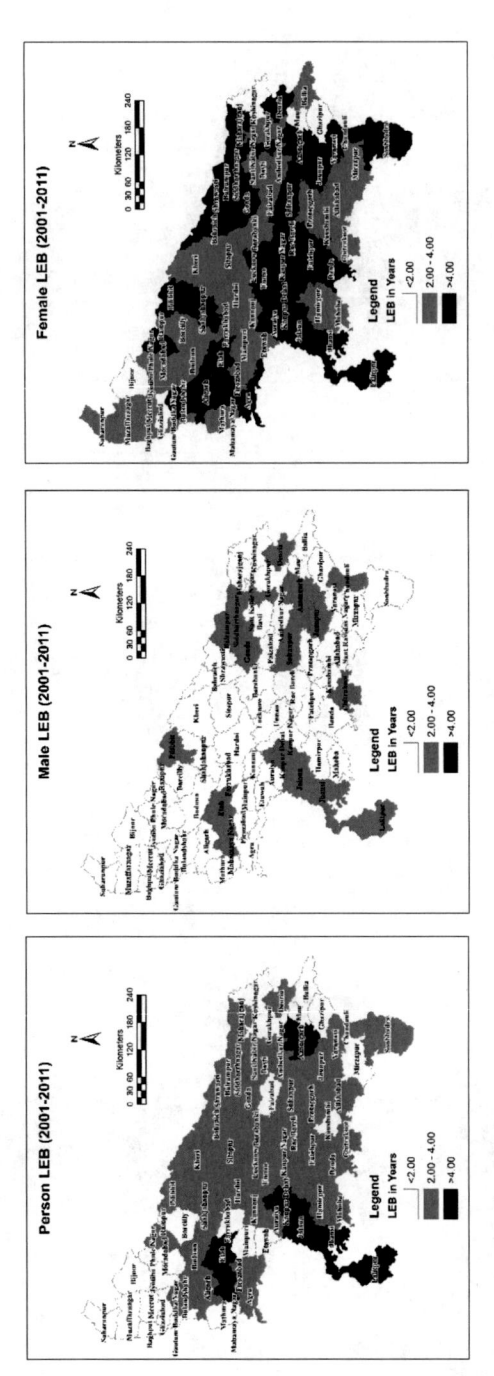

Fig. 2 Change in life expectancy at birth in all persons, male and females in the districts of Uttar Pradesh during 2001 and 2011

Table 2 Absolute and relative inequality measures of health status across the districts by gender, 2001–11

Inequality measures	Persons			Male			Female		
	2001	2011	Change	2001	2011	Change	2001	2011	Change
DMM	47.75	42.42	5.33	45.7	40.8	4.92	51.4	46.6	4.84
AID	23.88	21.21	2.67	22.9	20.4	2.46	25.7	23.3	2.42
Gini index	0.39	0.34	0.06	0.38	0.33	0.05	0.43	0.36	0.06

Source Authors' estimates based on Census 2001 and Census 2011 data (Office of RGI 2001, 2011)
Note DMM dispersion measures of mortality, AID average inter-district difference

4.2 Catching-up Process

The catching-up process is examined by plotting the change in LEB during 2001–2011 for districts of Uttar Pradesh by LEB levels in the initial period, 2001. The results reveal that LEB of males in the initial period and its change over the period showed a negative relationship that districts with a higher level of LEB registered comparatively lower growth as compared to their laggard districts with lower initial LEB levels. But, a considerable number of districts have also shown lower improvements with relatively lower levels of LEBs, while a few districts with higher levels of LEBs also have shown a better progress in it. Thus, here we interpret that although results suggest a catching-up process in LEB of males, females and all persons, the process is not very strong (Fig. 3).

4.3 Absolute β-Convergence

We have also assessed the convergence in averages of mortality rates. Convergence in mortality rates was measured based on LEB. The results of absolute β-convergence estimates showed statistically significant evidence of convergence in LEB of all persons (−0.089), males (−0.067) and females (−0.086) during the period 2001–2011. Table 3 shows that on an average, the LEB of all persons was converging by one unit per year towards the steady state across the districts. Moreover, the annual speed of convergence in LEB of males (0.69 years) is lower than that of females (0.90 years). Overall, the speed of convergence is very slow among both males and females. At this rate of convergence, the expected time for convergence based on the current levels of DMM was 45.5, 59.0 and 51.7 years for all persons, males and females, respectively.

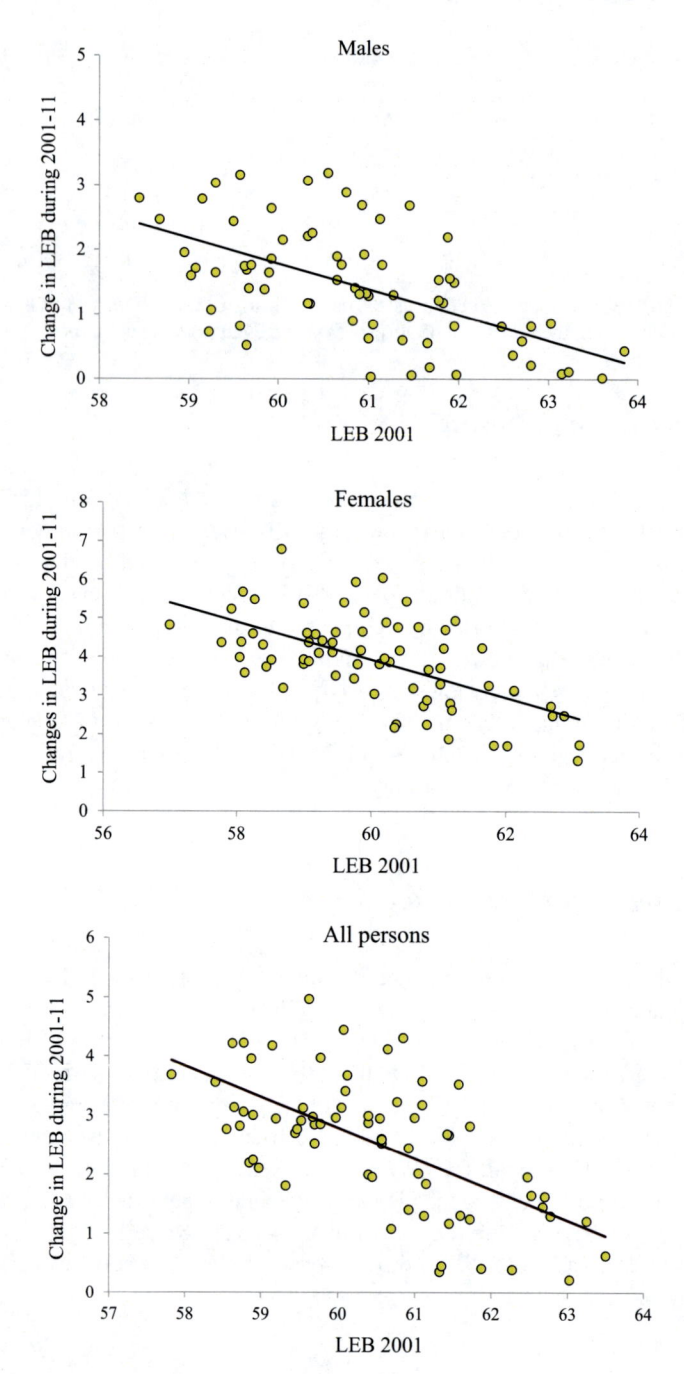

Fig. 3 Change in LEB during 1981–2011 for districts of Uttar Pradesh by LEB levels in the initial period, 2001, separately for males, females and all persons

Table 3 Absolute β-convergence estimates based on Barro regression model for LEB across the districts of Uttar Pradesh, 2001–2011

LEB convergence	Test of convergence (β-convergence)			
	Person	Male	Female	Male–female combined
β-coefficients (SE)	−0.08906*** (0.01248)	−0.06677*** (0.10873)	−0.08615*** (0.01223)	−0.11075*** (0.12562)
Constant	5.80053	4.2989	5.8032	7.1282
Number of observations	70	70	70	140
Degree of freedom	69	69	69	139
Adjusted R^2	0.4197	0.03473	0.4133	0.3557
Speed of convergence (annual)	0.932782	0.691036	0.900888	1.173769
Expected time for convergence in years (DMM)	45.5	59.0	51.7	36.1
Expected time for convergence in years (AID)	22.7	29.5	25.9	18.1

Source Authors' estimates based on Census 2001 and Census 2011 (Office of RGI 2001, 2011)
DMM and AID stand for dispersion measures of mortality and average inter-district difference, respectively
***$p < 0.01$
Note Districts: $n = 70$, df 69, standard error (SE) values in parenthesis for the beta coefficients at 95% confidence level

4.4 Sigma Convergence in LEB

Young et al. (2008) suggest that β-convergence is necessary but not a sufficient condition for sigma convergence. Therefore, we have examined sigma convergence based on a change in standard deviations of LEB over time for all persons, males and females across the districts of Uttar Pradesh (Table 4). The results for sigma convergence in LEB indicated a clear convergence in average LEB for males and females. The standard deviation in LEB of all persons declined from 1.32 years during 2001 to 1.07 years in 2011. Similarly, the standard deviation of LEB of males (0.22 years) and females (0.25 years) showed a moderate decline during the period of observation. Thus, results of the sigma convergence model are in collinearity with the findings of β-convergence. The parametric convergence metrics suggest that there is a convergence in LEB among the all persons, males and females across the districts of Uttar Pradesh, but its speed is very slow.

Table 4 Sigma convergence in gendered average LEB across the districts of Uttar Pradesh, 2001–2011

Sigma convergence			
Year	LEB all persons	LEB males	LEB females
2001	1.32	1.27	1.41
2011	1.07	1.05	1.16

Source Authors' estimates based on Census 2001 and Census 2011 (Office of RGI 2001, 2011)

4.5 Convergence Through Non-parametric Measures

Romer (1986), Bloom and Canning (2007) and Strulik and Vollmer (2015) have suggested testing convergence hypothesis using non-parametric measures, especially to detect the convergence clubs. Moreover, non-parametric convergence metrics do not make any assumption regarding the distribution of data. Therefore, they are powerful enough to detect minute dispersions. We have examined the convergence clubs through kernel density plot of LEB in males, females and all persons for the year 2001–2011. Figure 4 reveals in the case of LEB in males over the years 2001 and 2011, the presence of twin peaks in the distribution of LEB across the districts. The secondary peak has a minimum number of districts with highest LEB, whereas the first peak suggested a sufficiently large number of districts with a comparatively lower level of LEB. Similarly, the kernel plots in the case of LEB in females showed an emerging pattern of twin peaks for the year 2011. The overall distribution of LEB among the districts showed a rightward shift in case of female LEB as compared to males during 2001–2011. Districts with higher life expectancy levels emerged as separate convergence club suggested a noticeable divergence among districts by their levels of LEB in Uttar Pradesh over the years.

4.6 Determinants of Convergence

Table 5 presents the results from panel data regression showing socio-economic, demographic and supply-side factors such as health infrastructure as probable determinants of progress towards convergence in LEB across the districts of Uttar Pradesh, 2001–2011. The reduction of IMR ($\beta = -9.35, p < 0.01$) showed a significant negative association with the increase in LEB, meaning a decline in IMR raises the LEB, while literacy rate ($\beta = 0.01, p < 0.01$), per cent of children fully immunised ($\beta = 0.01, p < 0.01$) and score of health infrastructure ($\beta = 0.21, p < 0.05$) showed a significant positive effect on the improvement of LEB. However, a log of GDP per capita showed a positive but insignificant association with an increase in LEB. Probably, this pattern reflects the fact that the economic growth in the country is not inclusive in nature as the fruits are not being received by all. Overall, the results suggest that rise in IMR, education, healthcare infrastructure and health care along with

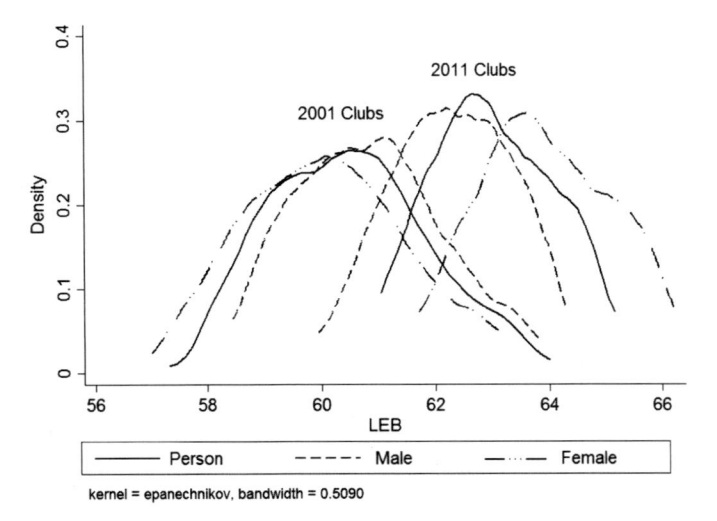

Fig. 4 Non-parametric test of convergence in health across the districts of Uttar Pradesh, 2001–2011

equitable distribution of fruits will help to raise the LEB levels across the districts of Uttar Pradesh.

5 Conclusion

The current exercise of assessment of convergence in progress of health status (measured in terms of LEB) across the districts of Uttar Pradesh during the last two decades has been the maiden effort to address inclusive growth in health status of the population in the state. Therefore, this is a timely attempt to fill the critical gap in the field of research on health policy and planning through addressing the concept of efficiency with equity in health progress in the state. We have applied various front-line methods for testing the convergence hypothesis for progress in the health status of both males and females at lowest possible administrative unit such as districts. Findings of this study propel numerous important conclusions. While the LEB trends suggest that although the number of districts with a higher level of LEB (above 63 years) has increased over the period, yet there was a huge variation in LEB transition across the districts in Uttar Pradesh. In particular, the gap between Eastern districts such as Balrampur, Bahraich, Barabanki, Gonda, Badaun and Western districts such as Ghaziabad, Moradabad, Meerut remains high despite substantial improvements in LEB among all the districts. This geographical gradient also holds true in gender-disaggregated LEB trends.

In general, although the study advances that the health status in the districts of Uttar Pradesh is converging, at a very slow pace, the conclusions differ in specific

Table 5 Results from panel data regression model (random effects)

Variables	β coefficients	Standard error	Confidence interval	
			Lower limit	Upper limit
IMR	−9.354***	0.222	−9.790	−8.919
TFR	0.078	0.070	−0.059	0.215
Population size	0.012	0.090	−0.164	0.189
Full immunisation	0.007***	0.003	−0.012	−0.002
Urban	0.003	0.003	−0.002	0.009
Literacy	0.014***	0.004	0.007	0.021
Log of GDP per capita	0.070	0.089	−0.245	0.104
Index of health Infrastructure	0.210**	0.104	0.006	0.414
Time dummy	0.112***	0.011	0.090	0.134
Constant	−121.062***	23.261	−166.65	−75.47
Number of observations	138			
R^2: Within	0.99			
R^2: Between	0.98			
R^2: Overall	0.98			
Wald Chi^2	7759.90***			

Source Authors' estimates based on Census 2001 and Census 2011 (Office of RGI 2001, 2011)
Standard error (SE) and upper and lower limits are at 95% confidence interval (CI)
*$p < 0.10$, **$p < 0.05$, ***$p < 0.01$

to convergence metric used. For instance, inequality-based measures of convergence suggest that convergence process is underway regarding both absolute and relative inequalities in LEB across the districts, during 2001–2011. Similarly, the findings based on catching-up plots and absolute β-convergence and sigma convergence measures affirm convergence in LEB across the districts of Uttar Pradesh. The presence of a strong evidence of convergence clubs indicates that growth process is not inclusive and is skewed to few district clusters of the state. LEB growth process has favoured some districts compared to others. The estimation of time required for convergence in LEB across the districts based on the current speed of convergence suggests that it would take as long as 45 years to see absolute convergence at a steady state of equilibrium across the districts. But, previous evidence suggests that the stability of the convergence process is not guaranteed. Convergence can replace divergence at any stage of the convergence process based on setbacks in progress or dissimilar progress of states in health indicators. These divergent mortality trends in districts can also re-converge as disproportionate improvements among laggard and advanced districts (Dorius and Firebugh 2010; Smith et al. 2009; Moser et al. 2005; McMichael et al. 2004).

On the other hand, the findings also suggest apparent gender differentials in the pace of LEB progress and rate of convergence: a higher rate of convergence among the female sex across the districts as compared to the males. Although the biological advantage of female sex had been historically offset through selective behaviour against females in developing countries in general and India in particular, however, over the time, through social, economic and political emancipation of females, the access to agencies through which females were claiming equal rights increased, being a catalyst to achieve the biological advantage in survival chances (WHO 2015). This connotation is well supported by the findings of this study in the context of Uttar Pradesh. Since the last one decade, females in the state are showing lower mortality, especially among children, adult ages and higher life expectancy as compared to their male counterparts. It is attributed to the reduction in maternal mortality ratio (MMR) and decreasing sex differentials in infant and child mortality (Office of RGI 2015). Thus, the findings also suggest that the highest contribution to an overall gain in life expectancy is contributed by a gain in female life expectancy. Similarly, findings suggest that decrease in infant mortality, progress in income level, improvement in literacy rate, full immunisation of children and health infrastructure would increase the health status across the geographical space in the state of Uttar Pradesh.

Moreover, achieving health goals of SDGs in Uttar Pradesh will not be possible unless speed and volume of the convergence in health status are achieved with inclusive growth process. The state should prioritise the agenda for reduction of IMR, a substantial increase in literacy rate and major investment in healthcare infrastructural availability and accessibility, universal access to immunisation services, especially in the laggard districts. The substantial contribution to IMR and female life expectancy in overall enhancement of life expectancy in the population of Uttar Pradesh suggests that improvement in maternal and child health, and reduction in maternal and infant mortality are the keys to future improvement in life expectancy of the state. Therefore, further enhancement of national and state programmes related to health and welfare of mother and children such as mother-baby package (MBP) services, saving newborn lives through improved management of birth asphyxia and essential newborn care (ENBC) services, nutritional programmes and reproductive and child health (RCH) programmes is required. Promoting outreaches of not only primary but also tertiary care treatment under national health mission (NHM) is also critical for enhancement of LEB. Prevention and treatment of communicable, non-communicable diseases, accidents, injury and falls through the installation of superior prevention and curative service delivery infrastructure and human resources are necessary for prolonging the life expectancy in a population (Blas and Kurup 2010; Whitehead et al. 2001). Also giving emphasis on laggard districts in these aspects will help to achieve convergence across the districts. In conclusion, convergence measures are important tools for timely monitoring of progress towards inclusiveness in a growth process. Convergence in averages of health status and its inequality not only reflects a sense of equity across the districts and between the sexes but also can be an effective summary measure for monitoring the progress in terms of absolute and relative distribution of health status.

References

Barro, R. J. (1991). Economic growth in a cross-section of countries. *The Quarterly Journal of Economics, 106,* 407–444.

Barro, R. J., & Sala-I-Martin, X. (1992). Convergence. *The Journal of Political Economy, 100,* 223–251.

Barro, R. J., & Sala-I-Martin, X. (1997). Technological diffusion, convergence and growth. *Journal of Economic Growth, 2*(1), 1–26.

Blas, E., & Kurup, S. A. (2010). Synergy for equity. In E. Blas, & S. A. Kurup (Eds.), *Equity, social determinants and public health programmes* (pp. 261–284). World Health Organization.

Bloom, D. E., & Canning, D. (2007). Mortality traps and the dynamics of health transitions. *Proceedings of the National Academy of Sciences, 104*(41), 16044–16049.

Census. (2001). Office of the Registrar General & Census Commissioner, India. 2001. Home/Population Enumeration/Final Population. New Delhi: Registrar General & Census Commissioner, India, Ministry of Home Affairs.

Census. (2011) Office of the Registrar General & Census Commissioner, India. 2011. Home/Population Enumeration/Final Population. New Delhi: Registrar General & Census Commissioner, India, Ministry of Home Affairs.

Coale, A. J., & Trussell, T. J. (1977). Estimating the time to which Brass estimates apply. *Population Bulletin of the United Nations, 10,* 87–89.

Deaton, A. (2013). *The great escape: Health, wealth, and the origins of inequality.* Princeton: Princeton University Press.

Dorius, S. F., & Firebugh, G. (2010). Trends in global gender inequality. *Social Forces, 88*(5), 1941–1968.

Drèze, J., & Sen, A. (2013). *An uncertain glory: India and its contradictions.* Princeton: Princeton University Press.

Feeney, G. (1980). Estimating infant mortality trends from child survivorship data. *Population Studies. A Journal of Demography Publication details, 34*(1), 109–128. https://doi.org/10.1080/00324728.1980.10412839.

Global Health Observatory [GHO]. (2017). *Monitoring health for SDGs.* Retrieved June 15, 2017 from http://www.who.int/gho/en/.

Goli, S., & Arokiasamy, P. (2013). Trends in health and health inequalities among major states of India: Assessing progress through convergence models. *Health Economics, Policy and Law.* https://doi.org/10.1017/s1744133113000042.

Goli, S., & Arokiasamy, P. (2014a). Maternal and child mortality indicators across 187 countries of the world: Converging or diverging. *Global Public Health, 9*(3), 342–360.

Goli, S., & Arokiasamy, P. (2014b). Trends in health and health inequalities among major states of India: Assessing progress through convergence models. *Health Economics, Policy and Law, 9*(2), 143–168.

Goli, S., Doshi, R., & Arokiasamy, P. (2013). Pathways of economic inequalities in maternal and child health in urban India: A decomposition analysis. *PLoS ONE, 8*(3), e58573.

Hill, K. (2013). Indirect estimation of child mortality. In T. A. Moultrie, R. E. Dorrington, A. G. Hill, K. Hill, I. M. Timæus, & B. Zaba (Eds.), *Tools for demographic estimation.* Paris: The International Union for the Scientific Study of Population. Retrieved June 30, 2017 from http://demographicestimation.iussp.org/content/indirect-estimation-child-mortality.

International Institute for Population Sciences [IIPS] and Ministry of Health and Family Welfare [MoHFM]. (2017). *National family and health survey: Fact sheet.* Government of India.

James, K. S., & Goli, S. (2016). Demographic changes in India: Is the country prepared for the challenge? *The Brown Journal of World Affairs, 23*(1), 169–188.

Lim, S. S., Allen, K., Bhutta, Z. A., Dandona, L., Forouzanfar, M. H., Pullman, N., et al. (2016). Measuring the health-related sustainable development goals in 188 countries: A baseline analysis from the global burden of disease study 2015. *Lancet, 388,* 1813–1850.

Marmot, M. (2015). *The health gap: The challenge of an unequal world*. London: Bloomsbury Publishing.

McMichael, A. J., Mckee, M., Shkolnikov, V., & Valkonen, T. (2004). Mortality trends and setbacks: Global convergence or divergence? *Lancet, 363,* 1155–1159.

Milanovic, B. (2016). Global inequality: A new approach for the age of globalization. *Panoeconomicus, 63*(4), 493–501.

Moser, K., Shkolnikov, V., & Leon, D. (2005). World mortality 1950–2000: Divergence replaces convergence from the late 1980s. *Bulletin of the World Health Organization, 83*(3), 202–209.

Office of the Registrar General of India. (2014). *Sample registration system year book*. New Delhi: Government of India.

Office of the Registrar General of India. (2015). *Sample registration system year book*. New Delhi: Government of India.

Office of the Registrar General of India. (2016). *Sample registration system year book*. New Delhi: Government of India.

Oxfam. (2017). *Oxfam briefing paper—Executive summary*. Retrieved June 15, 2017 from https://www.oxfam.org/sites/www.oxfam.org/files/file_attachments/bp-inclusive-growth-africa-020517-summ-en.pdf.

Piketty, T. (2014). *Capital in the twenty-first century*. Cambridge, MA.

Preston, S., Heuveline, P., & Guillot, M. (2000). *Demography: Measuring and modelling population processes*. New York, NY: Wiley Blackwell.

Quah, D. T. (1993). Empirical cross-section dynamics in economic growth. *European Economic Review, 37,* 426–434.

Romer, P. M. (1986). Increasing returns and long-run growth. *Journal of Political Economy, 94,* 1002–1037.

Shkolnikov, V. M., Andreev, E. M., & Begun, A. (2003). Gini coefficient as a life table function: Computation from discrete data, decomposition of differences and empirical examples. *Demographic Research, 8,* 305–358.

Smith, K. E., Hunter, D. J., Blackman, T., Elliott, E., Greene, A., Harrington, B. E., et al. (2009). Divergence or convergence? Health inequalities and policy in a devolved Britain. *Critical Social Policy, 29*(2), 216–242.

Stiglitz, J. (2015). *The great divide*. UK: Penguin.

Strulik, H., & Vollmer, S. (2015). The fertility transition around the world. *Journal of Population Economics, 28*(1), 31.

Torres-Reyna, O. (2007). Panel data analysis fixed and random affects using Stata (v. 4.2). In *Data & Statistical Services, Princeton University*.

United Nations. (1983). Estimation of child mortality from information on children ever born and children surviving, Manual X: Indirect techniques for demographic estimation. *Population Studies, 81,* 73–96.

Wagstaff, A. (2002). Poverty and health sector inequalities. *Bulletin of World Health Organization, 80*(2), e97–e105.

Wang, Y. (2004). A nonparametric analysis of the personal income distribution across the provinces and states in the US and Canada. *Regional and Sectoral Economic Studies, 4*(1), 5–24.

Whitehead, M., Dahgren, G., & Evans, T. (2001). Equity and health sector reforms: Can low-income countries escape the medical poverty trap? *Lancet, 358,* 833–836.

World Health Organization. (2015). *Monitoring health inequality: An essential step for achieving health equity* Updated 2015 version. http://www.who.int/iris/handle/10665/164530

Young, A. T., Higgins, M. J., & Levy, D. (2008). Σ-convergence versus β-convergence: Evidence form U.S. county-level data. *Journal of Money, Credit and Banking, 40,* 1083–1093.

Mohammad Zahid Siddiqui is a research scholar in Population Studies at the Centre for the Study of Regional Development, Jawaharlal Nehru University, New Delhi, India. He has done his master degree in Population Studies from International Institute for Population Studies (IIPS), Mumbai, India, with specialization in health economics. His core area of research are; economics of inequalities, economics of health service, health care utilisation, nutrition and child health, convergence in health status, new measures of economic inequalities and cost of income inequalities. He is currently working in the area of causation modelling of economic inequality and its consequences with special focus on Non-economic consequences of inequality. He has expertise in data analysis and experience in field surveys, sampling, data collection, data entry and data cleaning as well. He has work experience as a Research Assistant/Senior Research Assistant at Giri Institute of Development Studies (GIDS), Lucknow and Consultant in National Health System Resource Centre (NHSRC), New Delhi. He has published some articles on the above stated subject area in highly esteemed peer reviewed journals.

Dr. Srinivas Goli is an Assistant Professor of Population Studies at Jawaharlal Nehru University (JNU), New Delhi. He did his Masters and Ph.D. in Population Studies from International Institute for Population Sciences (IIPS), Mumbai, India. He is teaching Fertility Studies, Family Planning, Family Demography, Gender and Quantitative Methods in Social Science Research at JNU. He is consultant to various international and national research institutions. His research deals with Formal Demography, Family Demography, Inequalities in Health, Nutrition and Gender status and its Social Determinants. He has been working on modelling of fertility, mortality and health transition and convergence across the states and social groups in India. Currently, he is involved in collaborative research projects with Western Australia University, Australia, Bristol and Glasgow UK and University of Maryland, USA. Dr. Goli's future research interests are the transition in families and its implications, returns of family planning and fertility decline, and marriage dynamics in India.

Md Juel Rana is a doctoral student in Population Studies from the Centre for the Study of Regional Development, Jawaharlal Nehru University, New Delhi, India. His research interests include family planning, fertility, nutrition and health. He is currently working on Ph.D. research project entitled "Family Planning in India, 1951–2001: Outreach, Contraceptive Use Dynamics and Returns". He has several research collaborations with Population Council, New Delhi and International Council for Research on Women, New Delhi. Earlier, he was awarded M.Phil. degree on the dissertation entitled "Linkage between family planning and nutritional status of women and their children: Evidence from select South Asian countries". He has a good experience in survey data analysis especially in demographic health survey. He has published in his areas of interest in reputed national and international peer reviewed journals.

Swastika Chakravorty is a research scholar in Population Studies from Centre for the Study of Regional Development, Jawaharlal Nehru University (JNU), New Delhi, India. She did her Master of Science M.Sc. in Population Studies from International Institute for Population Sciences, Mumbai in 2014 after completing her B.Sc. (Statistics) from Delhi University in 2012. In her Ph.D. she aims to study the changing family demography in India and its role in reproducing inequalities among the vulnerable groups, i.e. women, children and elderly. She has worked as consultant for Evidence Action, India for monitoring and Evaluation of their health programmes and data in collaboration with MoHFW, India. She has also published some article in peer reviewed journals and some of her research papers are in peer review for publication in highly reputed journals.

Burden of Private Healthcare Expenditure: A Study of Three Districts

C. S. Verma and Shivani Singh

Abstract Provision of affordable health care to all, irrespective of their paying capacity, is the fundamental duty of a welfare state like India. However, the state has failed to fulfill its promise to provide health security to all. Post liberalization, there is a shift from welfare-oriented government health policies to market-oriented policies. This has further resulted in unregulated and unaccountable expansion of private health care sector. With the involvement of corporate players, the scenario has clearly shifted from 'mere privatization' to commercialization and corporatization of the healthcare sector. The new National Health Policy (2017) also promotes such health policies that will further promote the commercialization of services even within public facilities. Although the country has emerged as one of the leading destinations for high-end private healthcare facilities, the private healthcare sector is heterogeneous, widely mal-distributed, and is hardly able to provide minimum quality of care. In a state like Uttar Pradesh, the increasing out-of-pocket expenditure on health is among one of the biggest causes of impoverishment. This article analyzes the pattern of healthcare expenditure in public and private healthcare sectors in the state and how private healthcare market is flourishing at the cost of public healthcare sector. For this, out-of-pocket expenditure (OOPE) on ambulatory care and inpatient care in public and private sectors has been assessed across a sample of 3338 household spread across 47 villages and 13 wards in three districts of Uttar Pradesh. Recall period for inpatient care was 365 days and for outpatient care was 30 days. The findings from the study suggest that although majority of people prefer private healthcare, the choice of private provider depends on the economic status of the people. People from lower economic group seek care from RMPs, unregistered, and informal providers while people from higher income groups seek care from high-end private facilities. The OOPE is high in both public as well as private, more so in private sector. Lack of trained personnel, drugs, and equipment in public healthcare sector is the cause of high OOPE there. The high costs of good quality private healthcare services further deprive the people of lower economic strata from proper healthcare services because of their lack of affordability. Low coverage under health insurance schemes

---

C. S. Verma (✉) · S. Singh
Giri Institute of Development Studies, Lucknow, India
e-mail: verma.cs@gmail.com

© Springer Nature Singapore Pte Ltd. 2019
R. P. Mamgain (ed.), *Growth, Disparities and Inclusive Development in India*,
India Studies in Business and Economics,
https://doi.org/10.1007/978-981-13-6443-3_17

like Rashtriya Swasthya Bima Yojana (RSBY) and dominance of private hospitals in providing treatment under the schemes has also resulted in failure of health insurance in reducing OOPE. Lack of proper regulatory and monitoring authority and legal provisions further leads to exorbitant prices and corrupt practices in private sector. In order to provide universal health coverage and ensure healthcare for all, it is the need of the hour to promote private healthcare sector, but at the same time, it needs to be properly regulated and monitored. The government should strengthen public health system by increasing the public expenditure on preventive and primary healthcare in order to reduce the OOPE on health.

Keywords Utilization of healthcare facilities · Out-of-pocket expenditure on healthcare · Impoverishment

1 Background

Provision of affordable health care to all, irrespective of their paying capacity, is the fundamental duty of a welfare state like India. But, so far the state has failed to fulfill its promise to provide health security to all (Qadeer 2011). Access to basic healthcare services is a citizen's fundamental right that remains a distant dream in the current scenario. The State's failure has resulted in tremendous and unregulated growth of private healthcare sector. Ironically, the government's health policies have also been designed in such a way that they have ended up supporting the expansion of private health care sector. Thus, we see the healthcare industry growing at a tremendous pace owing to its strengthening coverage, services, and increasing expenditure, mostly by private players. Between 2008 and 2020, the industry is expected to record a CAGR (compound annual growth rate) of 16.5%. The total industry size is expected to touch US$ 160 billion by 2017 and US$ 280 billion by 2020 (IBEF Report 2017). The health expenditure in the country is estimated at almost six to eight percent of the GNP, and almost four-fifths of it is private expenditure, merely one-fifth being provided by the state. The deplorable condition of the public health facilities and the burden of demand for healthcare ensured the prolific expansion of private players who are unregulated, unaccountable, and out of the control of the State.

India's health sector has one of the largest medical human power and physical infrastructure, but most of it is in private sector. In recent decades, the health sector has undergone vast expansion, and the country has also emerged as one of the leading destinations for high-end diagnostic services with tremendous capital investment for advanced diagnostic facilities. Private health sector comprises secondary, tertiary, and quaternary care institutions, which are mostly concentrated in metros, tier I, and tier II cities (IBEF 2017). With 68.84% of the country residing in rural areas (Census 2011), it can be said that the private health sector is grossly non-uniform in its reach, and standard of caregiving and is unable to provide quality healthcare to all sections of the society. More recently, with an ever-growing private sector and involvement of corporate players, the scenario has clearly shifted from 'mere priva-

Table 1 Demographic profile of Uttar Pradesh

Basic characteristic	Uttar Pradesh	India
Total population	199.8 million	1.21 billion
Population growth rate	20.24%	17.64%
Sex ratio	912	943
Child sex ratio	902	919
Density per sq. km.	829	382
Literacy rate	67.68%	74.04%
Male literacy rate	77.28%	82.14%
Female literacy	51.36%	65.46%
Life expectancy at birth*	64.1	68.3
Life expectancy at birth (males)*	62.9	66.9
Life expectancy at birth (female)	65,4	69.9

Source Census (2011)

tization' to commercialization and corporatization of the healthcare sector such that we are witnessing commercialization of services even within public facilities. The prohibitive costs of services result in further deprivation of the poor and marginalised from availing essential healthcare.

Uttar Pradesh, the most populous state in India, is one of the poorest states with poor development and health indicators (Table 1). Although the state has an extensive health infrastructure, the human health indicators show that the state is among the poorest in the country. Infant mortality rate (IMR) is 48 in the state and 51 in the rural areas (SRS Bulletin 2014). The maternal mortality ratio (MMR) was 285 in 2011–13 (SRS, 2011–13). Unregulated growth of private healthcare sector and poor performance of public healthcare sector adds to the plight of people. It is ironical that in one of India's poorest states, 'out of pocket' payments are the major source of financing healthcare. High level of out-of-pocket expenditures poses higher economic burden on households and an impoverishing effect on their living standard (Ghosh 2011; Bhojani et al. 2012; Shahrawat and Rao 2011). There are only a few studies which have attempted to assess the situation at the grassroots level. This chapter attempts to assess the pattern of healthcare expenditure in public and private healthcare sectors in U.P. and how the private healthcare market is flourishing at the cost of public healthcare sector.

2 Methodology

In order to analyze the pattern of healthcare expenditure in public and private healthcare sectors in the state, Out-of-pocket expenditure on ambulatory care and inpatient care has been assessed. For this, a study has been conducted during July and

December 2015 in three districts of Uttar Pradesh: Kushinagar, Hamirpur, and Aligarh. Distribution of sample across the districts is done by multistage-stratified random sampling. The total sample size is 3338 households spread across 47 villages and 13 wards of the selected districts. Recall period for inpatient care was 365 days and for outpatient care was 30 days. The healthcare providers have been classified under five categories. First category includes subcenters, PHCs (primary health centers), and CHCs (child healthcare centers). Second category includes area/subdistrict/taluk hospital, district hospital, medical college hospital, ESI hospital, CGHS (central government health services). Third category includes private doctors, clinics, and nursing homes, while the fourth category includes private hospitals, charitable hospitals, and super-speciality hospitals. Fifth category includes RMPs (registered medical practioners), traditional healers, and other informal healthcare providers. Monthly per capita consumption expenditure (MPCE) has been taken as proxy of income level, and data have been collected on the set of questions based on National Sample Survey Organisation (NSSO) rounds on health care.

The impoverishment effect of healthcare cost has been measured using pre- and post-poverty headcount.

$$\text{Pre } H_p = 1/n \sum 1(X_i \leq \text{PL}_s)$$

$$\text{Post } H_p = 1/n \sum 1((X_i - \text{OOP}) \leq \text{PL}_s)$$

where,

H_p Poverty headcount,
X_i Per capita consumption expenditure,
PL_s State-level poverty line,
n Number of individuals, and
OOP refers to out of pocket expenditure on health.

3 Results and Analysis

3.1 Demographic Profile of Sample Households

The average household size in the study area is almost equal to the state average (Table 2). About 81.2% households belong to rural areas except in Kushinagar, where 90.8% of people are from rural areas. Majority of the households, i.e., 86.9% are Hindus, while only 12% are Muslims. The distribution of sample in terms of social groups depicts that 48.5% households belong to other backward classes (OBCs). About 29% are general and 22.6% are from scheduled caste (SC) and scheduled tribe (ST) categories. The share of households below poverty line is 17.5, 36.7m and 44.7% in Aligarh, Hamirpur, and Kushinagar, respectively, as against 39.8% in the

Table 2 Demographic profile of the sample households

Household characteristics	Category	Aligarh (n = 1117)	Hamirpur (n = 1104)	Kushinagar (n = 1117)	Total (n = 3338)	Uttar Pradesh[a]
Household size	Average household size	5.24	5.01	6.08	5.44	6.0
Place of residence (in %)	Rural	75	77.8	90.8	81.2	77.89
	Urban	25	22.2	9.2	18.8	22.11
Religion (in %)	Hindu	77	94	84.8	86.9	79.7
	Muslim	21.6	5.6	14.1	12.1	19.3
	Others	1.4	0.4	1.2	0.95	1
Caste (in %)	SC/ST	25.7	16.4	25.5	22.6	20.5
	OBC	30.3	57.9	57.4	48.5	50
	General	44	25.7	17.1	29	29.5
Literacy (in %)	Literacy rate	56.51	64.03	54.01	57.89	67.7
Share of BPL population	Households below BPL (percentage)	17.5	36.70	44.7	–	39.8[b]

Source Field survey data.
[a]Census (2011); [b]Planning Commission (2014)

state; this also reflects that the households in western region districts of Uttar Pradesh such as Aligarh are comparatively better off than the households from Bundelkhand and eastern region districts.

3.2 Utilization of Healthcare Facilities

A rapidly increasing cost in healthcare and associated affordability in the state is an increasing cause of concern. The demand for healthcare has tremendously increased in recent years and has resulted in an exponential increase in the share of private healthcare providers (Shah and Mohanty 2010). Likewise, the share of informal healthcare providers such as RMPs and traditional healers has also increased leading to further deterioration in the quality of healthcare.

The utilization pattern for outpatient care by various ailments depicts that majority of patients seek private health care in the case of infections. A sizable number of people suffering from infections like diarrhea or dysentery seek care from private doctors and clinics (Table 3). Almost 27.63% seek care from private hospitals, while almost 10% people seek care for the same from informal providers and RMPs. In

Table 3 Ailment-wise utilization of health facilities for ambulatory care in the study area

Type of health facility	Diarrhea/ dysentery	Gastritis/ gastric or peptic ulcers	Worm infestation	Amebiasis	Cataract	Total
Subcenters/PHCs/CHCs	196	5	19	6	3	229
	(6.35)	(1.98)	(6.99)	(5.26)	(10.00)	(6.10)
Public hospitals	331	21	31	11	3	397
	(10.72)	(8.33)	(11.40)	(9.65)	(10.00)	(10.57)
Private doctors/nursing homes	1331	126	115	60	11	1643
	(43.12)	(50.00)	(42.28)	(52.63)	(36.67)	(43.73)
Private hospitals	853	85	93	24	12	1067
	(27.63)	(33.73)	(34.19)	(21.05)	(40.00)	(28.40)
Informal providers	311	11	10	13	1	348
	(10.07)	(4.37)	(3.68)	(11.40)	(3.33)	(9.26)
None	65	4	4	0	0	73
	(1.23)	(1.59)	(1.48)	(0.00)	(0.00)	(1.94)
Total	3087	252	272	114	30	3757
	(100.00)	(100.00)	(100.00)	(100.00)	(100.00)	(100.00)

Source Field survey data

the case of other infections like amebiosis and worm infestations, more than 80% of people seek care from private providers. It is to be noted that 9.26% people seek care from the informal healthcare provider, viz. RMPs and traditional healers, which is a considerable share. This further reflects how lack of access and affordability results in low quality of care.

Our findings reflect overwhelming use of private healthcare services by the sample households. The same is corroborated by the NSSO June–July 2014 data which state that 85% of UP population seeks ambulatory care from private providers (NSSO). Private health sector is not a homogenous unit. It has different types of service providers who not only vary in terms of cost of care, but also the quality of care. The difference is substantial in the quality of service as well as its cost. Almost 88% people in Kushinagar district seek healthcare in private-sector establishments, whereas in Hamirpur and Aligarh districts these figures are around 75%. This is significant because Kushinagar has much higher ratio of people living below poverty line than other two districts. However, it is also important to know that public health facilities are much less in availability in Kushinagar than in Hamirpur and Aligarh. More use of private healthcare services in Kushinagar, therefore, is not by choice rather a compulsion. The place of living and socio-economic status also has a significant effect on the choice of healthcare provider. The survey shows that the utilization of public healthcare declines with an increase in income level, although the choice of public provider further changes with change in income (Table 4). Majority of

Table 4 Pattern of utilization of healthcare facilities for ambulatory care

Background characteristics	Level of care					Total
	Category	Health center/ PHC	Public hospital	Private doctor/ clinic	Private hospital	
District	Kushinagar	6	5.8	44.1	44.1	100
	Hamirpur	9.9	10.7	37.9	41.6	100
	Aligarh	3.7	17.2	51.6	27.6	100
	All	6.7	10.7	44.1	38.5	100
Gender	Male	6.4	11.2	43	39.4	100
	Female	7.3	9.5	46.5	36.6	100
Age	Children	6.7	10	37.8	45.6	100
	Adults	6.5	10.9	43.6	39	100
	Older population	7.3	10.2	45.9	36.6	100
Caste	ST/SC	7.4	11.1	44.5	37	100
	OBC	6.8	9.8	42.9	40.4	100
	General	6	11.8	45.7	36.5	100
Quintile	1	14.1	12	46.1	27.8	100
	2	8.7	11.4	42.7	37.1	100
	3	5.9	9.4	42.7	42	100
	4	3.3	7.4	48.2	41	100
	5	2.4	11.2	41.6	44.7	100
Place of residence	Rural	11.2	13.6	43.3	32	100
	Urban	4.4	11	48.1	36.4	100

Note The figures here show the percentage distribution of spells of ailments treated during last 30 days by level of care ($n = 18,182$)
Source Estimated from field data

people from lower income quintiles seek ambulatory care from peripheral public health facilities, while those from richer income quintiles prefer secondary- and tertiary-level public healthcare facilities. Majority of people seek care from private providers; however, the type of private provider depends on their affordability. Their lack of ability to pay for expensive private health care often forces people from lower income quintiles to seek care from quacks, less-qualified, or unregistered medical practitioners, and traditional healers. On the other hand, people from higher income groups are easily able to afford high-quality expensive private healthcare. Hence, lack of affordability forces the people from the weaker economic strata to seek poor-quality private healthcare despite making relatively higher out of pocket expenditure as compared to public healthcare (Scott and Jha 2014; Das and Mohpal 2016).

In the case of inpatient care as well, almost 69% people seek care from private providers. As per NSS 71st Round (NSSO 71st), nearly 59% seek private providers for inpatient care in Uttar Pradesh (Sundararaman and Muraledharan 2015). Except for obstetric care, for all other ailments, people prefer private healthcare over public healthcare. In the case of genito-urinary ailments, more than 90% people seek care in private sector. However, a significant share of people seek care for cardiovascular (heart and blood related) disorders, mental illness, and infections in public hospitals, and the share of people seeking care in private sector for the same is manifold higher.

Almost 37.8% women seek care in primary healthcare facilities, while almost 17.8% seek care in public hospitals, which is much higher than that for males. This may be mainly because obstetrics have been included in inpatient services. Likewise, larger share of people from SC/ST category (34.58%) seek care in public healthcare facilities as against 32.77% from other backward classes and 26.23% from general category. The preference toward private healthcare sector for inpatient care also increases with an increase in education level. Likewise, 66.8% people in rural areas and 65.91% people in urban areas seek care from private hospitals. However, people from rural areas generally visit primary healthcare (PHCs) facilities, while people from urban areas seek care from public hospitals. The impact of economic status on the choice of provider is also more evident in the case of inpatient care. Almost 45.3% of the people from lowest income quintile seek care in primary health centers, while 26.4% seek care in public hospitals. Only 19.9 and 8.4% people from the lowest quintile seek care from private doctors/clinics and private hospitals.

It is evident that the utilization of private healthcare services across all sections of society is above 80% of total usage of healthcare services.

3.3 Analysis of Cost of Healthcare

3.3.1 Outpatient Care

In the period of 30 days, the mean out-of-pocket expenditure (OOPE) on ambulatory care is Rs. 2461. The mean OOPE for informal healthcare providers is Rs. 899, while the median OOPE is Rs. 400 (Table 5). The mean OOPE in public healthcare facilities is Rs. 2182, while the median OOPE is also Rs. 851, almost half of the private facilities. The mean OOPE for private healthcare facilities is the highest among all (Rs. 2563). For further analyses, the OOPE under various heads, viz. service/bed charges, diagnostic tests, and medicines from the facility or outside have been estimated. The mean OOPE for informal healthcare services is the least under all heads. OOPE on medicines from outside and service charges are the major contributors to the OOPE for informal healthcare. However, in the case of public healthcare sector, which is considered less expensive, it is noted that the expenditure on medicines and diagnostics from outside is Rs. 1089 and Rs. 496, respectively. One of the biggest reasons for this high OOPE even in public health facilities is lack of availability of medicines and equipment.

In all the three districts, the OOPE on informal providers is the least while that of private providers is the highest (Table 6). A considerable share is spent on drugs

Table 5 Expenditure under various heads on OOP payments by type of healthcare facilities for outpatient care (in Rs.)

Type of healthcare facility	Service charges	Diagnostics test from the hospital	Diagnostics test from outside	Medicines from the hospitals visited	Medicines from outside	Total
Public	127	161	496	292	1089	2182
	(50)	(46)	(250)	(50)	(670)	(851)
Private	621	416	710	759	923	2563
	(250)	(295)	(350)	(410)	(554)	(1200)
Others	262	139	168	108	275	899
	(70)	(50)	(90)	(30)	(110)	(400)

Note Figures in parentheses are the median cost for the same
Source Estimated from field survey data

and diagnostics from outside in public hospitals in all the three districts. The OOPE on user charges, drugs, and diagnostics from the facility and outside is lower in rural areas as compared to urban areas for all the health facilities. In the case of public providers, the mean OOPE in rural areas is 839 as against Rs. 1376 in urban areas. For private providers, the OOPE in rural areas is Rs. 1339, while that in urban areas is 1648. In NSS 71st Round, the mean OOPE for non-hospitalized care in rural areas is Rs. 503, while that in urban areas is Rs. 629 (NSS, 71st Round). The reason for comparatively higher OOPE in our study is the difference in recall period. In NSS 71st round, the recall period for ambulatory care is of 15 days, while in this study the recall period of 30 days has been taken into consideration.

Income level is a significant factor in determining the level of OOPE on healthcare. The OOPE for people from lowest income quintiles is lowest for all types of health facilities. The OOPE on drugs and diagnostics in the private health facility is almost four to five times less than that in the highest income quintile. The results further depict that people from 4th and 5th income quintiles do not seek care from informal providers. However, for lowest income quintile, the expenditure on drugs from the facility and outside for informal providers is Rs. 60 and Rs. 55, respectively, which is two to three times less than that in the case of private providers. The OOPE on informal providers is even less than that in the case of public healthcare facilities. Although the OOPE is supposed to be low in the case of public health facilities, it is noted that a substantial share of OOPE is on drugs and diagnostics from outside even for the most vulnerable sections of the society. This further reflects the failure of public healthcare system to cater to the requirements of the poor and down-trodden sections of the economy. The average OOPE on drugs and diagnostics in private healthcare facilities for the lowest income quintile is much lower than that for the highest income quintiles which depicts the heterogeneity in the private healthcare sector.

Table 6 Out-of-pocket expenditure on ambulatory care by household characteristics

Background characteristic	Type of facility	Components of out of pocket expenditure (in Rs.)				
		Service charges	Diagnostics test from the hospital	Diagnostics test from outside	Medicines from the hospitals visited	Medicines from outside
District						
Kushinagar	Public	123	117	174	54	368
	Private	247	257	274	416	351
	Others	60	7	129	78	66
Hamirpur	Public	54	94	340	106	510
	Private	202	261	361	484	341
	Others	88	30	110	127	60
Aligarh	Public	120	122	420	116	553
	Private	239	508	389	466	415
	Others	71	69	135	118	91
Place of residence						
Rural	Public	35	79	134	34	253
	Private	366	238	165	267	336
	Others	51	59	128	112	93
Urban	Public	79	158	184	77	366
	Private	229	356	274	320	360
	Others	120	212	150	188	131
Income quintiles						
1	Public	1	35	150	–	182
	Private	50	107	158	155	180
	Others	35	0	110	60	55
2	Public	1	58	230	35	145
	Private	110	147	158	195	230
	Others	50	85	117	81	84
3	Public	30	100	280	50	350
	Private	258	250	384	410	250
	Others	78	100	141	150	113
4	Public	35	158	350	65	465
	Private	350	309	416	540	387
	Others	0	0	0	0	0
5	Public	54	259	412	72	549
	Private	410	409	450	597	402
	Others	0	0	0	0	0

Source Field survey data

Table 7 Mean expenditure under various heads on OOP payments by type of healthcare facilities for inpatient care (in Rs.)

Type of healthcare facility	Service charges/bed charges	Diagnostics test from the hospital visited	Diagnostics test from outside	Medicines and consumables from the hospitals visited	Medicines and consumables from outside	Total
Health center/PHCs	64	34	242	293	526	1264
Public hospitals	213	563	2697	1246	2611	5180
Private doctors/clinics	2589	4484	3987	6095	4455	13,658
Private hospitals	8629	10,129	10,776	38,221	38,595	38,202

Source Estimated from field data

3.3.2 Inpatient Care

In the case of inpatient care, for the facilitation of the analysis, health facilities have been categorized as subcenters, PHCs, and CHCs, public hospitals, private clinics, nursing homes, and private hospitals. The mean OOPE for hospitalized care in primary health facilities is Rs. 1264, while that for public hospitals is Rs. 5180 (Table 7). In the case of private clinics and nursing homes, the mean OOPE is Rs. 13,658, while that in the case of private hospitals is Rs. 38,202. The OOPE in private hospitals is manifold higher than that in public healthcare facilities.

The mean OOPE on hospitalized care as per NSS 71st Round is Rs. 18,268 in the country which is almost three times higher than Rs. 6643 in 60th Round (Table 8), which reflects the exponential increase in the cost of hospitalized care and increasing dominance of private healthcare sector in the country. The situation is even worse in U.P. as the mean OOPE is Rs. 22,540, which is among the highest in the country.

Further analysis of the cost components depicts that although the expenditure on service charges, drugs, and diagnostics from inside in the case of primary healthcare facilities is nominal, the expenditure on medicines and diagnostics from outside (Rs. 526 and Rs. 242 respectively) adds to the OOP. Similar trends are seen in public hospitals, where the expenses on medicines and diagnostics from outside are even higher (Rs. 2611 and Rs. 2697, respectively). In the case of private clinics and nursing homes, and large private hospitals, the expenditure under all heads is humongous. However, majority of the cost is incurred on drugs and diagnostics from inside the private health facilities, which exponentially increases the OOPE. The unregulated functioning of private health sector, lack of regulation in the case of price determination of medicines and diagnostics are the biggest reasons for it.

The average OOPE in Kushinagar for both public as well as private facilities is Rs. 5949 and Rs. 26,830, which is lowest among all the three districts (Table 9). This may be mainly because of the poor quality and lack of proper health infrastructure in the

Table 8 Average total medical expenditure per hospitalization case at inpatient care (in Rs.)

Place of living		Average total medical expenditure per hospitalization case at inpatient care in the last 365 days (Rs.)		
		Male	Female	Person
Rural	U.P.	22,134	15,765	18,693
	India	17,528 (5946)	12,295 (5406)	14,935 (5695)
Urban	U.P.	33,498	30,150	31,653
	India	28,165 (9535)	20,754 (8112)	24,436 (8851)
Total	U.P.	25,451	20,096	22,540
	India	21,223 (7004)	15,292 (6237)	18,268 (6643)

Note Figures in parentheses are corresponding from 60th Round NSS
Source NSSO 71st Round, key findings

Table 9 District-wise mean OOP expenditure on inpatient care (Rs.)

District	Public hospitals	Private hospital
Kushinagar	5949	26,830
Hamirpur	8982	45,075
Aligarh	8795	45,248

Source Estimated from field data

district. The OOPE on private healthcare is highest in Aligarh (Rs. 45,248) closely followed by Hamirpur (Rs. 45,075). This further reflects the huge inter-regional disparities in the availability of public as well as private healthcare in the state.

The average OOPE for the lowest income group is Rs. 1550 for public facilities and Rs. 12,300 for private facilities, with a difference of almost ten times (Table 10). This on one hand reflects how proper availability of public healthcare facilities can reduce the healthcare burden on households. But on the other hand, it also reflects the shortcomings of the public healthcare facilities, which forces people from lower income quintiles to seek care from private healthcare sector. The OOPE on public facilities for higher income quintiles is also higher than that for lowest income quintiles. The OOPE on private facilities for 4th and 5th quintiles is Rs. 42,300 and Rs. 108,990, respectively. There is a huge gap in the OOPE pattern for all the income quintiles. This is because many times, people from lowest income quintile have to forego medical treatment because of lack of affordability. Even if they are able to seek the treatment, they are forced to cap their expenditure on drugs and diagnostics according to their ability to pay. This is not only limited to drugs and diagnostics, but also to the type of provider visited and the duration of the treatment. Thus, on the one hand people from the lowest income strata limit their healthcare consumption

Table 10 Income-group-wise OOP for inpatient care in public versus private healthcare

Income groups	Public facilities	Private facilities
1	1550	12,300
2	2240	17,640
3	2690	24,500
4	7500	42,300
5	10,800	108,990

Source Estimated from field data

while people from higher quintiles are charged according to their capacities (Prinja 2012; Verma et al. 2017).

3.4 Impoverishment Due to High OOPE

There is enough evidence to support the argument that a large number of people find themselves in the poverty trap as a result of spending substantial part of their income on treatment of illness. In this study, an attempt has been made to assess the extent of impoverishment on the household due to high OOPE on healthcare. For this, poverty headcount ratio (H_p) has been estimated using pre-poverty headcount[1] and post poverty headcount[2]. For this, initially the fraction of people living below official state poverty line before expenditure on health and the fraction of people below poverty line after health payments have been calculated (Hooda 2014). The state-specific poverty line for rural as well as urban areas as adopted by Planning Commission for the year 2011–2012 has been used (Planning Commission 2014). The results depict that an episode of hospitalization almost doubles the poverty headcount, which increases from 12.76 to 21.26% (Fig. 1).

Although health insurance has been introduced by the government to provide coverage to the BPL households in the state against high OOPE on health, the insurance coverage is very low (Table 11). Only 4.85% households in the study area are enrolled under Rashtriya Swasthya Bima Yojana (RSBY) or national health insurance scheme, and almost 94% households are not insured under any health insurance scheme.

---

[1] Pre poverty Headcount = Pre $H_p = 1/n \sum 1\,(C_i \leq PL)$, where C_i is per capita consumption expenditure, PL is official state poverty line, and n is number of individuals.
[2] Post poverty Headcount = Post $H_p = 1/n \sum 1\,(C_i - OOP \leq PL)$.

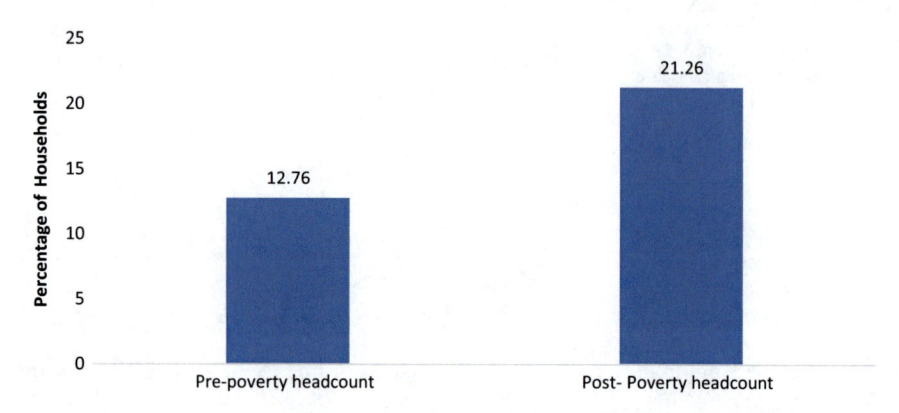

Fig. 1 Impoverishment effect of cost of healthcare. *Source* Estimated from field data

Table 11 Insurance coverage under different schemes in the project area

Type of insurance scheme	Percentage of households
Community health insurance scheme	0.07
Health insurance provided by an MFI	0.05
ESI	0.01
Insurance provided by employer	0.01
RSBY	4.85
Government sponsored health scheme	0.83
Private health insurance policy	0.05
Others	0.02
Not insured	94.14

Source Estimated from field data

4 Discussions

Falling incomes and rising healthcare expenditures particularly in the rural population are the new phenomena of the post-1990s, as an outcome of market-led health policies. During these decades, in the name of austerity measures, public health sector has been starved of finances, leading to poorer functioning of public healthcare facilities. That has given ample scope to the corporate-led private health sector. The decline in public health expenditure has also impacted preventive health measures by further leading to low access to safe drinking water, sanitation, and nutritional facilities. This further leads to high prevalence of water-borne and other communicable diseases among people from lower socio-economic strata (Hooda 2013). This raises the cost of treatments making health care unaffordable for people from lower social and economic strata, which are in fact the neediest.

An analysis of the expenditure shows that expenditure on medicine and diagnostics accounts for the largest component of OOP in both public and private facilities. Lack of human resources, medical equipment, and medicines at government facilities forces people to seek drugs and diagnostics from the private healthcare market, even while seeking treatment in public facilities. This further increased the OOPE in public healthcare facilities also (Saksena 2010; Basu et al. 2012; 8th CRM Report 2014).

The cost structure in private sector is also not standardized and the quality of care available is much diversified. This is mainly because of the non-homogeneity of the private healthcare system in the country. The private healthcare sector can be further classified as for-profit and not-for-profit; traditional and modern providers, who often practice cross-method medicine (Mills et al. 2001; Qadeer 2011). Individual registered and unregistered practitioners and private hospitals are mostly concentrated in urban areas and almost entirely provide curative care (Duggal 2006).

Hence, a large rural–urban divide is also visible as the rural counterparts are only dependent on primary health centers and subcenters, which deliver preventive and promotive healthcare to the people, mostly through their paramedical staff (Das and Mohpal 2016). Government's tendency to use isolated technological interventions without looking at the various inter-linkages of human environment and its curative policies has made the health services organisations top-heavy with most of the human and material resources concentrated on top. This has led to establishment and development of medically well-equipped major health institutions in the urban areas, while public health centers and peripheral units of district remain starved. As a result, people from urban areas have access to better health facilities as compared to rural people (Qadeer 2011; Iyengar and Dholakia 2012).

However, not all the people from urban areas have access to quality healthcare. This is mainly because government facilities are under-staffed and overburdened, while the good quality private healthcare is highly expensive and not affordable by all. Thus, people from lower socio-economic areas in urban areas are forced to avail the services of these less or least trained unregistered medical practitioners. Thus, the poor seek health care in private sector in spite of lack of resources which further increases their cost of care and pushes them toward impoverishment. In fact, poorer households have to spend a larger share of their household resources on health care than the rich (Dilip 2010).

The extremely high costs in private health sector are basically due to high service charges and prohibitive costs of drugs and diagnostics. With the emergence of big corporate players in this sector, the for-profit health sector is completely dominating the healthcare industry. They charge exorbitant prices for drugs, diagnostics, and medical treatment. On the other hand, the unregistered medical practitioners and informal providers deliver healthcare at very low costs. Thus, the private sector offers a wide range of quality of care, from globally acclaimed super-speciality hospitals to facilities that deliver care of unacceptably low quality (Shah and Mohanty 2010; Mohanan et al. 2016).

Although there is no particular definition of high-quality medical care, the Institute of Medicine provides its six key features: safe, effective, patient-centered, efficient, timely, and equitable. However, recent evidence\suggest that there are substantial deficiencies in these aspects in our healthcare sector (Scott et al. 2014). Various studies suggest that private providers are more responsive and patient-centered than public providers, which is one of the biggest reasons that even the people from marginal sections of the economy prefer private over public healthcare (Mills et al. 2001; Scott et al. 2014). However, this does not always hold true as there are wide gaps in costs and quality of care, which are mainly due to lack of regulation and government intervention in private sector.

The private healthcare sector is also allegedly engaged in various corrupt practices such as irrational prescriptions, commissions for referrals, and unnecessary investigations, and treats the patients as revenue generators, without rationality (Gadre and BMJ 2015). The lack of regulations, monitoring authority, and legal provisions on pricing of medicines, diagnostic charges, and surgical charges further provide private players a free hand to exploit the people.

Various studies have suggested that the private healthcare sector should expand and increase its sectoral efficiency so as to reduce the burden on government (World Bank 1987). But the recent commercialization and corporatization of private healthcare have led to a situation of market failure, as a major section of the society is unable to avail their fundamental right of healthcare due to exorbitant costs in private care. In order to redress this market failure, government intervention is the need of the hour.

However, government health policies, including the latest National Health Policy, 2017, have been designed in such a way so as to promote private healthcare in public facilities as well. The collaborations with private sector are becoming a new trend in the healthcare sector. The new National Health Policy also focuses on providing a larger role to private sector in place of regulating it. It plans to reinforce its support for public–private partnerships with not-for-profit and private-sector organizations through contracting and strategic purchase of services as a 'short term' measure to plug critical gaps in the health system. However, the duration of the 'short term' remains unspecified. The introduction of private providers within the public healthcare system further changes the legal basis, raising concerns over equity, cost of care, quality, and health rights and also creates further scope for private healthcare insurance providers to take off. The complex structure of PPPs and range of healthcare providers further aggravate the task of monitoring and regulating them. Lack of trained personnel in public facilities leads to outsource contractual workforce in PPPs, who are paid less and have to work in extremely poor working conditions. This has a further impact on quality of care provided to patients and on worker's rights as well (Roy 2017).

The study on PPPs in many countries like U.K. and U.S.A. show that such arrangements have their accountability to private investors and offer little assurance in providing universal and affordable healthcare to all. Various studies have concluded that the private sector only serves higher income groups with an underlying risk of providing low-quality and less-efficient healthcare at higher costs. In this context, how good an idea is promoting private sector in healthcare is yet to be seen.

5 Conclusions and Recommendations

India's private healthcare sector has become one of the fastest growing sectors in recent decades. It has also earned the reputation of being a much-preferred destination for investment. Corporatization of healthcare sector has been a major factor for such developments. Low priority for improving the much needed public health sector has created a vast opportunity for the corporate players to fill in the gaps and earn huge profits.

Majority of the people prefer private healthcare over public healthcare, despite their economic status. Although the out-of-pocket expenditure is high in both public as well as private facilities, yet in private healthcare sector it is exorbitant. Lack of trained personnel, drugs, and equipment in public facilities further forces the people to seek care in private sector. Public healthcare sector is also dependent on private healthcare market for drugs and diagnostics, which substantially increases the cost of care there. The high costs of good quality private healthcare services, however, deprive people of lower economic strata from seeking proper healthcare services because of their lack of affordability. Government healthcare policies are also designed in such a way so as to strengthen private healthcare sector. Despite the introduction of health insurance schemes like Rashtriya Swasthya Bima Yojana (RSBY), the government has failed to reduce OOPE because of low coverage and dominance of private hospitals in providing treatment under the schemes. Lack of proper regulatory and monitoring authority and legal provisions further leads to exorbitant prices and corrupt practices in the private sector.

In order to provide universal health coverage and ensure healthcare for all, the government should strengthen public health system by increasing public expenditure on healthcare, streamline structures, and human resources in facilities to improve efficiency as well as rationalize cost of care based on actual needs. Free availability of generic drugs and diagnostic facilities should also be ensured. Government health insurance policy needs to be revamped. There is also a need of effective regulation of private healthcare sector to contain healthcare cost, ensure quality, and prevent unethical practices.

References

8th Common Review Mission, Uttar Pradesh. (2014). *NRHM, Ministry of health and family welfare*. Government of India.

Basu, S., Andrews, J., Kishore, S., Panjabi, R., & Stuckler, D. (2012). Comparative performance of private and public healthcare systems in low- and middle-income countries: A systematic review. *PLoS Med, 9*(6), e1001244. https://doi.org/10.1371/journal.pmed.1001244.

Bhojani, U., et al. (2012). Out-of-pocket healthcare payments on chronic conditions impoverish urban poor in Bangalore, India. *BMC Public Health, 12*(1), 990.

Das, J., & Mohpal, A. (2016). Socioeconomic status and quality of care in rural India: New evidence from provider and household surveys. *Health Affairs, 35*(10), 1764–1773. https://doi.org/10.1377/hlthaff.2016.0558.

Dholakia, R. H., & Iyengar, S. (2011). Access to rural poor to primary health care in India. *Review of Market Integration, 4*, 71–109. April, 2012. Sage Working Paper No. 2011-05-03. Ahmadabad: Institute of Management.

Dilip, T. R. (2010). Utilization of inpatient care from private hospitals: Trends emerging from Kerala, India. *Health Policy and Planning, 25,* 437–446.

Duggal, R. (2006). Utilization of health care services in India. In S. Prasad & C. Sathyamala (Eds.), *Securing health for all, dimensions and challenges*. New Delhi: Institute for Human Development.

Gadre, A. (2015). India's private healthcare sector treats patients as revenue generators. *BMJ, 350*, h826, https://doi.org/10.1136/bmj.h826 (Published February 24, 2015).

Ghosh, S. (2011). Catastrophic payments and impoverishment due to out-of-pocket health spending. *Economic and Political Weekly, 46*(47), 63–70.

Hooda, S. (2013). *Changing pattern of public expenditure on health in India: Issues and challenges* (Working Paper Series 1, ISID-PHFI Collaborative Research Programme).

Hooda, S. K. (2014). *Out of pocket expenditure on health and households wellbeing in India: Examining the role of health policy interventions* (Working Paper No. 165, ISID-PHFI collaborative research programme).

India Brand Equity Foundation Report. (2017). *Healthcare Industry in India, 2017*. Retrieved July 23, 2017 from https://www.ibef.Org/industry/healthcare-india.aspx.

Iyengar, S., & Dholakia, R. H. (2012). Access of the rural poor to primary healthcare in India. *Review of Market Integration, 4*(1), 71–109.

Mills, A., Bennett, S., & Russel, S. (2001). *The challenges of health sector reform: What must governments do?*. New York: Palgrave Macmillan.

Mohanan, M., Hay, K., & Mor, N. (2016). Quality of health care in india: challenges, priorities, and the road ahead. *Health Affairs, 35*(10), 1753–1758. https://doi.org/10.1377/hlthaff.2016.0676.

National Sample Survey Office (NSSO). (2014). *Economic characteristics of... Ministry of statistics & programme implementation*. Government of India.

Planning Commision. (2014). *Report of the expert group to review the methodology for measurement of poverty*. New Delhi: Government of India.

Prinja, S., et al. (2012). Health care inequities in North India: Role of public sector in universalizing health care. *Indian Journal of Medical Research, 136*(3), 421–431.

Quadeer, I. (2011). *Public health in India: critical reflections*. New Delhi: Daanish Books.

Roy, B. (2017). Why public private collaboration is bad news for healthcare in India. The Wire. Retrieved March 20, 2017 from https://thewire.in/117527/ppphealthcarehealthpolicy/.

Saksena, P., et al. (2010). *Health services utilization and out-of-pocket expenditure at public and private facilities in low-income countries* (World Health Report, Background Paper 20, World Health Organization).

Scott, K. W., & Jha, A. K. (2014). Putting quality on the global health agenda. *The New England Journal of Medicine, 371*(1), 3–5. https://doi.org/10.1056/nejmp1402157.

Shah, U., & Mohanty, R. (2010). Private sector in Indian healthcare delivery: Consumer perspective and government policies to promote private sector. *Information Management and Business Review, 1*(2), 79–87.

Shahrawat, R., et al. (2012). Insured yet vulnerable: Out-of-pocket payments and India's poor. *Health Policy and Planning, 27*(3), 213–221.

SRS Statistical Report. (2014). *Maternal mortality ratio. Bulletin 2011–13*. SRS Bulletin.

Sundararaman, T., & Muraledharan, V. R. (2015). Falling sick, paying the price; NSS 71st round on morbidity and costs of healthcare. *Economic and Political Weekly, 50*(33), 17–20.

Verma, C. S., Singh, Shivani, Ranjan, Alok, & Sundararaman, T. (2017). Healthcare consumption in Uttar Pradesh; Iniquitous growth and the social factors contributing to impoverishment. *Economic and Political Weekly, 52*(9), 73–81.

The World Bank Annual Report. (2007).

Dr. C. S. Verma is a senior faculty at Giri Institute of Development Studies, Lucknow. He has taught Economics in different Universities for over two decades and superviseded M.Phil and PhDs. He is engaged in full time research since December 2013. His current area of research includes Public Health, Health Economics, Poverty and Development issues. He has also worked on projects supported by ICSSR, DFID, UNDP, Unicef, WHO and other international agencies. He has also contributed as member of various academic societies and civil society organizations. Dr Verma has authored and edited books, policy briefs and research papers for reputed national and international journals. His most recent paper titled, "Healthcare Consumption in Uttar Pradesh", was published in Economic and Political Weekly. Before taking up Academics and research, Dr Verma worked as journalist in the National Herald New Delhi. Dr Verma did his M.Phil on "Sino-Soviet Trade in the Eighties" and Ph.D. on "Reform of Soviet Foreign Trade Sector, from JNU, New Delhi.

Shivani Singh is a Senior Research Associate at Giri Institute of Development Studies, Lucknow. She has done her Ph D in Economics from BBAU Ambedkar University, Lucknow with specialization on Environmental Health. She is engaged in full time research for last two years and has been part of several studies in Public Health including Evaluation Studies on Community Health. She has half a dozen papers in reputed research journals to her credit including in Economic and Political Weekly.